Lordship and Community in Medieval Europe

Selected readings

Lordship and Community in Medieval Europe

Selected readings

Edited by
Fredric L. Cheyette, *Amherst College*

Holt, Rinehart, and Winston, Inc.

New York · Chicago · San Francisco · Atlanta
Dallas · Montreal · Toronto · London

Cover illustration: Oseberg lion head, from eighth-century Viking ship (Norwegian Embassy Information Service, 1967).

The maps "Medieval Brioude," "Medieval Moissat," and "Medieval Sauxillanges" are adapted from maps appearing in Gabriel Fournier, *Le Peuplement rural en basse Auvergne durant le Haut Moyen Age* (Paris: Presses Universitaires des France, 1962), pp. 167, 531, and 492.

Cartography: Joseph Stonehill

Library of Congress Catalog Card Number 67-25887

2650455

Printed in the United States of America
1 2 3 4 5 6 7 8 9

To Oren, Dina, and Tamara

Preface

This anthology makes available in English a selection of recent scholarship, European and American, on the growth of the nobility and the development of communities in medieval Europe. Although historians of medieval society have devoted their attention to these subjects for several decades, it has been difficult to present the results of their research to students, for textbooks do not yet give these problems adequate space and much of the original work has not been published in English. It was in order to make this scholarship available to my own students of medieval history that I undertook many of the translations in this volume.

The articles collected here have been chosen to supplement the standard textbooks. Particular attention has therefore been given to the development of aristocratic society in northern Europe and in the crusader kingdom during the eleventh and early twelfth centuries and at the end of the Middle Ages. Nine of the selections, grouped under the heading "Community," explore the development of villages and parishes, and communities of provinces and kingdoms throughout Western Europe. The Introduction and the first three essays place these developments in a context that will be familiar to the student—that of feudalism. They also suggest the nature of the continuing dialogue between concepts and empirical data that is the explicit concern of many of the authors and must be the explicit or implicit concern of all historians of medieval society.

Although this is not a "problems" book in the ordinary sense, I have selected essays that complement one another and that are concerned with a certain number of common themes. First, that the political organization of medieval Europe was not fixed but was constantly changing—in terms of those who exercised power and those who were subject to it, in terms of the way it was exercised and of the values that legitimized it. Second, that medieval lordship existed in a community apart from which it cannot be fully comprehended. Third, that for the historian to understand the structures of medieval social organization, the shared patterns of behavior, he must also understand the ideas and values that gave meaning to those patterns. The essays reprinted here show the diverse ways American and European scholars have developed these themes.

In translating I have tried to capture the thought of the original in readable English prose. For this reason, I have sometimes been forced to paraphrase, especially when faced with stylistic devices in French, German, or Italian that are not allowable in English. Where footnotes have been omitted or reduced to simple reference citations, this has been indicated. Editor's notes are clearly identified, and insertions in the text are enclosed in brackets.

For their help in putting this anthology together, I would like to thank the publishers of the articles and books from which the selections were taken and the authors who kindly let me use their work. I extend my thanks in particular to Hans Baron, Jean-François Lemarignier, and Joseph R. Strayer, who revised their articles for this anthology; to Joshua Prawer, who allowed me to see his essay "Estates, Communities and the Constitution of the Latin Kingdom" while it was still in page proof and who made valuable suggestions for improving my translation of his "Nobility and the Feudal Regime in the Latin Kingdom of Jerusalem"; to Léopold Genicot, who read my translation of his essay with great care and made several suggestions for its improvement; to Gabriel Fournier, who helped me choose an appropriate and coherent selection from his thesis; to Miriam Sambursky, who translated some very difficult German scholarly prose with considerable success; to Giuseppe Galigani for his translation of the article by Antonio Marongiu, and to Professor Marongiu for arranging to have this translation made; to Floyd Merritt and the reference staff of Frost Library, Amherst College, for the innumerable occasions on which they assisted me with bibliographical details and interlibrary loans; to Margaret Rocasah for her patient and expert typing; and to Shulameth Oppenheim and William Hunt, Jr., for their assistance with proofreading. Finally, I extend my warmest thanks to my friend and colleague Howell D. Chickering, Jr., who read the introduction and all the translations with a fresh and expert eye. Thanks to his careful reviewing there are fewer ambiguous sentences, graceless phrases, and glaring Gallicisms and Germanicisms than there otherwise would have been. The faults that remain are, of course, my own.

FREDRIC L. CHEYETTE

Amherst, Massachusetts
September 1967

Contents

Maps

Abbreviations Used in the Notes

BEC *Bibliothèque de l'Ecole des Chartes*

DA *Deutsches Archiv für Erforschung des Mittelalters*

EHR *English Historical Review*

H. Fr. Académie des Inscriptions et Belles-Lettres *Recueil des historiens des Gaules et de la France*

HZ *Historische Zeitschrift*

Jaffé Philippus Jaffé (ed.), *Bibliotheca rerum Germanicarum* (1864–1873)

Mansi G. D. Mansi, *Sacrorum conciliorum nova et amplissima collectio* (1759–1798)

MGH *Monumenta Germaniae historica*

- ***SS*** *Scriptores*
- ***AA*** *Auctores antiquissimi*
- ***SS rer. Merov.*** *Scriptores rerum Merovingicarum*
- ***Cap.*** *Legum sectio II: Capitularia regum Francorum*
- ***Const.*** *Legum sectio IV: Constitutiones et acta publica imperatorum et regum*
- ***Form.*** *Legum sectio V: Formulae*
- ***Dipl.*** *Diplomata*
- ***Dipl. Imp.*** *Diplomata regum et imperatorum Germaniae*
- ***Epp.*** *Epistolae*
- ***SS rer.*** *Scriptores rerum Germanicarum ad usus scholarum*

Migne J. P. Migne, *Patrologia cursus completus. Series Latina* (1841–1864)

PRO Public Record Office

RH *Revue Historique*

RHD *Revue historique de droit français et étranger*

Zs. *Zeitschrift*

ZRG GA *Zeitschrift der Savigny-Stiftung für Rechtsgeschichte. Germanistische Abteilung*

Introduction

What is feudalism? The history of Western thought, even in recent years, has known more important, more profound, and certainly more troubling questions than this. Yet, the problem was once—and not too long ago—of major political importance in the Western world; and "feudalism" is still a favorite term of political polemics in countries that today are beginning to "modernize" and wherever Marxist movements face well-entrenched privileged classes. The continuing difficulties that historians of medieval institutions face in trying to resolve this question are, in fact, closely related to the use of "feudalism" in political polemics, as Otto Brunner shows in this anthology. But this is not the only reason for their difficulties —difficulties which, although they have long been realized,[1] still remain unresolved.

Thus Joseph R. Strayer, in the first article reprinted here, argues that "Western European feudalism is essentially political—it is a form of government," one in which "rights of government (not mere political influence) are attached to lordship and fiefs, . . . in which political authority is monopolized by a small group of military leaders, . . . [and in which] public authority has become a private possession."[2] To this, Lynn White has replied that "European feudalism was essentially a way of organizing society for instant warfare, with emphasis upon local forces. In the ninth century, when the Carolingian realm decayed, vassals and fief-holders inherited the debris of public authority exactly because their society had already been reorganized in such a military way that they were in a position to pick up the political pieces."[3]

Bryce Lyon has seen the essence of feudalism in yet a different fashion. In a review of *Lord Hastings' Indentured Retainers, 1461–1483* by William

---

1 See Strayer, "Feudalism in Western Europe," below, p. 21, note 1.

2 *Ibid.*

3 Lynn White, *Medieval Technology and Social Change* (Oxford: Clarendon Press, 1962), pp. 135–136.

H. Dunham, Jr. (the Introduction and first chapter of which are included in this anthology),[4] Lyon argues that the indenture system described by Dunham should not be called "feudal" "because [it] did not involve homage. . . ."[5] It is no wonder that Dunham should comment, in his review of Bryce Lyon's book, *From Fief to Indenture,* "Disagreement might be reduced if words like 'feudalism,' now less a term of convenience than a cover of ignorance, were expunged from the historical vocabulary."[6]

These authors are not debating whether feudalism is to be defined in terms of economic exploitation or political privilege; their concerns are far from those of Sieyès, Hegel, and Marx. They are debating how a word that has been part of our common historical vocabulary since the early eighteenth century ought to be used by historians of the Middle Ages. Why, after two and a half centuries, should there be no agreement?

The reasons, aside from normal academic disputatiousness, are not hard to find. First, the uncommon amount of baggage the term "feudalism" carries with it: continuing overtones from political polemics; the consequence of scholarly polemics at the turn of the century on the relationship of feudalism to the growth of constitutionalism;[7] and the assumptions of nineteenth-century political philosophy, which made feudalism a stage of social development and the terms "state" and "sovereignty," as well as the distinctions between "economy," "political organization," and "society" part of the standard vocabulary for all subsequent discussions of institutional history. (These important assumptions are fully discussed by Brunner in the third selection in this anthology.)

A second reason for the disagreement among historians is a pervasive uncertainty as to precisely what is meant by "What is feudalism?" Is it simply a question about the form of medieval government? Or does it concern medieval political structures in general? Does it bear upon medieval economic structures? Or all of medieval society? In many cases, the way the question is interpreted depends upon the theoretical bias of the author.

For the word "feudalism" is not a simple universal concept like "table" or "unicorn." The confusion that surrounds it is not simply a consequence of vagueness around its edges. "Feudalism" is really a "concept-theory." When a historian defines it, he may bring into play—directly or by implication—a theory about what were the essential elements in the structure of medieval society, a theory about the causes of medieval social structure, a theory about the stages of European or universal social development, a general theory of historical causation, or several or all of these. To define

---

[4] See Dunham, "The Feudality of Retaining," below.

[5] *Speculum,* 32 (1957), 558.

[6] *Speculum,* 33 (1958), 304.

[7] See C. H. McIlwain, *Constitutionalism Ancient and Modern* (Ithaca, N.Y.: Cornell Univ. Press, 1940).

this concept-theory he must consciously, and (in part) arbitrarily, choose what to include and what to leave out. And in making that choice, he cannot avoid theoretical issues.

Lynn White's comment on Strayer's definition suggests yet a third reason for scholarly disagreement. When eighteenth-century political philosophers first used the word "feudalism" for a form of government, they conceived of it as a form parallel to the three Aristotelian forms (the rule of one, the rule of the few, the rule of many).[8] Feudalism, like monarchy, aristocracy, or polity, had a fixed, definable character. To be sure, Montesquieu was perplexed because feudalism as he defined it, unlike the other three forms of classical Aristotelian theory, did not develop in only one direction; it did not fit into the cycle of decay and regeneration that led society from monarchy to democracy and back again. On the contrary, feudalism led in quite contradictory directions; it produced "rules that tended towards anarchy, and anarchy that tended towards order and harmony."[9] Montesquieu had glimpsed what Marc Bloch two centuries later would call the "paradox of feudalism."[10] Thus, Montesquieu had already realized that a static definition of feudalism could not *by itself* explain the way medieval society had developed. But eighteenth- and nineteenth-century political philosophers were interested in other subjects; and for their discussions of the stages of social development, of the origins of capitalism and the nation-state, a static definition was satisfactory.

For a medievalist now to use a static definition to explain the development of medieval society, however, creates enormous difficulty. For when the historian defines feudalism as a particular set of institutional "characteristics," he is, in effect, proceeding by exclusion. He is cutting these characteristics out of their total context and suggesting either that as long as they existed they remained unchanged, or that whatever changes took place are to be explained only in terms of those characteristics. To the extent that the historian attempts to define the essence of feudalism, to list the characteristics that institutions must have in order to be called "feudal," he is making any explanation of change, of the dynamics of medieval society, difficult if not impossible; for he is eliminating, by the process of definition, factors that may have effected change. Lynn White's comment is just such an attempt to bring a dynamic element into a picture from which it had been excluded.

All the selections in this anthology are concerned with the dynamics of medieval society, with the way society changed and why it changed. Each of the authors has approached his own particular problems in his own special way. Few have guided their research or their remarks by the

---

8 Aristotle, *Politics* 3. 7.

9 Montesquieu, *De l'Esprit des Lois* **30**, 1.

10 Marc Bloch, *Feudal Society* (Chicago: Chicago Univ. Press, 1961), pp. 231–240.

traditional picture of medieval "feudal" society. Yet all, directly or indirectly, have something to say about that picture. What new insights do they give? What new questions have they asked?

Until recently, most people have seemed to assume that the "sovereign state" is the "natural" or "normal" form of political organization. Since the appearance of the sovereign state is normal, the supposition continues, it need not be explained. On the other hand, a political organization from which the sovereign state is absent *does* need to be explained and related in some way to the normal form. Probably for this reason, medieval society has long been explained in terms of a breakup or fragmentation of the state, of "public powers" being made "private," and of the subjects of the state being "mediatized" by the great nobility. What happens if we do not assume any natural or normal form of the state or of political power? What if we assume that *any* form of domination requires explanation? Not because domination of man by man is abnormal, but because the possible forms such domination might take are very numerous and the reason why one form developed rather than another is really the problem of interest. Many eighteenth- and nineteenth-century political theorists—those who promoted the idea of social contract, Adam Smith and his nineteenth-century followers, and socialists of all shades—made much of the distinctions between political, social, and economic organization (if they then proceeded to describe what were, or ought to be, the connections between them). They frequently implanted these distinctions in a single, much more fundamental one: between "state" and "society." It is probably because these distinctions were so fundamental to nineteenth-century thought that they seem almost a matter of course today. But there is nothing natural about them. Invented to analyze certain problems or to promote particular political ideals, they need not be considered the only possible vocabulary for social analysis. Indeed, recent studies, of which this anthology presents a sample, have sought ways to avoid these categories, producing notions such as "lordship," or "solidarity grouping" to cut across them, to grasp past human action in a new way.

In so doing, the authors have pushed their investigations of political life and of institutions into the realms of religion, moral values, military tactics, town planning, and church architecture (to name but a few of the themes they have touched on). As a result, they have been less inclined to reify such abstractions as "feudalism," "sovereignty," or "manorialism" (still so prevalent among textbook writers)—that is, less inclined to turn them into definable objects or impersonal forces—or to make of them the boundaries by which all discussions of medieval institutions must be limited.

The authors of the essays reprinted in this book have sought both to expand our present knowledge of the causes and direction of medieval institutional change and to construct with care the concepts by which to do so. For this reason, discussion of terminology plays a rather large role in many of the selections. To see how the authors have gone about doing this, we may take a look at one traditional way of dealing with medieval society—in terms of fief and vassalage—and ask how these essays might alter the picture this traditional approach has given.

Fief and vassalage have been associated with the term "feudalism" since that word and its French and German counterparts (*féodalité, Lehnswesen*) first came into use. The feudists of the seventeenth and eighteenth century—men who made their living drawing up inventories of landlords' charters—and the lawyers who tried, when possible, to give those charters cash value in court or out, used the term to refer to the legal system of landholding into which their documents appeared to fit. The term came naturally, for many of the charters concerned fiefs (*feuda*). Neither feudists nor lawyers were much interested in the historical development of this "feudalism"; they were even less interested in its role in medieval society. Their sole concern was to use the rotting parchments in their clients' archives to support their claims of the moment. They therefore fit the contents of those documents into what they imagined to have been the legal system of the past, a construction closely related to the system of their own day. Continuity, indeed rigidity, not change, was essential if a thirteenth-century document was to serve as evidence in an eighteenth-century lawsuit. Political writers soon took over both term and content to describe a form of government, and then, as the content became fuller and more fluid, to describe a form of society. And so it passed into the historian's vocabulary. For the feudists and lawyers of the eighteenth century, "feudalism" served a technical purpose. But if a historian approaches medieval society primarily in terms of fief and vassalage, he must make an important empirical assumption. He must assume, explicitly or implicitly, that fief-holding and vassalage were in fact of primary importance in medieval society, indeed, that they determined its nature.

Since this is an empirical assumption, how can we test it? One way would be to look at the medieval nobility. What was the position of the noblemen in medieval society? Of what importance was fief-holding and vassalage among them?

Other questions follow immediately from these: Who were the nobility? Where did they come from? From what, or whom, did they derive their power? What made their power legitimate in the eyes of those over whom they exercised it? This question is particularly important. For the other side of command is obedience, and as Karl Bosl remarks, we can ask questions either about those who give commands or about those who obey them. Was noble power derived by delegation or usurpation from the state? Or are such terms inadequate to describe what took place?

What was the relation of noble power to other power centers, such as the monarchies and the Church?

The articles by Walter Schlesinger and Jean-François Lemarignier are two recent attempts to answer some of these questions. Schlesinger's, already a classic of German medieval scholarship, represents one predominant view of the nature of the early Germanic nobility. To Schlesinger, these questions can be answered, in part, by looking at the Germanic cultural inheritance (using as sources both classical historical texts such as Tacitus and Caesar and the resources of philology and archeology), at the ideas and forms of lordship among early medieval Germanic peoples. Of particular importance is his emphasis on the close connection among the various varieties of lordship. Lemarignier, on his side, approaches these same questions by looking at the circumstances attendant on the disintegration of the Carolingian Empire and at the new forms of secular and ecclesiastical political leadership that emerged in the crucial half-century after the year 1000. Both describe the cultural environments that could put legitimate power into the hands of the high nobility and both explore some of the connections between this noble power and royal and ecclesiastical power. Clearly, religious history and the history of the Church cannot be divorced from the "general" political history of the Middle Ages.

Both Schlesinger and Lemarignier are primarily concerned with the highest ranks of the nobility: those who in the early Middle Ages were on their way to becoming kings, those who formed the "imperial aristocracy" under the Carolingians, and those who later became the heads of independent or quasi-independent principalities.

One of the major achievements of medieval scholarship since 1945 has also been the investigation of the lower nobility that began to emerge in the late stages of Carolingian disintegration. The dispersed nature of the sources, the differences in the rate at which various parts of Europe developed, and regional peculiarities in the way they developed—the typical problems encountered in any study of medieval institutions—have forced this research to be regional, rather than country-wide or European-wide. The selections by Georges Duby and Joshua Prawer are two examples of these local case studies, the former dealing with Burgundy, which some have called the "heartland" of feudalism, the latter with the Latin Kingdom of Jerusalem, the prime medieval example of an exported "colonial" society. These authors have done much to clarify the stages by which the lower nobility emerged and the precise role played by fief-holding and vassalage in the relations of the members of this new class to one another and to their social superiors. Both studies suggest that the importance of fief-holding and vassalage in shaping society was quite variable; that their importance depended upon political circumstances and upon the personal wealth, values, and ideas of the people involved.

These studies moreover show that the importance of fief and vassalage changed with time and varied widely from one level of the aristocracy to another. Only when we have such local studies for much of Europe will we know the extent to which fief-holding and vassalage truly shaped medieval society. Meanwhile, these essays provide a needed corrective to overhasty generalizations. The article by Léopold Genicot is a synthesis of the results of recent research on this question.

By thus focusing attention on the origins of the noble class, the sources of its power, and the forms of personal relationships that structured it, Schlesinger, Lemarignier, Genicot, Duby, and Prawer have, in effect, asked a different set of questions from those raised by earlier generations of medievalists. Their research makes it clear that, within this class, possession of a fief might be a major factor in determining an individual's power or it might be no factor at all; similarly, vassalage might exert a major influence over a man's behavior, a minor influence, or none at all, depending upon the individual, the period, and the place.

Fief-holding and vassalage did not by themselves shape medieval society. Yet dominion and dependence, command and obedience, fellowship and service—relationships that traditionally have been explained in terms of vassalage—still permeated it. How might these relationships be explained?

One way to do so would be in terms of the attitudes, values (including the values associated with vassalage), and desires of the people involved; in terms of the ideas their culture made available to them; that is, in terms of the "social psychology" of medieval men. Here we are in both novel and difficult territory. For what is involved is neither biography nor history told in terms of great men. Our concern is with institutions and thus with the habitual ways in which medieval men acted. Our concern is with the ideas and attitudes of the various groups that composed medieval society. The methodology this involves, especially the use of literature as a source for institutional history, still has to be worked out. The selections by Georges Duby, Adalbert Dessau, Arno Borst, and Maurice Keen, grouped here under the heading The Aristocratic Mind, are recent studies on this theme, in which the authors explore both the way in which social conditions formed concepts of loyalty, obedience, service, and knighthood and the way these concepts formed the nobility's response to their society.

The way noblemen behaved and their relations to one another, to their superiors, and to their subordinates were shaped by the many changing parts of a cultural kaleidoscope. What the historian must thus attempt to grasp, as precisely as possible, are the steps by which that culture altered its shape and, simultaneously, changed the way men behaved. He must fix the lines of the complex matrix formed by human institutions and their cultural environment.

This is true when studying any period of time, but it is particularly applicable to the late Middle Ages; for in this period society was becoming more fluid. Europe was shaken by plague, by repeated famine and continued warfare; governments were making new, and ever greater, demands on their subjects. Notions of nobility, service, chivalry, and fidelity reacted to all these events. Yet the institutional history of the period is all too often summed up by the simple assertion that feudalism was "dead" or "dying," and that monarchy was "rising." Such an assertion is ultimately based on the assumptions that fief-holding and vassalage determined the political behavior of the nobility from the tenth to the thirteenth century and that after 1300 fief-holding and vassalage were in some sense replaced by the king's command and by the action of his officials. But if fief-holding and vassalage are put in their proper historical place, the changes taking place in later medieval society become more complicated than feudalism's premature obituary would suggest. The articles by Eduard Perroy and J. R. Major, as well as the selection from William H. Dunham, Jr. explore various aspects of this problem in France and England.

In comparison with the modern nation-state or the Roman Empire, medieval "political" institutions were highly fragmented. This contention, it is fair to say, runs through almost all the selections collected under the title Lordship and Nobility. It would be a gross error, however, to consider medieval society either a fragmented or an anarchic one, to imagine that it was held together simply by contracts between otherwise isolated individuals or by the exertion of force, or threats of force, by those above on those below. Medieval society actually contained an enormous variety of "solidarity groupings"—permanent groups that consciously engaged in common activity—from the family, the village, and the town quarter on the smallest scale, to the "community of the realm" on the largest. The nature and history of this development, especially on a scale smaller than the kingdom, have only recently become the subject of historical investigation. The selections under the general title Community are a sampling of some of this research.

In his article on ruler and ruled in medieval Germany, Bosl suggests the general nature of medieval communities. Almost every lordship, whether exercised by the head of a household or a village or by the territorial prince or the king, had a community as its counterpart. Ties of vassalage also formed a community: the "solidarity" of lord and knights, the Flemish *potentia* discussed in the selection by Jan Dhondt. These communities were much more than a mere grouping of those subject to a common lord. As the articles by Helen Cam on the *vill* and by Pierre Duparc on the confraternities show, they had a very powerful autonomous life of their own.

The forms such communities took were as diverse as their processes of development. Many questions about them are still far from settled.

How old was the basic village community and its institutions? To the extent that the village was identical with the parish, the conclusions of Gabriel Fournier's study run contrary to some accepted opinions; the institutions of the village may be less rigid and immemorial than is sometimes thought.[11] What was the connection between village institutions and lordship; village institutions and patterns of settlement; and, thus, between village institutions and the building of churches and castles? How did economic changes affect those institutions? (We have many studies of medieval cities, from this point of view, but very few of medieval villages.) How did the legal renaissance and the growth of centralizing powers affect them?

Diversity was probably the most outstanding characteristic of medieval society. Of this, the study of medieval communities leaves little doubt. Yet, despite their diversity, the various communities, from the village to the kingdom, often used the ideas that were Europe's common inheritance in strikingly similar ways. Christianity and the remains of classical learning reached everywhere, touching the poor and illiterate, as well as kings and prelates. To villagers, these two influences eventually provided the lever for prying a modicum of independence from their lords. To the inhabitants of the fast-growing towns, they provided the "civic spirit" whose origins and influence Hans Baron describes—a justification for a life that was neither clerical nor knightly. To princes and kings, they provided maxims useful for justifying a novel and growing power. To the extent that Europe had a common culture—that it was the "Christian commonwealth"—it developed everywhere along common lines. The variety of sources and the variety of places where Antonio Marongiu has found "*quod omnes tangit . . .*" are but one example. The parallels between developments in the Latin Kingdom (described by Joshua Prawer) and developments in England at the other end of the European continent (discussed by Helen Cam) are yet another.

The historian may look at these communities in numerous ways. His imagination is his only limitation. Medieval men lived close to the soil, close to the elements. Their communities were shaped, first of all, by the land and the requirements it imposed. They were shaped also by religious attitudes and by the institution, the Church, that structured their religious life. They were shaped by moral values and economic drives and by the images men had of themselves as a community, whether it be one of village, city, province, or kingdom. In studying medieval communities, the historian can therefore look at the physical environment, the nature of the economy, the values and goals of the people, and the way they became conscious of themselves as a group. And this is only a beginning.

---

[11] See most recently, *Vorträge and Forschungen*, T. Mayer, ed. *7, 8* (Konstanz: Thorbeke, 1964).

There is no single set of conclusions to be drawn from the essays in this anthology. Different contexts will bring different themes to the fore. Nonetheless, these essays show that medieval society was too complex, too changing, for the historian to subsume it under one or two concepts, especially concepts drawn from nineteenth-century political or social philosophy. Diversity and change were the fundamental characteristics of medieval society, not rigidity or uniformity, and the historian's vocabulary must take this into account.

This is not to say that synthesis is impossible or wrong-headed. History should not be reduced to antiquarianism. However, to make an empirical generalization about the predominant characteristics of medieval society is not to define the essence of that society or the essence of feudalism. To be sure, there is a place for imaginative ideal-typical constructs, for "models" (to use the currently fashionable term), of which Otto Hintze gives one example; but they should be used as bench marks, as imaginative patterns to help empirical research uncover new relationships, new connections. They are not the end but a beginning to research. The same is true of empirical generalizations, such as those offered in the essay by Joseph R. Strayer, which mark only a stage in the continuing enterprise of scholarship.[12]

In his empirical investigation or synthetic description, the historian must now use terms that allow him to comprehend the fundamental diversity and fluidity that recent investigations have revealed in medieval society. His concepts should connect, rather than compartmentalize; rather than divide politics, economics, religion, and intellectual life into so many windowless tunnels, they should emphasize the continuity of social forms across many areas and many periods of activity. For institutions are habitual shared ways of acting, and the influences that shape such habits at any given moment include the entire culture. The task of the historian investigating institutions is not to define their essence, or to label one form as "true" or "classical" while shunting others into the shadows of "proto-" or "late," but to describe the various shapes these habitual ways of acting took and to search out the strands connecting them to the culture in which they were embedded.

---

12 Strayer himself has revised his views; see his most recent pamphlet, *Feudalism* (Princeton, N.J.: Van Nostrand, 1965).

FEUDALISM: TWO VIEWS AND A CRITIQUE

FEUDALISM IN WESTERN EUROPE*

Joseph R. Strayer

Feudalism, in Western European history, is a word which has been given many meanings,[1] but most of them can be brought into two general categories. One group of scholars uses the word to describe the technical arrangements by which vassals became dependents of lords, and landed property (with attached economic benefits) became organized as dependent tenures or fiefs. The other group of scholars uses feudalism as a general word which sums up the dominant forms of political and social organization during certain centuries of the Middle Ages.

There are difficulties with both usages. In the first category there is no agreement on the relationships which are to be considered typically feudal. Is it the act of becoming a vassal, or the act of granting a fief, or a combination of the two which makes feudalism? Retainers, clients, armed dependents of a great man—all these we have in both Germanic and Roman society from the fourth century on, but does that entitle us to speak of Late Roman or primitive German feudalism? Under Charlemagne there are vassals, and these vassals receive dependent tenures. Yet the king still keeps close control over all men and all lands, and the relationships of dependency are not necessarily hereditary. If this is feudalism, then we need another word to describe conditions in the eleventh century. In the seventeenth century, in both France and England all the technical forms of feudalism survive—most nobles are vassals and much of their land is held as fiefs. Yet it is only the form which has survived; the ideas which control the relationship of king and noble no

* Reprinted from *Feudalism in History* ed. by Rushton Coulborn, pp. 15–25, by permission of the Princeton University Press. Copyright 1956, by Princeton University Press.

longer conform to the feudal pattern. In short, the difficulty in concentrating on the technical aspects of feudalism is that it sets no chronological limits and provides no standards by which feudalism can be clearly distinguished from preceding and succeeding types of organization.

In the second category this difficulty is overcome by assuming at the outset that there is a "feudal age," a "feudal period" with definite chronological limits. The limits may vary, but there is general agreement on the core of the period—all authorities would admit that feudalism reached its height in the eleventh and twelfth centuries. But while this approach clears up the chronological confusion, it introduces a functional confusion by applying the feudal label to all social phenomena between the tenth and the thirteenth centuries. For example, the class structure of the late Middle Ages was very different from that of the early Middle Ages—are they both feudal? Lords used a different technique in exploiting their lands in 1200 from that in vogue in 1000—which technique should be accepted as typical of feudalism? We meet the sort of difficulties here that a modern historian would find if he assumed that the factory system were an integral part of democracy.

To obtain a usable concept of feudalism we must eliminate extraneous factors and aspects which are common to many types of society. Feudalism is not synonymous with aristocracy—there have been many aristocracies which were not feudal, and many lesser vassals would not have been considered members of the aristocracy in the early days of feudalism. Feudalism is not a necessary concomitant of the great estate worked by dependent or servile labor—such estates have existed in many other societies. Feudalism is not merely the relationship between lord and man, nor the system of dependent land tenures, for either can exist in a non-feudal society. The combination of personal and tenurial dependence brings us close to feudalism, but something is still lacking. It is only when rights of government (not mere political influence) are attached to lordship and fiefs that we can speak of fully developed feudalism in Western Europe. It is the possession of rights of government by feudal lords and the performance of most functions of government through feudal lords which clearly distinguishes feudalism from other types of organization.

This means that Western European feudalism is essentially political—it is a form of government. It is a form of government in which political authority is monopolized by a small group of military leaders, but is rather evenly distributed among members of the group. As a result, no leader rules a very wide territory, nor does he have complete authority even within a limited territory—he must share power with his equals and grant power to his subordinates. A fiction of unity—a theory of subordination or cooperation among feudal lords—exists, but government is actually effective only at the local level of the county or the lordship. It is the lords who maintain order, if they can, who hold courts and determine what is the law. The king, at best, can merely keep peace among the lords and usually is unable even to do this.

The men who possess political power also possess important sources of wealth—land and buildings, markets and mills, forests and rivers—and this wealth is naturally useful in maintaining or increasing their political authority. Yet wealth alone does not give political power—loyal vassals and courageous retainers are more important. Any sensible feudal lord will surrender much of his land in order to increase the number of his vassals, and the most powerful lords, such as the Duke of Normandy, actually possess relatively few estates. It is also true that political and economic rights do not always correspond. A lord may have rights of government where he has no land and may hold land where some other lord has superior political authority. No one finds this inconsistent, because the distinction which we have been making between political and economic rights has almost no meaning for the early Middle Ages. Public authority has become a private possession. Everyone expects the possessor of a court to make a profit out of it, and everyone knows that the eldest son of the court-holder will inherit this profitable right, whatever his qualifications for the work. On the other hand, any important accumulation of private property almost inevitably becomes burdened with public duties. The possessor of a great estate must defend it, police it, maintain roads and bridges and hold a court for his tenants. Thus lordship has both economic and political aspects; it is less than sovereignty, but more than private property.

Effective feudal government is local, and at the local level public authority has become a private possession. Yet in feudalism the concepts of central government and of public authority are never entirely lost. Kingship survives, with real prestige though attenuated power, and the Church never forgets the Roman traditions of strong monarchy and public law. The revival of Roman law in the twelfth century strengthens these traditions and by the thirteenth century most lawyers insist that all governmental authority is delegated by the king and that the king has a right to review all acts of feudal lords and, especially, their administration of justice.

Feudal lordship occupies an intermediate place between tribal leadership and aristocratic government. It differs from tribal leadership in being more formalized and less spontaneous. The feudal lord is not necessarily one of the group whom he rules; he may be a complete stranger who has acquired the lordship by inheritance or grant. It differs from aristocracy in being more individualistic and less centralized. The feudal lord is not merely one of a group of men who influence the government; he *is* the government in his own area. When feudalism is at its height, the barons never combine to rule jointly a wide territory but instead seek a maximum degree of independence from each other. One of the signs of the decay of feudalism in the West is the emergence of the idea of government by a *group* of aristocrats.

As the last paragraphs suggest, we must distinguish between an earlier and a later stage of Western feudalism. In the early stage feudalism was the dominant fact in politics, but there was almost no theoretical explanation or justification of the fact. In the later stage feudalism was competing with and slowly losing ground to other types of political organization, and many able writers tried to explain how and why it functioned. The great law-books of the thirteenth century—the Norman *Summa de Legibus,* Bracton, Beaumanoir—fit the facts of feudalism into a logical and well-organized system of law and government. Naturally most writers of secondary works have relied on these treatises and as a result the modern concept of feudalism is largely that of feudalism in the late twelfth and thirteenth centuries—a feudalism which was much better organized, much more precise, and much less important than that of the earlier period.

The first period of feudalism is best exemplified by the institutions of northern France about 1100. In northern France in the eleventh century the one basic institution was the small feudal state dominated by the local lord. He might bear any title (the ruler of Normandy was called at various times duke, count, or marquis) and he was usually, though not always, the vassal of a king. But whatever his title, whatever his nominal dependence on a superior, he was in fact the final authority in his region. No one could appeal from his decisions to a higher authority; no one could remain completely indifferent to his commands. His position was based on his military strength. He had a group of trained fighting men in his service; he held fortified strategic positions throughout his lands; he possessed sufficient economic resources to pay for both the army and the fortifications. There might be lesser lords within his sphere of influence who had accepted his leadership in order to gain protection or because his military power left them no choice but submission. Some of his retainers—not necessarily all—would have fiefs for which they rendered service, in which they had limited rights of government. Relations between the lord and these subordinates were still undefined. The exact amount of service to be rendered by the vassal, the rights of government which he could exercise, the degree to which these rights could be inherited by his descendants depended far more on the power and prestige of the lord than on any theory of law. It was up to the lord to defend his territory and his rights; if he failed he would either lose his lands to a stronger neighboring lord or to his more powerful subordinates. There could be great fluctuations in power and in amount of territory controlled, not merely from one generation to another, but even from one decade to another. The only thing which was relatively stable was the method of government. The customs of a region remained the same, even if the lordship changed hands, and every lord had to govern through and with his vassals. They formed the core of his army; the made up the court in which all important acts of government were performed; they performed most of the functions of local government in their fiefs.

The second stage of feudalism—the stage described by the great lawyers of the thirteenth century—bears a closer resemblance to the neat, pyramidal structure of the textbooks. The bonds of vassalage have been tightened at the upper and relaxed at the lower level; the ruler of a province now owes more obedience to his superior and receives less service from his inferiors. Early feudalism might be described as a series of overlapping spheres of influence, each centered around the castles of some strong local lord. Later feudalism is more like a series of holding corporations; the local lord still performs important functions but he can be directed and controlled by higher authority. Appeals from the local lord to his superior are encouraged; petty vassals are protected against excessive demands for service or attempts to seize their fiefs; the central government in some cases deals directly with rear-vassals instead of passing orders down a long chain of command. Royal law-courts play a great role in this reorganization. The institution of the assizes at the end of the twelfth century in England protected the rear-vassal and brought him into direct contact with the king. The development of appeals to the king's court at Paris gave the same results in thirteenth-century France. In this much more highly organized feudalism rights and duties are spelled out in great detail. The amount of service owed is carefully stated, rules of inheritance are determined, the rights of government which can be exercised by each lord are defined and regulated. Force is still important, but only the king and the greatest lords possess sufficient force to gain by its use; the ordinary lord has to accept judicial solutions to his controversies.

There is obviously a great difference between these two stages of feudalism, and yet the transition from one to the other was made so smoothly, in many places, that it was almost imperceptible. It is true that in the later stage rulers were aided by concepts which were not derived from early feudalism, such as the revived Roman law and the Church's ideas of Christian monarchy. Yet, giving due weight to these outside influences, there must still have been some principle of order and growth in early feudalism which made possible the rapid development of relatively advanced systems of political organization in the twelfth and thirteenth centuries. Early feudal society, turbulent as it was, was never pure anarchy. There was always some government, even if rudimentary and local; there were always some centers of refuge and defense. Early feudal government, primitive as it was, was still more sophisticated and complicated than tribal government. There was a higher degree of specialization—the fighting men and the men with rights of government were clearly marked off from the rest of the group. There was a little more artificiality in political organization. Feudal government was not (necessarily) part of the immemorial structure of the community; it could be imposed from the outside; it could be consciously altered by the lord and his vassals. Early feudalism was rough and crude, but it was neither stagnant nor sterile. Flexible and adaptable, it produced new institutions rapidly, perhaps more rapidly than more sophisticated systems of government.

To understand the real vitality of feudalism we shall have to consider briefly the circumstances in which it first appeared in Europe. The Roman Empire had collapsed in the West, largely because none of its subjects cared enough for it to make any great effort to defend it. The Germanic rulers who succeeded the Emperors were not hostile to Roman civilization. They preserved as much of it as they were able; they kept together as large political units as they could. They were not entirely successful in these efforts, but they did preserve real power for the central government and they did thwart the growth of independent local lordship. The greatest of the Germanic rulers, Charlemagne, even united a large part of Western Europe in a new Empire. This was a *tour de force* which has impressed men for over a thousand years; he made his bricks not only without straw but very nearly without clay. The Latin and Germanic peoples he united had no common political tradition, no common cultural tradition and very few economic ties. Their interests were predominantly local, as they had been for centuries; only the clergy remembered with longing the peace and good order of Rome. With the moral support of the Church and the physical support of the army of his own people, the Franks, Charlemagne held his Empire together, but it was always a shaky structure. The Church profited by its existence to extend the parish system and to improve the education of the higher clergy. These developments helped to soften some of the cultural differences among Western European peoples, and to lay the foundations for a common European civilization, but the forces of localism were still stronger than those which worked for unity. Local government was in the hands of counts, men of wealth and high social position who held their authority from the king but who were not always fully obedient to him. The counts, in turn, were not always able to dominate the great landowners of their districts. Vassalage was becoming common and something very like fiefs held of the king or of lords appeared about the middle of the eighth century. Charlemagne tried to reinforce the doubtful loyalty of local magnates by making the great men his vassals, but this expedient had only temporary success. The ties between the magnates and their retainers were far closer than those between Charlemagne and the magnates, for the retainers lived with their lords while the lords visited the imperial court only occasionally. As a result the magnates had great power in their own provinces, subject only to the intermittent intervention of the king. This was not yet feudalism: there was still public authority, and the great men held political power by delegation from the king and not in their own right. But it was very close to feudalism; a strong push was all that was needed to cross the line.

The push came in the fifty years which followed Charlemagne's death.

His heirs were less competent than he and quarreled among themselves. The magnates took advantage of these quarrels to gain independence; they began to consider their offices private possessions, to be inherited by their sons. Meanwhile invasions from outside threatened the security of all inhabitants of the Empire. The Saracens raided the south coast of France, the west coast of Italy, and even established a permanent fort at Garde-Frainet which interfered seriously with overland travel between France and Italy. The Magyars occupied Hungary, and from this base sent great cavalry expeditions through southern Germany, eastern France and northern Italy. Worst of all were the Northmen. For over a century their shallow-draft ships pushed up all the rivers of northern Europe and sent out raiding parties which plundered the countryside. The central government was almost helpless; it could not station troops everywhere on the vast periphery of the Empire and it could seldom assemble and move an army quickly enough to catch the fast-moving raiders. Defense had to become a local responsibility; only the local lord and his castle could provide any security for most subjects of the Empire.

It was in these conditions that feudal governments began to appear in northern France—a region which had suffered heavily from both civil war and viking raids. We could hardly expect these early feudal governments to be well organized and efficient—they were improvised to meet a desperate situation and they bore all the signs of hasty construction. But they did have two great advantages which made them capable of further development. In the first place, feudalism forced men who had privileges to assume responsibility. In the late Roman Empire, the Frankish kingdom, and the Carolingian monarchy wealthy landlords had assisted the central government as little as possible while using their position and influence to gain special advantages for themselves. Now they had to carry the whole load; if they shirked they lost everything. In the second place, feudalism simplified the structure of government to a point where it corresponded to existing social and economic conditions. For centuries rulers had been striving to preserve something of the Roman political system, at the very least to maintain their authority over relatively large areas through a hierarchy of appointed officials. These efforts had met little response from the great majority of people; large-scale government had given them few benefits and had forced them to carry heavy burdens. Always there had been a dangerous discrepancy between the wide interests of the rulers and the narrow, local interests of the ruled. Feudalism relieved this strain; it worked at a level which was comprehensible to the ordinary man and it made only minimum demands on him. It is probably true that early feudal governments did less than they should, but this was better than doing more than was wanted. When the abler feudal lords began to improve their governments they had the support of their people who realized that new institutions were needed. The active demand for more and better government in the twelfth century offers a sharp contrast to the apathy with which the people of Western Europe watched the disintegration of the Roman and the Carolingian Empires.

Feudalism, in short, made a fairly clean sweep of obsolete institutions and replaced them with a rudimentary government which could be used as a basis for a fresh start. Early feudal government was informal and flexible. Contrary to common opinion, it was at first little bound by tradition. It is true that it followed local custom, but there were few written records, and oral tradition was neither very accurate nor very stable. Custom changed rapidly when circumstances changed; innovations were quickly accepted if they seemed to promise greater security. Important decisions were made by the lord and his vassals, meeting in informal councils which followed no strict rules of procedure. It was easy for an energetic lord to make experiments in government; for example, there was constant tinkering with the procedure of feudal courts in the eleventh and twelth centuries in order to find better methods of proof. Temporary committees could be set up to do specific jobs; if they did their work well they might become permanent and form the nucleus of a department of government. It is true that many useful ideas came from the clergy, rather than from lay vassals, but if feudal governments had not been adaptable they could not have profited from the learning and skill of the clergy.

Feudalism produced its best results only in regions where it became the dominant form of government. France, for example, developed her first adequate governments in the feudal principalities of the north, Flanders, Normandy, Anjou and the king's own lordship of the Ile de France. The first great increase in the power of the French king came from enforcing his rights as feudal superior against his vassals. Many institutions of the French monarchy of the thirteenth century had already been tested in the feudal states of the late twelfth century; others grew out of the king's feudal court. By allowing newly annexed provinces to keep the laws and institutions developed in the feudal period, the king of France was able to unite the country with a minimum of ill-will. France later paid a high price for this provincial particularism, but the existence of local governments which could operate with little supervision immensely simplified the first stages of unification.

England in many ways was more like a single French province than the congeries of provinces which made up the kingdom of France. In fact, the first kings after the Conquest sometimes spoke of the kingdom as their "honor" or fief, just as a feudal lord might speak of his holding. As this example shows, England was thoroughly feudalized after the Conquest. While Anglo-Saxon law remained officially in force it became archaic and inapplicable; the law which grew into the common law of England was the law applied in the king's feudal court. The chief departments of the English government likewise grew out of this court. And when the combination of able kings and efficient institutions made the monarchy too strong, it was checked by the barons in the name of the feudal principles expressed in Magna Carta. Thus feudalism helped England to strike a happy balance between government which was too weak and government which was too strong.

The story was quite different in countries in which older political institutions prevented feudalism from reaching full development. Feudalism grew only slowly in Germany; it never included all fighting men or all lands. The German kings did not use feudalism as the chief support of their government; instead they relied on institutions inherited from the Carolingian period. This meant that the ruler acted as if local lords were still his officials and as if local courts were still under his control. In case of opposition, he turned to bishops and abbots for financial and military aid, instead of calling on his vassals. There was just enough vitality in this system to enable the king to interfere sporadically in political decisions all over Germany, and to prevent the growth of strong, feudal principalities. But while the German kings of the eleventh and twelfth centuries showed remarkable skill in using the old precedents, they failed to develop new institutions and ideas. Royal government became weaker, and Germany more disunited in every succeeding century. The most important provincial rulers, the dukes, were also unable to create effective governments. The kings were jealous of their power, and succeeding in destroying, or weakening all the great duchies. The kings, however, were unable to profit from their success, because of their own lack of adequate institutions. Power eventually passed to rulers of the smaller principalities, not always by feudal arrangements, and only after the monarchy had been further weakened by a long conflict with the papacy. Thus the German kings of the later Middle Ages were unable to imitate the king of France, who had united his country through the use of his position as feudal superior. Germany remained disunited, and, on the whole, badly governed, throughout the rest of the Middle Ages and the early modern period.

Italy also suffered from competition among different types of government. The German emperor was traditionally king of (north) Italy. He could not govern this region effectively but he did intervene often enough to prevent the growth of large, native principalities. The Italian towns had never become depopulated, like those of the North, and the great economic revival of the late eleventh century made them wealthy and powerful. They were too strong to be fully controlled by any outside ruler, whether king or feudal lord, and too weak (at least in the early Middle Ages) to annex the rural districts outside their walls. The situation was further complicated by the existence of the papacy at Rome. The popes were usually on bad terms with the German emperors and wanted to rule directly a large part of central Italy. In defending themselves and their policies they encouraged the towns' claims to independence and opposed all efforts to unite the peninsula. Thus, while there was fedualism in Italy, it never had a clear field and was unable to develop as it did in France or England. Italy became more and more disunited; by the end of the Middle Ages the city-state, ruled by a "tyrant," was the dominant form of government in the peninsula. There was no justification for this type of government in medieval political theory, and this may be one reason why the Italians turned with such eagerness to the writings of the classical period. In any case, the Italian political system was a failure, and Italy was controlled by foreign states from the middle of the sixteenth to the middle of the nineteenth century.

There are certainly other factors, besides feudalism, which enabled France and England to set the pattern for political organization in Europe, and other weaknesses, besides the absence of fully developed feudalism, which condemned Germany and Italy to political sterility. At the same time, the basic institutions of France and England in the thirteenth century, which grew out of feudal customs, proved adaptable to changed conditions, while the basic institutions of Italy and Germany, which were largely non-feudal, had less vitality. Western feudalism was far from being an efficient form of government, but its very imperfections encouraged the experiments which kept it from being a stagnant form of government. It was far from being a just form of government, but the emphasis on personal relationships made it a source of persistent loyalties. And it was the flexibility of their institutions and the loyalty of their subjects which enabled the kings of the West to create the first modern states.

NOTES

1. Pollock and Maitland, *History of English Law,* 2nd edn. (Cambridge, 1923), I, 66–67: ". . . *feudalism* is an unfortunate word. In the first place it draws our attention to but one element in a complex state of society and that element is not the most distinctive: it draws our attention only to the prevalence of dependent and derivative land tenure. This however may well exist in an age which can not be called feudal in any tolerable sense. What is characteristic of 'the feudal period' is not the releationship between letter and hirer, or lender and borrower of land, but the relationship between lord and vassal, or rather it is the union of these two relationships. Were we free to invent new terms, we might find *feudo-vassalism* more serviceable than *feudalism*. But the difficulty is not one which could be solved by any merely verbal devices. The impossible task that has been set before the word *feudalism* is that of making a single idea represent a very large piece of the world's history, represent the France, Italy, Germany, England, of every century from the eighth or ninth to the fourteenth or fifteenth. Shall we say that French feudalism reached its zenith under Louis d'Outre-Mer or under Saint Louis, that William of Normandy introduced feudalism into England or saved England from feudalism, that Bracton is the greatest of English feudists or that he never misses an opportunity of showing a strong anti-feudal bias? It would be possible to maintain all or any of these opinions, so vague is our use of the term in question."

THE NATURE OF FEUDALISM*

Otto Hintze

The following observations spring from the need to understand a problem of historical terminology that contains within itself a problem of historical facts. They are concerned with the concept of "feudalism," which so often is given a vacillating and ambiguous meaning and which so badly needs to be clarified. Long research in the sources has established the facts about the institutional history of the Frankish kingdoms and their successor states, from which this concept has been taken; but its meaning is still subject to dispute, and even Georg von Below's fundamental work[1] has not eliminated wide discussion. People speak of feudalism occurring in countries like Poland and Russia, ancient Egypt and ancient China, India, Turkey, and Japan. Many historians and sociologists often start with the assumption that feudalism is a stage in the historical development of institutions, through which every state and every people must once have passed, whether the present-day historian can find evidence of this stage or not. Others, such as Von Below, have been inclined to restrict feudalism to the Germanic-Roman world and to doubt the need for a comparative study that would point out its existence elsewhere. Caution and critical prudence are certainly very much in order, but we do not get very far by limiting feudalism to the Frankish kingdoms and the German Middle Ages. Whoever wants to engage in universal constitutional history must face the question whether, and on what grounds, the term "feudalism" or "feudal state" can justifiably be applied to other

* From Otto Hintze, "Wesen und Verbreitung des Feudalismus," *Sitzungsberichte der Preussischen Akademie der Wissenschaften, phil.-hist. Klasse,* **20** (Berlin, Jahrgang 1929), 321–330. (Reprinted in Otto Hintze, *Staat und Verfassung* (2d ed.; Göttingen: Vandenhoeck und Ruprecht, 1962), 84–95. Trans. by the ed.

people and other cultures. The following essay will seek to answer this question.[2]

If it were possible to give a conceptual definition of "feudalism," all this debate would be unnecessary. But it is impossible to grasp the complicated circumstances of historical life, so laden with unique occurrences, in a few universal and unambiguous concepts—as is done in the natural sciences. We must turn rather to intuitive abstractions, to the creation of Ideal Types, for such types underlie our scholarly terminology. I can therefore do nothing better than, first of all, to describe the Ideal Type that underlies our concept of feudalism. This Ideal Type must naturally be based upon the individual historical phenomenon from which the name has been taken; that is, on the feudal institutions of the Frankish kingdom and its successor and neighbor states, the area inhabited by the Germanic and Romance peoples during the Middle Ages. But naturally, we must do more than simply describe an individual case. We can either define a static essence, a closed, interrelated system of institutions—this then becomes the type of fully "feudal state". Or we can conceive the Ideal Type dynamically, functionally, as a more or less autonomously operating tendency, as a representative principle of state and Estate formation—this is closer to what is commonly meant by "feudalism." In my opinion, the proper thing to do is to combine these two ways of comprehending the phenomenon, a move made easier by the fact that they do not oppose each other but, rather, are complementary.

I must preface my search for an ideal-typical conceptualization of Roman-Germanic feudalism with a short criticism of Von Below's interpretation, for though he has clarified the problem with acuteness and depth, his views on several important points must be opposed. Von Below interprets feudalism—which he distinguishes, as a broad concept, from the narrow concept of "the feudal system" proper (*Lehnswesen*)—as a political and institutional development by which the wealthy "mediatized" the subjects of the state and thus brought them under their private authority. In my opinion, this is too narrow. For military, as well as social and economic functions are comprehended in the term "feudalism"; feudalism is a principle of military institutions and of economic and social institutions. Otherwise, it would be applicable to the German Empire alone. And even German constitutional development remains fundamentally incomprehensible if one proceeds from Von Below's presupposition that the Frankish and German kingdom was originally a true state in the sense of a civil association of subjects (*staatsbürgerliche Untertanenverband*) with an institutional character (*Anstaltscharakter*) and legal personality. A state that is divided up like the Frankish kingdom, whose supreme power is transformed like that of the medieval German kingdom, cannot possibly be comprehended as an "institution" (*Anstalt*) with legal personality. From the beginning it had a patrimonial character, even if Von

Below most decisively rejects this description. Feudal degeneration was not the first to denature, or rather overturn, the kingdom; the whole feudal development is understandable only on the supposition that the Frankish kingdom was not a true state in Von Below's sense, but something essentially different.

In the Frankish kingdom and the German kingdom that grew from it, feudalism did not yet exist, but these kingdoms prepared the ground for feudalism's growth. Their nature, I think, can be characterized by the following three traits, which are already suggested in the *Admonitio ad omnes regni ordines* (823/825) of Louis the Pious:[3]

1. A particularistic tendency, appearing as a premonition of the future constitution of Imperial Estates. It did not result from planned decentralization, but rather from an incomplete integration of the diverse constituents of the kingdom into a complete state. As a result, what remained from the old tribal constitution, with its particularistic, federalistic spirit, carried great weight. This particularistic tendency revealed itself especially in the way state power was divided between the king and the individual men of authority. It was divided in a way that is foreign to the modern state but was typical of the feudal: not according to the functions of state power (as in the modern state), but according to the physical things over which that power was exercised—over land and people. The constituent parts of the kingdom with their authorities at the summit did not form a unified centralized state, but rather a "put-together state," a simple personal union under the king, whose "person" alone held the whole together.

2. The predominance of the personal over the institutional in the exercise of dominion. Underneath this lay the Germanic conception of lordship as the personal right of a lord as member of a clan gifted with an inherited charisma. Max Weber sought to explain feudalism as above all the result of what he called "charismatic dominion" becoming everyday (*Veralltaglichung*). This is a very fruitful point of view, but must be enlarged upon—as will be done later in the essay. I see feudalism as above all a system of personal means of lordship which offered itself as a way to rule a vast kingdom in a time of a predominantly natural economy and little developed commerce, a system brought about by the lack of rational institutional arrangements. Under these conditions, the king used his personal lordship most efficaciously in connection with his power as household lord and as lord of a landed domain. This led to the reification (*Verdinglichung*) of dominion, instead of to its objectification as in the modern state. This reification typifies the traditional, patrimonial state, while objectification typifies the rational, institutional state. The administration of the former remains extensive; that of the latter shapes itself more and more intensively, a development that leads to the rationalization of the state. This predisposition explains that peculiar division of state power according to the things over which power is exercised, following the *partes*

regni instead of its functions; one is thought of patrimonially and traditionally, the other rationally and institutionally. Connected to this is a lack of a sharp distinction between public and private law.

3. A hierarchical trait, resting on the tight bonds that tied state and Church together, without any fixed boundaries between spiritual and temporal powers. After the Cluniac reform carried the day, the state was fitted into place in the hierarchic system of the Church; its order presupposed that all dominion came from God and that those who governed on the various levels of society held their power only as a grant of God. This concept is directly contrary to the idea of the sovereign state, which rests on the principle that state power comes either from the people or from him who governs, that the state has exclusive rules within its boundaries and is independent outside its boundaries. This hierarchic characteristic culminated in the theory of supreme papal rule over all Christianity.

The Roman and Germanic culture on which the Frankish state rested explains all these traits. Whatever was institutional in this state was predominantly of Roman origin. The personal character of political lordship and means of rule were above all Germanic. And it was this personal character of lordship that, under the circumstances, led to feudalism. A brief history of the Frankish institution of countship will clarify this.

The entire administrative organization of the Frankish kingdom leaned on the model of the Roman Empire and on the Church that the Roman Empire had influenced. Initially, the counts received a written grant of office following Roman formulas (this we know from Marculf and Cassiodorus). But the spirit of ancient administration was not handed over with the document. What survived and moved through these forms was first a charismatic mission. The initial character of the count's office, as a commission whose holder served only at the king's will, proves this. (Charismatic mission is, in any case, the deepest root of rule by commission.) When charismatic lordship became everyday, the counts began trying to assure their personal position. They sought, and were granted, the right to hold their offices for life; they were guaranteed against arbitrary deposition; here and there they made their offices hereditary. In time, this led to such confusion (under the Merovingians) that the Carolingians could find nothing to do but create personal ties; as a rule, the office of count was given only to those who became the Carolingians' vassals. Thus, the office became a fief, and the step was taken that would later lead to territorial principalities.

This example shows how the Frankish office organization interwove its antique inheritance with the personal impulse to power willed it by the Germanic tribal states and their leadership. The feudal system was a technique of personal lordship that sought to make effective an institution inherited from the spirit of the Roman bureaucratic state.

Roman-Germanic feudalism must be considered as much from the standpoint of the Roman Empire as from that of the Germanic tribal state. From the point of view of the Roman Empire, it appears as a continuation of the process of dissolution of political and military institutions that had begun in the third century, the collapse into a natural economy, the creation of landed lordships and *coloni,* the enrollment of foreign mercenaries, and private armies in the hands of great landowners. From the point of view of the tribal state, it appears as a mid-point in the transformation of crude and youthful warrior tribes from a weak tribal and clan constitution into a strong state and social order; for the tribes, once they were fully and definitively settled, were inclined with a certain regularity to establish such states.

This mid-point may be characterized by three typical transformations that changed military institutions, economic and social institutions, and political institutions. I use these three factors in place of the distinction Von Below makes between the "feudal system" and "feudalism." We must now take a brief look at these transformations.

1. Those subject to the ancient Frankish war duty were displaced by a new, professional fighting class composed of highly trained, mounted, individual fighters who answered the strategic needs of contemporary warfare, particularly at the time of the Saracen invasion. This fighting class was maintained by a typical form of private contract, which necessarily contained both a personal and a real legal relationship—vassalage and the benefice.

Vassalage was a transformation of the ancient Germanic free retinue, under the influence of the originally unfree, servant relationship of the Gallo-Roman *vassi* and private soldiers. By the eighth century, vassalage was used as a noble relationship of military service, founded on mutual fidelity; the vassal received the lord's protection and was guaranteed economic support appropriate to his position either as member of his lord's household or as usufructuary of land the lord had granted to him. This land, over which the vassal did not have full proprietary rights, was called a *"beneficium,"* or, in popular speech, *"feudum"* (from the Frankish **fĕhu-ôd* [cattle-owned].[4] The person who held the *feudum* owned only the chattel on the property, not the property itself. From this kind of land grant, the entire institution took its name, though it was only an external trait and in no way revealed the profound social processes peculiar to the entire institution. The name, however, gives us a glimpse at the sociohistorical relationships from which feudalism grew. It points back to a time when the chief use of a piece of land was for pasturing cattle rather than for agriculture. It is thus older than the allod, its conceptual opposite, and older than the full private ownership on which both the true peasant agricultural economy and the manorial institutions of the village rested. It thus goes back to the time when clan ownership was disintegrating. It served, like the Roman *precarium,* as a model for the *beneficium.*

In the Frankish kingdom, not only the king had vassals, but originally, many great lords had them as well. These military professionals were held on a purely private basis, and the use of vassalage for state purposes by Charles Martel was, in a certain sense, an attempt to bring these private military enterprises within the state (*Verstaatlichung*). Middlemen were thus unavoidable. From this came subinfeudation and the whole feudal hierarchy. The feudal system was a reordering of the entire set of military institutions—a reordering that the kingdom's expansion, the predominance of a natural economy, and the Moslem threat to routes and commerce had made a pressing political necessity.

Vassalage also went back to the time when the family as a protective group was disintegrating, for the vassal in fact renounced the protection of his family when he entered a lord's household retinue. The functions of the clan were disappearing; those of the lord of the household were growing. From the legal viewpoint the feudal relationship was a contract, but a contract of a peculiar kind; it was a contract that created a new status. It was important for Frankish and all Roman-Germanic feudalism that this status did not annul that of a free man; it enhanced it. Thus, the social value attached to knighthood turned the servants known in Germany as *"ministeriales"* (who had their French counterparts in those people performing liege homage)[5] from unfree servants into the social equals of free noble vassals. The knightly calling and the knightly way of life was what gave social rank; no longer was it conferred simply by free or unfree birth.

2. With the knight, the peasant (the free Germanic peasant, in contrast to the Roman *colonus*) first appeared. The peasant, no longer a simple cattle breeder, but a man involved in settled agriculture, became one with his soil. He became indispensable and, thus, economically unprofitable for regular military service. With few exceptions, he was weaned away from military practices; he became unwarlike and, in these troubled times, needed someone else's protection. With the collapse of clan institutions—which had given their members the necessary protection, and support, had avenged injuries, and had also provided security to the public authorities for their members' good behavior and the performance of public duties—a need arose for new communal groupings on the one hand, and for the protection of a powerful lord on the other. The village community did not guarantee protection. Many free peasants thus gave themselves, by an act of commendation, to the protection and command of a powerful lord, who often took over their land and became their landlord. Sometimes the peasants were forced into such acts by necessity. The lords who gave protection were usually ecclesiastical rulers, but temporal lords, especially those who possessed supreme powers (*obrigkeitliche Gewalt*), did so too. Thus, the peasant became subject to a landed lord; his status approached that of the Roman *colonus*. He finally fused with the

latter, becoming attached to the land in one of the age's infinitely gradated ways. We need not go into the details here. The important point is that a deep chasm opened up between a knightly military class and a more and more dependent peasant class; the knight was a landlord and the peasant, more and more, was the subject of either a knight or a sanctuary.

From then on, lordship over the land was the economic basis of the privileged classes. The knight could not live and work as a peasant; his fief was a small estate of at least four to six *mansi*,[6] whose exploitation was assured by dependent people. Thus, lordship over the land was not a product of feudalism. It already existed in Roman Gaul. But it spread to Germany along with feudalism, where the collapse of clan institutions and their transformation into village communities had prepared the ground. Lordship over the land developed next to the village community without absorbing it. Lordship over land was what was new, however; and it was the characteristic economic and social institution of feudalism. The picture *Domesday Book* gives of the structure of the English countryside in the eleventh century—an entire country divided into manors—is surely an artistic simplification on the part of the commissioners charged with drawing up this land and tax survey, a simplification of what in reality were very complicated relationships. But precisely because of its schematic nature, it is especially significant for an ideal-typical construction—as much so as the French schematic statement that a third of the land belonged to the king's domain, a third to the Church, and a third to the nobility, or the legal cliché, *"nulle terre sans seigneur"* [no land without its lord]. These statements do not entirely match reality, but they allow the fundamental Ideal Type to shine through.

For the Middle Ages, the landlord-peasant economy had the same significance as capitalism has for modern times. It formed the economic side of feudalism and was its most tenacious and enduring component. It lasted until the French Revolution and beyond. In its earlier stages (up to the twelfth century), it appeared in the form of a domain worked by those who owed labor service combined with small dependent peasant exploitations, as in the Carolingian *villa* [large estate]; later, after the abolition of the lord's direct domain, it took the form of sharecropping arrangements or leasehold. The landlord more and more became a simple collector of unearned rents. Finally, at the end of the fifteenth century, a new form of landed economic organization appeared in many areas, especially in eastern Germany and Poland: a form of agricultural management that might be called early agrarian capitalism.

3. A further important point is the way the lords of the land, particularly the knights, made rights of dominion their own, whether they received them as direct grants from the king (as fiefs or as security), or usurped them and then had them recognized either by later privileges or by tacit acceptance. The principal source was the immunity which, along

with landed lordship, was part of the Gallo-Roman inheritance and had nothing to do with the actual granting of fiefs. The old Frankish immunity remained within the bounds of a form of landed lordship; it founded mainly a patrimonial court and dominion. But then the offices of count became heritable fiefs, and, especially in tenth-century Germany, rights of dominion were granted to an increasing degree to ecclesiastical and temporal lords. Many court districts, many counties, were turned into private possessions by means of immunities. Whoever acquired high justice made himself a statelike power and, in so doing, enhanced his own status. In France he became a *seigneur haut justicier* [a "lord possessing rights of high justice"]; in Germany, a prince. The new princely class in the German empire after about 1180 was founded, not on office, but on feudal law. The members of this new class attempted to form states within a state.

With this, we have arrived in the area of political feudalism. Here, developments in the different states within the lands of the Germanic and Romance peoples and in different periods are so dissimilar that it is hardly possible to find a common way to express their peculiarity and the single aspect that distinguishes them from the modern state. The Ideal Type is most sharply marked where, as in Germany and predominantly in France, offices became fiefs. Here we grasp that "leakage" of subjects away from the state which Von Below sees as the particular essence of feudalism. The positive side of the development is more important, for we can see in it a tendency to form new states on a narrower basis and with more intensive forms of administration. This is the peculiar fundamental tendency of political feudalism. In Germany, it led to miniscule states and, finally, to a formal federalism; in France, to provincial regionalism, falsely tagged "federalism" during the Revolution. Only in England can one properly speak of "decentralization," given the stringent Norman centralization of the kingdom. The term would be false if applied elsewhere, for this tendency was much more the result of an incomplete integration of personal and corporative privileges into a unified state, which did not yet rest on a universal and common civil law. There is no more appropriate name than "political feudalism" for this loose structure of the state—more an exterior linking than an inner mixing of the various parts. Its essential trait remained the division of state power between head and members according to the physical things over which power was wielded (over land and people), rather than division according to its functions. It was frequently bound up with an institution of Estates, which were as much a support as a limitation on the monarchy. In England, monarchical absolutism existed before Magna Carta, and feudal parliamentary government existed during the "Lancastrian experiment" of the fifteenth century. Dynastic interests thoroughly dominated political feudalism. The household power or the domain was the special basis of state control. Among the personnel who staffed the "administration," the clerical Estate, who played a large role especially in the chancery, far outweighed the knightly nobility. This feudal class, together with the clergy, ran the state. Political feudalism may thus be considered as much a preparation for military absolutism as for the parliamentary government of a landed aristocracy.

These then were the three factors that together gave feudalism its total effect—we might even say, the three functions within which feudalism operated: (1) The military—the appearance as a separate group of a highly trained, professional, military class bound to a lord by fidelity, founded on private contract, who won for themselves a privileged position. (2) The social and economic—the development of a landlord-peasant form of economy assuring this privileged military class an unearned rental income. (3) The local position of these warrior noblemen as lords, and their predominant influence within the state (or even separation from it, to form their own)—within a state that was predisposed toward such influence because of its loose structure; because of the predominance of personal means of rule, rather than institutional; because of the tendency toward patrimonialism; and because of very close ties with the Church hierarchy.

If we glance over the history of the Germanic and Romance peoples, we will see that feudalism developed in three major stages, each of which was dominated by one of these characteristic factors. First, the period of early feudalism, in which the military factor predominated; this lasted until about the end of the twelfth century. Then the period of high feudalism, in which the warrior nobility brought its political influence to its highest point, in the form of particularistic separation from loose state structures, in the form of princely lordship (as in Germany), or in the formation—as counterweight to the monarchy—of corporate Estates within a tighter state structure (as in England). This period lasted until the sixteenth or seventeenth century. Third, a period of late feudalism, in which the predominant interest of the nobility was concentrated on maintaining and utilizing its members' economic and social position as lords of the land; this lasted until the French Revolution and until the old institutions involving the land disintegrated in the nineteenth century. The military function of feudalism was the first to disappear, with the appearance of mercenary troops and the standing army (in whose officers corps it long survived, however). Then the political functions disappeared, frequently under the color of Estates, in the period of absolutism and parliamentary government. Finally, the economic and social functions, the most tenacious of all, vanished under the impact of the principle of civil equality before the law and under the impact of capitalism.

NOTES

1. Georg von Below, *Der deutsche Staat des Mittelalters* (1914).

2. This translation includes only that part of the essay concerned with Western feudalism.—Ed.

3. *MGH Cap.* 1. 303.

4. Max Weber, *Wirtschaft und Gesellschaft,* **1,** 148 ff.

5. H. Pirenne, "Qu'est-ce qu'un homme lige?" *Bull. de l'Académie royale de Belgique, classe des lettres* (1909). New research has demonstrated that Pirenne's thesis of the ministerial origin of liege homage is not tenable. *See* in general Mitteis, *Lehnrecht und Saatsgewalt* (1933), 556 ff. The similarity between French and Norman liege homage and Germanic ministerial service is thus reduced to the tighter bonds between vassal and his own lord which strengthened the French monarchy and, in England, led to the political concept of allegiance. In Germany it benefited the spiritual and temporal territorial princes more than the emperor.

6. The amount of land sufficient—in theory—to support one household.—Ed.

FEUDALISM
The History of a Concept*

Otto Brunner

I

The historian who deals with the phonemenon called "feudalism" will normally turn, first of all, to books such as Marc Bloch, *La société féodale,*[1] François Ganshof, *Qu'est ce que la féodalité,*[2] or Heinrich Mitteis, *Lehnrecht und Staatsgewalt*[3] and *Staat des hohen Mittelalters.*[4] These books tell exactly what we ought to understand by "feudalism" and "feudal society." Although Bloch extends his discussion to include the relationship of the lord of the manor to his peasants, these authors largely agree with one another. The most precise description of the phenomenon appears to be Ganshof's. He concentrates on feudal law in its "technical," legal sense and consciously restricts himself only to the social structures it determined. These authors likewise agree on the chronological and geographical limits of their subject. To be sure, they deal with feudalism's preliminary stages and with its aftereffects in later periods, but they place their main emphasis on the period from about 900 to 1250, the "classical" period of the feudal system (*Lehnswesen*), the "feudal age." The feudal system developed in the territory between the Rhine and the Loire and spread out from there, changing and weakening in the process. It reached the border countries of Europe only in a weakened form, or not at all. In Poland and Hungary, countries to which a "feudal" character is often attributed, feudalism was unknown. Thus, it is not possible to equate feudalism—in this narrow sense—with the European Middle Ages, as is commonly done.

---

* Otto Brunner, "'Feudalismus'—Ein Beitrag zur Begriffsgeschichte," Akademie der Wissenschaften und der Literatur in Mainz, *Abhandlungen der geistes- und sozialwissenschaftlichen Klasse,* no. 10 (Mainz, 1958). Trans. by Miriam Sambursky; revised by the ed.

Can we guarantee a scholarly treatment of the subject simply by excluding such popular, prescientific, and nonscientific notions? Or do they consciously, or unconsciously, influence our scholarly approach? In fact, we already find in the books of Bloch, Ganshof, and Mitteis a more comprehensive idea of feudalism. For Mitteis, feudalism is a widespread phenomenon; he presents the "landed lordship" (*Grundherrschaft*) of late antiquity as an important example; the Frankish feudal system—feudalism in its more restricted sense—he regards as a special case of the general phenomenon of feudalism, which he defines in approximately the same way as Otto Hintze.[5] This is a most interesting methodological process. A concrete historical object is used to construct a fully developed, intuitive Ideal Type; this Ideal Type, through comparison with analogous phenomena, is then generalized to such an extent that in the end the original object that gave the Ideal Type its name appears as a special case. But it is precisely those characteristics that constitute the uniqueness and the historical function of this special case, that distinguish it from other "feudalisms." The specific meaning of Western feudalism cannot be made sufficiently precise by a general concept of feudalism.

Like Mitteis, Max Weber uses a general concept of feudalism. But among the many "forms called 'feudalism' " he singles out two "authentic forms": a feudalism involving fiefs (*Lehensfeudalismus*) and a feudalism involving benefices (*Pfrundenfeudalismus*).[6] "Fief-feudalism" (*Lehensfeudalismus*) is Western. The word "feudalism" by itself possesses a wider sense. The distinction Weber makes has proved very fruitful, even if one were to call the phenomenon he named "benefice-feudalism" by a different name.

Many other examples could be given. But those I have mentioned should suffice to show that, even in scholarly writings, we are dealing with a many-layered concept of "feudalism." This is necessarily so in all attempts at a comparative view. There are, thus, far-reaching differences of opinion about what may be considered to be feudalism and whether certain phenomena should be called "feudal."

Although the world of antiquity (or at least its classical period) is hardly ever characterized as "feudal," Ronald Syme calls Rome of the late Republican era a city-state in which "a feudal order of society still survived."[7] Others have seen landed lordship (*Grundherrschaft*), that is, local lordship over peasants within a larger political unit, as the prime characteristic of feudalism. Starting from here, nobility and feudalism could be equated in an even more indefinite way, especially at a time when the nobility had lost its ancient dominion. And so the word "feudal" survived in everyday language and in political journalism—especially that of the nineteenth century. Social groups composed of nobility or owners of landed property, that is, political leadership by the nobility or by landed proprietors, are "feudal." Its use indeed extends even to vague phrases about "feudal manners" or a "feudal way of life," expressions that parallel the *"zivil"* [inexpensive, "civil"] prices of a "bourgeois" restaurant; for in this vague sense, the opposite of "feudal" is "bourgeois" (*zivil*).[8] The real meaning of such opalescent terms, which belong to scholarship as well as to everyday life, can be determined only when we know against whom they were directed, for they were born in precise political situations.

Popular and journalistic usage has deeply influenced the language of scholarship.[9] Hintze, for example, speaks of a feudalism of great landlords surviving into the nineteenth century, at least in an economic and social sense.[10] And Maxime Leroy, in his *Histoire des idées sociale en France,* writes: "The revolution was an immense social revolution to the extent that it destroyed feudalism which in 1789 was nothing but an enormous landed domain."[11] "Feudalism" becomes a name for the world of lordship and nobility that went under in the great upheavals of the decades about 1800, but whose influence was felt for a long time after. Feudalism is distinguished from "bourgeois" society, the middle class, the industrial bureaucratic society of the nineteenth century; it is contrasted with "bourgeoisie" or "capitalism." Often, "feudal" is applied to any form of government not based on the principles of modern democracy.[12] And so, we must ask to what extent this basic situation affects the concept of feudalism as it is used in everyday language and in scholarly work.

The same is true of the contrast between "Estate" and "class," which is closely related to the contrast between "feudal" and "bourgeois." The extent to which this terminology is current, even today, can be seen in Heinz Markmann's analysis of the concept of Estate (which he rightly describes as "historically determined"): "The system of Estates which developed out of feudal, hierarchic-aristocratic structures and forms of government in the West during the early Middle Ages, was principally a system of rights and privileges that gave institutional definition to the social framework and regulated the flow of social processes along well-defined paths. Through the delegation of sovereign powers of an authoritative and legal-administrative nature, a hierarchically arranged group of vassals came into being. Through a process directly correlated to the decline of universal political power, they were transformed into the nobility who, supported by its *de facto* might, enforced its privileges."[13] In what follows, we shall discuss these concepts and shall show how they originated in the European situation about the year 1800.

Friedrich Ludwig von der Marwitz, who rightly or wrongly is known as a typical early nineteenth-century feudalist, described in his memoirs the ceremony in which the assembly of the Electorate of Brandenburg, the Estates, did homage to King Friedrich Wilhelm III on July 6, 1798—a classic act from the feudal world, in the sense of that word at that time. The citizens of Berlin assembled in the *Lustgarten;* the noble Estate, in the White Room of the Berlin Palace. The diplomatic corps was also invited. With them "the recently arrived ambassador of the French Republic [entered the hall], who was none other (says Marwitz) than the notorious Sieyès, a rabble-faced character with a black head (everyone was then still powdering his hair) and an enormous tricolor sash. A terrible omen of the time we experienced eight years later." We can well understand that "his appearance provoked great murmurings and nearly caused a fracas."[14]

Two completely contrasting worlds here physically confronted each other. The assembled *Junkers* obviously knew exactly who Emmanuel Sieyès was—the influential Revolutionary pamphleteer, the member of the Convention who had voted for the execution of Louis XVI. His pamphlet, *What Is the Third Estate?*, written in 1789 and republished in an even more antiaristocratic version in 1796,[15] had appeared the same year in a German translation. In Germany he was known as the most representative publicist of Revolutionary principles.[16] Had he not said, in the version of 1796: "In all countries the rabble belong to the aristocracy"? The Third Estate, so he had written, the sum total of bourgeoisie and peasantry subject to the royal administration and thus entitled to vote for the Estates-General, make up the nation. The nation is "a body of associates living under a common law [namely that of the state] and represented by the same legislature." The first two Estates (the clergy and the nobility) and especially the nobility, the "plenipotentiaries of feudalism," have privileges "which stand distinct from the rights of the great body of citizens. It [the noble Estate] does not belong to the common order, nor is it subject to the common law. Thus its civil rights already make it a people apart in a great nation"; so do its political rights. "The Third Estate contains everything pertaining to the nation; while nobody outside the Third Estate may be regarded as part of the nation." Freedom does not come from privilege, but from rights that are common to all.

The model of society on which this thesis rests is obvious: freedom is universal equality before the law of the state.[17] We can well understand the murmurings of the Brandenburg knights when the man who had so lucidly formulated these theories entered the room. However, the absolute state, especially Enlightened Absolutism, had already laid the foundations for the idea that the nation is the totality of those who are equal before the law. The great codifications of Enlightened Absolutism, so imbued with the spirit of modern natural law with its notions of the unalienable rights of man, were based on this idea. This was true in Prussia as well. The Civil Code, drafted by Karl Gottlieb Svarez, was enacted in 1794, after royal resistance and the Provincial Diet, alarmed by the French Revolution, had considerably diluted it.[18] Even so, the Code had been developed from a principle that would have led to the abolition of "privilege," were the principle taken to its logical conclusion. In it, the traditional structure of the Three Estates (nobility, towns, countrypeople) "had been rationalized into a system of professional obligations in the sense of a rational division of labor in the state."[19]

Sieyès had asked by what right the aristocrats could keep the people in subjugation. The only right the aristocracy could refer to was the right of conquest. If this were true, the Third Estate could meet force with force: "Why should it not repatriate to the Franconian forests all the families who wildly claim to descend from the race of the conquerors and to inherit their right of conquest?" "Could nobody reveal to [our fellow citizens] that it is at least as good to be descended from the Gauls and Romans as from the Sigambrians, Welch and other savages from the woods and swamps of ancient Germany?"[20]

These statements belong to a view of history that Sieyès did not invent. They first developed in the late sixteenth century during the controversies between the Estates and the monarchy.[21] Francis Hotmann in his *Franco-Gallia* (1573) was the first to claim that liberty—"the rights and liberties" the Estates were fighting for in their conflict with a monarchy striving toward absolutism—was derived from the Franks; liberty came from the Germanic forests (as Montesquieu later formulated it). To this, the protagonists of absolute monarchy opposed the thesis that the king derived from the *imperium Romanum* a legitimate rule over the Gallo-Roman people. The controversy became particularly lively in the last decades of the seventeenth century and the first half of the eighteenth.[22] The opposition that had fought the absolutism of Louis XIV after 1688 was an aristocratic opposition. But this aristocracy was not what it had once been. It had developed into a "corporation" distinct from the state.[23]

Legally it still was an *État,* an Estate. In the late Middle Ages and in early modern times, Estates were associations of local authorities, landlords, and city communes. In France, however, the royal bureaucracy had dissolved seignorial and communal rights. No longer did the Third Estate consist, as before, of the royal communes (*bonnes villes*); it included all the bourgeoisie and peasants who were directly subject to the king and his officers. Already in 1484 they could elect their representatives directly to the Estates of the *bailliages.* The same happened to clergy and nobility in the sixteenth century. Here are the origins of the corporate Estates, of a society composed of Estates.[24] This is particularly important. For the "feudal" society, the society of Estates, that existed in France before 1789—given its special form by the early and continual influence of the monarchy and its offices—was frequently the model for general interpretations of feudalism. Here was, indeed, a corporate estate, a "feudal society," distinct from the state. When the ambiguous concept of class was applied to this society, these classes were then seen to be determined, not (as elsewhere) by profession, property, or private dominion[25] originating in property or capital, but by rights of lordship now regarded as illegitimate "privileges."[26] These classes were legally organized as *États,* as Estates.

The concepts of "Estate" and "class" even today appear related to each other. Scholars explain them by pointing to their past connections or by contrasting them.[27] The society of Estates of the Old Regime, gradually changing into a class society, has clearly become a model. But this relationship of Estate to class was largely limited to Germany. For there the transformation into a class society was a much slower process and older forms that could be defined as "Estates" kept their influence for a longer time. One must thus be all the more careful not to equate the Estates within the bourgeois society of the nineteenth century, or the society of Estates of the Old Regime, with the political structures of earlier centuries, especially of the Middle Ages.

The Old Regime also gave rise to the concept of "feudalism." The word *"féodalité"* appeared only in the seventeenth century[28] and at first designated only the body of feudal law. It was a legal concept, not a political or a social one. *"Féodalité"* or *"gouvernement féodal"* [feudal government] in the sense of feudalism, as an *état de civilisation,* a form of culture, appeared for the first time in a posthumous work (published in 1727) by the Comte de Boulainvilliers, the most important literary champion of the thesis that noble liberty stemmed from the Franks. Montesquieu, especially, was responsible for defining the term and giving it currency. The French Revolution was familiar with it. "The National Assembly has completely abolished the feudal regime," said the decree of August 11, 1789.

What did the Revolution achieve and what were its aftereffects? On the famous night of August 4, 1789, the two higher Estates—which together with the Third Estate, had already constituted the *Assemblée Nationale*—renounced their rights of lordship. At the same time, all corporations—communes, townships, guilds, and all other associations—were dissolved. From this moment, there was only the state, borne by a nation of free and equal men, a state that absorbed all governmental powers within itself and no longer recognized any autonomous right to rule based on privilege, right, or "liberties." The seigniory, in its broadest sense, disappeared. For, in French, *"seigneurie"* meant the individual dominion of secular or ecclesiastical lords, as well as the collective lordship of the communes; the term was generally used for all authorities below the king. The same process took place in central Europe and beyond, though at a much slower rate. It had already begun in the period of absolutism, with the policy of peasant protection and state control of the towns; it continued in various degrees until 1848 and the years following.[29] The result was everywhere the same; seignorial rule and old-style autonomous towns disappeared. The state developed its administration; it absorbed all local authorities, allowing towns and rural communities, *départements* and provinces, only a state-controlled form of self-administration limited to well-defined areas of competence.[30] No more were there rights, liberties, privileges, or autonomous powers. The individual citizen and his family stood directly under the state, its administration, and the forms of self-administration it organized. But here, too, far-reaching changes took place. For the great codifications of the decades before and after 1800 substantially limited the power of the *pater familias* over his wife, children, and servants. A contemporary observer, Ignaz Beidtel, could claim that these measures "aimed at the liberty of the individual and the extension of the rights of the government."[31]

The abolition of slavery, the most radical form of the rule of one person by another, belongs to this movement. Slavery had been possible since antiquity. To one degree or another, it had always existed. Until the eighteenth century, a Christian could be a slave and a non-Christian could be enslaved. In the eighteenth century all great thinkers had allowed slavery—had even justified it. Now this changed radically.[32] Slavery was first abolished in Europe, then overseas, after long disputes and battles that extended into the second half of the nineteenth century. Clearly, in a world where slavery was possible at least in principle, there existed a different kind of rule over human beings from that which later came into existence. Here is the root of the eighteenth-century tendency to reduce the different forms of peasant dependency to forms of "bondage," and to equate this with slavery, especially when the right to move from place to place was restricted.

In the years immediately preceding and following 1800, Europe rejected on principle the idea that rule was a form of personal dependence whose harshest form was slavery, rejected autonomous seignorial rights independent of the state. This rejection originated in the modern state's monopoly of supreme power, in the idea of sovereignty. Here the distinction between state and society in the modern sense began. This, in theory, had been the goal of absolute monarchy. And what absolute kings had nearly attained, or at least had prepared the way for, the Revolution fully accomplished. Sovereignty of the prince and sovereignty of the people both excluded autonomous powers. Wherever such powers still existed, they were transformed into local authorities, appointed and controlled by the state.

To Boulainvilliers and Montesquieu, the most striking characteristic of feudalism was the "parceling out of sovereignty" to small, and still smaller, local authorities.[33] The "feudal system" organized these local authorities into the "feudal state." Sieyès and his precursors and adherents regarded this form of government as evil, believed that it had originated in conquest and rude force, and demanded that its surviving remnants be abolished. To them, legitimate power was vested only in the state, borne by the nation in accordance with the principle of popular sovereignty. It was with this assumption that they and their successors then analyzed the feudal state. They presupposed the concept of sovereignty within the state, the concept of a unified supreme government, of "the monopoly of legitimate power" (Max Weber), of the "state's legal monopoly of legislation."[34] In the feudal state, these existed, but "parceled out." For many years, the publicists for absolute monarchy had worked to destroy the moral basis of the seigniory. They provided rich material for the Revolution to use in its battle against feudalism.[35]

The feudalism the *Assemblée* abolished in 1789 had lost its original position much earlier, however. Only the ruins of "feudal rights" remained, now regarded as absurd.[36] Feudal dues were demanded, and no recognizable service was given in exchange; these dues could be considered nothing but forms of "exploitation." As Maxime Leroy says, in 1789 feudalism seemed to be an enormous landed domain.[37]

But what was the real basis of "feudal society"? Was it what was left over after feudal rights had been abolished, what had always been owned—landed property? Was "feudal society" essentially a landowning class in contrast to the "class" of artisans and tradesmen, the class of the bourgeoisie? Thus, out of the situation in 1789, the problem of the feudal state and feudal society appeared. Historians interpreted earlier centuries using the distinction between state and society drawn from their own times. This distinction has been the starting point for all examinations of the historical foundations of the present. We must now ask whether, by using it, we can really grasp the basic categories of this world of lordship that was going under.

II

Let us look first at the notion of "feudal society." To see the structural change that took place here, we can look at the way the meaning of the term "civil society" changed. Since antiquity the *"koinonía politiké,"* or *"societas civilis,"* had meant a "political" constitution modeled on the antique city-state, the *polis,* or *civitas.* It was normally set in contrast to the household, the *"societas domestica." Societas civilis* was identical to *"res publica"* and *"populus";* thus "politics" was the theory of the *societas civilis;* "economics," that of the household in its broadest sense.[38]

Then the concepts of "political" and "civil" (or "bourgeois") parted ways. Civil society in the modern sense separated itself from the state. It became an economic society; a social, nonpolitical structure. The society of citizens made up the nation, the embodiment of the sovereignty of the people, the sum total of all those equal before the law and thus free; the citizens also formed the "civil," economic society. This antithesis was formulated most strongly in Germany following Hegel, in the form of the antithesis between "political science" and "social science." For in Germany the nation was not yet politically organized; and the apparatus, the governmental bureaucracy, of the individual German states was clearly not identical with "civil society."[39]

During the eighteenth century the ambiguous concept of *status,* of

"Estate," a concept that was not simply "sociological," was still current. The imperial and territorial diets were divided into Estates as Estates-General and provincial Estates; and this was but one of the many possible examples of *status* known to Christian ethics. Clergy and laymen, old and young, single and married—each had his *status* with its own special ethical demands. The distinction of rich and poor, which we find in every century, also had its place here. Since each man had more than a single *status,* both rich and poor appeared within each of the different Estates and corporations. Sometimes this distinction designated a ruler-ruled relationship; the dependents, the subjects, were called "poor people," though the term meant nothing about their wealth.[40]

When "privileges" were abolished and the "nation" was created as a civic society composed of men who were equal before the law of the state, wealth and poverty became the decisive characteristics that stratified the new civil society distinct from the state. Though now no relationship of political dependence existed, no "lordship" in the old sense, there were nevertheless "private," domestic, forms of dependence in the agrarian and industrial sectors, most clearly in the factories; in the management of industry; and in the capitalistic management of agriculture. Eventually, the antithesis "rich/poor" was transformed into "bourgeois/proletariat": the capitalist who owned the means of production and the worker, the proletarian, who sold his labor. But only later did people see this. During the French Revolution, Gracchus Babeuf and his followers were the first to notice that equality before the law did not do away with the inequality of property. But Babeuf, a feudist by training, saw it mainly as inequality of landownership brought about by "feudalism" and he demanded an "agricultural law" to distribute land equally.[41]

Already for Sieyès, however, far in advance of his time, the nation was a *"nation commerçante et industrielle"* [a nation that works]; its members were "the true stockholders in the great corporation of Society." Sieyès saw in France a "commercial and industrial enterprise," where the decisive factors were not wealth, but labor and production. His concept of society was more economic than political.[42]

Growing industrialization during the Napoleonic era brought forth the opposition of bourgeoisie and proletariat.[43] Like *"citoyen,"* the word *"bourgeois"* originally meant "burgess" [a member of a town corporation]. But in the seventeenth and eighteenth centuries, it acquired the meaning of master artisan or industrial entrepreneur, which soon led to its being equated with "capitalist."[44] The proletariat were first discovered by H. Simonde de Sismondi, who in 1819 defined the members of this class as "the men who work without owning."[45] Political economy, developed in England especially by Adam Smith, now became the study of the laws of the market society. The "economy" became an autonomous sphere within the state rather than, as it had been, within the household.

Eventually this led people to search out the economic foundations of feudalism. They found them in the "natural economy"—in "landownership," large estates, and "property." Now, it is true that the phenomenon called "feudalism" occurred in an era of what is called "natural economy," an era when agriculture predominated. The commercial economy was limited and had a special character. There was no unified system of market quotations; as a result, money did not follow the market.[46] It is equally true that the "economic" substratum of feudalism, at least of Western fief-feudalism, was landownership. This landownership, however, was not the same as that which existed when the catchword "feudalism" was developed; it was really "rule over land and people."[47] We are not dealing in the Middle Ages with a ruling class in the nineteenth-century sense; we are dealing with a class of rulers. But since the old meaning of lordship was forgotten, it was not only traced back exclusively to conquest, but was also seen exclusively in terms of force and exploitation. When looked at from a purely economic point of view, power could have been based only on property, on landownership,[48] just as in modern "bourgeois" society, it is based on ownership of capital in communications, banking, trade, and industry.

Lordship in the old sense, furthermore, needed a religious basis in order to be "legitimate." This religious basis was decisively shaken in later centuries, in particular by the modern natural-law theory of Christian Thomasius, and, finally, by the Enlightenment. Theories of society and history became "secularized," a new philosophy of history replaced the old Christian doctrine of salvation and its theology of history.[49] Behind this lay the Western trend toward specific rationality,[50] toward empirically demonstrable reason. Science and reason, modern science modeled on mathematics and mechanics, with their particular concepts of "reason," replaced the theological-historical meaning of the Christian tradition. "World history" became the history of the "spirit" or of "society"; and large fields, such as political history, were excluded as meaningless. It was a history of "progress" through a succession of stages like "feudalism" and "capitalism" that characterized whole periods.[51] Turgot was the first to develop the well-known "law of three stages" in his history of the sciences. Condorcet, in his *Tableau du progrès de l'esprit humain* declared the free exercise of fundamental liberties to be the goal of history.

We encounter these problems most clearly in the writings of the early French socialists after the Revolution.[52] The goal of Claude Henri de Saint-Simon (1760–1825) was to abolish all rule, all government (even that now concentrated in the state), and to replace it with a "scientific administration." World history had progressed from antiquity, characterized by slavery, to the "theocratic-feudal" institutions of the Middle Ages, where slavery was replaced by "serfdom."[53] Feudalism, which had originated in conquest, and feudalism's martial spirit were then, in turn, gradually overcome by peaceful labor, by "industrialism." Labor was the central theme of world history. After Saint-Simon's death, his often inconsistent views were taken over by his followers, the Saint-Simonians, and further developed. The *Exposition de la doctrine de Saint-Simon* published in 1829/1830 (which Maxime Leroy called one of the principal works of French socialist thought), put forward as its goal an *Association universelle,* a classless and rulerless society in which the administration of things replaces the government of men. Neither birthright nor right of conquest nor force, but only labor, would determine one's place within this society. For all property is the source of exploitation; masters and slaves, patricians and plebeians, lords and serfs, landowners and tenants, idlers and laborers—these have determined the history of mankind up to now. The relationship of master to employee is the last stage in the transformation of slavery.[54] For his judgment on feudalism, Saint-Simon adopted the view of French history that had developed in the sixteenth century. Since the Frankish conquest, two classes had existed: the Franks as masters and the Gallo-Romans as slaves who worked for their masters in agriculture and trades.[55]

Augustin Thierry (1795–1856), for several years Saint-Simon's secretary, was able to make the past come alive. But he wrote his *Récits des temps mérovingiens,* his works on the medieval history of France and England, to take revenge "on the nobility for all the injustice and oppression suffered by his ancestors." Foreign conquerors—who later became the nobility—had robbed the indigenous people of their independence, he argued; this was the origin of the feudal constitution and of the conflict between the nobility of the Old Regime and the bourgeoisie. From the twelfth until the eighteenth century, an indissoluble alliance had united the monarchy and the Third Estate. This had determined the progress of history, whose immanent goal was the transformation of the Third Estate into the nation. This theory of an "alliance" between monarchy and bourgeoisie had strong aftereffects. German historians often expressed regret that such an alliance had never existed in Germany.[56]

François Guizot, a representative "bourgeois" liberal historian, also described the debate over the part played by the Franks and Gallo-Romans and considered this, and other factors in the barbaric Dark Ages, to be the seeds of all later relationships. Physical force had frequently been used, but it was the idea of justice, of "political legitimacy" carried by the monarchy, that in the end won out. The feudal constitution had originated in barbarism. It was always hateful, because it allowed the "capricious arbitrariness of the individual" to be decisive—not justice, but power in the form of self-help.[57]

The opposite view also survived, however. In 1814, commissioned by Napoleon to write *De la monarchie francaise,* the Comte de Montlosier presented in it "the point of view of a presumptuous aristocrat conscious of his Germanic descent." And Chateaubriand was proud of his Frankish ancestry. Count Arthur Gobineau (1816–1882), in his *Essai sur l'inégalité des races humaines,* in the end carried the thesis to excess in his historical theory of races. He saw history as a decline through miscegenation, beginning with the Romans; France reached her high point in the feudal era.[58] It is not by chance that Gobineau made enormous use of the book of Boulainvilliers, the main representative of the Frankish theory, the man Marc Bloch called a "Gobineau *avant la lettre.*"

The concept of classes and (to a lesser degree) the political concept of race were to some extent determined in the nineteenth century by the argument over the historical part played by Franks and Gallo-Romans, a discussion that in France went back to the sixteenth century. But the argument lost its political relevance about the middle of the century,[59] an attrition certainly due in part to Alexis de Tocqueville. This aristocrat believed that there was an unavoidable tendency toward equality in modern democracy. At the same time, he described, in his *L'ancien régime et la révolution* (1865), how absolute monarchy had transformed the internal structure of France and prepared the ground for the Revolution. He showed quite clearly that the "feudalism" the Revolution abolished had long since ceased to be identical with earlier structures bearing the same name. Interested in analyzing the present, De Tocqueville had no reason to enter into the details of feudalism, although he took its origin in "conquest" as a matter of course.[60]

In Germany, Hegel tried to master the situation created by the French Revolution. Historians have recently pointed to parallels between his point of view and that of Saint-Simon and Saint-Simon's pupil, Auguste Comte.[61] Today, we know how strongly and lastingly Hegel's thinking was shaped by the French Revolution and the revolutionary period that followed; but it was also shaped by his knowledge of contemporary political economy and by the industrial revolution spreading out from England.[62] From the latter, he derived his concept of civil society as a "system of needs" standing between the state and the family. This civil society is "the society which alone—in axiomatic emancipation from all traditional norms of human life—has as its content the nature of the needs of man as an individual and their satisfaction in the form of abstract labor and the division of labor."[63]

Like the French philosophers of history in the eighteenth and nineteenth centuries, Hegel saw world history as those past events in which freedom realized itself, as stages in the development of the World Spirit. In doing so, he followed a path common to post-Voltairian philosophy of history. The French Revolution raised human liberty "universally . . . to be the principle and the goal of society and the state."[64] Its necessary presupposition was the modern society of labor. Former times, in contrast, were determined by "the relationship of domination and slavery."[65] Hegel was here apparently thinking of ancient slavery, the form of slavery that together with serfdom was regarded in his time as the harshest and most despicable form of dominion.[66] Hegel discussed slavery repeatedly; but in feudal rule as well he saw only masters and slaves.[67] We should remember, however, that the word *"Knecht"* [which Hegel used] had more than one meaning in earlier centuries. It should not be equated with "slave" or "serf." The *gute Knechte* [good servants] who, according to the *Sachsenspiegel,* confirmed the public peace, were the Saxonian princes and nobles; in the lower nobility were *edle Knechte* [noble servants, compare English "knight"]; merchants' clerks and artisans' apprentices were called *"Knechte,"* as were male servants in rural and other households—all definitely freely contracting parties. The word *"Knecht"* was not used, however, for villeins who were permanently bound to the landowner. When Hegel took the slave to be the prototype for the *Knecht,* when he referred to the difference between the slave and "today's servants,"[68] he showed the fundamental change in the concept of government that had occurred in his time. For Hegel, servitude, slavery (and, we may add, feudal rule) were historical phenomena which the French Revolution's breakthrough toward general liberty had deprived of all present justification. "Slavery occurs in man's transition from the state of nature to genuinely ethical conditions; it occurs in a world where a wrong is still a right. At that stage wrong has validity and so is necessarily in its place."[69]

Hegel, like his French contemporaries, rejected older forms of lordship, which he called "servitude," and gave the central role to labor. But he did not treat feudalism in the sense of a feudal society, as we have done here. Though he spoke of civil society as a "system of needs" and of the individual's striving for gain, his thoughts were directed toward the state, the bureaucratic state of his time,[70] in which he saw the realization of the ethical. Thus, in his *Philosophy of History,* Hegel talks only about the "feudal state" of the Middle Ages, as he conceived it to have existed after the ninth century, and about the "transition from feudal sovereignty to monarchy." "In feudal sovereignty we see nothing but lords and serfs; in monarchy, on the contrary, there is one lord and no serf, for servitude is abrogated by it, and in it Right and Law are recognized."[71]

These theses, so obviously important for German historical thought,[72] will be re-examined later in this essay. It is not by chance that among the thinkers influenced by Hegel only those who had a thorough knowledge of early French socialism dealt with "feudal society." This was true both of Lorenz von Stein and Karl Marx.

Von Stein,[73] like Hegel, was concerned with the relationship between "civil society," which he conceived as a class society, and the state. Beginning in 1842, Von Stein introduced the Germans to a detailed knowledge of French social structure and early socialism. He seemed to regard France as the model for the development of society from feudalism to capitalism.[74] The central theme of his *Geschichte der sozialen Bewegung in Frankreich von 1789 bis auf unsere Tage* (1850) is liberty and the absence of liberty. Freedom is absent when a "ruling class," legally fixed by privileges, Estate, and caste, controls the government. The ruling class in France, the nobility, sprang from the feudal system. It relied on its landed property, acquired mainly by force of arms, from which it derived its unearned income, held by force of privilege. The conflict between this class and the rising capitalist society created a revolutionary situation.

Like Von Stein, Karl Marx had no reason to delve deeper into the past. Both were concerned with analyzing the present and predicting the future. They could thus use "feudalism" of the period before 1789 as a screen against which to contrast their own times. For this they needed no detailed description of its historical character and its transformations.

Karl Marx took over, practically unchanged, the formulations we have seen in the works of Saint-Simon and the Saint-Simonians.[75] The categories that had emerged in the French Revolution formed Marx's early writings. The "so-called usages of the privileged" were "usages against the law." Mankind is divided into "animal races," whose "connection is not equality but inequality."[76] "Feudalism in the widest sense is the world of animals, the world of divided mankind, as against the world of differing human beings, whose inequality is only the reflected colors of their equality." Thus Marx could say in his critique of Hegel's *Philosophy of Law:* "The Middle Ages are the animal-history of mankind, its zoology."[77]

Marx took his concept of capitalism, defined in terms of ownership of the means of production instead of drawing on vague notions of wealth or property in general, from contemporary political economy. He adopted Hegel's historical conceptions which, as is well known, he proceeded to invert. He was the first to give the concept of class a full meaning; history became the history of "class struggles." The ownership of the means of production leads to domination and exploitation in the capitalistic system (for in industrial society, "capitalism" is the expression of the relationship of ruler to ruled); the ownership of land did essentially the same in feudalism. As Joseph A. Schumpeter has shown, for Marx "it was essential for the logic of capitalism . . . that it grew out of a feudal state of society. . . . [He] accepted the bourgeois view that feudalism was a reign of force in which subjugation and exploitation of the masses were already accomplished facts. The class theory devised primarily for the conditions of capitalist society was extended to its feudal predecessor. . . . The feudal exploiter was simply replaced by the capitalist exploiter."[78]

For Marx, feudalism was also a necessary stage between slave economy and capitalism. Like Saint-Simon, he founded his theory on an old view of history confined to Europe: slave economy (antiquity), feudalism (Middle Ages), capitalism (modern times). Even so, feudalism remained a general category in the framework of world history. In capitalism there was no direct lordship or direct force, only an indirect one arising from the ownership of the means of production. The feudalism of 1789—which could still be observed—was nothing but landownership. This, the decisive factor in an agricultural society, was regarded as the basis of feudalism. For this reason one could speak of feudalism anyplace in the world where there are large estates with dependent people on them, where there are systems of leasehold, for example. The different forms were secondary, were "superstructures."[79] Marxist history has extended the notion of feudalism as a preliminary stage to capitalism, to the whole world. The article *"Feôdalnij stroj"* ["Feudal order"] in the *Great Soviet Encyclopedia* (1956), which defines feudalism in this way, states that feudalism lasted in Western Europe until the seventeenth and eighteenth centuries; in Russia, until 1861, in Soviet Asia, until 1917; and in China, until the twentieth century.[80]

In Germany, despite revolution and reform, the old "feudal society," the old society of Estates, continued to exist with only minor changes. The formation of a "bourgeois society" was a process that extended well into the second half of the century; landlordism and some provincial diets of the traditional type still survived. In contrast to the violent breakthrough of the French Revolution, older social forms were still effective in Germany despite far-reaching changes; but the representatives of continuity and tradition were conscious of the changes taking place. In 1806 Karl D. Hüllmann published his *Geschichte des Ursprungs der Stände in Deutschland.* In the preface to the second edition (1830), he wrote that the first edition had been published in the fateful year when the old empire ceased to be and the foundations of civil order and tradition collapsed. But in the order established in 1815, Hüllmann saw a continuation of the four Estates—clergy, nobility, burgesses, and peasants—with only the medieval element uprooted. The "transformation of the society of the state" had incorporated the bourgeoisie into the state; the state had ceased being the sum total of corporations. For the peasants, the nineteenth century signified civic birth.[81] Obviously following Justus Möser, he wrote the history of the older "civil order" (which for him still meant the *societas civilis*), the history of landed property. Hüllmann's concept of Estate corresponded in all essentials to contemporary ideas. Take, for example, the well-known trend toward enlarging the provincial diets by adding representatives of townspeople and peasants. Hüllmann thought the medieval concept of Estate, based on seignorial or guild rule, to be a thing of the past. In this he was not alone.

Although Friedrich Ludwig von der Marwitz was familiar with the elements of the old constitution, the "feudal constitution," he described them in detail because he knew that in his time it had disappeared. The feudal constitution was gone, he said. It should be replaced by a "society of citizens"[82] in whose Estates' organization the nobility should have its place, somewhat in the spirit of the *Allgemeines Landrecht* [Prussian Civil Code].

Adam Müller, the most important theoretician of the Restoration-Romantic school, was once close to Marwitz. In his *Elemente der Staatskunst* (1809), he dealt with a concept of central significance for him: the idea of "community" in the organization of property and in the national economy, without distinguishing between state and society. "Feudalism" was for him a kind of private property. The model for the society of Estates he desired was the English society of his time.[83]

In Hegel's *Philosophy of Law,* the Estates appeared as organic parts of "civil society" as "private Estates" that acquired "political importance and influence" when their members participated in the legislative power, though they participated in a "system of mediation" not one of representation.[84] At mid-century, Wilhelm Heinrich Riehl saw civil society as "the people considered from the point of view of labor and property." It was organized, Riehl said, into four Estates—the nobility and peasants being the forces of inertia, the middle class and the proletarians, those of movement. The nobility had been transformed from a "political corporation" into a "social Estate."[85]

Despite differences in detail, the modern concept of civil society appeared in the works of all these conservative authors. This concept in turn formed those of Estate and feudalism. Nor do more recent ideologists of Estates, writing in the nineteenth and twentieth centuries, have a true notion of the old order that they like to refer to as their model.[86]

Therefore, it is not astonishing that the typical formulas with which we are already familiar recur in the works of liberal historians. "In prehistory the individual was free and, in the main, equal; then came semibarbarism with the privileged free and the worker in bondage; only since our towns have grown large do we have civilized states in this world, and since then the secret has been revealed that only free labor makes people's lives great and secure and permanent." These sentences, with their formulas reminiscent of Sieyès, are spoken by the merchant in Gustav Freitag's novel *Soll und Haben.*

It is impossible to follow in detail, here, the way these concepts developed in German historical scholarship; we would also have to give attention to a secondary issue: the debate with Marxism. I will refer only to some recent examples which clarify the basic conception of feudal society. Franz Oppenheimer has founded his *System of Sociology,* and the social and economic history included in it, on the contrast between "political means" of conquest and the "closing off" of the great landed estates that resulted from it, on one side, and the "economic means" of a peaceful bourgeois "society of barter" on the other.[87] Alexander Rüstow, in his *Ortsbestimmung der Gegenwart,* considers rule originating in conquest and stratification as the Original Sin of world history. Freedom is directly contrary to it.[88] In Otto Hintze's very complex idea of feudalism, the most permanent factor is the relationship between landowner and peasant in an "economic-social" sense.[89] And Bloch's extension of the concept of feudal society to include seignorial relations leads us to suspect similar influences at work.

Thus, "feudalism" in this sense seems defined as the ownership of the most important means of production in an agrarian society—the land—an ownership originating in force and injustice. Feudalism is in all essentials identical with landed lordship. Schumpeter has expressed his astonishment at a sociology which "displays uncritical confidence in the explanatory value of the element of force and of the control over the physical means with which to exert force."[90] A critique of this one-sided approach would have to begin with some questions about the nature and function of landed lordship, as well as about the nature of medieval lordship in general. The question immediately arises, "What is the relation of lordship to those organisms that might be called 'state'?"

III

Certain concepts of the "feudal state" also go back to the era of absolutism, although the theory of the feudal state is less strongly influenced by anti-feudal sentiments. (Such sentiments were directed primarily against the "feudal society" of Estates as it existed before 1789 and against its continuing influence in the nineteenth century, not against the feudal state which had long since ceased to exist.) Boulainvilliers and Montesquieu, we will recall, saw in the parceling out of sovereignty, the dominant characteristic of feudalism. In France, about 1640, the absolutist theoretician Charles Loyseau had distinguished in principle between the *seigneurie publique* of the king (the state) and the *seigneuries privées* (the lordships). The exercise of sovereign rights by these "private authorities" Loyseau could explain only by delegation or usurpation. Thus they were regarded—rightly or wrongly—as derived from the undivided sovereign authority of the state and, as such, contestable, while the defenders of feudal rights tried to operate with the thesis of the "parceling out" of sovereignty.[91] In Germany historians spoke of private authorities, patrimonial powers, and "purchased," sovereign rights.[92] In any case, the absolute state defended its claim to sovereignty; its administration covered over these local authorities, emptied them of their contents, and eventually abolished them. Whereas "feudal society" and its rights, reduced to great landed estates, continued to present a very real problem, the feudal state had disappeared. It was only a memory. If one were interested in attacking the concept of sovereignty, he could use the "feudal state" as the antithesis of the modern state or regard it as a preliminary historical step leading up to the bureaucratic state of modern times. Both ways have been followed.

The Bernese patrician Karl Ludwig von Haller, in his *Restauration der Staatswissenschaften* (1816), took issue with the modern concept of "sovereignty" and denied the existence of a "state" in the Middle Ages; in those days, only private seigniories had existed, he wrote. Haller's theories were of practically no political influence. His continued effect on scholarly writing is thus all the more astonishing. Even in the twentieth century, there have been polemics against him and the way he denied the existence of a medieval state.[93] Evidently, his theses had questioned a point of central importance for German historical studies. Hegel, starting from entirely different presuppositions, was likewise of the opinion that in the period of "feudal rule" there had been no state[94]—no state such as that which in the present represented for him the last stage of the World Spirit.

Assertions of this kind took their bearings from the contemporary concept of the state. Since certain characteristics of modern states were not found in the association called "feudal state," one could deny its statehood, treat it as a preliminary stage, or generalize the concept of "state" to such an extent that it also became applicable to the feudal state.

Interest in the feudal state was fostered primarily by legal and constitutional historians. Understandably, they worked with contemporary political and constitutional concepts, such as were to be found in 1815: the undivided authority of the "monarchic principle" and the concept of "constitution." The categories they developed were influential for a very long time, indeed, up to the present.[95] Georg Waitz's still indispensable *Deutsche Verfassungsgeschichte,* which drew on a vast quantity of sources, was based upon the constitutional concept of the nineteenth century.[96] Paul Roth, in his theory of the *Untertanenverband* [association of subjects], interpreted the oath of allegiance, especially in the Carolingian era, as the way a "State-people" in the modern sense was created. This association of subjects had then been broken up by feudal institutions which he regarded as "barbarism of the worst kind, covered by a little civilization."[97] Outlooks as diverse as those of Rudolf Sohm and Otto von Gierke had one question in common: "What date can be set for the beginnings of the 'state,' and what forms of government must be called 'private'?"[98] Even a first-rate expert like Georg von Below was still part of this tradition. He defined feudalism as the withdrawal of subjects from the ruler by "mediatization" under private authorities.[99] The notion of the feudal state as a hierarchy of feudal relationships proved very suitable for understanding this process of mediatization under private authorities, at least for understanding its origin in the granting or delegation of sovereign rights.

The legal and constitutional historians who concerned themselves with the medieval state necessarily had the state of their own times in mind and compared it to conditions in earlier centuries. They focused on two phenomena: the "administration"—the highly developed officialdom of these states with their bureaucratic organization—and the "constitution" in its nineteenth-century sense. In Germany, of course, more stress was laid on the bureaucracy, whose social prestige by far surpassed that of the bourgeoisie. Hegel said of the Prussia of his own times, "Government rests in the world of the official."[100] Although the personal decision lies with the monarch, "under the established laws and the precise organization of the state, that which is left to the sole decision of the monarch . . . has to be regarded as little." Thus Hegel can say, about "the transition from feudal rule to monarchy" that "vassals become officers of state, whose duty it is to execute laws."[101] What Hegel spoke of here has remained a basic theme until today: the relation of feudalism to bureaucracy. (This is not meant to assert any literary connection between Hegel and modern writers, though reminiscences of Hegel can be shown even in the latest histories of the law.[102]) Given the historical importance of bureaucratic organization for the modern state, given the social predominance of the administration in nineteenth-century Germany, it is not surprising that much more stress was laid on the relation of the "feudal state" (whatever this was thought to mean) to the bureaucracy, especially since the scholars concerned with legal and constitutional history were involved in training that bureaucracy; it is not surprising that more stress was put on bureaucracy than on the significance of the feudal state, or state composed of Estates, for the modern "constitution" of the nineteenth century.

"Feudal system and governmental power" was a theme of central significance for the important scholarly work of Heinrich Mitteis. As we have said, he distinguishes feudalism in general from the Frankish feudal system in particular. "It was the feudal system and feudal law that turned feudalism, which had originated in non-state elements, into a state (*eingestaatet*), and divested it of its centrifugal tendencies. The feudal system was feudalism turned positive. Feudal law also regulated political relations, guaranteed services to the state in return for participation in political prerogatives. The king stepped onto the apex of the feudal pyramid; his position as a ruler was strengthened by his position as the supreme liege lord. Feudal law became the administrative law of the medieval state, its form of personal rule, its organization of noble power. The feudal state became the constitutional state (*Rechtsstaat*) of the Middle Ages. The feudal system and feudal law were the contribution of the Germanic mind to the general history of feudalism. The feudal system led feudalism toward the objectified modern state."[103] In these words from the preface, Mitteis outlined the conclusions of his book, *Der Staat des hohen Mittelalters,* on the flowering of the feudal system in the twelfth century. Its foundations lie in the extension of feudal law to an administrative organization, a characteristic of western, Frankish feudalism. "Already in the ninth century, feudal law was increasingly becoming the legal form of administration in the medieval state."[104] In the thirteenth century, "the feudal state began its tranformation into a system of objective organizations. Feudal law as a principle of organization disappeared; dependent, permanently salaried officials took the place of vassals. Where the feudal system survived until modern times, it became an empty form; as a moving force in the state it had played its part by 1300."[105]

Mitteis's point of view is clear. We do not want to dispute, as this point, whether it is correct. But it seems questionable that this one-sided approach really allows us to understand the inner structure of the medieval "state" or even to explain the background of modern constitutional history.

According to Mitteis, the feudal system led from "feudalism" or "rule of the nobility"[106] to the modern administrative state. Was this, however, a tendency innate in the feudal system (*Lehnswesen*)? Or was it rather an instrument that could be put to use under certain conditions, conditions that might be foreign to the feudal system itself? Although Mitteis, as an historian of law, was primarily concerned with working out the specific dynamics of a legal system (in this case that of feudal law), he was, nevertheless, well aware of other factors. He knew that the feudal system exerted centrifugal as well as centripetal forces. He knew how important the monarchy and its sacral foundations were, especially in France, which provided him with his paradigm. One also must take into account that France had one single dynasty which enforced succession by primogeniture and that the royal domain steadily expanded. Only the king's extraordinarily powerful position made his feudal suzerainty a centripetal force and an instrument of royal authority. The feudal state became fully effective because the king ruled a large and constantly growing part of France *directly* and not simply as supreme liege lord. Thus, even in the heyday of feudalism, France was only partly a feudal state. At that very time, the basic forms of the administrative state were being created in the royal domain. People did not first have a concept of the feudal state which they then replaced with the administrative state. The rising monarchy used feudal laws to develop a feudal state; at the same time, in its narrower sphere of lordship, it created the administrative state, the "institutionalized territorial state," and used the Estates as a way of organizing local authorities into a complementary element. Thus, it is simply not the case that the feudal system by itself led to the feudal pyramid and to the activation of royal suzerainty. It is rather that the rise of royal power led to these results. A makeshift, serving to maintain at least a formal tie between kingship and the king at a time when it was of hardly any practical significance, was successfully transformed into an effective instrument of royal rule. The feudal state, understood in terms of a feudal pyramid, was but temporarily significant. It was never the exclusive principle. The feudal state achieved its real significance from the differently organized, and more limited, royal domain; it was here that the foundations of the administrative state were created. The rudiments also existed in the feudal principalities,[107] which the king could keep only if they reverted to the crown. What this means is clearly shown by the German example. We cannot say that the feudal state led to the objectified modern state; we can say only that it was replaced by the administrative state. There have been European states, like Poland and Hungary, where the road led from the rule of the nobility to the administrative state and that of Estates without passing through feudal law.[108] But the idea of a feudal state characterized by a feudal pyramid lends itself to romantic treatment and at the same time to treatment as a rational, pellucid hierarchy of delegated authority. This picture has obviously been formed around the bureaucratic state with its successive layers and its prescribed competences. As we have seen, Mitteis regarded feudal law as the administrative law of the Middle Ages.

Mitteis conceived of the feudal state at the height of the Middle Ages—with its relatively rational organization, represented as the "feudal pyramid," and its systematized feudal law—as a first step toward the modern state. Werner Näf set the "feudal state" over against the state of modern times.[109] The latter, Näf says, is the "postfeudal state," which came into existence in the thirteenth century; its oldest form is the "State made up of Estates" (*Ständestaat*). The structure of the medieval state was feudalistic; it led to the parceling out of the state, to its splintering; the competences of the ruler became private property. The modern state replaced this feudal state. Its earlier stage, at about 1200–1500, was the *Ständestaat,* which was characterized by a dual authority because the monarchy (the one holder of power in the state) had not yet succeeded in appropriating the rights that feudalization had splintered, or in bringing state tasks into the state (*verstaatlichen*) sufficiently quickly, securely, and completely. Thus there was room, even need, for a second authority which was embodied in the imperial and provincial diets: *Cortes, États,* and *Stände.* This *Ständestaat* came into being through contracts, such as Magna Carta. Duality did not exist in the state; the state had come into existence in, and through, this duality (by means of the contracts). The ideas of this Swiss historian are obviously shaped by the history of the Estates and, thus, by the history of more recent representative constitutions. For Mitteis, on the other hand, the bureaucratic element of the modern state definitely took first place. The same applies to the antithesis *Personenverbandsstaat* [state formed by personal ties] and *institutioneller Flächenstaat* [institutionalized territorial state], suggested by Theodor Mayer.[110] Here the feudal state appears as the last embodiment of the *Personenverbandsstaat;* while the *Flächenstaat,* government by officials, designates the beginnings of bureaucratic administrative organization.

Even clearer is Max Weber's approach, centered on "bureaucracy."[111]

For us, the important point is that Weber consciously took as his starting place the problem of the peculiar "rationality" in European history, the problem of rational government.[112] This rationality is legal; it is bound by normative rules and laws. But the purest type of legal government is exercised through a bureaucratic administration. The concrete historical object around which the Ideal-Type bureaucracy was developed, was the modern constitutional administrative state. Weber himself, again and again, cited the specific example of European bureaucracy, with its legally trained, expert officialdom, and the basic difference between European bureaucracy and that of other civilizations. "Bureaucractic administration is . . . the most rational type of government. . . . It is the kernel of the modern Western state." He then compared this Ideal Type with other forms of government, to see what characteristics of rational dominion were missing in their administration.[113]

According to Weber, feudalism, on the other hand, is one of the forms of traditional dominion, a "feudal form of administration." He developed a typology of forms of government according to the basis of their legitimacy,[114] distinguishing three pure Types: the rational belief in the legality of legislated normative rules; the traditional, resting on an established belief in the sanctity of immemorial traditions; and the charismatic, "resting on the devotion, heroism, or exemplary character of an individual person, and on the normative patterns or order revealed or ordained by him."[115]

It must be pointed out that these distinctions can be applied only after the breakthrough to the "modern world," in which the phenomenon "dominion" has undergone a basic change.[116] Only at the beginning of the nineteenth century does legitimacy appear as a problem.[117] Only then do we find any mention of traditional, of "historically developed" values handed down to posterity. In opposition to the rational constitutional and administrative state around them, historians become concerned with the part played in history by great individuals. Previous centuries did not regard "tradition" or "history" as the only forms of legitimation; they lived in an order that seemed "old" to them, because they were convinced that it was good and just and that it had been valued for these reasons in the past as well as in the present.

Of course, we must remember that Max Weber's types of government are "pure Types," which in historical reality, appear only in mixtures. Nevertheless, it is necessary to say something about the historically conditioned nature of Weber's concept of "traditional." Starting from his central idea, the importance of the rational in history—especially in Western history—Weber sees tradition as the "negative" of the rational. Tradition, so it seems, has no concrete objective content peculiar to it; it exists because rationality is lacking. Thus, Weber sees feudalism as a traditional form of government in contrast to a rational, bureaucratic one.

This concept of the "feudal state," developed as an antithesis to "bureaucracy," led to a one-sided overestimation of dominion and did not do justice to communal, cooperative, corporative elements in village, town, and country. These were presented as counterpoles to dominion, whereas, in reality, both were closely intertwined in the Middle Ages. One cannot be conceived without the other. It must again be emphasized that the feudal state was transformed, not only into the bureaucratic and administrative state, but simultaneously into the state made up of Estates. When we inquire into the historical foundations of modern constitutions, we have to consider, not only bureaucratic "administration" but also parliamentary "constitution." And the background of the latter is the *Ständestaat.* For this reason, one is not justified in disregarding the institutions of Estates[118] in a bureaucratic view of history, even though in many absolutist states of modern times they were repressed, robbed of their political power, or paralyzed in their functions. The tendency to disregard them is clearly visible in Mitteis's thought when he says that "the *Ständestaat,* as a rule, was only a transitory form and was overcome everywhere by the monarchy."[119] With good reason, Werner Näf has commented that, although the absolute state to a large extent denuded the Estates of their power, it did not abolish them.[120] Even when institutions had been robbed of essential functions, their continued existence as such carried weight. So long as they existed, be it in name only, they prevented a radical break with traditional norms. This was the case in France in the years preceding, and following, 1789. Likewise, we cannot understand the fight about "constitutional" or "Estate" constitutions in the German states prior to the Revolution of March 1848—the *Vormärz*—if we do not also consider Estate institutions of an older type that were still in existence.[121] Despite the influence of the English model (which was given a different meaning on the continent), the knowledge of those institutions was of importance for the constitutional movement of the nineteenth century.

IV

Of what importance for the inner history of the European states was the early form of government implied by the catchword "feudalism"? To what extent can the roots of the specifically European idea of liberty be attributed to this early form? A great merit of Otto Hintze's study on the *Wesen und Verbreitung des Feudalismus*[122] is that it is only one part of a comprehensive constitutional history of Europe in which he deals equally with the bureaucratic organization of the modern state and with "representative governments."[123] Heir to the tradition of the great German historians of the nineteenth century, Hintze starts with the "military constitution," which provides him with a comprehensive viewpoint that includes foreign policy. It is not surprising that he does not analyze earlier forms of "lordship," but, by making a critical assessment of the historical and sociological literature,[124] tries to unite the different points of view presented by the theses of feudal society and feudal law.[125] This shows considerable progress. It is not yet a final assessment.

Hintze also tries to apply to other civilizations the complex concept of feudalism he has developed. To do this, he has to relinquish certain essential features peculiar to the social structure of Europe. This watering down of the concept appears even more clearly in the collection of essays *Feudalism in History*,[126] which seeks to find "conformities" in different civilizations. Its authors understand feudalism, not as "an economic and social system," but as a "method of government," as a political structure. The Ideal Type of the feudal state and its feudal pyramid are plainly the standard applied. The civilizations examined from this viewpoint often show analogous phenomena, conformities, but the essays cannot claim to describe the whole political and social structures of such worlds. Furthermore, extant sources are often insufficient for sure conclusions.

Whoever tries to find conformities in different civilizations will have to ask whether they do not also exist in the nonfeudal elements of these civilizations, whether the difference between various "feudalisms" or feudal phenomena is determined by differences in such elements as religion, monarchy, or city. The concept "feudalism" is too narrow for such comparisons. There is a danger that certain feudal institutions (landlordism, administration, etc.) will appear uniform because they were earlier examined in isolation.[127] In order to compare the West with other civilizations, one would first have to present the whole inner structure of the Western Middle Ages with both its feudal and nonfeudal elements and their inner connection. On the other hand, the concept of feudalism is too complex for such a comparison. It is not by chance that studies on non-European civilizations speak of feudal "traits" or "principles," of individual phenomena which are also encountered in European feudalism. Would it not be better to examine these individual structural elements first—be they "feudal" or not? Would it not be better first to investigate their conformities or differences, their functions within the different civilizations, and the way they spread from one to the other?[128]

There are difficulties in such an enterprise, and there is much uncertainty about the categories to be used. However, E. Rothacker's article on the comparative method in the humanities[129] will help to clarify the issues and to show the way in which our question has been historically determined—as we have tried to do in this essay with regard to the categories "feudal state" and "feudal society." Scholars in other fields, not conversant with such difficulties, might well ask whether it would not be more useful to get rid of all this ballast and go right to the subject itself. This approach would not give us history, however. At best it would yield simply a collection of antiquarian notes. History is possible only when related to the present—to each present. Our questions are rooted in the present. But these questions solidify and decline into catchwords. They survive into a present that is different from the one in which they originated. The transformation of inner structures is a lengthy process and requires a long time to be understood. All we can do is analyze the questions life itself brings to us and recognize that these questions are historically determined and need to be renewed.

It might appear that a concept like "feudalism"—if defined more widely and indeterminately—might be made more serviceable and of greater general validity. This is true, but its apparent universal validity would result from its having lost all meaning. It could then contribute nothing to our understanding of the inner structure and dynamics of the individual forms it included. It is useless to discuss whether a certain case concerns feudalism or not, if one cannot define its precise meaning. As long as we deal with the "feudalism" of a definite time or a definite place, its meaning is usually evident or can be deduced from the context. The situation is more difficult in comparative studies. Here we have to give a precise definition of the concept of feudalism used in each case; we have no choice but to apply more or less generalized Types. In each case, we must ask ourselves if they are useful to perform the job and how much generalization is useful in the construction of each Type.

NOTES

1. Marc Bloch, *Feudal Society* (1961). Trans. by L. A. Manyon.

2. François Ganshof, *Feudalism* (1952). Trans. by P. Grierson.

3. Heinrich Mitteis, *Lehnrecht und Staatsgewalt* (1933).

4. Heinrich Mitteis, *Staat des hohen Mittelalters* (4th ed., 1952).

5. *Ibid.,* 16 ff.; also, H. Mitteis, *Die Rechtsidee in der Geschichte* (1957), 86 ff.

6. Max Weber, *Wirtschaft und Gesellschaft,* J. Winckelmann, ed. (4th ed., 1956), 148 ff.

7. R. Syme, *The Roman Revolution* (1939), p. 12; on the terminology see A. Heuss, "Der Untergang der römischen Republik und das Problem der Revolution," *HZ,* **182** (1956), 1 ff.

8. Schulz-Basler, *Deutsches Fremdwörterbuch,* **1** (1913), 210 f.

9. Especially clear in the sociology of literature and art, where the contrast "feudal/bourgeois" is used. See A. Hauser, *Sozialgeschichte der Kunst und Literatur* (1953); A. Mazaheri, in *So lebten die Muselmanen im Mittelalter* (1957), divides Islamic history into feudal and bourgeois periods.

10. Otto Hintze, "Wesen und Verbreitung des Feudalismus," *Staat und Verfassung* (1941), p. 85. [Translated in this volume.]

11. Maxime Leroy, *Histoire des idées sociales en France,* **1** (1946), 59.

12. Thus the American Vice-President Nixon opposed his country's foreign policy, because, against its own democratic principles, it "did not join the side of the people against their oppressors, but cooperated with corrupt feudal classes." *Die Weltwoche* (Zürich), 12 Sept. 1958.

13. H. Markmann, *Einführung in die Soziologie,* A. Weber, ed. (1955) 249 f.

14. Fr. L. v.d. Marwitz, *Lebensbeschreibung,* Fr. Meusel, ed. 1 (1908), 31 ff.

15. Emmanuel Sieyès, *What Is the Third Estate?* (1963). Trans. by M. Bloudel.

16. O. Brandt, "Untersuchungen zu Sieyès," *HZ,* 126 (1922), 410 ff.

17. S. Landshut, *Kritik der Soziologie, Freiheit und Gleichheit als Ursprungsproblem der Soziologie* (1929).

18. E. Wolf, *Grosse Rechtsdenker* (3d ed., 1951), 410 ff.

19. R. Smend, *Staatsrechtliche Abhandlungen* (1955), p. 315.

20. Sieyès, *What Is the Third Estate?* p. 60.

21. M. Göhring, *Weg und Sieg der modernen Staatsidee in Frankreich* (1946), 87 ff.; E. Hölzle, *Die Idee einer altgermanischen Freiheit vor Montesquieu* (1925); E. Weis, *Geschichtsschreibung und Staatsauffassung in der französischen Encyclopädie* (1956), 24 ff.

22. This view of history did not go unopposed. In the great *Encyclopédie,* the contributors of the pertinent articles (*"Fief, Etat"*)—above all, Boucher d'Argis with his training in the history of law—gave a largely objective picture. They pointed out the difference between the feudalism of the eighteenth century and that of the Middle Ages and criticized the Frankish theory of feudal origins. Boucher d'Argis was of the opinion that seignorial courts were older than feudal law. Yet, at the same time, the editor, Diderot, spoke scathingly about "feudal government" in words that essentially corresponded to the views of Sieyès. Weis, *Geschichtsschreibung,* 33 ff.

23. P. Joachimsen, "Zur Psychologie des deutschen Staatsgedankens," *Dioskuren: Jahrbuch für Geisteswissenschaften,* 1 (1922), 106 ff.

24. Otto Brunner, "Die Freiheitsrechte in der altständischen Gesellschaft," *Aus Verfassungs- und Landesgeschichte. Festschrift für Theodor Mayer,* 1 (1954), 293 ff. On the many meanings of "Estate," see O. Brunner, *Land und Herrschaft,* (4th ed., 1959), 395 ff.

25. R. Dahrendorf, *Soziale Klassen und Klassenkonflikte in der industriellen Gesellschaft* (1957). People still attempt to define classes as "economically" determined, but mean a relationship involving dominion.

26. M. Bloch, *La société féodale,* 2 (1940), carries the subtitle: *Les classes et le gouvernement des hommes.*

27. Of the rich literature, see L. v. Wiese, *Gesellschaftliche Stände und Klassen* (1950). "Class" is defined (p. 47) as the type of social stratification existing from the French Revolution to the First World War. A. Weber, *Einführung in die Soziologie* (1955), 237 ff.

28. M. Bloch, *La société féodale,* p. 2; E. Littré, *Dictionnaire de la langue française* 2 (1872), 1642.

29. On the position of the nobility in the eighteenth and nineteenth centuries, see A. Goodwin, *The European Nobility in the Eighteenth Century* (1953); F. Martini, *Die Adlesfrage in Preussen vor 1806 als politisches und soziales Problem* (1938); O. Brunner, *Adeliges Landleben und europäischer Geist* (1949), 313 ff.

30. H. Heffter, *Die deutsche Selbstverwaltung im 19. Jahrhundert* (1950).

31. H. Conrad, *Individuum und Gemeinschaft in der Privatrechtsordnung des 18. und beginnenden 19. Jahrhunderts* (1956).

32. Ch. Verlinden, *L'esclavage dans l'Europe médiévale,* 1 (1955). The Prussian Civil Code of 1794 and the Austrian ABGB of 1811, codes whose history goes back far into the eighteenth century, expressly forbid slavery and serfdom.

33. Bloch, *La société féodale,* 1, 2 ff.

34. F. Wieacker, *Privatrechtsgeschichte der Neuzeit* (1952), p. 298.

35. K. Schmidt, *Das Jus primae noctis* (1881) is an instructive example; O. Brunner, *Adeliges Landleben,* 310 f.

36. Before the Revolution Gracchus Babeuf was a feudist; that is, his profession was to search for feudal rights and collect feudal dues. It was in the archives, he later said, that he had discovered "the horrid secrets of the usurpations by the noble class." See Leroy, *Hist. des idées sociales,* **2**, 55 ff.; Th. Ramm, *Die grossen Sozialisten,* **1** (1955), 131 ff.

37. Leroy, *Hist. des idées sociales,* **1**, 59; F. Olivier-Martin, *Histoire du droit français* (2d ed., 1951), 642 ff.

38. O. Brunner, *Neue Wege der Sozialgeschichte* (1956), 33 ff.; W. Conze, "Staat und Gesellschaft in der frührevolutionären Epoche Deutschlands," *HZ,* **186** (1958), 1 ff.

39. See the later discussion in this article.

40. Brunner, *Land und Herrschaft,* 263 ff.

41. Leroy, *Hist. des idées sociales,* **2**, 55 ff.; Th. Ramm, *Die grossen Sozialisten,* **1**, 131 ff.

42. Leroy, *Hist. des idées sociales,* **1**, 329 f.

43. *Ibid.,* **1**, 115, 16 *n.* 1.

44. C. Brinkmann, art. "Bourgeoisie," *Encyclopedia of the Social Sciences,* 1[2] (1943), 645 ff.; E. G. Barber, *The Bourgeoisie in 18th Century France* (1955).

45. Leroy, *Hist. des idées sociales,* **2**, 293 ff.; C. Jantke, *Der vierte Stand* (1955); W. Conze, "Vom 'Pöbel' zum 'Proletariat'," *Vierteljahrschrift für Sozial- und Wirtschaftsgeschichte,* **41**, (1954), 333 ff.

46. Brunner, *Neue Wege der Sozialgeschichte,* 80 ff.

47. Walter Schlesinger, "Herrschaft und Gefolgschaft in der germanisch-deutschen Verfassungsgeschichte," *Herrschaft und Staat im Mittelalter* (1956), 135 ff. [Translated in this volume.]

48. F. Olivier-Martin, *Hist. du droit français,* 66 ff. The idea that property was the basis of dominion and of class formation already existed in the eighteenth century; Ramm, *Die grossen Sozialisten,* **1**, 62 ff.; Dahrendorf, *Soziale Klassen und Klassenkonflikt,* p. 27.

49. Brunner, *Neue Wege der Sozialgeschichte,* 177 ff.

50. *Ibid.,* 17 ff.

51. Categories that possess some limited value in certain special fields of historical study, such as "stages" in economic history or "styles" in art history, are thus transferred to general history and invested with a claim to totality. See Brunner, *Neue Wege der Sozialgeschichte,* 54 ff.; M. Landmann, *Das Zeitalter als Schicksal* (1956).

52. Leroy, *Hist. des idées sociales,* **2**, 197 ff.; Ramm, *Die grossen Sozialisten,* **1**, 210 ff.; N. Sombart in A. Weber, *Einführung in die Soziologie* (1955), 81 ff.; E. Rothacker, "Philosophie und Politik im französischen Denken des frühen 19. Jahrhunderts," *Mensch und Geschichte* (1950), 103 ff.

53. Ramm, *Die grossen Sozialisten,* 258 ff.

54. M. Leroy, *Les précurseurs du socialisme français* (1948), 191 ff.: "L'homme a jusqu'ici exploité l'homme: Maîtres, esclaves; patriciens, plébiens; oisifs et travailleurs, voilà l'histoire progressive de l'humanité jusqu'à nos jours"; Th. Ramm, *Der Frühsozialismus* [Kröners Taschenausgabe, **223**] (1956), 81 ff.

55. Ramm, *Der Frühsozialismus,* p. 271.

56. Augustin Thierry, *Essai sur la formation et des progrès du Tiers Etat* (1853). See also E. Fueter, *Geschichte der neueren Historiographie* (3d ed., 1946), 448 ff.; F. Engel-Janosi, *Four Studies in French Romantic Historical Writing*

(1955), 88 ff.; on the survival of Thierry's thesis see H. de Man, *Jacques Coeur* (1950) and O. Brunner's comments in *Anzeiger der Österreichischen Akademie der Wissenschaften,* **88**, (1951), 127 ff.

57. F. Guizot, *Allgemeine Geschichte der europäischen Zivilisation* (1844), 44 ff., 74 ff.; Leroy, *Hist. des idées sociales,* **2**, 524 ff.

58. M. Leroy, *Hist. des idées sociales,* **2**, 2 ff.; on Gobineau, see E. Cassirer, *Vom Mythus des Staates* (1949), 284 ff.

59. The Germanist thesis was decisively shaken by Fustel de Coulanges who successfully destroyed the assumption that there was an institutional continuity between the popular Germanic assemblies, via the March- and May-fields of the Franks, and the Estates General, a theory that had played a central role in the Frankish thesis. Although Fustel de Coulanges one-sidedly stressed continuity with Rome, the problem from then on was confined to scholarly history. See Olivier-Martin, *Hist. du droit français,* 1 ff.

60. J. P. Mayer, *Alexis de Tocqueville, Prophet des Massenzeitalters* (1954).

61. N. Sombart in A. Weber, *Einführung in die Soziologie,* p. 81.

62. J. Ritter, *Hegel und die französische Revolution* [Arbeitsgemeinschaft für Forschung des Landes Nordrhein-Westfalen, **63**] (1957).

63. J. Ritter, *Hegel,* p. 36; H. Popitz, *Der entfremdete Mensch, Zeitkritik und Geschichtsphilosophie des jungen Marx (*1953), 117 ff.

64. Ritter, *Hegel,* p. 22.

65. *Encyklopädie des Geistes* § 433–435.

66. See the earlier discussion in this article.

67. *Philosophie der Geschichte, Sämtliche Werke,* **11**, 464 ff.

68. *Rechtsphilosophie* § 67, *Zusatz.*

69. *Ibid.,* § 57 *Zusatz.*

70. See the remarks of Th. Schieder in Ritter, *Hegel,* 67 f.

71. *Philosophie der Geschichte, Sämtliche Werke,* **11**, 464 ff., 504 ff.

72. See pt. III of this article.

73. L. v. Stein, *Geschichte der sozialen Bewegung in Frankreich von 1789 bis auf unsere Tage,* G. Salomon, ed. (1921) esp. **1**, 153 ff.

74. A. Weber, *Einführung in die Soziologie,* p. 455.

75. On Saint-Simon's importance for the young Marx, see G. Gurvitch, "La sociologie du jeune Marx," *La vocation actuelle de la sociologie* (1950). Compare the passage from the *Doctrine de Saint-Simon* cited here with the well-known passage in the *Kommunistischen Manifests* [Frühschriften, **2**], 575 f.

76. Karl Marx, *Die Frühschriften,* S. Landshut and I. P. Mayer, eds. **1** [Kröners Taschenausgabe, **81**], 209 f.

77. *Ibid.,* p. 126.

78. Joseph A. Schumpeter, *Kapitalismus, Sozialismus und Demokratie* (2d ed., 1950), 36 ff.; for a survival of this approach in a primitive ideological form, see I. Hindels, *Von der Urgesellschaft zum Sozialismus* (1950).

79. A. Timm, *Das Fach Geschichte in Forschung und Lehre in der sowjetischen Besatzungszone seit 1945* (1958), 80 f.; see the syllabus on "Gesamtüberblick und Periodisierung des Feudalismus."

80. Vol. 44 (1956). *Geschichte der UdSSR I. Feudalismus 9.–14. Jh.,* B. D. Grekow ed. (1957). *Zur Periodisierung des Feudalismus und Kapitalismus* [Supplement to the *Zeitschrift der Sowjetwissenschaft*] (1952). Although Marxists and some Western publicists see feudalism as surviving in China into the twentieth century, Sinologists restrict it to an early period, replaced later by "gentry society." D. Bodde, "Feudalism in China," *Feudalism in History,* R. Coulborn, ed. (1956), 49 ff.; W. Eberhard, *Chinas Geschichte* (1948).

81. K. D. Hüllmann, *Geschichte des Ursprungs der Stände in Deutschland* (2d ed., 1830).

82. W. Kayser, *Marwitz* (1936), p. 180.

83. Adam Müller, *Elementen der Staatskunst* J. Baxa, ed. (1922). The fourteenth lecture (**1**, 264 ff.), entitled "Von dem Wesen des Feudalismus," is a polemic against the strict absolute private property of Roman Law.

84. *Philosophie des Rechts* § 201 ff., § 303 ff. See Schieder in Ritter, *Hegel und die französische Revolution,* p. 68.

85. W. H. Riehl, *Die bürgerliche Gesellschaft* (6th ed., 1961).

86. C. Jantke, *Der vierte Stand* (1955), 86 ff.; H. Markmann in A. Weber, *Einleitung in die Soziologie,* 250 ff. The book of W. Schwer, *Stand und Ständeordnung im Weltbild des Mittelalters* (2d ed., 1952), does recognize the different nature of the medieval "ruling Estate," but as the editor, N. Monzel, says: Schwer remains tied to the popular "Marxist style."

87. F. Oppenheimer, *Sozial- und Wirtschaftsgeschichte Europas* [*System der Soziologie,* 4 (1929–1935)].

88. A. Rüstow, *Ortsbestimmung der Gegenwart* (1950–1957).

89. *Staat u. Verfassung* (1941), 74 ff.; Brunner, *Land u. Herrschaft,* 240 ff.

90. Schumpeter, *Kapit. Soz., u. Demokratie,* p. 37.

91. R. v. Albertini, *Das politische Denken in Frankreich zur Zeit Richelieus* (1951), 37 ff.

92. O. v. Gierke, *Das deutsche Genossenschaftsrecht,* 4 (1954), 204 ff.

93. G. v. Below, *Der deutsche Staat des Mittelalters* (2d ed., 1925).

94. *Sämtliche Werke,* **11**, 470 ff.

95. Vgl. Th. Ellwein, *Das Erbe der Monarchie in der deutschen Staatskrise* (1954).

96. See the remarks of H. Dannenbauer in *Herrschaft und Staat im Mittelalter* (1956), 60 ff.

97. P. Roth, *Feudalität u. Untertanenverband* (1863).

98. Brunner, *Land u. Herrschaft,* p. 111.

99. G. v. Below, *Der deutsche Staat des Mittelalters,* 282 ff.; H. Triepel, *Delegation und Mandat im öffentlichen Recht* (1942), who follows Von Below on the delegation of public rights through enfeoffment and grants of immunity.

100. *Sämtliche Werke,* **11**, 567 f.

101. *Ibid.,* p. 505.

102. H. Mitteis, "Über das Naturrecht," *Deutsche Akademie der Wissenschaften zu Berlin, Vorträge,* **26** (1948) and *Die Rechtsidee in der Geschichte* (1957).

103. Mitteis, *Der Staat des hohen Mittelalters,* p. 19.

104. *Ibid.,* p. 67.

105. *Ibid.,* p .424.

106. H. Mitteis, "Adelsherrschaft im Mittelalter," *Die Rechtsidee in der Geschichte,* 636 ff., esp. 649 f.

107. F. Lot and R. Fawtier, *Histoire des institutions françaises au moyen âge,* **1** (1957).

108. It must also be pointed out that even in the classical feudal state, France, feudal law was not all-pervasive; see Olivier-Martin *Hist. du droit français,* 642 ff.

109. W. Näf, "Frühformen des modernen Staates," *HZ,* **171** (1951), 225 ff.; F. Hartung, "Herrschafsverträge und ständischer Dualismus in deutschen Territorien," *Schweizer Beiträge zur allgemeinen Geschichte,* **10** (1952), 163 ff.

110. Th. Mayer, "Die Ausbildung der Grundlagen des 'modernen' deutschen Staates im hohen Mittelalter," *HZ,* **159** (1939), 463 ff.

111. M. Weber, *Wirtschaft und Gesellschaft,* J. Winckelmann, ed. (4th ed., 1955), 148 ff., 633 ff.; J. Winckelmann, *Staat und Gesellschaft in der verstehenden Soziologie Max Webers* (1957).

112. M. Weber, *Gesammelte Aufsätze zur Religionssoziologie,* **1** (1920), 1 ff.

113. M. Weber, *Wirtschaft und Gesellschaft,* pp. 128, 131.

114. J. Winckelmann, *Legitimität und Legalität in Max Webers Herrschaftssoziologie* (1952).

115. M. Weber, *Wirtschaft und Gesellschaft,* p. 124.

116. See earlier discussion in this article.

117. A conservative like Marwitz was of the opinion that the "legitimacy" of 1815 had replaced the relationship of "mutual duties," the form of government of earlier times, with a "one-sided, imaginary love." *Lebensbeschreibung,* **1**, 647. See C. J. Friedrich, *Constitutional Government and Democracy* (1950).

118. D. Gerhard, "Religionalismus und ständisches Wesen als Grundlage der europäischen Geschichte," *HZ,* **174** (1952), 307 ff.; K. v. Raumer, "Absoluter Staat, korporative Libertät, persönliche Freiheit," *HZ,* **183** (1957), 55 ff.

119. Mitteis, *Der Staat des hohen Mittelalters,* p. 434.

120. W. Näf, *Die Epochen der neueren Geschichte,* **1** (1945), 411 ff.

121. R. E. Huber, *Deutsche Verfassungsgeschichte seit 1789,* **1** (1957), 640 ff.

122. O. Hintze, *Staat und Verfassung, Gesammelte Abhandlungen zur allgemeinen Verfassungsgeschichte* (1941), 74 ff.

123. O. Hintze, "Typologie der ständischen Verfassungen des Abendlandes," and "Weltgeschichtliche Bedingungen der Repräsentativverfassung," *Staat und Verfassung,* 110 ff., 130 ff.

124. See the bibl. in Hintze's *Staat und Verfassung* and *Zur Theorie der Geschichte* (1942).

125. The problems discussed are mainly of continental origin, as can be seen from the materials used. English and American historical sociology has as its main concern the transition from "savage" to "civilized" society. In it, feudalism appears as a transitional stage. See H. E. Barnes, *Historical Sociology* (1940). The reasons for the difference in approach are obvious.

126. *Feudalism in History,* Coulborn, ed. (1956).

127. Thus F. Altheim uses the concept "feudalism" in a very general way when he finds "feudalism" at Attila's court, a pattern of tribal chiefs and bureaucracy in the form of "scribes"; *Attila und die Hunnen* (1951), 102 ff. He uses it in another form, in his studies on the Near East, *Utopia und Wirtschaft* (1957), esp. 103 ff., where he seems to be concerned with the prehistory of Max Weber's *Pfründenfeudalismus,* without really going deeply into it.

128. An example could be the appearance of "cataphracts," soldiers in full armor, which Altheim mentions in his various studies.

129. E. Rothacker in *Zeitschrift für vergleichende Rechtswissenschaft,* **60** (1957), 13 ff.

LORDSHIP AND NOBILITY

I. Dominion

LORD AND FOLLOWER IN GERMANIC INSTITUTIONAL HISTORY*

Walter Schlesinger

The German Middle Ages knew several kinds of lordship. The head of a household was "lord" of those who belonged to his house; the great landowner was lord of his dependents; the leader of an armed band was "lord" of his followers; the territorial prince was lord of his territory. With the development of feudal ties, a new form of lordship appeared; the lordship of a lord over his vassals, called "feudal" lordship. Those who looked after the regular and orderly proceedings of courts and who guaranteed enforcement of the judgments found by a court's assessors acquired a "court lordship." "Church lordship" grew out of the proprietary rights of church founders over their churches. Villages and towns were under village lords and town lords. So too, the position of the king in his kingdom was a lordship; "lord" was the suitable title by which to address him. And over

* From Walter Schlesinger, "Herrschaft und Gefolgschaft in der germanisch-deutschen Verfassungsgeschichte," *Historische Zeitschrift,* **176** (Munich, 1953), 225–275. Reprinted in W. Schlesinger, *Beiträge zur deutschen Verfassungsgeschichte des Mittelalters* (Göttingen, 1963), **1**, 9–52. Trans. by the ed. Portions of pp. 227–231, 233, 236, and 266–269, omitted in this translation by the kind permission of the author, have been signaled by ellipses.

all these earthly forms of lordship stood the lordship of God over heaven and earth, over time and eternity. God (and, similarly, Christ) was simply "the Lord."

To be sure, lordship was not the only creator of political order in the Middle Ages. No less effective was the creative power of the community. Every lordship had a particular communal element associated with it. Nor did lordship first create community. The latter grew from separate roots; its origins were autonomous. The kin group took the form of a community; so did the cult group (which lived on in the guild); so did the vill and the town commune; and, finally, so did the territory in the territorial Estate or as a "province." Perhaps all associations grew out of the cult-community, where every member stood in the same relation to the deity and the priest performed his functions, not by virtue of a divine mandate, but by a mandate from the community. The kin group was also a cult group, as was the early tribe, in which, to be sure, lordship was also an active force. Lordship and community penetrated each other in a variety of institutions; the penetration is clearly recognizable in the simplest form of association: the household. This essay will not deal with community; but, consciously one-sided, will be restricted solely to a discussion of lordship. Thus, it must not be taken as a description of the entire institutional structure of early medieval peoples and territories, but as a description of simply one aspect, an aspect that seems to me to be fundamental.[1]

We shall begin with a brief look at the linguistic evidence, at least at some of the Germanic materials (without any attempt to survey all the Germanic tongues).[2] The oldest known Old High German already had three words for "lord": *"frô,"*[3] *"truhtîn,"* and *"hêrro."* The same words appeared in Old Saxon: *"frô," "drohtîn," "hêrro."*[4] Did these words denote clearly distinguishable forms of lordship? The evidence gives no clue. Only *"truhtîn,"* an ancient *n*-form (like Latin *domus* > *dominus*) shows an original well-defined special meaning. The word came from the world of the warrior band; *"truhtîn"* was the lord of the band. The Goths must already have used this word in this sense. But very early, the word *"hêrro"* took on this same meaning; it was already used this way in the oldest piece of Old High German poetry, the *Hildebrandslied* (verse 47), and frequently in the *Heliand*. . . . It is important to note that all these words were used especially to designate the king, including the heavenly king, God and Christ. Apparently, this was especially true of *"frô,"* whose genetive plural form, *"frôno,"* was used as an indeclinable adjective meaning *"publicus"*: "public" was that which was related to the lord. In the *Ludwigslied* (verse 5) *"frônisc githigini"* appeared as an equivalent for the *"trustis dominica"* of the *Lex Salica*. *"Hèrro"* finally displaced the other words, a development we need not be concerned with here.

Hêrro" began to combine with other words only very late.[5] With the exception of *"skefhêrro" (nauclerus)* which belongs to the relatively early Monseer glosses, composite forms such as *"hûshêrro"* [house-lord], *"kirihhêrro"* [church-lord], *"lanthêrro"* [landlord] appeared only in the eleventh and twelfth centuries, *"lêhanhêrro"* [fief-lord] and *"munthêrro"* [lord giving protection], in the thirteenth. Although the evidence is quite fragmentary, one is forced to the conclusion that the various kinds of ancient lordship were consciously differentiated only relatively late.

The results are the same when we look at the Latin expressions used in early medieval sources. The word *"dominus,"* which had long since lost all connection with house (*domus*), was used to denote a "lord" in a general sense. There is even evidence of its early use merely as a form of polite address, applied to an ever-widening circle of people. It is used too frequently in this way for us to be able to draw any distinctions from its application. It is worth pointing out, however, that the king appeared as *dominus* without any modifier; thus, *"dominium"* many times meant royal lordship, and significantly, *"dominicus"* in the *Lex Salica* meant "pertaining to the king," as it did in the so-called synodal laws of the Wends.[6] But both *"dominium"* and *"dominicus"* also generally meant "lordship" and "pertaining to lordship"—and referred to lordship of many gradations. Naturally the word was applied to God, on the example of the Vulgate. Besides *"dominus"* and its forms, the later Latin word *"senior"* was used. It later became the special name for the feudal lord; but before the development of feudal relationships, it appeared as a word for king.[7] As far as I know, it was used only very rarely to refer to God, though in the form *"senior ecclesiae"* it had already appeared in the sixth century.[8]

Latin and German words for "lord" thus developed along similar lines. All could refer to the king. Likewise (it is important to note), all could be applied to God and Christ. Used thus, the words referred to the biblically founded kingdom of God and Christ, the kingdom of the King of Kings and Lord of Lords, of the *"allero cuningo craftigost,"* as He is called in the *Heliand.* In Germanic lands the *"dominus"* of the Vulgate and church liturgy could be conceived of only as parallel to earthly kings. Thus lordship was the essence of kingship. Kingship, according to linguistic evidence, was not a lordship *sui generis;* it was of the same essence as the lordship of other lords, though of a more exalted kind. . . .

The household in Germanic territories had the legal form of both lordship and community.[9] Here we will speak only of lordship. The lord of the household was its head: he answered for it; he ordered its life. He possessed broad powers over those in his household who did not have full standing in law: over his wife and children, over unfree and (to a lesser extent) free servants. His power of disposal over the unfree in his household was unlimited, although softened by custom—especially where the unfree did not live in the house itself but, as Tacitus already observed, were given land on which they owed a rent and were economically self-sufficient, like the late-Roman *coloni*.[10] Thus, already at this time, a kind of "landlordship" or landed seigniory was developing out of the lordship of the household, a landlordship rooted in personal servitude rather than in the renting of land. The "house" included more than the lord's living quarters with its outbuildings; it included a complex of habitations which ought to be called a village. Tacitus reports that Civilis, the leader of the Batavi revolt, controlled several *villae* on the Lower Rhine, by which the Roman historian undoubtedly meant estates with *coloni* attached to them—and surely not *coloni* of Roman origin.[11] (Whether such forms are to be recognized in the archaeological evidence, in differences in grave contents, for example, cannot be discussed here.) We should not forget these "unfree" roots of later village lordship. . . .

The lord of the household also had a power of discipline over wife and children, even the right to sell them in case of extreme necessity. Above all, he had the power to demand that all members of the household, free and servile, take part in feuds, even when blood vengeance was not involved. He had the power to command, as well as the power to protect. The lord of the house not only assured its members the necessities of life, as their *"hlaford"* [breadwinner] as the Anglo-Saxons called him; the lord also answered for them in court and upheld their rights against attacks from outside. He was moreover responsible for everything they did on his order and even, in part, for those things they did without his order. The power that belonged to the lord of the household was called *"munt"*; the person to whom that power belonged was called—in the *Heliand*, for example—*"mundboro,"* in Anglo-Saxon *"mundbora."* This power extended far beyond the simple duty of protecting one's blood group; it stretched over those who did not have full standing at law. Thus it was not rooted in the clan (*Sippe*). . . .

How did lordship over free men develop? This question raises the problem of the origins of the "state" among the ancient Germans, one of the "greatest puzzles of early institutional history."[12] We can attempt only a partial answer here, beginning not with the clan but with the household.[13] How did it happen that the *munt* of the household lord came to be extended over free men not originally belonging to the house?

When a free man sought the protection of the lord of a household, he renounced a part of his free standing in law and thus required someone's *munt*. For example, in ancient times the free German recognized no general military duty in the modern sense. Should an enemy invade the land, every able-bodied person naturally joined in the fight to expel the invaders. Indeed, this was more a right than a duty. The obligation to obey a general levy of fighting men, however, did not exist except in the case of "holy war."[14] And in times of holy war, as Tacitus tells us, the free German did not appear in obedience to the order of a war leader (who had no authority like the Roman *imperium*), but rather "by the mandate of the god, whom they believe inspires the warrior."[15] The individual who was personally dependent on another, however, did owe obedience to such a general levy of fighting men. This kind of personal dependence was created when someone living in the vicinity of a fortification (*Burg*) sought the protection of a powerful lord in cases of necessity.[16] A great number of these rampart-enclosed places (*Wallburgen*) dating from the Germanic period have been found; and, undoubtedly, more small fortified lords' houses will be found in the future, for they were always the site of later construction. As places of refuge, these strongholds already existed at the time of Tacitus.[17] Those who sought refuge there simultaneously undertook the obligation to help with its upkeep and defense. Thus the lord could *order* them to contribute to its upkeep and defense. As far as I know, events of this kind are not related by the evidence we have for the earliest period. We must assume they occurred, however, or else the nature of the Germanic fortified place, which the sources testify to, becomes incomprehensible. I doubt, however, if it is valid to distinguish between fortified places belonging to a lord (*Herrenburgen*) and those belonging to the community (*Genossenschaftsburgen*).

The nature of these fortified places appears clearly in one source where one would not expect to find it: in the Old Saxon Genesis. When the poet describes the destruction of Sodom and Gomorrha, he takes great liberties with the biblical text. Clearly, he has his own world in mind. He speaks not only of the destruction of the city of Sodom but also of the destruction of *Sodomaland,* also called *"Sodomarîki."* The principal center is *Sodomaburg,* a fortified place with at least one tower. The inhabitants of this land are the *Sodomoliudi* or *Sodomothiod.* For the sake of the just among them, Abraham asks to be allowed to settle in the territory and to live near the fortified places (*bûan an them burugium*); thus, there are others besides *Sodomaburg.* In these fortified places there are "ports" (*wic*), living quarters; a collective plural, *"brêd burugugisetu,"* designates the entire complex of the settlement.[18] The poet perhaps pictures the Saxon situation in the ninth century, but a comparison with England indicates that its essential aspects must be much older. English historical documents of the most traditional type show an arrangement that resembles the one described by the Saxon poet. Kent is inhabited by the *Cantwara.* (The last syllable is similar to the first in *"wergeld";* the word must mean "men of Kent.") The district is called *"Centland,"* or *"Centrice,"* and the chief town of the territory is called *"Cantwarabyrig"* [Canterbury]. The settlements around them are called *"port,"* a word that in England is known to have replaced the earlier *"wic."*[19] In comparing the Anglo-Saxon with the Saxon, we are led back to the time before the two were divided. Moreover, *Beowulf* (verse 53) and the *Heliand* (verses 1203, 2825) confirm these conclusions by speaking of fortified places around the territory and by mentioning the *wic* in connection with them (*Heliand,* verse 2827).

Even in non-Saxon Germany, a similar situation seems to have existed. . . . These fortified places in the *Heliand* belong to lords; for both Solomon and Herod appears as *burges uuard* [protector of the *burg*] (verses 1678, 2772). Historical evidence again confirms this with Saxon place-names formed from individual names, as Brunsburg or Hiltifridesburg. . . . But a sharp distinction between district fortified centers (*Gebieterburg*) and refuge centers (*Fluchtburg*) is as little justifiable in Germany as would be a distinction between places belonging to a lord and those belonging to a community. The word *"burges uuard"* is sometimes replaced in the *Heliand* by *"folctogo"* [folk leader] (verses 5407 ff.). The commander of the *burg* and the leader of the people are thus identical. . . .

It is understandable how, very early, the power of a lord whose residence was in or near a fortified place extended out over the free people living in the surrounding area. One can no longer call this power *"munt,"* but it is clear that it was an extension of the lord's household *munt* or at least was constructed along the same lines.[20] The power of command belonging to the lord of a fortified place, later called the *"burgban"*—as we find at Corvey, Gandersheim, Seeburg, Greene, and Magdeburg as well as along the Middle-Rhine[21]—was something that split off from the *munt* of the household lord. The fortified place was in effect the lord's house, even when he did not continuously live there. Thus, among the Anglo-Saxons the lord's house was called *burg*, but the peasant's house was not.[22]

When a free man came under a lord's protection in this way, his free status was not lessened. Coming under someone's protection could lead to a loss of freedom, but did not necessarily do so. To be free did not mean to be fully free to do everything. Wife and children were without question as free as the head of the house, yet at the same time, they were under his *munt*. Thus, subjection to a *munt* did not by itself mean a lessening of freedom. On the other hand, a lessening of duties brought with it a lessening of rights. To the extent that one took an active part in the tasks established by the community he enjoyed various rights. Here is the point where might and right met. In any event, whether through voluntary subjection or forced subjection by a greater power, the free might gradually come under the lordship of another person. In a later age the exercise of lordship over free men would be the most important sign of nobility.

The group of armed followers (*comitatus*) was built on this same foundation: free men subjecting themselves to a lord for military purposes. A variety of relationships could be involved, however.[23] In the following discussion we will be concerned with the relationship between lord and follower, a relationship freely entered upon, based on fidelity, and obligating the follower to give counsel and military aid, the lord to give protection and largesse. We will not be concerned with the relationship between a superior and the subjects who obey his orders.

The free German knew no obedience, at least no unqualified obedience. Bonds of friendship and fidelity tied the lord and his follower together. In a later age, the follower swore *trustem et fidelitatem* to his lord [faith—that is, help—and fidelity]. Fidelity was both an all-encompassing relationship and a mutual relationship; the follower owed it to his lord and the lord to his follower, his man. For the lord to act against right, that is, against his follower's rights, was not permitted. Should he do so anyway, he could no longer count on his demands being executed. The follower was always as free in his decision as was the lord; the follower did not have to do whatever his lord demanded, but only what he was convinced was the right thing to do. There is much evidence, not only that the lord asked his followers' advice, but also that he followed it, even against his own original decision.

The foundation for the bond between lord and follower was the oath of fidelity, for whose existence we have evidence as far back as the old Germanic period.[24] The follower placed himself under the lord's protection, entered his household, and became his "table-companion." Mainly young men entered this kind of service (which, as we shall see, was not the only kind of lord-follower relationship). Tacitus, at the end of his description of the coming of age of Germanic youth, the ceremony in which they received the arms of adulthood, relates how a band of exceptional youth (*iuvenes*) grant their "virtue" and might to a leader.[25] The author of the *Heliand* uses *"jungiro,"*[26] [youth] as a word to designate the armed follower, in contrast to *"hêrro,"* [the elder]. . . . Many of those who entered a lord's household as followers were thus children. Beowulf was seven years old when he entered the household of King Hrethel.[27] The word *"degen,"* sometimes used to designate a follower, is etymologically related to the Greek *"téchnon,"* [child]. When the follower entered the lord's house, he came under the lord's *munt,* which he left only when he had proved himself in the use of arms. For only a deed of arms could demonstrate his excellence. When the follower had accomplished this, he was taken into the circle of true warriors. The lord gave him weapons and horse, clothing, and above all the ring that plays such a large role in the epics. To the Germanic mind, this gift made visible the lord's "blessing."

Tacitus also speaks of ranks within the group of followers. These must have mainly involved a division between the "youth" and the proved warriors (*robustiores ac iam pridem probati*). *Beowulf* mentions the distinction between *geoguð* and *duguð* [youth and virtue]. Great is the pride, says Tacitus, of the man who stands next to the lord. This "elder" of the group plays a major role in many epic poems. Think of Hildebrand, Hagen, Wate. Since it was always possible to dissolve the bonds of the *comitatus,* it was a matter of honor not to desert the lord before a battle or in misfortune.

Among themselves, the followers formed a very tight association, with mutual obligations to give aid and counsel. Like the members of a clan, they called each other "friend"; thus the word *"nôtfriunt,"* [battle-friend]. *Beowulf* also contains words such as *"maguthegnas"* [young kin retainers]; and, even, *"magas"* [kinsmen] for the followers (verse 1015); and, for the band of followers, *"sibbegedryht"* [band of kinsmen] (verses 3, 87, 729). Thus, the association among followers seems to have followed the pattern of the family group (*Sippe*).[28] The murder of a member called for blood vengeance; feud between members was not allowed: differences were settled by the lord.

Any free German could collect a retinue around him, provided his reputation was sufficiently great to attract followers and provided he had the means to support them and to give them gifts. These lords of retinues were called *"principes"* by Caesar and Tacitus. What the Germans called them, we do not know. In a later age, the Latin *princeps* translated the Old High German *"furisto," "hêrôsto,"* and *"hêrro."* In the age of Caesar and Tacitus, however, the German equivalent must have been *"truhtîn,"* which, as we saw, originally meant the lord of an armed band. Tacitus gives *"princeps"* this same special meaning in his *Germania*.[29]

These *principes* have sometimes been strangely misconceived as "dukes" who held elective "offices." We must first ask what meaning the word *"princeps"* had to the Romans of Tacitus' time; for, in using this word Tacitus must have wished to make clear to his readers what Germanic lords were like. In Rome at this time *"princeps"* designated a man of high standing, of superior rank, who imposed himself by his authority, not by virtue of any office. The leading example was Augustus, who styled himself *"princeps,"* to indicate that he ruled because of his prestige and authority, not because of any office, and above all, not as king. When Tacitus wrote, "In these same councils they elect *principes* to render law in the villages and lands" (*per pagos vicosque*),[30] he could not have meant that they elected people to be *principes,* but only that those *principes* were chosen who were to render law. If read thus, it is all the same whether *pagi* and *vici* [lands and villages] are to be understood as court districts or not. (It is clear only that if one thus interprets *pagus,* he must do the same for *vicus.*) Only *principes* were able to preside over the courts, as Ceasar already indicates. In peacetime, Ceasar says, the *principes regionum atque pagorum* [the *principes* of the regions and territories] render law among their people (*inter suos*) and settle disputes. A *magistratus* is chosen only in time of war.[31] The ability to hold a court was a privilege of the *principes.* The emphasis should be placed, not on the election of the judges, but on the fact that only *principes* could be chosen. These *principes* received free gifts from members of the clans and from individuals. In the assembly of people they had the most important voice. On lesser matters they could decide by themselves; on important matters, they first conferred among themselves and then presented their conclusion to the assembly to accept or reject.

The *principes* did not form a closed caste. Noble birth was very important, to be sure; there was a nobility by birth—"They elect their kings from among those with noble blood" (*reges ex nobilitate sumunt*). In the second century B.C., Livy spoke of "noble youths and the children of kings" among the Bastarnae.[32] Insofar as anything is known about their origins, the *principes* came from noble families. Tacitus likewise spoke of *nobiles* who seem to be identical with the *principes*.[33] (Now and then he also used the very unspecific expression, *"proceres."*)[34] If, on the other hand, the war lord was chosen *ex virtute,* he also must have had the status and prestige of a *princeps,* but not necessarily noble birth, as the opposition to *"ex nobilitate"* in the relevant sentence undoubtedly indicates: ["They select their kings from those with noble blood, their war leaders from those with prowess" (*ex virtute*).][35] Here we have the original nobleman: the man who acquired his position not by birth, but by his actions. Exceptional prowess not only raised the individual above the others, but gave him a heritable status as well; a father's exceptional action gave his son a share in *dignatio;* a father's prowess ennobled his son.[36] This outlook was connected with the belief in the grace belonging to the clan (*Sippenheil*) and was one of the roots of heritable "kingworthiness" found later on. Even before the migrations began, the class of nobility must have gradually become fixed—all in all, a class of lords, to whose exceptional quality the right to have an armed retinue belonged. "The *principes* vie with each other as to who shall have the most numerous and the bravest followers. It is an honor and a source of strength always to be thus surrounded by a large troop of picked youths, an ornament in time of peace, a guard in time of war."[37]

To the extent that it went beyond the household, ancient Germanic lordship was lordship of a retinue. At the same time the latter was closely related to household lordship and, to a large degree, grew out of it. As *Beowulf* demonstrates in its description of King Hrothgar's followers, these originally were members of the household. We can also see the connection of house and armed retinue in another way. It is doubtful whether there existed in the earliest period any comprehensive "clan peace" or "folk peace." Nordic sources especially, suggest conditions quite different from such a "peace." In these areas, because of the continuous family blood feuds and the desire for vengeance and booty, the relation of lord to house must have acquired many of the characteristics of lord and military following. Hans Kuhn has even suggested that one of the roots of the group of armed followers is to be found in the extended peasant family.[38]We must be very cautious, to be sure, in generalizing from Icelandic materials; but the picture Tacitus gives of the conditions among the Cherusci ("they had lost all their nobles in civil war, and only one was left from the royal family, who was living in Rome"[39]) does not say much for the folk peace; and the detailed lists of *wergeld* contained in the so-called folk laws suggest circumstances similar to those in the Nordic countries. Nor, finally, does the importance of the blood feud, even in much later times,[40] suggest the existence of an early folk peace. Had such a thing ever existed, it disappeared during the long, war-filled period of migration.[41] All this suggests that, in addition to the "noble" retinue described by Tacitus, there must have existed peasant armed retinues on a lower level. The entire tribe, or if one prefers, the entire people, must have been fundamentally divided into such groups of armed followers. The word *"Gesinde,"* which originally designated the follower, was used to refer to peasants; since the word means "road companion," its warlike roots are evident. Besides the landless *Gesinde* (*"Gesinde"* in the narrow sense), dependent small peasants also appeared very early: wandering serfs or freemen who placed themselves under the *munt* of the wealthy peasants. Undoubtedly, there was also something of an armed-follower relationship between the Icelandic *Gode* and *Dingmann*.[42] Similarly, in Saxony where Germanic conditions remained in a relatively pure state, Erich Molitor has suggested that peasant bands of armed followers existed—even though, in the ninth century, the *nobiles* appeared almost everywhere as the lords of the *liberi* [the free].[43]

The way the *comitatus* gave its form to the household even found an echo in marriage law, where the married woman appeared as the "companion joined to her husband by the ties of a follower" (*Gefolgschaftsband*).[44] It is therefore not suprising that the later power of lord over his peasants was not one-sided, but, as has been well said, was a quasi-contractual relationship.[45] This thoroughly expressed the essence of the ancient band of followers.

We cannot here discuss the extent to which the period of migrations was the heyday of the band of followers. The Germanic epics are its precipitate—though only of its noble form. (For these were aristocratic poems; we cannot expect them to show the life of the peasantry.) The religious poems of a later time were also linked to this form of organization through their vocabulary, which, to an astonishing degree, was the vocabulary of the armed following and its lord. So much did the armed following permeate society.[46]

During the migrations, another special kind of following developed, one that Caesar described among the migrating Germanic tribes rather than the settled ones.[47] It was not a new invention of the period of migration. A *princeps* rose in the folk assembly to say that he wished to lead a raid for booty: whoever wanted to join him should make himself known. Those who wanted to join spoke up and immediately gave their fealty to the leader; whoever then backed out was a deserter and traitor. The Viking expeditions must have begun in the same way. So, too, must those expeditions in search of foreign lands to conquer, the *princeps* gathering a retinue around him with their women, children, and all their belongings in their train and setting off to found a new permanent settlement. Ariovistus must have brought together the kernel of his group in this way. When such a vast undertaking was involved, recruiting must have been done beyond the folk assembly and the recruits must have come from more than one small clan. Not only individuals, but also *principes* with their followings reinforced for the occasion, joined in the special undertaking They arranged themselves freely under the leader, to whose safety they pledged their faith, much as the leader's own following had done. The leader thus became a war king. If the undertaking was successful, the settlement achieved, and the kingdom founded, then the war troop became a new tribe and the war king a tribal king. In this way, royal power was rooted in lordship over an armed following. This was especially the case among the Alemanni, who were ruled, according to Ammianus, by a multitude of *reges, regales,* and *reguli,* that is, petty kings whose dominion could not have come from anything but the leadership of an armed retinue. Expressions such as "kings and their people," "all of Gundomadi's people," "Vadomari's people," "the kings and people of the Alemanni," "Hortari's realm," and the like, speak clearly enough.[48]

The story of the Batavian rebellion of A.D. 69 is conclusive.[49] Civilis, a member of a royal family, sought to establish a kingdom, though not by leading a migration or by settling people bound to him in a foreign territory. At the start of the rebellion, Civilis called an assembly of the *primores gentis et promptissimi vulgi* [the chiefs of the people and the boldest of the lower class] who, "following barbarian custom," swore an oath—an act in which we must see the oath-taking of the band of armed followers. Several tribes were involved from the beginning; the Canninefates elected their leader by raising him on a shield, a ceremony that was later used especially for royal elections. (Again, the connection between kingship and the institution of the armed following is clear.) In the battle each tribe was placed separately, "so that each might make clear its own prowess," as Tacitus says.[50] The tribes were under a common leader, however—a leader who, had the revolt not failed, certainly would have become king. Thus, the tribes had their own separate life, as much as they did in the later Frankish and German kingdoms. Apparently, "personality of law" had already taken root.

Once again the Old Saxon Genesis presents a lively expression of the ideas that lay behind such kingdom-founding, in the verses where the poet describes the Angel's Fall (verse 278 ff.). Although the relation of Lucifer to God is not drawn specifically in terms of the armed follower to his lord, but rather, in terms of the relation of a servant to his household lord, it is with an armed following in mind that the rebellious Angel throws off God's grace. Lucifer has more *folcgestealna* than He. Also, God the Father is clearly thought of as both the heavenly household lord and the lord of a retinue. In the following passage, Lucifer thinks of founding his own power. Without a biblical model, the poet gives free rein to his own invention:

> Why must I strive? he said. / It pleases me little,
> To have a lord. / I can with my own hands as many
> Wonders work. / I have power enough
> To build / a statelier throne
> One higher yet in heaven. / Why must I serve for his grace,
> Give to him such allegiance? / I can be God like him.
> Strong companions stand by me. / In a fight they will not fail.
> Strong-minded heroes; / they have chosen me lord,
> Famous warriors. / From such one has good counsel,
> Takes good counsel with such folk-supporters. / They are my ready friends,
> They are brave in their minds' intention. / I can be their Lord,
> Rule this kingdom. / It does not seem right to me,
> That I / should have at all to implore
> God for any gifts; / no longer will I be his follower.[51]

Lucifer prowls around the *stôl,* the throne in the great hall of the house. He has had his fill of being subject to a lord (*heárran*) whose favor (*hyldo*) he must serve; he would rule the kingdom himself.[52] He would himself be lord, the "Old one," not the "youth." The word is never said, but the meaning is clear: he would be king in place of God. Unambiguously, the lordship that Lucifer seeks is over a band of followers. It is borne by strong fellows, courageous heroes, famous men, *folcgesteallan* [roughly translated, "folk-fellows"], that is, the members of the folk who have formed a retinue. They are his friends (*frŷnd*) and dear to him; the grace and favor that binds lord to man here shines through. They will not desert him in battle and will aid him with good counsel; thus, they will fulfill the twin duties of the follower, aid and counsel. These comrades (and this is important) have elected Lucifer their lord (*tô hearran gecorene*). It remains unclear whether this phrase means (1) the election of a leader in the manner described by Tacitus among the Canninefates; (2) an act for a well-defined single purpose, as with Civilis; or (3) that the followers have attached themselves to Lucifer one by one (for this is also described in Old Saxon as "electing a lord").[53] The procedure of the election is not essential, however. What is important is that the man who sought to erect a royal lordship depended on his followers; these were the chief props of his future power, the only ones mentioned. One cannot doubt that the emergence of kingdoms among the early Germans was preceded by events of this kind, that kingship was claimed by war. Historical sources show this clearly. Again, might and right were closely entwined. Victory was decisive.

Victory brought not only a considerable increase in a king's power, but in his authority as well. The kingly grace (*Königsheil*) had stood the test and the king's sacred consecration grew with his outward might. Widukind gives a beautiful example of this mentality. The Saxons, after their victory over the Thuringians, proclaimed that their battle leader must possess transcendent valor and the spirit of God.[54] The Germans did not have to be forced to follow such a leader. They elected him leader and swore to him their fidelity. In the kingdoms of the period of migrations the *principes,* the king's followers were closest to the throne; as the king's power grew, so did theirs. The lord's largesse, of which the poets so often sang, expressed itself in great, sometimes gigantic, assignments of land, which the lord's followers in turn divided among their own followers, their peasants. Already, such land division is spoken of in *Beowulf.*[55]

Thus, settlements were, at least in part, of the lords' foundation from the first—above all because the lords had always to count on a fixed subject population. There were also peasant settlers who received their land directly from the king (apparently referred to in title 45, *De Migrantibus,* of the *Lex Salica*). As the kin groups must have stayed together in war and migration, so they must have settled together. The community of the wealthy peasant and his small peasants and household servants must also have weathered the hardships of migration. Kin groups and "peasant migration communities"[56] were mirrored in the immensely varied nature of settlement.[57] Along with the villages that grew from households, various group settlements were founded in the period of migrations. Those place names formed from a personal name and an "-ing" ending suggest that one individual must have led the settlement, in contrast to the communal union of the settlers. The rich peasant became lord of one village; lords of several villages were the immediate followers of the war king and thus the successors to the *principes* of ancient Germany. These lords too, had their followers, so that the various retinues formed a gradated social structure. This was already so in the time of Tacitus, who relates how Inguiomerus with his followers (*cum manu clientium*) went over to Maroboduus because he felt it beneath him to be subject to the young Arminius.[58] The voluntary nature of such subjection to the lordship of a rising king could not be clearer, nor could it be clearer that the ties of follower to lord were stronger than those of kin to kin: the Cherusci followers of Inguiomerus fought without hesitation on the side of their own people's enemy.

Later, this gradated social structure is most clearly recognizable in England.[59] Here the petty kings maintained earlier ways much better than the continental kings, for in England no living Roman institutions survived, to be taken account of. Beneath the kings were subkings (*subreguli*), for whose existence among continental tribes we also have evidence.[60] In addition to the kings and subkings, a host of so-called *duces* existed in these petty kingdoms; Bede reports that no less than thirty *duces regii* came to the aid of Penda of Mercia.[61] The king's followers played an important role in the institutional life of the country, and it is clear that these followers had their own retinues, as had been the case with Inguiomerus. Thus, in the list of witnesses to a charter of 738, we find: *"Ego Vilbaldus commites meos confirmare et subscribere feci,"* [I, Willobald, have my retinue confirm and subscribe] and six others of the same kind.[62] In the seventh century we find the members of the king's group of followers (*gesithcund*) in possession of extensive territories worked by their peasants.[63] Peasant groups of followers also remained. Even in the time of Alfred both *eorl* and *ceorl* had people under them, by whom they might be betrayed. The *ceorl* like the *eorl* was a *hlaford,* a lord.[64]

It would not be mistaken to assume that the same situation had originally existed on the continent. As the monarch rose, so did the nobility. This joint emergence was clearest among the Lombards, whose *duces* were the immediate successors of the older *principes* and, perhaps, was also what lay behind the five "genealogies" in the *Lex Baiuvariorum.* Marked differences separated the development of different tribes, depending on each tribe's particular destiny; but in general, the small lords of Tacitus' time became great lords in the course of settlement. As they had once lived in a lord's house, so they now lived in the king's court (this did not exclude their having a household under them; in fact, they usually did). They did the judging in the king's court; with their aid and counsel, they helped the king to govern;[65] and whenever they could, they tried to assert the right to elect the king themselves.[66] Inevitably, opposition very soon developed between this noble order and the king. For, implanted in Roman land, kingship was now gaining strength from the soil of Christian antiquity, in a way that must have appeared foreign and shocking to Germanic ideas—though, to be sure, the great men were also putting to use the ruins of the Roman provincial world.

That the noble order of the Frankish kingdom became the germ cell of the West was an event of world-historical significance. The armed retinue, whose nature derived from the period of migrations, was the basis of this noble power; now this group became the private army, and one must assume that military service continued to be demanded of the free peasantry as well. The Carolingians rose to power at the head of a private army. It followed that the noble families coming from the territories between the Maas and the Mosel, the home of the Carolingians, rose to power with them. The Frankish kings did not succeed in breaking the power of these noblemen; along with the kings, they remained the carriers of Frankish history. They ruled from the North Sea to the

Mediterranean: under the king, next to the king, and, often enough, against the king. In the documents, they appear as *optimates, potentes, maiores, seniores, primi, principes, primates, maiores natu, nobiles,* and *nobiliores.* Besides the word used to translate *"nobilis"* in particular (*Adel*), the German word that sufficed to translate all the rest was *"hêrro"* (although it must be remembered that our evidence for this word comes only from the late Frankish period). Notker[67] and the glosses translate the Old High German *"hêrro"* with the Latin *magnates, proceres, magni, senatores, possessores, principes,* and *potentes,* as well as with *magistratus, patres curules,* and *domini;* the entire stock of Latin words was used to refer to the members of the Frankish nobility. The word *"hêrro"* was used in Old Saxon before the Frankish conquest, as the *Heliand* testifies, and it was used to mean the leader of an armed following. If the word was taken over by the Saxons from the Franks (a possibility its absence from Anglo-Saxon suggests), then we have another argument that the Frankish nobility were essentially lords of armed followings.

Royal lordship and noble lordship were originally as little distinguished from each other as were royal law and folk law. According to both prologues to the *Lex Salica,* the Frankish *proceres* were those men who "found" the law to be recorded (at least such was the pretense); in other codifications, the cooperation of the great men was, at the least, imagined. For instance, the seventh-century laws of King Wihtred of Kent were found by the great men: *"ða eadigan funden,"* says the prologue.[68] Sacred blood (*Geblütsheiligkeit*) ran in the veins of the nobility as well as in that of the royal family;[69] on this basis, any noble family could take the kingship. The *stirps regia* [the royal race] that Tacitus speaks of among the Cherusci was the family of Arminius who, though not yet a king, was clearly on his way. The same was probably true of Civilis.[70] Among the Anglo-Saxons the *dux* (*heretoga*) possessed the same victory-bringing virtue as the king.[71] Likewise, the "older" and "younger" ducal dynasties of the German tribes did not consider themselves essentially different from the king. One, like the other, was raised up by the great followers.

Sources that are sometimes considered of little value make this clear—a passage in the *Vita Mathildis antiquior,* for example. The *principes* as a tribal assembly (*regni consilium*) discuss who is to have the *heroum principatum.* They elect Heinrich duke; he later becomes king. He even expresses the wish to become king.[72] At the time of Henry II, the *Bavarii,* that is, the Bavarian nobility, had the right to elect their duke.[73] It is also known that in 919 they claimed the right to make their duke a king.[74] Ekkehard von Meissen was elevated Duke of Thuringia "by the election of all the people" (*communi totius populi electione*).[75] He, in turn, made the Duke of Bohemia his *miles* (again a glimmer of the law of the armed retinue). Whatever the term *"miles"* might mean here, clearly, the Margrave already before 1002 was claiming rights as lord of the powerful

Duke of Bohemia, rights that by our conceptions should have been reserved to the king; and we should not be surprised that the Margrave eventually laid claim to the royal crown. Already once before, in the seventh century, a duke of Thuringia had pretended to such a title. According to Pseudo-Fredegar, Duke Rudolph styled himself "King in Thuringia."[76]

To put the sparsely scattered evidence together: the step from duke to king was possible in the Frankish, as in the Ottonian, period without moving from one realm of law into another. The duke had his *herzogrîche* [dukedom],[77] as the king had his *kunigrîche* [kingdom]. In Widukind's famous description of the election proceedings of 936, Otto the Great was called *"novus rex"* [new king], twice called *"novus dux"* [new duke], and occasionally called *"princeps."* No distinction seems to have been felt.[78] Thus there was no distinction between the nature of king and that of duke, but only a difference of degree, and Widukind, who had only the lord of a retinue in mind, beclouded even this. This original similarity in ducal and royal power still appeared in the *Sachsenspiegel:* "Saxony, Bavaria, Franconia and Swabia were all kingdoms; later the names were changed and they were called duchies."[79] Furthermore, there were noble dynasties—such as the Konradin in Franconia, and others[80]—who exercised lordships similar to those of the dukes; whose members were sometimes styled "duke"; but who, in fact, were not tribal dukes. The various forms of lordship passed without a break from one level to another.

The German kings, however, already were striving to turn the rank of duke into an office; or at least, with the aid of ties of vassalage, were striving to turn the dukes into royal dependents. Royal lordship laid claim to a predominance over all the others. A difference of degree was being turned into a difference in kind.

All that the Frankish kings adopted from ancient government to shape their own position—ideas, instruments of dominion, powers of office (we cannot here discuss them at length)—appeared most clearly in the Empire of Charlemagne. The Germanic king of whom Tacitus spoke—the king who had no unlimited or unfettered power, who had to rule by persuasion rather than by command[81]—by this time is hardly recognizable. One thing above all is striking: the way conversion to Christianity had won for the Germanic kings an unprecedented increase in their authority.[82] The transformation of pagan "blood holiness"—for centuries a fixture of the folk mind—into a Christian divine grace was one of importance, not only in the history of ideas but in the history of institutions. The king's position changed from one among the people, as in Germanic times, to one over the people. When Alcuin wrote to Charlemagne, "By royal decree the people are to be led not followed," he expressed a sentiment totally alien to Germanic thought.[83] To the same extent that the power of the Christian God—of the *"alowaldand"* of the *Heliand*—vanquished the power of the pagan gods, the authority grew of the king whom He had established[84] as ruler of the earthly kingdom. It was this theocratic idea of office joined to assumptions derived from the world of the armed following, that lent to this kingship a good part of the special quality that some historians have glorified. From it derived what was now a qualitative rather than quantitative distinction between kingship and lordship—but a distinction that could become real as well as theoretical, only if the nobility recognized its existence.

Already in the Merovingian period, some were asserting that the king was to be served "as the vicar of our Savior."[85] In the expression *"fideles Dei et nostri"* [God's faithful and ours], which kings from Pepin to the Hohenstaufen were accustomed to use in their charters to refer to their subjects, the identity of kingdom and Church is clear.[86] Faith in God and faithfulness to the king were the same. The relationship of the faithful to God was conceived of in terms of the retinue; the *fideles Dei* were called *"gotes holdon"* in the *Ludwigslied* (verse 36). But the king, according to this song, had the authority to order them into battle, for he had the direct commission of God: *"Hluduîg, kuning mîn(!), hilph mînen liutin"* [Ludwig, my king, help my people] (verse 23). The word *"liuti,"* latinized as *"leudes"* in Frankish sources (where it was used as a synonym for *"holdon"*), once again stems from the armed retinue. These *leudes* were the same faithful who were called *"gisellion"* [blessed], *"nôtstallon"* [fellow in time of need], *"dugidi"* [troop], and *"frônisc githigini"* [noble retainers] (verse 5), with respect to the king. Charlemagne's division of the Empire in 806 spoke of his "kingdom given us by God."[87] In the *Ludwigslied* this kingdom appeared as a following bestowed by God. The intimate connection of kingdom to following could not be clearer. God's retinue and the king's retinue were identical. They were the *fideles Dei et regis,* God's faithful and the king's.

But God could demand obedience, not simply (as originally was the case with the king) the reciprocal tie of fidelity. The *Heliand,* in which the relationship of God to man was expressly shaped in terms of the following, already made clear this fundamental inner difference.[88] Thus, the king as vicar of God could give orders and demand obedience. ". . . [A]ccording to the will of God and our command," as a capitulary of Charlemagne put it.[89] Royal authority to legislate, so foreign to Germanic law "finding," was derived from God's will, made known by the king's pronouncement. If this notion found its way with relative ease into people's minds, it was only because it was inextricably mixed with the ancient pagan notion of sacral kingship. There can be no question that royal lordship over the Church, if it was rooted in the Germanic proprietary church, also drew nourishment from the idea that the king was God's vicar. The king's lordship over the Church and the proprietary church-lordship of the nobility slowly became two different things.

The Frankish and German nobility did their best to maintain their position next to this rising royal lordship.[90] The latter's pre-eminence was recognized, to be sure: the care with which Einhard founded the transfer of kingship from the Merovingians to the Carolingians, and with which Widukind repeated it, in describing the transfer from the Franks to the Saxons, is revealing.[91] (For Einhard the bearer of this royal lordship was a family, for Widukind it was a tribe; it would be worthwhile to investigate this change more closely.) In the long run, however, the kings did not succeed in gaining a unitary lordship, although they constantly sought it. The concentration of power in the state, today a simple political necessity and recognized as such by not a few Frankish and German kings, appeared to the nobility, whenever it went beyond a certain point, as injustice. Thus Bruno put it in a simple and well-turned phrase in his history of the Saxon war: "In wishing alone to be lord of all, he (Henry IV) wished no one else in his kingdom to live as lord."[92]

This opposition of king to aristocracy fills the history of the Frankish and Germanic kingdoms. It is the theme of the violent reversals in Merovingian and Carolingian history, and it decided the fate of the German Empire in the age of the Investiture Controversy. Because of this opposition the power crises in the medieval kingdoms were always constitutional crises as well.

In the beginning the Frankish aristocratic class clearly had the quality of a retinue: the *antrustiones* and *leudes,* the king's bodyguard, formed its nucleus, to which the other components were joined. *Optimates* and *antrustiones* were still paired in an edict of Chilperic (573/575) and were clearly distinguished from "all the people."[93] It appears that the Frankish kings for a time claimed as their exclusive privilege the right to have an armed following. This claim was one of the measures by which the kings sought to create a subject society (*Untertanenverband*) in which the intermediate power of the nobility would be eliminated and the legal position of every individual determined solely by his relation to the king. For the same reason the kings created a single class of free men, whose model was the freedom of the military colonists on royal lands.[94] The group of free men were to serve in place of the royal retinue of great men. The king made himself the immediate lord of a group of followers that included the entire kingdom; all free men were his *leudes;* they took an oath of allegiance in the form of an oath of a follower; the word *"populus"* was used in the sense of a retinue. At the same time, the army was transformed.

The kings went further yet. They strove to make themselves household lords of their kingdoms.[95] Heritability replaced the principle of election. The principles of real property inheritance—division among heirs—were applied to the entire kingdom. The shield-raising that expressed the election of a war band's leader was replaced by the enthronement: the occupation of the chief seat by the heir to the house. To the king now belonged the right and duty of peace-keeping throughout the land, rather than simply in the army.[96] Moreover, the kings took on the priestly functions of the Germanic household lord. Just as any other lord considered the duties pertaining to divine service within his household-lordship to be his special possession (notably, the rights to choose a priest and to treat the church he founded as his own), so did the king in the kingdom that was his enlarged household. There was no conception of a royal or Imperial Church in an institutional sense; such a concept would have been alien to the nature of the Church and foreign to a mentality so lacking in abstract notions. The Frankish and German kings had at their disposal only a proprietary lordship over individual churches, including many of episcopal rank. To obtain such lordship over all the churches in their kingdom—at least over all that did not belong to the nobility—was continuously their object, an object impossible to disentangle from their claims to be God's earthly vicar.

As soon as the kings had learned to use the remnants of late Roman administration they attempted to turn the nobility into officers, to establish as a fundamental rule that royal service ennobles, whereas originally only the nobility had a right to serve in the most intimate circle of the royal retinue. The kings tried to transform the nobility by birth into a nobility by service. Men who had the king's trust, whatever their social origins, were taken into royal fellowship. Romans became *convivae regis* [the king's companions], and even the unfree won power and influence. It was the same phenomenon that Tacitus had found among those German tribes ruled by kings: the freed men rising higher than the free and even higher than the nobility.[97] In this fashion men of low birth, as well as the heirs of Roman senatorial families and of Burgundian, Alemannic, Thuringian, Bavarian, and Saxon noble dynasties, entered the Frankish nobility. It was not without compulsion that they won recognition of their rights. And they soon let it be known that they were sprung from ancient nobility by birth.

In Carolingian times, the most powerful families of this noble class were tied with special closeness to the king. Most were of Frankish origin, but their possessions were scattered across the length and breadth of the gigantic empire and their commissions sent them on official functions into all its territories. As the "imperial nobility" (*Reichsadel*), as they are called,[98] they considered themselves above the common run of noblemen whose standing was based only on their landed possessions. But to whatever extent closeness to the king and participation in the royal government enhanced these families' nobility, that quality was not in itself derived from the king or the kingdom; simple executors of royal orders they never became. From the ninth century on, they strengthened their ties to the land as landed property increasingly determined their status. Many families were able to hold their high position and took the title of "duke"; others sank in the social hierarchy or died out. These were replaced at the top by new families, especially in the eastern parts of the Empire. But the noble class remained: now in the German Empire a closed caste, alone allowed to use the rights of the "state."[99]

From this noble class the Carolingians drew their counts. In principle, these positions were royal offices as they had been under the Merovingians,[100] but it was a principle few kings succeeded in sustaining. Continuously, the countships that were offices became countships that were lordships. Notker reveals much when he translates the word *"dignitates"* with *"herscaft."*[101] Only those who belonged to the noble class were worthy to have the highest places. Only those who already possessed the powers of lordship could take on the authority of office. And if the most powerful kings did not bend to this rule, their example was not lasting. In Alemania, for example, countships by right of lordship already existed at the time of the final annexation of this region, before the middle of the eighth century; and some have argued with good reason that countships had existed even before the Frankish introduction of the system of government through counts.[102] If in 721 St. Boniface met two brothers who had commands (*cui praeerant*) in the Merovingian territory of Amöneburg, these brothers must have had their power by inheritance rather than by the authority of an office. The situation was not different at the end of the ninth century, although there was an intervening period when the counts were more strictly dependent on the king.

Charlemagne named as count whomever he wished. Temporarily he succeeded in damming up the power of the nobility, in making the great men truly dependent on himself, in creating a royal administration that turned those under him into true "subjects"—even if he did not succeed in extending his measures into all the corners of his kingdom. Charlemagne attempted to create a genuine adminisrative state. Soon after his death, however, as if nothing had happened, the nobility returned to their ancient power, although the form of that power had slightly altered.

The extent to which the Ottonians managed to cover their empire with a network of counts who acted as officials has not been resolved; nor has the extent to which these offices were related to Carolingian institutions been determined. We know nothing about the extent of noble possessions at this time or the extent to which they came under the power of the counts. Nor is it known whether this was usually the case. The counts' power must have rested on the royal fisc in its most general sense, that is, on those portions of the kingdom over which the king had exercised a direct lordship. But how much and for how long it was restricted to this base, are questions that remain to be explored. Some, by arguing back from later sources, have concluded that the nobility exercised the power of jurisdiction, even high justice, over their subjects by virtue of their own right; and some have seen this jurisdiction as stemming from the judicial rights of the ancient Germanic *principes*.[103] This cannot be proved by our sources, however, nor can the contrary. With all due caution, given the present state of our knowledge, one can say only that the nobles, like the king, derived their jurisdictional lordship out of the past and that here, as elsewhere, no original qualitative difference can be found.[104]

The tie that bound nobleman to king was originally the fidelity of the follower to his lord. But one must not romanticize. The history of the period of migrations and of the Frankish kingdom is full of infidelity and treachery—on the side of both lords and men. Naked lust for power only too often overcame the customary power of moral ties; its significance as a force in institutional history cannot be overrated. In the Middle Ages also, worldly might made institutional right. What jurists call the "normative power of fact" was a major force, although the idea of a general juridical order was not abandoned. The idea of a follower's fidelity, the recognized pre-eminence of royal blood, the theocratic notion of office, and the natural power of forceful personalities all contributed; but in the long run it was the enormous means of power at the kings' disposal, their purely quantitative predominance, that made royal dominion a rightful one.

From this it follows that feudal law alone could not have been the creator of royal lordship, that feudal law cannot be taken as the chief, the most particular legal creation of the Western Middle Ages, as the "Ideal Type of an entire cultural epoch."[105] For feudal law contained both centripetal and centrifugal forces. In one place the former, in another the latter, triumphed. It was less the judicial order than the distribution of power that determined the structure of institutions.

The origins of feudalism[106] and its later development lie beyond the limits of this paper. We will note only that both royal and noble lordship took on the form of feudal lordship, that feudal lordship replaced the ancient lordship of a following. In this fashion the latter was given form.

Two things must be considered. If it is true that the origins of feudal organization are to be found in the mixing of the Gallo-Roman clientele with the Germanic *comitatus,* then the "feudal hierarchy," a pyramidal structure with the king at its summit, derives without question from the *comitatus.* For long before feudal relations were introduced into England, such a hierarchic structure, based solely on the Germanic band of followers, existed. Second, this mixing of Germanic and Gallo-Roman institutions presupposes an identical economic and social base to both, a peasant "way of life." Yet in no way can the commendation of a poor man for life to a great landed lord, as we know it from the often-cited text of the Tours Formulary,[107] be equated with the entrance into the Germanic retinue, for the latter was possible only for distinguished young men, was undertaken only for a period of time (and for purely military ends), and existed only in the sphere of the kings and great lords. Even the dependent peasants must have been rather like followers of their lord. We must therefore imagine the mixing process as one in which the Frankish lords took their Gallo-Roman *vassi* into their retinues and used them together with their Germanic peasant followers as fighters in their feuds.

This brings us to the subject of the so-called landed seigniory (*Grundherrschaft*).[108] The landed seigniory is a modern concept, foreign to the Middle Ages. Neither in Latin nor in ancient Germanic tongues was there an exact equivalent. In Germanic lands, the possession of land brought with it no rights of lordship over people. In the late Roman Empire, it was quite otherwise. Here the ownership (*dominium*) of land did develop into a lordship based on land. The history of late antique landed dominion is beyond the scope of this article, but it must be noted that this form of dominion served as a model of considerable influence for the structuring of landed lordship in the Frankish kingdom. In conquered Gaul, the Franks had sufficient opportunities to learn Roman methods of organizing landed possessions. The Frankish lords must have frequently stepped into places vacated by great Roman landlords, and the acceptance of the Roman *potentes* into the Frankish noble class must also have done much to assimilate this form of dominion.[109] The annexation of territories east of the Rhine introduced it into Germany as a matter of course. If we remember, moreover, that these eastern lands were a "colonial" territory for the Franks, we must allow the possibility that it was here given a markedly purer character than in the Frankish heartland (as is so often the case with colonial territories). To be sure, the sources reveal nothing. It is also to be assumed that in the Germanic east, indigenous Germanic forms of landed lordship lived on to a greater extent than west of the Rhine.[110]

Already in the time of Tacitus, as we have seen, types of relationships existed among the Germans which one might call a landed seigniory developed from the household and from serfdom. Furthermore, the peasantry was also involved in the institution of the armed following, and it was usual to bestow land on one's followers. Thus, a kind of lordship based on land could develop over free men.

A fully developed form of landed seigniory already existed in central Germany by the year 700. There is evidence for it in the heart of Thuringia, in Arnstadt, Mühlberg, and Mondra (near the eastern edge of Germanic settlement toward the Slavs), and in Hammelburg on the Franconian Saale.[111] We must suppose a similar institution existed in Würzburg. Many of these seigniories consisted of an undivided "demesne" with peasants attached to it; but some had one-family tenements (*hobae*) with "domiciled" serfs (*casatae*). Characteristically, in Mühlberg and Hammelburg, the lord's house was called *"burg" (in castello Mulenberge, ad Hamulo castellum*). In Mondra there must also have been a lord's *burg,* for a nearby locality is called "Monraburg." The Thuringian Duke Heden, perhaps of Frankish origin, was "landlord" in both places. (His chief residence was in Würzburg.) Western influence is thus not excluded, as the name Mühlberg itself suggests. An indigenous development must already have taken place, of the kind associated with the institution of the *burg* discussed earlier in this article. But if lordship throughout Germany in time became derivable from a grant of land, whereas originally land had been granted because of ties of lordship, if personal ties came to be drawn from ties of real property, then this without question resulted from the influence of the Roman pattern. In many cases, observation of the kinds of effects produced by lordship leads us also to western Frankish models. As a result of this complicated process, which paralleled the "realization" of feudal relationships, lords intensified their control, even over subject classes that originally had been free.

Historians have often described the process by which lords rounded out their territories and leveled their subject population to the same legal status, the process by which landed seignorial lords added the power of command to their possessions. To do this, they have almost exclusively used ecclesiastical sources, for such sources are the most evident of those which time has left us. But we cannot in this manner discover the origins of legal attachment to the soil, to which were subjected not only the successors of the ancient unfree but the heirs of the ancient free men as well. Our sources unequivocally demonstrate that the so-called landed seigniory was highly developed by ecclesiastical lords in Germany; but these lords did not originate it, nor did they bring it into the territories east of the Rhine. To be sure, it would be difficult to overestimate the importance of ecclesiastical landed seigniories for public institutional development. The extent of ecclesiastical holdings, the system of proprietary churches, the institution of the church "advocate" and the *servitium regis,* and the involvement of the Church in feudal ties all brought the Church into the midst of the struggle for secular institutional power. But, without question, the Church took over the institution of the landed seigniory in Germany as something already at hand.

For the early period, the extant charters and customals reveal something about noble possessions and their attached peasantry only at the moment these possessions were given to the Church. Nevertheless, we can see that there were some among the mass of donors, even in the eighth century, who disposed of lands and peasants in numerous and often widely scattered villages. At the same time, within single villages there were often a large number of donors whose holdings in any one place were quite small, but who possessed land elsewhere and thus must have held their possessions as landed seigniors. If the division of village lands is understandable in terms of Germanic laws of land inheritance, which must have rapidly led to extensive fragmentation, the scattering of possessions remains to be explained. The best assumption is that this scattering was a consequence of royal grants of land given to provide centers of support for royal service, a policy the kings followed in various parts of their realms. If this was a very expedient policy east of the Rhine for the Carolingians above all, the equivalent must have occurred earlier, for the scattering of possessions to which our sources testify even before the middle of the eighth century, cannot have taken place overnight. Probably the transfer of landed property played a greater role in an earlier period than we commonly imagine. Perhaps it goes back to the pattern of land seizure at the time of the Frankish conquest or at the time of first settlement, as has already been suggested.

There were also villages that belonged largely or entirely to one lord. Here we must distinguish between villages in territories anciently settled and newly assarted land, a distinction that has already proved fruitful in tracing the history of lordship.[112] In the case of newly assarted land, villages belonging to one lord are easily explained. Exclusive village lordship in lands of ancient settlement may go back to the period of original settlement, as place names formed from personal names make clear. (To be sure, the historian must not use documents of the later Middle Ages as a springboard into a period one thousand years earlier, as has sometimes been done.)[113] It remains to be explained, however, why there was no fragmentation. Only a minute investigation of the history of individual villages and the possessions of individual persons and seignorial families, an investigation in which are used all the techniques developed for tracing the history of land settlement, will be of help here.[114] We will then be in a position to know whether, from the beginning, great seignorial holdings were widely spread across the countryside, vast holdings clearly different from the small seigniory of a village or parts of neighboring villages, the latter being hardly comparable to the former.[115]

From what has preceded, we may conclude that the rights of a lord over his subjects did not derive simply from his power of disposition over land. This is especially true of the lord's power of jurisdiction and of those rights of village lordship that were known in southwest Germany as *"Zwing und Bann"* [constraint and command] and as *"dominium villae"* in the eastern part of central Germany (where the phrase appears as early as the twelfth century). In these new settlements, the "colonial lands" of the east where landed lordship imprinted itself most clearly and most firmly, these rights could not have been either gifts or usurpations. They flowed from the powers of lordship itself. Scholars are now inclined to recognize these rights as an "autogenous immunity."[116] By its own authority, the lord exercised powers that included jurisdiction. Today, we would call his functions those of the "state."[117] Thus, to call these powers a "landed seigniory" is not very revealing.[118] They were rather powers of lordship over land and people.

The king was likewise lord of land and people; and, as must be added, so was Christ, insofar as He was King. In the *Heliand,* Christ, the

King of the world, was called "Lord of all lands and peoples" (verses 2287 ff.). The notion that royal lordship originally derived from landed lordship, or developed parallel with it (a notion today almost one hundred years old), must now be considered out of date.[119] If we do away with the old idea of landed lordship—in the field of institutional history (not that of economic history, where it is still useful)—and replace it with the idea of "lord over land and people," we will be able to show the close connection of royal lordship to other forms of lordship. But first we must correct one misunderstanding.

It might appear from what has been said, that it was the influence of Roman landed dominion that added lordship over land to lordship over people. And in fact, some have argued, in opposition to older conceptions, that the "state" of the early Middle Ages was a group of peoples (*Personenverbandstaat*) in contrast to the territorial state (*Flächenstaat*) of later times.[120] The intended meaning is not that the king's power was based solely on personal ties—for clearly there was some territorial notion of "state"—but the realm was ruled, so it is argued, through the possession of strategic routes and localities, "on the pattern they inherited from the Roman state."[121] On the other hand, the essence of the modern state is not seen as exclusively "territorial"; it is rather an "institutionalized territorial state." That is, the rule of the state not only extends throughout its territory, which gives it body, in which it is "reified" (*verdinglicht*); it is also objectified (*versachlicht*). The "state" is an idea and a goal, an objective thing that creates its own organs. In this form the distinction has been uncommonly fruitful. Nevertheless, it has recently been oversimplified, reduced to the mere contrast of peoples and territory.[122]

There cannot be the slightest doubt that the royal lordship of the early Middle Ages had a territorial character, one extended to "land" as well as people. Lordship over an area, that is, "the power to lead the inhabitants of a geographically defined area without respect to their tribal law,"[123] certainly existed before the eleventh and twelfth centuries. The so-called personality of law of the early Middle Ages had no influence on this. Once again, we may learn from Old High German poetry.

The first lines of Otfrid's poem read:

> Ludwig the Brave, full of wisdom,
> Ruled all of the eastern realm, as a king of the Franks should do;
> His power spread over all the lands of the Franks to such an extent
> That his power, as I tell you, ruled over all.[124]

Personal and territorial elements are tightly linked. The "lands of the Franks" are not the lands where the Frankish people settled, but rather—since "the eastern kingdom" is used as a variant for it—"eastern *Francia*," the kingdom of Louis the German. From this king himself we have proof that he conceived of his lordship territorially. From 833 on, Louis dated his charters by the year of his reign "in eastern *Francia.*" His rule had previously been restricted to Bavaria, and, accordingly, the great *Salzburg Annals* called him "king of the Bavarian territory" (*rex Baiowarie regionis*).[125] . . .

This territorial conception of lordship was nothing new. It was already to be found in Gregory of Tours, who had Clovis say before the war against the Visigoths, "It is truly disagreeable to me that these Arians hold a part of Gaul. With God's help, let us go and bring the land under our rule."[126] One might be tempted to think that only the intended expulsion of some inhabitants was meant here or that the expression was a legacy of Roman political thought in the mind of a bishop from a senatorial family. But an edict of Chilperic spoke of things *"in regione nostra"* [in our territory], and even more clearly, an edict of Gunthram refers to things *"infra regni nostri spatia"* [within the breadth of our kingdom], and *"universa regio nostrae pacis et concordiae"* [the entire area of our peace and union].[127] So, likewise, in 581 Marius of Avenches wrote of a *"marca Childeberti regis"* (March of King Childebert)—thus, of a bounded district[128]—and in 612 a submission was executed with the words, "We and our land are now yours."[129] The examples could be multiplied. . . .

The center of this territorial lordship was the lord's house, the *burg.* From the history of Henry IV and the Hohenstaufen, we know that the construction of such *burgen* provided the means for obtaining intensive territorial control.[130] But *burgen* had existed before, and their institutional function had been the same. Widukind related the submission of the Bavarian Duke Arnulf to Henry I with the words, "handing over himself with all his realm" *(tradito semet ipso cum omni regno suo)*.[131] By "people" (*populus*), Widukind commonly meant the armed retinue.[132] This and the *burgen* composed Burchard's realm; to the personal element was added the territorial, represented by the *burg.* Even in the speech that Widukind put in the mouth of the dying Conrad I, the fortified centers were not forgotten. Along with plentiful fighters, they were required for the glory of the realm.[133] The significance we have given the *burg* on the basis of other evidence is thus confirmed.[134] And one can go even further.

The *burg* was not only a strategic locality in the early Middle Ages; it was also, as later on, a means for extending territorial control. In the Ottonian period, the commanders of fortified places along the Saale and Middle Elbe divided the land into contiguous territories; and earlier, at the end of the eighth century, the same must have happened in southern Hassegau, in the angle formed by the Unstrut and the Saale. The former was land conquered from the Slavs and thus a "colonial area"; the latter was apparently an area of military settlement on the eastern border of the Empire, but directed more against the Saxons than against the Slavs. These were exceptions, to be sure, for in these frontier territories the monarchy's planned measures for territorial control could not hem in the power of lords by their own right. But these exceptions must still be recognized. One cannot speak of an early medieval "state" formed by ties of man to man as if there existed no impetus to territorial control. One can say only that this territorial control could not be fully achieved because the king's lordship over land and people, if not bounded, was at least restricted by the power the nobility exercised by its members' own inherited authority. It is at this point that the hierarchically ordered structure of society, later repeated in the feudal state, becomes relevant. The ties that bound these lords over land and people to the king were primarily personal. Only feudal law began to associate them with landed tenure, and sufficient allodial possessions always remained. Here was undoubtedly a state held together by personal ties. The king could not exercise immediate lordship over the men and subjects of the nobility; noble lordship inserted itself in between. The king, therefore, did not rule the entire territory of his realm *in the same way* as the modern state governs within its boundaries. In this sense the modern state is a "territorial state," whereas the medieval state was not. In this sense one may speak of a state based on personal ties as well as of lordship over land and people.

If our argument is correct, the nobleman's power of lordship over land and people grew out of his household lordship and his lordship of a retinue. The power of the king grew from the same roots, but, fed by antique and Christian traditions, reached exceptional heights. Nobleman's and king's: both go back to a very ancient, unitary lordly power—power over land and people—often given form through an armed retinue and only later splitting into noble lordship and royal lordship. If this was the case, we should not be surprised to find both *"res publica"* and *"dominium villarum"* [village lordship] translated by *"hertuom"* and *"publicus"* by *"frôno,"* which also appears in combinations such as *"frônhof"* and, thus, is connected with landed lordship.

The distinction between private and public law thus appears to be irrelevant to early medieval lordship. To be sure, medieval men knew the difference between public and private; they used the words *"publicus"* and *"privatus"* often enough. But they saw the boundary between the two rather differently than modern men. A *"burgstrâza"* was a *privata via,* but not a private road in the modern sense; and a *"hêrstraza"* was a *publica vel regia via* (*Gl.* 3, 118). The distinction was most clearly made by Notker: "They call private all that is not royal."[135] "Public" (*publicus*) in the Middle Ages was what belonged to the power of the king as lord; but the historian must not conceive of the rights springing from this in the light of our notion of public law, nor as belonging to the Roman concept of *"res publica."* Only in the light of this conclusion may we construct a distinction between king's law and folk law—and we must be carefully aware that this was only a secondary phenomenon. The seignorial power of the nobility, similar to that of the king and made subject to it only as the result of a complicated historical development, cannot be termed "private" in our sense or in that of Roman law. For the rights coming from the nobility's seignorial powers, like those coming from the king's, had both a private and public nature.

The territorial lords of the high and late Middle Ages inherited their powers from this earlier seignorial nobility. They took over royal rights, to be sure, but not to the extent that they derived their territorial lordship exclusively from such acquisition or usurpation. For their territorial lordship was also lordship over land and people, like royal lordship and seignorial lordship. Its development is outside the scope of this article, however. What follows are only some general, and by no means exhaustive, observations on the later development of the processes we have been considering.

The emergence of territorial lordship was ultimately a question of personal ability and a question of power. The starting points were quite diverse. Dukes such as the Wittelsbachs became territorial princes; so did *ministeriales* such as the Reuss. What mattered was the ability to use noble lordship over land and people. In the course of the twelfth and thirteenth centuries, and in part earlier, *ministeriales* also succeeded in doing this. The decisive issue was whether one succeeded in making his land and people free from the power of a "foreign" lord—aside from that of the ever-weakened monarchy. The future territorial lords had to battle not only those above (to win emancipation from royal and, where necessary, from ducal power), not only those below (to intensify and concentrate their seignorial powers over their future subjects), but also on all sides, against those who were doing the same thing. In the thirteenth century these lords succeeded in breaking their ties to the monarchy, a monarchy by that time decisively weakened by the Investiture Controversy, which finally destroyed the ancient sacral personal ties. But the cities, and a lower nobility whom talent had raised from the class of *ministeriales,* resisted the growth of the territorial lords' rights over those below. And this resistance was not always overcome. In Swabia and Franconia especially, many of these cities and lower nobility as Imperial Cities and Imperial Knights kept themselves free of the territorial lords. Most lords over land and people failed, however, in their fight with their fellows along the road to territorial lordship.

To be a "state" in the Middle Ages meant to be free from "foreign" lordship. The territorial state had as its superior lord only a king whose lordship was at best restricted and, in the end, merely nominal. In exterior affairs a weak tie remained, but within his land the territorial lord recognized no royal authority. Only a few lords, however, succeeded in gaining such independence and in keeping it. The greatest number of noble lords met defeat in battle with their more powerful neighbors, to whose lordship (in one form or another) they finally had to submit. With this their dream of territorial lordship came to an end. For as a rule the neighbor transformed his lordship into territorial rule, even if he had begun with only a weak form of subjection. In this manner counts and lords in great number were reduced to simple landholders. Even the Imperial Princes depended more on their *de facto* power than on their imperial rank, with the result that the less powerful came to hold their land of the more powerful—not only abbots, but even bishops, such as those of Meissen, Merseburg, and Naumburg, who could not keep the Wettins away from their door. If the nobleman was not thus subjected to a "foreign" lord, he himself became a territorial lord, even if he did not seek to be one—and this is the best proof of what we have just said. Such were the Imperial Knights who, as leftovers from a time long past, could not be fit into the public-law concepts of the eighteenth century.[136] These miniature lordships never became "states" or even "territories." But neither did they belong to other states or territories. Thus, well into modern times, a form of lordship continued that was nothing but the private and public lordship over land and people descended unchanged from the early Middle Ages. The principalities of the Schwarzburgs and the Reuss were constructions of a similar sort, as was the principality of Waldeck whose nineteenth-century "sovereignty" should not deceive us; in reality, here was another undivided lordship from the Middle Ages that had not given way to a "modern" state. Such too was the lordship of Schonburg, swallowed up by the Electorate of Saxony in 1740 but retaining jurisdiction by right of its own authority until 1878—a medieval noble lordship that finally disappeared in the Bismarkian state.[137]

One cannot talk about the legal title by which a lord became and remained subject to a "foreign" one, for each case was different. Nor can one list the various rights of diverse origins that turned a lord who had collected them into a territorial lord, for this also varied everywhere. Thus the question is essentially a false one. The territorial states of the late Middle Ages were individualized constructions of history. They can be defined only by generalized concepts. It is impossible to point to an historical line and say, "Here they 'turned into' territorial lordships." The nobility's seignorial power over land and people in which "public" and "private" rights were inextricably mixed was the foundation. It developed in two ways: on the private side, into the landed seigniory (which would better be called the "*new* landed seigniory," if we adopt the term "landed seigniory" for earlier times); on the public side, into territorial lordship. The conceptual distinction of public and private spheres in our sense followed from the reception of Roman law. But German institutional developments met it halfway.

When a lord over land and people was subjected to a "foreign" lord, he was forced to give some of his rights to his superior lord and then receive them back, or at least to recognize that he held those rights as if by cession from his superior. These rights were then considered as delegated rights, although in reality they were not; they were held by virtue of a privilege, although actually they had not been transferred and in some cases a written privilege had neither been requested nor granted. What remained to the lower lord were then his "private" rights. From these grew the private landlord rights of the late Middle Ages and modern times: a body of economic rights more and more denuded of their political character (though the lord kept "public" rights, still considered to be delegated, in addition to his private rights).

Whenever a lord succeeded in avoiding subjection to another and subjugated others to himself, he necessarily tried to integrate his newly acquired rights into his own unified set of powers, to consider those rights as derived from his own. His lordship thus changed its character; it became a "public" territorial lordship. For the set of rights that the victorious lord took to himself was a limited one. He did not remove all rights from the lord who came under his sway, but only those rights whose use seemed necessary for the aims of his new form of lordship. Insofar as a lord set himself such conscious goals, he departed from custom; from his action came an objective, calculated, and willed political entity: the "institutional" state. "Political" aims now came to the fore; an apparatus was put together to help attain them, an apparatus that had only delegated power—the bureaucracy. The territorial lord, his ties to the Empire now extremely weak, appeared not only as the highest judge, but also as the highest lord. He was emperor in his own territory. His territorial lordship became territorial sovereignty; his power now touched all inhabitants equally; all foreign power he now excluded from his territory—it could no longer be "executed." The rights of the territorial lord were public insofar as they referred to the objective political body of the territory. The rest of the original noble lordship from which all this had sprung became the lord's private rights—the nucleus of his domain. This is the picture of the modern institutional territorial state, which in Germany, as is well known, was realized not in the Empire but in the princely territories.[138]

NOTES*

1. I hope this will counter one objection that this article cannot fail to engender. The essay is less a demonstration than a program and does not claim to present final answers. Given the current state of research, which has destroyed one picture of the past without replacing it with another, any final answers are impossible. For this reason, only a selection from the relevant sources and studies will be given. I have answered the criticism of H. Kuhn, "Die Grenzen der germanischen Gefolgschaft," *ZRG Germ. Abt.,* 73 (1956), 1–83, in "Randbemerkungen zu drei Aufsätzen über Sippe, Gefolgschaft und Treue," *Beiträge zur*

* Except for references to sources and bibliography, most of the material in the original notes has been omitted.—ed.

deutschen Verfassungsgeschichte des Mittelalters, **1** (1963), 296–316. See also K. Wührer, "Die schwedischen Landschaftsrechte und Tacitus' Germania," *ZRG Germ. Abt.,* **76** (1959), esp. 15 ff.; R. Wenskus, *Stammesbildung und Verfassung* (1961), 346 ff.

2. G. Ehrismann, "Die Wörter für 'Herr' im Althochdeutschen," *Zs. für Wortforschung,* **7** (1905/1906), 193 ff.; G. Lagenpusch, *Das germanische Recht im Heliand* (1894); K. Guntermann, *Herrschaftliche und genossenschaftliche termini in der geistlichen Epik der Westgermanen* (1910); A. Bartels, *Rechtsaltertümer in der angelsächsischen Dichtung* (1913); H. Beer, *Führen und Folgen, Herrschen und Beherrschtwerden im Sprachgut der Angelsachsen* (1939); E. Richter, "Senior-Sire," *Wörter und Sachen,* **12** (1929), 114 ff.; W. Stach, *DA,* **9** (1952), 352.

3. Only in the vocative; compare Old Saxon *"frôio," "frôho," "frâho."* [From the text.]

4. A fourth, "waldand," is clearly recognizable as a participle; its substantive form is more recent, though in the composite *"alouualdo,"* we have a non-participial form. [From the text.]

5. What follows comes from the documentation of the Althochdeutschen Wörterbuch in Leipzig, which E. Karg-Gasterstädt kindly made available to me.

6. *Zs. für Kirchenrecht,* 4 (1864), 162.

7. *MGH SS rer. Merov.* **1**. (2d ed.) 188 (Childebert, 575).

8. *MGH Cap.* **1**. 11.

9. F. Kauffmann, "Altdeutsche Genossenschaften," *Wörter und Sachen,* **2** (1910), 26 ff.; Otto Brunner, *Land und Herrschaft* (4th ed.; 1959).

10. Tacitus *Germania* [hereafter, *Ger.*] 25. (F. Lütge, in *Studi in onore di Armintore Fanfani,* **1** [1962], 516, has misunderstood my reference to this. I am of course also of the opinion "that the self-sufficient unfree was lord in his own house." Any other translation is impossible. But he is still unfree. See Brunner, *Land und Herrschaft,* 254 ff.)

11. Tacitus *Historiae* [hereinafter, *Hist.*] **5**. 23.

12. Heinrich Mitteis, "Staatliche Konzentrationsbewegungen im grossgermanischen Raum." *Festschrift Adolf Zycha* (1941), p. 58.

13. *Ibid.,* p. 58.

14. Tacitus *Annales* [hereinafter *Ann.*] **1**. 59 ff., 55 gives an example of a nonholy war.

15. Tac. *Ger.* 7.

16. For what follows, see H. Dannenbauer, "Adel, Burg und Herrschaft bei den Germanen," *Grundlagen der mittelalterlichen Welt* (1958), 121–178. No archeological evidence for premigration *burgen* has been found. What I have to say is valid only for the period after the migration, although, of course, new finds may change these conclusions.

17. Tac. *Ann.* **1**. 57.

18. I do not know if this expression is connected with one found in an Anglo-Saxon law of the seventh century, *"XII hida gesettes landes,"* [referring to land held by peasants]; F. Liebermann, *Gesetze der Angelsachsen* **1**, 118 par. 64.

19. The *portgerefa* of London was first called *"wicgerefa";* Liebermann, *Gesetze der Angelsachsen,* **1**, 11 par. 16, 16.2.

20. A. Waas, *Herrschaft und Staat im deutschen Frühmittelalter* (1938); E. Molitor, *ZRG Germ. Abt.,* **64** (1944), 112 ff.

21. *MGH Ottonis I Dipl.* 27, 300; *Ottonis II Dipl.* 214; F. Beyerle, "Zur Wehrverfassung des Hochmittelalters," *Festschrift Ernst Mayer* (1932), 31 ff.; Walter Schlesinger, "Burg und Stadt," *Festschrift Theodor Mayer,* **1** (1954), 97 ff.

22. Liebermann, *Gesetze* **2**/2, 330, art. "Burg."

23. Waitz has constructed a much narrower concept than Brunner. [From the text.]

24. Tac. *Ger.* 14 and *Hist.* 4. 15.

25. Tac. *Ger.* 13–15.

26. F. Kauffmann, *Zs. für Deutsche Philologie,* **32** (1901), 250 ff.; Schönbach, *Zs. für deutsches Altertum,* **40** (1896), 122.

27. Compare Tac. *Ger.* 13, on the meaning of which see Dannenbauer, "Adel, Burg u. Herrschaft," *Grundlagen,* pp. 131–132; H. Mitteis, "Formen der Adelsherrschaft im Mittelalter," *Festschrift Fritz Schulz* (1951), p. 230; R. Much, *Die Germania des Tacitus* (1937), 154 ff.

28. K. Kroeschell, "Die Sippe im germanischen Recht," *ZRG Germ. Abt.,* **77** (1960), 1–25; W. Schlesinger, "Randbemerkungen," *Beiträge z. Verfassungsgesch.,* **1**, 286–296.

29. Tac. *Ger.* 13, 14. On the problem of translation, fundamental to early medieval institutional history, see W. Stach, "Wort und Bedeutung im mittelalterlichen Latein," *DA,* **9** (1952), 332 ff.

30. Tac. *Ger.* 12.

31. Caesar *Bello Gallico* **6**. 23.

32. Livy **45**. 5, 10.

33. Tac. *Ger.* 38, 25.

34. Tac. *Ann.* **1**. 55.

35. Tac. *Ger.* 7. (See K. Bosl, "Reges ex nobilitate, duces ex virtute sumunt," *Frühformen des Gesellschaft im mittelalterlichen Europa* [1965], pp. 62–73.)

36. Tac. *Ger.* 13.

37. Tac. *Ger.* 13.

38. *Germanische Altertumskunde,* H. Schneider, ed. (2d ed., 1951) p. 101.

39. Tac. *Ann.* **11**. 16.

40. Brunner, *Land und Herrschaft* (4th ed.; 1959).

41. Even Mitteis, *Festschrift Zycha,* p. 59, calls the clan a "peace group" *(Friedensverband).*

42. F. Boden, *Die isländische Regierungsgewalt in der freistaatlichen Zeit* (1905).

43. *ZRG Germ. Abt.,* **64** (1944), 136; Nithard *Historiarum libri IIII,* IV 2 (Müller, ed., *MGH SS rer. Germ.* [1925], 41 ff.); *Lex Saxonum,* 8, 18, 50, 64.

44. A. Schultze, "Uber westgotish-spanishes Eherecht," *Akademie der Wissenschaften, Leipzig, Berichte der philologische-historischen Klasse,* **95** [1943], Heft 4 (1944), 51, 63.

45. K. S. Bader, "Staat und Bauerntum im deutschen Mittelalter," in *Adel und Bauern im deutschen Staat des Mittelalters,* T. Mayer ed. (1943) p. 119.

46. Guntermann, *Herrschaftliche und genossenschaftliche termini* gives the essential material, although it is not exhaustive from all points of view.

47. *Bello Gallico* **6**. 23.

48. A. Bauer, *Gau und Grafschaft in Schwaben* (1927). The Alemannic *Huntaren* and *Baaren* also signify the lordship districts of such petty kings; see H. Dannenbauer, *Historisches Jahrbuch* **62**/**69** (1949), 177 ff.; T. Mayer, "Baar und Baarschalken," *Mitteilungen des oberösterreichishen Landesarchivs,* **3** (1954), 143–156 and "Staat und Hundertschaft in fränkischer Zeit," *Rheinische Vierteljahrsblätter,* **17** (1952), 343–384; F. Steinbach, "Hundertschaft, Centena und Zentgericht," *Rheinische Vierteljahrsblätter,* **15/16** (1951-1952), 121–138; J. Jänichen, "Baar und Huntari," in *Vorträge und Forschungen,* T. Mayer, ed., **1** (1955), 83–148.

49. Tac. *Hist.* 4. 12 ff.

50. *Ibid.,* 16–23.

51. O. Behaghel, *Heliand und Genesis* (6th ed., 1948), p. 213. [My thanks to my colleague Howell D. Chickering, Jr., who translated this.]

52. The relationship of subordination is denoted by the word "*geongordôm*"; Lucifer is God's "*geongra*." [From the text.]

53. See *Heliand* vv.1186 ff., 1199.

54. Widukind *Rerum gestarum saxonicarum libri tres* **1**. 12 (*MGH SS rer. Germ.,* P. Hirsch, ed. [1935], p. 21.) Compare *Beowulf* vv.64 ff., 859 ff.

55. Vv. 2489, 2606 ff. See in general H. Brunner—C. von. Schwerin, *Deutsche Rechtsgeschichte,* **2** (2d ed., 1928), 350 ff.

56. The expression is from A. Helbok, "Volk und Staat der Germanen," *HZ,* **154** (1936), 234 ff. (I cannot agree with other views put forward in Helbok's article.)

57. An often cited passage in Libanius is irrelevant here; see W. Göz, *Klio,* **17** (1921), 240.

58. Tac. *Ann.* **2**. 45.

59. See F. M. Stenton, *Anglo-Saxon England* (2d ed., 1950), 298 ff. R. G. Collingwood and J. N. L. Myres, *Roman Britain and the English Settlements* (2d ed., 1937), 347 ff. also point to the fundamental importance of the retinue. The opinions expressed here are above all those of A. Bauer, *Gau und Grafschaft* concerning the settlement of the Alemanni. For the opposite view see J. E. A. Jolliffe, *The Constitutional History of Medieval England* (1937), who adopts the views of older German scholarship.

60. H. Brunner, *Dtsche. Rechtsgeschichte,* **1** (2d ed., 1906), 164.

61. Bede *Historia Ecclesiastica* **3**. 24 (Plummer, ed. p. 178).

62. W. de G. Birch, *Cartularium Saxonicum,* **1** (1885), no. 159.

63. Leibermann, *Gesetze,* **2**/2, 330, art. "Burg."

64. *Ibid,* **1**, 50, par. 4.2.

65. H. Zatschek, "Germanische Raumerfassung und Staatenbildung in Mitteleuropa," *HZ,* **168** (1943), 27 ff., esp. 43 ff.

66. I have elsewhere tried to demonstrate that royal election, stemming from the "election" of a leader by his retinue, was legally equated with entrance into a retinue: *ZRG Germ. Abt.,* **66** (1948), 381 ff. See also W. Schlesinger "Über germanisches Herrkönigtum," *Beiträge z. dt. Verfassungsgesch.,* **1**, 53–87; "Karlingische Königswahlen," *Beiträge z. dt. Verfassungsgesch.,* **1**, 88–138. On the noble class: A. Bergengruen, *Adel und Grundherrschaft im Merowingerreich* (1958); R. Sprandel, "Struktur und Geschichte des merowingischen Adels," *HZ,* **193** (1961), 33–71; R. Wenskus, "Amt und Adel in der Merowingerzeit," *Mitteilungen des Universitätsbundes Marburg* (1959) **1**/2, 40–56.

67. A tenth-century monk of the monastery of St. Gall and master of the monastery's school, he translated a number of the Latin philosophical works into German.—Ed.

68. Leibermann, *Gesetze* **1**, 12.

69. K. Hauck, "Geblütsheiligkeit," *Liber Floridus. Festschrift für Paul Lehmann* (1950), 187 ff.

70. Tac. *Ann.* **11**. 16; *Hist.* 4. 13. It is possible that an earlier kingship had disappeared among the Batavians, among the Cherusci, and, indeed, among all the Germanic tribes with a princely constitution; see R. Wenskus, "Amt und Adel," 409 ff.

71. Beer, *Führen und Folgen,* p. 227.

72. *MGH SS* **10**. 576. See J. O. Plassmann, *Princeps und Populus* (1954).

73. Thietmar *Chronicon* **5**. 14 (R. Holtzmann, ed., *MGH SS rer. Germ. nova series* **9** [1935], p. 236).

74. *MGH SS* **30**. 742.

75. Thietmar, *Chronicon* **5**. 7 (Holtzmann, ed. p. 228).

76. *MGH SS rer. Merov.* **2**. 165. See H. Zeiss, *Wiener Prähistorische Zeitschrift,* **19** (1925), 145 ff.; W. Schlesinger, "Germ. Heerkönigtum," *Beiträge,* **1**, 72 ff.; A. Hömberg, *Westfalen und das sächsische Herzogtum* (1963).

77. W. Schlesinger, *Die Entstehung der Landesherrschaft,* **1** (1941), 121.

78. Widukind *Rer. gest. Sax.* **2** 1 (Hirsch, ed. 63 ff.). See also J. O. Plassmann, *Princeps und Populus.*

79. *Landrecht,* **3**, 53 par. 1.

80. G. Tellenbach, "Vom karolingischen Reichsadel zum deutschen Reichsfürstenstand," *Adel und Bauern im deutschen Staat des Mittelalters,* 22 ff.; I. Dietrich, *Das Haus der Konradiner* (unpubl. diss., Marburg: 1952).

81. Tac. *Ger.* 7, 11.

82. Mitteis, *Festschrift Zycha.* 69 ff.; W. Berges, *Die Fürstenspiegel des hohen und späten Mittelalters* (1938); W. Hamel, *Reich und Staat im Mittelalter* (1944), 26 ff.; G. Tellenbach, "Germanentum und Reichsgedanke im frühen Mittelalter," *Historisches Jahrbuch,* **62/69** (1949), 117 ff.; F. Heer, *Die Tragödie des heiligen Reiches* (1952); H. Büttner, "Aus die Anfängen des abendländischen Staatsgedankens," *Historisches Jahrbuch,* **71** (1952), 77 ff.

83. *MGH Epp.* 4. 199.

84. For example, *MGH Dipl. Karol.* 58, and numerous other places.

85. *MGH Epp.* **3**. 198.

86. H. Helbig, "Fideles Dei et regis," *Archiv für Kulturgeschichte,* **33** (1951), 227 ff.

87. *MGH Cap.* **1**. 127.

88. E. Grosch, *Das Gottes-und Menschenbild im Heliand* (unpubl. diss., Leipzig: 1947); W. Ebel, *Geschichte der Gesetzgebung in Deutschland* (2d ed., 1958), 26 ff.

89. *MGH Cap.* **1**. 131.

90. O. Freiherr von Dungern, *Adelsherrschaft im Mittelalter* (1927); H. Mitteis, *Festschrift Fritz Schulz,* 226 ff.

91. H. Beumann, "Einhard und die karolingische Tradition im ottonischen Corvey," *Westfalen,* **30** (1953), 150–174.

92. Bruno *Liber de bello Saxonico* (H. F. Lohmann, ed., *MGH kritische Studientexte,* **2** [1935], 55).

93. *MGH Cap.* **1**, 8. The single class of free men spoken of here is not the same as the so-called King's free men (*Königsfreien*) who have been the subject of much recent debate. See T. Mayer, "Bemerkungen und Nachträge zum Problem der freien Bauern," *Mittelalterliche Studien* (1959), pp. 164–186; C. Baaken, "Königtum, Burgen und Königsfreie," *Vorträge und Forschungen,* T. Mayer, ed. **6** (1961), 9–95; on the critical side is F. Wernli, *Die Gemeinfreien des Frühmittelalters* (1960) and *Die mittelalterliche Bauernfreiheit* (1959). Much more comprehensive is F. Lütge, "Das Problem der Freiheit in der frühen deutschen Agrarverfassung," *Studi A. Fanfani.* H. Grundmann, "Freiheit als religiöses, politisches und persönliches Postulat im Mittelalter," *HZ,* **183** (1957), 23–52, does not deal with the institutional problem.

94. W. Schlesinger, *Die Entstehung der Landesherrschaft,* 127 ff.; T. Mayer, "Königtum und Gemeinfreiheit im frühen Mittelalter," *DA,* **6** (1943), 329 ff.

95. *ZRG Germ. Abt.,* **66** (1948), 413 ff.

96. Later this is clearly recognizable among the Normans: Dudo of St. Quentin *De moribus et actis primorum Normanniae ducum* **2** 31/32 (Lair, ed., *Mémoires de la Société des antiquaires de Normandie* **23** [1865] 171 ff.).

97. Tac. *Ger.* 25.

98. G. Tellenbach, *Königtum und Stämme in der Werdezeit des deutschen Reichs* (1939) and "Einführung," *Studien und Vorarbeiten zur Geschichte des grossfränkishen und frühdeutschen Adels* (1957); P. Classen, "Die Verträge von Verdun und von Coulaines 843 also politische Grundlagen des Westfränkischen Reiches," *HZ,* **196** (1963), 1–35.

99. O. v. Dungern, *Adelsherrschaft;* Mitteis, *Festschrift Fr. Schulz;* R. Sprandel, "Dux und comes in der Merowingerzeit," *ZRG Germ. Abt.,* **74** (1957), 41–84.

100. E. Freiherr von Guttenberg, "Iudex h.e. comes aut grafio," *Festschrift Edmund E. Stengel* (1952), 93 ff.

101. *Boethius* 2. 17.

102. Bauer, *Gau und Grafschaft,* pp. 73, 79: *MGH SS rer. Merov.* **1.** 137 (2d ed.).

103. Mitteis, *Festschrift Fr. Schulz,* pp. 230, 248.

104. T. Mayer, "Die Ausbildung der Grundlagen des modernen deutschen Staates im hohen Mittelalter," *HZ,* **159** (1939).

105. H. Mitteis, *Der Staat des hohen Mittelalters* (3d ed., 1948). See also his *Lehnrecht und Staatsgewalt;* W. Kienast, *HZ,* **158** (1938), 3 ff.; W. Keinast, *Untertaneneid und Treuvorbehalt* (1952); F. Ganshof, *Feudalism* (1961); F. Olivier-Martin, *Histoire du droit français* (2d ed., 1951), 80 ff.; "Studien zum mittelalterlichen Lehnwesen," *Vörtrage und Forschungen,* T. Mayer, ed., **5** (1960).

106. The dominant ideas are opposed by H. Krawinkel, *Zur Entstehung des Lehnwesens* (1936) and *Untersuchungen zum fränkischen Benefizialrecht* (1936).

107. *MGH Form.* 158.

108. R. Kötzschke, *Allgemeine Wirtschaftsgeschichte des Mittelalters* (1924), 220 ff.; F. Lütge, *Deutsche Sozial-und Wirtschaftsgeschichte* (1952), 44 ff. Of the almost inexhaustible literature, I can mention only G. Seeliger, *Die politishe und soziale Bedeutung der Grundherrschaft im frühen Mittelalter* (1904); G. Seeliger, *Staat und Grundherrschaft in der älteren deutschen Geschichte* (1909); F. Lütge, *Die Agrarverfassung des frühen Mittelalters im mitteldeutschen Raume vornehmlich in der Karolingerzeit* (1937); and A. Dopsch, "Die Grundherrschaft im Mittelalter," *Festschrift Zycha,* 87 ff.

109. K. F. Strohecker, *Der senatorische Adel im spätantiken Gallien* (1948). For the area east of the Rhine, I am not in total agreement with the conclusions of R. Sprandel, *Der merowingische Adel und die Gebiete östlich des Rheins* (1957).

110. Lütge, *Agrarverfassung,* 145 ff., 106 *n.* 2.

111. *Regesta diplomatica . . . historiae Thuringiae,* O. Dobenecker, ed., 1 (1896), no. 5, 7.

112. T. Mayer, *Geschichtliche Grundlagen der deutschen Verfassung* (1933); A. Helbock, *Grundlagen der Volksgeschichte Deutschlands und Frankreich* (1935 ff.).

113. Above all in the works of Viktor Ernst, *Die Entstehung des niederen Adels* (1916); *Mittelfreie* (1920); *Die Entstehung des deutschen Grundeigentums* (1926).

114. H. Dannenbauer, "Fränkishe und schwäbische Dörfer am Ende des 8. Jahrhunderts," *Festgabe für K. Bohnenberger* (1938), 53 ff.; K. H. Ganahl, "Langen-Erchingen," *ZRG Germ. Abt.,* **58** (1938), 389 ff.; J. Sturm, *Die Anfänge des Hauses Preysing* (1931); H. Dachs, "Germanischer Uradel im frühbairischen Donaugau," *Historischer Verein von Oberpfalz und Regensburg, Verhandlungen,* **86** (1936), 119 ff.

115. R. Kötzschke, "Salhof und Siedelhof," *Akademie der Wissenschaften, Leipzig, Berichte der philologisch-historischen Klasse,* **100** (1953).

116. See the bibl. in T. Mayer, *Fürsten und Staat* (1950), p. 278.

117. See Brunner, *Land und Herrschaft,* 276 ff., esp. 292 ff.

118. A. Dopsch, *Herrschaft und Bauer in der deutschen Kaiserzeit* (1939), 1 ff.

119. G. von Below, *Der deutsche Staat des Mittelalters* (1914).

120. See T. Mayer, "Grundlagen d. modernen dt. Staates," *HZ,* **159** (1939) and its rich bibliography.

121. *Ibid.,* p. 464.

122. F. Rörig, "Geblütsrecht und freie Wahl in ihrer Auswirkung auf die deutsche Geschichte," *Akademie der Wissenschaften, Berlin, Abhandlungen der philologisch-historischen Klasse,* 1945/1946 no. 6, pp. 22, 41, 43; W. Holtzmann, *Das mittelalterliche Imperium und die werdenden Nationen* (1953), p. 17. Even Mitteis has not escaped this one-sidedness; he finds the beginning of district lordship (*Gebietsherrschaft*) only in the High Middle Ages; *Festschrift Fritz Schulz,* p. 247. Similarly in *HZ,* **163** (1941), 478. See also Zatschek, "Germanische Raumerfassung," *HZ,* **168** (1943).

123. Mitteis, *HZ,* **163** (1941), 478.

124. Trans. by Edward P. Nolan, Indiana Univ.—Ed.

125. *MGH SS* **30**. 742.

126. *MGH SS rer. Merov.* **1**. 85 (2d ed.).

127. *MGH Cap.* **1**. 8, 11 ff.

128. *MGH AA* **11**. 239.

129. *MGH SS rer. Merov.* **2**. 308.

130. K. Bosl, *Die Reichsministerialität der Salier und Staufer* (1950–1951).

131. Widukind, *Rer. gest. Sax.* **1**. 27 (Hirsch, ed. p. 40).

132. This is one of the main conclusions of Plassmann, *Princeps und Populus.*

133. Widukind, *Rer. gest. Sax.* **1**. 25 (Hirsch, ed. p. 38).

134. See also Dudo of St. Quentin, *De moribus* (Lair, ed., p. 159).

135. *Die Schriften Notkers und seiner Schule,* P. Piper, ed., **1** (1882), 76.

136. T. Mayer, "Analekten zum Problem der Entstehung der Landeshoheit, vornehmlich in Süddeutschland," *Blätter für deutsche Landesgeschichte,* **89** (1952), 93.

137. W. Schlesinger, *Die Landesherrschaft der Herren von Schönburg. Eine Studie zur Geschichte des Staates in Deutschland* (1953).

138. The theory of territorial lordship advanced here has received but little echo; it has been neither rejected nor accepted. The problem is as important for the history of German institutions as that of the relation between the institution of the band of armed followers and the growth of the early medieval empire. See now H. Patze, *Die Entstehung der Landesherrschaft in Thüringen,* **1** (1962).

POLITICAL AND MONASTIC STRUCTURES IN FRANCE AT THE END OF THE TENTH AND THE BEGINNING OF THE ELEVENTH CENTURY*

Jean-François Lemarignier

The Carolingians conceived of a well-articulated state in which the authority of the king or emperor found support in an administrative hierarchy that penetrated well down the social ladder. To this state was tied a secular Church, equally hierarchical, in which the bishop, the head of the diocese, became, as it were, the pivotal power. If his powers were strengthened, his wealth and prerogatives extended, there was no reason to gainsay it, for the right to invest the bishop with his office assured the king the most efficacious of controls.

Monasticism also had its place. Its way had been prepared long before, a century before 751;[1] it was a monk, St. Boniface, who had raised up the monarchy of Pepin. Forming an island of withdrawal and work, a center of culture where the elites were trained, the monastery was, in a way, the soul of the "liturgical civilization" that was the civilization of the Carolingians.[2] Favored and regulated by Charlemagne, it rendered a sure profit with no risk, molded itself marvelously well to the structures of state and Church, bent willy-nilly to royal tutelage (grounded particularly in the servitudes placed on abbatial election), and accepted its subjection to episcopal control. Independent of one another, the monasteries were each dependent upon their bishop.

---

* Jean-François Lemarignier, "Structures monastiques et structures politiques dans la France de la fin du Xe et des débuts du XIe siècle," *Il monachesimo nell'alto Medioevo (Settimane di studio del Centro italiano di studi sull'alto Medioevo,* 4) (Spoleto, 1957), 357–400. Revised by the author for this anthology; trans. by the ed.

All in all, this regime was workable. St. Benedict of Aniane had for the most part accommodated himself to it, trying only to reduce royal control—and even episcopal jurisdiction—by gaining freedom in abbatial elections and autonomy in administering monastic lands. The regime, however, was tied to the political and ecclesiastical structures of the times. It implied at the top a prince who had a high idea of his mission and enough authority to bring it to realization, a prince whose outlook was likewise broad enough to exercise a worthy influence on the choice of bishops. Both were threatened, particularly after 843, by the "checkmate of Charlemagne,"[3] a defeat that threw political life into ever more serious difficulties. The Empire was fragmented into kingdoms and, after 888, the kingdoms into territorial principalities.[4] Leadership fell to lower hands; and hostile clienteles, raised up by the play of successive allegiances, bred a growing anarchy. A monk echoed the universal suffering.[5]

Anarchy, in turn, gave rise to a thirst for order. In the second and third decades of the tenth century this desire took the form of monastic renewal —with Cluny, Gerard of Brogne, and John of Gorze. But renewal, even in the early days of Cluny, and more clearly in the case of the two reformers from Lorraine, still followed the model of Carolingian structures. The personal union of the monasteries under the rule of Gerard and John would not have been disavowed by St. Benedict of Aniane. Episcopal jurisdiction was not excluded, and in Flanders Gerard of Brogne even went so far as to accept the interference of the Count.[6] The Ottonian monarchy, which gave political expression to this renewal in Germany, took on the same Carolingian, or, if one prefers, neo-Carolingian coloration. Man is an animal who walks facing backward; whenever he can, he imagines a return to order in terms of a return to the past. The Ottonian Church, secular or regular, was the very image of the preceding century. If the Ottos favored the exemption of a few monasteries and the direct attachment of these monasteries to Rome, it was for reasons that were peculiar to each case, and always temporary. At the beginning of the eleventh century Burchard of Worms sketched the true outlines of his contemporary German church, when he affirmed in his collection of canons that monasteries were subject to their bishops. No alternative was imaginable.[7]

The high quality of an episcopacy whose recruitment was one of the major concerns of the emperors made this possible. But was royal authority in France strong enough to realize the same goal? Can the year 936, marked by the restoration of Louis IV d'Outremer, signify, as in Germany, a political renovation? To be sure, this was not an ephemeral restoration, for the next half-century saw three kings from the old dynasty succeed to the throne from father to son. But the similarities east and west stopped there —that is to say, at very little. The last Carolingians failed where the Ottonians succeeded. In France the decline grew worse, and the year 936, rather than signifying a renovation, appears as the dividing point in the comparative history of France and Germany, a dividing point with far-reaching consequences.

After 987 and the arrival of the first Capetians on the throne, the gap became even wider. A fall of one more step, a fall that expressed itself in a genuine revolution in the structure of politics and that provoked in reaction a revolution in the structure of monasticism—this is what the generation of Hugh Capet and Robert the Pious (987–1031) witnessed. And this is what we must now trace.

I. THE DECLINE OF POLITICAL STRUCTURES

The monarchy became weaker; territories splintered even more; ties of vassalage began to weaken.

The young Capetian monarchy, which in 987 had definitively replaced the last Carolingians, tried as best it could to maintain the prerogatives of the old dynasty for its own profit. Legally, nothing changed: the new dynasty claimed the same sacral character, born of the same rituals, founded on the same texts, creating the same duties and the same powers, protected by the same sanctions. Abbo of Fleury, although not without a tinge of skepticism as to its true efficacy, recalled this sacral character in the times of Hugh Capet;[8] and Aimon, a few years later, underlined it in his own fashion when he inserted the legend of the Holy Ampulla, the miraculous origins of the oil used for anointing at the coronation, into his story. But did this halo with which the king was thus glorified, this halo which the monk Helgaud would soon burnish by giving his hero the power to heal lepers, have any point other than to compensate for a weakness that was only too real?[9]

In fact, Hugh Capet, no longer supported even by the feeling of legitimacy from which his predecessor had benefitted, saw his field of activity become progressively smaller.

The southern regions fell away. In the days of the last Carolingians, people in *Gothia* and in the Spanish March still knew that a royal act was necessary, or useful, if they wished to obtain a gift or confirmation of goods or privileges, such as an immunity or the right to elect an abbot freely. Indeed, people in the South requested royal diplomas often enough that a full one sixth of those extant dating from 936 to 987 concern these regions.[10] After 987 there were none until 1108. Their absence was complete south of a line that approximately coincides with the boundary separating the *langue d'oil* from the *langue d'oc;*[11] it was the sign of a loss in royal prestige, of an inability to give protection. In 988, Count Borel of the Spanish March, gravely threatened by an offensive of the Emir Al-Mansur, still sought the support of High Capet (or rather renewed a request earlier made of Lothar and Louis V); but Hugh made only some slight and erratic preparations and, finally, did not go. After his failure, the Spanish March sought support elsewhere—at Cluny and at Rome. At the end of the eleventh century the Count of Barcelona would become vassal of the Holy See.[12]

The king's failure led others to exercise certain prerogatives that had previously been his. Was there any prerogative more specifically royal in Carolingian times than that of maintaining the peace (*pax et justitia*), of preventing brigandage and repressing those *latrones* whom Charlemagne and Louis the Pious had so often menaced with punishment in their capitularies? Now it was the bishops who, in the king's absence, instituted the "peace of God." The movement began in Aquitaine (Chartroux, 989) and Septimania (Narbonne, 990) before spreading elsewhere. Places and dates underline the moment and its common cause: the king's retreat.

This royal absence from the South had its counterpart at the royal court, where the Southern princes appeared little or not at all. Among the *proceres,* the royal vassals whose names at the bottom of royal diplomas signal their presence at court, neither the Duke of Gascony, the Count of Toulouse, the Duke of *Gothia* and the princes of this region, nor the Count of the Spanish March appeared even once from 987 to 1108 (if for a moment we extend our investigation to this date). The Duke of Aquitaine appeared only rarely—on very great occasions. Exceptionally, the Count of Auvergne and the Count of La Marche would appear; and that was all from south of the Loire.[13] Abbo of Fleury, going into Gascony about the year 1000 to visit the priory of La Réole said jokingly to the monks who accompanied him, "Look! I am more powerful in this country than the King of France, for no one here fears his domination."[14]

The South was not the only area affected. A list of royal diplomas from 898 to 1108, drawn up reign by reign and by the location of their beneficiaries, would show a gradual narrowing of royal influence, in which the reigns of Hugh Capet and Robert the Pious appear only as stages along a path of ever-steepening decline. In the last decades of those two centuries (1077–1108), there were hardly any diplomas for lands outside *Francia.*

The nature of the royal diploma itself changed. Until 987 all royal diplomas uniformly received the chancery's subscription which, along with the king's subscription and signs of validation, gave these acts the quality of public acts grounded solely in royal authority. After 987 there was a change. The king had his diplomas, or at least some of them, signed by those around him when they were issued. This practice was borrowed from the style of private charters, which were signed in the same fashion. It was a sign that royal authority alone was no longer enough to maintain the decision expressed in the diploma or to guarantee its value. The first diploma thus signed was dated 988,[15] the year of dynastic change. The coincidence proves that the change in dynasty brought with it the change in style. All the same, we must not believe that the new habit immediately took firm root. Conservative elements sought to curb its spread. A major problem, perhaps *the* major problem, is to determine how the practice slipped in and by what successive stages. Under Hugh Capet diplomas of this new type are only a small proportion (about one sixth) of the total still known (if to the diplomas having multiple subscribers, we add one non-royal charter, a private charter the king witnessed sometime between 992 and 996, along with other witnesses—a practice that also reveals a decline).[16] For the first part of the reign of Robert the Pious, such diplomas reach one third of the total. Then, after 1025, there is a sudden rise, which increases during the following half-century. From one third they become one half; then two thirds under Henry I (1031–1060); and seven eighths from 1060–1077.[17]

The social rank of the witnesses to these acts suggests the same development, marked by the same dates.

It began at the top. Under Hugh Capet, two out of three witnesses were bishops, and under Robert, they remained a strong majority until about 1025. With them appeared several counts and, on rare occasions, one or two territorial princes. For the moment, there were hardly any less important lords.[18] All these bishops, princes, and counts were from Langued'oil, almost all of them from *Francia*. In these regions where the king retained whatever remained of his power, the ruling group attempted, despite everything, to keep up the practices of the last Carolingian century, in which the episcopacy supported the monarchy and the king governed from the midst of a court of his faithful who were men of high esteem and superior social rank. Expressions such as the king having his acts subscribed *"manu fidelium nostrorum"* [by the hand of our faithful], *"consilio procerum nostrorum"* [with the advice of our great men], *"a fidelibus nostris"* [by our faithful], or invoking his "common counsel with the great and first-ranking men of our palace" recall the decisions of the end of the ninth century which the king promised to take "with the common counsel of our faithful."[19] A court session such as that of June 9, 1017, when three archbishops, twelve bishops, the Count of Poitou, the Duke of Normandy and three counts from *Francia* put their names to an act—a session that coincided with the coronation of Hugh, Robert's eldest son—recalls the coronation of Louis IV in 936 when twenty or more bishops, two or three territorial princes, and several counts of *Francia* were present.[20] The rank of those signing the royal acts corresponded to the importance of the meetings at which they were issued. These meetings were illustrious occasions, fundamental events in the military, political, and judicial life of the realm: the siege of Avallon (1005); the synod of Chelles, convoked and presided over by the king to judge the murderers of his palatine Hugh of Beauvais (1008); the coronation of Hugh (1017); the Council of Orleans, where heretics were condemned (1022); the coronation of Henry, the future

Henry I (1027).[21] These acts testify to a government of the high aristocracy.[22]

About 1028 the social rank fell. The names of a half-dozen bishops, a half-dozen counts of *Francia,* and the counts of Flanders and Poitou were to be found that year, as they might have before, at the bottom of one of Robert's diplomas; but they were far from being alone. Twelve or thirteen castellans and viscounts from regions of royal influence slightly overshadowed them: the lords of Montfort, Montmorency, Beaugency, and Gallardon and the viscounts of Nogent and Dreux, etc., whom six knights also joined. These castellans, viscounts, and knights appeared suddenly in the royal diplomas and almost all of them, for the first time. Never before had they appeared in such number or formed so large a proportion. The finest flower of the French aristocracy, perhaps, but of a middling aristocracy, and even a rather low one, putting the bishops and counts dangerously into the minority.[23] The tendency increased under Henry I and Philip I.[24]

Yet another sign of decline was tied to this. Were all these lords of lesser social rank the king's vassals? Was it as his vassals that they attested to his diplomas? Sometimes, to be sure, but not always. A royal act shortly before 1030, which two bishops, two castellans, and about ten knights signed, called all of them *"testes"* [witnesses].[25] The practice grew under Henry I, and still more under Philip I, to welcome an ever-lengthening list of names to the bottom of royal acts solely for the sake of having them as witnesses, should the need arise. It was again an influence of the private act, and its consequences were serious. To associate the royal court with a diploma was one thing; to accumulate witnesses was quite another. The practice suggests that men placed more faith in the listing of witnesses to give acts some value and assure their execution than they did in the special character of a royal act.

At precisely the same time, and signifying the same thing, the queen's *Laudatio* [approval] appeared in 1030; in two acts of 1031 the "approval" of the queen and of the king's two sons, Henry and Robert, appeared, the three subscribing immediately after the king.[26] What some have called "the Capetian trinity" thus went back to these last years of the reign of Robert the Pious, defining a kind of familial government at the very moment (as Georges Duby has well demonstrated) when kinship solidarity was replacing the ancient solidarities of public law, weakened by the demise of Frankish institutions.[27]

All these practices, especially the appearance of castellans among the witnesses, were at the same time directly connected to the division of territory into smaller and smaller fractions, a breakup that now reached a crucial point.

Up to the last years of the tenth century, the power of the political leaders may have faded bit by bit until at times, in the hearts of some fragmented territorial principalities, it had been gathered into the hands of a count governing a single *pagus*—for instance, the counts of Anjou, of Maine, of Mâcon; but it had fallen no further. The *pagus* had resisted. From a former administrative district, which the *pagus* had been in Carolingian times, it had perhaps become a political unit, if its lord had been capable of grasping his independence. In any event, it had remained a territorial unit, had kept its cohesion, its frontiers, and its judicial and administrative organization. Social life had been structured within its frame. And this façade giving the illusion that the Carolingian regime lived on, had often served to mask political decline, since men more often judge a regime by the administrative structures affecting their daily lives than by the political structures that dominate them. As long as the *pagus* had not been touched, Carolingian public institutions had not received the *coup de grâce*.

At the end of the tenth and during the first third of the eleventh century, the *pagus* in turn was affected. The phenomenon was a general one. (This has been a major discovery by Belgian and French medievalists of the last twenty years in independent studies that have led to generally similar conclusions.)[28] It is in the Mâconnais that this change has been most recently observed and masterfully described.[29] In the time of Otto-William (982–1026) comital authority collapsed, and the counts retained only Mâcon and its surroundings. The *pagus* of Mâcon was divided among five or six castellans—the lords of Beaujeu, Brancion, Uxelles, etc.—and two or three immunist churches, of which Cluny was one. The castellans freed themselves of the coercive power of the Count (the last example of his using it occurred in 1019); churches fortified themselves by the peace of God and strengthened their own justice (as Cluny began to do in 1016). Around the castles and the immunities, the level of the leaders went down one notch.

Approximately the same facts and certainly the same dates can be found in Maine, where the castles and castellans of Sablé (last third of the tenth century), Château-du-Loire (before 1007), Mayenne (before 1014), Duneau (between 1016 and 1025), and Bellême, on the Norman border,[30] etc., rapidly rose. In 1014, Hamelin of Château-du-Loire and Haimon of Mayenne appeared as the principal vassals of the count.[31] These castellans were hereditary,[32] had their own policy, fought their own wars,[33] and modeled themselves on the Count; like him,[34] the castellans had their courts and their circles of vassals who witnessed their acts.[35] The same was true in *Francia,* in the region of the royal domain where disintegration seems to have profited first the viscounts—the viscounts of Vexin, who became counts of Meulan (990) and the viscounts of Mantes (*circa* 1006)—and then the castellans, those lords of the Ile-de-France whom we have already met at the court of Robert the Pious.[36] It was during this prince's reign that these castellans created their castles and affirmed their dynasties. Of this there is no better witness than a late eleventh-century chronicler of St.-Germain-des-Prés who, in relating the events of Robert's reign at the end of his universal history, retained for his story nothing but these creations, spoke only of the castellan families of the Paris region, of their genealogies and their relations— the Montforts, the Meulans, and the Montlhérys.[37]

About this same time, Poitou was likewise broken up into viscounties and castellanies governed by "castellans who were sovereign in their seigniory and often in conflict with the count."[38] In Anjou conditions were about the same at precisely the same time, and they menaced the count's authority in the same way. It was only a menace, however, for the count reacted with greater efficacy and finally disciplined his turbulent baronage.[39] The Angevin example suggests a little less disorder; it was similar to the two principalities of Normandy and Flanders, which, in the end, did not disintegrate, where order was saved at the level of the duchy and the county. The danger was great in Normandy during the last years of the tenth century, however, and was thwarted just in time by Richard II.[40] In Flanders, during the reign of Baldwin IV, the danger was even greater.[41]

Can Langued'oc be included in this inventory (despite the absence of equally detailed study)? Analogous developments have recently been found in Gascony,[42] in Comminges,[43] and in Auvergne[44] and Velay;[45] they have even been suggested for the county of Besalu, in the heart of the Spanish March,[46] not to speak of Provence.[47] But here the checkerboard was less dense, and the situation demands study in greater depth.

Not only did the framework of political activity contract; the nature of the rights of public power became, in a way, degraded, as the word *"consuetudo"* [custom] proves—a word that people began to use about the year 1000 to denote public powers. The sources called by the name of *"consuetudines"* the public rights that once had been the king's: in the first place the *bannum,* which step by step had fallen into the hands of the castellans and other "banal" lords.[48] The sudden frequency of *"consuetudines"* proves that "what had been essentially regalian powers were no longer founded on the express delegation of the sovereign, but in habit and the testimony of collective memory,"[49] a sign of decline quite analogous to those lists of witnesses at the end of the diplomas of the counts and territorial princes, and which, as we have seen, would soon appear affixed to diplomas of the king. The word *"consuetudines"* not only denoted the rights of public power, but in addition extended to rights whose origins were purely private, such as manorial dues. The two were mixed, a sign that public and private power were less clearly distinguished.

All this gives the impression of a certain confusion and, in any case, of a scattering of lords and a mosaic of political territories subject to their authority. Did coherent ties of vassalage at least unite these territorial lords among themselves and in some way compensate for the territorial anarchy?

Vassalage and feudal practices always carried within themselves the yeast of anarchy and a threat of disorder for society. This the leaders—those whom we would call the "public" powers—had always tried to remedy, with differing means at different times. In the French kingdom of the first half of the twelfth century a feudal hierarchy was conjured up: a parallel hierarchy of persons and lands, in which the real element predominated, in which one fief was held of another, that fief of yet another, and so on in order up to the *regnum* and the king—a coherent pyramid inspired, it seems, by Gregorian ideas that Suger echoed,[50] a masterpiece of the political and juridical imagination which powerfully served the unifying designs of the French monarchy. But this hierarchical design supposed that the notion of one fief being held of another had already been conceived, and this had not yet happened in the first third of the eleventh century. The common mind was not at all yet ready for it. Vassalage was thought of, above all, in terms of personal devotion; the economic consideration, the grant of a benefice, implied no chain linking these benefices among themselves.

Is this to say that in this first state of things there was no way to turn feudal practices toward the goal of order? The Carolingians had sought to do so and had imagined that they had found the way by incorporating some of the rigor of the tie of vassalage into the oath of fidelity due the king,[51] or by charging their *vassi regales* (and even all *seniores*) with judicial and military responsibilities over their own *vassi:* that is, by using them as intermediaries.[52] These plans, these attempts, led to a hierarchical arrangement, or at least to the skeleton of a multileveled hierarchy. Such a hierarchy could still be found in tenth- and eleventh-century Germany, when the Abbot of Gorze led his vassals to the royal army, or when the Abbot of Lorsch placed the military service due the emperor on twelve great vassals who were obligated each to furnish one hundred armed fighting-men;[53] it also lived on in eleventh-century Normandy.[54] For any effectiveness, however, it presupposed both authority at the summit and devotion at the base, the two being closely linked. Authority did exist in Germany and Normandy; but in France it had disappeared in most regions and at the level of the kingdom, as we have seen.

As for devotion, it required for its effectiveness that a vassal have but one lord. All vassals did, during the Carolingian period, and almost all of them still did in eleventh-century Germany.[55] But in the Western kingdom, rarely at the very end of the ninth century and the beginning of the tenth, but more and more often after that, vassals were to be found who did homage to several lords in order to increase the number of their benefices.[56] The appearance of castellanies, which multiplied the chances for territorial lords to increase their power, favored the practice of multiple vassalage, whose frequency suddenly soared. Already in 975 Geoffroy Grisegonelle, count of Anjou and a vassal of Hugh Capet, was also vassal of the Duke of Aquitaine from whom he had received Loudun and Mirebeau in fief; and, still in the days of Hugh Capet, Bouchard of Vendôme, one of the vassals on whom the king most depended, received in fief from Sifroi, bishop of Le Mans, the episcopal rights over sixty-four parishes along the Loir as the price for his military aid against the Count of Maine.[57] A number of the territorial princes and counts who appended their names to the diplomas of Robert the Pious as royal vassals were involved in other ties of fealty and had rendered homage elsewhere: Hugh of Beauvais, Robert's palatine,[58] was also a vassal of the Bishop of Orleans;[59] Eudes II of Blois[60] had Count Rainard of Sens give him the castle of Montereau in fief in 1015;[61] Fulk Nerra, Robert's vassal for Anjou,[62] was also, as his father had been, vassal of the Duke of Aquitaine for the castellany of Saintes;[63] Baldwin IV, count of Flanders,[64] was vassal of Emperor Henry II who had given him Walcheren and Valenciennes in fief;[65] Otto-William, count of Mâcon, was vassal of Rudolph of Burgundy for certain possessions east of the Saône;[66] and Dreu, count of Vexin, held *in beneficia* of St.-Germain-des-Prés, five villages in the region of Mantes over which he claimed to exercise the *consuetudines*.[67]

Of all the territorial lords who drew royal vassals into dependence on themselves, Eudes II, count of Blois and Troyes, was certainly the principal one and the one most to be feared. In any case, multiple vassalage did not frighten him. The house of Champagne, which Eudes—more than anyone—helped to construct, was founded on a play of multiple holdings, many of which probably went back to his time.[68] Encircling the royal domain to the point of threatening it with extinction, he arranged to acquire vassals in the very heart of the group of royal vassals: among the counts, Galeran of Meulan, Mannassès of Damartin, and Hilduin of Breteuil; among the castellans (for multiplicity of ties had, as a matter of course, extended to this level of the political and social ladder) Hugh Bardoul, lord of Nogent-le-Roi and of Broyes-en-Champagne, and Ganelon of Montigny.[69] Eudes thus prepared the revolts that darkened the last two years of Robert's life and yet more gravely threatened the beginning of the reign of Henry I.[70]

The practice—which, of course, was not limited to the world of royal vassals, even if we restrict our examples to them—became so current that churchmen, who had greeted it with hostility,[71] resigned themselves to accept it. Not only was Bishop Renaud of Paris, the son of Bouchard of Vendôme, in the king's fealty for the Vendômois and his bishopric, but Fulbert of Chartres forced him to enter the fealty of the church of Chartres as well for various lands he held of that church. Fulbert likewise required the knights to whom Renaud had subinfeudated parts of this fief to render homage to himself. But he had too much of a sense of order, as well as too much legal sense, not to measure the dangers of such interweaving and he sought to counteract these multiple fealties by a system of priorities. Renaud would render homage only *salva fidelitate Roberti* [without prejudice to his fealty to Robert]; and the knights, homage without prejudice to their fealty to Renaud.[72] These reservations of fealty, which had a bright future before them,[73] testify both to the spread of multiple vassalage and to the anarchy it engendered.

Men were not only vassals of several lords, but became so successively over time. This too contributed nothing to the coherence of feudal ties. Territorial lords passed from the allegiance of one to that of another, following the stronger side, seeking an ally or as the result of a war or a treaty of peace. It was an ancient practice, already far spread at the end of the ninth and in the tenth century,[74] and it remained undiminished in the days of Hugh and Robert. Thus the counts of Nantes had found themselves tossed among several contrary allegiances: to the counts of Rennes; to the counts of Anjou; and, as the outcome of alliances sealed by oaths of homage, to King Lothar and the counts of Blois, who were taking Anjou from the other side. In the same way the counts Rennes had sought support against the counts of Anjou, first from the counts of Blois and then, it appears, from Hugh Capet. They finally found their best protection in the fealty of the Duke of Normandy, to whom Alain III did homage about 1030.[75] In the same region (so Richer tells us) Fulk Nerra, the count of Anjou, defeated by Count Eudes of Blois, was forced as a condition of peace to do homage to his enemy's son.[76] Several decades later Maine was torn between Norman and Angevin allegiances.[77] In Burgundy the oaths of fealty collected by Robert the Pious, beginning with Otto-William, had no purpose other than a political one.[78]

That these ties sometimes took the form of homage of peace or frontier homage[79] could only accentuate their fragility. Where would these vassals of several lords, these temporary vassals, have found a source of devotion to their lord? Some princes reached the point where they were not very sure what the obligations of their vassals were. Duke William of Aquitaine felt the need to have them specified by Fulbert of Chartres, whose famous letter of 1020 was a kind of legal opinion and would become a source of law. It is worth noting that in this letter Fulbert insisted upon the negative obligations of the vassal; as for positive obligations, aid and counsel, he tended to attach them, at least to a certain extent, to the grant of a fief.[80] At exactly the same time, and from somewhat the same point of view, Dudo of St. Quentin, writing in the entourage of the Duke of Normandy, by means of a tendentious narration of the events of the tenth century, defended the thesis that the Duke owed the king nothing but simple personal homage creating bonds of friendship, harmony, and peace but carrying no obligation of service. According to Dudo, Normandy was not held in fief but possessed allodially (*in alodo et in fundo*)—a Norman evasion of vassal service, expressed and enlarged for the first time into a kind of total theory.[81]

All these texts present an image in which hierarchy is quite absent. If a particular text granting authorization to manumit a serf allows the historian to reconstruct a chain of personal relations to which the serf's lord is subject, it does not suffice to suggest the idea of hierarchical coordination.[82] It is rather anarchy that the texts give witness to, an anarchy with its train of insecurity and troubles—which a famous story of Raoul Glaber allows us to measure[83]—and also with its search for remedies and for new forms of solidarity. The peace of God developed; oaths of peace multiplied, begetting an obligation for those who took them not to violate the peace; and soon associations were formed, obligating those who joined to respect it.[84]

The peace movement was linked to the three aspects of decline that we have tried to distinguish. It was linked to *feudal anarchy*—one oath of peace was given in almost the form of a vassal's oath of fealty, including even the clause reserving the vassal's allegiance to his lords;[85] another included the vassal's obligation not to betray his lord (*ne homo tradat seniorem suum*), the oath becoming a support for the vassal's fidelity.[86] It was linked to *territorial fragmentation*—Duby has shown that in Burgundy the development of monastic jurisdictions, of monastic immunist seigniories, was tied to the development of the peace of God.[87] It was linked to the *decline of the monarchy*—it was the king's weakness (*imbecillitas regis*) that decided the bishops of Soissons and Beauvais to have the oaths of peace taken in their dioceses in 1023.[88]

In these oaths, in this search for peace, the monasteries' need for protection was not forgotten; for the monasteries were also victims of the troubled times. Threatened, attacked, they sought remedies for the evils that beset them in new supports and novel structures.

II. THE RENOVATION OF MONASTIC STRUCTURES

In two important ways the collapse of Carolingian political structures ruined the very base on which monastic life rested. First of all, royal protection had suffered the same fate as other regalian prerogatives; from the *tuitio* of a king who had a high idea of his mission and above all a broad and sympathetic point of view, a number of monasteries had fallen under the *dominatio* of territorial lords who were more jealous of their less legitimate and less well-assured power and whose power was exercised closer to home. The monasteries became the objects of power plays among these great "chiefs".[89] Second, as a result of a less direct but equivalent development, episcopal investiture escaped from the hands of the king in a similar but more limited way.[90] More than one episcopal office, and those among the richest and most powerful, such as the archbishopric of Reims, had become the plaything of political opponents.[91] The choice of occupants had been gravely affected. There were cases of nepotism, of simony, and of nicolaitanism, the one leading to the other in the manner that Humbert of Moyenmoutier would later denounce; examples could be found in the tenth century and at the beginning of the eleventh—although one should not exaggerate their frequency.[92] Did such prelates have the qualities necessary to exercise a beneficent control over the monasteries of their dioceses? Would not the monks, threatened if not hard pressed, seek to escape such bishops' grasp and turn toward Rome against them as well as against the laity (for the two were linked)? Would they not seek other supports leading to other structures?

This fight for liberty took on the scope of a revolution led by a general staff who planned it before acting and who realized their object, step by step. The major steps, those both most necessary and most difficult to take, were to win monastic exemptions from episcopal jurisdiction. They were taken in a bitter struggle against an episcopacy that was united, much feared, and well armed. First exemption for a few pivotal monasteries was secured, then for an order, the Order of Cluny.

For almost a quarter of a century (from about 991 to 1016), the effort was contained within the circle of former habits, limited to a monastery—the building, its lands, its goods, its monks, and its abbot. In itself this was no legal novelty: privileges of this kind had been granted for a long time. Nonetheless, for a long time, as a result of Carolingian hostility, there had been extremely few of these privileges, with the exception of those already mentioned in Ottonian Germany. The withdrawal from Carolingian political positions meant, all in all, a similar withdrawal from Carolingian monastic positions.

What was new was the sudden swelling of a movement that would drown, like a wave, what the Carolingians had built and would bring to the top a few key monasteries. It began at Fleury, or rather it was begun by Abbo of Fleury; for at the beginning it was one man's action that did all. He was evidently a powerful man, involved in all the monastic reforms of his time (many of which he himself inspired) and involved in politics as well. He played a role of prime importance at the council of St. Basle de Verzy in 991, at which it all began. Convoked by the king in accordance with Carolingian methods, directed by the king or by his representatives, and composed of archbishops and bishops, the council's mission was to judge Archbishop Arnoul of Reims, who was accused of felony. The prosecution's thesis, presented by Bishop Arnoul of Orleans was that the episcopacy was competent to render judgment; that of the defense, supported by Abbo of Fleury, was that the case should go to the Pope. Arnoul of Orleans was the diocesan bishop of Abbo, abbot of Fleury. The two men clashed on a question of principle, that is, one that could not be compromised. The subject of their fight had already opposed Hincmar to Nicolas I, a confrontation that could not but aggravate its vehemence; it would later pit Henricans against Gregorians. Here at the council, the fight was transposed to the level of relations between a bishop and an abbot of his diocese, to a problem of everyday life, and this made it intolerable. The bishop would not be satisfied with less than the abbot's destruction and would even attempt his assassination. Abbo would not rest in peace until he had obtained an exemption for his monastery, obtained it from the papacy whose cause he had championed at the Council of St. Basle.

To acquire this exemption, Abbo methodically set to work, step by step. First he put together his arguments in two collections of texts. The first, the more famous, he composed between 991 and 993–994—a collection to serve for combat rather than as a general compendium. Here he gave the starring role to the texts on monastic liberty, notably those of Gregory the Great, such as the letter to Marinianus protecting a monastery from the "prejudicial and injurious acts" of the bishop and providing for appeal to Rome in case of conflict between bishop and abbot. This perfectly suited Abbo's preoccupations and formed his strongest weapon. A new conflict between Abbo and Arnoul in 993–994 induced the abbot to add to his first group of texts another letter of Gregory that he had neglected—the letter to Castorius forbidding the bishop to celebrate public masses in a monastery of his diocese without permission of the monastery's abbot—and to draw up a second collection, the *Epistola XIV,* in which this letter was given predominance. Armed with these texts, Abbo set off for Rome, where he obtained from the Pope—although not without battle and delay—a privilege giving Fleury essentially what his collections had claimed: exemption from the bishop's coercive power and from episcopal public masses, with appeal to the Holy See allowed in case of conflict (996 or 997).

It remained to extend this privilege to other monasteries and to other liberties, especially to exemption from episcopal control over ordination. After an attempt by the canons of St. Martin of Tours, it was finally the monks of Cluny who breached this last line of episcopal resistance and obtained from Gregory V in 998 or 999 a privilege exempting them from the bishop's coercive power and from his control of ordination: they were allowed to ask any prelate they wished to perform ordinations, to bless the abbot, and to consecrate churches. The matter had been astutely linked to the question of public masses; the letter to Castorius, which Abbo had thrown into the debate a few years before, had not gone unused. The diocesan bishop was totally excluded from Cluny. To a large extent, the monks owed this supreme freedom to their temporal statute as a monastery given to the Holy See, constituting Rome's property and owing the Pope an annual rent to symbolize that proprietary dependence.

A few years later, William of Volpiano laid down as the condition for the reform he was undertaking the grant of the same kind of privilege, if not for all the monasteries he controlled, at least for the principal ones—for those which served as centers of action in the three major areas of his influence: Normandy, northern Burgundy, and Lombardy. William obtained them for Fécamp (1006–1016), St. Bénigne of Dijon (1012) and Fruttuaria (1006) and established these monasteries as islands of withdrawal and study, as seedbeds of abbots and bishops, sheltered from episcopal interference.[93]

Fruit of a defiant monasticism that was successfully carrying through an autonomous plan of reconstruction, these extensions could not but raise a reaction on the part of a disturbed episcopacy. Already at the synod of Chelles (993 or 994), the bishops had decreed that "if the Roman Pope makes a decision contrary to the Fathers, that decision will be null," a statement that simply meant opposing to pontifical privileges the principle of the Council of Chalcedon that monks should be subject to their diocesan bishops. In 1008, on the occasion of a new conflict between Fleury and the Bishop of Orleans, another prelate, Fulbert of Chartres, certainly one of the most authoritative and perhaps one of the most moderate bishops of his time, sided against the monks. The privilege given by Gregory V to Fleury he found untenable. Though he searched, he said, he could find neither canonical text (*legem*) nor any subtle reason (*modum ratiocinationis*) to justify this claim to exemption from episcopal authority. Undoubtedly, in order to find them one would have to be "a new rhetor, who did not descend, but rather fell from heaven."[94] The monks triumphed, but solely because the Pope acted just in time to save them.

The bishops only stiffened their backs. The consecration of an abbatial church by a papal legate about this time roused their indignation. They cried sacrilege; accused the Pope of transgressing the canons; recalled that it was an ancient rule, founded in ancient authority, that a bishop could not exercise any power in the diocese of another without his permission. To the thesis of effective papal primacy they opposed, without qualification, a thesis of episcopal equality granting the Pope only a precedence of honor. The quarrel over the structure of monasticism was calling into question the entire organization of the Church.[95] It would do so even more when, from the rung of exemption for a single monastery, monasticism reached up and grasped exemption for an entire order, the Order of Cluny (1016–1027).

The year 1016, which seems to have been the point of departure for these efforts, was a year of major events for Western Christendom, events that put monasticism in the limelight and thereby enabled it to profit.

The Moslems of the Emir of Majorca launched an attack on the coast of Italy. Pope Benedict VIII organized a counteroffensive. Some of Cluny's lay protectors and some Norman knights joined in; and, as it would appear from a series of concordant pontifical privileges, some monasteries also became involved in the undersides of papal politics.[96] It was at the height of these intrigues, in September 1016, that Benedict VIII launched the most energetic and wide-reaching of his prohibitions, addressed to all the bishops of Burgundy, Aquitaine, and Provence, to defend the monks of Cluny against all the evils from which they were suffering.

These evils were the consequence of the decline of political organization, indeed, doubly so. Cluny's possessions had been plundered. Who were the guilty? The lords of Berzé and Brancion, Guichard de Beaujeu (and others whose names the Pope does not hesitate to mention), castellans of the Mâconnais, who at precisely this moment were affirming their authority.[97] Which possessions had been their victims? The lordships (*poestés*) Cluny held, Laizé and others (also listed in full by the Pope), whose *consuetudines* the castellans had usurped—immunist seigniories that were also on the rise. Without intending to, Benedict VIII reveals the fights involved, the anarchy that territorial fragmentation had engendered, and the competition between castellans and immunists that was its fruit.[98]

Benedict proposed to remedy this anarchy, or at least to protect from its ravages the monastery of Cluny, which belonged to Rome. His means of defense was to tighten this temporal link, a first step on the road toward the idea of a Cluniac Order enlarged at the base and finding support at the summit at Rome. Three elements above all seem to have combined to produce this order: the tie of temporal subjection, spiritual exemption, and Roman primacy.

Benedict VIII strongly emphasized the first. He recalled this dependence, which the papal chancery called Cluny's *"libertas,"* and gave it precision. It covered "Cluny itself and all the other places belonging to it situated in Burgundy, Aquitaine and Provence, whether monasteries, priories, or domaines."[99] He could have put a list of names under these categories, as we can ourselves. Thirty-four monasteries and priories in these three regions were accounted for in 1016, and their names inscribed on the parchment: thirteen in southern Burgundy, sixteen in Provence, four in Auvergne and one in Gascony, foundations at the grass roots, reaching through Cluny toward Rome.[100]

The second element was spiritual exemption. Benedict VIII did not yet go so far; he did not say that the Cluniac establishments were exempt—it was only the proprietary rights of the Holy See that he laid claim to. But one can feel that he was heading that way. Drawing up the list of those guilty of injuring the monks, the Pope vowed them to malediction and anathema and ordered the bishops to whom the bulls were addressed to excommunicate them and to have their own clergy respect this punishment under pain of divine retribution. To be sure, the bishops were not yet threatened, should they decide to resist these orders, with the same punishments that the Gregorians would inflict; the Pope did not yet have the means. But he treated the bishops as subordinates and interfered with their jurisdictions. This act of 1016 was one that led to exemption.

Eight years later the step was taken. In 1024, John XIX, renewing the privilege of Gregory V, repeated the clause that sheltered the monks of Cluny from episcopal coercion and extended it to all the monks of Cluny "wherever they are" (*ubicumque positi*). It appears ill fitting, he argued, that someone other than the Pope might declare "a son of the Holy Apostolic See" anathema, like the disciple of a "subject church" and "without our judgment." If anyone believes, the Pope went on, that he has a just reason for condemning a Cluniac monk to such a penalty, let him call upon the justice of the Holy See. Thus the monks of Cluny, whether they resided in the mother abbey or in one of the dependent houses, and even if they were on the road from one to another, were no longer justiciable before the bishop of the diocese.[101]

What powers did diocesan bishops retain over the foundations dependent on Cluny? They had neither the power to coerce the monks nor the right to promote them to holy orders. These were two major blows at their spiritual authority. But what the bishop no longer did, someone else had to do. The development of exemption led straight to monastic centralization, straight to the organization of an order.

It was the Pope who supported the order and he, in turn, established that support on the primacy of Rome—the third element. The occasion was the bishops' violent opposition to Cluny, which the monks could vanquish only with the help of Rome. The conflict broke out in 1025. Abbot Odilo had called on the Archbishop of Vienne to perform the ordination of some monks; the Bishop of Mâcon protested at the Council of Anse. These ordinations, he declared, performed in his diocese and without his authorization, were contrary to the canons. Odilo in reply produced the papal privilege granting the monks free choice of a prelate to perform consecrations. The bishops retorted by citing the rule of the Council of Chalcedon. The "piece of parchment" (*charta*)—an inexact and pejorative term—that Odilo had produced was contrary to this rule, they said, and thus null and void.

In the end Odilo won only by appealing to the Holy See. At the Council of Rome in 1027, John XIX used all his energy for the abbot's defense and confirmed Cluny's privileges in their entirety. He advanced two arguments. Cluny belongs to the Pope; it is, he said, *"nostrum monasterium singulare,"* a member of a body of which the Roman Church is the head, and one may not "separate a member from it." The Roman Church has primacy over all the others, it is "head and heart of all the churches"—a borrowing from pseudo-Anacletus which the Gregorians would again place in the limelight when they used it to found their own claims.[102]

If this success, these solutions, these arguments and this quotation presaged the Gregorian centralization of the Church a quarter of a century beforehand, they also consecrated the success of a thoroughly new type of monastic hierarchy. The former structure, composed of monasteries that were independent of one another and each subject to their diocesan bishop, was replaced by another composed of monasteries that were each independent of the bishop and subject, beyond the framework of the diocese, to the head of their order who himself depended on the Pope. For the autonomous monastery was substituted the affiliated monastery. This is the idea of the monastic order. To be sure, the *ordo,* the common rule, was not foreign to it; the word itself is proof.[103] But this was a necessary, not a sufficient condition. Can one speak of an order of Richard of St. Vanne or of William of Volpiano?[104] The monasteries subject to them followed a common rule, but no real ties united them.

We must make a second reservation to our conclusions. This real tie already existed sketchily in tenth-century Cluny; certain monasteries, such as Charlieu, Sauxillanges, and others, some of which would form part of the group of thirty-four listed in 1016,[105] were already attached to it. The tie was purely temporal, however, and did not suffice to create a monastic order in the true sense of the word, in the sense it was understood in the early years of its history—at Cluny and Cîteaux. These are the reasons one cannot truly speak of a Cluniac Order until after 1024–1027.

This is not to say that from this time on the Cluniac Order would know only a rise with no falls and that the Cluniac centralizers would suffer no reverses. There was something in the movement that was too new for it not to meet with resistance. It had to wait until the Gregorians, perhaps drawing their inspiration in part from Cluny, had shaped the common outlook and habituated the mind to the idea of a pyramidal hierarchy connecting all the churches to one another and to Rome; it remained for Cîteaux in the twelfth century to realize an order even more highly structured than Cluny. Cluny was but a prototype.

It was a prototype that owed nothing to the feudal hierarchy. Whether Cluny was feudal, antifeudal, or a-feudal is a question that has recently been much debated.[106] What we have said about feudal anarchy—at some length—allows us now to conclude that Cluny was not symmetrical to feudalism but opposed to it. Ties of dependence of man to man, purely personal and ending in anarchy as a consequence of multiple vassalage, are one thing; the real tie of dependence of one church on another is something else: a tie that can only be unique.[107]

It is not from the viewpoint of legal analysis alone that monastic hierarchy and feudal anarchy opposed each other in France during the first third of the eleventh century. One might also say that the former was the fruit of a reaction against the evils of the latter, or rather against the evils of anarchy of any sort, including all three elements that we have tried to distinguish. There is no need to repeat what we have said about the relation of monastic hierarchy to territorial fragmentation in our discussion of the events of 1016. Its relationship to the decline of the monarchy is equally clear.

Would the monks of Cluny have sought papal support if the king had been able to provide some help? The gradual waning of royal aid on their behalf, of the same kind and at the same time as we have found in general, is revealing. About 1016, at the height of the crisis, Cluny informed Robert the Pious of the evils from which its members suffered. Robert was still able to act in northern Burgundy, and the monks of St. Bénigne of Dijon had sought and won his help against the dangers that threatened the very heart of the region over which they exercised their power—Dijon and its surroundings.[108] Odilo asked Robert for a diploma, which the king granted between 1017 and 1023; in it were mentioned certain of the seigniories defended by Benedict VIII, such as Laizé and Trades. But where Benedict protected the monks and acted, Robert simply confirmed their possessions—a negative attitude, a sign of good will and impotence.[109] Furthermore, he intervened only in favor of Cluny's domains in the Châlonnais and the Mâconnais. Compared to the bull of Benedict VIII which included Aquitaine, the geographical extent of Robert's act was very narrow—as we might expect, given what we have seen of the royal absence from Langued'oc.

After this diploma conditions deteriorated, the royal withdrawal was complete. There would be no more diplomas for Cluny from a king of France until the twelfth century.[110] Robert would grant none during the crisis of 1025–1027, although his aid was solicited. In a rather detached manner, John XIX asked him for one, suggesting the course of action for the King to follow and practically dictating even the words he should use.[111] But Robert did nothing. He refused to choose sides between the Pope and the bishops and took refuge in silence.

A disillusioned episcopacy also suffered from this progressive weakening. Old Bishop Adalberon of Laon echoed their complaints soon after the Cluniac success of 1027. In a poem dedicated to Robert the Pious, written in the mediocre manner of the satirists of the times, he mockingly criticized the king and his policies.[112] "The state is dragged to its ruin, the laws abolished," he wrote.[113] It is not the King who governs but a *procurator regis,* a substitute king.[114] The monks are chiefly responsible for this lamentable situation, those of Cluny first of all. They are the ones who make the law; they usurp the place of the episcopacy.[115] "Odilo went to Rome and asked salvation for his monks"[116] (an allusion to the events of 1027, which exasperated Adalberon), he has turned his monks into a brawling militia under his command. They are his *milites*. "Me, I am no longer a monk," says a monk. "I fight under a king's orders; my master is King Odilo of Cluny."[117] Robert is his accomplice; out of weakness, he lets it all be done. The poisonous arrow that Adalberon let fly from his satire can be summarized something like this: it is no longer Robert who is King, it is Odilo of Cluny.

Adalberon might also have taken the papacy for his target, since the papacy also gained by the overthrow of the old order. For the future, monasticism promised devoted troops who would provide support in the days of Gregory VII. For the present, Cluny's progress was the papacy's own. The expansion of Cluniac seigniories, because they belonged to the Holy See, profited its patrimony. The growth of the Cluniac Order in Langued'oc preparing the way for expansion into Spain, in the end favored Roman influence as well.

All this constituted the balance of a victory whose continuation after 1027 was certain. Further victories came rapidly, and almost always brought changes in social life in their train. The truce of God appeared in 1027 in Roussillon, where Cluny had penetrated. The peace of God progressed. One and the other were made possible by the efficacy of judicial sanctions. A letter was addressed to all the bishops of Gaul in 1041 to further both institutions; Odilo was one of the principal signers. Monastic growth extended well beyond the areas controlled by Cluny. In Normandy and England it was after 1027–1030 that intelligent princes began to confer powers of justice and police on important monasteries to bring order and peace to the most vulnerable parts of their maritime states—to the estuaries, along the coast and rivers, and on the islands—a prelude to political "take off" and, in any case, its condition.[118]

Certain regions, however, reacted less rapidly if they did not benefit from the authority of a powerful prince or found themselves off the main road of a federative monasticism such as that of Cluny or of William of Volpiano. It even happened that the dislocation of political structures led first to a kind of monastic dispersion. But everywhere, sooner or later—and never after too long a time—a centralizing foundation succeeded in regrouping the monasteries in the spirit of the new structures. It was thus in Maine where, in the first years of the eleventh century, the castellans founded tiny monasteries such as Tuffé; priories of abbeys of Le Mans, such as Solesmes; and, above all, collegiate churches serving a castle, such as Sablé and St. Guingalois of Château-du-Loir. In this area the centralizing movement would be the work of Marmoutier. From Dunois (about 1040–1050) and from Vendômois (where it competed with La Trinité of Vendôme) its influence reached into Maine after 1050 and especially about 1066–1067 when, one after another, several collegiate churches (and not the least important)—Sablé, St. Guingalois, St. Martin of Bellême—became its prioires. Marmoutier at that moment was favored by William the Conqueror who furthered its expansion not only on the Norman frontiers but in England as well. Mormoutier paved the way for the Plantagenet Empire.

In the royal domain developments were somewhat the same. First a scattering of small monasteries and collegiate churches appeared in the period of territorial fragmentation and once-great royal monasteries, such as St.-Germain-des-Prés, became weaker. St.-Germain suffered from the monarchy's decline to such an extent that William of Volpiano made it but a stage on the route to Normandy. Then (although not before the reign of Philip I) a centralizing movement began, profiting a royal abbey, such as St.-Denis; or a Norman abbey, such as Le Bec; or even more, the Cluniac priory of St.-Martin-des-Champs—in the days when St. Hugh introduced Cluny into this area (1079).

Although the sketch we have made far from exhausts the richness of the scene, these events, as late as they were,[119] nonetheless were the distant continuation of those we have related in detail. By 1030 the monks had won enough; the new structures they had put together with patience and tenacity over a generation had been sufficiently perfected and given solid enough foundation for the success of their plans and the result of their fight to be certain.

This allows us, indeed requires us, in conclusion to place what the monks did into the general historical picture.

A principal problem of medieval history is to establish the line separating a West in decline, crossed by invading hordes or threatened by pagans, weakened by anarchy, and half-asphyxiated by a sclerosed economy, from a West in progress, whose structures are being strengthened, whose political ideas are taking wing, whose economy is opening up. Marc Bloch gave a name to this contrast: "the two ages of feudalism." But where should we place the line? Bloch suggested the middle of the eleventh century; and when we look at the three elements discussed in this essay, it is precisely in the middle of the eleventh century that we begin to discern enough of an upturn to ascertain the direction the West will take. This is so true that, if we were forced to select only one moment, it is indeed this one that we would feel constrained to take. But was there only one? Bloch was too sensitive a historian ever to have made such a claim, and it was only with decided nuances that he made his choice.

Everything depends, first of all, upon the level one chooses. At the top of the political and social structures? Or at their base? The answer is not the same for each case. It took time for the movement to spread itself from one level to another. Duby, in his excellent study of the Mâconnais, has found the dividing line appearing only about 1060. Even if we concentrate exclusively on the summit of society, we would find different dates in different places. The French monarchy began its movement of renewal, roughly, only after 1108 and more so in 1120 with Louis VI and Suger. This means that only at this moment did the monarchy begin to profit from the currents that, elsewhere and higher up, had penetrated earlier—in the Church of the Gregorians, for instance, where after 1049, 1059, and more so in 1077, it had become irresistible.

But did not what happened in Rome in the last third of the eleventh century, and what came out of Rome, have any precedents? Can one look to an earlier period? It is in this sense that the years 1020–1030 can be viewed as a step on the road, as a first step—not only in terms of what is ending, of the past that disappears (in 1013–1014 the last invasions of Scandinavian pagans against a Normandy turning toward Rome, in 1016–1018 the last great Moslem offensive) but also, and above all, in terms of what is beginning, of a future half-seen. This was particularly the case with the perfection of the idea of an exempt monastic order, an idea pregnant with revolutionary implications.[120] Until this time, privileges had been granted to individual sanctuaries and their saints. This remained the practice for some time yet, so much did the mind of the times rebel against change. The idea of an exempt order, however, led to a kind of privilege that one might call "administrative." And one of the characteristics of the second feudal age is precisely the expansion of administrative structures, which, supported by firmly established political structures, little by little brought coherence into Church and state.

NOTES

1. Jean Hubert, "Saint-Riquier et le monachisme bénédictin en Gaule à l'époque carolingienne," *Il monachesimo nell'alto Medioevo* (Spoleto, 1957), pp. 293–309.

2. E. Delaruelle, "La Gaule chrétienne à l'époque franque. L'Epoque carolingienne," *Revue d'histoire de l'Eglise de France,* **38** (1952), 64-72.

3. F. L. Ganshof, "L'échec de Charlemagne," *Comptes-rendus de l'Académie des Inscriptions et Belles Lettres* (1947), pp. 248–254.

4. J. Dhondt, *Etudes sur la naissance des principautés territoriales en France (IXe–Xe siècle)* (1948).

5. Dom J. Leclercq, "Le florilège d'Abbon de Saint-Germain," *Revue du Moyen-Age Latin,* **3** (1947), 113–140.

6. E. Sabbe, "Deux points de l'histoire de Saint-Pierre au Mont-Blandin," *Revue Bénédictine,* **47** (1935), 52–61.

7. Jean-François Lemarignier, "L'exemption monastique et les origines de la réforme grégorienne," *A Cluny . . . travaux du congrès . . . de Cluny* (1950), pp. 299–301, 316.

8. *Coll. can.* **3**. Migne, *PL* **139**, *c.* 477.

9. J.-F. Lemarignier, "Autour de la royauté française du IXe au XIIIe siècle," *BEC,* **113** (1956), 10–11.

10. J.-F. Lemarignier, "Les fidèles du roi de France (936–987)," *Recueil de travaux offert à M. C. Brunel* (1955), **2**, 157.

11. J.-F. Lemarignier, *Le gouvernement royal aux premiers temps capétiens (987–1108)* (1965), pp. 38–40 and the maps of sanctuaries benefiting from royal diplomas, 898–1108 (no. 1–5). The boundary passes through St.-Jean d'Angely,

Lusignan, Preuilly, Bourges, then, heading south, through Thiers (see Lemarignier, map 3), and, as an exception, la Chaise-Dieu (1052) (see Lemarignier, map 4).

12. Lemarignier, "Les fidèles dus roi de France," pp. 159–160, 162, and *Le gouvernement royal,* p. 40.

13. Lemarignier, *Le gouvernement royal,* pp. 47–48, 173. The Duke of Aquitaine subscribed to the following diplomas: (Robert the Pious) W. M. Newman, *Catalogue des actes de Robert II* (1937), 46, 68, 72; (Henry I) F. Soehnée, *Catalogue des actes d'Henri Ier* (1907) 92; (Philip I) M. Prou, *Recueil des actes de Philippe Ier* (1908) 84, 86. The Duke of Aquitaine, as well as the counts of Auvergne and La Marche, attended the coronation of Philip I (*H. Fr.* **11**. 33). Count Audebert of La Marche subscribed to Prou 84; Count Robert of Auvergne, to Prou 135; see the tables of subscribers to royal diplomas under Robert the Pious, Henry I, and Philip I in Lemarignier, *Le gouvernement royal.*

14. Aimoin, *Vita S. Abbonis* 20. (Migne, *PL* **139**, *c.* 410); see Pfister, *Etudes sur le règne de Robert le Pieux (996–1031)* (1885), p. 228.

15. Newman 2 (988).

16. *Ibid.* 8.

17. Lemarignier, *Le gouvernement royal,* p. 189 and table 1 (categories of diplomas).

18. With the exception of Newman 24 (1005), to which a viscount and a castellan (Bouchard de Montmorency) subscribed, and of Newman 30 (1007), to which subscribed the Archbishop of Tours, the Bishop of le Mans, Eudes II of Blois, five castellans, and seven knights. To Newman 58, there subscribed, besides three sons of the king, two archbishops, three bishops, as well as a count of *Francia*; a castellan (Amauri de Montfort), and three knights. Apart from these three acts, before 1025 and even before 1028 (Newman 72, 13 May 1028), only royal sons, archbishops, bishops, abbots (very rarely), territorial princes and counts of principalities (few in number), and counts of *Francia* subscribed to royal diplomas. See Lemarignier, *Le gouvernement royal,* p. 47 and n. 28, the tables of subscribers to the diplomas of Robert the Pious and the general table of categories of subscribers.

19. " . . . *manu nostra nostrorumque fidelium subterfirmavimus*"—Newman 24; ". . . *consilio procerum nostrorum*"—Newman 31, 17 May 1008); ". . . *commune consilium cum proceribus et primoribus palatii nostri* . . ." is found a little later in Soehnée 92, 1052 (*H. Fr.* **11**. 588). References for the ninth century: *Annales Bertiniani,* Waitz, ed. p. 139 (877) and Capitulary of Quierzy; see Lemarignier, "Autour de la royauté," p. 8 n. 1. and *Le gouvernement royal,* pp. 55–58.

20. Newman 46: archbishops of Reims, Sens, and Tours; bishops of Beauvais, Amiens, Noyon, Chartres, Laon, Soissons, Troyes, Meaux, Senlis, Thérouanne, Orléans, and Auxerre; the Count of Poitou, the Duke of Normandy (probable), Counts Eudes II of Blois, Fulk of Anjou, and Gautier of Amiens-Valois-Vexin. On the assembly of 936 see Lemarignier, "Les fidèles du roi de France," pp. 142–144. The assembly for the coronation of Henry I (Newman 68, 15 May 1027) is of the same order as that of 1017: the Archbishop of Reims, bishops of Beauvais, Amiens, Laon, Soissons, Noyon, Troyes, Châlons, Langres, and Châlon-sur-Saône; Abbots Odilo of Cluny, Evrard of St. Remi of Reims and Richard of St. Médard of Soissons. These assemblies should be compared with the royal councils of the same period, attended by the prelates of the same region: St. Basle de Verzy, 991 (F. Lot, *Etudes sur le règne de Hugues Capet,* p. 31); Chelles, 993–994 (Richier 4. 89, Latouche, ed. **11**, 288 ff.)

21. To which correspond Newman 24, 31, 46, 58, 68, which form the majority (five out of nine) up to 1027 and are, far and away, the most important.

22. See note 24.

23. Newman 72 (following the facsimile).

24. DIPLOMAS OF ROBERT THE PIOUS

	996–1028 (NEWMAN 9–70)		1028–1031 (NEWMAN 71–108)	
Archbishops and bishops	58	= 79	15	= 33
Abbots	3		0	
Territorial princes and counts of principalities	5		4	
Counts of *Francia*	13		14	
Archdeacons and minor ecclesiastics	0	= 18	3 / 23	= 46
Castellans and viscounts	8			
Knights and unidentified lords	10		20	

Before 1028 the high aristocracy was in the great majority (79 : 18); afterward, it was in the minority (33 : 46).

25. Newman 86. On the date, see Lemarignier, *Le gouvernement royal,* p. 73 n. 15. Newman 58 (1022–1023), a diploma for St.-Mesmin de Micy, must be left aside. The copies that alone preserve it have on the same line, *"Nomina testium"* and *"locus sigilli."* These phrases and their arrangement prove that they were added by the copyist, as my wife proved in her unpublished thesis on the cartularies of St.-Mesmin de Micy: Marie-Marguerite Lemarignier, "Les cartulaires de Saint-Mesmin de Micy," *Ecole des Chartes, Pos. des thèses* (1937), pp. 110–113. See Lemarignier, *Le gouvernement royal,* p. 73 n. 18.

26. Newman 83 (1030), see Chevrier and Chaume, *Chartes et documents de Saint-Bénigne de Dijon* (1943), 2, 79 n. 296; Newman 87 (Chevrier and Chaume, 49 ff. n. 260). On the text see Lemarignier, *Le gouvernement royal,* p. 75 n. 30, pp. 194–195.

27. Georges Duby, *La société aux XIe et XIIe siècles dans la région mâconnaise* (1953), 272 ff.

28. Works of Aubenas, Dhondt, Duby, Garaud; bibl. in J.-F. Lemarignier, "La dislocation du *pagus* et le problème des *consuetudines,*" *Mélanges . . . Louis Halphen* (1951), p. 401 n. 3.

29. Duby, *Société.*

30. R. Latouche, *Histoire du comté du Maine pendant le Xe et le XIe siècle* (1910), 59 ff.; J. Boussard, "La seigneurie de Bellême aux Xe et XIe siècles," *Mélanges . . . Louis Halphen,* 43 ff.

31. They subscribe as *fideles* to an act of Hugh III—Latouche, *Histoire du comte du Maine,* Catal. d'actes, p. 140 n. 13.

32. Latouche, *Histoire du comte du Maine,* p. 62.

33. *Ibid.,* p. 66.

34. *Ibid.,* pp. 24, 33.

35. *Ibid.,* pp. 70, 65 n. 3.

36. On the viscounts see J.-F. Lemarignier, *Recherches sur l'hommage en marche et les frontières féodales* (1945), p. 14 and n. 16.

37. Lemarignier, "Autour de la royauté," pp. 35–36.

38. M. Garaud, "L'organisation administrative du comté de Poitou au Xe siècle et l'avènement des châtelains et des châtellenies," *Bull. de la Société des Antiquaires de L'Ouest,* ser. 4, 2 (1953), pp. 411–454.

39. L. Halphen, *Le comté d'Anjou au XI*[e] *siècle* (1906), pp. 152–165.

40. Michel de Boüard, "Le duché de Normandie," in Lot and Fawtier, *Histoire des Institutions Françaises au Moyen Âge,* 1 (1957), 6–12 (and bibl.); Jean Yver, "Le developpement du pouvoir ducal en Normandie de l'avènement de Guillaume le Conquérant à la mort d'Henri Ier (1035–1135)," in *Atti del Convegno Internazionale di Studi Ruggeriani* (1955), pp. 183–204.

41. F. L. Ganshof, "La Flandre," *Histoire des Institutions,* **1**, 343 ff.; on the crises of the reign of Baldwin IV, see J. Dhondt, "Note sur les châtelains de Flandre," *Mémoires de la Commission départementale des monuments historiques du Pas-de-Calais,* **5** (1947), 43–51.

42. Ch. Samaran, "Les institutions féodales en Gascogne au moyen âge," *Histoire des institutions,* **1**, 187.

43. Ch. Higounet, *Le comté de Comminges de ses Origines à Son Annexion à la Couronne* (1949); P. Ourliac, "L'origine des comtes de Comminges," *Rec. de trav. offert à M.C. Brunel* (1955), **2**, 313–320.

44. A. Bossuat, "L'Auvergne," *Histoire des institutions,* **1**, 104.

45. Delcambre, "Géographie historique du Velay. Du 'pagus' au comté et au baillage," *BEC,* **98** (1937), 33.

46. J. A. Brutails, *Etude sur la condition des populations rurales du Roussillon au moyen âge* (1891), p. 269.

47. G. de Manteyer, *La Provence du I*[er] *au XII*[e] *siècle* (1908), p. 341, 353 ff.; R. Busquet, "La Provence," *Histoire des Institutions,* **1**, 251.

48. Lemarignier, "La dislocation du *pagus* et le problème consuetudines."

49. Duby, *Société* p. 207.

50. Lemarignier, *Le gouvernement royal,* pp. 7–10, 171–176.

51. Ganshof, "Charlemagne et le serment," *Mélanges . . . Louis Halphen,* pp. 259–270, 267.

52. P. Petot, *"L'hommage servile," RHD,* 4me sér., **5** (1927), 100.

53. Guilhiermoz, *Essai sur l'origine de la noblesse* (1903) p. 263 n. 21, p. 174 n. 10.

54. In two forms: (1) reserving fealty to the duke—Kienast, *Untertaneneid und Treuvorbehalt in England und Frankreich* (1952), 234 ff.; and (2) reserving military service due to the duke by his rear-vassals—Haskins, *Norman Institutions,* 7 ff., esp. 11–12. See Lemarignier, "Autour de la royauté," p. 22.

55. F. L. Ganshof, "Les relations féodo-vassaliques aux temps post-carolingiens," *I problemi comuni dell'Europa post-carolingia* (1955), p. 112.

56. F. L. Ganshof, "Depuis quand a-t-on pu, en France, être vassal de plusieurs seigneurs," *Mélanges Paul Fournier* (1929), 261 ff.

57. *Ibid.,* p. 266; *Gesta pontificum Cenomanensium,* Busson and Ledru, ed. pp. 353–354.

58. He is called *"fidelis"* of the king in a diploma of Robert (Newman 31, *H. Fr.* **10**. 591; 17 May 1008).

59. *H. Fr.* **10**. 105 *B* (Helgaud); Newman 32.

60. Subscribes as *fidelis* of the king; Newman 46, 55, 68, 72.

61. J. Hubert, "La frontière occidentale du comté de Champagne du XIe au XIIIe siècle," *Recueil de trav. offert à M.C. Brunel,* **2**, 20. He is also vassal of the Bishop of Auxerre—Lemarignier, *Recherches sur l'hommage en marche,* p. 135.

62. Newman 46 and 72.

63. Halphen, *Le comté d'Anjou au XI*[e] *siècle,* p. 29 n. 3, p. 54.

64. And by this title, Robert's vassal. He subscribed to Newman 72 at the time of the marriage of his son Baldwin to the king's daughter. See F. Lot, *Fidèles ou vassaux?* (1904), pp. 12–13; Flach, *Les origines de l'ancienne France,* **4**, 68–71.

65. F. L. Ganshof, "Les origines de la Flandre impériale," *Annales de la société royal d'archéologie de Bruxelles,* **46** (1945), 99–137.

66. R. Poupardin, *Le royaume de Bourgogne (888-1038)* (1907), p. 225. That he was a vassal of Robert the Pious is proved by Newman 24 (Chevrier and Chaume n. 233 [1005]): ". . . *terram . . . quam comes Otto ex nobis tenet beneficiali dono. . . .*" Vassalage for the lands beyond the Saône goes back to Count Aubri, who lived about 930; Poupardin, *Royaume,* 212 ff. and Duby, *Société,* p. 90.

67. Newman 85.

68. Lemarignier, *Recherches sur l'hommage en marche et les frontières féodales,* 127 ff., 143–144, 155 ff.; J. Richard, *Les ducs de Bourgogne et la formation du duché du XI*[e] *au XIV*[e] *siècle* (1954), 21 ff.

69. Galeran de Meulan is one of the *fideles regis* whose aid Fulbert of Chartres solicited in 1015 against Count Rainard of Sens (*H. Fr.* **10**. 452 *ep.* 18); in 1031 Manassès, called *"noster a secretis . . . comes"* by Robert, and Hilduin, Manassès' brother, *"necnon et proceres palatii,"* subscribe to a royal diploma, apparently as king's *fideles* (Newman 88); this does not prevent Eudes II from calling all three *"curiae nostrae . . . primates"* in 1034–1036 and having them in this quality subscribe to one of his diplomas (Martène and Durand, *Thesaurus novus anecdotorum* (1717) **1**, *c.* 175–176; see H. d'Arbois de Jubainville, *Histoire des ducs et des comtes de Champagne,* **1**, 327-330). The royal vassalage of Hugh Bardoul is demonstrated by several texts cited by J. Devaux, "Essai sur les premiers seigneurs de Pithiviers," *Annales de la Société historique et archéologique du Gâtinais* (1887), 68–70; the following texts are mutually corroborative: *H. Fr.*, **11**. 160; *Miracula Sancti Benedicti,* **6**, 18 (De Certain, ed. pp. 244–245); diploma of Henry I (Soehnée 69, 3 May 1044) indicating that Hugh, defeated by Henry I, was deprived of the fiefs he had previously held of the king; he subscribed in 1028 to Newman 72. On the Champenoise vassalage of this same Hugh, see D'Arbois de Jubainville, *Hist. des comtes de Champ.,* **1**, 357, 362; **2**, 40; also A. Duchesne, *Histoire de la maison de Broyes, Preuves,* pp. 7–8: charter of Hugh (before 1060), in which the subscription of Count Thibaud can be explained only by vassal dependence. As for Ganelon de Montigny, that he was a vassal of Eudes II is proved by a charter of this Count (circa 1032–1037) to which Ganelon subscribed as *fideles* (Mabille, *Cartulaire de Marmoutier pour le Dunois* 4. 5); he called Henri I *"dominus meus rex Francorum Henricus"* in a charter to which the monarch has him subscribe (Mabille, *Cartulaire de Marmoutier pour le Dunois* **22**. 22-23 [A.D. 1044–1060]; Soehnée 71); in addition, Ganelon subscribed to Newman 30.

70. J. Dhondt, "Quelques aspects du règne d'Henri Ier, roi de France," *Mélanges . . . Louis Halphen,* pp. 199–208.

71. Thus Odo of Cluny—Ganshof in *Mél. Fournier,* p. 270.

72. Fulbert, *ep.* 5, 6, *H. Fr.* **10**. 447; Esmein, "Nouvelles théories sur les origines féodales," *RHD* (1894), pp. 532–535; also Ganshof, "Les relations féodo-vassaliques aux temps post-carolingiens," p. 106.

73. Kienast, *Untertaneneid.*

74. Lemarignier, "Les fidèles du roi de France."

75. F. Lot, *Etudes sur le règne du Hugues Capet,* pp. 198–199; L. Halphen, *Le comté d'Anjou,* 17 ff.; Lemarignier, *Recherches sur l'hommage en marche,* pp. 116–119.

76. Richer 4. 91 (Latouche, ed., **2**, 294). This is possibly only an invention of

Richer (Latouche, p. 295 n. 3 and Halphen, *Le comte d'Anjou du XIe siècle,* p. 27 n. 3); but that possibility is of little importance. If Richer imagined it, it was because it could have been true, given the customs of the times.

77. Latouche, *Histoire du comté du Maine,* 31 ff.

78. And also the fealties that Otto-William won in the *Lingonense;* Chaume, *Les origines du duché de Bourgogne,* **1**, 488.

79. Thus the Breton homage to the Duke of Normandy; see Lemarignier, *Recherches sur l'hommage en marche.*

80. *H. Fr.* **10**. 463, *ep.* 38. As the words *"sed non ideo casamentum meretur"* indicate and, a little later on, *"si beneficio dignus videri velit"*; but here, in this second phrase, Fulbert has apparently gone back on his first presentation and adds, *"et salvus esse de fidelitate quam juravit,"* betraying an uncertainty in his mind, an uncertainty that perhaps takes on full meaning if one compares it with the thesis of his contemporary, Dudo of St. Quentin (see note 81). On Fulbert's letter see Ganshof, "Les relations féodo-vassaliques," pp. 87–88; H. Richardot, "Francs-fiefs." *RHD,* 4me sér., **27** (1949), 233.

81. See Lemarignier, *Recherches sur l'hommage en marche,* 79 ff., 98.

82. Newman 79 (996–1029); Lemarignier, *Le gouvernement royal,* p. 172.

83. Raoul Glaber **4**, 5 (Prou, ed. p. 104).

84. Bonnaud-Delamare, "Fondement des institutions de paix au XIe siècle," *Mélanges . . . Louis Halphen,* p. 19 and "Les institutions de paix dans la province ecclésiastique de Reims au XIe siécle," *Bull. philologique et historique du Comité des travaux historiques,* années 1955–1956 (1957), pp. 143–200.

85. Oath imposed by Gerard of Cambrai (1023), *Gesta episc. Camer.* **3**. 41 (*MGH SS* **7**. 481); see Kienast, *Untertaneneid,* p. 29 n. 2.

86. *Breve recordationis de treuva Domini,* Duc, ed. "Documents," *Miscellanea di Storia italiana,* **24** (1885), 369 (first half of the eleventh century, undoubtedly 1025–1040).

87. Duby, in *Le Moyen Âge* (1946), 174 ff. and *Société,* pp. 159–160.

88. *Gesta episc. Camer.* **3**. 27 (*MGH SS* **7**. 474.) Text of Guerin's oath in Pfister, *"Etudes sur . . . Robert le Pieux,"* p. LX.

89. E. Lesne, *Histoire de la propriété ecclésiastique en France,* **2**[3].

90. J.-F. Lemarignier, "Les institutions ecclésiastiques en France du Xe au milieu du XIIe siècle," in Lot and Fawtier, *Histoire des institutions* **3**, *Institutions ecclésiastiques* (1962), p. 54 and n. 1 (bibl.).

91. A. Dumas, "L'Eglise de Reims au temps des luttes entre Carolingiens et Robertiens," *Revue d'histoire de l'Eglise de France,* **30** (1944), 5–38.

92. Lemarignier, "L'exemption monastique et les origines de la réforme grégorienne," p. 302; and Lot and Fawtier, *Histoire des institutions,* **3**, 54–55.

93. Lemarignier, "L'exemption monastique," p. 301–319.

94. *H. Fr.* **10**. 448, *ep.* 8 (Migne, *PL* **141**, *c.* 208, *ep.* 16).

95. Lemarignier, "L'exemption monastique," pp. 323–325.

96. *Ibid.,* pp. 328–329.

97. Duby, *Société.* [Translated in this volume.]

98. Jaffé, 4013. On this competition, see Duby, *Société,* 214 ff.

99. *". . . tam de ipso loco* [Cluny] *quam de omnibus ad se pertinentibus, in Burgundia, Aquitania, Provincia constitutis, videlicet monasteriis, cellis, terris . . ."*—Jaffé, 4013.

100. Lemarignier, "L'exemption monastique," pp. 319–320. List of thirty-four establishments, p. 319 n. 6. See also the map in Simone Berthellier, "L'expansion de l'ordre de Cluny et ses rapports avec l'histoire politique et économique du Xe au XIIe siècle," *Revue archéologique,* **11** (1938), 319–326.

101. Lemarignier, "L'exemption monastique," 321 (Jaffé, 4065).

102. *Ibid.*, pp. 325–326 (Jaffé, 4079, 4081–4083).

103. Dom J. Hourlier, "Cluny et la notion d'ordre religieux," *A Cluny . . . Travaux du congrès . . . de Cluny,* pp. 219–226 has quite rightly emphasized this point. See Dom K. Hallinger, "Zur geistigen Welt der Anfänge Klunys," *DA,* **10** (1954), 444, for bibl. and the same author's important *Gorze-Kluny* [Orbis Catholicus, Studia Anselmiana, **23–24, 24–25**] (1950–1951), where the opposition between the imperial type of monasticism of Gorze and the monasticism of Cluny is so well illuminated. Dom Hallinger has studied it from very different points of view, including and going beyond the problem of constitutional organization. He has developed ideas completely in accord with those of this article. On the origins of the idea of monastic order see Lemarignier in Lot and Fawtier, *Histoire des institutions,* **3**, 58-59 and above all the very important study by Cinzio Violante, "Il monachesimo cluniacense di fronte al mondo politico ed ecclesiastico (sec. 10 e 11)," *Spiritualità Cluniacense* [Convegni del centro di studi sulla spiritualità medievale, **2**] (1960), 155–242, esp. 192–193.

104. Dom Hourlier has seen this very well, "Cluny et la notion d'ordre religieux," p. 225.

105. *Ibid.*, p. 223.

106. Hallinger, "Zur geistigen Welt der Anfänge Klunys," esp. pp. 436–444, partially translated in the *Revue Mabillon,* **46** (1956), 117–140.

107. A precedent may be found in the precarial act, Lemarignier, "L'exemption monastique."

108. Chevrier and Chaume, *Chartes et documents,* n. 260 (Newman 87).

109. *Chartes de Cluny* (Bruel ed.), n. 2711 (Newman 59).

110. Diploma of Louis VI, in 1119, Bruel, n. 3943; see Jean Richard, *Les ducs de Bourgogne,* p. 183; Lemarignier, *Le gouvernement royal,* p. 78 n. 40.

111. Jaffé, 4081.

112. G. A. Huckel, "Les poèmes satiriques d'Adalbéron," *Bibliothèque de la Faculté des lettres de l'Université de Paris,* **13** (1901), 49–184. The *Carmen ad Rotbertum regem* (pp. 129–167) was written between 1027 and 1030: after 1027 because allusion is made (v. 131, p. 142) to Odilo's trip to Rome in that year to defend Cluny's privileges:

Hic (Oidelo) Romam petiit monachis orare salutem

and before 1030, the date of Adalbéron's death. On the mediocre type of satire during this period and in this area, see L. Musset, "Le satiriste Garnier de Rouen et son milieu," *Revue du Moyen Âge Latin,* **10** (1954), 237–266.

113. V. 64–66, p. 136, see p. 96.

114. V. 69–70.

115. V. 36, p. 133 with commentary; also p. 98.

116. V. 131.

117. V. 113–115:

Miles nunc; monachus diverso more manebo;
Non ego sum monachus, iussu sed milito regis:
Nam dominus meus est rex Oydelo Cluniacensis.

118. Details and bibl. in Lemarignier, "L'exemption monastique," p. 327.

119. Lemarignier, *Le gouvernement royal,* 94 ff., 141 ff.

120. On the whole group of problems posed by Cluny and the Cluniac movement, see—in addition to the essential article of Violante, "Il monachesimo cluniacense"—Th. Schieffer, "Cluny et la querelle des investitures," *Revue historique,* **61**, (1961), 47–72, and J. Wollasch, H.-E. Mager, H. Diener, *Neue Forschungen über Cluny und die Cluniacenser,* G. Tellenbach, ed. (1959).

II. The Growth of the Noble Class

THE NOBILITY IN MEDIEVAL *FRANCIA*: Continuity, Break, or Evolution?*

Léopold Genicot

As soon as a medievalist turns to his documents, he meets the *nobiles,* the nobility. If he opens Gregory of Tours, he soon finds *"nobiles"* mentioned—a person *"nobile genus"* [nobly born], another *"nobilissimus in gente sua"* [of most noble birth].[1] If he runs through the Frankish capitularies, he will soon find an article applying to *"omnes homines laïci, tam nobiles quam ignobiles."*[2] Whether he turns to narrative sources or to acts and charters, he immediately runs into the problem of the "nobles." And the more he leafs through his documents, the more deeply he gets into his subject, the more convinced he becomes of the importance of this problem. For the "nobility" are present everywhere and they always play the

---

* Léopold Genicot, "La noblesse au moyen-âge dans l'ancienne 'Francie': continuité, rupture, ou évolution?" *Comparative Studies in Society and History,* 5 (Univ. of Mich., Ann Arbor, 1962), 52–59. By permission of the editors of *Comparative Studies* and of the author. Trans. by the ed.

leading roles. They give to the times their fundamentally aristocratic character.

For this reason, during the last twenty or twenty-five years, historians have devoted numerous studies to them. These studies, which have multiplied in all those countries that are heirs to Merovingian and Carolingian *Francia,* have neither brought about nor imposed a solution; but they have established a great many facts, facts that allow us to put forward—with prudence, and as an hypothesis rather than a certitude—a tentative solution.[3] I shall try to sketch out such a solution in the following pages.

I will first of all attempt to define the *nobilitas* of the High Middle Ages and, then, to describe the development of the thing itself, of its idea, and of the word, from the eleventh century to the threshold of modern times.

"Nobilis": the word is ambiguous. It can connote something individual, social, or legal; can apply to people of great personal value, to the members of a superior class, or to members of a legally privileged group. And the most serious question raised by its presence in early medieval documents is: "What does it mean?"

The first possibility is excluded. In the minds of the scribes, chroniclers, and hagiographers of the Merovingian, Carolingian, and post-Carolingian periods, being "noble" did not mean, or did not *only* mean, being distinguished by eminent personal qualities. Fundamentally it meant belonging to a group. Without fail charters and narrative sources attribute a class and even caste spirit and attitude to the *nobiles.*

A few signs demonstrate how real and how relevant is this class cohesion. Arrogance above all or, to use the expression of the biographer of St. Columbanus, *"tumor"* [swelling], translated by the nobility's refusal to mix with the rest of the population.[4] Living, they marry among themselves. Dead, they can rest in peace only among themselves. The *Historia Walciodorensis monasterii,* written about 1150, but confirmed by acts of the eleventh century, reveals that this Meuse abbey had set up a "noble cemetery" within its walls.[5] Generosity is another sign, freedom with material things: a "gift worthy of a nobleman"—in the most ancient monastic cartularies, this expression keeps coming back like an old song.

Identity of thought and action does not necessarily mean complete homogeneity. One scholar has recently maintained that he could distinguish two practically sealed-off strata in the noble class of mid-ninth-century Touraine: some very great families who owned lands and held high offices in various part of the Empire (for which reason another scholar has called them the *"Reichsaristokratie,"* the imperial aristocracy) and the regional aristocracy, itself divided into two strata—counts and viscounts in one, *vassi dominici* and *vicarii* in the other. Whatever we make of these conclusions, Sigebert of Gembloux, one of the best eleventh-century historians, speaks of the *"altitudines nobilitatis,"* the heads of the nobility.[6]

The precise composition of this group is less easy to discover than its existence, or even its structure. Are its members descendants of the *principes* immortalized by Tacitus? Are they the right-hand men of the barbarian kings and Carolingian sovereigns? Or are they the last descendants of Roman or Gallo-Roman senatorial families? All three hypotheses are possible and, undoubtedly, all are valid to a certain extent, depending upon the region. Apparently most of the nobles of "inner Germany," Saxony, Thuringia, and Bavaria, areas that did not experience the mixing of the fourth- and fifth-century invasions, were the heirs of the *Ethelfreien,* the noble free. In the basins of the Meuse, the Scheldt, and the Seine, which the Franks occupied and in which the Frankish kings established their centers, the nobles were *homines novi,* self-made men or their descendants. South of the Loire, in lands where the Germanic tribes established few settlements, they were representatives of the native Gallo-Roman nobility.

Thus undoubtedly the nobility was a social class. But the connections that most of the documents draw between nobility and birth, *nobilitas* and *genus,* make one wonder if even at this early period the nobility was not also a legal class, a class with heritable privileges. And the more one looks, reflects, and compares, the more he is inclined to answer "yes."

A special noble legal status must have existed. Were French scholarship to free itself from pre-conceived theses (and especially from those to which Marc Bloch mortgaged French rural history, whatever their exceptional merits), it would certainly join in the categoric conclusions of German scholars. The special status came from Germanic lands; the disintegration of the Late Empire eased the way for its diffusion throughout Gaul. The *de facto* situation of fourth-century *potentes* hardly differed from the *de jure* position of the *principes* in Tacitus' *De Germania.* This status can be summed up in one word: "liberty."

This liberty was perhaps partially modified during or immediately after the invasions. According to a Dutch specialist, it must at this time have lost that absolute character that had made every free German a state in himself and every group of Germans a confederation.[7] During the transition from antiquity to the Middle Ages the great men, it is claimed, promised fidelity to the king and thus recognized a public authority. Nevertheless, they still remained, and from now on would remain, even more distinguished from the class of simple freemen who were obliged to obey a functionary, who were enclosed in an administrative framework, who were "mediatized." The nobility's liberty may have become relative; it remained, or rather became, specific because its members' link with the sovereign was direct. In any event, noble liberty retained its most important attributes, its essential corollaries: immunity and the right to have an armed following.

The Germanic "prince" and his heir by idea if not by blood, the early medieval noble, was an immunist because he was really and fully free—

free personally and free in his patrimonial possessions, his allods. He owed nothing to anyone, either for himself or for his lands. He had sovereign disposition over both. He thus ruled those who settled on his land and worked it for his benefit, or for their own. He commanded them. He judged their disputes and their dealings; as a later age would say, he possessed *"bannum"* and *"justitia"* [command and justice] over them; he was their *dominus,* their lord. His authority, furthermore, transcended his own domain. With his peers he formed the *mallus* [court] and decided conflicts among peasants who were not his tenants. In exchange for dues and "gifts" he assumed protection over them—in times of danger he shielded them in the vast open area enclosed behind the palisade of his *castrum;* he defended them at the head of his armed followers.

For he had the right to create a personal "militia." Along with some less interesting rules concerning, for example, the rituals to be followed in transferring real property or the way conflicts were to be settled, this right to have a *comitatus,* to have a *Gefolgschaft,* completed the definition of noble status and described his physiognomy: lord, judge, and captain.

That these were perpetuated privileges and that they were perpetuated by inheritance, seems barely disputable. *"Genere nobilis,"* noble by birth —the texts repeat it to satiation, but never *"divitiis nobilis,"* noble by wealth. Two points are less clear, however. What blood? And did blood alone suffice? Was nobility transmitted by one's mother or by one's father? By either? Or conjointly by both? The first hypothesis, seemingly the most astonishing, should not be excluded; it may even be the most plausible. The *Historiae Francorum* cites a *"Tetradia nobilis ex matre, patre inferiore."*[8] The *Vita Wicberti,* from the eleventh century, records that the hero's mother married several times and *"longe lateque pullulante prosapia, se paene totam repleri et nobilitari gaudet Lotharingia,"* [her family multiplying far and wide, Lotharingia rejoiced that by her it was almost completely peopled and ennobled].[9] Even if the question is not superfluous (and the passage from Gregory of Tours shows that it is not), it is more theoretical than practical; for most often the nobility married among themselves.

Certain phrases in charters and chronicles, particularly *"praedium libertatis"* [land of a free man], force us to consider an equally, or even more delicate problem. Was birth the only important element? Did it not have to be associated with the ownership of an allod? Probably the acquisition of such real property did not bring with it noble status. But the question remains whether the absence of such property or its loss meant exclusion from that class, at least from the benefits it granted. This question we cannot answer.

All in all, the early medieval nobility appears as a legal class characterized by two traits: (1) enjoyment of a liberty that brings with it immunity of person as well as patrimony and the right to have an armed following, a liberty that thus confers on its possessor a public role, political, judicial, and military; (2) transmission of these privileges by inheritance, perhaps on condition that ownership of an allod go along with it.

At certain periods, under the pressure of men and events, society changes more rapidly and more profoundly than at other times. Thus it was with the West after 950, 1000, or 1050. The continued growth of population, the development of all kinds of trade brought about or sustained by this growth, the political activities of kings or of those such as princes or lords who acted as kings made the rhythm of evolution more rapid. There was no break, no reversal. There was a transformation whose mainsprings, whose character and limits, we must attempt to grasp.

At the beginning of the second millenium several factors influenced the social structure. Noble families, more prolific, multiplied, threw out branches, weakened themselves economically, and often maintained themselves only with great difficulty. The younger branches especially, less endowed, resisted less well;[10] they alienated their estates, then their rights —notably the command and justice whose possession had been the privilege and mark of their class. Or they gave in to the maneuvers of princes trying to monopolize these rights over as large a territory as possible. Sometimes they even renounced their liberty and fell into the ranks of the *cerocensuales* or the *ministeriales*. Among the elder lines some, trying to avoid the fragmentation of their patrimony, limited the number of their offspring, and thus risked extinction by illness or combat.[11]

Facing an aristocracy that frequently lost its leaders and many of whose members were in difficult material straits, were political and economic forces, not to speak of the spiritual forces of the clergy or, more precisely, of the priests who succeeded in retaining liberty and in acquiring the honorific titles granted to knights: *"dominus"* or *"messire."* Political forces: at the top the princes; at the bottom the *ministeriales* and among them, most notably, the *milites,* the knights. The princes tried—almost always successfully—to appropriate the powers of command and jurisdiction exercised by the nobility, or at least to get the nobility to hold them in fief. The *ministeriales,* coming from lower layers of society and often (especially in Germanic lands) even from the servile class,[12] had as their ambition equality with the nobility; they succeeded sooner or later and more or less completely—again, depending upon the region. They performed a task, or to state it better, they filled an office—*defendere, tueri* [to protect]— that was doubly honorable: it was the traditional activity of the great since the days of the *principes* and their *comites;* it was an activity exalted by a Church wanting peace and order. As vassals, the *ministeriales* rubbed elbows with members of the greatest lineages who, according to some, had already become involved in feudal relations in Frankish times, and who were certainly involved—at least since the tenth and eleventh century—for part of their land. These *ministeriales* were supported by the princes they served. Sometimes they carved out a solid fortune for themselves by acquiring lands and rights abandoned by aristocrats who were out at the pocket. They married their children into aristocratic houses. Not astonishingly, they acquired personal liberty and transmitted it to their descendants in perpetuity, or at least for several generations.

Economic forces: the inhabitants of newly born or reborn cities. Collectively, these people demanded "liberties": exemption from seignorial dues, especially from the "exactions" levied as a price for protection and from charges deriving from the *ban;* the privilege of being summoned before no court other than that of the franchise and the right to be a member of that court; the right to create an urban militia. When added up, these liberties almost equaled the "liberty" of the nobility, especially of the nobility that had lost its powers of command and jurisdiction. Acquisition of these liberties raised the cities almost to the level of the nobility. Individually, the newly enriched bourgeois, his fortune made, put his money into land, bought domains, and lived as an aristocrat.

This complex evolution entailed some changes in the position and structure of the nobility. If the nobleman was not already integrated into a feudal order in the fifth and sixth centuries, he was so now, and thus into a political formation. He was now no longer staunchly independent, absolutely sovereign. In the North he was also no longer exclusively rural. The analogy between his status and that of some of the bourgeoisie facilitated the creation of ties between them; in the thirteenth and fourteenth centuries many an important nobleman acquired a house in the city and sometimes a wife as well. In addition, the growing number of nobility and the diversity of their origins, of their wealth and power, provoked a reorganization of the noble class. Groups formed within it, above all in those areas where the barriers between ancient lineages of *nobilitas* and young families of the *militia* fell most rapidly. Social groups formed, each enjoying more or less high consideration usually translated by a more or less honorable title: the group of those who possessed rights of justice, who were perhaps *the* nobility, strictly speaking; the group of knights to whom protocol reserved the title *"messire";*[13] the wealthy, who were called "bannerets," their impressive following lined up behind their oriflamme; the simple "gentlemen." Legal groups formed also, endowed with certain prerogatives, above all with jurisdictional prerogatives: peers, for example, who judged one another (at least in certain matters); later on, barons and counts.[14]

Did the exhaustion of the traditional aristocracy and the push of new strata force more fundamental modifications? Did noble status itself change, especially in its two most essential points: the rules by which belonging to the class—the acquisition, transmission, and loss of its privileges—were determined; and the nature and extent of those privileges? Yes and no.

Noble condition remained fundamentally a question of blood. Normally it was inherited; when someone's nobility was denied, his best strategy was to prove he was of noble birth. But apparently, the paternal line was now on the ascendant: in a growing number of customs it alone counted. This was undoubtedly the result of the growing prestige, especially since the year 1000, of knighthood, an exclusively masculine affair. On the other hand, it was precisely knighthood that could replace birth. First in Capetian territory, then, undoubtedly under its influence, in the remainder of former *Francia,* knighting conferred heritable noble privileges. Where the heritability of these privileges was unlimited, the knight became part of the nobility; where it was limited to two, five, or seven generations, he was very nearly assimilated. Finally, before the end of the Middle Ages, the letter of ennoblement appeared.

Legal status still centered on the word "liberty," but on a liberty that was more concrete and probably less broad. The nobleman of the Late Middle Ages remained a *liber* and thus a "public person." He could make contracts under his own seal, whose appearance on the act guaranteed it was genuine. He retained his mission of judging and protecting; he presided over his tribunal, or, if he had none, sat as an *homme de loi* in a royal or territorial court; he struck the decisive blow in battle in the open countryside, welcomed the local clodhoppers into the courtyard behind his castle walls or inside the moat that surrounded his house, withstood the attack on his battlements and his fortified tower. But with the economic exploitation of the *ban* and the imposition of numerous "banal" charges on all those "breathing the lord's air," with the development of parish organization, with the setting up of administrative districts and tribunals, the noble's liberty became in some ways more precise. It now appeared primarily as a privilege of escaping from dues and taxes, as the right to receive the sacraments and a burial in the church of one's choice, as the right not to be judged by ordinary functionaries and judges, as, in short, the right to stand above all those institutions that now began to envelop the masses more and more tightly. If, as was earlier suggested, noble liberty demanded the possession of an allod and implied immunity, it was similarly narrowed. Even the principal nobility were forced to turn much or all of their patrimonies into fiefs. To be sure, they usually took one piece in fief of one prince and another in fief of another and thus retained an "international" character. But if they were not completely and exclusively incorporated into a single territory, they were nevertheless, for the most part, integrated into one or another. They had to assist its head with their coin and their arms and go to justice before his court. Their less fortunate fellows frequently abandoned their powers of command and justice to their peers or their elders, ceded them willy-nilly to the prince, or simply sold them. The idea of liberty was thus detached from allod, command, justice, and immunity.

This dissociation posed a problem for the period, one revealed by a peculiar uncertainty in terminology. There were many now to be found whose ancestors were noble but who had no allod, or in any case no *ban* and justice, and who were not knighted. Were they still to be considered nobles? Juridically yes. But socially? There was hesitation. Sometimes they were called noble; sometimes the title *"noble homme"* was reserved for knights. Most often the title was reserved for those holding a high seigniory, a "banal" or judicial seigniory (the name hardly matters), and the other blue bloods were called simply "gentlemen," *"francs hommes," "Welgeborenen,"* or "men of lineage." There was no lack of titles.

Thus, from the early to the late Middle Ages there was no break but simply adaptation. After the eleventh century as before, nobility remained a matter of blood. However, one could also obtain it by being knighted and, later, by letters patent. Public activity was still its price and liberty its reward. Liberty, however, was no longer so broad: it removed its beneficiary from seignorial, parish, administrative, and judicial subjection, but not from a political framework nor from subjection to the state now forming, with its high courts and its demands.

As a result of these changes the nobility of modern times was emerging —a nobility with new or retouched rules, rules that were more detailed and rigorous. It was, however, a nobility that offered the same fundamental traits as that of the Middle Ages, perpetuating itself by inheritance, holding public functions, and in this way justifying, if not its complete independence, at least its own privileged place.

NOTES

1. *MGH SS rer. merov.* **1**, 1 (2d ed.); see the index.

2. *Capitulum Vernense* 15 (*MGH Cap.* 14).

3. In this article reference will be given only to the most recent works and to a few sources. See, for further bibl., the author's earlier writings, especially his review of the principal theories, in "La Noblesse au moyen-âge dans l'ancienne Francie", *Annales, E.S.C.,* **17** (1961), 1–22 and his monograph on *L'Economie rurale namuroise au bas moyen-âge,* **2**, *Les hommes—la noblesse* (1960).

4. *Vita Columbani* (*MGH, SS rer. merov.* **3**. 132).

5. *MGH SS* **14**. 532.

6. *Gesta Abbatum Gemblacensium* (*MGH SS* **8**. 508).

7. It would be better to say, more rigorously, "every free German family," for the German is contained by his family and can do nothing without it.

8. [Tetradia, noble from her mother's side, whose father was of lower rank . . . .]—*MGH SS rer. merov.* **1**. 1 (2d ed.), 489.

9. *MGH SS* **8**. 508.

10. Georges Duby in "Une enquête à poursuivre: la noblesse dans la France médiévale," *Revue historique,* **226** (1961), 1 ff., proposes calling these families of secondary stature *"basse noblesse de souche"*; the expression is vivid but dangerous, for it easily leads to confusing these authentic nobles of lower rank with the *niederer Adel* from the *ministeriales,* of whom we will soon speak.

11. The general table annexed to the most recent Belgian study of a noble family [R. de Liedekerke, *La Maison de Gavre et de Liedekerke* (1961)] illustrates this practice of elder branches and its dangers.

12. P. Petot, "Observations sur les ministériales en France," *R.H.D.* 4[me]s., **38** (1960), 493.

13. In Forez, as in other regions of France and Lotharingia, *"dominus"* is a title of knights and only knights, to judge by a statement of M. Gonon, "La vie religieuse en Forez au XIVe siècle et son vocabulaire d'après les testaments," *Archivum Latinitatis Medii Aevi* **30**. 250, 252: "le titre [de dominus] précede une fois le nom d'un donzeau, par erreur."

14. J. Richard, "Erection en dignité de terres bourguignonnes (XIVe et XVe siècles)," *Mémoires de la Société d'histoire du droit et des institutions des anciens pays bourguignons, comtois et romands,* **21** (1960), 25–41.

THE NOBILITY IN ELEVENTH- AND TWELFTH-CENTURY MÂCONNAIS*

Georges Duby

In 980 the disintegration of Frankish political structures had not yet touched the institution of the count in the Mâconnais. Uncontested head of the aristocracy, protector of the immunist churches, the Count of Mâcon preserved a pre-eminent command over all free men within the *pagus*.[1] But in the years that followed, the profound disease that had been undermining the Carolingian monarchy for a century reached its terminal phase and attacked the superiority of the count. The count lost his authority over those powerful persons who held his castles and were thus the principal supports of his power; he lost his rights over the immunist churches, he became one private lord among others. This disintegration carried off with it the very idea of public law and redivided the powers of command anew. . . .

With the loss of control over castles and immunities, the Count of Mâcon by imperceptible stages lost his sovereign power over the entire breadth of the *pagus*. At the death of his grandfather, Otto-William [in 1026], Count Eudes had command of the free men, rich and poor, only in the immediate surroundings of the fortress of Mâcon. To the south, at Dracé and Fleurie; to the west, at Pierreclos and Scissé; to the east, at Replonges, he ran into the power of the lords of Beaujeu, Berzé, Brancion, and Bâgé. Even within this narrow territory, every great ecclesiastical domain was an enclave where his power was contested; in the heart of the city, at the very gate of his castle, the cathedral church had installed its

* From Georges Duby, *La société aux XIe et XIIe siècles dans la région mâconnaise* (Paris: Librairie Armand Colin, 1953), pp. 155, 170–172, 185–195, 230–245. Trans. by the ed.

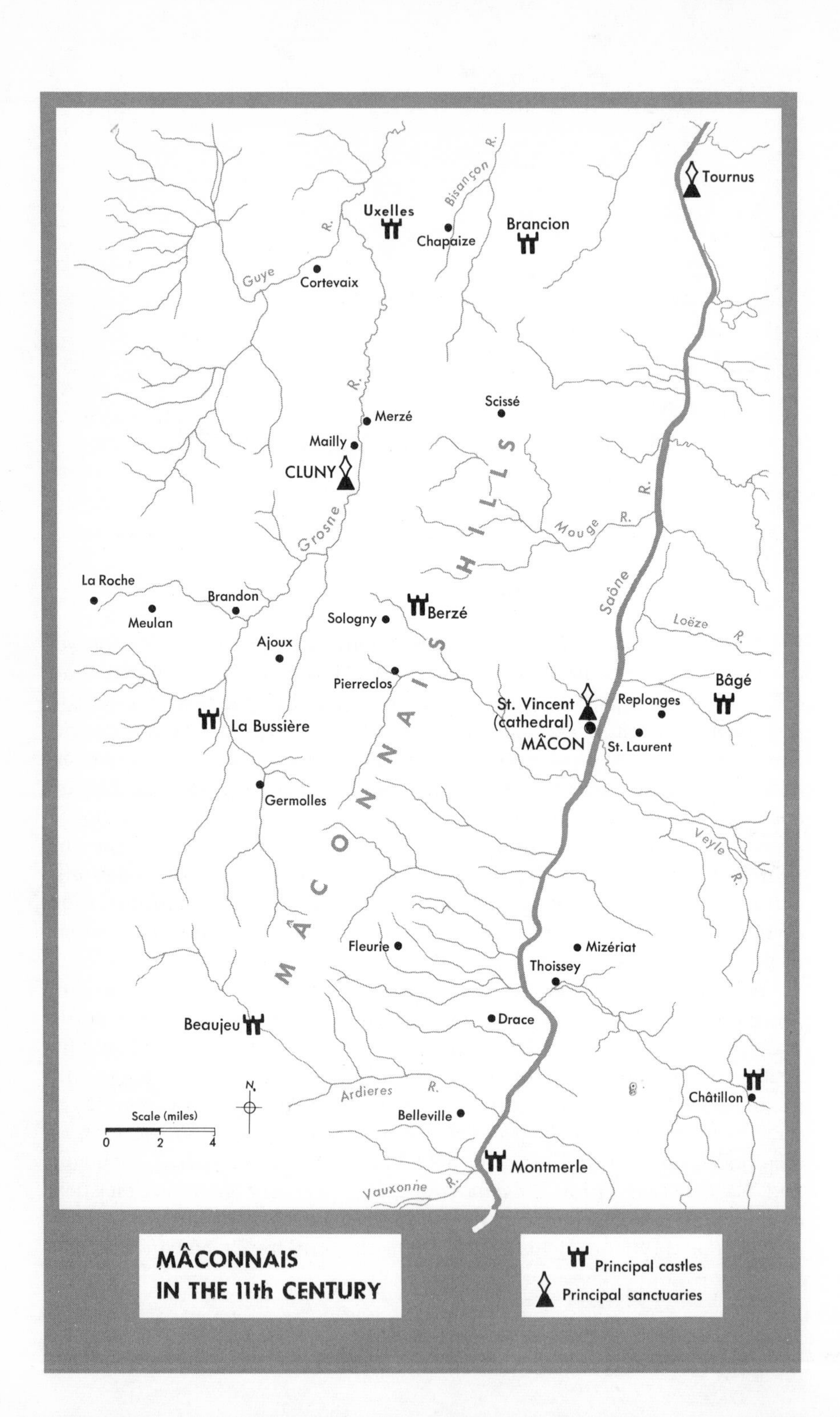
Tournus
Uxelles
Bisançon R.
Brancion
Chapaize
Guye R.
Cortevaix
Grosne R.
Merzé
Scissé
Mailly
CLUNY
MÂCONNAIS HILLS
Mouge R.
Saône R.
La Roche
Brandon
Meulan
Berzé
Sologny
Loëze R.
Ajoux
Pierreclos
Bâgé
St. Vincent (cathedral)
Replonges
La Bussière
MÂCON
St. Laurent
Germolles
Veyle R.
Fleurie
Mizériat
Thoissey
Beaujeu
Drace
Ardières R.
Châtillon
Scale (miles)
0 2 4
N.
Belleville
Montmerle
Vauxonne R.
MÂCONNAIS IN THE 11th CENTURY
Principal castles
Principal sanctuaries

sauveté, the seat of an independent tribunal. This attrition was of fundamental importance for the history of society. For, in effect, along with the pre-eminence of the count the public institutions of the Frankish period had disappeared. The nature of power had been transformed; no longer was the distinction made between the *ban* (the power to command which once had flowed from the power of the king) and *de facto* domination privately exercised over one's own dependents. Count, castellans, immunists, lords of vassals, and masters of serfs or of free men who had commended themselves—all those who protected and directed—were placed on the same level. A juxtaposition of competitive clienteles replaced a hierarchy of powers, while precise and general duties toward the entire community gave way to particular promises of varying kinds of limited service: the devotion of a vassal to his *senior,* the submission of a humble dependent to his lord. With this sweep of the brush, all social classifications were put into question; the idea of liberty faded, while the opposition between rich and poor, "noble" and peasant, grew strong. Within these two classes political relationships would be rebuilt along different lines. The aristocracy would be organized only by feudal institutions; free men of lower condition would find themselves subject to domination of a stricter sort and would melt into the class of serfs.

The failure of comital authority liberated the free and the richest from the military and judicial duties to which their ancestors had been subject. The greatest lords, those whose power and wealth equaled the count's, simply refused to obey, to appear at his court, and, undoubtedly, to serve in his army. All the holders of allodial land who were affluent enough to bear arms and to attend the count's assemblies, who were subject to the jurisdiction neither of a *vicarius*[2] nor of an immunist, escaped the constraints with which, after the year 1000, the great lords—lay and ecclesiastic—bound their subject peasantry. Most broke all relations with the count and placed themselves under the protection of the nearest castellan or sanctuary—but in the very supple form of ties of vassalage. As for those neighbors of the castle of Mâcon who remained tied to the count, they found it easy to gain equal treatment by threatening to pick up their fealty and carry it elsewhere. Within the aristocracy only relations of vassalage controlled political ties. These relations were slowly built up during the course of the eleventh century. . . .

I. FEUDAL RELATIONS AT THE END OF THE ELEVENTH CENTURY

The Count of Mâcon, finding it impossible to force the castellans to submit to his *ban,* to his command, tried to obtain at least their homage and service. But since the benefices that the castellans' ancestors had received in earlier years had become allodial holdings, the Count was forced to grant them new fiefs sliced out of his own domain. The viscountial "honor" [the lands and rights attached to the position of viscount] was an exception; it continued to be held of the county. By means of this "honor" the count kept the Blanc family, lords of Montmelard, Matour, and Bois-Sainte-Marie, as his vassals. At the end of the twelfth century Viscount Artaud held of the count the customs he collected on the lands of St. Pierre of Mâcon; his brother Hugh, who succeeded him, held the *vicariae* of the district of Charlieu and seignorial rights at Mouhy in fief; their uncle Stephen had earlier received the mills at Chevignes.[3] The other great lords were won over by gifts. In 1040 Count Geoffrey granted the *condaminiae*[4] of Reneins to the Castellan of Montmerle, Robert Enchainé, to gain Robert's support; Count Guy won the friendship of the lord of Uxelles, Josseran Gros, by allowing Josseran to acquire the ecclesiastical revenues (*abbatia*) of St.-Laurent-lès-Mâcon; the castellans of La Bussière received Mont d'Ajoux in the lands of Brandon in fief; and, finally, the Beaujeu became vassals of the count in return for certain tenures.[5] By means of these concessions the Count of Mâcon received the homage of the region's castellans during the time of the First Crusade. However, the fiefs that formed the wages of their devotion were of but small value. In the Mâconnais the count's domain was not large enough to allow him to show great generosity without dangerously impoverishing himself. It was easier to settle his vassals on his great forested allods in the Jura; and it was there, among the "gentry" of Revermont, that he recruited his best clientele.[6] The castellans of the county of Mâcon were much less solidly held than those of the Charolais where the Count of Chalon had extensive and barely cleared woods at his disposal to pay for their fidelity.

Furthermore, these great lords were vassals not only of the count: homage and fiefs had also tied them to one another and to the principal sanctuaries. Oaths alone, without the grant of land, were often a guarantee of mutual friendship; Gautier, lord of Berzé, became the vassal of the Abbot of Cluny without receiving anything—without promising anything either, except faithfully to keep the peace that had just been concluded. There is no evidence that he ever appeared at the abbot's court or rendered the abbot any military aid. Between the two neighboring and rival powers, homage sealed a security pact.[7] Often, likewise—when a castellan still held some precarial tenures that an ecclesiastical establishment had once granted his ancestors, precarial tenures that had turned into fiefs—the contract of vassalage only continued an older land-holding relationship. Such were the ties that bound the lords of Bâgé to St. Vincent of Mâcon and the lords of La Bussière to Cluny.[8] Through homage the Church maintained its rights over the most endangered parts of its temporal possessions. Feudal grants also allowed lords to consolidate their territorial seigniories. Frequently castellans possessed allods or rights in districts belonging to another fortress; to avoid squabbles it was better to abandon their use to the lord with whom one was in competition, in return for his fealty and some reciprocal favors. Thus the Bâgés, who still held powers of command in the neighborhood of their domains in the Mâconnais hills, gave these powers in fief to their cousins, the Berzés, masters of the neighboring castle.[9]

As a result, feudal relations among the high aristocracy criss-crossed one another. Between lords of equal power they created no true subordination and did nothing to reduce the independence of the castellans. There is no evidence in the texts from the end of the eleventh century that the Count of Mâcon received from his great vassals either military service or attendance at court. He expected from them only either temporary aid, such as that which Robert of Montmerle gave to help him carry off the patrimony of Viscount Guigue, or partial devotion, such as that rendered by Josseran Gros, who was retained elsewhere by the more munificent "benefits" he had received from his other lords, the Count of Chalon and the Bishop of Mâcon.[10] It was only on rare occasions, for exceptionally solemn events, that the elite of society assembled of their own free will around the count, for one day bringing back to life the ancient assemblies of the city.[11] The Count of Chalon seems to have been able to force the castellans of the Charolais, who held better fiefs of him, to submit to stricter discipline; the Busseuils, the Chigys, and the Digoines regularly came to act as escort to him and to sign his acts. Their dependence was still very loose, however. A great lord such as Lébaud de Digoine was first of all concerned with his personal interests, with those of his men, and even with the service of his other lord, the Bishop of Mâcon.[12]

The homage that tied the castellans to the counts was far from replacing the older Frankish fidelity; it was not an instrument of submission. Nor did it allow a castellan or an immunist church to control its neighboring lords. When Oury of Bâgé placed his hands between those of the new bishop and placed an *écu*'s worth of candles which he owed for his fief on the altar of St. Vincent, he felt he was quit of other obligations toward the church, which for its part, appears to have expected nothing more from him. In any case, what means would a lord have employed to impose obligations on a vassal against that vassal's will, if the lord was neither stronger nor richer than his "man"? For the great landed proprietors who held vast allodial holdings, the desire to obtain or hold a fief was not strong enough to make them give up their freedom for it. And if such vassals did not observe their sworn faith, how were their lords to confiscate their fiefs? At the beginning of the twelfth century the lord of Bâgé refused to do the homage he owed St. Vincent. The Bishop and the chapter, finding it impossible to confiscate his fief, bought his oath of fealty for one thousand shillings and two marks of silver. It was a high price to pay for a purely formal promise; for, several years later when the lord of Bâgé again showed himself unsubmissive, the lords of the church of Mâcon were forced to call in the Archbishop of Lyon to arbitrate.[13]

In the higher ranks of the nobility a vassal recognized neither the judicial nor, undoubtedly, the military authority of his lord. At this level homage and fief were only the means to consolidate and calm the often very tense relationships among competitive and fundamentally foreign powers.[14]

The feudal tie was much more strict when it attached a member of the lesser nobility to the count, to a castellan, or to an ecclesiastical power. In such cases the lord dominated his vassal sufficiently to demand more extensive services: he could give his "man" enough support for the latter not to be niggardly with his devotion. The vassal with only modest allodial lands welcomed a fief as a considerable addition to his resources, even if the fief was not itself of great value; and the fear of confiscation, which he could hardly evade, maintained his obedience. Between the higher ranks of the nobility and the lower, feudal institutions truly structured political relations. They assured the organization of the petty nobility.

In the last years of the tenth century a certain number of free men of moderate means had already commended themselves to powerful neighbors from whom they expected material or spiritual aid. After the year 1000 the weakening of comital authority and the development of feudal custom consolidated and extended these clienteles. Willy-nilly, those who were isolated chose a patron, but their motives for commendation remained the same. They carried their homage to the nearest castle or sanctuary. At the end of the eleventh century all the knights of surrounding villages were thus attached to the master of a fortress; Hugh of Germolles, Artaud of La Ferdière, Guy of La Roche were the vassals of the lord of La Bussière; Bernard of Mépillat, Bernard of Jayat, Geoffroy of Mizériat, André of Niermont were vassals of the lord of Bâgé.[15] These were the *milites castri,* the knights of the castle.[16] Often, like Létard of Feugères at Beaujeu or Létaud of Cortambert at Lourdon, they possessed their own houses where they lodged during their periods of guard-service.[17] So too, by granting fiefs, the great immunist churches kept the descendants of precarial tenants in their homage and won new fidelities; in this way the knights of Merzé, Mailly, Saint-Nizier, Bière, Sologny, and Meulin, whose allods bordered the lands of St. Pierre, became vassals of the abbey of Cluny.[18] These networks of dependence woven around the castles and principal sanctuaries had a territorial character. They bound all the little lords residing in a castle district or in the interstices of an immunist's domain to the chief local power.

Between a knight and his lord, the relationship of vassalage was still, as it had been in the tenth century, a tie of mutual friendship similar to that which bound the family together. Those who had commended themselves formed a great family; a scribe drawing up a charter in 1100 found no better phrase to designate the common lord of a list of vassals than *"caput mansi,"* the head of the house, the same name that was given the eldest member of a family community.[19] Private allegiance, however, seems to have absorbed some formerly public duties. After 1000 the *milites castri,* the knights of the district, vassals of the castellan who directed their military activity, were undoubtedly led to feel that their ancient duties of *chevauchée* and castle-guard were part of the services of their fiefs. On the other hand, the jurisdiction a lord had over his tenures authorized him to call his vassals to special court sessions whose jurisdiction, legally limited to settling disputes, might greatly expand in cases involving confiscation of a fief. In every castle and immunist church, a judicial court developed to arbitrate not only disputes between the lords and their "men" but among neighboring knights as well. The vassals of a fortress or a sanctuary were normally justiciable because of their feudal tenure. The laymen who sat on the court of Cluny about the year 1000 were for the most part the abbey's precarial tenants;[20] their successors of the eleventh century held fiefs of St. Pierre.[21] The earliest litigants were expressly called *"vassi"* in the records.[22] And some sessions of this judicial organ were without question feudal courts, such as the assembly of the monastery's enfeoffed knights who forced Lambert Deschaux to abandon his father's benefice in 1064, or the one of similar composition that eight years later decided to confiscate the fief of Geoffroy of St.-Nizier.[23]

Thus, about the time of the First Crusade military and court service seem to be added to the "familial" obligations of the small vassal. These duties tightened the feudal ties, already reinforced by the strong feelings of affection and gratitude and the frequent contact which attached the knight to his lord. When the vassal's rights were threatened, the lord came to his aid, took the dispute in hand, supported his vassal with all his own influence. In return the vassal helped him as best he could, not only refraining from doing the lord harm but also serving him in his private wars and acting as witness or guarantor for him whenever necessary.[24] It was a tight and profitable alliance. Consider, for example, the attitude of Humbert le Hongre, a knight of the upper Mâconnais whose allods lay between Cortevaix and Chapaize: He held a fief of the Gros family, masters of the nearby castle of Uxelles, and was entirely devoted to their service. He gave them aid and counsel, witnessed their acts, appeared for them in court, and gave himself as a hostage to be confined to their fortress as security. To their care, he confided his son who followed them to the court of the Duke of Burgundy. And when Josseran, one of the brothers Gros, became a monk and chamberlain of Cluny, Humbert le Hongre went over to the monastery's clientele. All his actions, like those of his relatives and neighbors, Artaud of Bussières, Engilbert of Cortevaix, and Elie of Cray, were determined by the oath of fealty he had taken to the castellan of Uxelles.[25]

One should not, however, exaggerate the rigor of these ties of dependence. In the eleventh century the smaller vassals' subordination remained imperfect for two reasons. The first was the small value of the fief. The Mâconnais remained a land of allods.[26] Rich in free land, the knight did not need his fief to subsist; his patron could exercise no genuine economic constraint over him. The second and main reason was the plurality of homage. Along the vague frontiers of military districts and immunist territories, castellans and ecclesiastical lords fought for the knights' allegiance. They offered them protection and fiefs and proposed greater advantages in return for lighter duties. Free to carry his fealty wherever he wished, the small nobleman clearly chose the patron who would have the least control over him and, certain of easily finding another protector ready to welcome him and grant him an equivalent fief, was ready to haggle with his own lord over the services he owed. Furthermore, inheritance and exchange of tenures complicated personal relationships. Through the fiefs they inherited from their ancestors, Geoffroy of St.-Nizier and Josseran of Bière were attached both to the lord of Berzé and to the abbey of Cluny. Humbert le Hongre himself, so solidly attached to the lords of Uxelles, held a fief of Cluny and another of the castellan of Bourbon-Lancy.[27] At the end of the eleventh century there undoubtedly were no longer any knights who were not vassals of two or more lords. The enfeoffed knight, belonging to several bands of vassals, protected by each of his patrons against all the others, was virtually free of the strictest of military and judicial obligations. He was, in fact, not subject to distraint. Feudal duties without question weighed more heavily on the petty aristocracy than on the great. They did not succeed in genuinely subjecting the vassal to his lord. . . .

In the last analysis, feudal institutions were adapted to the previous structure of the upper class, without significantly modifying it. Homage taken by one great lord to another or by one knight to another was simply a guarantee, a promise not to injure; taken by a petty nobleman to a powerful one it was a genuine allegiance, a promise to serve. Vassalage and fief, customary practices born of private usage, organized the relationships already imposed by an unequal division of wealth and power. They did not create new ones. In eleventh-century Mâconnais there was no feudal pyramid, no "feudal system."[28] The count, the castellans, and the ecclesiastical powers were so many "heads" (*capita*)[29] independent of one another despite feudal ties, each the center of a knightly clientele. These vassal troops, recruited in the castle district or in the immunity's neighborhood, had a territorial character; but their frontiers were not clear. Plurality of homage made them flow into one another; their shapes constantly varied with the inheritance and sale of fiefs. In spite of their power and their ability to confiscate the fief of a faithless vassal, the lords had little grip on their men—allodial holders with other resources, other patrons, other shelters. After the collapse of the court's authority in the eleventh century the aristocracy, now restricted only by feudal institutions, found itself free of all true constraints. The most powerful enjoyed total independence. The lesser nobles, more restricted by the service owed for their fiefs, still had an air of great freedom; for if they committed a crime, there was no definite court to judge them nor power to punish them. For the upper class feudalism was a step toward anarchy.

II. THE FORMATION OF THE KNIGHTLY CLASS

(A) The Title

In 971 the word *"miles,"* the Latin translation of the word "knight," was (as far as we know) used for the first time by a Mâconnais scribe to designate the member of a particular social class.[30] To be sure, the term had been used before in popular speech and its appearance in an archival document does not mean that a new conception of society was born at precisely this moment. The men who drew up charters and other documents had their own jargon, sanctified by tradition, and this new expression was forced on them from the outside, by current usage.[31] Church chanceries were slow to follow the movement, and it was inadvertently and against his desire to write classical Latin that the chronicler Raoul Glaber twice used the word *"miles"* to express a social quality rather than the military function.[32] When notaries adopted the Latin equivalent for the word "knight," the social transformation had been completed. It was evident to everyone. The date of first adoption is nevertheless important; for it was the date when this transformation was officially recognized and juridically consecrated. We will try to explain this event by looking for the now-obsolete terms that *"miles"* replaced and the reasons for this replacement.

Guilhiermoz, in his magnificient book on the origins of the French nobility, argued that in the eleventh century the idea expressed by the word *"miles"*—"knighthood," let us say—and the three concepts of liberty, vassalage, and nobility were equivalent. *"Miles,"* Guilhiermoz said, took the place of *"liber," "vassus,"* and *"nobilis."* Do the texts from the Mâconnais justify his conclusions?

Scholars a long time ago rejected the first of these propositions by demonstrating that the quality of knighthood was not the same as the status of freeman.[33] In fact, extant charters clearly show that the words *"liber"* and *"francus"* did not disappear beneath the knightly title, that throughout the eleventh century there were laymen who, without deserving to be called knights, were no less free men. To be sure, knighthood was incompatible with servitude. Some rich men of great influence, such as the *prévôts* of the great Cluniac deaneries who rubbed elbows with the nobility and lived an aristocratic life, had no right to the title. They were serfs. In the Mâconnais there was no ministerial class of the German type. Still, "*miles*" was not a synonym for free. It designated a particular category of free laymen and it did so from its very earliest use; one cannot argue that its use was gradually restricted over time.

Guilhiermoz, resting his argument on the Carolingian military capitularies and on a quantity of charters and literary texts, tried to prove that in the eleventh century military service was transferred from allods to fiefs and that the vassal, the soldier *par excellence,* naturally received the title "*miles.*" On this point his proof has never been seriously attacked. It is commonly admitted that knighthood equaled dependent vassalage.[34] On first sight the documents of the Mâconnais seem to confirm this view; the moment the term for knight began to spread was the same moment that feudal institutions began to structure the aristocracy. Above all, in many charters, "*miles*" seems to replace Latin words like "*vassus*" and "*fidelis,*" which clearly express personal dependence. When one sees the preamble to a precarial title, "*Adiit quidam vassus . . . , quidam fidelis . . .*" [a certain *vassus* took . . .], become about the year 1000 "*Adiit quidam miles . . . ,*" when in the accounts of judicial pleas the formula "*Proclamaverunt se . . . de quodam milite*" [so-and-so complained about a certain *miles* . . .] replaces "*Proclamaverunt se de quodam vasso,*" he easily becomes convinced; all the more so as these acts concern precarial holdings turning into fiefs and public courts turning into feudal courts—institutions that were thoroughly imbued with the influence of vassalage.[35] Was knighthood thus nothing but vassalage?

If one looks more closely, however, three facts make one suspect that the two ideas were not identical. First, all vassals were not *milites;* thus the Count of Mâcon by a charter of 1107 allowed the monks of Cluny to acquire lands that "his knights or his men" held of him in fief.[36] Therefore, the title of "knight" applied only to certain vassals, a qualification rather restricting the scope of Guilhiermoz' deductions. The second fact is of a grammatical nature. In all the formulas in which "*miles*" designates a dependent—both in the texts we have collected and in those gathered by Guilhiermoz—the relation of man to man is signified not by the substantive itself, but by a special grammatical device involving the possessive form. Thus, when Guilhiermoz concluded that the phrase "*militare alicui*" had a sense of vassalage, he was not wrong; but personal dependence and the idea of service was expressed by the word "*alicui*"—"*militare*" was there only to show the particular kind of service and the social status of the dependent.[37] To be sure, the same is true of the words "*vassus*" and *"fidelis"*; but, unlike these two terms, *"miles"* could be employed by itself and, in such cases had no connotation of vassalage. This leads to our last remark.

"Miles" was often used as a personal title—indeed this was its most novel usage. Men glorified in its honor, insisted, "I *N.*, knight . . . ." If the word evoked only the idea of personal submission, why would they so insist on it? There was nothing particularly honorable in proclaiming oneself the man of another, unless one was vassal of a very important individual whose patronage was extremely advantageous. But in such cases one mentioned it, as those ninth- and tenth-century nobles had done when they flattered themselves at being not just vassals, but vassals of the king or of the count.[38] This appears to be sufficient reason not to accept the second equation of Guilhiormoz, whose thesis was based on a conception of eleventh-century society which overestimated the importance of feudal relations and neglected the allod. *"Miles"* expressed, not a personal tie, but a social quality. Undoubtedly, most vassals had that quality and their lords underlined it, calling them, not their faithful or their men, but "their" knights, just as they might say "my cleric" without anyone supposing that *clericus* implied personal dependence. "Knight" was no more the synonym of "vassal" than it was of "free man." Knighthood was not vassalage.

Thus, all that remains of Guilhiermoz' thesis is the identity of knighthood and nobility. This, at least, the documents well demonstrate. If we go over the formulas in which *"miles"* seems to replace *"vassus,"* we find upon examining them a bit more thoroughly, that the new expression takes the place of *"nobilis"* or its equivalent. In precarial charters the scribes had written about fealty only on exceptional occasions, and beneath their pens "knight" came to replace adjectives for nobility—as certain redundancies prove.[39] In the same way, when *"miles"* came into use in judicial records, "noble" had already replaced the adjective "faithful."[40] In formulas of exchange where ideas of vassalage had never appeared, *"miles"* again replaced *"nobilis."*[41] Last of all, if numerous expressions for ties of man to man subsisted throughout the eleventh century, after 1030 the old epithets for nobility disappeared. The last known text from the Mâconnais in which the word *"nobilis"* appears as a title was dated 1032.[42] These adjectives were still used from time to time to honor certain knights,[43] but they expressed social rank only when applied to women of high birth. The fact is revealing: there was no word to use as a substitute, for *"miles"* was an essentially masculine term.[44] The adoption of the chivalric title thus did not mark a change in the idea of liberty; contemporary with the spread of feudal relationships, it was not a direct effect. It meant above all that the nobility had taken on a new character.

It is not surprising that the men of the eleventh century used a military term to designate the "nobility." Undoubtedly, up to this time the word had been understood in a very precise sense; men had applied it to those who fought and thus could have applied it to any free man, at least to any who had not cut his hair and "untied his baldric" to become a cleric. In the tenth century, *milicia* was lay liberty.[45] But for a long time, as is well known, warfare had been reserved to men of substance who could arm themselves properly, maintain horses, and thus alone play an effective part in combat.[46] Only the members of the aristocracy, those who were generally called "nobles," were genuinely men of arms; it was already an ancient practice to consider the use of a horse and sword as the outward sign of nobility.[47] As the year 1000 approached, the movement for the peace of God perhaps accentuated this natural tendency of men's minds. When, in order to confine disorder, carrying arms was forbidden to men of lesser quality and when the peasants, considered unwarlike and unarmed, were put under special protection, the military specialization of the wealthy was confirmed. The synonymity is thus explained. But why the preference?

The two terms, *"nobilis"* and *"miles,"* do not have the same grammatical function. The first is an adjective; the second, a noun. It is a slight shade of a difference, to be sure, but one that reflected a profound modification in social outlook. If men stopped using the word "noble," they did so because it was no longer possible to use this adjective of comparative force, which connoted only a quality of variable intensity, to designate the members of the superior class. A noun was necessary, a title with definite meaning, that applied to an entire group, that could, like *"clericus"* or *"servus,"* translate a status and not simply a relative and changeable superiority. For, in fact, *"miles"* was originally used as a title; it was used because people felt a need for a personal title.[48] It was no longer enough to be thought more noble than one's neighbor. One now had to be able to proclaim his quality, to state on all occasions that he belonged to a well-defined social category. The adoption of the noun *"miles"* by scribes drawing up charters not only signified a juridical recognition of the ancient *de facto* identity of wealth and the fighter's calling, it was also the first sign, the most characteristic sign, of a class consciousness being born. It is the proof that an undefined and evasive "nobility" at the end of the tenth century found its boundaries, became a true class whose members, like other legal groups—clergy or serfs—shared a common status.

This transformation of vocabulary took place at exactly the same time as the political revolution. Completed between 971 and 1032, it occurred during the same period that the comital court became a private court and the first customs appeared in the banal seigniories. The coincidence is too clean to have happened by chance; the adoption of this military term and the delimitation of an aristocracy which it implies must be related to the new conditions of political life. As long as public institutions under the direction of the count maintained the legal unity of the class of freemen, nobility remained relative and adjectives such as *"nobilis," "strenuis," "inluster,"* which marked only a moral illustriousness, were perfectly suited to expressing a superior shade of freedom. The collapse of the count's power, however, changed the entire social structure. The new conception of authority traced a clear line through the class of freemen, dividing those subject to the seigniory from those who escaped its grasp. Henceforth this was the frontier of the noble class. On one side stood those, more or less noble, who possessed the same privileges. A title, rather than a comparative, was needed to name them. And since it was precisely their military capacities that allowed them to escape seignorial exploitation, that exempted them from banal customs, it was quite natural that these men should display their combatant's status as the sign of their nobility. The knights were those free men of the upper class who were subject to no constraint except vassal obligations. The knighthood of the year 1000 was the former "nobility" now supplied with a shape and a definition, crystallized around the profession of arms and the legal privileges it brought with it.

(B) The Inheritance of Knighthood

The title *"miles"* was a legal recognition of economic superiority. In tenth-century society the most noble were the wealthiest; to be a professional fighter, to attend the count's court rather than the *viguier*'s, one had to be a man of means. The precise limit that the assuming of a knightly title marked, about the year 1000, corresponded to a certain level in the hierarchy of wealth. Which level? We must now define it, now that it was clearly underlined and clothed with legal value.

Commonly, historians refer for this purpose to the ancient regulations of the capitularies of 806 and 807 which required military service from all persons possessing four *mansi* and full armor from all landed lords enjoying the revenues of more than twelve *mansi*.[49] It seems foolhardy, however, to imagine that such ideas were maintained during the two centuries of troubles that shook the Carolingian edifice to its foundations, it seems yet more dangerous to generalize regulations that were only local and exceptional.[50] It is better to use only contemporary documents. What, first of all, was the cost of equipment? Horses were not rare in the Mâconnais, where peasants willingly raised them and any moderately prosperous landholder could easily turn himself into a horseman. From one end of the eleventh century to the other a horse was worth from twenty to fifty shillings, depending on its quality, that is, about five times more than an ox.[51] Arms cost more. The average price of the cuirass alone, the essential part of a man's armor, was apparently one hundred shillings. It was the price of a good *mansus*.[52] Thus, anyone wanting to equip himself for the profession of arms had to have liquid capital amounting to several pounds at his disposal, something beyond the reach of most peasants who, in order to assemble a patrimony, took years to save a handful of pennies. Moreover, simply to have the arms was not enough. Leisure was required; at the first alert the knight had to abandon his fields. Thus knightly life was reserved for those who could depend entirely upon others to work their domains: reserved for those who could lead the life of a lord.[53] Landed seigniories of quite variable content could assure the requisite economic independence; since tenant holdings brought in little, what was most needed was a substantial reserved domain and enough servants to work it. Generally a knight's domain grouped about ten *mansi* around his farmyard. Fromald, the brother of a knight, *"nobilis homo,"* who withdrew to the cloister of St. Vincent of Mâcon without taking religious Orders, gave all his goods to his fellow canons—about fifteen *mansi*.[54] At about the same time, Arlier the Bald possessed three *mansi*, five *courtils*, three serf families, and a good reserve composed of various scattered holdings in the valley of the Grosne.[55] In 1080 Létard of Feugères, a knight from the Beaujolais, divided a landed seigniory of about the same size among his relatives.[56] These three men belonged to the most petty knighthood. Entrance into the class of knights was thus reserved for men holding great landed possessions—at least 350 acres—that is to say, it was reserved for a very small number.

No statistics allow us to count exactly how many were able to honor themselves with the knightly title around the year 1000. However, the five parishes of the *ager* of Merzé, a territory particularly privileged by rich documentation, where we know with certainty all the people of importance, supported seven knights at the end of the tenth century.[57] If we assume that the density of nobility was equal throughout the 150 parishes of the Mâconnais, we may guess that, at the moment it came into being the class of knights[58] included about two hundred heads of families. Our research into the origins of those knights of Merzé also reveals that all the members of this class were the heirs of the wealthiest landholders of the tenth century.

But if wealth made the knight, then knighthood at its beginning was an open class. Whoever had arms and the desire to use them, whoever had the time to train at swordplay on horseback and could without an afterthought leave his domain in mid-harvest to go off on a military campaign or do castle-guard in the local fortress, immediately became a member. Wealth—landed wealth—was the sufficient condition. Any enriched peasant came near nobility. Wealth was also the *necessary* condition. Any noble son whose patrimony lost value immediately lost his social status. Nothing could be more movable than such a group: sales, purchases, gifts, and inheritance constantly changed its membership. Such, at least, was the opinion of Marc Bloch, who wondered how many twelfth-century knights were descended from fortunate adventurers or from peasants who had slowly hoarded together strips of land.[59]

Actually, economic conditions left little chance for the knightly class to welcome newcomers into its midst. Exchange of agricultural products gave the peasantry small profit, as we know, and allowed them little hope of quitting their plows for military adventures. As for grants of fief, they were too small by themselves to raise a man without means into the knightly class. For the economic tendency was toward the gradual impoverishment of the laity. It was surely the case that in the year 1000 there were fewer men capable of fighting on horseback than there had been fifty years earlier; more than one descendant of a noble family, impoverished by his ancestors' pious donations, could not take on the title of "knight." And after 1000 this patrimonial disintegration would force the poorest *milites* to give up the fighter's profession and by the same token, nobility. As an economic class, knighthood ran less risk of filling up at the top than of draining out at the bottom.

It was a serious danger for its members. When nobility was nothing but an illustrious coloration whose brilliance might gradually fade, a man could descend the steps of the social hierarchy without really noticing it—simply at the cost of some of his pride. If such a man no longer joined the comital troop, if he confined his activity to village life and carried his suits to the vicarial court, he did not really lose class: he stayed a free and independent man, financially pressed perhaps, but one whom chance might one day pull from obscurity. In the eleventh century this was no longer so. If one was no longer capable of fighting, he immediately fell under the domination of a powerful neighbor, was forced to answer the demands of his *prévôts*. He suffered a dependence infinitely more degrading than the free promises of a vassal; he became hereditarily dependent. It was a brutal and irremediable fall.

Now that a precise boundary separated the knights from the others, to cross that boundary was to lose the most precious social and political advantages. What must have been the torment of impoverished noblemen whose income barely allowed them to keep up a front, as they saw their too numerous sons crowd one another on their meager patrimony? Clearly, they dreamed of passing on to them, even in poverty, the privileges they owed to their relative wealth.[60] Most probably, the desire to assure one's heirs the title of "knight," if not a sufficient fortune, was born at the same time as a class consciousness, as the feeling that one belonged to a group whose frontiers were clearly fixed and whose privileges were defined. The development of political institutions conferred too many advantages on the new nobility for it to remain open very long. It must rapidly have closed itself off, at least in one sense; for if it was essential to prevent one's descendants from slipping out of the nobility, there was as yet no great need to oppose a massive influx of newcomers. A reversal in the economic cycle, the appearance of a new phenomenon—the enrichment of the lesser classes—was necessary to bring about a total closing of the class.[61] But from the beginning, knighthood carried the seed of inheritance.

The idea took some time to impose itself. In the first decades of the eleventh century the knightly class still lost some of its members. Of the seven knights living in the *ager* of Merzé in the year 1000, one, Aidoard, died without heirs; two others, Seguin and Engeaume, did not leave enough to their sons for them to maintain their station; the sons were reduced to peasant condition: in 1080 their descendants exercised the honorless functions of *prévôts* in their native villages for the account of the distant castellans of Bourbon-Lancy. At the end of the eleventh century only four lineages—richer and above all less prodigal of alms—kept the title of "knight," the Merzés, the Arliers, the Maillys and the Burdins, and no poorer families rose to fill the gaps.[62]

Between 1050 and 1075, however, many signs indicate that knighthood stopped being the mark of economic superiority to become a strictly hereditary quality. First of all, the use of the title "knight" became much more frequent. Previously, it had been used only from time to time, like the titles of nobility, if the scribe drawing up an act felt like using it; Ancy d'Oblé, for example, who is named in thirteen extant documents, is called knight in only two of them.[63] But after 1060 everyone who had the right to the title constantly paraded it. It was a wall preventing a man from falling from his class. The phrase *"quidam miles"* was a genuine social criterion in the cartularies drawn up at the end of the century, such as that of Paray-le-Monial. The only names it does not follow are the names of peasants or of *ministeriales.*[64] Furthermore, this title, at first simply an added appendage, about 1050 began to be incorporated into the family name. The form *"N.,* knight of *N."* gradually came to be preferred to *"N.* of *N.,* knight." It thus became inseparable from the family name, the property of the entire lineage claimed by all heirs.[65] By 1075 the development was complete. From that time on, one was a knight from father to son, whatever the family's economic vicissitudes. The title of "knight" was taken by all male heirs who were not clergy. Better yet, it honored the entire family, male and female.[66] And when Achard of Merzé (the son of a knight), having taken the tonsure and abandoned all military activity called himself *"clericus et miles,"* cleric and knight, the title clearly no longer had anything to do with a style of life, with a personal aptitude for the profession of arms.[67] It had become a social title distinguishing the members of a social class.

In the last quarter of the eleventh century the limit surrounding knighthood had become a fence preventing its members from leaving. *Milicia* was no longer a class open to all who could lead a certain style of life, but a privileged hereditary class, a true nobility in the legal sense of the term. This small group, which definitively brought together the descendants of the few lineages who were affluent enough to equip their sons about 1030, was a solid crystal around which grew, under the effect of political revolution, the large and changing nobility of the High Middle Ages.

NOTES*

1. The Carolingian local administrative district.—Ed.

2. Formerly, a delegated official of the count.—Ed.

3. *Recueil des chartes de l'abbaye de Cluny* [hereinafter *Cluny*], A. Bernard and A. Bruel, eds. (1876/1903), 572 and 3067; *Cartulaire de Saint-Vincent de Mâcon, connu sous le nom de Livre Enchaîné* [hereinafter *Mâcon*] C. Ragut, ed. (1864), 11; *Cartulaire du prieuré de Paray-le-Monial* [hereinafter *Paray-le-Monial*] U. Chevalier, ed. (1890), 108.

4. Unparceled lands belonging to the domain.—Ed.

5. *Cluny,* 3577, 3475, 4244; Mâcon 631. According to L. Aubret, *Mémoires pour servir à l'histoire de Dombes,* 1 (1865), 273, 276: the Beaujeu held the domain of Cenves in fief of the Count of Macon in the eleventh century.

6. *Cluny* 3682.

7. *Ibid.* 2895, 3324.

8. *Ibid.* 919, 2087; *Mâcon* 2, 18, 37, 265, 543, 548; Archives départementales [hereinafter AD] Saône-et-Loire *G* 222 no. 1.

9. *Cluny* 2124, 3062.

10. *Ibid.* 3577, 3920; *Mâcon* 18, 26; *Recueil des pancartes de l'abbaye de la Forte-sur-Grosne,* Georges Duby, ed. (1953), p. 111.

11. *Cluny* 3726.

12. *Paray-le-Monial* 45, 64, 87, 152, 167; *Cluny* 3067, 3340; *Mâcon* 26.

13. AD Saône-et-Loire *G* 81 no. 1, *G* 222 no. 1.

14. Jean-François Lemarignier, *Recherches sur l'homme en marche et les frontières féodales* (1945).

15. *Cluny* 2769, 3829, 3841; *Mâcon* 11, 456, 471, 589.

16. *Cluny* 3822, 3827; *Paray-le-Monial* 90, 111.

17. M. C. Guigue, *Cartulaire Lyonnais* (1893), 10; *Cluny* 2195; see F. Kiener, *Verfassungsgeschichte der Provence seit der Ostrogothen bis zur Errichtung der Konsulate* (1900), p. 111.

18. *Cluny* 2784, 3038, 3159, 3161, 3321, 3400, 3503, 3685. Thus, the monks knew how to use feudal institutions, contrary to the opinion of G. de Valous, *Le monachisme clunisien des origines au XVe s.* (1935), p. 85.

19. *Cluny* 3784. On the meaning of this expression see J. Flach, *Les origines de l'ancienne France* (1886–1917), 2, 446–454, 483.

20. *Cluny* 1837, 2296, 2380, 2422, 2549.

21. *Ibid.* 3262, 3666, 3685, 3821, 3828.

22. *Ibid.* 941, 1528, 1723, 1759, 1821, 1852, 1885, 2296, 2508, 2848, 2975, 3221, 3262, 3400.

23. In the same way the precarial tenants of St. Vincent appeared before the episcopal court: *Mâcon* 30, 31. *Cluny* 3822; *Paray-le-Monial* 166. See G. Duby, "Recherches sur l'évolution des institutions judiciaires pendant le Xe et XIe s. dans le Sud de la Bourgogne," *Le Moyen Âge,* 2 (1946), 161, 167, 177.

24. *Cluny* 2869, 3577, 3744, 3784, 3896; *Mâcon* 456.

25. *Ibid.* 2995, 3104, 3302, 3440, 3574, 3703, 3784, 3809, 3986, 3926: *Mâcon* 27.

26. See G. Duby, *La société . . . mâconnaise,* pp. 291–305.

27. *Cluny* 3640, 3642, 3824.

28. We do not share the opinion of L. Verriest, *Institutions médiévales* (1946),

* Except for source and bibliographical references, most of the material in the original notes has been omitted—Ed.

1, 30, based on texts from the early Middle Ages, that there was a hierarchical organization of military service within the framework of the county.

29. "Caput et dominus, de cujus capite erat"—*Cluny* 2979, 2994, 3067, 3577, 3640, 3703, 3759, 3862, 3867; *Necrologium Sancti Petri Matisconensis,* C. Guigue, ed. (1876), 8; AD Saône-et-Loire *H* 142 no. 2; *Mâcon* 21; *Cartulaire de l'église collégiale de N.D. de Beaujeu* C. Guigue, ed. (1864), 8.

30. Cluny 1297.

31. Ibid. 1297, 1915, 2532.

32. Raoul Glader *Histoires* (M. Prou, ed. 1886) **4.** 2, 5; **2.** 10, 21. Compare the preceding with **1.** 3, 7; **3.** 2, 7; **3.** 9, 38; **4.** 9, 26; **5.** 4, 21.

33. Marc Bloch, "Liberté et servitude p rsonnelle au moyen-âge," *Anuario de historia del derecho español,* **10** (1933), 19–115 and "Sur le passé de la noblesse française," *Annales d'histoire économique et sociale,* **36** (1936), 366.

34. M. Bloch, "Le problème de l'or au moyen-âge," *Annales d'histoire économique et sociale,* **33** (1933), 369 and *La société féodale* (1939–1940), **2,** 15; F. Lot, *L'art militaire et les armées au moyen-âge en Europe et dans le Proche-Orient,* **2** (1946), 421.

35. Mâcon 9, 391, 398, 410, 475, 505; *Cluny* 912, 920, 1723, 1759, 1821, 1842, 1852, 1855, 1887, 1978, 2087, 2195, 2406, 2407, 2517, 2552, 2846, 2924, 2950, 3246, 3262, 3323, 3472, 3577, 3829; *Paray-le-Monial* 86, 111.

36. Cluny 3862, 3867; *Paray-le-Monial* 8.

37. A. Guilhiermoz, *Essai sur les origines de la noblesse en France au moyen-âge* (1902), pp. 342, 344.

38. Cluny 271, 272, 1297; *Mâcon* 204.

39. Mâcon 391.

40. Cluny 2552. *"Fidelis"* was last used in 997–1007—*Cluny* 2406. For *"nobiles,"* see *Cluny* 2719, 3342, 2992.

41. Old formula: *Cluny* 271, 1374, 2532; *Paray-le-Monial* 96. New formulas: *Cluny* 2532; *Paray-le-Monial* 96.

42. Cluny 2883.

43. Cartulaire de N.D. de Beaujeu 19; *Cartulaire du prieuré de Saint-Marcel-lès-Chalon,* M. and P. Canat de Chizy, eds. (1894), 6, 48; *Paray-le-Monial* 2, 8, 15, 26, 45, 107—all from the end of the eleventh century.

44. Cluny 315, 2014, 2678, 2853, 2883, 3734; *Mâcon* 498; *Cartulaire de St.-Marcellès-Chalon* 56; *Cartulaire de N.D. de Beaujeu* 19.

45. Cluny 802, and above, n. 32.

46. Lot, *Art militaire,* **1,** 91–94.

47. Migne, *PL* **133** col. 647; *Cluny* 2255. At Cluny, tenants arriving on horseback, more "noble," were better received than those on foot and were put up in a special building—E. Lesne, *Histoire de la propriété ecclésiastique en France* (1910–1943), **6,** 123.

48. Cluny 911, 1297, 1915, 2532, 2573, 2574; *Mâcon* 260.

49. MGH Cap. **1.** 134–137, 123. See A. Déléage, *La vie rurale en Bourgogne jusqu'au début du XIe s.* (1942), p. 445. [The *mansus* (*pl. mansi*) was the house and fields sufficient, in theory, to support one family.]

50. H. Halphen, *Charlemagne et l'empire carolingien* (1947), p. 171.

51. Cluny 3789. For prices, *Cluny* 1769, 1848, 2334, 2957, 3789.

52. Ibid. 3034.

53. P. Heck, *Beiträge zur Geschichte der Stände im Mittelalter* (1900–1905) **1,** 296–297.

54. Mâcon 473, 494; Bibliothèque de l'Académie de Mâcon, *Manuscrit pour l'histoire de Mâcon,* **2,** fo 33.

55. Cluny 227, 1773, 1816, 1883, 2429, 2430, 2556, 2775.

56. *Cartulaire Lyonnais* 10.

57. Duby, *La société . . . mâconnaise,* pp. 57–64.

58. Lot, *Art militaire,* 1, 94–113.

59. Bloch, *La société féodale,* 2, 10.

60. The closing-off of the knightly class ought to be related to the tightening of the family group—Duby, *La société . . . mâconnaise,* pp. 263–280.

61. Mâconnais documents contain no mention of *"adoubement."*

62. Seguin gave a large funerary donation to Cluny—*Cluny* 2427; about 1080, the children of his three sons were peasants at Taize—*Cluny,* 3034, 3642. See also *Cluny* 3262, 3277, 3301, 3641, 3642; *Mâcon* 31.

63. *Cluny* 2996, 3026, 3030, 3032, 3078, 3082, 3204, 3189, 3685, 3753, 3758, 3795; *Mâcon* 10, 26.

64. Before 1050, when persons of different ranks are listed together, everyone has his due title and the knights have precedence only over other laymen; later, men are divided into clearly distinguished categories: *milites* and *burgenses et servientes*—*Cluny* 3874, or more often, *rustici*—*Cluny* 3726; *Mâcon* 548, 598; AD Saône-et-Loire *H* 24 no. 8.

65. *Cluny* 2992, 3340; *Mâcon* 483.

66. *Cluny* 3677, 3758, 3822; *Mâcon* 31.

67. *Cluny* 2975.

THE NOBILITY AND THE FEUDAL REGIME IN THE LATIN KINGDOM OF JERUSALEM*

Joshua Prawer

The purpose of this study is to bring out the main lines in the development of the nobility of the Latin Kingdom of Jerusalem—a nobility that changed profoundly during the first hundred years of its existence—and to outline the relationship of that class to the political order of the crusader kingdom. We have tried to show elsewhere[1] that the commonly held notion of the crusaders' society as a "pure form of feudalism" stems from an anachronistic use of historical sources and that the royal power of the first kings of Jerusalem in no way resembles that of their Capetian contemporaries. If we are looking for an analogy, we would find it more easily and with more justification in the power of the princely houses of Normandy, Anjou, and Flanders.

On what social base was the royal power of the kingdom erected? What determined its evolution during the first century of its history? These questions immediately bring us to the social structure of the nobility of Jerusalem (an almost totally neglected field of research)[2] and to the study of changes in the constitutional life of the kingdom. Since the problem has never been considered from this point of view, this essay will provide a broad preliminary sketch, to be filled in with detail and proper shading by later studies.

---

* Joshua Prawer, "La noblesse et le régime féodal du royaume latin de Jérusalem," *Le Moyen Âge,* **65** (Brussels, 1959), 41–74. Trans. by the ed.

I. THE FORMATION OF THE NOBILITY AND THE DOMINANCE OF THE ROYAL POWER

Two main factors determined the character of the oldest nobility of the kingdom: the chronic state of war against Islam and the continual wave of immigrants to the Holy Land during the first three decades of its existence. Obviously, the kingdom could not sustain itself against Islam without a large number of immigrants to replace the losses on the battlefield.

The First Crusade left only a thin deposit of settlers. Chronicles inform us that in 1100 there were no more than 300 knights and 1200 *sergents.* Who were these knights? Certainly not the members of the great families of the West, since these left the country after the conquest. The majority of these knights were either European vassals of the house of Bouillon,[3] or men who had entered the service of that family during the First Crusade. Fed by the stream of new immigrants, this original seed grew with time. It is unfortunately impossible to know these new colonists any better. We know, it is true, that several great lords of the West sailed to the East. But we should not be misled: these lords, with very rare exception, did not stay in the Holy Land but, after touring the holy places and taking part in a few skirmishes against the Moslems, returned home. We are sometimes told that the younger sons of great families left for the Middle East. This would appear logical, but, we must admit, we have insufficient proof that it was true.[4] On the contrary, that the surnames of the immigrants, as the documents of the kingdom attest, are Syrian or Palestinian (a fact that greatly astonished their contemporary, the chronicler Fulcher of Chartres)[5] seems to prove that these settlers were of rather modest origins and had no reason to retain surnames drawn from their European possessions.[6]

The first concern of the kings was to use these knights in the arduous task of securing the country from the Moslems. They therefore took them into their service as royal vassals. Some of the great lords who remained in the East after the First Crusade, such as Tancred, did the same. But the flood of newcomers had to be supported. The "normal" method would have been to give the conquered territories as fiefs. The kings acted otherwise, however; Godfrey of Bouillon, for example, preferred to give town and city revenues as fiefs. Furthermore, many knights were simply retained directly in the service of the royal house. Even in the time of Baldwin I the chronicles still speak of knights belonging to the "house of Godfrey."[7] It is impossible to say whether the hesitation of the princes to enfeoff their land is a consequence of the small size of the royal domain at the beginning of the conquest, or the result of a far-seeing policy aimed at putting a tight rein on the knights, at restraining their freedom of action.[8] The Normans, conquering England, did the same thing; and forty years after the conquest, the kings of England preferred to pay salaries or to grant sources of revenue to their knights rather than to enfeoff them with lands.[9] However, the inevitable process of infeudation could not be arrested; and under Baldwin I, with the expansion of the frontiers and the integration of the lands of independent lords into the kingdom, the land began to be granted in fief. These grants drew the first lines of the future feudal map of the kingdom and at the same time formed the basis of its political organization.

The origins of the feudal seigniory, it must be said, are extremely obscure. Thus we do not know the principle by which a simple fief, destined to remain such in the royal domain, was distinguished from the fief that would become a barony or an independent seigniory. Was it the size of the fief? We have no way of telling, since the earliest acts of investiture have disappeared. In the thirteenth century jurists would maintain that any lord having enough vassals to make up a court could have his own justice.[10] Did they mean that every lord having the three vassals necessary to make up a court became *ipso facto* a justicer lord, a lord with rights of justice? If this was the jurists' intention, the explanation does not fit the first enfeoffments very well. We should prefer to imagine that the creation of a seigniory in the Latin Kingdom was expressly accompanied by the grant of feudal rights of justice and that elsewhere, where lands were conquered independently of the king (such as the principality of the Galilee), feudal justice was automatically retained when the land was integrated into the kingdom. Yet others probably won these rights through *de facto* evolution. In 1120, however, the king continued to possess the right to interfere in seignorial justice.[11]

While the feudal regime was crystallizing during the first two or three decades of the kingdom's history (1100–1130), the noble class was taking shape.

If continual immigration and colonization explain the creation of baronies and seigniories, it was the continual state of war that accounts for the most characteristic trait of the knightly class: the instability of its families and of their possessions. It is astonishing to note the tiny number of seignorial landholders who succeeded in handing their estates on to their descendants between 1100 and 1130. Hebron, for example, conquered in 1099, had its revenues enfeoffed to Gerard of Avesne. By the middle of 1100 it was again in the hands of King Baldwin I, who enfeoffed it to Gaudemar Carpinel (whose descendants remain unknown); the city later belonged to Roger of Haifa (1102), Hugh of Rebecq (1104), and Gautier Mahomet (1107–1115), persons apparently unrelated. Only in 1115 did a seignorial family of Hebron appear.[12] This case is extreme, but not exceptional, as the history of Haifa proves. First promised by Godfrey of Bouillon to Gaudemar Carpinel, the city was taken away from him by Tancred in 1100, then given back to Baldwin I after Tancred's departure.

The king then gave it to Rohart (who died in 1107). In 1109 it was again in Tancred's hands for a short time, then returned to the royal domain. Only under Baldwin II was Haifa linked to the name of Vivien, the father of Payen II (*circa* 1138) who became lord of the city.[13] The history of the principality of the Galilee had no fewer ups and downs. After its conquest the territory was turned into a principality by Tancred (1099); then enfeoffed by Baldwin I to Hugh of St.-Omer (1100). Upon Hugh's death (1106), Baldwin gave it to Gervais of Basoches, who was captured by the Moslems in 1108; given to Tancred in 1109, the Galilee soon returned to the royal domain and was then enfeoffed to Jocelin of Courtenay in 1113. The three next lords of the principality belonged, so it appears (but it is not certain), to the family of Bures (until 1168). The principality then went back to the family of St.-Omer until in 1173 it came into the domain of the famous Raymond of Tripoli.[14]

These incessant changes of seignorial families explain the obscurity that surrounds the early history of the seigniories. The later possessors, who were not related to their predecessors, did not bother to keep a record of their genealogies. For proof one only need look at the case of Beyrouth. Fallen to the Christians in 1110 and enfeoffed to Fulk of Guines, Beyrouth's lord is not cited in a text before 1125—Gautier I Brisebarre, who was no relation to Falk of Guines. Gautier's brother, who succeeded him in 1127, was the true founder of the seignorial family.[15] Sometimes these seignorial changes were the result of fights with the king, as was the case with the lord of Jaffa from the family of Le Puiset,[16] or the lords of Oultre-Jourdain from the family of Le Puy.[17] Under these conditions, it was the family that took solid root—such as the Garniers of Caesarea-Sidon (appearing around 1108), both of whose branches continued for nearly a century—that was the exception.[18]

Warfare, which took its heavy toll of prisoners and dead, was the main cause of these changes. But one should not neglect the character of the immigration itself, the work of younger sons or of young men, very few of whom were married when they left for the East. Economic motives not being among the main reasons for immigration, the immedate departure of entire families from their European homes was not necessary. It was only when the married knight was well established in the Latin Kingdom that he thought of bringing over his family.[19]

It was to this society, formed by successive waves of immigrants, that the earliest legislation applied. Its purpose seems to have been to help the knightly class put roots down in the conquered country. Only an analysis of this legislation—which has not previously been done with this in mind—will allow us to delimit more clearly the shape of the noble class and the problems its existence created.

The earliest legislation chiefly concerned rights of succession and infeudation.[20] An early *assise* allowed women to inherit land in the absence of male heirs.[21] This decision moved in a direction opposite to contemporary tendencies in Europe, but suited the conditions and demands of life in the Latin Kingdom. The knight who had devoted his life to the service of the king and the country was assured that if chance did not grant him a male heir, he could leave the fief he had acquired through hardship and danger to his daughter. He was thus more strongly attached to his new country; and that also served the state.

Another *assise* (an early one, although we cannot precisely fix its date) established the terms and conditions of infeudation. According to John of Ibelin, "Ancient fiefs descend to all heirs;"[22] in other words, investiture assured possession of a fief to the knight who received it and to all his descendants, direct and collateral.[23] This was of the greatest importance, for it enlarged the right of succession at a time when such tendencies were not common[24] and by this, again, helped the knightly class to establish itself. Since many of the new immigrants were not married and death and captivity worked their ravishments, nothing was more natural than to compensate those who fought by guaranteeing that their family, even distant family, might enjoy the fruits of their bravery. At the same time the *assise* induced relatives both near and distant to join the immigrant in the hope of inheriting his fief.

Still another *assise* fixing the rules of succession to fiefs had the same object: no knight who already possessed a fief could enter into possession of another one due him by the common law of succession. The second fief went to his younger brother if the brother had as yet no fief, or even—as a result of the enlargement of the group who could inherit—to any other relation who did not yet have a fief.[25] Evidently, the concern here was that as large a number of knights as possible should establish themselves within the confines of the small kingdom. This *assise* prevented the accumulation of fiefs in the hands of a small number of noble families; it facilitated the establishment of a large number of knights belonging to the same line. Another one with the same intent prohibited the subinfeudation of parts of fiefs unless the lord retained more than the total of the land subinfeudated;[26] thus the lords were obliged to support a large number of household knights without weakening the economic potential of their fiefs.

The oldest legislation of the kingdom thus throws some light on the formation of the noble class. It was, furthermore, the work of a strong central power, which found its most complete expression in the *assise* on the dispossession of vassals by the king, promulgated under Baldwin II (1119–1130) or Baldwin III (1143–1163).[27] As yet there was nothing to limit that power. The knights were gradually establishing themselves as a class; they undoubtedly had some kind of class consciousness, but not enough to form the basis for a baronial opposition. Its members changed too often, their roots in the country were too weak, and new waves of immigration shook the weakly mortared structure too often for any noble opposition party to have a chance against the king.

In contrast to this weak and heterogeneous class, the king drew strength from his position as commander in time of war and as the source of honor and favor in time of peace. His domain at the time was quite large: the great ports and the revenues from commerce belonged to him, as well as vast territories (all of Judea and Samaria). The principality of the Galilee, the only one that could compare to his domain, cut a poor figure next to Jaffa, Tyre, and St.-Jean d'Acre.[28] The king therefore had at his disposition both land and money, not to speak of the fiefs that so often returned to him on the failure of seignorial lines. Nor ought we to forget that feudal wardship of minors and widows gave the king still other means to reward his vassals' services. Philip of Novara[29] informs us that the rule allowing noble women to choose their husbands freely, the rule in force immediately after the conquest, was replaced by arbitrary royal choice, imposing on noble widows the knights chosen by the king. This change, which probably occurred under Baldwin II (1119–1130) or shortly thereafter,[30] still further enlarged the king's power and his grip on the knightly class, whose fortunes depended almost entirely upon him.

II. THE PERIOD OF TRANSITION: THE GROWING IMPORTANCE OF THE NOBILITY

The moment when this primitive structure began to change, when a greater social cohesion began to turn this political regime in a new direction is impossible to fix with any certainty. We think that sometime during the reigns of Fulk of Anjou (1131–43) and Baldwin III (1143–1163), the change took place that brought about a lessening of royal power; the period of Amalric I (1163–1174) opened a new period in the constitutional life of the kingdom.

About 1130 one can discover the first signs of opposition to royal power and at the same time a new stability among seignorial families. Almost immediately after Fulk of Anjou came to power, two great revolts broke out: one led by Hugh of Le Puiset, count of Jaffa, and the other by Romain of Le Puy, lord of Oultre-Jourdain.[31] Twenty years later the country was again in the throes of a civil war; the support of aristocratic factions decided the disputed succession between Queen Melisende and her son Baldwin III. To be sure, royal power was not completly shaken; the king was still the head of the kingdom, but the revolts, a phenomenon unknown at an earlier period, marked a change in the balance of power between king and vassals.

This change will be shown by analysis of the development of the noble class during the thirty years that separate the beginning of Fulk's reign from the beginning of that of Amalric I.

The first impression one receives is that of stability. In startling contrast to the preceding period, we see the noble families now firmly established in their seigniories. Succession has become regular; genealogies are continuous and clear—proof that the seignorial families have become rooted in their patrimonies. There remains no trace of any important line becoming extinct and thereby escheating an important fief back to the royal domain. On the contrary, fiefs were passed to related families when there was no male heir, or at the time of a marriage.

New seignorial lines came into being as new seigniories were created: Casal Imbert (*circa* 1123), the fief of Joffroi le Tort (*circa* 1125), Caymont (*circa* 1139), Ibelin (1141), Scandalion (*circa* 1148), the fief of the Chamberlain (*circa* 1149), Blanchegarde (1166), etc. Colonization by the knightly class became more dense. To settle the knights, means of support had to be found. These means were the royal domain, handed out in large slices. Under Amalric I this effort stopped (unless one considers his Egyptian expeditions to be colonizing movements); the creation of the seigniory of Jocelin of Courtenay, formed by bringing together fiefs of different origins (*circa* 1179–1192), was a late and altogether exceptional case. By 1150 the feudal map of the kingdom had been fixed and would hardly vary until the end of the First Kingdom.

New problems now had to be faced. The kingdom had reached its saturation point. New arrivals found it difficult to place themselves in a now rigid feudal hierarchy. The only way for the crown to win the allegiance of the new members of the noble class was to grant yet more fragments of the royal domain, which was becoming too small for comfort. From time to time the king managed to reconstitute a reserve, as when he bought the seigniory of Beyrouth from its impoverished possessor, giving in return the unimportant fief of Blanchegarde (1166).[32] But the gradual impoverishment of the royal domain was not noticeably slowed—think only of Nablus, given in dowry to Queen Mary, Amalric's wife, which passed in 1176 into the hands of the Ibelins,[33] or of the rich fief of Oultre-Jourdain, which had left the royal domain and had belonged since 1160 to the Millys.[34] This shrinkage of the royal domain meant the weakening of the crown, which could strengthen itself against the great lords only by acquiring new vassals; and this could be done only by cutting yet more fiefs from the royal domain. The king's means of action became dangerously reduced.

At the same time a caste spirit began to form among nobility and knights while the noble class, socially more and more differentiated, split into two distinct groups. A caste spirit had already existed in latent form among the nobles and knights of the First Crusade; one may see it in the first efforts to organize the kingdom. Godfrey of Bouillon[35] or Baldwin I had established a special court for the nobility, distinguished from the court of the bourgeoisie by its clientele, its procedure, and its penalties. But the conscious formulation of this caste feeling appeared only with the rise of aristocratic dynasties around which it could crystallize.

Two *assises* expressed this new spirit. First, "an *assise* that a lord may arrest neither knight nor lady for debt"[36]—probably promulgated on the occasion of a general discussion of debts—which made a characteristic distinction: whereas neither a knight nor a noble lady nor anyone who had pledged faith and rendered homage could be imprisoned for debt, one of the bourgeoisie could be imprisoned and even forced to work until his debt was completely paid. This double standard was a legal recognition of the caste spirit. This *assise,* which goes back to the twelfth century, was undoubtedly promulgated after 1146 (for at this date nobles were still being arrested for debt).[37] It probably dates from the reign of Baldwin III or Amalric I.

The same spirit inspired the so-called *assise* of Bilbeis (1168), which distinguished nobles from non-nobles serving on horseback; the former were not required to dismount during an attack on a besieged city.[38] The *chevauchée,* the arisocratic form of combat, became the monopoly of a caste, even if it immobilized the cavalry beneath the walls of a besieged fortress. Such was the behavior required by the knightly code.

The formation of a new class of great lords—a class whose rise was marked by rebellions at the beginning of this period and by intervention in a disputed succession to the crown at its end—reinforced this spirit. Everywhere that it existed, this upper stratum of the nobility manifested itself by similar signs, by rules tending to favor the accumulation of land in its hands. In Europe this was achieved by several means: by the *Leihezwang,* which forced the prince to grant out immediately any fief that fell into his hands by the disappearance of a noble line; by restricting marriages of the nobility to a narrow circle of families; by rules of succession favoring the concentration of landed wealth in a few hands. The Latin Kingdom was no exception, for special legislation facilitated the same development. These various *assises* following the first period of conquest all belong to the twelfth century, although one cannot date them exactly. We are inclined to place them about the middle of the century, an estimate that seems to be corroborated by the general direction of developments as well as by indications drawn from independent sources.

Accumulation of fiefs in the hands of the high nobility had been restricted by old legislation whose intent was contrary to noble interests. These acts had sought to colonize the country densely and had opposed concentration of fiefs all the more, since as immigration continued unabated, the pool of available fiefs slowly evaporated. In this first conflict between the interests of the nobility and that of the kingdom, the nobility came out on top. Abrogating the earliest legislation, a new *assise* allowed a vassal already holding a fief to succeed to another as long as he hired a fighting-man to do military service for it.[39] This reform served the interests of eldest sons who, usually already fief-holders, could inherit other lands, accumulate several fiefs, and thus establish a foundation for a growing family fortune.

Rules concerning the wardship of widows were modified in the same sense. Although the power of the king to choose a second husband for a noble widow might often have wounded the sensibilities of the woman concerned, it was the noble houses themselves that led the opposition. The widow's "friends" (that is, family), says Philip of Novara, were wronged because the king asked neither their counsel nor their consent. Under their pressure a new rule was introduced: the king was to propose three barons to the widow, from among whom she was obliged to choose her husband.[40] A small concession, to be sure, but one that left the widow's family a limited choice and undoubtedly presupposed their advice and consent. Meanwhile the nobility prepared a new weapon. Although obliged to choose her husband from the three candidates proposed by the king, under pain of losing her fief by *commise,* the widow (adds Philip of Novara) could refuse all of them on the grounds of disparagement or misalliance. The king thus found himself forced to propose to the heiress candidates of her own social rank and of similar wealth, or else the widow, with the advice of her family, might refuse the marriage.[41]

The results were clear. Not only did the king lose control of wealthy heiresses and thus of one means to reward his followers; the new rules moreover favored the confinement of noble marriages to a very small number of families and helped a few houses of high nobility to accumulate great wealth. The upper stratum of the nobility closed itself off. The knights, legally members of the same class, became a lower order.

These high nobles, who could be described—in the words of Gislebert of Mons—as *"potentes parentela et turribus fortes,"* [the powerful, strong in family and in towers] began to lay claim to power in the kingdom, made themselves the guardians of a kind of Palestino-Syrian national feeling, and looked upon all newcomers as intruders and foreigners. Their xenophobia was the common factor connecting the opposition to Manasses of Hierges, constable and favorite of Queen Melisende; the opposition to Thierry of Flanders, the eternal crusader who never succeeded in carving out a seigniory for himself in the East; and the opposition to Renaud of Châtillon, Milo de Plancy, and the two Lusignans —of whom one nevertheless became the Tragic King. To the nobles these newcomers were nothing but rivals who could find a place for themselves in the Eastern sun only by marrying a rich heiress. And royal support was not always enough to assure their success. Some, like Châtillon and Lusignan, achieved their object; others, like Manasses of Hierges, were forced to leave the country, even after marrying an heiress and receiving her dowry; others, such as Milo de Plancy, were simply assassinated.

Beneath this choice aristocracy crowded the mass of small knights, "noble" by birth—an anonymous mass about whom the chroniclers tell very little and the documents nothing at all. The kingdom's service list (unfortunately twenty or thirty years later than the period with which we are here concerned)[42] only half reveals them, but it can be of some use if we correct it in matters of detail. In any event, an analysis of this list is indispensable for an understanding of the reign of Amalric I, during which these ordinary knights played an important role in the constitutional life of the kingdom.

From the viewpoint of feudal ties the knights can be divided into royal vassals and seignorial vassals, the latter being rear-vassals of the king. Toward 1170, 257 knights were attached to the royal domain, 402 to the lay seigniories, and sixteen to ecclesiastical seigniories. Thus, about 40 percent were connected to the royal domain and 60 percent to seignorial domains.[43] The information available concerning the knights of the royal domain allows us to define with some precision the structure of this social class, a class that was not perfectly homogeneous.[44] We may generalize these conclusions to cover the seignorial domains; for there is no reason to suppose a different social structure there and, furthermore, we have a few additional pieces of information that allow us to verify these conclusions.

Of the 213 knights of the royal domain,[45] 59 owed only their own service; sixteen owed, in addition, the service of one vassal; eight owed their own service and that of two vassals; six their own and that of three vassals; two their own and that of four vassals; two their own and that of six vassals; one his own and that of seven vassals. The fief of Le Chamberlain, serving with six knights, was exceptional, as were the Constable's fief, serving with seven, and the fiefs of the Viscount of Nablus and of Balian of Ibelin at Nablus, which served with fourteen knights.

The preponderance of those holding "fiefs of one knight" and of knights serving with but one or two vassals (who hardly differ from the first) is striking. Thus, to sense the reality of this feudal hierarchy we must know what this "fief of one knight" was and what was the economic situation of these knights who served "with their own body."

In an earlier study we have shown that very few of the knights mentioned in these service lists actually held landed fiefs.[46] Most had only *fiefs en besant,* fief-rents assigned on royal revenues, markets, customs, or maritime ports. This type of fief must have been more common in the seigniories and the parts of the royal domain near the coast than in the interior. For it was in the maritime cities that economic life offered the best conditions for the creation of money-fiefs, even though in the cities of the interior, such as Tiberius in the Galilee and Nablus in Samaria, commerce was developing because of international trade routes and the traffic in rural products on their way to the markets of the maritime cities.

Unfortunately, it is impossible to know the percentage of fiefs that were money-fiefs. Only the frequency with which they appear in the texts and the place they hold in the works of the jurists (who consider them the equals of landed fiefs, consider them, so to say, as "normal" fiefs)[47] indicate their great diffusion. Saladin's attacks and the loss of territory that followed meant that money-fiefs became preponderant in the thirteenth century. One has only to compare the number of knights recruited in the Latin Kingdom with that raised at the same time in France. The "knights of the French kingdom"[48] who owed service to the king in 1216 numbered about eight hundred; the French army that took part in the battle of Bouvines, three-fifths of the total contingent, counted the same number of knights and a few less sergeants than the Latin Kingdom threw into the battle of Hattin.[49] To be sure, France recruited three or four times the number of knights that owed service to the king. But how could the arid earth of Palestine, whose breadth was no greater than that of a French province, support some 675 knights[50] if it had disposed of only its landed revenues?

The average value of the money-fief seems to have been an income of four hundred to five hundred *besants*.[51] What was this worth? No study gives the answer, but according to a source published (and forgotten) a long time ago,[52] the daily wage of a knight in the mid-thirteenth century amounted to approximately 7 *s.* 6 *d.*, an amount about equivalent to a gold *besant* of the Latin Kingdom.[53] The annual upkeep of a knight thus cost about three hundred fifty *besants,* not counting such extraordinary expenses as the costly replacement of a sick or dead horse. The margin between the revenue of a 400-*besant* fief and a knight's expenses was therefore minimal, if it existed at all.

The noble class in the third quarter of the twelfth century was thus composed of an exclusive circle of barons and justicer lords at the summit. There existed hardly more than twenty-four important seigniories, which as a result of marriage and inheritance within a small group were held by no more than ten lords, of whom many possessed several seigniories—thus, less than ten families held these twenty-four seigniories, since several lords belonged to the same houses (without mentioning family alliances, close or distant). Between this small number of great lords and the mass of knights there existed no intermediate class, no well-off knights in possession of large enough fiefs to be able to enfeoff, in turn, a number of their own vassals. The feudal hierarchy in the Latin Kingdom was thus greatly simplified: there existed scarcely more than one degree of vassalage. The royal domain at Jerusalem consisted of twenty vassals and twenty-one rear-vassals; at St.-Jean d'Acre, apart from the fiefs of the officers of the kingdom, of twenty-three vassals and nine rear-vassals; at Tyre it comprised fourteen vassals and fourteen rear-vassals; at Nablus, not counting the fief of an Ibelin, thirty-five vassals and thirty-five rear-vassals. On the lay seigniories, whose extent was less than that of the royal domain, subinfeudation must have been even rarer.

This populous class of *chevaliers d'un écu* [sixty-shilling knights], afforced by mercenaries recruited for the great campaigns, occupied a social and economic position that was manifestly inferior. A few of them held landed fiefs; most had only their money-fiefs. For one and the other, income barely exceeded expenses. Their outlook and their conduct must, as a result, have been profoundly marked. Enjoying the prestige their rank conferred among the conquered population and the bourgeoisie, they did not have the means to lead an aristocratic way of life (Weber's *Herrenwesen*). Furthermore, their fief-rents denied them the privilege of true nobility that Marc Bloch called "the right to command." The slenderness of their means made them strictly dependent on their immediate lords and, thus, in no way comparable to the English squire, the lord of the manor, pillar and foundation of Plantagenets' administration.

III. THE PERIOD OF AMALRIC I AND THE PREDOMINANCE OF THE GREAT FAMILIES

Under Amalric I the Latin Kingdom achieved its political apogee, while feudal legislation continued to adjust to the new social and economic realities. During his reign the most famous statute of the Latin Kingdom, the so-called *assise* concerning liege homage (*assise sur la ligece*), was enacted. At the same time probably, far-reaching changes in the rules of infeudation were taking place.

The first fiefs of the kingdom had been conferred on vassals and their entire family lines both direct and collateral. Later, as both Philip of Novara and John of Ibelin inform us,[54] infeudation was restricted to a vassal and his direct descendants born of his legitimate wife. (The jurists give no date for this change, but we may date it approximately, for an act of infeudation of 1152 already contains the formula[55] that treatises of jurisprudence will later reproduce.)

Whom did this change profit? The king, now able to take back fiefs from those lines that disappeared? But what advantage could the king possibly have from the return to his domain of a simple knight's fief? He needed knights more than land and rents. He would have to infeudate the escheated land immediately, in order to assure military service. The advantage would be clearer in the event one of the great seignorial houses was extinguished. But this was not a very probable occurrence. The old families, deeply rooted in the country, whose wealth eased the way to marriage alliances, did not expire so easily. And even if a direct line did disappear, the king could not profit because the great families remained enfeoffed according to the old law rather than the new: their fiefs descended to all possible heirs or heiresses. If anyone profited from the change in the law, it was the possessors of the great seigniories, within which a single knight's fief counted more than in the royal domain. But still the real object of this new *assise* remains unclear.

Another *assise* of Amalric I, conceding important privileges to the class of great lords, testifies to the way their relations were developing. Maritime affairs held a particular interest for the king; it was he, in all probability, who gave the kingdom the *Cour de la chaîne,* a special commercial and maritime court. Among the chapters of the *Livre des assises des bourgeois* on maritime questions, the following statement appears: "Whenever a ship may wreck, the lord of the land must have the mainsail and tiller of a ship broken up on the sea or on land, for King Amalric gives this liberty to all the Kingdom of Jerusalem."[56] This is irrefutable evidence that the Crown had retained until the mid-twelfth century the right to wreck on the entire coast, as it had, until 1130, a monopoly of the ports. Infeudation of large coastal stretches had certainly reduced the king's powers, but baronies and great seigniories had not been closed to royal intervention—at least in cases of shipwreck. Now, faced with the increasing power of the high nobility, Amalric was forced to give up this last vestige of his rights. One recalls the *Charte aux Normands,* which Louis X granted in 1315 to the coastal lords of Normandy.

What about the *assise* concerning liege homage? The circumstances of its promulgation remain obscure, and the manner in which it was applied, even more so. Nevertheless, in the light of the social climate that we have described (and without the aid of new documents) we can reach some conclusions that are quite different from those usually accepted.

According to all the sources, the *assise* concerning liege homage was issued after a war between Amalric I and Gerard, lord of Sidon, a war whose apparent cause was the arbitrary dispossession by Gerard of one of his vassals.[57] Can we accept this explanation?

We must remember, first of all, that when Amalric I came to the throne, he had to face violent opposition. Even the chronicler William of Tyre, usually so discreet when it comes to anything that might embarrass the court of Jerusalem,[58] does not hide the fact that only a few barons, backed by the clergy and the people, supported the king against all the remainder of the nobility.[59] The nobility was contesting Amalric's right to succeed to the throne: a characteristic feature of the social evolution that had taken place, a result of the shift in the balance of power in favor of the noble families. Even the support of the clergy and the people had its price: Amalric was forced to repudiate his wife.[60] In these circumstances, did the king have the means to promulgate an *assise* that, as a matter of course, required the consent of the great men of the kingdom and that, at the same time, had the diminution of their power as its object?

Another difficulty: Amalric carried on his war against Gerard with the aid of a feudal army. Would the nobility have fought one of the most powerful of its members in order to put a minor rear-vassal back into his fief? Furthermore, it is rather difficult to imagine the hard-headed, greedy Amalric going to war for some abstract notion of justice.[61]

In reality, although it was the avowed aim of the war, neither the king nor the nobility were fighting for the rights of a minor rear-vassal. The nobility certainly expected some profit from the venture. (E. Meynial has suggested that the king, to gain their support, had agreed that fiefs falling to noblemen already enfeoffed might be served by a paid warrior,[62] a change we prefer to ascribe to an earlier period.)

If the nobility took part in the war against Gerard of Sidon, it was rather because this war meant a tacit abrogation of the ancient *assise* of Baldwin II (or Baldwin III) that allowed the king to dispossess his vassals at will.[63] The war punished a lord who had dispossessed his own vassal without judgment. It followed that the rule ought *a fortiori* to apply to the king's vassals, to his noble tenants-in-chief. In fact, Gerard, a lord who had gone so far as to make Sidon a nest of pirates[64] lost little. The nobles finally stepped between the combatants; peace was re-established, the lord of Sidon made his due show of humility, and the rear-vassal was restored his rights. More importantly, the judicial precedent was immediately confirmed by an *assise* that was vowed to long life.

The *assise* concerning liege homage had many facets and many ramifications. Historians, however, have paid little attention to anything but the oath of liege homage it required from all rear-vassals of the Crown. To be sure, the liege homage now given by all fief-holders created a direct link between the mass of knights and the king. One should not forget, however, that the primary object of this oath was to make all rear-vassals members of the royal High Court and to allow them to demand justice there if their immediate lord did not give it to them. This new link, we are told, was directed, or could have been directed, against the great nobility. But we never see it applied in this fashion: the explanation that it could strengthen a strong king and weaken a weak one is insufficient.

To a certain degree, it is the superficial analogy between the oath of liege homage in the Latin Kingdom and the famous Oath of Salisbury taken by the English and Normans to William the Conqueror in 1086, that has influenced historians' commentaries. If the English oath was the foundation of Anglo-Norman royal power, then it is plausible to believe that the oath of liege homage played an analogous role in the Kingdom of Jerusalem. But this was not so.

The *assise* concerning liege homage is known to us almost uniquely through thirteenth-century sources. At this times its influence was felt throughout the judicial and constitutional life of the kingdom. But the documentation does not allow us to claim without fear of error that this was so immediately after the *assise*'s promulgation. In the thirteenth century its influence was manifested above all in three large areas:

1. In the area of *politics:* all fief-holders, being the king's liege men, could take part in the deliberations of the High Court, whose competence extended to political as well as administrative and judicial questions.

2. In the *judicial* field: a lord's vassal dispossessed without judgment of the court of his seigniory had the right to proceed against his lord before the king.

3. In the field of *feudal relations:* every vassal, doing liege homage to the king, from now on owed him fealty against all. Liege homage could be rendered only to the king; it became a royal monopoly.[65] At the same time, all noblemen and knights holding fiefs became peers with respect to the king, for all vassals of the same lord formed a community of equals with respect to their common lord.

But in fact, the *assise* could not have had any real political influence. All we know of the Kingdom of Jerusalem and of every other medieval state allows us to affirm with certainty that neither the king nor the great lords could draw any advantage from having the knights join in the deliberations of the royal court. A medieval *parlamentum* was not an anticipation of a modern national assembly; even in the East votes were weighed rather than counted. From time to time simple knights might play a determined role. During certain military expeditions the group the chroniclers call the "*populus*"—knights and non-nobles—forced a decision on their leaders. But the "people in arms" had already played this role during the First Crusade, and its force was not augmented by the *assise* concerning liege homage.

The judicial side of the problem is quite different. The war that Amalric I won over his vassal did not result in a constitutional victory for the monarchy: quite the contrary. Victory signified the safeguarding of a vassal's rights against his lord's arbitrary proceedings and, as explicit or tacit corollary, an identical guarantee to the tenants-in-chief against their own lord, the king.

As a further consequence, a rear-vassal, if injured, could in principle call all the fief-holders from his seigniory to sit in judgment with his lord on the case and ask his fellow vassals to refuse their service to their common lord, if he did not do justice. Furthermore, the rear-vassal could now call on the king, his liege lord, to force his immediate lord to do justice or to execute the judgment of the court. If the immediate lord refused, he lost for life his rights of jurisdiction. In principle, then, this was a victory for the rear-vassals. But was not this victory more apparent than real? To decide this we must first discover the men concerned and how they acted.

Note first of all that a rear-vassal could not present his complaint before the High Court except in two very well-defined situations: when his immediate lord refused to do justice, or when his lord had condemned him without judgment. The High Court was never a "court of appeal" in the modern sense. Its doors opened to rear-vassals only when the doors of their own lord's court had remained closed. If the seignorial court gave a judgment the vassal thought wrong, he could not carry this case before the High Court but could only accuse his judges of "false judgment"—and engage in single combat with each of them before the seignorial court, to prove his accusation. In other words, a lord could easily prevent a vassal from appealing to the king's court by judging the case himself.

In this seignorial court—composed of knights largely without independent means, whose fiefs were usually money payments from the lord's treasury—the lord enjoyed unequaled prestige. His vassals had neither the power nor the ability to resist strong pressure from his side. Of course it does not follow that the lord could openly dictate the sentence of his court or openly disregard the prescriptions of custom. In everyday affairs, however, the lord's opinion must have weighed heavily. Against his lord's opinion, a rear-vassal had hardly any recourse. Calling his peers to sit in judgment was no aid, and he could neither appeal to the High Court nor call the vassals of another lord to sit in judgment. Here is the most important effect of the *assise* concerning liege homage: the knights of the kingdom did not become peers at all times nor everywhere; their "peerage" was neither absolute nor universal; they became peers only vis-à-vis the king. They received no right to involve themselves in the business of any seignorial court other than their own; seignorial affairs remained the business of the lord and his own vassals.

It is obvious that the *assise* concerning liege homage was not a general remedy for the difficulties of rear-vassals; it did not correct and probably was not issued with the intention of correcting anything but the most crying abuses. It had preventive value—no lord would have liked to be cited before the High Court by one of his own vassals who would have then had the right to call the vassals of other seigniories. It was a salutary threat hung over the heads of the great lords, but not a dangerous one.

The king, however, had more immediate vassals than did the nobles; the menace that was partially effective against them must have been much more effective against him. His immediate vassals, the justicer lords, could call all the members of their class, of their "Estate," to take part in giving judgment—against him. For all nobles were peers in relation to the king. And in all the known cases in which the *assise* concerning liege homage was invoked, it was invoked not against a justicer lord but against the king. Raoul of Tiberias, dispossessed by Amalric II for treason, without judgment of the High Court, called the nobles of the kingdom to sit in judgment (then, faced with the obstinate refusal of the king, renounced his case and quit the kingdom).[66] It was different with the famous lord of Beyrouth who, dispossessed by order of Frederick II, called on his peers and succeeded in depriving the Emperor of his vassals' service.[67] The same Emperor's *baile,* Balian of Sidon, having received an order not to execute a judgment of the High Court in favor of the Princess Alix against the Teutonic Order, found himself deprived of the service of the nobility and knights, who had been called upon to aid the Princess. Even in this case, however, the Princess found herself obliged to absolve her "peers" of their obligation.[68] Again, Henry II, king of Cyprus and Jerusalem, saw his knights withhold their service until his vassal, Philip of Gibelet, received the fief-rent due him.[69] On another occasion, led by a certain Guillaume Raymond, Henry's vassals—described as "a great mass of men, most of whom were sergeants, more than there were of knights"—demanded their pay which had been too long delayed and threatened to renounce their service. Only the aged lord of Beyrouth, the finest jurist of his age, rid the king of this menace by finding that the vassals' procedure had been faulty.[70] In all these cases, the only ones we know, it was always the king who was threatened; it was his immediate vassals, justicer lords, knights of his house and domain, who used the *assise* concerning liege homage through which every knight became "peer" of his lord and his fellow knights, but only with respect to the king.[71]

The importance of the *assise* for feudal relations came from the obligation it imposed on vassals to quit the service of their immediate lord if he refused to be judged by the High Court (if the lord rebelled) and to join the king's service. This royal "advantage" (as it was called), while important, remained limited—as the interpretation of its content by contemporary jurists demonstrates. Those vassals who left their lord's service to join the king were within forty days to be paid a recompense equal to the revenues they lost. If the king could not pay this indemnity, they could return to their lord and the king thus lost their support. What this meant in practice, since the royal treasury was usually empty during the thirteenth century, was that the king had to suppress a rebellious vassal within forty days or lose the support of his rear-vassals. Neither chronicles nor jurists, however, mention any case that would allow us to gauge the real import of this clause. Its true value must have resided less in its judicial form than in its moral force: it was a means of prevention, giving a prospective rebellious lord a subject for reflection before he dared defy the king and his High Court.

The *assise* concerning liege homage contains another clause that has never attracted historians' attention. If the king has reason to suspect one of his men of possible rebellion "all the people of the towns and castles of the king's vassal must, at the king's request or command, swear fealty to the king."[72] Thus, after the war against Gerard of Sidon the inhabitants of Sidon and Beaufort (another castle of the seigniory) swore fealty to the king. Although we know of no other example of this oath after the promulgation of the *assise* concerning liege homage, one is to be found—curiously enough—in 1155, about ten years before the *assise* appeared: the subjects of the canons of the Holy Sepulchre swore fealty to the canons, but reserved the *fidelitas regis,* their fealty to the king.[73]

We can probably detect an even older example of this kind of oath in a text of 1142 in which Count Raymond of Tripoli gave Raphana to the Knights of St. John, "in peace, freely in alms and dominion and liege fealty of all men, both knights and bourgeois, holding these lands and possessions."[74] Thus an oath of liege homage, obligatory on all possessors of land, whether vassals, rear-vassals, or bourgeois, existed in the county of Tripoli nearly twenty years before the *Assise* concerning liege homage. Was this a usage peculiar to Raphana or to the county of Tripoli? It is impossible to say. However, the oaths of fealty taken by the colonists of Mahomaria[75] in 1155 show that an analogous usage existed in the Latin Kingdom in the days of Baldwin III, the predecessor of Amalric I.

Another document emanating from the court of Baldwin III (1161) shows that the oath of liege homage to the king was already being taken by a rear-vassal. When Philip of Milly acquired the great fief of Oultre-Jourdain from the King, he was required to safeguard the possessions of John Gomman, who until this time had been vassal of the King. The King, furthermore, stipulated "that the aforesaid John, for the land he holds beyond the Jordan, will do homage to me the aforesaid king and service to Lord Philip."[76] Since this newly created seigniory of Oultre-Jourdain was autonomous, like all the great seigniories, and since its lord became a justicer lord, it is possible that this was a special case in which liege homage was given the King to protect a former vassal, now "mediatized," against any possible injury from his new lord.

These facts lead us to conclude that the most striking clauses of the *assise*—liege homage from rear-vassals and oaths of fealty from the bourgeoisie of the great seigniories to the king—were not so revolutionary as some would like to think. At the most, the *assise* now generalized and rendered obligatory for the entire kingdom a technique used in exceptional circumstances during the previous twenty years.

In conclusion, the *assise* concerning liege homage appears to have a different import from that ordinarily ascribed to it. It did not strengthen the king nor the position of the knights and rear-vassals. Its only beneficiaries were the members of the high nobility, the lords holding rights of justice. A union of the king and the mass of knights was conceivable only if the king were a Machiavellian prince (inconceivable in the thirteenth century) and the knights were like the English gentry. The knights of the Latin Kingdom had poor fiefs or modest rents, however, and therefore could not form a serious opposition to the high nobility.

The heroic but sad reign of Baldwin IV (1174–1185) marked the final collapse of royal power. From then on, the fight for power was not between the king and the nobility, but between two parties, two factions of the nobility, one of which received the support of a few members of the royal court.[77] It was the great families, rich and powerful, who disputed the crown. A historical accident, the succession of a child to the throne (Baldwin V), and the worsening of the political situation put the future of the country into the hands of the nobility. Saladin did not allow the royal power any time to reconstitute itself; and the battle of Hattin (1187) simultaneously marked the end of the First Kingdom and the complete annihilation of royal power.

During the Third Crusade the Western sovereigns, Philip Augustus and Richard the Lion-hearted, would be able to divide up their future conquests in advance, without giving a thought to the King of Jerusalem. Twenty years later, a papal legate, Pelagius, refused to give the King of Jerusalem command of the ill-fated crusade against Damietta (1218–1221).

Only the great families remained. In their honor, Philip of Novara made himself herald of the war against Frederick II. And Marino Sanudo, writing the history of the kingdom in the thirteenth century, did not even think it necessary to divide his narrative according to royal reigns.

NOTES

1. Joshua Prawer, "Les premiers temps de la féodalité dans le royaume latin de Jérusalem" *RHD,* 4me sér., **22** (1954), 401–424.

2. These questions have only in recent years become the object of historical study, in particular in the works of C. Cahen, C. R. Smail and J. Richard. See C. Cahen, "La féodalité et les institutions politiques de l'Orient latin," Accademia Nazionale dei Lincei, Fondazione Alessandro Volta, *Atti dei Convegni,* **12** (1957), 167–191. No useful information is to be found in the old works of Beugnot, Dodu, and Hayeck. However, the works of H. Prutz, *Kulturgeschichte der Kreuzzüge* (1883) and J. L. La Monte, *Feudal Monarchy in the Latin Kingdom of Jerusalem* (1932) explain many important points.

3. On the vassals of Godfrey of Bouillon, see J. C. Andressohn, *The Ancestry and Life of Godfrey of Bouillon* (1947) and C. Moeller, "Les Flamands de Ternois au royaume latin de Jérusalem," *Mélanges P. Fredericq* (1904), pp. 189–203.

4. R. Fawtier, *Les Capétiens et la France* (1942), pp. 193–196, has already attracted attention to this point. Is it not surprising that in Flanders, one of the greatest centers of the crusading movement, no noble family disappeared during the two hundred years of the crusades? See P. Feuchère, "La noblesse du Nord de la France," *Annales, E.S.C.,* **6** (1951), 311 *n.* 4.

5. Fulcherius Carnotensis, *Historia Hierosolymitana* **3**. 37 (*Académie des Inscriptions et Belles-Lettres, Recueil des Historiens des Croisades* [hereinafter *H.Cr.*], *Historiens occidentaux* **3**. 467–468).

6. *Ibid.* p. 468: *"Nos nostri sequuntur de die in diem propinqui et parentes, quaecumque possederant omnino reliquentes, nec etiam volentes. Qui enim illic erant inopes, hic facit eos Deus locupletes . . . qui non habuerat villam, hic . . .*

jam possidet urbem. Quare ergo reverteretur in Occidentem, qui hic taliter invenit Orientem?" [Our relatives and families followed us, willingly leaving behind whatever they had. For those who in their homeland were utterly destitute God here made rich in lands; those who had not even owned a manor, here possessed a city. Why then go back to the West when they had such good fortune in the East?]

7. On the infeudation of town revenues by Godfrey of Bouillon, see Albertus Aquensis, *Historia Hierosolymitana* **7.** 37 (*H.Cr., Hist. occid.* 4. 532), and J. Prawer, "The 'assise de teneure' and the 'assise de vente'—a study of landed property in the Latin Kingdom," *Economic History Review,* 4 (1951), 82 n. 2.

8. A conqueror who was independent of the king, such as Tancred, assured himself the services of knights by distributing tithes of ecclesiastical establishments in the Galilee: *Cartulaire de Mont Thabor* in *Cartulaire de l'ordre des Hospitaliers de Saint-Jean de Jérusalem,* Delaville Le Roulx, ed. (1894–1906) **2,** 898; see also *ibid.,* p. 826, no. 2831.

9. A. L. Poole, *From Domesday Book to Magna Carta* (1951), p. 13.

10. *La Clef des Assises de la Haute Cour,* 60 (*H. Cr., Lois* **1** 584): *"Partout là où le seignor et trois de ces houmes ou plus est, si sont court."* [Wherever there are a lord and three or more of his vassals, there a court exists.] See John of Ibelin, *c.* 164 (*H. Cr., Lois* **1** 254). Feudal jurisdiction is defined in the kingdom by the expression *"droit de court, coins et justice."* On the meaning of this expression see Chandon de Briailles, "Le droit de coins dans le royaume de Jérusalem," *Syria,* **23** (1943), 244–257. See J. Richard, "Les listes des seigneuries dans le Livre de Jean d'Ibelin," *RHD,* 4me sér., **32** (1954), 566 ff. and J. Richard *Le royaume latin de Jérusalem* (1953), p. 85.

11. See J. Prawer, "Les premiers temps de la féodalité." This right to intervene in the independent jurisdiction of baronies and seigniories represented a transitional phase in the growth of absolute seignorial independence.

12. G. Bayer, "Die Kreuzfahrergebiete von Jerusalem und S. Abraham," *Zeitschrift der deutschen Palästina-Vereins* (hereinafter *ZDPV*), **65** (1942), 165 ff. It appears that St.-Abraham did not leave the royal domain until 1161 when the de Milly family acquired it.

13. Du Cange, *Les Familles d'Outremer, s.v. Haifa.*

14. R. Grousset, *Histoire des Croisades,* **2** (1936), appendice, 837 ff.

15. E. Rey, "Les seigneurs de Barut," *Revue de l'Orient Latin,* 4 (1896), 12 ff.; M. E. Nickerson, "The seigneurie of Beirut in the 12th century and the Brisebarre family of Beirut-Blanchegarde," *Byzantion,* **19** (1949), 141 ff.

16. J. L. La Monte, "The Lords of Le Puisset on the Crusades," *Speculum,* **17** (1942), 100 ff.

17. E. Rey, "Les seigneurs de Montréal et de la Terre d'Outre le Jourdain," *Revue de l'Orient Latin,* 4 (1896), 19 ff.

18. Even Caesarea was not originally a fief of the Garnier family, but the fief of one Harpin, viscount of Bourges (died 1102). Eustace Garnier appeared only six years later. See J. L. La Monte, "The Lords of Caesarea in the Period of the Crusades," *Speculum,* **22** (1947), 145 ff. and "The Lords of Sidon in the 12th and the 13th centuries," *Byzantion,* **17** (1944/1945), 183 ff.

19. This explains the severe and frequently repeated legislation against bigamy in the Holy Land.

20. It is impossible to date this legislation exactly. However, as M. Grandclaude has proved, these *assises* belong to the oldest legislation of the kingdom—M. Grandclaude, "Liste d'assises romontant au premier royaume de Jérusalem," *Mélanges Paul Fournier* (1929), 329 ff.

21. Philip of Novara c. 71 (*H.Cr., Lois* **1** 542). M. Grandclaude, "Liste d'assises," p. 335, thinks that this *assise* goes back to Godfrey of Bouillon.

22. John of Ibelin *c.* 150 (*H.Cr., Lois* **1** 233, 235); Philip of Novara *c.* 66 (*ibid.*, p. 537).

23. Philip of Novara *c.* 66 (*ibid.*): *"celui don de tous heirs peut venir et escheir a toz ceaus qui sont heirs de ses biens, soit frere ou seur ou parent, ja ne soit il descendu de la souche dou conqueror, mais qu'il seit de cele part dont le fie muet."* [That which is given 'to *X* and all his heirs' can descend to all those who are heirs to his goods, where brother, sister or other relative, even if they do not come from the same line as the first possessor, as long as they are related to the person who holds the fief.]

24. Collateral succession was not accepted in Germany until the end of the twelfth century under Henry VI. See P. Guilhiermoz, *Essai sur l'origine de la noblesse en France au moyen-âge* (1902), p. 199.

25. Philip of Novara *cc.* 68, 71 (*H.Cr., Lois* **1**. 538, 542); John of Ibelin *cc.* 148, 187 (*ibid.*, pp. 223–224, 297–299). This problem was studied in an excellent article (unfortunately almost forgotten) by E. Meynial, "De quelques particularités des successions féodales dans les Assises de Jérusalem," *RHD*, **16** (1892), 408–426.

26. Philip of Novara *c.* 81 (*H.Cr., Lois* **1**. 553–554); John of Ibelin *cc.* 142, 143, 148, 150, 182 (*ibid.*, pp. 216–217, 223–227, 284–285); *Livre au roi cc.* 38, 46 (*ibid.*, pp. 633–634, 640).

27. On the royal power in this period see J. Prawer, "Les premiers temps de la féodalité" and "Etude sur le Droit des *Assises de Jérusalem*: Droit de Confiscation et Droit d'Exheredation," *RHD*, 4me sér., **39** (1961), 520–551, **40** (1962), 29–42.

28. The best description of the royal domain is given by J. Richard, *Le royaume latin de Jérusalem*, p. 72.

29. Philip of Novara *c.* 86 (*H.Cr., Lois* **1**. 588).

30. See Prawer, "Etude sur le Droit des *Assises de Jérusalem*."

31. Like J. Richard, *Le royaume latin*, p. 90, we think that there were really two revolts, probably contemporaneous and related to each other, and not one revolt as the chronicle of William of Tyre would have one believe.

32. See Bayer, "Die Kreuzfahrergebiete," 165 ff.

33. G. Bayer, "Neapolis und sein Gebiet," *ZDPV*, **63** (1940), 155 ff.

34. Bayer, "Die Kreuzfahrergebiete," 165 ff.

35. Following the famous prologue of John of Ibelin and all the sources that derive from it. See the peculiar discovery of G. Recoura in *Mélanges d'histoire et d'archéologie de l'École française de Rome*, **42** (1925), 147–166.

36. John of Ibelin *c.* 188. (*H.Cr., Lois* **1**. 300–301).

37. M. Grandclaude recognized that the *assise* belonged to the twelfth century—M. Grandclaude, "Liste d'assises." In 1146 Walter of Caesarea sold part of his possessions to the Knights of St. John *"pro liberatione mea et hominum meorum qui pro debitis meis apud Acon saepissime tenebantur capti"*: [to free myself and my men, held prisoners for my debts at Acre. . . .]—Delaville Le Roulx, *Cartulaire*, **1**, 118.

38. Richard, *Le royaume latin*, p. 78; *H.Cr., Lois* **1**. 455, note *c*.

39. Philip of Novara *cc.* 67–70 (*ibid.*, pp. 538–541). See E. Meynial, "De quelques particularités des successions féodales."

40. Philip of Novara *c.* 86 (*H.Cr., Lois* **1**. 558–560).

41. The date of this *assise* is unknown. M. Grandclaude, "Liste d'assises," shows that the king offered a widow a single candidate in 1177, but Grandclaude rightly refuses to draw any conclusions. The case was perhaps an exception, and we would prefer to place this *assise* in the middle of the twelfth century. It seems to us that the promulgation of the new *assise* must have occurred at the time when the great seignorial families, such as the Ibelins, were contracting marriages with the royal family of Jerusalem and even with the imperial family of Byzantium.

42. For the date of this list, see most recently J. Richard, "Les listes de fiefs dans Jean d'Ibelin," *RHD,* 4me sér., **32** (1954), 566 ff. and his bibl. The problem of the date does not appear to us to have been resolved.

43. John of Ibelin *c.* 271. (*H.Cr., Lois* **1**. 422–426).

44. On the list of John of Ibelin, the descriptions of seignorial contingents give no detail but simply the total number of knights due from each seigniory; the lists from the royal domain, on the other hand, are detailed and give the names of the knights from each locality.

45. We have subtracted the contingents of Haifa, Scandalion, and Blanchegarde (21 knights all together) from the sum of 257 knights in the royal domain. These seigniories no longer belonged to the royal domain when the lists were drawn up and, as a result, we have for them only the total size of their contingents, insufficient information for detailed analysis. We do not know the details of the contingent from Beyrouth (23 knights).

46. For the seigniories of Tyre and Arsuf, see J. Prawer, "Etudes de quelques problèmes agraires et sociaux d'une seigneurie croisée au XIIIe siècle," *Byzantion,* 22 (1952), 19, 23.

47. See, for example, John of Ibelin *c.* 182 (*H.Cir.,* Lois **1**. 284–285): *"Que qui a II. M. besanz, et il doive servise de son cors et de un autre chevalier ou de deus sanz son cors."* [. . . that whoever has 2000 besants, and must himself serve along with one knight, or with two knights if he himself does not serve. . . .] See also Philip of Novara *c.* 46 (*H.Cr., Lois* **1**. 521).

48. F. Lot, *L'art militaire et les armées au moyen-âge,* **1** (1946), 219.

49. E. Audouin, *Essai sur l'armée royale au temps de Philippe Auguste* (1913), p. 3.

50. This is the new estimate calculated by C. R. Smail, *Crusading Warfare* (1956), p. 89.

51. J. L. La Monte, *Feudal Monarchy,* p. 150. Fiefs of 600 besants and more, apparently, were to be found. But the calculations by La Monte on the fluctuations in value of these fiefs do not appear to us to be well founded. The fact that a lord received 1200 or 2000 besants annually for the service of two knights (see *n.* 47) does not prove that a simple fief was worth 600 or 1000; for one must allow something for the lord's profit. In direct investiture, the fief was from 400 to 500 besants. (See Philip of Novara c. 67.) Furthermore, we have an irrefutable proof in the colonization of Cyprus by the Lusignans at the end of the twelfth century. According to the "continuator" of William Tyre, *L'Estoire de Eracles Empereur,* **26**, 12 (*H.Cr., Hist. occid.* **2**, 192), *"Et furent establi le fié à quatre cens besanz blanz le chevalier, et a trois cenz besanz blanz li Turquoples, a II. chevaucheures et hauberjon."* [Fiefs were created paying 400 white besants per knight and 300 white besants per lightly armed soldier with two horses and a coat of mail.]

52. I hope soon to publish a study of this source.

53. Practically the same wages as were customary in the army of Philip Augustus and St. Louis. See E. Audouin, *Essai sur l'armée royale,* 51 ff. Our source is contemporary to St. Louis.

54. Philip of Novara *c.* 66 (*H.Cr., Lois* **1**. 536–537); John of Ibelin *c.* 150 (*ibid.,* pp. 225–227).

55. Pons, abbot of Mount Tabor, enfeoffed Hugues de Bethsan (1152) with the formula: *"do et concedo Hugoni de Bethsa . . . heredibusque suis legitimis, legitime de eo natis."* [I give Hugh of Bethsa . . . and his legitimate heirs, born legitimately of him. . . .]—Delaville Le Roulx, *Cartulaire,* 2, 903 no. 11. In an act of enfoeffment by Amalric I in 1169: *"confirmo tibi . . . et heredibus, quos ce filia Jozelini Piselli habebis."* [I confirm you and the heirs you will have from the daughter of Jozelin Piselli. . . .]—*Tabulae Ordinis Theutonici,* E. G. W. Strehlke ed. (1869), no. 5. In another act by the same king from 1174 is to be found, in all probability, the original phrase of the *assise*: *"Confirmo tibi . . . et heredibus tuis quos de uxore legitime desponsata genueris."* [I confirm you . . . and the heirs you will procreate with your legitimately married wife. . . .]—*Tabulae Ordinis Theutonici,* no. 7.

56. *Livre des assises de la cour des bourgeois c.* 49 (*H.Cr., Lois* 2. 47).

57. See the sources cited by Grandclaude, "Liste d'assises," p. 339 n. 44, and J. Richard, *Le royaume latin,* pp. 78, 81.

58. William of Tyre, as is well known, wrote his chronicle at the request of Amalric I.

59. William of Tyre **19.** 1 (*H.Cr., Hist. occid.* **1**[2], 883).

60. William of Tyre **19.** 4; **21.** 1 (*ibid.,* pp. 888–890, 1004).

61. William of Tyre **19.** 2 (*ibid.,* p. 886): *"Interventu munerum auferebat saepe, differebat saepius, aliter quam censurae rigor et juris modestia pateretur."* [Induced by money, he often stood aside and more often delayed acting, rather than doing what strength of judgment and obedience to law required.]

62. Meynial, "De quelques particularités."

63. See Prawer, "Les premiers temps de la féodalité," and "Etude sure le Droit des *Assises de Jerusalem.*"

64. Richard, *Le royaume latin,* n. 81.

65. In glaring contrast to European usage; see John of Ibelin *c.* 195 (*H.Cr., Lois* **1**. 313–314).

66. Philip of Novara *c.* 42 (*ibid.,* 518); John of Ibelin *c.* 203 (*ibid.,* p. 325).

67. Philip of Novara *c.* 52 (*ibid.,* p. 528; John of Ibelin *c.* 203 (*ibid.,* p. 325).

68. John of Ibelin *c.* 203 (*ibid.,* p. 326).

69. John of Ibelin *c.* 203 (*ibid.,* p. 326).

70. John of Ibelin *c.* 239 (*ibid.,* p. 384); see also *cc.* 236–237 (*ibid.,* pp. 376–382).

71. From a strictly legal point of view, everyone who possessed a fief in the kingdom would have had the right to intervene in cases before the High Court, even if it concerned only a knight of the royal domain (for the seignorial court of the king was the High Court). However it appears to us to be highly improbable that the jurists of the kingdom would have drawn these consequences from the *assise.*

72. Philip of Novara *c.* 51 (*ibid.,* p. 527); John of Ibelin *c.* 140 (*ibid.,* p. 215), *c.* 199 (*ibid.,* p. 320); Jacques of Ibelin *c.* 10 (*ibid.,* p. 457).

73. The formula of the oath is conserved in *Cartulaire de l'église de Saint-Sépulchre de Jérusalem,* E. de Rozière, ed., 1849), no. 131: *"ego . . . juro fidelitatem Deo et sanctissimo Sepulcro et conventui eiusdem S. Sepulcri ad custodiendum et manutenendum vitam et membra eorum et omnia quae ad S. Sepulcrum et ad predictum conventum pertinent, salva fidelitate regis Jerusalem. Sic Deus me adiuvet et istud sanctum evangelium"* (1155). [I swear fealty to God and the most Holy Sepulchre and the monastic community of the Holy Sepulchre, to guard them in life and body and all that belongs to the Holy Sepulchre and the aforesaid monastic community, reserving my fealty to the King of Jerusalem. So help me God and these Holy Gospels.] See J. Prawer, "Colonization activities in the Latin Kingdom of Jerusalem," *Revue Belge de Philologie et d'Histoire,* **29** (1951), 1096 ff.

74. "*. . . quiete, libere in elemosinam et dominationem, et ligietatem omnium hominum, tam militum quam burgensium, ibidem terras habentium et possessiones.*" [. . . peacefully, freely in alms and lordship, and with the liege homage of all men having lands and possessions there, whether knights or townsmen.]—Delaville Le Roulx, *Cartulaire,* 1, 117, no. 144.

75. Now al-Bira, to the north of Jerusalem.

76. "*. . . quod praefatus Johannes pro terra, quam ultra Jordanem tenet, michi predicto regi faciat hominium et domino Philippo servicium.*" [. . . that John do homage to me, the king, for the land he holds beyond the Jordan, and perform his service to lord Philip.]—Strehlke, *Tab. Ord. Theutonici,* no. 3.

77. M. W. Baldwin, *Raymond III of Tripoli* (1936) and J. Richard, *Le royaume latin,* 134 ff., give excellent accounts of these fights, taking into consideration the family ties among the noble factions.

III. The Aristocratic Mind

Knighthood in the High Middle Ages: Ideal and Reality*

Arno Borst

"Du nennest ritter; waz ist daz?" [You are called "knight"; what is that?] asks young Parsifal. Into the mouth of an older knight, Wolfram von Eschenbach puts only an imprecise answer: King Arthur confers *ritters namn,* the name of "knight," on those who are of a knight's kind, *ritters art.* Thus "knight" is a title. One is not born a knight, yet must be born to knighthood; for *ritters art* is found mainly in noble families, like the heroes of the *Nibelungenlied* who are "highborn" (*von arte hôh geborn*). Nevertheless, it is not his ancestry that makes the knight, but the way he proves himself in *aventiure,* in errantry, as Hartmann von Aue explains in his epic of Iwein. The knight rides armed into the world, seeking out his equals in arms and rank with whom to cross swords, not to fight over specific differences but to prove, again and again, his knighthood. There is no rest, even for him who is already called "knight." High in the background the strong castle rises, but he does not hide behind its

* From Arno Borst, "Das Rittertum im Hochmittelalter—Idee und Wirklichkeit," *Saeculum* (Munich, 1959), **10**, 213–216, 224–231. Trans. by Miriam Sambursky; revised by the ed. [The bibliographical footnotes have been omitted, by permission of the author.]

walls; he rides down into the wilderness to face fantastic adventures, surrounded by Death and the Devil—unafraid, in shining armor, on his steed. In 1513 Albrecht Dürer engraved him thus in copper.

When we look more closely at Dürer's engraving, we see that this vast castle, townlike in extent, is not a knight's dwelling but, rather, a princely residence. The heavy, finely chased plate-armor resembles the parade armor of Maximilian I and belongs more to an imperial than to a knightly armory. Here rides not a medieval knight but the subsequent embodiment of a way of life long past, a glorified ideal figure. Only such a figure could encounter horrid Death with his snake's head and the shaggy, goatlike Devil in this forceful way. And the knight described by Hartmann and Wolfram—is he, too, not such a phantom? He lives in a small castle, his armor is a modest coat of mail, but he too, like Dürer's knight, rides into the pathless wilderness to fight dragons and villains as a member of King Arthur's Round Table or a Knight of the Holy Grail. What twelfth-century nobleman really left family and manor to fend for himself for years on end, simply to fight for honor's sake in a wilderness to which he had neither been summoned by an oath of fealty nor lured by territorial gain? Who could raise to knighthood the nobleman who had proved himself, if King Arthur was only a legendary figure and real kings forbade feuds among the nobles? Who were the knights? Hundreds of times the designation "knight" and its Latin equivalent *"miles"* appear in the documents, but they appear in a way that signifies neither the ideal glorified by the artist nor a social group. A military reality is all these words mean. Every warrior on horseback is called "knight," the free and noble lord as well as the unfree *ministerialis.* "Knight's kind" is in no way dependent on birth. Is knighthood therefore nothing but a name and a phantasmagoria, the creation of an artist's imagination, without any real basis and form?

Scholarly literature could make one believe it. Medieval historians have labored long and intensively at the constitutional, legal, and social history of the nobles and serfs; but where we could expect a historical description of this vague knighthood, they are even more reticent than Wolfram von Eschenbach. Meanwhile, historians of culture fritter away their efforts in collecting colorful details about armor, tournaments, and castles and are hardly conscious of the spirit that infused life into these relics. Philologists, on the other hand, use literature to play grammatical games on knightly systems of virtue and accord themselves a dispensation from reality. They describe the knight as the hero of an ideal civilization without mentioning the misery of his daily life or his domestic worries. French *savants* show us the most Christian *chevalier;* German researchers transform the "Knight of Bamberg" into a Germanic hero; and, in the end, the Marxists regard all this as an insignificant ideological superstructure that barely manages to conceal the material interests of the exploiting Junkers.

This separation of facts and ideas, of basis and superstructure, of social, cultural, and intellectual history, suits the ideologies of the nineteenth and twentieth centuries—of the materialists and idealists, the nationalists and occidentalists. But do not such divisions cut the life line of the Middle Ages, at least that of medieval knighthood? Behind the images of Dürer and the poets is a higher idea—an idea of freedom as the voluntary acceptance of ties of dependence by the upper class—an idea which corresponded to a social reality, to a layer between rulership and service. Such a being—hard to define, hovering between idea and reality—is distorted by crude, one-sided interpretations. Was knighthood in the High Middle Ages a reality embedded in the conditions and circumstances of the period? Were its poetry, its ideals and ceremonies answers to, or demands upon, this reality? Has medieval knighthood a real history? We shall deal with three aspects of this question: I, the historical roots of knighthood before the twelfth century; II, the reality of the lesser nobility in the twelfth and early thirteenth century;† III, the ideal images of knighthood in this period, the flowering of chivalry and of the Middle Ages. We will then conclude with IV, reflections on the idea and reality of knighthood in general.

I

According to the prevailing view, wherever there are mounted troops and an aristocracy—among Homer's Greeks, the Germans of Tacitus, the Japanese Samurai, Saladin's Moslems, in Russia and among the Zulus—there we find knights. Everywhere in world history since nomadic equestrian peoples attacked the sedentary river-civilizations of the Near and Far East in the second millenium B.C. and forced them into battle, there have been mounted warriors. And nearly everywhere, cavalry in battle has been intertwined with a feudal structuring of the aristocracy, with a phase of political life when, after heavy internal disturbances or external threats, political order could be safeguarded—as far as it was possible at all—only through personal bonds between lords and those who served. From the times of the later pharaohs, the Greeks, and the Persians, noble lords in armor frequently defended their country from war chariot, horseback, and castle. Chariot, horse, and castle were instruments of the lords duty to protect and at the same time attributes of their rulership. Although they rode horses and were prototypes of the *ethos* of nobility, they were not knights but nobles first of all, members of a rank that was entitled to rule by right of birth. In Byzantium, Japan, and elsewhere, the ruling class let its dependent unfree serfs participate in defense; they were

† Most of section I and all of section II have been omitted in this translation.—Ed.

equipped with armor and horses; sometimes they were settled in castles and made economically free through grants of land so that they should always be ready in case of war. But even with horse and castle they were not knights but only servant retainers. Often, too, in the early Western Middle Ages, nobles and servant retainers together rode to war. The customary name for both, found so often in the sources, was *"milites."* This *miles* of the early Middle Ages also was not a knight but, generally, a mounted warrior. By position, either he belonged to the nobility, the gentry (was an *Edelfreier, nobilis, senior, seigneur, lord*) or he was a retainer (*serviens, ministerialis, sergeant*). Lords and serfs met as fellows-in-arms; but politically, legally, and socially, rulership and service remained sharply divided, as they had been in nearly all forms of older feudalism.

Thus, knighthood as a combination of rulership and service was not an ancient and widespread phenomenon, but something peculiar. Not tradition but a historical situation produced it. The system of lords and followers among the ancient Germans and Celts—whose importance is so often exaggerated—was no more the root of knighthood than was Charles Martel's victory over the Saracens. Knighthood was born in the ninth century, the period of the dissolution of the Carolingian Frankish state, when Germany and France began to separate. In this period there developed a new aristocracy and the occidental form of feudalism, distinguished from earlier feudalisms by a new correlation between rule and service. . . .

III

If we try to reconstruct—without preference or prejudice—the ideal image of the knight from the courtly literature of the Western High Middle Ages, we must concede that there never existed in the High Middle Ages a general, binding ideal of chivalry. The expert swordsman, the gallant knight, the courtly knight, the Christian knight are contradictory motifs. All of them made their impression on the nobleman, but he neither carefully selected suitably matching details nor exclusively adopted one of these ideal types. Moreover, the form these types acquired depended on the real situation of the lesser nobility—which differed from country to country. Our discussion will be limited to a few comparative elements drawn from French and German literature of the twelfth and early thirteenth century.

The oldest ideal of knighthood, already making its impression on the pugnacious French nobility before the twelfth century, was the rough warrior. The earlier *chansons de geste* told of the mighty deeds of past heroes and paid no attention to delicate ideals, *courtoisie,* or religion. Beginning about 1100, these epics opened themselves at least to the ideal of the *miles christianus,* the Christian knight—first of all in northern

France, the home of the first crusaders. From this period came the Old French *Chanson de Roland.* Although it was probably written by a Breton cleric, it was not wholly Christian but preserved the style of the wild heroic epic. The knight loves battle and bloody slaughter in which he finds glory and loot; his feats of arms earn him a place in heaven. He fights for honor and renown in the service of his feudal lord, worrying little about transcendental aims, not wrestling with God. Sweet France and Christendom are nearly identical; religion is something robust and tangible. When Roland dies, he extends his glove toward heaven and becomes God's vassal, after having faithfully served his Emperor on earth. The principal virtue of the Christian knight is *vasselage,* the unthinking courage and unconditional fidelity of the vassal. It does not always get its proper reward; the traitor Ganelon holds the blind obedience of his vassals who therefore meet his fate and are hanged together with him. Life is rough and merciless; there are no tender emotions, not even toward women. The old feudal order has been robed in a religious garb but hardly changed; the paragon is still the muscular hero. One hesitates to apply the epithet "knightly" to it just yet; but knightly it was, although it lacked decorum, manners, and everything courtly.

In the German *Rolandslied* there were also only weak traces of courtly decorum and service to womankind, yet stress was laid on points different from those in its immediate French model. It was also composed by a cleric belonging to a precourtly circle—the court of the Guelf Henry the Lion, about 1170, where noble poetry was fostered in a slightly old-fashioned spirit and where people enjoyed the past. But the virtues the French poem gave its Christian champions were attributed in the German one to the hated heathens—they are chivalrous fighters for home, country, and glory. It is the traitor Ganelon who speaks most impressively about feudal loyalty. The true Christian knight fights neither for material, temporal aims nor even out of feudal loyalty: he is bound to his emperor by religious zeal and by a readiness to sacrifice all for his religion. This turn toward the spiritual and religious may have been less ecclesiastical and more Germanic than is usually thought. The readers of the German poem were enclosed in solid structures that needed neither praise nor inculcation. The reality of their life was well enough framed to give them security. But they lacked the continuity of aristocratic consciousness, they lacked a tradition of ease, and these were replaced and compensated for by high-aiming demands, by sublimation and education.

The motif of the Christian knight, even in the writings of clerics, was thus manifold and bore distinctive local historical hues. This motif was also neither the only nor even the most important one. Beside the heroic poetry there appeared a chivalric lyric that presented quite a different picture of the true knight. Most of these poems sought to glorify the courtly lady and the knight's love for a mistress who is another's wife. They were ephemeral compositions, graceful, singable, speaking to the soul. They developed first in France—beginning about 1100—and survived longest in the politically divided South, in the lands fought over by France and England, in Aquitaine and the neighborhood of Toulouse, at many small courts, in castles and the haunts of the robber-barons. The poets were reigning princes like Count William IX of Aquitaine-Poitou and poor upstarts like Bernard of Ventadour. Beneath a harsh sun, on poor soil, in the midst of bizarre mountains, these troubadours sang of the shining joy of life. Bertran de Born despised the cowardly monk, the clever diplomatist, and the temperate ruler; his only political maxim was: "*A lor!*" at it! Woman's beauty did not charm him. He praised, he loved the intoxication of battle where many a colorful helmet and sword, many a spear and shield are hewn to pieces; where horses who have lost their masters rove the forests and red blood covers the green meadow, "and many a one lies on the ground, the shaft still in his heart." Many of his companions may have used their freedom for licentiousness and looting; others looked for higher delights. Bernard of Ventadour glorified only the beautiful mature woman, the woman who belonged to another and did not love the poet. Each of his beloveds is beautiful; each poem shows them with the same sweet smile. He tells us the real name of not a single one of them. They are not individuals but pretexts. Like fishes jumping at the bait, the knight lets himself be taken prisoner unresistingly; he matures while he endures, while he serves a lady who never responds. It is the tingling excitement of the forbidden, the unattainable, the unresolved tension that trains the lover to true knighthood. When the desired object refuses to give herself, self-discipline forces a man to be upright. It does not matter whether individual troubadours here or there received a clandestine reward for their songs; the reality of love was transformed into the playful suspense of a festive moment, into a gay, floating "as-if" where every glance already was the happiness of fulfillment—in short, into gallantry. The troubadours did not omit religious themes. But when the wildest among them became devout at the end of their lives, they entered a monastery; they did not become Christian knights protecting widows, orphans, or, still less, church property. Most of the time they lived only for the day and its extremes—for burning passion, battle, and love—not for political forms or for spiritual values. Among the 460 known troubadours, hardly ten are original; most of them are only imitators. But exactly this is characteristic: real or possible experiences did not create ethical demands but exchangeable *topoi,* glittering forms and a pleasing game.

The themes of the troubadours' songs traveled from France to Germany, but in the process their spirit changed. The years about 1170 were the springtime of the *Minnesang,* of German chivalric poetry, in the Hohenstaufen territories adjoining France.The authors wrote in High German, even if they had been born on the Lower Rhine or in Thuringia. When the Babenberger's Court of the Muses at Vienna and the Wartburg of the Thuringian Landgraves were at last deserted, the Hohenstaufen kings of the thirteenth century remained surrounded by poets. Most of these poets were *ministeriales* and they raised knighthood to a world-view which, although not homogeneous, was always elevated in principle and spirituality and weighty in language and form. The Aleman Hartmann von Aue put little value in thoughtless battling and amorous dreams—the true knight was the crusader who turned from service to a lady to the service of God, from the transitory to the eternal. The Thuringian Heinrich von Morungen, on the other hand, had been a crusader and traveled as far as India, but his song was given wholly to *Minne.* To him, however, it was not a frivolous and gallant game; woman is the symbol of every high ideal. Heroic asceticism educates by denial; a brillant radiance raises the loved one, and love itself, into the sphere of devoted, blissful contemplation. This "high *Minne*" was soon divorced from love for the earthly wife, the beautiful maid, or the buxom peasant girl as it was then taught by Wolfram von Eschenbach, Walther von der Vogelweide, and Neidhard von Reuenthal. In France the poet lightheartedly loved danger and the chance of the tempting moment; in Germany he aspired on principle toward the eternally denied or toward the intimate.

The chivalric epic, recited in the castle during long evenings, already sometimes quietly read, sought to harmonize incompatible motifs by way of a drawn-out and complicated plot. Poets tried their hand again and again at the same familiar subjects of the legend of King Arthur; sought a noble and harmonious language, and courtly behavior. Here too, themes and forms were brought to Germany from France and transformed in the process. In France the epic did not flourish in royal Paris, the citadel of of theology, nor in the troubadours' South, but in the rich principalities of the North, in Champagne and Flanders. At these courts, in the sphere of influence of the lively Eleanor of Aquitaine and her daughter Marie of Champagne, there reigned a mild moderate order (politically as well as spiritually), a code of courtly conventions full of wisdom and temperance. We find this spirit in the Arthurian epics of the burgher-poet Chrétien de Troyes. Their arena is limitless, like a fairy tale; their season, an eternal spring; their heroes are presented gracefully, elegantly and gloriously framed in precious armor, with purebred horses and choice gowns. They are always, and unalterably, the same. Conflict of duties hardly bothers them, even when they must sentimentally choose between honor and love. They engage in senseless, adventurous, wonderful deeds, not for King Arthur, but for an exclusive society of their equals, and especially for a beloved lady. Untroubled, they serve the earthly powers, war, and, at the same time, love—God and the cosmic order, much less. Their attitude is *mesure,* the golden mean of sensible steadiness, the harmony of values, and the noble gesture.

The German epic poets were also mostly small officials, often from the Hohenstaufen's territory if not in their service. Hartmann von Aue composed a German version of Chrétien's Arthurian romances. He, too, taught the *mâze* between the extremes, but his arbiter was not court society. For him true knighthood was part of a transcendental world-order composed of dream and dignity. Serving one's lady, lord, and God are neither unrelated nor irreconcilable. They are hierarchically ordered. Yet they are not rungs in a static scale of virtues, for the world and man are a task, not a condition. What is demanded is not a conventional norm but an inner attitude. When Wolfram's Parsifal neglected to ask the compassionate question, he behaved like a horseman, not like a knight. Wolfram's Parsifal and Hartmann's Iwein do not start out as heroic paragons; they soon lose the acclaim of Arthur's Round Table. Even God turns from them. Painfully, through self-education and self-alienation, through madness, they find their way to the protecting mission that God demands—and to the beloved woman. It is reached only by knight-errantry, by experience. The taboos of the real world of the nobility were removed. What Hartmann portrayed was not the contemporary nobleman. Sometimes one can catch a corner of reality, as in his description of a rustic cabbage-baron; but then one sees dark shadows. Wolfram's digressions into reality, with their familiar humor, also show the gap between poetry and the real world. In Hartmann's poem, Gregorius can be a gallant knight even without *geburt* and *guot*,‡ although he thereby imperils his soul's salvation, which the monastery had protected. *Arme Heinrich,* "Poor Henry," after his bitter experiences, in the end marries the serf who saved him, without any consideration of rank or lowering of his standing. The chastened knight goes out into a world which is neither a shining nor oppressive cosmos, but chaos; whenever he can, he imposes the proper order as God's aid, as the friend of the weak, the animals, the peasants, and even the heathens—serving a utopian ideal. Never was there such a historical reality, not even under the Hohenstaufen.

All these motifs of knighthood, with all their differences, with all the uncertainties about their origins, stem from the striving of the noble stratum, caught between lordship and service, to erect a higher ethos that would correspond to its real situation and enhance it: the noble giving service to God, to his overlord, to his lady, instead of suffering overweening pride or despondency. Only the blind chauvinist can find the harmonious play of the French and the laborious efforts of the Germans to be in sharp contrast. In reality they complement each other; they were the effects of the same spirit in different circumstances. Roughly speaking, the chivalric literature of the twelfth century mirrored in France the reality of the aristocracy; in Germany, an ideal image of man. The ruling class of

‡ Birth and possessions.—Ed.

France, powerful and secure, loved the harmony of convention in the spiritual sphere; because of its fortunate position, it had little cause for melancholy. From its freedom it drew its own laws and measures, while it lived in the fullness of the moment, celebrating its social existence in its literature. In Germany chivalric culture was mainly the product of the Hohenstaufen *ministeriales.* Their efficacy, traditions, and self-consciousness were shaky; a program of indoctrination reinforced them. Because the *ministeriales* were forced into a structure given by tradition, because they lived by second-hand power, their poets broke through the barriers of rank and conventions and demanded, dreamed of, an eternal image of man. German chivalric literature was the product of a crisis, yet its criticism was directed neither against the Hohenstaufen nor against the princes. It aimed beyond reality. Reality had provoked an escape into the ideal.

IV

In the High Middle Ages the connection between knightly ideal and aristocratic reality was thus closer than historical research has generally maintained. This connection contains the essence of medieval knighthood. Not that poetry simply described reality—if so, it would have been history; nor did it want to change conditions—if so, it would have been political polemic. The ideals of knighthood were utopian exaggerations; nobody, not even a poet, could live them. But they were not just mental experiments floating away into the mist. As demands and incentives addressed to the stratum of noble retainers, these ideals defined freedom as a voluntary bond and service as the proof of nobility. As ideals they were not uniform; their effect on the Western world was to construct contradictory images in answer to the questions, "Serving whom?" "Bond to what?" No one could simultaneously serve God, king, glory, and woman. Even Walter von der Vogelweide did not succeed in reconciling these heterogeneous motifs.

In the various European countries, moreover, these ideals took on the coloring of local reality. Many peoples contributed their variations to the theme. Knighhood thus developed a different individuality in each country: in England, among the Normans, in Portugal and Spain, in Italy, in the Scandinavian countries, in Poland and Hungary. "Knighthood" was not immediately at home everywhere. It prospered only in countries whose structure was shaken, not where the indigenous territorial structure of a rural aristocracy was still intact. Nor did it succeed where a strong monarchy already attracted all forces. It flourished only in the intermediate stratum between lordship and service and only in the period between the arbitrary rule of a nobility and that of state power, between 1100 and

1250. It flourished only as long as the idea of knighthood agreed with the social reality of the lesser nobility. Between the curtailment of aristocratic power and its uprooting by king, princes, and bourgeoisie, in the moment between brutality and spirituality, the lesser nobility helped to achieve a balance, helped to make the transition. Its ideal was just this—balance, *mesure, mâze.*

This knightly principle of balance was, of course, the product and symptom of a transitory situation, a formal ideal not immovably tied to any content. For just this reason it was so widely effective—from the sphere of religion to that of gallantry, from Portugal to Hungary; but for this reason also, it remained superficial. Such a formal and utopian ideal could be realized in only one way: as a playful, highly stylized way of life. This was what made knighthood immortal. It obliged the nobility to rise above everyday life, to replace selfishness with measure and discipline; thus it was more than a few gestures, ceremonies, and conventions. It was an attitude, the same attitude with which the aristocrats calmly mounted the scaffold in the French Revolution.

A nobleman's childhood was unfettered; education was given only to the man within the child. He was not overfed with mental nourishment. The young page had to prove himself in a strange court over many years—in war, at the hunt, in courtly service to his lord and to guests. Then he received the sword, his fief, and a wife. In his castle he had plenty of leisure, which he filled with hunting, dancing, and play. Play, however, was not only a pastime but indeed a way of life—one could say a second life above the real one, a way of life enclosed by rules and stylized attitudes. Even meals and fashion were subject to the rules of the game, halfway between provocation and reserve. Ladies and guests were courteously and hospitably honored, but reserve accompanied the conviviality. The castle, the center of noble life, was both fortress and feast hall, the place for the social life of an elite. The noble proudly displayed himself in his shining armor and his colorful coat of arms; he scorned disguise and all far-reaching weapons. War for him was also a game with rules, played by the elite in hand-to-hand fights and duels without ambushes and without large armies. The tournament turned war into something even more gamelike. Peacetime too was dangerous. One played with life. The older man got little attention; twenty years during which every moment was a feast—then it was over.

This way of life was more easily realized than were the diverging ideals of knighthood. There was the court feast in Mainz (1184) for instance, when, before ten thousand guests, Barbarossa knighted his sons and then himself took part in the jousting, and Heinrich von Veldeke and French poets sang. This splendid game of the elite was not an abstract idea but part of the reality of Western medieval society when lordship and fellowship, nobility and service, were woven together under the sign of freedom as a voluntary tie of dependence. That it was once a social reality shaped the European nobility thenceforth. From then on nobility rested—at least so it was claimed—less on inherited charisma and birth than on disposition, on having proved oneself, on cultivation and convention, on ethos and learning.

The decline of knighthood in the late Middle Ages did not signify a breakup of the chivalric way of life. On the contrary, it was enthusiastically taken over by kings and bourgeoisie. But they now forgot that knightly ideals were unattainable; they took them for reality. Three hundred years before Don Quixote, errant knights really began to roam the forests and the English kings established King Arthur's Round Table. The ideal of knighthood became detached from the lesser nobility to which it corresponded. *Politically* the nobility were overwhelmed by the absolute power of the state and by civil administration. *Militarily* the knights were vanquished by the mercenaries with their tactical maneuverability, their great numbers, and their new weapons: crossbows, longbows, and cannons. Even the heavy plate-armor these now made necessary, even the thickest castle walls, could not withstand the new weapons for long. *Economically* the nobility, depending on its unchanging land-rent, lost the race against government finance and bourgeois capital. The noble became a courtier, an official in royal pay, a merchant, or even a farmer. He became the "Poor Knight," the *Arme Ritter*—since the fourteenth century a very simple dish, bread soaked in milk and fried, bears this name. Many nobles left their castles, which fell to ruin; robber-barons nested there until the police strung them up to the nearest tree. *Socially* the nobility became one class among others, a member of the *Ständestaat,* an inherited "estate." Haughtily exclusive, organized in associations of knights, they fought for their rights when they had lost their task. The noble had to tolerate the king's raising his bourgeois advisers to knighthood. The old nobles laughed at them. These knights of the new order, they said, had never in their lives been in greater peril than while stewing prunes over a hot stove. The orders of knighthood now became orders of merit, the forerunners of our modern badges of distinction, medals worn on a chain or ribbon. No longer were the knights communities of people infused by the same spirit; at most they were a court society enhancing royal splendor with their playful conviviality and their glamour—the Order of the Golden Buckle, the Order of the Garter, the Order of the Porcupine . . . The chivalric way of life was no longer universally binding; the nobility acquired learning, the page was taught manners on the dance floor instead of while bearing his knight's shield; being dubbed a knight became a formality. Tablemanners and etiquette lost their freedom and amiability, became formal and stiff. One knew too precisely what was right and proper. The social duties of the knight were taken over by the cavalry man; what had been courtly now became just pretty. Fashion became lascivious and shrill, armor showy and impractical, tournaments less and less dangerous and more and more luxurious. Knightly behavior in wartime was hardly more than fiction. The Emperor Maximilian, sometimes called "the last knight," was much more interested in infantry, cavalry, and artillery. The literature of chivalry became anemic and high-flown, the more there was of it. Meanwhile the nobility tried to conjure death by tearful piety and lived out its morbid life in melancholy.

Yet, although knighthood had long since died, the idea of knighthood still remained alive at the beginning of the modern era. For Dürer's etching stands at the beginning of the modern age. Under absolute monarchy, the European aristocracy repeatedly infused life into the ideal of the noble servant. All its guiding images were influenced by that of knighthood: the Italian *cortegiano,* the Spanish *hidalgo,* the French *honnête homme,* the English gentleman. In literature the garland of knightly figures reached from Ariosto's *Orlando furioso,* by way of the *Don Quixote* of Cervantes, to Goethe's *Goetz von Berlichingen*—the free knight who is dependent only on God, his Emperor, and himself. In real life, too, knights still remained—from Bayard, the fearless knight above reproach, to Prince Eugene, the noble knight. The old world of the nobility disappeared only with the French Revolution. It was then that Edmund Burke exclaimed, "Now the era of knighthood has ended." He was not mistaken. In the romantic revival, in Novalis, Arnim, and Scott, the knight became even more of an ideal, a symbol of nostalgia for a lost past. In 1810, Madame de Staël wrote: "For the moderns, knighthood is what heroic times were for the ancients. All the noble memories of the European nations are bound up with it." Convulsively, and in blatant contrast to historical reality, people tried to hold on to the chivalric spirit. In an era of industrial revolution and of "knights of industry," men brought together knightly panoplies of war in museumlike armories and restored romantic castles. In the midst of mechanized war with far-reaching weapons and motorized tanks, the "cross of the knight" was still conferred. And today, while the last cavalry captains are dying, the cultivation of horsemen flourishes.

Should we not at last let these spirits rest? History has better things to do than to nurse doleful dusty traditions. The history of knighthood could teach us more than a few empty formalities and curiosities. It contains some maxims of great relevance for understanding history and mastering the present—that rule is ennobled only by service; that the elite needs the community; and first and foremost, that only mental discipline can subdue the chaos of life and the fanaticism of power.

THE IDEA OF TREASON IN THE MIDDLE AGES*

Adalbert Dessau

As is well known, the ideas that feudal society held about treason were not the same as our own; for the Middle Ages saw treason as above all a crime against the ties of dependence and mutual obligation between lord and vassal that formed the central element in all feudal law.

The history of the terms used for traitor can serve to describe the development of those ideas. The technical term is *"fel/felon,"* clearly defined in *Girart de Roussillon:*

> *Ne dei estre de droit ne fel ne bles,*
> *Car qui dreit fauserei faus traices es. . . .* (vv. 1809–1810)
> [And must be rightfully neither felon nor injuror,
> For who falses right a false traitor is.]

and in the *Song of Roland:*

> *Guenes est fel d'iço qu'il le trait.* (v. 3829)
> [Guenes is a felon in that he betrays.]

In the *Passion du Christ* of the tenth century, the words *"fel/felon"* generally serve to characterize the Jews, who, according to medieval ideas, had betrayed their lord. Similarly, *"fel/felon"* plays a role in the Provençal *Boèce* and in Latin texts from 858 on, generally expressing (in the tenth century) the idea of a crime against the ties between lord and vassal. In this sense *"fel/felon"* is still the usual name for a traitor in the *Song*

---

* Adalbert Dessau, "L'idée de la trahison au moyen âge et son rôle dans la motivation de quelques chansons de geste," *Cahiers de civilisation médiévale,* 3 (Poitiers, 1960), 23–26. Trans. by the ed.

of Roland; only about 1130 does its semilearned synonym *"traître/traîtour"* begin to play a role, thus revealing a certain participation of "learning" in lay literature.

Under the influence of courtly literature and its ideology, *"fel/felon"* later takes on a moral connotation—"wicked," for example (the *Dictionnaire* of Godefroy gives numerous examples)—while the same word keeps its specifically legal meaning in other branches of medieval literature.

The legal idea of feudal treason, for which we have witness as early as the tenth century, has considerable ideological import because it was applied to other aspects of life; it was reflected in some archaic religious traditions, for example. Thus, many twelfth-century texts show the hero—whether a saint or a nobleman—as God's vassal fighting in judicial combat for his lord against traitors. In *Ogier le Danois* Ogier says in prayer to God before rejoining combat with a Saracen:

> *Et ke vos drois soit par moi maintenu.* (v. 11357)
> [And may your right be upheld by me.]

Likewise, after having struck down a pagan, Guillaume affirms in *Aliscans:*

> *Deu si vengié. si m'en set molt bon gré.* (v. 1062 *a*)
> [God is thus avenged, and will be very pleased with me.]

The last words, like many other texts, show that God's vassal, looking on his relations with his Supreme Lord according to the principle of *do ut des* [I give that you should give], expects a *guerredon.* Naturally, God never breaks the ties of mutual obligation. One cannot, of course, say the same for the pagan gods who, because they themselves are traitors, themselves betray their men. The latter draw the proper conclusion from this sad experience, deny their false and felon gods, and commend themselves to the true and faithful God of the Christians.

Following this ideology, the universe itself is seen through the lens of feudal law. Thus, Satan by his betrayal of God becomes the supreme head of all traitors, whose acts are comprehended in his crime. Grouped in the ranks of his vassals are, on the one hand, all those who are not Christians, and on the other, all those who betray their ties of vassalage: the Jews, as murderers of Christ; the great persecutors of the first Christians, such as Nero; the pagan gods; and naturally the Saracens, along with the traitors of the *chansons de geste.* In this fashion Ganelon and his followers are criminals against man and against God; and for this reason one so often finds that the loyal hero's victory is explained by the fact that "God and right" were on his side. This opinion is formulated in an exemplary manner in *Yvain:*

> *Deus se retient devers le droit,*
> *Et deus et droit a un se tienent.* (vv. 4444–4445)
> [God stood on the side of right,
> And God and right made common cause.]

On the other hand, the fact that the pagans are all traitors against God absolutely guarantees that universal order, having been troubled by treason, will be re-established by a Christian victory, as expressed in the *chanson* of *Guy de Bourgogne:*

> *Escrit est en la loi, por voir le puis conter,*
> *Que le paiens ne puet vers le François durer.* (vv. 2396–2397)
> [It is written in the law, to be seen and told,
> That the pagans cannot last against the French.]

What role does this ideology of the first feudal age play in the motivation of certain groups of *chansons de geste?* What role has this ideology that tends to embrace the universe in a conception of treason equated with a crime against the ties of vassalage? Numerous *chansons de geste* describe an instance of feudal betrayal in which the *loiaus om,* the faithful vassal, fights against the traitor; in such epics, this judicial battle, whether duel or not, constitutes the main subject and frame of the poem's action. It is interesting to note that in most conflicts thus described, the guilty party is not the vassal.

In one group of *chansons de geste*—now generally considered the product of a traditional development of historical materials—treason committed by a lord is portrayed with what is incontestably a juridical motivation.

The war between Ogier and Charlemagne breaks out because Charles refuses to render justice to his vassal after Charles's son has killed Ogier's son. The fight between Renaut de Montauban and the Emperor begins because the latter likewise has refused to render justice to his vassal and has aggravated the dispute by slapping Renaut in the face. The first conflict between Girart de Roussillon and Charles Martel arises from Charles's plan to deprive Girart of lands that are presented as allodial. The conflict between Raoul de Cambrai and Bernier, on which the entire song of *Raoul de Cambrai* is focused, springs from Raoul's attack on the vassal's mother, his refusal to render justice to her, and his slapping Bernier's face. These motivations are not arbitrary. Quite the contrary: they represent situations in which the vassal has an immediate right to proceed to war against his felon lord. These cases were already defined in a capitulary of Charlemagne:

> No one should leave his lord after he has accepted from him anything worth one *solidus;* except if the lord should wish to kill him, or strike him with a stick, or violate his wife or daughter, or take his inheritance from him.[1]

Later on, denial of justice, which plays a preponderant role in the *chansons,* was added to the list.

The lord's guilt was so notorious in such cases that in *Ogier le Danois,* Charlemagne says to his son:

> *Ogiers a droit, si me puist Dex aidier:*
> *Ocesis li son fil que il ot chier.* (vv. 9137–9138)
> [Ogier is right; so may God help me;
> His son is killed whom he held so dear.]

To appreciate the full import of that admission, we must compare it with a phrase in the *Assises* of Jerusalem: "Between lord and man there is only faith, and that faith must be recognized and kept between them."[2]

If the motivation of these *chansons de geste* is incontestably juridical, the way the texts solve their central conflict is of a quite different character. Charles and Ogier are reconciled after divine intervention prevents Ogier from killing the young Charlot. Renaut renounces his warrior life to die as a saint. The first war between Girart de Roussillon and Charles Martel is ended by divine intervention, and after the second war Girart leads a life so difficult that he nearly becomes a saint. Bernier renounces his good right and hands himself over to the mercy of his enemies.

How are these striking contradictions to be explained? In the case of *Raoul de Cambrai,* I have demonstrated elsewhere, through an analysis of content and style, that at the beginning of the twelfth century the poem ended with the death of Raoul, that is to say, with the vassal's victory, thus keeping the epic's juridical character. The remainder of the rhymed part—from the death of Raoul to the destruction of Paris—is, as Gaston Paris long ago supposed, an addition composed about the middle of the twelfth century, an addition that neutralizes the poem's ending and substitutes a moral condemnation of the vassal's right to take vengeance on his lord in place of the original juridical solution hostile to the traitorous lord. A corresponding neutralization is to be found in a passage of the *Roman de Thèbes,* dating from about the same period, in which, during the trial of Daires, some of the nobles allow that Daires had the right to make war on his traitorous lord and others, although admitting that he had the right to do so, say that nevertheless one ought not to fight his lord.[3] This transformation of *Raoul de Cambrai,* by the addition of the newer ending, reveals a profound change in ideas, a change the consequences of which can also be detected in the Ogier legend. Matellus von Tegernsee reveals the juridical character of this poem about the middle of the twelfth century. It still retains this character toward the end of the century in the *chanson Ogier le Danois,* in which Ogier's right to fight Charlemagne is expressly recognized. But several years later Ogier is included, along with Renaut de Montaubon and Girart de Roussillon, in a *chanson de geste* about traitors entitled *Doon de Mayence.* Like the transformation of *Raoul de Cambrai,* this change attests to a change in public opinion that began to occur at least by the fourth decade of the twelfth century, a change that completely overturned the public evaluation of some of the epic heroes and their legendary actions.

In accounting for this change, the origins of which are perhaps to be found in the idea of the peace of God, we probably ought to consider the neutralization of the solution to each poem's central conflict as a conscious fabrication. This does not mean that each poem once ended like *Raoul de Cambrai.* René Louis has come to analogous conclusions about *Girart de Roussillon* on the basis of other arguments. This hypothesis, founded on changes in public opinion, is in agreement with traditionalist theory; but at the same time it allows us to examine closely the mechanism of change in the structure of the epic poems because this change of opinion is revealed in a whole group of *chansons de geste.*

During the second half of the twelfth century poets begin to compose *chansons de geste* that, being entirely the product of their author's fantasy, are heroic romances rather than true *chansons de geste.* It is important to note, however, that for nearly a century, from the *gestes* of Nanteuil and St.-Gilles to *Gaidon,* the construction of these newer *chansons* follows a strict structural and compositional schema. In all these poems the conflict is motivated by the action of a traitor, all descendants of Ganelon. These *traitres losengiers,* these lying traitors denounce the faithful vassal and thereby trouble the normal order of feudal relations. What follows is a long fight, rich in adventures, but ending always with a victory of the *loiaus om* over the traitors that re-establishes legal order.

It is worth noting that the neutralization of epic conflict in these *chansons* has influenced their motivation. The lord, although he lends his ear to traitorous calumnies (usually explained by Charlemagne's senility), is no longer guilty. Having more or less excluded the lord from the motivation of the epic's conflict, these *chansons* no longer need to neutralize its solution. Consequently the solution is completely juridical; in most poems it is presented as a trial according to strictly regulated procedures, ending in a duel in which the traitor dies, since "God and right" are on the side of the faithful vassal. As a result, this group of *chansons* neutralizes the entire epic action and thereby allows the portrayal of a strictly juridical case; the historical *chansons,* already known to the public, had to have their solutions neutralized, and this created a very strong conflict in their structures. These two phenomena had the same effect, an effect that reveals their common cause—a moral condemnation of war against one's lord—caused by a change in opinion that, about the middle of the twelfth century, forced minstrels to modify the structure of their poems.

The causes of this change in opinion must be sought in a profound change in the structure of society, in the feudal centralization brought about by kings and great feudal lords. The change is reflected in antique and courtly stories as it is in *chansons de geste.* The stories of *Alexander* and of *Partonopeus de Blois* picture a royal counselor of non-noble origin whose evil actions have tragic consequences; in the end the counselor is defeated by faithful vassals. Here we see a whole class fighting a bad counselor who comes from a lower class.

This result allows us to classify the *chansons de geste* we have discussed within the framework of medieval society. Because they picture a judicial war by a vassal to re-establish the juridical order of feudal ties, they reveal themselves as the literature of vassals of the first feudal age and therefore as the literature of the entire noble class—inasmuch as in the feudal hierarchy every noble was the vassal of another. By helping to dissolve the earlier hierarchical system, thus modifying the situation of most of the vassal nobility, historical development brought about profound changes in the structure of the *chansons de geste,* changes one can consider the cause of the decline of the epic.

The structural changes studied here also allow a few conclusions concerning the mechanisms by which epic poetry traditionally developed. Aside from the constantly renewed development of epic style, it would appear that the development of the content of these poems depended not only on the minstrels' more or less arbitrary inclusion of themes and events but also—and in the first place—upon the development of opinion among the epic's public. This last development, in turn, reflects changes in that public's social structure and exercises a decisive influence on the structure of epic poetry. Thus, epic poetry develops with epic society and disappears with it.

These are the conclusions one can draw from a study of the idea of treason in the motivation of some of the *chansons de geste;* naturally these conclusions are valid only for this one group of French epics. No claims should be made that these conclusions are universally valid; for some very important *chansons de geste* such as the *Song of Roland* or the *Chanson de Guillaume,* although they also underwent a traditional development, were not touched by the structural changes we have outlined. The relation between the *chansons de geste* just examined and the other epics needs to be investigated. Other studies may, perhaps, contribute to a solution of this problem.

NOTES

1. *MGH Cap.* I. 189.
2. *Assises de Jérusalem* I. 315.
3. Vv. 8167 ff.

IN NORTHWESTERN FRANCE
The "Youth" in Twelfth-Century Aristocratic Society*

Georges Duby

In the twelfth-century narratives written in the northwestern portion of the French kingdom,[1] certain well-born men are styled "youth," either individually by the adjective *"juvenis"* or collectively by the substantive *"juventus."* Clearly, these are precise qualifying terms, used to indicate that the people concerned belong to a particular social group: Sometimes they are used to designate churchmen, particularly a certain portion of a monastic community.[2] Most often, however, these terms apply to warriors and serve to place them in a well-defined stage of their lives. We must first try to determine the limits of that stage. It is clear that the individual called a "youth" is no longer a child, that he has passed the stage of education and of the exercises that prepare for military activity. The authors of these twelfth-century narratives use other words to qualify the sons of the nobility still learning the skills their estate requires: *"puer," "adulescentulus," "adolescens imberbis."* These nouns are used to refer to young men who have clearly left what we call "childhood," who have passed their fifteenth, seventeenth, or even nineteenth birthday, but who have not yet finished their apprenticeship. The "youth," on the other hand, is a man, an adult. He is part of the warrior group; he has received his arms; he has received the *adoubement.* He is a knight.[3] It is to be noted, furthermore, that knights are called "youth" until they are married, and

* Georges Duby, "Dans la France du Nord-Ouest. Au XIIe siècle: les 'jeunes' dans la société aristocratique," *Annales, Economies-Sociétés-Civilisations,* **19** (Paris, 1964), 835–846. Trans. by the ed.

even afterward. In the *Historia ecclesiastica* of Orderic Vitalis married knights without children are called "youth" while others, younger but already fathers, are no longer *"juvenis"* but *"vir."*[4] In the warrior world, then, the man of arms is no longer held to be a "youth" once he has become the head of a household, established, rooted, and the founder of a family. "Youth" can thus be defined as that part of a man's life between the ceremony of knighting and fatherhood.[5]

The sources indicate that this portion of life could be very long. For most individuals its duration is extremely difficult to establish, for the texts are very poor in biographical indications that can be precisely dated. I will cite two examples, however. About 1155, at the age of eleven or twelve years William the Marshal left his paternal home to become *puer* in the house of his uncle, William of Tancarville. He was armed knight in 1164, did the tournament circuit in 1166–1167, then led a life of "adventure and prowess."[6] He took a wife in 1189 when he was about forty-five. His "youth" had lasted a quarter of a century. Undoubtedly this was an exceptional case. But Arnold of Ardres, son of Count Baldwin of Guines, knighted in 1181 and married in 1194 remained a "youth" for thirteen years. What was known then as "youth"—being of a particular age and having a certain situation in military society and in the familial structure—could cover a large part of knightly life. The "youth" were considerable in number. They thus had considerable influence on the aristocracy of this region.

Their importance stemmed not so much from their number as from their behavior—"youth" appears in these narratives as a time of impatience, turbulence, and instability. In the preceding and following stages of his life the individual was fixed—in his childhood at his father's home or at the house of the patron who reared him, in his own house when he himself was married and a father. Between these two stages, he wandered. This refusal to stay, this wandering, appears in every description of the life of the "youth" as its most fundamental character. The youth leaves; he is moving; he crosses provinces and countries; he "wanders through all the lands."[7] For him the "most beautiful life" is to "travel in many lands seeking rewards and adventure,"[8] "to seek honor and rewards." It is thus a period of quest—for glory and reward in war or, even more, in tournament.[9]

From its beginnings, this errantry was considered a necessary addition to one's education, a "study," *studia militiae*—such as that followed by the young Arnold of Pamele "in imperial and royal wars" (until he suddenly entered a monastery, later becoming bishop of Soissons and a saint).[10] The "youth" therefore did not generally wander alone. In the earliest period of errantry, the "youth" was accompanied by a mentor chosen by his father, a knight also a "youth," but more experienced. The latter's task was to counsel the young man, to restrain him, to perfect his education, to direct him toward the most profitable tournaments. This was Ogier's role with Roland in the *Chanson d'Aspremont;* in real life that of William the Marshal in the company of Henry, son of Henry II of England. When Arnold of Ardres was knighted, his father and his father's lord, the Count of Flanders, gave him a mature man as his counselor *"in torniamentis et in rebus suis disponandis."* The counselor, since he himself could not go wandering, sent as instructor in arms his nephew who had been a companion of the "young" Henry of England.[11] More frequently, the "youth" was incorporated into a group of "friends," who "love one another as brothers."[12] This "company," this *"maisnie"* (these are the terms used by vernacular texts), was sometimes formed the day following the ceremony of knighting, by all those young warriors who had received the "sacrament of knighthood" on the same day and who then remained together.[13] Most often it formed around a leader who "retained" the youth, gave them arms and money, and directed them to adventure and its reward.[14] Sometimes this leader was an established individual, but almost always he was himself a "youth." Often, in this case, the company grouped the "youth" of vassal families around the lord's newly knighted son. Orderic Vitalis shows Robert Courteheuse thus bringing with him the sons of his father's vassals, sons who were Robert's own age and who, up to this time, had been "fed" and "armed" by his father.[15] A swarm of "children," arrived at adulthood, left the great seignorial house in this way, led by the seignorial heir who had just attained chivalric status, all escaping toward the errantry of "youth." The cohesiveness of vassal ties that joined the fathers together was reconstituted among the "youth"; in the heart of the youthful band it was prolonged for another generation. Ordinarily, however, the company's structure was more complex—in the *familia* maintained by Hugh of Chester, the *pueri* still in their apprenticeship, clergy, and courtesans mixed together with knights, all of them *juvenes*.[16] Who were the "youth" whom Arnold of Ardres led off to adventure? Two very close friends, his inseparable companions; knights who had come not from his father's house but from far away, such as Henri le Champenois, and, finally, all the tournament-goers of his father's principality.[17]

In these bands, joy reigned supreme. The leader spent freely and delighted in sex, gambling, players, horses, and dogs.[18] Morals were loose.[19] The band's business, however, was fighting "in tournament and in wars." One day a group of French knights turned from its route to see Clairvaux. It was three days before Lent, and St. Bernard exhorted them to refrain from fighting. But "as they were youth and strong knights, they refused" and, after drinking, left to seek military sport.[20] The companies of youth thus formed the cutting edge of feudal aggressiveness. On the lookout for any adventure from which they could wrest "honor" and "reward" and, if possible "return wealthy,"[21] always mobile and ready to leave, they kept up the agitation of war. They fanned the fires of trouble in areas of instability and provided the best contingents for distant expeditions.[22] A "youth" directed the military action of the Erembald clan during the Flemish troubles of 1127. The "youth," the "poor bachelors," were those whom William of Orange harangued when he organized an expedition against Nîmes in order to "endow his household." And how many youth there must have been among the armed pilgrims, among the crusaders.[23] Devoted to violence, the "youth" formed the organ of aggression and tumult in the body of chivalric society. But for just this reason it constantly affronted danger. Aggressive and brutal, the "youth," by their situation, were a decimated group. On this point we are abundantly informed. In the texts I have used, the most numerous references to the "youth" concern their violent deaths. Death came on them accidentally while they were hunting or practicing with their weapons, but most often, it came in military confrontations.[24] At times it mowed down whole groups of noble families' offspring; it constantly tore large holes. Two sons of the castellan Henry of Bourbourg died in their "youth," while a third came back blind from a tournament.[25] When Lambert, the author of the *Annales Cameracenses,* in a very curious passage drew up his own genealogical table, he recalled the ten brothers of his grandfather Raoul, all killed in battle the same day, whose memory "the poets' songs" had carried down to his own time; and of the other fifteen men of his blood he mentioned, three had died in combat, a fourth by falling off a horse.[26]

The military profession of the aristocracy, biological stimulation, and all that went with the age of these men help to explain their behavior. But in order to grasp the deeper springs, I think we must also consider the familial life within which this group of "youth" existed; for the structure of the family did much to sharpen their greed and to throw them into adventure and turbulence. A statistical sampling based on a large number of genealogies leads one to think that within the twelfth-century aristocratic society of northwestern France, the average number of years between generations was some thirty-odd. At the end of the twelfth century the eldest son normally came of age and received his arms when he was between sixteen and twenty-two, that is, at a time when his father (in his fifties) still held his patrimony well in hand and felt quite capable of caring for it himself. Propriety demanded that wealthy fathers and those careful of their family's glory provide the eldest son with what was necessary to lead a group of wandering "youth" for a year or two after knighting.[27] At the end of those wander-years we find the "youth" back at his father's house. He is bored. He finds the place stuffy. His tour has given him a taste of economic independence and free spending; now deprived of it, he strongly feels its absence. He casts an envious eye on the revenues that belong to him. If his mother is dead, bad counselors prick him into asking for his part of the inheritance, as one persuaded Arnold of Ardres, for example.[28] Long discussions ensue: a first confrontation with the father, who sometimes must give in. But even then the "stay" weighs heavily. Tensions rise against the father's powers. The history of the greatest lineages is full of such disputes; sometimes they provoke the son's new departure, this time an aggressive one. The "young" eldest son, surrounded by his young companions, opens battle with the old lord.[29] In any event, "*long sejour honnit jeune homme,*" a long stay dishonors a young man. Even if the family's peace is not violently troubled, the young heir, incapable of satisfying himself with domestic activities, takes to the road.[30] His father, relieved, gives him leave to depart,[31] to recall him only in senility.[32] Everyone thought it normal that a knighted son, neither settled nor married, put the open fields between himself and his father's house.

The rules by which aristocratic patrimonies were managed thus provoked the eldest son to go off in quest of adventure. But he had brothers and, ordinarily, a lot of them. Orderic Vitalis leads one to think that five, six, or seven boys normally survived to adulthood in a noble family. These also felt pushed to leave and even more strongly than the first-born. As early as the beginning of the eleventh century, the eldest son's privilege of receiving his father's succession and his seignorial powers was firmly established among the highest noble lineages, the kings, the counts, and the castellans. Undoubtedly, this privilege was more slowly admitted among families of lesser status. By the end of the twelfth century, however, primogeniture obtained throughout chivalric society in this area where allods had become rare and feudal law opposed the division of fiefs. Our witness is the care that writers took to specify the eldest boy, and even the eldest girl, in their genealogical lists.[33] What then happened to the younger sons? Two or three might hope to be well provided for in the Church. To the others sometimes came a small part of the inheritance, generally provided out of recent acquisitions or from the maternal side of the family.[34] But in these cases the possession was precarious. And these remnants promoted discord among the brothers, fed their greediness, and sharpened their temptation to grab another brother's or a nephew's portion by force.[35] Deprived of any hope of a certain inheritance, the younger sons saw only one way out—adventure.

The source of those impulses throwing the knights of the twelfth century into a wandering life must therefore be placed in the customs regulating the descent of inheritances and the distribution of family resources. But in order to shed more light on the situation of the "youth," we must closely examine the play of matrimonial practices and their repercussions, since (as we have seen) "youth" continued until marriage and, in practice, ended with it. There is no need to insist on the fact that every marriage was a transaction negotiated, decided, and concluded by the father and the older members of the lineage.[36] These people of course were most concerned with the marriage of the eldest son. But since this union involved the future of the house, they acted with considerable prudence; they waited for the really good chance to appear, and this prolonged "youth" yet more. Where the other sons were concerned, they were yet more circumspect—for other reasons. It was very important not to allow too many younger sons take wives, for fear that lateral branches of the lineage would multiply excessively and eventually choke out the main stem. Furthermore, and most important—to marry a son meant always to amputate a part from the family patrimony in order to establish the new husband upon it and to guarantee the *dot,* the wife's dower.[37] For the eldest, they perforce resigned themselves to do this. For another son they were much more reluctant. The younger son was destined for a longer "youth." Another roadblock: there were very few marriageable girls in the neighborhood. Former marriages had made the entire knighthood of a land cousins to one another. The age's ideas of incest, the formal probibitions of the Church against consanguinity, erected an unbreachable obstacle. This obstacle was re-enforced by the play of successive marriages. Genealogical tables show that heads of households went through several widowerhoods; in order that the marriage might bear financial fruit, a young man might be given a widow older than he, or the sickly offspring of a lineage fallen into biological decrepitude. Then there were always the dangers of childbearing. Once widowers—for whatever reason—well-established, fixed, these men sought new wives in their neighborhoods. Their positions, their prestige, their worldy wisdom favored them in the race for marriages. They won the best prizes and took the opportunities away from the "bachelors" without wives. All added thus to prolong "youth" and to push the "youth" into distant adventures.

These adventures, in effect, also (and perhaps above all) turned out to be quests for wives. Throughout their years of wandering, the band of "youth" were enlivened by hopes of marriage. They know that their leader, once he himself was established, would hold it his first duty to marry off his companions.[38] All the *juvenes* were on the lookout for a rich heiress. Should they espy one, they sought to reserve her, even if she were barely nubile. Sometimes they took the child along in their wanderings, free to restore her to her father if they should find a better match along the way or if another "youth" demanded her with too great insistence. I shall take another example from the *History of the Counts of Guines.* A certain adventurer had taken the daughter of the castellan of Bourbourg—promised to him as his wife—to England. Baldwin of Ardres, having gained the father's friendship by his military activities, succeeded in getting the castellan to talk about bringing the heiress back and ended by marrying her.[39] The intention to marry seems to have ordered the "youth's" entire behavior, inciting him to shine in combat and to show off in sporting matches. Thus Arnold of Guines first tried by his prowess to seduce the Countess of Boulogne; then he promised himself to the daughter of the Count of Saint-Pol; then, breaking all his previous engagements, he threw himself on the heiress of the castellans of Bourbourg as soon as he knew she was ripe for taking.[40]

The hunt for the rich girl, for the good settlement, was thus not always in vain. But its dangers and its profits can be explained only by the relative abundance of the game, that is to say, by the frequent wilting of noble lineages, by which entire inheritances fell into the hands of an heiress. And this phenomenon itself was closely tied to the life of the "youth," to its particular situation, to its adventurous life, and to the dangers it risked, dangers that decimated its ranks. Once again we must return to a consideration of aristocratic demography. An analysis of seignorial genealogies is here both instructive and convincing. Here are two cases, neither of them exceptional. First, the descendants of the Norman lord Hugh of Grentemesnil. Ten of his children survived to adulthood, five sons among them. Two died young (in the usual sense of the word). Two others went off in search of adventure; one established himself in Apulia, a second, nearer, in England, where he had two sons. Both of these latter died on a "youthful" trip, in the sinking of the *Blanche Nef*. Only one son remained on the patrimonial estates—the eldest, Robert, perhaps because he was married earlier and, thus, was earlier removed from the dangers of "youth." Robert, however, had only a daughter, and through her the family fortune passed to another lineage.[41] Second, the case of the castellan Henry of Bourbourg. It is certain that, in twenty-four years, his wife gave him twelve children who survived to maturity (such facts suggest that we should not exaggerate the effects of infant mortality in this social stratum). Among Henry's offspring, seven sons were provided with church livings; the eldest held the castle at his father's death and, although married twice, had no children; three others died or became invalids as youths; the last-born was castellan after his brother, married, but saw his son die in infancy; the entire inheritance went to his daughter who was pounced upon by Arnold of Ardres.[42]

These "youth," as one can see, this tempestuous band excluded by so many social conditions from the body of established men, of *patres familiae,* of heads of households, this unstable border that brought about and supported the great crusading undertakings, the taste for tournaments, the propensity for sexual promiscuity and concubinage, these "youth" exercised a decisive influence on the demography of this region's nobility and on the development of its patrimonial holdings. By maintaining most young men unmarried and in danger, this structure clearly reduced the danger of divided inheritances. But it also lowered the chances that lineages would survive, hastened the extinction of many families, and favored the renewal of the high aristocracy through the chance matrimonial successes of adventurers of lesser lineage. Thus, whoever asks questions about the behavior and destiny of the knighthood must examine this social group very closely.

Furthermore, the presence of such a group in the heart of aristocratic society maintained certain mental attitudes, certain displays of collective psychology, and certain myths, whose reflection and models are to be found in the literary works written for the aristocracy during the twelfth century and in the exemplary characters they present—literary works that in turn supported, prolonged, and stylized the group's spontaneous intellectual and emotional reactions. We must first of all note that the "youth" formed the primary audience for all the literature that is challed chivalric and which was undoubtedly composed principally for its enjoyment. I have already mentioned the mimes that Hugh of Chester maintained in his household and the bards who recalled to Lambert—the author of the *Annales Cameracenses*—the memory of his ten great-uncles killed in combat. When bad weather held the "youth" Arnold of Ardres in the boredom of domesticity, he had stories told to him. His relative, Gauthier of L'Ecluse, to amuse the band, recounted the legends of Gorment and Isembart, of Tristan and Iseult and also of the deeds of former lords of the castle.[43] It should not be astonishing that the typical situation of the "youth," the adventurous quest, and prowess in arms, furnished structure and motives to the epic poems and romances and even to sermons composed for these groups; for Gerald of Avranches, priest to the *familia* of Hugh of Chester, took for the theme of his sermons (which had an effect) the *emendatio vitae,* the reform of life of military saints—Demetrius and George, Maurice and the martyrs of the Theban legion, Eustache and Sebastian.[44] It would be interesting to reconsider the themes of chivalric literature as a function of the tastes, the prejudices, the frustrations, and the daily behavior of the "youth." I will limit myself to two specific points.

First, the transference of the hopes and dreams of the *juvenes* into the genealogical literature written in twelfth-century northwestern France—the model of the young adventurer who conquers the love of a rich heiress by his prowess and thus establishes himself in a strong seigniory far from his native land, eventually to become the founder of a powerful lineage. K. F. Werner has shown how, among the great lords of this region, the collective memory recalled a genealogical past that always ran blank in the ninth and tenth centuries. Beyond it, no ancestors were known. They invented. The writers who specialized in this genre imagined, as the first ancestor of great princely families, a foreigner young and brave, *"miles peregrinus,"* noted for his military qualities, and sometimes conquering his lordship by means of marriage.[45] Such cases are known for families of Anjou, Blois and Bellême; such was imagined by Lambert of Ardres, a priest in the service of the "youth" Arnold, a cleric impregnated with all the literature for which the "youth" had a taste. When Lambert traced the line of the counts of Guines back to the tenth century, he put there the figure of Siegfried the Dane. This ancester is a "youth"; he rides in search of adventure. His quest leads him to the household of the Count of Flanders. There he loves the Count's sister. He cannot marry her, but gives her a bastard son who becomes the founder of the counts of Guines.[46]

My second remark about the literary transpositions of the mental attitudes peculiar to the "youth" concerns the development of courtly love. These considerations force me to leave northwestern France for the South, for the troubadours of the generation of approximately 1150. Cercamon, Marcabru, Allegret all exalted the idea of *"jovens."* By this term they apparently designated less an abstract virtue than the ideal that animated the group of "youth." "Youth," for whom the troubadours themselves spoke, appeared in their songs as victims of society. The youth find no women to welcome them; they are all married. And when a woman gives herself to the game of adulterous love, her partner is not a "youth," but himself a husband. What appeared then in the love songs of the second half of the twelfth century was a proposal of a new kind of love relationship, better suited to the position of the *juvenes.* Husbands ought not to court the ladies, nor to prevent their wives from welcoming the "youth" and their service of love. For the triangle husband-wife-married lover, the poets of the "youth" proposed to substitute the triangle husband-lady-young servant of courtly love. For the profit of the "youth," they sought to break through the established circle of erotic relationships.[47] The success of this ideal theme is well known. In fact the game went on in reality as well, although then it somewhat changed its hue. To conclude, I come back once again to Lambert of Ardres and to his patron and hero, Arnold the "youth." Arnold's quest for prowess brings him to the attention of the Countess Idax of Boulogne who, as mistress of a seigniory, appears to him a magnificent godsend and the promise of an admirable situation. With her, Arnold exchanges secret love messages; he loves her—or pretends to. In fact *"ad terram tamen et Boloniensis comitatus dignitatem, veri vel simulati amoris objectu, recuperata ejusdem comitisse gratia, aspiravit."* [Winning the countess's grace by putting forward a true or pretended love, he hoped to claim the land and dignity of the county of Boulogne.][48]

Such was the aristocratic "youth" of twelfth-century France: a pack let loose by noble houses to relieve their surplus of expansive power—off to conquer glory, profit, and feminine prey.

NOTES*

1. I am using them in a general study of the aristocratic family in feudal society. This essay is a preliminary sketch of some ideas.

2. Thus, Orderic Vitalis, *Historia ecclesiastica* [hereinafter *Hist. eccl.*] (Leprévost and Delisle, eds., **2**. 47, 94). My remarks about books 3 to 7 of the *Hist. eccl.* rest on the unpublished study by J. Paul "La famille et les problèmes familiaux en Normandie au XIe siècle d'après l'*Historia ecclesiastica* d'Orderic Vital" (1960).

3. *Hist. eccl.* 8: Robert of Rhuoddan is called *"puer"* until he is *"miles."* Baldwin VI, son of the Count of Hainaut is *"juvenis etiam miles"*; H. d'Arbois de Jubainville, *Histoire des comtes de Champagne* (1859–1866), **7**, pt. 1, 70.

4. *Hist. eccl.* 4 (**2**. 219); 3 (**2**. 25).

5. *"Bachelier"* seems to have been the exact equivalent expressing in Romance the idea of *"juvenis"; L'Histoire de Guillaume le Maréchal* (P. Meyer, ed.), v. 1477; *Charroi de Nîmes* vv. 23–25; *Chanson de Roland* vv. 3018–3020.

6. *Guil. le Maréchal* vv. 1895, 1901.

7. *Guil. le Maréchal,* vv. 2399, 2444. V. 1890:

> *Que nus qui velt en pris monter*
> *N'amera ja trop long sejor . . .*
> *. . . Ainz s'esmoveit en meinte terre*
> *Por pris e aventure quere*
> *Mais souvent s'en reveneit riches . . .*
> [No one wishing to rise in esteem/ Likes to stay too long . . ./ Thus he went through many lands/ Searching reputation and adventure/ And often he returned rich . . .]

See also Lambert d'Ardres, *Historia comitum Ghisnensium* 91.

8. *Guil. le Maréchal* vv. 754; 2997–2998; 1513–1517:

> *Puis mena si très bele vie*
> *Que plosors en orent envie*
> *En torneiemenz e en guerres*
> *E erra par totes les terres*
> *Ou chevaliers deit pris conquerre.*
> [He led such a wonderful life/ That many envied him for it/ Going to tournaments and war/ And wandering through all the lands/ Where knights must win renown.]

9. Note that young men of good family who did not receive the *adoubement* but were sent off to study fell into a very similar kind of wandering, in which scholastic disputation, an occasion for prowess and prizes, played the role of the tournament. The young Abelard's behavior, even the vocabulary he uses in the first pages of his *Story of My Calamities,* are very expressive of this.

10. *Acta sanctorum,* 15 Aug. 3. 232 *A*.

11. *Aspremont* vv. 7515–7516; *Guil. le Maréchal* vv. 2427–2432, 1959–1967; *Hist. com. Ghis.* 92.

12. *Guil. le Maréchal* v. 15884.

13. *Hist. com. Ghis.* 91.

---

* Except for source and bibliographical references, most of the material in the original notes has been omitted.—Ed.

14. *Guil. le Maréchal* vv. 2673–2675, 2679–2685.

15. *Hist. eccl.* 5 (**2**. 381), 7 (**3**. 190).

16. *Hist. eccl.* 6 (**3**. 4).

17. *Hist. com. Ghis.* 92.

18. Hugh of Chester, *in militia promptus, in dando prodigus,* kept minstrels and prostitutes in his *familia*—*Hist. eccl.* 6 (**3**. 4).

19. When Roger and his companions left the *maisnie* of Hugh of Chester to convert, Orderic Vitalis describes them returning "as though from the flames of Sodom"—*Hist. eccl.,* 6 (**3**. 16); see also Guibert de Nogent, *De vita sua* **1**. 15 (Bourgen, ed. p. 57), **3**. 19 (p. 220).

20. "Fragmenta Gaufredi," *Analecta Bollandiana* **50** (1932), 110.

21. *Guil. le Maréchal* v. 1897.

22. *Hist. eccl.* 3 (**2**. 54).

23. *Charroi de Nîmes* vv. 641–646.

24. Richard, son of William the Conqueror, killed while hunting—*Hist. eccl.* 5 (**2**. 391); Hugh, son of Giroie, *"juventute florens,"* died wounded by a javelin in sport—*Hist. eccl.* 3 (**2**. 29); see also *Hist. eccl.* 3 (**2**. 25); *Hist. com. Ghis.* 72, 134.

25. *Hist. com. Ghis.* 122.

26. *MGH SS* **16**. 511–512.

27. *Guil. le Maréchal* v. 2444; *Hist. com. Ghis.* 91.

28. *Hist. com. Ghis.* 92.

29. Robert Courteheuse, *Hist. eccl.* 5 (**2**. 381); The eldest son of William the Marshal, accompanied by another youth, supported the side of the King of France against his own father—*Guil. le Maréchal* v. 15884; in the eleventh century the son of Robert the Pious, with a troup of associates his own age, ravaged his father's lands—Raoul Glaber, *Historiarum libri quinque* **3**. 9.

30. In *Hist. com. Ghis.* 93, Arnold of Ardres prefers to go to countries *propter torniamentorum studium et gloriam,* rather than stay in the country where there is no war. *Guil. le Maréchal* v. 2391: the "young" Henry, his father, and their companions,

> *En Engletere sojurnerent*
> *Près d'un an qu'il ne s'atornèrent*
> *A nule riens fors a pleidier*
> *Ou a bois ou a torneier*
> *Mais al giemble rei pas ne plout*
> *Tel sejor, anceis li desplout,*
> *A ses compaignons ensement*
> *Ennuia molt très durement,*
> *Car a esrer plus lor pleust*
> *Qu'a sejorner, s'estre peust*
> *Quer bien saciez, ce est la somme*
> *Que lonc sejor honist giemble homme.*
> [In England they remained/ For almost a year they did nothing but engage in *pleids*/ Or hunt or fight in tournaments./ But to the young king/ Such a stay was not pleasing. Thus it displeased him.
> His companions likewise/ It bothered very much./ For to wander would have pleased them more/ Than to stay./ For you should know—this is it in short—/ A long stay dishonors a young man.]

31. *Guil. le Maréchal* vv. 2404, 1391–1394.
32. *Hist. eccl.* 5 (**2**. 457, 463).
33. *Hist. com. Ghis.* 63; *MGH SS* **16**. 511–512.
34. In the southwest, the old lord settled the *dispositio* of his succession while still alive—*Historia pontificum et comitum Engolismensium* 26, 31, 36.
35. *Historia pontificum et comitum Engolismensium* 30.
36. *Hist. com. Ghis.* 149.
37. *Hist. com. Ghis.* 149.
38. *Aspremont,* vv. 5572–5573; *Hist. com. Ghis.* 64.
39. *Hist. com. Ghis.,* vv. 39, 60.
40. *Hist. com. Ghis.,* vv. 93, 149.
41. *Hist. eccl.* 11 (**4**. 167 *n*. 2).
42. *Hist. com. Ghis.* 122.
43. *Hist. com. Ghis.* 96.
44. *Hist. eccl.* 3, 3–18.
45. K. F. Werner, "Untersuchungen zur Frühzeit des französischen Fürstentums," *Die Welt als Geschichte,* **20** (1960), 116–118.
46. *Hist. com. Ghis.* 9–11.
47. R. Nelli, *L'érotique des troubadours* (1963), 108 ff.
48. *Hist. com. Ghis.* 93.

The Laws of War in the Late Middle Ages*

M. H. Keen

"The notion of a law of nations was preceded and prepared for by the chivalric ideal of a good life of honour and loyalty."[1] The conclusions which stem from a study of the law of arms form in effect an extended commentary on this statement of Huizinga. For this military law of the fourteenth and fifteenth centuries bridges the gap between his two theses. It reveals the chivalrous obligations of a soldier formalised in a law, which was applied in the courts as a part of what was then understood to be the law of nations, the ancient *jus gentium*.

Because it bound men irrespective of their allegiance, one may perhaps call the law of arms an international law. But it was very different from any international law known to the modern world. The extraordinary variety of the legal matters which it regulated make this clear, and make it clear further that in the late middle ages the categories into which laws were classified were different from those now in use. The law of arms governed alike the conduct of soldiers towards enemies (a matter now regulated by agreed international convention), the discipline of armies (military or martial law in our sense), rules concerning rights in spoil (which appear to be modelled on the law of property), and armorial disputes (which would probably now be regarded as a branch of peerage law). Of the distinction which today is drawn between public and private international law there is no hint here. The rulings of the law of arms quoted by individuals who were claiming, for example, rights in ransoms,

---

* Reprinted from *The Laws of War in the Late Middle Ages* by M. H. Keen with the permission of the University of Toronto Press (Ont., Canada) and of Routledge and Kegan Paul, Ltd. (London). The selection is the concluding chapter, pp. 239–247.

suggest that it was an early prototype of private international law. But when Charles VII's advisers told him that by law of arms the English seizure of Fougères in 1449 constituted a *casus belli*,[2] they were applying this law to a public issue, and labelling the English action (to use modern phraseology) a breach of public international law. The same law was taken to govern public and private relations in war.

What this apparent confusion of terms indicates is the difficulty of applying a definition such as "international law" to the customs of a society which did not think in terms of nationality. The distinguishing feature of a nation, as we understand the word, is its independent sovereign status, which makes it, legally, a unique and self-sufficient society. In legal theory, the kingdoms and principalities of the later middle ages were neither unique nor self-sufficient. The only society which was so was the society of Christendom, a supra-national society of which Christian kingdoms were dependent members. His allegiance to this society was the one overriding obligation of the Christian soldier. Various ties of personal loyalty might attach him to a whole series of secular masters; to one man, perhaps he was bound by a sworn contract to serve him for a stated period, to another because he wore his order of chivalry, to others again by the tenure of fiefs. Each of these allegiances was based in an individual relationship, and for this reason conflicts of loyalty were a problem for the individual, defying resolution on the basis of any guiding principle of nationality. The only obligations which were universal were those which bound all Christian men alike, such as the rules of chivalrous conduct, for allegiance to the honour of knighthood was not limited by place or time. The rules of chivalry applied, in Ayala's words, "wherever there was war."[3]

This points the way to a first and most important conclusion. Because the society called western Christendom had no visible head, its unity (at least in the later middle ages) is often treated as chimerical. That one law could be accepted as binding on soldiers throughout its length and breadth shows that this was not the case. This law was something more than a vague set of principles of loyalty and honour. It was a law which was accepted and enforced in properly constituted courts, and whose intricacies were argued by trained lawyers. It had a sound authoritarian basis in the written laws of Rome, the canon and civil laws. These laws had general validity because the equation of Christian society and the Roman people was assumed as a historical fact. The absence of any visible head to this body politic did not matter, since its members were bond together by their common obedience to "mother church," whose lord was God himself. The sovereignty of this unseen master did not seem remote or ineffective to men who believed that the direct interplay of natural and supernatural forces was the key to historical causation. Thus, just as the principle that kings should rule under God's law was the rallying cry of constitutionalists among their subjects, so too the principle that *dei lex est major legi principis*[4] gave force, in the late middle ages, to the belief that the relations of the subjects of one king with those of another ought to be "constitutional" also.

As has been said before, chivalry in the fourteenth and fifteenth centuries was regarded as a Roman institution. To the people of that period, the difference between the rules of chivalry and the discipline of imperial Roman armies was merely chronological. The law of arms was thus a professional law, the common law of all soldiers in the world of Roman Christians. But these people viewed Roman history through the distorting lens of contemporary conditions. To the descendants of the barbarian invaders of the Roman world profession and status went hand in hand, and were alike hereditary. Thus when Charles VII's council, spurred to reflection by the outrages of the *écorcheurs,* attempted to diagnose reasons for the general indiscipline of his soldiers, they attributed it to the fact that of late the King's armies had become filled with "artisans, labourers and other idle folk," who could never be expected to live up to the high standards of chivalry.[5] Fighting was a business for those of gentle birth. This is why armorial disputes came within the view of the military courts; for men of this age, banners and blazonry, which were inherited, had the same sort of significance as badges of rank today. This brings us to a second important conclusion about the law of arms. It was not just the law of a certain Christian profession, but also the law of a hereditary noble class.[6]

This is a quite different idea of what an international law may be to any with which we are now familiar. It does, however, serve to illustrate how real the unity of Christendom seemed in those days; class solidarity transcended the boundaries of kingdoms. It also helps to explain why the law of arms was respected. "In the middle and lower classes," said Taine, "the chief motive of conduct is self-interest; with an aristocracy the mainspring is pride."[7] As regards the greater nobility, at least, of the later middle ages, there is much truth in this statement. Princes, such as Philip the Good or Henry V, were jealous of their good fame, and punctilious in discharging obligations in which their honour was involved.[8] It is true, no doubt, that it was chiefly the very great who were as careful as they, and that this was partly because they had to play to a wide audience—they knew that every action they took would be observed, and judged by severe critics. Obligations upon honour clearly weighed much more lightly with ordinary knights and professional captains, as is shown by the subterfuges which they adopted in order to avoid them. Nevertheless, the example of their social superiors was not completely lost on them. Nowadays we hear so much of class strife as an overriding force in history that we may sometimes forget how strong, in most periods, has been the natural urge of men to ape their betters. Certainly, just as they were often more impressed by the outward appurtenances of rank than by its obligations, professional soldiers were as a rule more concerned with the letter of their chivalrous code than with its spirit; but this does not mean that chivalrous obligations meant nothing to them. When Seguin de Badefol, one of the worst of the *routiers,* swore to keep his treaty with the Dauphin of Auvergne, or otherwise 'to be held forever false and wicked, attainted of treason and perjured on his faith in all courts and before all lords',[9] he may not have intended to keep his word, if he could find an excuse to break it. But it is surely significant that even in dealings with a man of his stamp, the Dauphin still regarded a solemn promise on knighthood to be the best guarantee he could get.

In fact, in their dealings with their equals and superiors, the conduct even of the free companies and the *écorcheurs* will stand up to scrutiny. Here at least pride of place had its beneficial effect, and not surprisingly, for it was in this sector of society that ambitious soldiers wished to impress. For those in arms generally, the law of arms did a great deal to ensure a humane standard of conduct. Gentlemen prisoners were usually treated well, and allowed to go free on parole. The practice of taking men for ransom also helped to prevent unnecessary bloodshed in the field. But the story was different in the case of the noncombatant. The civilians, and above all the humble, suffered untold hardships in war. The awful tales in descriptions of the *écorcherie* of men hung, roasted, or dragged behind horses in order to extract a few pennies of ransom from them, testify to conduct which can only be described as barbaric and inhuman. One or two exceptional commanders (Henry V is a famous example) acquired a good reputation for enforcing the rules which protected the common people of the country over which war was raging; the average captain simply did not regard them. "A man may not torture a prisoner to extort money from him by way of ransom," says Paris of Pozzo, "but it is different in the case of peasants, at least according to the custom of mercenaries."[10] This is a very wide exception, and a very important one. In its light, the whole theory of chivalry, of an order of knighthood whose Christian duty is the protection of the needy and defenceless, becomes meaningless.

The trouble with professional soldiers was not that they failed to take the obligations of their chivalrous rank seriously, but that they did not take them seriously enough. Rank can indeed foster in a class a sense of obligation, but it can also foster a sense of exclusiveness. Too many soldiers treated their obligations as such as applying only to their relations with their equals in the field of battle. This attitude is understandable, but it is not endearing. For here there were stronger grounds for taking their responsibilities in earnest; it was very much in their interest to do so. If one did not pay one's own ransom to the man who took one prisoner, he or his friends might all too easily serve one in one's own coin. One observed enemy safe-conducts, because to infringe them without excuse might easily lead to reprisals. Pride was a potent force in keeping soldiers to their word of honour, but it was clearly much more potent when it was backed by self-interest.

One cannot, indeed, help wondering whether the law of arms would have meant anything if it had not been for the financial stakes at issue in battle. In all the legal problems of war, as we have studied them, the question of profit has been in one way or another involved. Among other things, this is the reason why matters of discipline and disputes between soldiers of different allegiance were governed by the same law; in contemporary conditions, such questions were inseparable. It was essential for a commander to have power to limit the plundering of his soldiers; otherwise his army was likely, in the hour of victory, to dissolve into a disorderly rabble in the quest for loot. Thus disobedience of standing orders could be held to invalidate a man's title to a ransom, because by law of arms a captain was entitled to make ordinances which his soldiers were bound to obey.[11]

This matter of the spoils of war may have had a still more crucial importance. Financial interest was not only a reason why the law was obeyed; it seems likely that it was the key factor in its development and achievement of general recognition. There had always been local rules about conduct in war, such as those which are recorded by Beaumanoir for the Beauvaisis, or the thirteenth century customs of the March of Scotland. But in the fourteenth and fifteenth centuries war had become a commercial concern at the international level; the ransoming of prisoners and villages, the sale of safe-conducts and strategically placed forts had become a legitimate means of making a living. Soldiering too had become international. A captain like Francois de Surienne had on his muster rolls men born in England, France, Brittany, and Germany, and they might find themselves equally easily fighting in any one of these lands, or in Italy or Scotland. In these circumstances, the need for a common soldiers' law was one which was felt. It was met by applying to the problems which conduct in war presented the principles of the only laws known to be generally accepted, the canon and civil laws. Where these laid down no rules, difficulties were resolved by applying principles drawn from other known laws. Thus for instance the rules governing rights to ransom were assimilated to those governing the tenure of fiefs. But if ransoms had not been so profitable, it is unlikely that any learned doctor would have bothered about defining these rules.

The law of arms was thus a product of the international wars of the late middle ages. As has already been said, though, the word "international" must be used with caution with reference to this age. Its legal theories were dominated by ideas of "right" which made little distinction between the rights of public bodies and those of private persons, its political relations by ideas of allegiance based in the sworn promises of one man to another. Its wars were fought over the rights of persons, rather than the interests of nations, and its soldiers fought as members of an order pledged to the defence of such rights. The rights which they in turn acquired in war, to ransoms and such-like, were allowed to be theirs individually, as the fair reward of the risks which they had run therein. It was this which made their profession so profitable. The rules of the law of arms were appropriate to this condition of things. They were formulated and applied with a view to the protection of the rights of individual soldiers, not to regulating the conduct of the troops of warring nations. In a society in which, under God, personal loyalties and heritable personal rights meant more than anything else, these rules gave the code of chivalry tangible force, sanctioning agreements made for private gain by allegiance to the honour of knighthood. Their effectiveness was due to their appeal to two most potent human motives, pride and profit.

Circumstances, however, were changing at the end of the Hundred Years War. The idea of chivalry, of a united order of Christian soldiers pledged to the armed defence of justice, was a legacy of the age of the crusades; it had little significance in the contemporary world of emergent nation states. By this time the open profiteering of professional soldiers had debased the old principle, that the spoils of war were the equitable reward of the man who risked his life in a just cause. It was not easy to justify their sort of profit on moral grounds, or to take much pride in the way it was won. From the very beginning of the Hundred Years War, moreover, signs of the pressure of standards quite other than those in which chivalry was founded had been apparent. The courts had always enforced the rule, that only rights won in a war waged on the authority of a "public" power were recognised as justly acquired. This standard of judging the justice of war was a purely conventional one, and its recognition implied that there were more important calls on the loyalty of a soldier than his allegiance to an order of knighthood, pledged to defend eternal right. Once this supra-national allegiance no longer took priority, chivalry had no more purpose.

The law of arms, however, had more to it than a set of chivalrous ideals. It was a formal and generally accepted law, and its currency helped to establish two very important legal principles, which were remembered long after the idea that soldiering was the Christian vocation of a noble class had been forgotten. One was that war, in its proper sense, could only be waged by sovereigns. The consequences of this view were, in the period of the Hundred Years War, unclear, because it was not then clear what the precise definition of a sovereign ought to be. In early days, the word was taken to denote an individual whose high personal status entitled him to special rights, but more and more, as time went on, these special rights were associated with those whose status entitled them to speak on behalf of a collective body of men. Here are revealed essential links in the pedigree by which Grotius's principle, that only sovereign states may legitimately make war, may be traced back to its ancestry in the *droit de guerre* of the feudal *seigneur*. The other principle, which the enforcement of the law of arms by the military courts of the fourteenth and fifteenth centuries helped to establish, was that in war soldiers, though they served different lords, were yet bound by certain general and known rules of conduct. Once again it was on this belief, that there are general laws binding on all men regardless of nationality, that Grotius founded his theory of international law. Huizinga was right: the chivalrous conceptions of honour and loyalty of an age when the idea of nationality was not fully understood prepared the way for the notion of a law of nations.

NOTES

1. J. Huizinga, "The Political and Military Significance of Chivalric Ideas in the late Middle Ages," *Men and Ideas* (translated James S. Holmes and Hans van Marle, London, 1960), p. 203.

2. R. Blondel, *De Reductione Normannie,* pp. 37–8 and 41.

3. Keen, *The Laws of War,* ch. IV, pp. 52–53.

4. See *Laws of War,* ch. II, p. 18.

5. Document quoted by Tuetey, *Les Écorcheurs sous Charles VII,* Tome I, p. 131.

6. It is very difficult to distinguish the professional from the hereditary elements in the factors which made soldiering a noble profession. On this, see *Laws of War,* Appendix II, *The Peerage of Soldiers.*

7. Quoted by Huizinga, *cit. supra,* p. 205.

8. See *Laws of War,* ch. XI, especially p. 190, n. 6 and 7 (Henry V), and p. 203, n. 1, p. 205, n. 1, p. 211, n. 3 (Philip the Good).

9. *Spicilegium Brivatense,* ed. A. Chassaing (Paris, 1886), p. 366.

10. Paris of Pozzo, *De Re Militari,* Lib. IX, cap. 2 (Zilletus, *Tractatus Juris Universi,* Tome XVI, fo. 421vo).

11. Cf. Upton, *De Officio Militari,* Lib. I, cap. 16, and Lib. IV (ed. Bysshe, p. 32 and p. 133); see also B. Mus., Stowe MS. 1047, fo. 248 (on the powers of a commander, heraldic MS.), "quinto datur [principali capitaneo] potestas faciendi statuta, et proclamationes faciendi, et executionem demandandi." A good example of a disciplinary ordinance being quoted in a dispute over ransom is the case of Chamberlain *v.* Gerard in the Court of Chivalry, in which Chamberlain called the Marshal of Despenser's host of 1383, who testified that the ordinances he had made about taking prisoners made it impossible for Gerard to have taken the prisoner in dispute legitimately (P.R.O., C47/6/5).

III. The End of the Middle Ages

FEUDALISM OR PRINCIPALITIES IN FIFTEENTH-CENTURY FRANCE*

Edouard Perroy

I shall start the present discussion with a question of phraseology. But I hope to be able to show that there is in it more than a mere question of words, and that behind the words lies a very substantial matter.

One of the outstanding factors of the political life of both England and France in the second half of the fourteenth and during the whole of the fifteenth century, is the existence of a group of landed magnates of an entirely new type, with entirely new political ambitions. Yet, all French historians are content to call this group of princes "feudal lords." They see in their struggles with the crown a new aspect of the old feud between monarchy and feudalism. We are told that both Charles VII and Louis XI had to fight with feudal coalitions. Occasionally, to distinguish this form of feudalism from the one prevalent in earlier centuries, they speak of "féodalité apanagée." The phrase is not altogether satisfactory, since many of these princes were not holding apanages (Armagnac and Foix in southern France), while others, although holding apanages, had other

* Reprinted from Edouard Perroy, "Feudalism or Principalities in Fifteenth-Century France," *Bulletin of the Institute of Historical Research* (University of London, 1943–1945), **20**, 181–185.

lands far more important that were not apanages (this is the case for Bourbon and, of course, Burgundy).

In England, where the baronage played a similar although slightly different part, phrases like "new feudalism" or "bastard feudalism" have been coined by modern historians. But they cover something more than the constitution of large principalities, as in France. They define the new relationship between patron and client, through contracts of retinue, which do not seem to have existed on the other side of the Channel. Restricting the present paper to France, I come to wonder if the word "feudalism" ought not to be discarded once for all, for it creates a regrettable confusion as to the real character of the new baronage that takes a prominent part in the life of the nation from the time of Charles V right to the close of the Middle Ages.

That all the princes and magnates were, theoretically, vassals of the crown, is of course beyond discussion. It remains to be seen if this "vassality" was the deciding factor of their policy or if, on the contrary, their opposition to, and their attempts at the control of, the crown were not the outcome of conceptions entirely alien to the decadent feudal system of the time.

First, let us note that all these magnates had, by the end of the fourteenth century, created in their principalities an administrative machinery exactly similar to that of the state. Their political programme could not be, like that of their ancestors of the thirteenth century, to put a check to the growth of influence of the king's officers and machinery of state, since this machinery they had readily accepted and converted to their own use. The chronology of these changes has not yet been precisely examined; it is worth taking the trouble. One will note that some of the smaller feudal states were among the first to create this machinery, while, on the other hand, very great and powerful houses waited a long time before enacting the measures which transformed their lordships into miniature modern states.

A few instances will suffice. The county of Forez, in central France, was by no means a large territory, about the size of a modern French department. Yet, from the end of the thirteenth century onwards, very rapid changes were effected in its internal organization. Before 1300 the count had a regular appointed council with sworn councillors; a chancery, copied from the king's. His judges held two courts, one for ordinary cases, the other for the appeals from the vassals' courts, thus escaping the danger of too frequent appeals to the king's courts. The household was also fully organized, as can be seen from accounts dating from 1325. Further, as early as 1317, was created a new financial department, which very soon afterwards was called the Chamber of Accounts. Ordinances were enacted to define the way in which the count's treasurer and other officials were to account to the Chamber. It was a small affair, with only two or three clerks, but its duties and work were exactly similar to those of the king's Chamber of Accounts, the birth of which is placed by Borrelli de Serres in 1303 or 1304. In some ways, the work in Forez was done more thoroughly than in Paris; the filing of acts of homage from the vassals, the investigation of homages not rendered, the keeping of the count's archives, the appointment and pledging of new local officials, can be illustrated by a series of registers, still extant, which show how efficient it was from the start. Let us note that the then count of Forez, John I, was a prominent councillor of Philip the Fair and of his three sons. In his official missions he realized the usefulness of the new royal administration and immediately copied it for the government of his smallish fief.

The instance of a late development will be given by Burgundy. Recent research (by M. Pocquet du Haut-Jussé) has shown that up to 1350 the dukes of Burgundy kept a very archaic financial organization, with a very inefficient accounting system. When King John took the government of the duchy in the name of his stepson Philip of Rouvre, some of the more modern methods then in use in Paris were brought in, but very timidly. The accession of Philip the Bold in 1363 was not even the occasion for startling changes. The new duke waited till 1386 to adjust his administration to that of the king. M. Pocquet tells how he simply borrowed some of Charles VI's civil servants, and put them in charge of the creation and organization of the Chamber of Accounts of Dijon. But, by the end of the fourteenth century, the change was everywhere effected. It had been more easily made in new apanages than in old feudal principalities, for in a newly created apanage the recipient simply took charge, so to speak, of all the king's officials, who automatically became his own servants. We shall see in a moment what strength the princes gathered from this personnel of devoted officials and how they pushed them in the king's services.

These rival administrations might not have been very dangerous for the king, had the princes carried on their government on strictly old-fashioned lines. Theoretically, the king's overlordship was still observed, with judicial appeals to Parliament, the right to levy feudal contingents, and the right to collect taxes. But all these rights were subtly and gradually annihilated. Often the princes evaded appeals to Parliament by the creation of an intermediate appeal court, such as the Jours Généraux which Philip the Bold organized at Beaune. More often, all the regal rights were in fact given to the prince, who, besides being the feudal lord of the principality, was also holding the title of king's lieutenant in the same district and thus exercising the king's rights. The gradual growth of the institution of the king's lieutenancy in the fourteenth century ought to be carefully scrutinized. At first it seems to have been a temporary delegation of power for reasons of emergency and convenience. Languedoc was the first province, owing to its distance from Paris, to have permanently a king's lieutenant. Then, under Charles V and chiefly Charles VI, the practice was extended to other provinces till it spread to practically the whole territory of the kingdom.

Lastly, the right to collect taxes was also very precariously exercised by the king's servants. The princes, having great personal ambitions, could not "live of their own." It was difficult for them to ask local Estates to grant them subsidies, since these could only be levied after and over the king's aids. The simplest way to replenish their treasuries was to obtain from the crown a part, one-third, half or even the total amount of the aids. "Gift of the aids" was their main preoccupation. As the right of the king to levy taxes in the great fiefs, even after the vote of a subsidy by the Estates, was never completely recognized, the barons could easily barter with the king. In the case of Burgundy, M. Pocquet has again shown that the decisive steps in the matter were taken not by the feeble Charles VI, but by the wise Charles V, who finally consented not to collect any taxes in the duchy, without even getting from his brother the smallest gracious aid. In a monograph published in 1935, M. Lacour pointed to similar facts relating to Berry. By the end of the fifteenth century all great principalities, including Burgundy, Berry, Anjou, Orleans, Bourbon and the rest of them, were in the habit of converting for their own use and for long periods at a time the total amount of the king's taxes.

This was not enough for the princes. Even under stern monarchs like Charles V, they were normally employed in diplomatic missions, sent as king's lieutenants, put at the head of armies, etc. For these services they were given salaries, at first proportionate to the duration of the mission. Soon these indemnities were paid in advance by monthly instalments and thus became regular pensions. The princes tried to get even more: extraordinary gifts, sometimes very substantial, with or without any pretext, had to be bestowed on them if they wanted to "keep their estate." M. Pocquet tells us that in the case of Burgundy they were so enormous that the receipts of the duchy, which amounted to about 100,000 francs a year in 1375, had swollen to over 500,000 at the beginning of the fifteenth century.

This vital necessity of keeping open and well furnished the flow of money and gifts entailed important political consequences. The princes must keep control of the crown—not only by being permanent members of the king's council, but by placing their protégés and own officials in all the services of the state; and there we return to the question of administrative personnel. It could be shown by many individual instances that, under Charles VI, the normal career of the state official started in the services of a prince, from which the official was gradually promoted through the royal departments; he remained a client of the prince, had to see that his patron's wishes and interests were carried out and protected; his allegiance to the crown was only secondary. Furthermore, as all the princes could not be served at the same time, both in regard to gifts of money and to appointment of their protégés, it was inevitable that they should vie for the first place each against the other. From 1380 to 1418, every time one prince took the lead over another, a complete *épuration* of all the services was effected by the victor, who placed his protégés in all responsible posts. The administrative anarchy which culminated in the Cabochien movement has its root in this constant upheaval of the machinery of state.

Thus we see that the political problem of fifteenth century France is not a feudal one: the state is swallowed by rival and smaller states; competitions between the magnates' officials and the king's servants, the appropriation of the king's revenues by the princes, and lastly the systematic appointment of the princes' officers to state functions are the most important aspects of this problem. Others ought to be added, which lack of space and also of good detailed studies prevent me from more than mentioning here. We do not see yet very clearly how in France the princes developed their retinue; how they enrolled the services of the smaller nobility, how they built up private armies, how they paid the services of their retainers. This needs being gone into more thoroughly than has been done hitherto. May I mention, for instance, that M. Rey, who is just putting the finishing touch to an important book on the finances of Charles VI,† intends afterwards to use his notes for a study of what I should term the king's pensioners, trying to trace the origin and activity of all the persons who got a pension from the insane king, and to what prince they were chiefly devoted.

Lastly, I must point out that, in the civil wars that were the outcome of such social and economic changes, the magnates, however powerful, could not count on their own forces to keep permanent control of the monarchy. They tried to enlist popular support by pretending that they favoured reforms. The culmination of this came in 1465, with the war of the Public Weal. But it can be traced back as early as 1405, when John the Fearless of Burgundy took the lead of what Coville justly termed the Party of Reforms. It can be followed up by the Cabochiens of 1413; it is seen again in the Praguerie of 1440 and again in the frustrated coalition of 1442, which clamoured for the calling up of the Estates General.

Thus, we have gone very far from feudalism. Indeed the question of how the crown and the magnates were going to adjust their opposite ambitions in fifteenth century France is more akin to that which confronted Richelieu and the *Grands* or Mazarin and the Fronde in the seventeenth century, than to the feudal leagues of 1315. In less than a century after 1315, the character of both the state and the baronage had changed so much that, in my opinion, we must rule out all reference to feudalism.

---

† Maurice Rey, *Le domaine du roi et les finances extraordinaires sous Charles VI, 1388–1412* (1965); Maurice Rey, *Les finances royales sous Charles VI; les causes du déficit, 1388–1413* (1965).

THE FEUDALITY OF RETAINING*

William Huse Dunham, Jr.

I. ARGUMENT: THE FEUDALITY OF RETAINING BY INDENTURE

To dub the politico-military system of feed retainers in fifteenth-century England "Bastard Feudalism"[1] does not seem very enlightening—no more so than to brand Britain's Baldwinian economy "Bastard Capitalism." Actually, neither system was illegitimate, that is unlawful, even though acts of parliament regulated aspects of each. A happier view is to construe the peers' practice of retaining companies of knights, esquires, and gentlemen as a refinement, and not a degeneration, of an earlier feudal custom. Its continuance as an effective social procedure would seem to prove, not decay, but viability. Likewise, the notion that the years 1399–1485 marked "the decline and fall of English feudalism" reflects a pessimistic attitude towards feudal retaining—the result of evaluating the institution from its defects rather than from its purpose and achievements. The misuse, largely through unlawful maintenance, of the power that liveried retainers provided, led to wrongs aplenty. This happens when any institution, like the Stuart monarchy, is abused. But overmuch concern with the evil consequences of these abuses has produced moral indignation and a denigration of retaining, rather than an historical understanding.

An optimistic point of view towards Yorkist society, and one freed

---

* Reprinted from William Huse Dunham, Jr., *Lord Hastings' Indentured Retainers, 1461–1483* (Transactions of the Connecticut Academy of Arts and Sciences, no. 39), (New Haven: 1955), pp. 7–26. By permission of the Conn. Academy of Arts and Sciences and of Professor William Huse Dunham, Jr.

from Tudor propaganda,[2] may lead to a more judicious conclusion. Did not the so-called "pseudo-chivalry" of Edward IV's reign produce, in fact, more sophisticated arrangements for war and politics than had the socially primitive tenurial feudalism of Norman England? After all, the practice of retaining men by oath or indenture was founded upon the most sacred of English constitutional principles—that of contract. Even after the personal relation between a "lord" and his "man" had become separated from the tenure of land, it still rested upon a bi-lateral contract. Whether a contractual arrangement not based upon land and tenure is strictly "feudal" may be a matter of debate; but to Maitland feudalism before 1300 meant:

> "a state of society in which the main social bond is the relation between lord and man, a relation implying on the lord's part protection and defense; on the man's part protection, service and reverence, the service including service in arms. This personal relation is inseparably involved in a proprietary relation, the tenure of land . . ."[3]

Once this personal relation has been severed from the proprietary relation, some will argue, it has lost its "feudal" character. But during the fifteenth century, men translated the Latin word for fief, *feodum,* into "fee", the thing that supplanted the land fief. Recent research has traced the *fief-rente* (a fief consisting of an annual payment in pounds, shillings, and pence) back to Henry I's time, the year 1103. Henry II, too, used the *fief-rente* to procure military service from continental nobles, and "literally hundreds" of "feudal contracts" survive from the reigns of John and Henry III.[4] Here, surely, was an antecedent of, though perhaps not "the model for, the indenture system." By Edward I's time, lords, as well as the king himself, were using *fiefs-rentes* to procure reserves of fighting knights. An agreement in 1297 between Sir Aylmer de Valence, the lord, and Thomas, lord of Berkeley, the man, substituted cash—a £50 annuity—for land as the substantive bond between them.

This use of money, often derived from particular lands named in the indenture, in place of the land itself may have marked a change in the form, but not in the substance of the conractual principle. The reciprocal quality of the contract persisted. On through the fourteenth century cash fees, still called *feoda* in contemporary documents, annuities, and the giving of cloth for livery, *robe,* supplanted land as the nexus between a lord and his retainers, as his "men" came to be styled.[5] N. B. Lewis has already analyzed the organization of these indentured retinues and described the terms of fourteenth-century contracts by which a lord procured military and other services in return for cash annuities, livery, and military equipment. The domestic discord of Edward II's reign and the foreign wars of Edward III's provoked a need for soldiery, at the kings' expense, and this prompted lords to increase the number of men they retained in peace as well as for war. The greater amount of money current at this time made it more convenient and more economical to fee a retainer than to endow with land a knight. The lord's control over his retainer was firmer, for how easy to stop payment on an annuity and how cumbersome to recover a land fief either by a private war or through a lawful, but protracted, process in the king's court. As the magnates' revenues became greater on through the fifteenth century, so did the size of their retinues of feed retainers. Even in Edward IV's reign, some peers still were paying cash annuities; but a change was taking place, and only two of Lord Hastings' 69 extant indentures (1461–1483) record money fees. Instead, this peer contracted to be a "good and favorable lord" to his men who were neither tenants nor, literally, "feed" retainers. The final substitution of what medieval men called good lordship—aid, favor, support, and preferment—for the fee created a more refined, certainly a more subtle, relationship, one that could be advantageous and effectual only in a more sophisticated society. And yet, paradoxically, these less tangible gifts by the lord gave fifteenth-century feudal retaining a close resemblance to the Anglo-Saxon institution of lordship. Perhaps there was a continuity through the intervening centuries, by means of things-taken-for-granted, custom, and traditions, which the surviving written records do not make evident. Certainly by 1483 the practice of retaining, replete with good lordship, had become an institution far richer socially than the arid phrase, "the indenture system," can possibly connote.

Parallel to the process whereby fiefs gave way to fees, and fees to favor, was an elaboration of the services rendered by the retainer, no longer a tenant "involved in a proprietary relation." Service in arms, the original *raison d'être* of Norman and Angevin feudalism, still continued as the essential function of the fourteenth-century retainer. But he performed peace-time services, too, as Lewis has demonstrated, attending the lord at tournaments, parliaments, and public assemblies; joining in the lord's recreations; and being "in the household at the lord's will," though not a permanent resident. This comparatively civil tone is even more conspicuous a century later in Lord Hastings' contracts though they still required the retainers to fight for their lord. But they describe fighting in euphemistic terms—to ride and go, defensibly arrayed, at Hastings' call. By Edward IV's reign, the retainer's commitment to take his lord's part and quarrel against all men, except the king, had come to mean more than just fighting with him on the field of battle.

In actual practice, the retainer now supported the lord in county politics and, occasionally, in the national arena of parliament. The recent identification of some members of the fifteenth-century house of commons as peers' retainers has led to the contention that the lords of parliament dominated the lower house by "placing" therein their "servants." But the history of Lord Hastings' 88 retainers fails to confirm this assertion. His men constituted, at the most, no more than 2.2% of the members of

Edward IV's six parliaments; and seven, perhaps ten (2.4% or 3.44% of the whole house) was the largest number of his servants to sit at a single parliament. Furthermore, all but 3 or 4 of Hastings' 14 retainers who sat in any parliament were elected to the house before, and not after, they signed indentures with him. However, his company of knights, esquires, and gentlemen did give Lord Hastings political influence, the "rule" of the midland shires of England. Many of his men were sheriffs and justices of the peace in Derby, Leicestershire, and Stafford. By capturing county offices, they performed political services which complemented their military functions and established their lord's local ascendancy. In the same way the earl of Northumberland's retainers, among whom were 38 knights, account for his dominance in the north. Such a company of gentry, tied by indentures to a peer of the realm, through their position in county society and by their connection, through their lord, with one another, seems a progenitor of those associations of lords and country gentlemen which were to produce the parliamentary factions of the future.

The peers' bands of non-resident retainers survived into the sixteenth century, and even the most order-conscious of the Tudors, Elizabeth I, had to dispense with those acts of parliament that prohibited livery and retaining. She licensed not only the peers, but courtiers and civil servants, even her chief justice, to retain men and to give them liveries. The reason why was that this politico-military system still had a place in Tudor England for it supplied the sovereign with manpower. The royal government needed men for both war and peace; and the lords' retainers provided captains for the contract armies and officials for county governance. There they guarded the king's, as well as the lord's, parochial interests, and on occasion they satisfied the vanity and enhanced the worship of both lord and sovereign by parading, while dressed in parti-colored liveries, up and down the countryside or along the streets of London. Their part in Tudor pageantry disguised, but it did not eliminate, the original military purpose of retaining. Retainers constituted a potential military force in Mary Tudor's time; and even if the threat of force was used more frequently than its application, a company of retainers might enable a peer to speak more forcefully in national as well as local affairs.

The monarch's problem was to control this institution and to use it to his and the kingdom's advantage. To do this, he had to command the lords' allegiance, and this meant a mastery of the art of politics—guiding, checking, driving, and cajoling men high-spirited, ambitious, and selfish. Henry VI's complete inability to do so explains not only his failure but why the lords seized his government and why the practice of retaining got so out of hand. Nevertheless, during the two centuries, 1399–1603, the vast majority of peers usually were constant to the reigning sovereign as were their own retainers to them. Even the Tudors, with all their talk about law, order, and the cult of kingship, condoned retaining. Like the Yorkists, they, too, depended upon the system far too much to try seriously to stop the peers from binding men by oath, promise, or indenture. Militarily, the lords and their companies provided the king with a skeleton, if not a standing, army. They constituted an organization through which the monarch might recruit, under the royal contract system, armed forces to meet domestic emergencies or to make foreign expeditions. Until the Tudor dynasty was secure, if ever it was—certainly not until after Norfolk's rebellion in 1569 or perhaps even Essex's in 1601—the most that the sovereign could hope to do was to control the lords and their retinues. Gradually he gained ascendancy through statutory regulation, through personal politics, and by the centripetal magnetism of his court over a system that determined the structure of both war and politics.

The statute of 1390 was the first major attempt to regulate and control retaining and to restrict it to the presumably dependable members of society, the peers of the realm. Who designed the act is not certain, but its consequence was to give a monopoly on retaining companies of knights and esquires to the lords temporal. Furthermore, to do so lawfully, the lord must retain by indenture, and the retainer must contract for the term of his life and for peace as well as for war. Such a permanent connection, the legislators hoped, would prevent peers from admitting into their companies irresponsible men, wrongdoers, or criminals, and it might even make the lord responsible for his followers. The retainers, too, were to be recruited from the gentry. Only knights and esquires were eligible to be retained, for other than household or legal service, and to wear the livery of a lord's company. The 1390 act not only prescribed the conditions under which peers might retain, but it also determined in large part the terms of the contracts and the course of future legislation.

Subsequent acts of parliament regulated retaining by trying to eliminate the abuses of the institution, chiefly maintenance, champerty, and embracery. They also sought to restrict ancillary practices like the retainer's wearing of livery—badges, cognizances, tokens, jackets,—the insignia which identified the retainer's lord. This later legislation distinguished between maintenance (the evil to be eradicated), livery (the psychological stimulus to many of the abuses), and retaining itself (the institution to be preserved). Statutes repeatedly prohibited unlawful, though not lawful, maintenance; then they restricted the wearing of livery to various categories of persons—household servants, and king's and the prince's retainers, officers in the universities, and the lords' non-resident retainers, but only on those occasions when they went with their lord on the king's service. Actually, not a single act of parliament until that of 1468, despite the commons' petitions and their speakers' requests, denied the peers' right to retain by oath, promise, or indenture. But the act of 1468 forbad any person of whatsoever rank or degree to do so; and when construed literally, this statute would seem to apply to peers. However, not only did the lords temporal continue to retain non-residents, but they drew up elaborate indentures like those signed and sealed by Lord Hastings and his retainers.

Beneath all of these laws, statutes, and contracts, there was of course a code of social conduct, a romanticized version of Edward III's rules of chivalry, to govern retaining in practice. This code, like all unwritten ones, consisted of traditions, attitudes, and convictions all taken for granted. Seldom were the rules written down, and now they are hard to come by. Even Hastings' contracts state so little and assume so much. The very concept of good lordship in Yorkist England needed no definition; and even the "faith and honor of knighthood," by which Sir Simon Montfort swore to be Lord Hastings' servant, were words easier to understand in 1469 than to define today. Fidelity and trust, man to man, was at the heart of the lord-retainer connection. Granted that the promise of faithful service was not always kept in Yorkist and Tudor England, still feudal retaining would not have survived for a decade, let alone two centuries, had not the vast majority of a lord's company been true and stuck to him for term of life. Just this, we know, Lord Hastings' men did until his death at Richard III's command drove them to seek a new lord. The values which governed this politico-military system were honor and integrity, good faith and the keeping of contracts. But its genius was the combining of the high ideals of Plantagenet chilvary with Yorkist-Tudor opportunism. The mutual advantages to both lord and retainer account for its success, and they enabled the institution to survive even Thomas Cromwell's "Revolution in Tudor Government."[6]

The rise and fall of a retainer, as William, Lord Hastings' career may be styled, demonstrates the opportunities that the institution offered an ambitious man on the make. Richard, duke of York, had retained William's father, and he himself first became the duke's servant and then the retainer of his son, Edward, earl of March. When Edward became king of England in 1461, Hastings became his councillor, his chamberlain, and a baron. Thereafter, he went on from power to power and built up his own company of retained knights, esquires, and gentlemen, the well-willers who constituted the true foundation of a peer's prestige. Without his personal attachment to Edward IV and without his permanent position at the Yorkist court from 1461 to 1483, Lord Hastings, a nouveau peer, might not have drawn and held together his company of men; but without their support, both political and military, his career at court might have been less profitable and certainly less long. Ironically, Hastings' fall resulted from his fidelity to his own lord, King Edward IV, and his loyalty to his lord's son, Edward V. A seasoned councillor and no novice at palace politics, this lord balked at Richard III's usurpation of his nephew's throne. Unlike the earl of Warwick's death in battle which ratified his treason to Edward IV, Hastings' execution sanctified with blood his loyalty to his lord. While the fidelity of a single retainer cannot obliterate the bar-sinister imposed upon fifteenth-century feudalism, it may in part redeem feudal retaining from the charge that it was only

> "a parasitic institution . . . cut off from its natural roots in the soil, and far removed indeed from the atmosphere of responsibility, loyalty and faith which had characterized the relationship of lord and vassal in the earlier middle ages."[7]

II. LORD HASTINGS AND HIS LORD: A RETAINER'S RISE AND FALL

On Friday-the-thirteenth of June, 1483, "close upon noon," William Lord Hastings was beheaded. Scarcely an hour before, he, the king's chamberlain, had sat in the Tower of London at a council with the protector of the realm, Richard, duke of Gloucester. There the duke accused him of treason and swore by St. Paul not to go to dinner until his enemy was dead. A squad of armed men hustled Hastings from the White Tower onto the Green "beside the chapel"; a priest near at hand shrived "him apace"; and Hastings' head was "laid down upon a log of timber and there stricken off." Just a fortnight later the impetuous duke seized Edward V's throne and became Richard III.

The nature of Hastings' treason is not yet clear. Supposedly, he refused to go along with Richard's plan to usurp his nephew's crown. "Undoubtedly, the protector loved [Hastings] well, and loath was to have lost him," Sir Thomas More later wrote, for Hastings had supported Richard, after Edward IV's death in April 1483, against Queen Elizabeth and her Woodville kinsmen. First, he had joined the duke's faction which had enveloped the boy-king; and then he had helped to make Gloucester the protector of the realm until Edward V should come of age. However, in order to contain Richard's ever-increasing power, Hastings had effected a reconciliation with the queen. Together with Bishop Morton of Ely and the chancellor, Archibishop Rotherham of York, he sought to maintain a balance between the rival factions. But the chamberlain, like many a moderate in time of crisis, merely made himself suspect to each side and fell victim to their feuds.

However, the protector had given Hastings his chance for he had sent a common friend, William Catesby, to win him over to "their party." But Catesby had "found him so fast [firm] and . . . heard him speak so terrible words" that he dared disclose no more of Richard's scheme. Hastings, doubtless, had learned enough, or perhaps too much. And so he, with Rotherham and Morton, had to go—the bishops into confinement and the chamberlain, with no cloth to save him, to the block. Later on Richard allowed Hastings' head and body to be buried together in St. George's Chapel at Windsor Castle.

The fall of Hastings, like his rise to power, probably resulted from his adherence to the cult of lordship. He himself had been Edward IV's retainer, and fidelity, good faith, was in theory at the very heart of the system of retaining men by oath or indenture. In the case of Lord Hastings, contemporaries recognized in him an "honorable man, a good knight and a gentle, of great authority with his prince." Here in the personal attachment between lord and man is, I believe, a clue to Hastings' conduct between Edward IV's death in April and his own on 13 June. Otherwise, why should Hastings have stuck at a change of monarchs, one that would advance his own erstwhile friend? Even a stranger, a cynical Italian cleric visiting England in 1483, caught the point of Hastings' fidelity to Edward IV and to his heir. Dominic Mancini, in a cold, Machiavellian analysis of Yorkist politics and personalities, explains that after the protector had gotten into his power all the blood royal, his prospects were not sufficiently secure "without the removal or imprisonment of those who had been the closest friends of his brother [Edward IV] and were expected to be faithful to his brother's offspring." The three most conspicuous of Edward's *fideles,* according to Mancini, were Morton, Rotherham, and Hastings.

However, the chamberlain's relations with Edward IV had been more intimate than those of the bishops. All three men had "helped more than other councillors to form the king's policy and besides carried it out." "But Hastings," Mancini noted, "was not only the author of his sovereign's public policy, as being one that shared every peril with the king, but was also the accomplice and partner of his privy pleasures". Thomas More, too, believed that Queen Elizabeth's special grudge against Hastings resulted not just from Edward's "great favor" towards his chamberlain but from his being "secretly familiar with the king in wanton company," meaning, John Stow explained, "wanton doings with light women." But Hastings was also a "man of great feelings (*sens*) and prowess (*vertu*)," the French chronicler, Commines, declared and he had "great authority with his master, and not without reason for he had served him well and loyally." Upon his death the *Great Chronicle of London* recorded how "this noble man was murdered for his truth and fidelity which he firmly bore unto his master." And Thomas More, on Bishop Morton's authority, finally characterized Hastings as "a loving man and passing well beloved. Very faithful and trusty enough, trusting too much."[8]

Trusting too much, perhaps, but the first Baron Hastings was no novice in the sophisticated politico-military machinations of 1483. His own rise to power and wealth proves that. He caught the main chance in 1461 and thereafter he grasped lands, offices, fees, and favours. Ethically, Hastings seems neither better nor worse than his rivals at court; nor was he, a recipient of the king's cast-off paramours, noted for any peculiar moral sensitivity—except for his fidelity to Edward IV, a virtue not wholly distinct from self-interest. Throughout Edward's reign, Hastings had succeeded in manipulating men and women; he had mastered many an intrigue at home and abroad; and in 1471 he had outmaneuvered and outfought his brother-in-law, Warwick the kingmaker. Even if Hastings was, as More asserted, "easy to beguile, as he that of good heart and courage forestudied no perils," Mancini looked upon him as a hardened councillor, one "in age mature and instructed by long experience in public affairs." So old a hand in palace politics was not likely to stick quixotically to a boy-king without some strong conviction. Back in 1471, upon Edward IV's restoration to the kingship, Hastings had accepted Prince Edward to be the "undoubted heir" to the crown of England; and he, "as a true and faithful subject," had sworn to bear to the prince "faith and truth." But so had five dukes, thirty-one other earls and barons, and numerous knights, some of whom went along with Richard III or at least acquiesced in his usurpation.[9]

Hastings' will, dated at London 27 June 1481 when Edward IV still lived, suggests that conscience was what prompted him to oppose Richard's *coup d'état*. No copybook testament, this will is an intimate document marked by sincerity and candor. "In witness that this is my last will and testament," it reads, "I did write this clause and last article with mine own hand." The striking feature of the will is the recurrent mention of Hastings' connection with his personal lord, Edward, earl of March, duke of York, and then king of England. After commending his soul to God in a conventional manner, he tells how

> "the king of his abundant grace, for the true service that I have done and at the least intended to have done to his grace, hath willed and offered me to be buried in the College or Chapel of St. George at Windsor in a place by his grace assigned in the which College his highness is disposed to be buried."

Hastings then orders his "simple body" to be buried there and bequeaths 100 marks for a tomb and lands worth £20 a year to the dean and canons of Windsor for a "priest to say daily mass and divine service . . . for the king's prosperous estate during his life and after his death for his soul, for the souls of me, my wife, and for all Christian souls." Here is evidence of a special intimacy between Hastings and Edward IV, and of affection towards his earthly lord. For Hastings, not without pride, preferred to be buried at Windsor alongside the king rather than alongside his wife at Ashby-de-la-Zouche.

From Edward, Hastings sought one final favor. In his will he asks the king to care for his son and heir, for his wife and other children, and to "be good lord to" his executors. These last commissions, so reminiscent of Anglo-Saxon wills, conform to the centuries-old code of good lordship. To Edward, as to his personal lord, Hastings appeals for his family's protection. Then for the heir to his barony, his son, Edward (presumably named after the king) he writes, "also, I in most humble wise beseech the king's grace to take the governance of my son and heir; and as straightly as to me is possible, I charge mine heir on my blessing to be faithful and true to the king's grace, to my lord prince, and their heirs."

Here is Hastings' mandate to his son and successor to bear a true allegiance, not only to the king but also to Edward, prince of Wales. How, then, could Lord Hastings himself, within two years, forsake his lord's heir, Edward V, without becoming in his own son's eyes a notorious faith-breaker? Furthermore, he ends his will by asking the king to be good lord to his wife and children; and, in turn, he charges them to be their sovereign's true subjects. And then, writing the last article with his own hand, Hastings addresses Edward IV

"whose good grace in the most humble wise I beseech to be good and tender, gracious lord to my soul, to be good and gracious lord to my wife, my sons and mine heirs, and to all my children whom I charge upon my blessing to be true subjects and servants to you, my sovereign lord under God, and to your heirs, to all your issue; beseeching you, sovereign lord, also to be good lord to my surveyors and executors in executing this my last will and testament as my most singular trust is in your good grace above all earthly creatures, as well for my wife and children as to mine executors and surveyors in executing this my last will and testament. Signed with mine hand and sealed with the seal of my arms the day and year aforesaid."[10]

The temper of this will, admittedly a solemn matter made at a solemn moment, is that of honest devotion and genuine fidelity. Although "sentiment was not a fifteenth-century virtue, disloyalty to the king was a breach of feudal obligations and a challenge to authority besides which death was as nothing."[11]

If Hastings' fidelity to his lord was a factor in his fall, Edward's good lordship had been directly responsible for his rise. For over twenty years he remained the true friend and confidant, the companion-in-arms and chamberlain, and the faithful retainer of Edward as earl of March, duke of York, and king of England. Why William Hastings fared better than Edward's other retainers remains a mystery, that of personality. William's father, Sir Leonard Hastings, had been a retainer of Edward's father, Richard, duke of York. The duke granted him a £15 annuity for life in 1436 and by 1442 had made him his "beloved councillor." Six years later Leonard was knighted, and in 1449 Henry VI, perhaps under York's influence, granted him exemption for life from serving on assizes or juries and from being appointed sheriff, escheator, coroner, constable or collector. Such were the emoluments of good lordship, and his lord, the duke of York, in 1456 executed Sir Leonard's will.[12]

The year before, William, then about 24 years old and the duke of York's "beloved servant," was sheriff of Warwickshire and Leicester. York granted him, too, on 23 April 1458, a £10 annuity "in consideration of his good and faithful services done and to be done to the said duke." William agreed to serve York before all other men, except the king, and to attend him at any time. Almost immediately, in 1459 Hastings experienced the advantage of being a great lord's retainer. When Henry Pierpont complained that William and Thomas Hastings and Henry Ferrers were responsible for the slaying of his brother, Robert Pierpont, the duke of York arbitrated the case. To "appease" the variances between them, the parties "were put in the rule, ordinance, and judgement" of the duke. After hearing Pierpont's complaint and the Hastings brothers' "excuse," York made an "award" dated 17 October 1459. This required both sides "to keep the king's peace" and thereby to prevent the "great inconveniences which else were like to grow between them." Further, the Pierponts were to release, by writing, "all manner of appeals" for Robert's death and all "actions of trespass"; in return, the Hastings brothers were to forego "all manner of actions" against the Pierponts and to pay them in 5 installments between Christmas 1459 and Michaelmas 1462 a total of £40. Henry Pierpont was to find a priest "to sing divine service" during 2 years for Robert's soul. Thus the duke of York acted as the good and gracious lord of his retainer, and this arbitration saved the Hastings brothers a more costly, and perhaps a less successful, trial at common law. The Pierponts, too, probably found private mediation cheaper, speedier, and more rewarding than the king's justice might have been.

This same year, 1459, Hastings fought in the duke's army at Ludford, and for this the Lancastrian parliament at Coventry attainted him. The next year, he was with York's son and heir, Edward, earl of March, and so absent from the battle of Wakefield where the duke was killed. Upon York's death, Hastings presumably became Edward's retainer, and he marched with him from Gloucestershire to London where the new duke of York, on 4 March, 1461, was proclaimed King Edward IV. On Palm Sunday, 29 March, Hastings fought for Edward at Towton, and there the Yorkist king knighted him on the field of battle. A few months later, sometime after 13 June and before 26 July when he summoned Hastings to parliament, Edward created him a baron, Sir William Hastings, Lord Hastings.

Already preferment had begun to come Hastings' way. On 11 May, 1461 the king appointed him and his brother, Ralph, jointly constable of Rockingham Castle in Northamptonshire, and from this office they received wages of 12 pence a day. Lord Hastings also enjoyed many other emoluments—lands, offices, rewards, fees, and annuities granted by the king or by his fellow peers. He stood so high in Edward IV's esteem, Dugdale was to write in his *Historical Collections . . . of the Family of Hastings,*

> "that divers eminent persons taking notice thereof accumulated their favors on him. Amongst which John Mowbray, then duke of Norfolk, bestowed on

> him the stewardship of his manors of Melton Mowbray, Segrave, and others in county Leicester with the fee of £10 per annum during his life."

Other peers and peeresses—Anne, duchess of Buckingham, John, Lord Lovell, Lord Rivers, and Jacquet of Luxembourg, duchess of Bedford—favoured him with grants and annuities. Even more durable were the lands—those of Viscount Beaumont, the earl of Wiltshire, and Lord Roos—which the king granted Hastings in 1461 "for the better maintenance of his estate"; and on 17 February 1462, a royal letter patent declared his properties to constitute "the lordship, barony, and honor of Hastings." Edward IV further augmented the chamberlain's growing fortune in August 1467 by bestowing upon him a chain of manors and castles, including Folkingham in Lincolnshire—properties that were to be the territorial foundation of his grandson's earldom of Huntingdon.

Besides lands and annuities, the first Lord Hastings acquired many offices of profit. He was constable of several castles, steward of royal manors, honors, and lordships, a master forester, chamberlain of North Wales, receiver-general of Cornwall, chief steward of the duchy of Lancaster, keeper of the exchanges at the Tower of London and Calais, and master of the king's mints which were to pay him 4d. for every pound weight of gold and silver coined. There is no need to catalogue all the sources of Hastings' income; he had a plenty and his revenues constantly increased as Edward's reign wore on.

The king's favor also led to advantageous marriages for Hastings himself and later for his children. His own marriage, before 6 February 1462, to Katherine Neville, Lord Harrington's widow, the earl of Salisbury's daughter, and Warwick's sister, brought wealth, prestige, political connections, and apparently some degree of happiness. She bore him heirs, three sons and a daughter, who afforded opportunities for marriage alliances with old peerages. His daughter, Anne, her father's will provided, was to marry George, earl of Shrewsbury (whose wardship Hastings held in 1475); and if he should die "before carnal knowledge between the same earl and her had," then she was to marry his brother, Thomas, "if the law of the church will suffer or license it." His own heir, Edward, married, before 18 February 1481, Mary, the heiress of Margaret, Lady Hungerford, and in her own right Baroness Botreaux, Hungerford, and Moleyns. She brought to her husband her baronies and titles which passed on into the Hastings estate for their son, George, the first earl of Huntingdon.[13]

During Lord Hastings' own life, he held two major political appointments. He was the king's chamberlain from 1461 until his death, and in 1471 he was made "keeper, governor-general, supervisor, king's lieutenant of the town and castle of Calais, the tower of Rysbank, castle of Guisnes, and the marches thereabout." The former office brought and kept Hastings close to the king as one of his most secret councillors; while in the latter post, Hastings preserved for the Yorkist dynasty, and for England, the bridgehead to the continent so essential for Edward's expedition in 1475 to France. On this occasion Hastings augmented his estate by a pension of 2,000 *écus* from Louis XI. His refusal to give an acquittance for its payment, lest the English king's chamberlain be called publicly a pensioner of France, won for him, according to Commines, the French king's praise. With less regard for chivalric niceties, Hastings accepted a similar gift from Edward's ally, the duke of Burgundy.

Such gratuities helped Lord Hastings to meet the high cost of serving his king and of living at the royal court. The "robes" and "fees" which he, as chamberlain of the household, received annually were commuted at only £12 a year; but the king supplemented this salary with occasional "rewards". For Hastings' "great charges and costs, as well in his attendance upon our person in the office of our chamberlain as in the attendance and daily labor in our council and otherwise by our commandments," the king in 1468 ordered the exchequer to pay him £100 "by way of reward." The fruits accruing to Lord Hastings from his service to the king enabled him to avoid any financial embarrassment prior to his death. In 1483, however, his widow and his heir had to redeem gold and silver plate pledged for a loan of £360. Of this sum, £40 had been borrowed against "a collar of gold of King Edward's livery".[14]

This token of Edward's lordship, like the badge a lord gave to his retainer, also signified Hastings' obligations. He served his lord faithfully in a variety of ways, and throughout Edward's reign his loyalty was constant. When the earl of Warwick temporarily restored Henry VI and the Lancastrians to power in 1470, Hastings had managed Edward IV's escape and had crossed with him to Holland. The chamberlain was the man who brought the volatile duke of Clarence back from his defection and who organized the Yorkist return. He landed with Edward at Ravenspur in the spring of 1471, and his retainers, with their followers, were the first to rise in the Yorkist king's behalf. Hastings commanded the third division, said to include 3,000 horsemen, at the battle of Barnet on 14 April; then he marched on west with Edward to fight in the final victory in May at Tewkesbury. There one of Hastings' own retainers, Nicholas Longford, was knighted. Already, on 17 April 1471, the king had licensed Hastings to convert his houses at Ashby-de-la-Zouche, Bagworth, Thornton, and Kirby in Leicestershire and one at Slingesby in Yorkshire into castles. This permission to build walls, towers, pinnacles with holes for shooting, and machicolations points up the Yorkist dynasty's dependance upon those peers whom Edward could trust and also the king's confidence in Hastings' fidelity.[15]

Immediately after Edward IV's restoration, Hastings accepted fresh responsibilities. Right off in 1471, he became the king's lieutenant, the keeper, and the governor-general of Calais. In this post, he recruited soldiers to garrison the castles, clerks and gentry to administer the civil government, and engineers to repair the fortifications—and so prepare the way for Edward IV's French invasion of 1475. The English landings in France led to little more than verbal skirmishes and a truce. But for the next three years Hastings at Calais carried on negotiations with the French. Duties such as these fell to him as an officer of state, the king's lieutenant at Calais and his chamberlain; and yet underneath these formal appointments lay Hastings' close personal connection, as a feudal retainer, with Edward. After the king's death, he was one of the executors of Edward's will; and at once he sought to protect his lord's minor heir, Edward V, from his uncles, Rivers and Gloucester. Finally, Hastings' death at the duke of Gloucester's command—no longed for martyrdom it's true—sanctified with blood his good faith to his personal lord.

Hastings' "great authority with his prince," as Thomas More described it, may explain how he acquired power over other men. Conversely, his use of lordship—the practice of retaining men by indenture—may account in part for his influence with the king. The constancy and consequences of Hastings' affinity with Edward suppose something more than mere personal compatability. The chamberlain was not just a royal favorite, in the seventeenth-century sense, upon whom the monarch squandered his and England's wealth to slake his emotions. Nor can the chivalric cult of fidelity alone explain their mutual steadfastness. Yorkist England, as the many perpendicular parish churches still commanding the countryside recall, was a wealthy and a materialistic England, a land where power was the determinant. Wealth, both landed and commercial, as Hastings' affluence makes clear, could make a man powerful; but in fifteenth-century politics, man-power counted even more in both military and civil affairs. Time and again a lord's ability to raise men to serve in war or peace proved the decisive factor. Horsemen and archers in abundance determined which faction, or alliance of factions, was to gain the ascendancy. Men to staff the civil offices in shire and borough meant power to maintain both a magnate's personal sway over the territory where he had "the rule" and the peace of peaceless kings. Even if Hastings' authority with the king was the keystone of his power, that authority, in turn, depended upon the man-power that he could bring to his sovereign's service. No doubt Edward IV's trust and confidence enabled Hastings to build up a party of adherents, to reward his own faithful servants, and to hold their loyalty. However, he seems also to have had the talent to organize, into an effective political force, his "well-willers." Some of them he retained formally by written indentures; others were tenants on his lands; and the services of a few he procured for nothing more tangible than the hope of preferment to be obtained through the chamberlain's influence at Edward's court and in his council.

From the king's point of view, the benefits he bestowed upon Lord Hastings proved a sound investment politically, and politics, after all, was the essence of the regal enterprise. The king's business was to rule English society effectively, a thing the saintly and forlorn Henry VI had failed to do. To accomplish this, Edward IV needed loyal men to serve him and the kingdom, in effect, both a standing army and a civil service. In theory, Hastings, like every other peer of the realm was a counsellor-born; and in practice, he, like other magnates loyal to Edward, brought to the king's service his own band of faithful followers. Their collaboration in wartime worked to preserve the king's government, and in peace they helped to impose the regal policy throughout the kingdom.

Tudor propagandists dramatized the battles between Yorkists and Lancastrians and called them the Wars of the Roses. Thus they created the impression of a prolonged period of warfare. Actual fighting probably occupied less than 12 weeks between 1450 and 1485; and the battles, seldom lasting longer than an eight-hour day, were well dispersed among the English counties. So there was really no physical disruption of normal life for over 95% of the people for about 99% of the time. Similarly, the mythical red and white roses have supposed a two-party war. Actually English politics throughout the fifteenth century were conducted on a multi-party basis. The apparently dual alignment in the battles to gain possession of Henry VI's person or of the kingly office was illusory and often only temporary. Beneath the surface were many factions. Even when two opposing armies appeared upon a battlefield, the warriors wore neither the red rose nor the white, but the peers' many different badges. Alliances between the lords, many of them merely momentary, merged their bands of soldiers into armies; but their agreements sometimes lasted hardly long enough to win a battle and seldom longer than to serve the individual peer's political advantage. At Bosworth Field in 1485, the earl of Northumberland, who had indented in 1474 to be Richard, duke of Gloucester's faithful servant, withdrew and did not fight; and only towards the end did Lord Stanley and his contingent join battle for Henry Tudor.

Like other fifteenth-century magnates, Lord Hastings used the system of retaining by indenture to maintain a central corps of adherents. Around them he organized the manpower, civil as well as military, to support or to thwart the reigning king. These partisans constituted a body of reservists, men upon whom Hastings could count to champion not only his own quarrels but also his lord's. One of his retainers, Harry, Lord Grey of Codnor, signed indentures dated 30 May 1464 to take Lord Hastings' "full part and quarrel and to be with him against all" persons except the king. He proved faithful, during the critical spring of 1471, to both his lord and to his king by "attending in his own person upon us [Edward IV] in this our great journey [battle] as in bringing unto us a great number of men defensibly arrayed at his cost and charge." For this loyal and effective support, the king, on 24 May 1471, ordered the exchequer to pay Lord Grey of Codnor "£100 by way of reward."[16]As Hastings' retainer, Grey was in alliance with the chamberlain and brought to Edward's aid his own servants. Presumably Hastings' other retainers also brought men "defensibly arrayed," and they probably provided many of the 3,000 men whom he is said to have commanded at the battle of Barnet.

A decade earlier, in 1461, Hastings had begun to recruit retainers who were to form his company. As soon as he became a baron, he was eligible to retain men by oath, promise, or indenture lawfully. In the course of his career at least 88 knights, esquires, and gentlemen, and 2 peers, signed and sealed indentures to serve him for life in both peace and war. To prevent Lord Hastings from calling up to London this company of faithful retainers, men who had covenanted to take his part and quarrel, was probably the reason why Richard, duke of Gloucester, in June 1483, struck him down so quickly. Hastings' execution was reported to Sir William Stonor within the week: "with us is much trouble, and every man doubts other. As on Friday last was the lord chamberlain beheaded soon upon noon." And then below his signature, as a postscript, Simon Stallworth noted one immediate consequence in an unadorned statement:

> "All the lord chamberlain's men became my lord's of Buckingham men."[17]

Was this rank desertion, a running to cover under the protection of Gloucester's momentary ally? Or did it presage the duke of Buckingham's forthcoming revolt in October 1483 against King Richard III? How many of Hastings' retainers joined the duke is not known. But in 1485 Henry VII was to knight two of them, Humphrey Stanley and James Blount, for fighting against Richard III on Bosworth Field, land that had belonged to William, Lord Hastings.[18]

NOTES

Abbreviations Used in Footnote Citations

Cal. Close Rolls: Calendar of the Close Rolls, London.
Cal. Patent Rolls: Calendar of the Patent Rolls, London.
Eng. Hist. Rev.: The English Historical Review, London.
H.M.C. Report: The Reports of the Historical Manuscripts Commission, followed by the number of the report or the name of the collection when not numbered.
P.R.O.: The Public Record Office, London, followed by the "Reference" number of the manuscript cited.
Trans. Royal Hist. Soc.: Transactions of the Royal Historical Society, London.

1. A Victorian divine, the Reverend Charles Plummer, chaplain of Corpus Christi College, Oxford, seems to have coined this unedifying expression and to have contributed it, along with the unchivalrous term, "pseudo-chivalry," to the English historical vocabulary, *Sir John Fortescue, The Governance of England* (1885), p. 15. K. B. McFarlane resurrected it in 1943, but in 1945 he was willing to qualify it to mean only the "appearance of" or "resembling" feudalism. Helen M. Cam favors Holdsworth's refined, but hardly more historical, term, "new feudalism." Since this study discloses a continuity of feudal principles and attributes, the implication in the word "new" of a revival, or an imitation, of feudalism makes this term misleading. The most significant writings on retaining by indenture are: H. M. Cam, "The Decline and Fall of English Feudalism," *History,* XXV (1940), 216–233; K. B. McFarlane, "Parliament and 'Bastard Feudalism'," *Trans. Royal Hist. Soc.,* 4th Ser., XXVI (1944), 53–79; N. B. Lewis, "The Organisation of Indentured Retinues in Fourteenth-Century England," *Idem,* XXVII (1945), 29–39; K. B. McFarlane, "Bastard Feudalism," *Bulletin of the Institute of Historical Research,* XX (1943–45), 161–180; J. C. Wedgwood, "John of Gaunt and the Packing of Parliament," *Eng. Hist. Rev.,* XLV (1930), 623–625; *cf.* N. B. Lewis, *Idem,* XLVIII (1933), 391; J. S. Roskell, "The Knights of the Shire for the County Palatine of Lancaster," *Chetham Society,* vol. 210 (1937), 6; Bryce D. Lyon, "The Money Fief under the English Kings, 1066–1485," *Eng. Hist. Rev.,* LXVI (1951), 161–193; "The Feudal Antecedent of the Indenture System," *Speculum* XXIX (1954), 503–511; H. G. Richardson, "John of Gaunt and the Parliamentary Representation of Lancashire," *Bulletin of the J. Rylands Library,* XXII (1938), 175–222.

2. The extravagance of the Tudors' propaganda for authoritarianism, law, and order—doubtless as necessary as useful at the time—has been exceeded only by that of their twentieth-century idolators.

3. F. W. Maitland, *The Constitutional History of England,* p. 143.

4. B. D. Lyon, "The Feudal Antecedent of the Indenture System," *Speculum,* XXIX (1954), 503–511.

5. P. R. O. E101/411/13, fols. 36–38, the "account Book" of Sir John Fogge, keeper of the great wardrobe, in 1464 used the heading, *Feoda et Robe,* for the list of annual payments to the chamberlain of England, the steward of the household, the king's chamberlain, and other household officers.

6. Many of us have been unable to find any evidence that either Edward IV's or Henry VII's monarchy was either "new" or "strong." G. R. Elton, *The Tudor Revolution in Government* (1953), has provided positive affirmation of my belief that not until 1533–35 did the Tudor monarchy really acquire strength sufficient to distinguish it clearly from its medieval predecessor.

7. H. M. Cam, "The Decline and Fall of English Feudalism," *History,* XXV (1940), 225. Like N. B. Lewis, I feel that the permanency and the legality of the written bond made the indentured retinue "certainly a steadying influence in a society where old institutional loyalties were breaking down . . ." This is not to deny the evils obviously resulting from the abuses, defects and human frailties apparent in the institution's operation. But I find it very difficult to follow the argument of the enthusiasts for the twelfth and thirteenth centuries—in view of the civil wars under Stephen, John, and Henry III and the armed opposition against Henry II and even Edward I—that the tenurial tie afforded English society a greater stability than did the "personal ties" in Lancastrian and Yorkist England. N. B. Lewis, "The Organisation of Indentured Retinues in Fourteenth-Century England," *Trans. Royal Hist. Soc.,* 4th Ser., XXVII (1945), 39.

8. For Hastings' relations with Edward IV and Richard III, and for the analysis of his character, see: D. Mancini, *The Usurpation of Richard III,* ed. C. A. J. Armstrong; Thomas More, *The History of King Richard III,* ed. J. R. Lumby; Philippe de Commines, *Memoires,* ed. B. de Mandrot (1901) I, 205; II, 3, 6; *The Great Chronicle of London,* ed. A. H. Thomas and I. D. Thornley, p. 231; John Stow, *The Annals of England . . .* (1615), pp. 447–51.

9. In the parliament chamber at Westminster, 3 July 1471, those present swore this oath:

"I, Thomas, cardinal archbishop of Canterbury, knowledge, take, and repute you, Edward prince of Wales etc., first begotten son of our sovereign lord, King Edward etc. to be very and undoubted heir to our said lord as to the crowns and realms of England and France and lordship of Ireland, and promise and swear that in case hereafter it happen you by God's disposition to overlive our sovereign lord, I shall then take and accept you for the very true and rightwise king of England etc. and faith and truth shall to you bear; and in all things truly and faithfully behave me towards you and your heirs as a true and faithful subject oweth to behave him to his sovereign lord etc. So help me God and halidom and this Holy Evangelist." *Cal. Close Rolls, 1468–1476,* pp. 229–30, no. 858.

10. William Hastings' will was proved 12 August 1483 at Maidstone. Contemporary copies are at Somerset House, London, P.C.C., Logge, 7, and at the H. E. Huntington Library, MS. HA, Family Papers, 1464–83.

11. C. H. Williams, in *Cambridge Medieval History,* VIII, 439–40.

12. For Hastings' life and career, see: G. E. Cockayne, *The Complete Peerage,* ed. V. Gibbs; *Dictionary of National Biography*; William Dugdale, *Historical and Genealogical Collections of the Family of Hastings . . . ,* an unpublished manuscript history written in 1677, H. E. Huntington Library, MS. HA (hereafter cited as Dugdale, *History of Hastings Family*); *cf.,* Huntington Library Bulletin, V (1934), 52 and *H. M. C. Report,* Hastings MSS., IV, 348–51. Dugdale states (p. 13) that William was "born about the year 1431." For details about Sir Leonard Hastings, *idem*; for the record of the Hastings-Pierpont arbitration, MS. HA Family, 1400–62. *The Cals. of Patent* and *Close Rolls, 1461–83,* record Hastings' appointment to various offices and many were noted in Dugdale, *History of Hastings Family*. For the payment of arrears of Hastings' salary of 12 *d.* a day as constable of Rockingham in 1468, P.R.O., K.R. Memoranda Roll, E159/245/ mem. vii (Trinity Term 8 Edward IV). For the grant of Folkingham Castle, Lincs., *ibid.,* mem. 28 (Michaelmas Term).

13. H. E. Huntington Library, MS. HA Family, 1464–83 (2 June 1475) and William, Lord Hastings' will.

14. For Hastings' fees and robes as chamberlain, P.R.O. E101/411/13, fols. 36–38, the "Account Book of Sir John Fogge," for the year 4 Edward IV. For Hastings' "reward," 9 Nov. 1468, P.R.O., E404/74/11, a privy seal warrant. For the gold collar, *H. M. C. Report* No. 78, Hastings MSS. I, 305.

15. Henry N. Bell, *The Huntingdon Peerage* (1820), pp. 15–19, 19 *n.*

16. P.R.O., E404/74, a writ of privy seal, 24 May 1471.

17. *The Stonor Letters and Papers,* ed. C. L. Kingsford, II, 161.

18. Stanley and Blount were made bannerets after the king's victory over Lambert Simnel's adherents at the battle of Stoke, 1487, and 4 of Hastings' retainers were made knights after this battle: Henry Willoughby, Ralph Longford [Langforthe], Maurice Berkeley, and Ralph Shirley, *The Paston Letters,* ed. J. Gairdner, VI, 187.

THE CROWN AND THE ARISTOCRACY IN RENAISSANCE FRANCE*

J. Russell Major

The historian has been so bewitched by the disappearance of the great feudal nobles in France during the early Renaissance that he has frequently lost sight of the fact that it was not the kings, but the aristocracy that profited most by their passing. This aristocracy consisted of three elements: the landed nobility, the upper bureaucracy and judiciary who were often nobility of the robe, and the bourgeois patricians of the towns, some of whom had been ennobled by the municipal offices they held.[1]

This article will deal primarily with the composition, economic position, and organization of the landed nobility, the most important element in the aristocracy. The landed nobility must be divided into a greater nobility and a lesser nobility. Some of the great nobles were from ancient families; others were new men who had been recently advanced by royal favor, for between 1515 and 1600 twenty-eight new peerages were created. Lesser titles were handed out with even greater generosity; Henry III alone erected fifty-five counties, marquisates, duchies, and principalities.[2] These great nobles were the true successors of the feudal dukes, for the governors who were sent to administer the duchies that had escheated to the crown were chosen from their ranks. These governors exercised, or sought to exercise, nearly every nonjudicial prerogative of the king. Thus, when Burgundy escheated to the crown, the king did not personally assume the duties of the former dukes; nor was centralized control established from Paris. Rather the provincial customs and institutions were left much as they

* Reprinted from J. Russell Major, "The Crown and the Aristocracy in Renaissance France," *The American Historical Review* (Washington, 1964), **69**, 631–645.

were with a parlement replacing the feudal court and a governor the former dukes. Around these governors and other great nobles new centers of power emerged in every province, as will be indicated shortly.[3]

The lesser nobles consisted of the old seigneurial nobility and a new nobility composed of nobles of the robe and the bourgeois—patricians of the towns or their immediate descendants who had purchased fiefs. Some historians have looked upon this movement from the town to the countryside as marking the growing ascendancy of the bourgeoisie. This is a grave error. Between the years 1000 and 1300 thousands of the most enterprising serfs flocked to the towns where many prospered, but one does not speak of this phenomenon as marking the rise of serfdom; it is correctly referred to as the rise of the towns. One does not insist that the serfs brought with them a "serf mentality" that pervaded the towns for centuries, or that they revolutionized urban economic activities by applying to them their knowledge of agricultural techniques. Is it not probable, then, that when many of the ablest and most successful burghers decided to move to the country and live as nobles during the Renaissance, they strengthened the landed nobility, that they adopted the mental attitudes of the class they were joining, and that their urban knowledge had a limited influence on agricultural practices?

It is true that the bourgeois purchaser of a fief was not immediately welcomed by his new neighbors. It was especially galling to a noble with an established family position to learn that he had become the vassal of an overrich merchant; at the Estates-General of 1614 the deputies of the nobility asked that nobles be excused from rendering homage in person to non-nobles who had purchased fiefs.[4] But the fact that the newcomer's nobility was challenged made it all the more necessary for him to abandon his bourgeois ways and live nobly in every respect. When Molière wanted to amuse the court of Louis XIV by satirizing the bourgeois gentleman, he did not depict him as the hardheaded, grasping businessman who was seeking to change rural society and rural economic practices; rather he created Monsieur Jourdain. Indeed, if the newcomers from the town had not been accepted sooner or later by the old nobility, the ranks of the second estate would have been very thin, for the number of families in Burgundy, and presumably in the other provinces, who during the Wars of Religion could trace their gentility back before the Hundred Years' War was small, and some of them had intermarried at one time or another with the bourgeoisie.[5]

If one concedes that these newcomers must be considered part of the landed nobility, it becomes highly probable that this class was improving its economic position. It may be true that prices rose more rapidly in the sixteenth century than income from some landed estates, that some nobles were recklessly extravagant, and that others weakened their families by leaving part of their estates to younger sons, but it is also a fact that when a nobleman had to sell a fief, a purchaser, generally from the towns, was thereby enabled, sooner or later, to join the ranks of the landed aristocracy. Furthermore, the income per acre from land grew considerably,[6] and the aristocracy as a whole increased the size of its holdings. In this it was greatly aided by the enforced sale of a large part of the lands of the Church during the reigns of Charles IX and Henry III,[7] a little-known event that may have been nearly as significant as the sale of monastic lands in England. Income from Church lands that were not sold also found its way into the hands of the aristocracy as this class held nearly every bishopric and abbey in the kingdom. Even a dour Calvinist like the Duke of Sully drew about 45,000 livres per year from the abbeys he held in commendam.[8] Of importance also was the purchase by nobles of many peasant holdings.[9]

That it was possible for a noble to be frugal when the occasion demanded and to increase his income during the inflationary period of the Renaissance may be easily illustrated. The Count of Nevers, for example, reduced the size of his household in January 1468 because of heavy debts incurred by war, the provision of a dowry for his sister, and other extraordinary expenses. Later, during the inflationary period, the dukes of Nevers managed to increase their income from 115,085 livres in 1551 to 466,260 livres in 1612. Hard times followed, and by 1626 the ducal income had been reduced to 319,260 livres, but expenses had been correspondingly cut to 311,373 livres. The ducal debt in 1625 amounted to only 91,000 livres, or about 30 per cent of the annual revenue.[10] Whether the dukes of Nevers were the exception or the rule will not be known for sure until there are many studies of the finances of noble families—a type of research apparently nonexistent in France today[11]—but numerous Renaissance châteaux throughout the country suggest that on the whole the income of the landed nobility, including the newcomers to its ranks from the towns, was on the increase, and that there were sufficient funds available for an aggressive policy.[12]

The structure and organization of the landed nobility cannot be adequately described until much more research is done, but two facts seem clear. First, the feudal system was still important and enhanced the power and prestige of the great nobles. The archives of the dukes of Nevers contained literally thousands of documents on the homage rendered them by their vassals throughout the Renaissance.[13] In their correspondence nobles constantly alluded to the lord-vassal relation. In 1583 one woman who had inherited two fiefs wrote the La Trémoïlles for permission to render liege homage by procuration, and another woman requested permission to mortgage three baronies. Other letters explain delays in rendering homage.[14] In 1572 young Henry of Navarre told his vassals to be ready to accompany him to La Rochelle and in 1580 informed a supporter that he was dispatching a nobleman "with fifteen or twenty of my gentlemen to help you make war. . . ."[15] The households of the dukes of Nevers were made up largely of their vassals, who were also to be found among those who commanded their towns and châteaux.[16]

Second, the old feudal system was complemented during the Renaissance by a patron-client relation, a system comparable with what the English have called the "new feudalism" or, less elegantly, "bastard feudalism." The "new feudalism" differed from the old in that the client did not render homage to the patron and the patron did not provide the client with a fief or in most instances with specified money payments at regular intervals. It was similar to the old feudalism in that it was an honorable relation based on mutual loyalty and interests. Under the "new feudalism" members of the lesser nobility, ambitious for advancement, often entered the service of a great lord. They might begin with minor posts in the lord's household or as men-at-arms in his *compagnie d'ordonnance,* but if they proved able and loyal they could aspire to important household positions, the captaincy of châteaux, or, through the favor of their patron, positions at court or in the royal bureaucracy. Other nobles preferred to reside at home, but dispatched their sons to their patron's château to serve as pages and to receive modest educations. The patron in return would either provide for the pages when they reached manhood or use his influence with the king to get them positions. When a patron summoned his clients to accompany him into battle, on a journey to court, or for some other service, he expected them to come clad in his livery, or at least his device, and with a suitable number of followers, depending on their rank. If a client got into trouble with the law, the patron was expected to use every means possible to prevent his being punished.[17]

Historians have generally assumed that this system was not formalized by a special oath or indenture,[18] but this view is incorrect, although further research will be necessary before it is known whether indentures were common or were only used occasionally. On April 8, 1429, for example, Gilles de Rais took a written oath to serve his powerful cousin, Georges de La Trémoïlle, against all seigneurs and other persons without exception until death.[19] No specific mention was made in this indenture of De Rais's obligation to bring his retainers with him in case of war or of La Trémoïlle's obligation to reward him for his services. These matters seem to have been clearly understood, however, for De Rais served his lord faithfully, and La Trémoïlle won for his twenty-three-year-old client the post of marshal of France three months after the indenture was signed. As this indenture was made just before the dawn of the French Renaissance, it would be well to cite another, dated near the end of this period.

> We, duke of Rohan, promise to the queen mother on our honor to serve and defend her at the risk of our life . . . in whatever she will judge suitable to guarantee the king and his estate from the ruin which threatens them, binding ourselves from this hour never to leave the service of her majesty, but to follow her wishes in all things; her majesty having also promised us on the word of a queen to guarantee us from the evil that some will want to visit upon us in consideration of the above. Given at Angers, the 30th of May, 1620.
>
> Henry de Rohan[20]

A rebellion, of course, followed.

Thus a "new feudalism" based on the ties of mutual loyalty between patron and client had come into being by the dawn of the Renaissance and continued to thrive well into the seventeenth century. In some respects it was more dangerous to the crown than the old feudalism because under the old feudalism the lord was limited in the number of his vassals by the number of his fiefs, or if the money fief be included, by the size of his treasury. Under the "new feudalism" neither fiefs nor specific payments were required, and the number of clients a lord had was limited only by his prestige, influence, and the popularity of his cause. When Condé raised his standard of rebellion at Orléans in the spring of 1562, the nobles who answered his summons were, with a few exceptions, not his vassals, but they named him as their chief and took an oath not only to obey him, but also "to hold ourselves in readiness as far as we are able in money, arms, horses, and other required things, . . . to accompany him wherever he commands, and to render him faithful service. . . ."[21] This document, which might be called a collective indenture, tied Protestant and other disaffected nobles to Condé and ushered in the Wars of Religion.

Most clients rendered faithful service to their patrons, and most patrons reciprocated by looking after their clients' interests, even to the extent of defending them from the king's justice. When in 1615 a seigneur of Marsillac violated the code and abandoned Condé's service to assume that of the Queen Mother, the angered prince told the sieur de Rochefort to punish him. Marsillac was beaten nearly to death, but the Queen Mother, highly incensed at the treatment meted out to her new retainer, demanded Rochefort's head. A bitter quarrel ensued between Condé and the Queen Mother in the presence of the King. The haughty Prince, while hiding Rochefort from justice, even had the effrontery to present his case against Marsillac to the parlement of Paris. Here he won some support, to the anger of the Queen Mother, but on Marsillac's recovery an apparent reconciliation between the two patrons was achieved. Rochefort continued in Condé's service, and the following year the young Prince got the King to give him the post of councilor of state and a gift of 36,000 livres.[22]

François de Bonne, duc de Lesdiguières, governor of Dauphiné, was willing to go to equal lengths to protect his clients from justice. He had established Marie Vignon, the wife of a silk merchant of Grenoble, as his mistress. This woman, not content with her role, conspired with a Savoyard colonel temporarily in Lesdiguières' service to have her husband murdered. The deed was done, but the parlement of Grenoble mustered the courage to imprison the colonel. Furious at this affront the old duke returned to Grenoble and released his client, despite the concierge's argument that only an order from parlement could set the prisoner free. When the president of parlement protested, Lesdiguières sharply rebuked him for ordering the arrest without consulting him. In the end the colonel went free, and the powerful governor, instead of being punished by the king in council, was given a royal letter approving his conduct and a pension for his mistress. Two years later in 1617 Marie Vignon, plebeian-born widow of a silk merchant, achieved her ultimate goal of becoming the wife of Lesdiguières, marshal, duke, peer, and later constable of France.[23]

The above incidents were perhaps exceptional, but it is clear that the behavior of the great nobles' retainers was an object of concern to many. Special patrols had to be established at Tours in 1468 and 1484 during the meetings of the Estates-General with orders to arrest all unruly persons including the people of the princes and the king.[24] In the Estates-Generals of 1560, 1576, 1588, and 1614 the Third Estate included in its *cahiers* protests against the practice of gentlemen protecting from punishment those in their retinue who had committed misdeeds.[25] Royal ordonnances frequently forbade anyone to interfere with magistrates in the execution of justice, but to no avail. In the great ordonnance of 1629, near the end of the Renaissance, the crown had once more to prohibit nobles from protecting those wanted for crimes.[26]

Whatever the evils of the system from the point of view of the Third Estate, it had distinct advantages for the great nobles because it enhanced their prestige to have a large number of gentlemen in their service, and it gave them military power. Some nobles such as the Nevers and the La Trémoïlles relied primarily on their role as feudal lords supplemented by their positions as royal governors or lieutenant generals. As governors of Nivernais, the Nevers added the authority of the king to the wide powers they already wielded as dukes, and neither the inhabitants of the enclaves in the duchy nor the clergy could escape their authority. They owned and controlled a large number of castles and fortified towns which they garrisoned with captains and soldiers of their choice. In addition, they had a guard of archers and between 1615 and 1616 even a Swiss guard.[27] The La Trémoïlles, frequently lieutenant generals in Poitou and the surrounding provinces, were in an almost comparable position. In 1487 they had at least twenty-seven fortified towns and castles captained by their retainers, and in 1595 they raised from their lands five hundred gentlemen and two thousand foot soldiers at their own expense.[28] Other nobles such as the Montmorencys in Languedoc or the Guises in Burgundy used their posts as governors to establish large clienteles. Neither family owned a significant amount of land or had many vassals in their governments; thus it was necessary for them to rely on the techniques of the "new feudalism" to establish their position. Neither exercised powers as complete as the Nevers did in Nivernais, but the Guises drew strong support from Burgundy during the Wars of Religion. The biographer of one Montmorency has called him "the uncrowned king of southern France," and the provincial estates of Languedoc followed another Montmorency into rebellion in 1632.[29]

Cardinal Richelieu took advantage of his position as chief of the royal council to create a military establishment that consisted of a company of horse guards and a company of musketeers. Like the other great nobles, he insisted on personal fidelity. His intimate adviser, Father Joseph, is reported to have said that the cardinal wants "officers who will be faithful to him and only to him without exception and without reservation. He does not want those who serve two masters knowing full well he would not find fidelity in them. It is so rare to find men of this character that if it were necessary to buy them the Cardinal would pay their weight in gold."[30] That Richelieu found those who would serve him loyally even at the cost of incurring the hatred of the king's musketeers is well known to all readers of the romances of Alexander Dumas.

The situation would have been dangerous enough to the crown if the governors and other great nobles had drawn their clients entirely from the landed nobility, but they did not, and the "new feudalism" spread into the army, the judicial and administrative bureaucracy, and even into the towns. The much-vaunted army created by Charles VII was officered by the great nobles; even the mounted men-at-arms were generally of noble birth. Under such circumstances it is nearly certain that the great nobles assigned key subordinate positions in their companies to their vassals and clients and that the ambitious unattached noble in such a company soon found it advisable to adopt his commander as his patron. One is therefore not surprised to find that in the 1550's the lieutenant and the ensign in the Duke of Nevers' company were his vassals, and the guidon was a gentlemen in his household.[31] The Duke of Mayenne had many clients in his company in Burgundy.[32] This situation led the great nobles to consider the royal troops they commanded as their own. These troops, although paid from taxes levied on orders from the king, wore the livery or device of their commander, and his colors became the company standard. Royal ordonnances encouraged this practice because in an age before uniforms it provided the best means to identify troops in battle and to place the blame on those who pillaged.[33] The primary loyalty of these troops was generally to their commanders whom they followed into revolt in many instances throughout the Renaissance. The king's army really consisted of the companies of such nobles as could be persuaded to support him, plus some hired mercenaries. Perhaps it was the unreliable nature of these French troops that caused the monarchs to entrust their personal safety primarily to Swiss and Scottish guards.

The great nobles exercised considerable influence over the appointment and behavior of royal officials in their fiefs. The dukes of Nevers had the right to name all royal officials in their territories, and when offices were made hereditary in 1604 in return for an annual fee, it was the dukes, not the king, who got the payments.[34] The counts of Laval had the privilege of naming royal officials in their lands,[35] as did some other important nobles. Governors were often able to win support from the royal judicial and administrative officials in their province, especially during the Wars of Religion, and their clients included town officials and leading ecclesiastics.[36]

Great nobles also managed to place their clients in the judicial and administrative chambers of the central government. The practice was common by the time of Charles VI[37] and was continued by the nobility to the best of its ability in succeeding reigns. In 1540 one finds a vassal of the Duke of Nevers serving in the king's household.[38] Condé counted a president of the parlement of Paris among his loyal supporters during the minority of Louis XIII and got three of his followers named councilors of state in return for halting his rebellion in 1616.[39] The Duke of Rohan used his influence to get the governor of a town appointed to the king's household in 1617 and in 1620 sought to capitalize on this favor by having Marie de Médicis, his own patron, commission this old soldier to raise a regiment to aid in their rebellion.[40] The Guises were especially successful in the art of placement during the Wars of Religion. Indeed so great was the danger of the nobles penetrating into the government by getting appointments for their clients that the Duke of Sully later informed Cardinal Richelieu that the reason Henry IV made officeholding hereditary was to weaken the influence of the great nobles in the bureaucracy.[41]

One should not assume from the above that the great nobles exercised an all-powerful influence over the lesser members of the aristocracy. Often the reverse was more nearly true, a fact that can be best illustrated by a brief inspection of the relationship between the governors and the provincial estates. These estates, controlled as they were by the upper clergy, the nobility, and bourgeois patricians of the towns, regarded the governor as their agent at court. If they wanted a reduction in taxes, the suppression of newly created offices, or any other concession, they asked their governor to intercede with the king on their behalf. This the governor invariably did because the taxes to pay his salary and that of his military companies and guards were voted and generally collected by the provincial estates. A governor who was successful in winning special favors could expect further rewards. Thus in addition to voting Montmorency and members of his family their usual salaries and gifts, the estates of Languedoc in 1620 granted him 30,000 livres in consideration of his extraordinary expenses, 132,000 livres to reimburse him for the cost of his troops used to suppress a recent uprising, and 10,800 livres for "his great services." The same assembly flatly rejected one royal request for 25,000 livres for five years to repair the bridge at Avignon and refused to do more than to promise to consider at their next meeting a second request for 400,000 livres.[42] Small wonder Cardinal Richelieu complained that the authority of the king was scarcely known in Languedoc.[43]

On the other hand, the ineffectual Duke of Guise enjoyed so little credit at court and in his government of Provence that the estates did not vote his salary or taxes to support his two companies in 1629 or 1630.[44] So important was it to have a governor with influence that in 1630 the three estates of Brittany petitioned the King to name Richelieu their governor, and a few years later Provence asked for his demented brother.[45]

The aristocracy sought to influence the crown through other officials. Royal commissioners sent to negotiate with the provincial estates invariably received payment, and the Secretaries of State, those confidential advisers of the king who dealt with the various provinces, were not neglected. The same assembly of the estates of Languedoc as cited above voted 1,500 livres for the King's Secretary of State who handled the affairs of the province and 300 for his assistant.[46] In 1599 the three estates of Comminges received a letter from their deputy requesting money for distribution at court to ensure the preservation of their liberties, 1,000 *écus* being earmarked for Michel de Marillac who was already earning his reputation as an enemy of provincial liberties.[47] Secretaries and valets of important persons were sometimes remembered[48]; even the lowly historian did not escape notice. When the estates of Languedoc learned that the royal historiographer was planning to write a description of their province, they voted him 100 *écus* and promised him an additional sum if his book upon completion was found to be "useful." Enough mention was made of the privileges of the province at this point in the journal of the estates to leave no doubt in the mind of the most naïve member of our profession what kind of a book would be considered "useful."[49] Thus in Renaissance France the provincial estates levied taxes to pay royal officials to convince the king that they were unable to pay the taxes he requested and that their respective provinces had privileges that must not be overridden.

During the Renaissance about one-third of France did not have provincial estates that met periodically. In the provinces the landed nobility appears to have put direct pressure on its governors and patrons. The great noble who could not obtain enough concessions from the crown for his clients was faced with a choice of losing his influence over them or of revolting in the hope that the crown would purchase his submission. Thus, by rebelling, the Duke of Nevers increased his income from 401,003 livres in 1616 to 806,776 in 1617, but at the same time his expenses jumped from 400,345 to 808,520 livres, strong circumstantial evidence that the real winners of the revolt were his followers.[50]

The situation described above provides the basis for the contention that throughout the Renaissance the most powerful class was the landed nobility, just as it had been during the Middle Ages. This does not mean, however, that kings were necessarily ineffective. Just as the medieval king was the principal lord in the kingdom, so the Renaissance monarch was the greatest patron. The former governed with the cooperation of his vassals, the latter with the cooperation of his clients. To ensure this cooperation the king had at his disposal the highest offices of the Church, government positions, military commands, patents of nobility, and nearly every type of privilege. The great noble who wanted these things for himself or his clients usually found faithful service the surest path to success. To make doubly certain, the king distributed pensions and the right to certain royal taxes on an annual basis to the great nobles. Thus royal control over the nobility was based largely on a vast patronage. The king who administered it wisely and fairly could hope for enough cooperation from the great nobles and their clients to make the system work. But if the king was a minor or was weak and the control of the royal patronage fell into the hands of a faction, those nobles who were excluded revolted.[51] There was no exception to this rule during the Renaissance.

The Wars of Religion made the dangers of the "new feudalism" all too clear to the crown, and beginning with the reign of Henry IV serious attempts were made to mitigate its effect. The first step was to free the bureaucracy from the influence of the great nobles. This was accomplished in 1604 by making officeholding hereditary in return for the payment of an annual fee. Eventually this enabled royal officials to become as independent of the crown as of the nobility, but so long as the right to have hereditary offices was challenged by other elements of the Renaissance aristocracy, the bureaucracy stood loyally by the crown except when the crown curtailed or threatened to curtail its privileges.[52]

The second step was to get control of the tax-collecting machinery so that the provincial estates would no longer be in a position to reward or punish royal officials. Henry IV began to move in this direction in 1603 when he issued an edict substituting royal tax collectors for those of the local estates in Guienne. This attempt had to be abandoned in 1611 during the regency of Marie de Médicis, but was renewed in Guienne in 1621 and elsewhere between 1628 and 1632. In some provinces the result was the abandonment of the provincial estates and the appointment of obedient royal tax officials; in others the provincial estates were allowed to continue to exist under careful scrutiny from the crown and with sharply curtailed taxing privileges.[53]

The third step was to separate the mass of the Protestants from the great nobles. This was accomplished by persuading most of the great nobles to return to the Catholic fold during the seventeenth century and by issuing edicts granting a degree of religious toleration in 1598 and 1629.[54] The fourth step was to substitute intendants for governors as the principal royal officials in the provinces, an action that gradually took place after the middle of the seventeenth century.[55] The fifth step was to establish effective control over a large standing army, an accomplishment of Michel Le Tellier and the Marquis de Louvois during the reign of Louis XIV.[56] The final step was to separate the great nobles from the lesser nobles, a process that took place gradually during the seventeenth century and was nearly completed by the creation of the court at Versailles where the great nobles laughed at jokes about the country gentlemen upon whom their power had formerly rested. In this manner, the "new feudalism" of the Renaissance became as much a part of the past as the "old."[57]

NOTES

1. Jean-R. Bloch, *L'Anoblissement en France au temps de François 1er* (Paris, 1934), esp. 11–123.

2. Roger Doucet, *Les Institutions de la France au* XVIe *siècle* (2 vols., Paris, 1948), II, 462–63.

3. J. Russell Major, *Representative Institutions in Renaissance France, 1421–1559* (Madison, Wis., 1960), 5–7. If the governor was frequently absent, his lieutenant generally assumed the leading role in the province.

4. *Recueil des cahiers généraux des trois ordres aux États généraux* [hereafter cited as *Cahiers*], ed. Lalourcé and Duval (4 vols., Paris, 1789), IV, 193. For an example of trouble on this score, see Lucien Romier, *Le Royaume de Catherine de Médicis* (2d ed., 2 vols., Paris, 1922), I, 182–83.

5. On ennoblement by prescription, see Bloch, *Anoblissement en France,* esp. 54–56. Historians who have studied the genealogies of noble families emphasize social mobility in the Renaissance. (See, e.g., Henri Drouot, *Mayenne et la Bourgogne* [2 vols., Paris, 1937], I, 30–33; Roland Mousnier, *La Vénalité des offices sous Henri IV et Louis XIII* [Rouen, 1945], 58–63, 506–41; Fernand Braudel, *La Méditerranée et le monde méditerranéen à lépoque de Philippe II* [Paris, 1949], 619–24; Pierre Goubert, *Familles marchandes sous l'ancien régime: Les Danse et les Motte, de Beauvais* [Paris, 1959], 16–19, 79–85, 131–37; Raoul Busquet, *Études sur l'ancienne Provence, institutions et points d'histoire* [Paris, 1930], 320–26; and J. Russell Major, *The Deputies to the Estates General of Renaissance France* [Madison, Wis., 1960], 147.) Édouard Perroy has found that of 215 noble families in Forez in the thirteenth century only 5 survived until the Revolution. He estimated that the average duration of a noble line was from three to six generations. There would, therefore, have been virtually no nobility if newcomers had not eventually been accepted into its ranks. (See his "Social Mobility among the French Noblesse in the Later Middle Ages," *Past and Present,* XXI [Apr. 1962], 31.) Claude de Seyssel, the leading theorist of the French Renaissance monarchy, recognized the existence of and the need for the practice of elevating members of the Third Estate to the nobility. (See *La Monarchie de France,* ed. Jacques Poujol [Paris, 1961], 125.)

6. J. Russell Major, "The French Renaissance Monarchy as Seen through the Estates General," *Studies in the Renaissance,* IX (1962), 121; Braudel, *Méditerranée et le monde méditerranéen,* 624–37; Pierre Goubert, "The French Peasantry of the Seventeenth Century," *Past and Present,* X (Nov. 1956), 72.

7. Victor Carrière, *Introduction aux études d'histoire ecclésiastique locale* (3 vols., Paris, 1934–40), III, 423–26; Ivan Cloulas, "Les Aliénations du temporel ecclésiastique sous Charles IX et Henri III (1563–1587)," *Revue d'histoire de l'église de France,* XLIV (1958), 5–56.

8. Henri Carré, *Sully* (Paris, 1932), 356.

9. Pierre Cavard, *La Réforme et les guerres de religion à Vienne* (Vienne, 1950), 392–98; Louis Merle, *La métairie et l'évolution agraire de la Gâtine poitevine de la fin du moyen âge à la révolution* (Paris, 1958), esp. 49–95.

10. *Inventaire des titres de Nevers de l'Abbé de Marolles,* ed. Jacques Soultrait (Nevers, 1873), cols. 577–78, 528–29, 531. The Duke of Nevers was able to lend Henry III 100,000 livres in 1576 and 400,000 livres more in 1578. (*Ibid.*, cols. 524-25.)

11. French historians have written many superb economic and social histories since World War II, but these histories deal with selected geographical areas, not noble families. There is also need for works comparable to John M. Bean, *The Estates of the Percy Family, 1416–1537* (London, 1958); Alan Simpson, *The Wealth of the Gentry, 1540–1660: East Anglian Studies* (Chicago, 1961); and Mary E. Finch, *The Wealth of Five Northamptonshire Families, 1540–1640* (Oxford, Eng., 1955).

12. For example, a study of the construction and alteration of thirty-two châteaux in the Oise Department reveals that twenty-four were built or restored in the sixteenth and early seventeenth centuries, but only two during the period of economic decadence between 1643 and 1715. (Pierre Goubert, *Beauvais et le Beauvaisis de 1600 à 1730* [Paris, 1960], 534.)

13. *Inventaire . . . de Nevers,* ed. Soultrait, esp. cols. 52–379. The documents are now lost. Other sources are too numerous to cite. Doucet agrees that the lord-vassal relation was widespread, but argues that it was declining. More likely it was being slowly replaced by the "new feudalism." (See *Institutions de la France,* II, 458, 468–74, and for archival sources, II, 487.)

14. *Lettres missives originales du seizième siècle tirées des archives du duc de La Trémoïlle,* ed. Paul A. Marchegay (Niort, 1881), Nos. 193, 194, 205, 252.

15. *Recueil des lettres missives de Henri IV,* ed. Berger de Xivrey (9 vols., Paris, 1843–76), III, 48–49, 311.

16. Lists of the members of the ducal household in 1476 have been published in *Inventaire . . . de Nevers,* ed. Soultrait, cols. 47–48. Jean de la Rivière, Antoine d'Avril, Hector Berthelon, and Étienne du Pontot were captains of towns and châteaux and holders of fiefs in the duchy. (*Ibid.,* cols. 414–15, 757; fiefs in the duchy are listed *ibid.,* cols. 795–874.)

17. The patron-client system, or the "new feudalism," has never really been studied in France, but see the brief remarks in Romier, *Royaume de Catherine de Médicis,* I, 167–68, 208–22. For an account of Cardinal Richelieu's relation to his pages, see Maximin Deloche, *La Maison du Cardinal de Richelieu* (Paris, 1912), 327–62.

18. See, e.g., Édouard Perroy, "Feudalism or Principalities in Fifteenth Century France," *Bulletin of the Institute of Historical Research,* XX (1943–45), 181. Bryce D. Lyon recognized the existence of contracts in France that were identical to the English indentures except that there was no retaining fee, but he apparently saw them as being of purely military significance. (Bryce Lyon, *From Fief to Indenture: The Transition from Feudal to Non-Feudal Contract in Western Europe* [Cambridge, Mass., 1957], 255–58.) However, retaining fees were paid in France in the late Middle Ages, and indentures were often used for nonmilitary purposes. (B.-A. Pocquet du Haut-Jussé, "Les pensionnaires fieffés des ducs de Bourgogne de 1352 à 1419," *Mémoires de la société pour l'histoire du droit et des institutions des anciens pays bourguignons, comtois et romands,* VIII [1942], 127–50; André Leguai, *Les Ducs de Bourbon pendant la crise monarchique du xve siècle* [Paris, 1962], 35.) It is difficult to study indentures in France without thorough archival research because in their publications French historians generally refer to any sort of contract between two nobles as a "treaty of alliance." Thus Leguai published an indenture and a treaty between two equals without drawing any distinctions between them. (*Ibid.,* 195–96, 201–202.) Historians of the Renaissance frequently refer to treaties between nobles, especially during periods of rebellion, and to one noble entering the service of another, but the actual contracts, if any, have almost never been published. Further research is badly needed on this problem, but it is my impression that indentures were used without retainer fees in Renaissance France much as William H. Dunham, Jr., describes them in England. (See his *Lord Hastings' Indentured Retainers, 1463–1483* [New Haven, Conn., 1955]. For the contribution of the *fief-rente* to the theory of *rentes,* see Bernard Schnapper, *Les Rentes au* xvie *siècle* [Paris, 1957], esp. 43–44.)

19. Les La Trémoïlle pendant cinq siècles, ed. Louis, duc de La Trémoïlle (5 vols., Nantes, 1890–96), I, 183. On this relationship, see also *ibid.,* 202–203, 226–29.

20. Archives du Ministère des Affaires Étrangères, mémoires et documents, France, MS. 773, fol. 49.

21. Jules Delaborde, *Gaspard de Coligny, amiral de France* (3 vols., Paris, 1879–82), II, 70–74.

22. Henri, duc d'Aumale, *Histoire des princes de Condé* (7 vols., Paris, 1863–96), III, 42–45; *Négociations, lettres et pièces relatives à la conférence de Loudun,* ed. Louis Bouchitté (Paris, 1862), 788–89, 799. This post of councilor of state is perhaps a basis for Aumale's statement that Rochefort entered the King's service after this incident. (Aumale, *Princes de Condé,* III, 45.) More likely it was another case of a great noble's winning advancement for his clients. Note that two other clients of Condé were named councilors at the same time. (*Négociations,* ed. Bouchitté, 788.)

23. Charles Dufayard, *Le Connétable de Lesdiguières* (Paris, 1892), 375–79; Louis Videl, *Histoire de la vie du connestable de Lesdiguières* (Paris, 1638), 260–61, 297–99.

24. Major, *Deputies to the Estates General,* 144.

25. Cahiers, ed. Lalourcé and Duval, I, 324, II, 303–304, III, 224, IV, 311-12, 319, 322.

26. Recueil général des anciennes lois françaises depuis l'an 420 jusqu'à la révolution de 1789, ed. François-A. Isambert *et al.* (29 vols., Paris, 1822–33), XVI, 272. For references to other ordonnances against maintenance, see Philibert Bugnyon, *Commentaires sur les ordonnances de Blois establies aux Estats generaux convoquez en la ville de Blois* (Lyon, 1584), 297–307.

27. L. Despois, *Histoire de l'autorité royale dans le comté de Nivernais* (Paris, 1912), 229–40.

28. La Trémoïlle, *Les La Trémoïlle,* II, 108–10, IV, v; Charles Samaran, *Le Chartrier des La Trémoïlle* (Paris, 1930), 26.

29. Drouot, *Mayenne et la Bourgogne,* esp. I, 102–19; Paul Gachon, *Les États de Languedoc et l'édit de Béziers, 1632* (Paris, 1887), esp. 87–91, 225–49; Franklin C. Palm, *Politics and Religion in Sixteenth-Century France* (Boston, 1927), 125–56.

30. Deloche, *Maison de Cardinal de Richelieu,* 370.

31. The lieutenant was the sieur de Givry; the ensign, the sieur d'Espeuilles; and the guidon, the sieur de Saint-Simon. (François de Rabutin, *Commentaires des guerres en la gaule belgique. Société de l'histoire de France,* ed. Charles Gailly de Taurines [2 vols., Paris, 1932–44], II, 123, 281.) One also notes that Gilbert de Chevenon who held the fief of Saint-Amand from Nevers joined the company as a man-at-arms (*ibid.,* I, 115–16) and that another vassal, La Brosse, was a member (*ibid.,* II, 147). Many other names could doubtless be added if a roster of the company were available. For an example of the intermixing of the gentlemen of the household with the company, see *ibid.,* I, 172–76.

32. Drouot, *Mayenne et la Bourgogne,* I, 112–13.

33. Gaston Zeller, *Les Institutions de la France au* xvie *siècle* (Paris, 1948), 310–11.

34. Despois, *Autorité royale,* 273–76, 483–86. For a general account of the influence of the great nobles on the appointment of royal officials, see Mousnier, *Vénalité des offices,* 287–311.

35. La Trémoïlle, *Les La Trémoïlle,* IV, 117–19.

36. On the role of the governors, see esp. Gaston Zeller, "Gouverneurs de provinces au xvie siècle," *Revue historique,* CLXXXV (Jan.–June 1939), 225–56; Doucet, *Institutions de la France,* I, 229–44; and Drouot, *Mayenne et la Bourgogne,* esp. I, 73–77, 102–19, 293–313. The ambitions of the great nobles are indicated by the peace terms Mayenne suggested to Henry IV in 1594. (*Ibid.,* II, 362–63). Indeed, governors became so powerful during the Wars of Religion that the Estates-General protested in 1588 and 1614. (*Cahiers,* ed. Lalourcé and Duval, III, 53, 140–41, IV, 200–201, 309–11.)

37. Perroy, "Feudalism or Principalities," 181–85.

38. *Inventaire . . . de Nevers,* ed. Soultrait, col. 54.

39. Aumale, *Princes de Condé,* III, 53, 69; *Négociations,* ed. Bouchitté, 788.

40. "Lettres adressées de 1585 à 1625 à Marc-Antoine Marreau de Boisguérin," *Archives historiques du Poitou,* XIV (1883), 349–54, 361–63.

41. Mousnier, *Vénalité des offices,* esp. 63–66, 287–311; Cardinal Richelieu, *Testament politique,* ed. Louis André (Paris, 1947), 233–34.

42. Archives Départementales [hereafter cited as AD], Hérault, procès-verbal of the estates of Béziers, May–June 1620. The 10,800 livres voted Montmorency were actually for his *ustinsiles des étrangers,* a company that the estates knew no longer existed. Other examples of gifts by the estates to governors are: Provence to Guise in 1601, 15,000 livres for his services (AD, Bouches-du-Rhône, C 9, fol. 20–20v); Burgundy to Biron in 1602, 10,000 *écus* in addition to his regular salary "in recognition of the favors and good offices he had rendered the province" at court (AD, Côte-d'Or, C 3016, fol. 465); Dauphiné to Lesdiguières in 1621, 18,000 livres and to his son-in-law, 6,000 (AD, Isère, I C 4, No. 45). Condé was fortunate enough to be assigned the task of negotiation with the estates of Burgundy and Provence in 1631 concerning the abolition of the *élus.* For his services he was voted 100,000 livres by the estates of both provinces. (AD, Côte-d'Or, C 3080, fol. 2v; AD, Bouches-du-Rhône, C 16, fols. 127v–128). Provence also voted the two intendants 5,000 livres each. (AD, Bouches-du-Rhône, C 16, fol. 127v–128.)

43. *Mémoires du Cardinal de Richelieu: Société de l'histoire de France,* ed. Robert Lavollée (10 vols., Paris, 1907–31), IX, 302.

44. AD, Bouches-du-Rhône, C 16, fols. 66v–67, 127v–28v. In 1631 when the estates were in a desperate position Guise was voted 100,000 livres. (*Ibid.,* fol. 128v.)

45. Louis, Comte de Carné, *Les États de Bretagne* (2d ed., 2 vols., Paris, 1875), I, 288; AD, Bouches-du-Rhône, C 108, fols. 105v–107.

46. AD, Hérault, procès-verbal of May–June 1620. The estates of Provence voted the Secretary of State in charge of its affairs 800 *écus* in 1611 and his assistant, 200 *écus,* because of the importance of the affairs of the province being considered at court. (AD, Bouches-du-Rhône, C 10, fol. 263v.) The same amount was voted in 1612 and smaller sums thereafter. (*Ibid.,* fols. 336v, 404v; C 12, fols. 17, 51, 237, 281v, 354v–355; C 15, fol. 145v; C 16, fol. 96.) The estates of Burgundy voted the Secretary of State in charge of its affairs 15,000 livres in 1631. (AD, Côte-d'Or, C 3080, fol. 2v.)

47. AD, Haute-Garonne, C 3676, Nos. 53–54.

48. The estates of Provence frequently voted their governors' secretaries and servants money. (AD, Bouches-du-Rhône, C 10, fol. 404v; C 12, fols. 114, 236v, 277v–278, 354v–355.) The estates of Burgundy voted its governor's secretary 600 livres in 1605. (AD, Côte-d'Or, C 3017, fols. 37v-38v.)

49. AD, Hérault, procès-verbal of the estates of Pézenas, Dec. 1597–Jan. 1598.

50. Inventaire . . . de Nevers, ed. Soultrait, col. 528.

51. On the use the king made of the great nobles to control the lesser nobles, see Romier, *Royaume de Catherine de Médicis,* I, 208–10; on the award of pensions, see Mousnier, *Vénalité des offices,* 407–409. I do not believe that either the army or the bureaucracy added much to the king's strength because both contained many persons who were loyal to the great nobles, and both were quite small by modern standards. (See Major, "French Renaissance Monarchy," 117–19.) It is true the size of the bureaucracy increased during the Renaissance, but this increase was caused as much by the desire to raise money through the sale of offices as by the desire to increase royal power. This is illustrated by the practice of having officials take turns performing the same duties. (Zeller, *Institutions de la France,* 138–40; Mousnier, *Vénalité des offices,* 25–28.)

52. For an explanation of how the *droit annuel* strengthened the crown during the reigns of Henry IV and Louis XIII, see *ibid.,* 557–621.

53. I am engaged in a study of the decline of the provincial estates during the reigns of Henry IV and Louis XIII and will offer evidence to support this paragraph at a later date.

54. The Edict of Nantes (1598) and the Edict of Alais (1629). By his abjuration Henry IV had already won the support of most Catholics.

55. Roland Mousnier, "État et Commissaire: Recherches sur la création des intendants de province, 1634–1648," *Forschungen zur Staat und Verfassung: Festgabe für Fritz Hartung* (Berlin, 1958), 325–44. His recent "Note sur les rapports entre les gouverneurs de provinces et les intendants dans la première moitié du xviie siècle," *Revue historique,* CCXXVIII (Oct.–Dec. 1962), 339–50, indicates that the intendants were at first only the advisers and assistants of the governors. They did not supplant the governors in the provinces during the first half of the seventeenth century as was formerly thought.

56. Louis André, *Michel Le Tellier et Louvois* (Paris, 1942), 277–427.

57. The efforts of the crown to halt the practice of dueling and to demolish fortified châteaux have often been cited as weakening the nobility. Edicts against dueling, however, were designed to preserve the nobility, not to destroy it, and in the Estates-General of 1588 the nobles themselves asked that the death penalty be imposed on duelists. (*Cahiers,* ed. Lalourcé and Duval, III, 143.) Most nobles evidently did not regard the château-fort as a necessary ingredient for their power because from the dawn of the sixteenth century they generally preferred to build their châteaux in the more comfortable Renaissance style. During the rebellions between 1562 and 1629 many of the surviving châteaux-forts as well as some recently fortified places fell into the hands of Protestants or lawless persons who resisted local officials and terrorized the countryside. This situation led the deputies of the nobility at the Estates-General of 1588 to ask that owners of fortified places guard them carefully to keep them out of undesirable hands. (*Ibid.,* 143, 148.) The deputies of the clergy and the Third Estate were more vehement and advocated demolition. (*Ibid.,* II, 77, 295–96, 308–309, III, 55, 228, IV, 314-15.) The provincial estates with the concurrence of the nobility often asked that forts be demolished. Thus in 1622 the estates of Béarn asked that all châteaux and other fortified places in Béarn be demolished except those at Pau and Navarrenx. (AD, Basse-Pyrénées, C 708, fols. 303–308). The estates of Rouergue petitioned the King to destroy fortified places in 1596. (Archives communales, Millau, AA 12.) A similar request came from Provence in 1597 and was repeated many times thereafter. (AD, Bouches-du-Rhône, C 8, fols. 68v, 83v, 151–151v, 188v–189v, etc.) The estates of Burgundy did likewise in 1618, and among those compensated in 1631 for the demolition of a château was Cardinal Richelieu himself. (AD, Côte-d'Or, C 3017, fol. 203–203v; C 3079, fol. 6–7.)

COMMUNITY

I. Village, City, and Province

THE COMMUNITY OF THE VILL*

Helen Maud Cam

It is a commonplace to say that the vill and the manor are not synonymous in England of the high Middle Ages. The township was an entity both older and longer lived than the lordship, and even in the heyday of feudalism, the township, the *villata,* the community of the vill imposes itself on our attention—not only as an indispensable unit in the governmental system but also, in many parts of the country, as a community conscious and active in its own right.

As with the more conspicuous community of the shire, the Anglo-Norman and Angevin kings preserved and invigorated the township by making use of it. When facts were needed, as in the Domesday inquest and in numerous other inquests down to those of 1255 and 1274–5 recorded in the so-called Hundred Rolls, the township was called upon to supply them by four or six men, with or without priest and reeve. Similar deputations had to attend the shire and hundred courts periodically, and, if Miss Hurnard is right,[1] they were being expected to report the names of suspicious characters long before the Assizes of Clarendon and Northamp-

* Reprinted from Helen Maud Cam, "The Community of the Vill," *Medieval Studies Presented to Rose Graham,* V. Ruffer and A. J. Taylor, eds. (London: Oxford Univ. Press, 1950), pp. 1–14.

ton required every township of a hundred to present on oath the names of suspected criminals to the sheriffs and justices; a task fufilled, as the records prove, at the tourn, the county court, and the general eyre. In particular, from 1194 at least, the coroner, inquiring into sudden deaths, treasure-trove, and the like, always summoned the four vills nearest to the scene of the event, by four men from each vill, to report upon oath what they knew about the matter.[2] The decrees of 1233, 1242, and 1285 laid on the vill the duty of keeping watches by four or six of its number, and the following of the hue and cry by the whole township; it was responsible for seeing that every one of its members was in frank-pledge or tithing, and for the custody of any criminal committed to its keeping by the sheriff. Hardly separable from its police duties were its military obligations. Though Henry II's Assize of Arms had expressly excluded the villein from its scope, all men were liable for the defence of the realm,[3] and this responsibility was riveted on the township in a series of regulations. John's measures against threatened invasion in 1204 had provided for the registering and leading of the village forces, whilst the regulations of 1242 set up constables in every township; the regulations of 1253 made the township responsible for providing the arms required; and both men and weapons were to be ready for inspection by the shire authorities when demanded; an inspection held twice a year, according to the Statute of Winchester in 1285. An entry on the court rolls of Halesowen shows a village picking its own men for the call-up to the Welsh wars in 1295,[4] whilst for the same campaign a Lincolnshire vill contributed 4*s*. to the expenses of its soldiers[5] and "all the men" of a Durham vill were penalized for not compensating their fellows for their war service.[6] The invaluable *Nomina Villarum* of 1316 is the fruit of an inquiry arising from the provision in the Parliament of 1315 that one man should go from every whole vill of the kingdom for the Scottish war, as are the returns, preserved for three counties, of the weapons in the keeping of the constables of each vill for the use of the militia men.[7] The vill is also under the ancient obligations of keeping up roads, causeways, and bridges, referred to in Clause 23 of the Charter of 1215; the sheriff in his tourn will inquire into their discharge of such duties. Analogous, but of more recent origin, is the duty of keeping the walls of a royal park in repair, shared by ancient custom between a number of Northamptonshire townships whose names, according to an ancient deponent in 1548, are "engraven upon the stones upon the walles of said parke."[8]

Again, new forms of taxation made new work for the townships. The sheriffs had been accustomed to collect the ancient customary dues which went to make up the farm of the shire by hundred and vill;[9] when the regulations for levying the taxes on property began they fell into the same pattern.[10] In 1225 the payment was made by four lawful men and the reeve of each vill to the county knights;[11] and the fortieth of 1232 and the thirtieth of 1237 were assessed in the same way. Willard has shown that under Edward I the responsibility for assessment rested directly on the vill, with no intervention from the hundred; and the final assessment of 1334 was drawn up on the basis of agreement between the chief assessors and the communities of the cities, boroughs, and men of the vills.[12] Whilst Mr. Thompson has shown that the actual subtaxor in the vill was sometimes a villein,[13] Mr. Homans has found an instance in 1306 of the distribution by the vill itself among its own members of the war-time requisitions levied by the sheriff: an admirable instance of the common sense of the township. A substantial villager is assessed by the whole vill at half a quarter of oats for the use of the king "because he has more than he needs for his own sustentation."[14]

"The township," says Maitland, "is a community which, even if it has not rights, certainly has duties";[15] and he, like Madox before him,[16] gives illustrations from the reign of Henry II onwards of the money penalties inflicted on the vill for failure to discharge these duties and for other delinquencies—for taking no action when a man is found slain, for receiving a man who is not in frank-pledge, for exceeding its powers by putting men to the ordeal of water or hanging a thief, for infringing the Crown's monopoly of the great fish, for not raising the hue and pursuing the criminal, for ploughing up the king's highway, for failing to resist a Flemish raid, even for remaking a ditch before authorized to do so by the royal justices. In every case it is the *villata* that is amerced; in these matters the lord of the manor, if such there be, is ignored; the penalty, like the obligation, is on the community. But other records show the lord of the manor himself treating his tenants as a community. Study of the Durham halmotes, to which Maitland directed our attention, shows that commands to the vills are most frequently couched in the form *injunctum est omnibus tenentibus* [it is ordered to all tenants], whilst money penalties are inflicted on the *communitatem ville.* Financial obligation has a communalizing effect; and it is difficult, in view of the evidence noted above, to accept Maitland's suggestion[17] that the distribution of the financial burden was stereotyped by annexation to holdings so that no discussion was needed when the community had to find a sum of money for any purpose. Stenton has propounded the contribution of the primitive levies of Anglo-Saxon tributary rulers towards the growth of the earliest folkmoots;[18] there can be little doubt that collective financial responsibility was one of the causes of preservation of an active communal organization.

Another force, as is genearlly accepted, was the need for cooperation in agriculture, for though much may be stereotyped by custom the English climate is not, and emergencies of all sorts may demand initiative or innovation. The plainest evidence of communal agriculture action are the by-laws drawn up by common agreement. Mentioned from early in the thirteenth century by such names as Le Belawe (Wilburton 1222), *statutum autumpni* (Herts. 1228), *statutum villate,* Le Byelawe (Ely 1303–9), even the *plebicetum*[19] (Yorkshire 1297), found recorded in writing from 1329,[20] they are described as being agreed upon *inter communam ville* (Durham 1296) and as being enforced, in Yorkshire, by the *custodes statuti autumpni*.[21] A judge refers in 1370 to "the usage throughout the land called Bie-laws" by which neighbours can levy a sum by common assent, assess each man and distrain for non-payment.[22] Penalties for disobedience are frequently mentioned; sometimes they go entirely to the township or *communitatem plebiceti,* sometimes they are shared between the lord and the township.[23] In sixteenth-century Kingsthorpe, a long-lived community, they may be shared between the town officers and the town.[24]

Another well-known illustration of the township acting as a body in agrarian concerns is the practice of inter-commoning in fen or marsh country, mentioned by Maitland,[25] and very fully discussed by Nellie Neilson in her edition of the *Terrier of Fleet* in Lincolnshire.[26] Seven townships have rights of common in Gruntifen, and three in Thetfordheyfen along with the Templars of Denny Abbey.[27] As Miss Neilson observed, though most of the documentary material belongs to the period when the lord of the manor has assumed control, the villata still has its part to play," and it seems clear that the origins of such agreements go back far beyond the manorial origins.[28]

The township is indeed tough. Beatrice Lees in her edition of the Templars' inquest of 1185 comments on the fact that, apart from the *villa integra* whose entity is preserved by the enforcement of public obligations,[29] "the vitality of the ancient local group" asserts itself against both "the administrative organization of the preceptory and the feudal organization of the manor."[30] She cites the spirited protest of the small community of Lockridge, Wilts., against the innovations of the Order "when Osbert of Dover held the bailiwick";[31] the sworn statement of the men of Kerby, Yorkshire, who owe rent but no service, as to the customs of their court and as to the forfeitures which they retain intact and those which they divide with the brothers;[32] and the statement of the township of Willoughton, Lincolnshire, as to the Templars' lands in their village: "all this land is of the gift of Simon de Canci and Roger de Bussei. But the *villata* knows not how to separate the fee of Simon from the fee of Roger except for five tofts."[33] This incapacity to apply the complexities of feudal tenurial theory to the actual fields on which they lived is paralleled by a statement in the Hundred Rolls of 1255. The villagers of Oving, Buckinghamshire, asked to say who holds the vill of Oving, start off bravely with the statement that Robert of Oving is lord of the vill and holds one knight's fee of the honour of Doddeley and answers for three hides. They then proceed to enumerate four other tenants, three of them each holding one-seventh of the vill of a different lord, and the fourth holding one-fourteenth of the vill of yet another lord, and then break down. "Of this vill we know nothing else, nor can we discover anything, save that William de Bello has view of frank-pledge."[34] In such villages, as in the many Cambridgeshire villages of three, four, or five lords of manors described in the Hundred Rolls of 1279, "the villar unity persists."[35] It may be, as Joan Wake suggests, apropos of a Northamptonshire village with six lords, that "the sense of unity at Harlestone, its corporateness, has come from the very fact of its divisions which have forced on the village the necessity of centralization in what must have been a series of village meetings for the organization and administration of its corporate affairs."[36] The *villata* of Harlestone that sets up a joint committee to represent itself and the lords of the vill in 1410,[37] probably to tackle the changeover from a two-field to a three-field system of cultivation, has taken joint action before, notably in 1294 when it delivered an acre of land to the rector for providing adequate bell-ropes for the church.[38] Similar charitable actions by various Danelaw villages are noted by Stenton: the endowment of a chapel by the men of Hutthorpe, Northamptonshire, about 1155;[39] the endowment of a church at Keddington by the joint donation of the lord and the men of Keddington of an acre for every bovate of the vill;[40] the witnessing of gifts to Greenfield Priory by the townships of Driby and Holton in Lincolnshire, an action which he thinks was probably taken on behalf of the two townships by their representatives in the shire courts.[41] It is in connexion with one such transaction that we hear of a common seal of the township, when the whole community of the vill of Wellow in Nottinghamshire in 1250 bind themselves and their heirs and successors by a common oath to provide a chaplain for the chapel of Wellow, and provide for his support and the proper upkeep of the chapel, affixing to the two charters that record their pledge the seal of their community.[42] The whole community of the vill of Towcester, Northamptonshire, by a unanimous agreement of the vill, appoints proctors to collect alms for the repair of the bridge at the north end of the town.[43] Again, the levying of a sum to repair the roof of their church by the parishioners of an unnamed village in 1370 is the occasion of the judicial pronouncement as to the validity of bylaws cited above.[44]

The township can act in a less eleemosynary manner. The estate book of Henry de Bray registers a convention of *la commune de la vile* of Harlestone with Henry as to bull and boar in 1309.[45] The men of Toddington, Bedfordshire, by unanimous consent in an assembly grant some land to the prior of Dunstable at an annual rent of 6*d.*, and their grant is upheld by the justices of Novel Disseisin in 1293.[46] The community of the vill of Kingsthorpe repeatedly farms out the town mills,[47] and grants a vacant place for enclosure to two members of the community.[48] The whole community of the vill of Brightwaltham effects an exchange of common land with the abbot of Battle in 1294.[49]

We have seen the community of the vill acting with the lord and without the lord; we have next to consider it acting *vis-a-vis* the lord. Economic historians have found numerous instances of lords of manors letting the manors to the men of the township at farm. Sowerby is held of the Templars by the men of the vill for £10 as early as 1185;[50] the priory of Worcester has farmed out Hallow and Tibberton to the *villani* of those two townships by 1250;[51] Richard of Cornwall has farmed out Bensington to twenty-seven men of the vill by 1257.[52] Ramsey Abbey has farmed out Hemingford by 1280, and Elton by 1312 in like manner; and so on in Essex, Yorkshire, Somerset, Wiltshire, Herefordshre, and Berkshire.[53] And the king himself is the first to farm out the manors of his ancient demesne. Madox has noted many instances when a vill, most often a royal vill, farmed itself to the Exchequer; a process so near to that by which a borough paid its farm as to illustrate aptly the observation that the dividing line between a vill and borough was not easy to draw. In Chapters II-V of his *Firma Burgi* he gives numerous instances of unincorporated vills holding the vill at farm. His instances can be supplemented from the printed pipe rolls. In Northamptonshire alone there are seven royal manors whose men are farming them in 1242,[54] including Kingsthorpe, to which the farm of the hundred of Spelhoe was appendant.[55] As with the chartered borough, the right of a vill to pay its own farm at the Exchequer involves the right to appoint an agent who will be recognized by the Exchequer as its accredited representative. An interesting instance of the temporary commitment of vills to the administration of their own community has been pointed out by Mr. Homans; it would seem that when Kirtlington, Oxfordshire, escheated to the Crown as a Norman fief in 1203 it was handed over to the reeve and four men for the time being until the manor was granted out to a new tenant. He notes a parallel instance in Oxnead, Norfolk, in 1290.[56] The vills further resemble the boroughs in purchasing privileges from the king; to take one of several instances which have been pointed out to me by Mr. H. G. Richardson, the men of Lothingland, Suffolk, in 1230 request a charter from the king granting them the farm of the manor of Lothingland, and also other special privileges, very likely the hundred of Lothingland as appendant to the manor, for which they are prepared to pay £160. There have been protracted negotiations; the representatives of Lothingland have had to return to their fellows at home for fresh instructions.[57] Unincorporated vills may hold charters from the king, and the men of a vill may hold a charter of privileges from their lord.[58]

The community of the vill, then, besides being compelled to accept "public" responsibilities in matters of taxation, militia, police, criminal liability, road and bridge service, and the like, is in a position voluntarily to accept fresh responsibility, to bind itself to the fulfilment of obligations, and to incur financial liabilities. In an age when the legal principles of incorporation had not yet been worked out, its legal status is not easy to define. Both Madox and Maitland, however, have noted instances where vills sue or are sued.[59] But it would seem that medieval legal writers have not pronounced on the matter, and this lends some interest to an entry on the Close Roll of 39 Henry III which, so far as I know, has not hitherto been discussed in print by any legal historian:

> *Pro hominibus Imberti Pugeys.*—Rex ballivis B(onifacii) Cantuariensis archiepescopi de Cantuaria salutem. Quia secundum legem et consuetudinem regni nostri hucusque optentum est quod villate et communitates villarum ejusdem regni nostri querelas et querimonia suas per tres vel per quatuor ipsorum in curiis nostris et aliorum possint prosequi, vobis mandamus quod, si homines dilecti et fidelis nostri Imberti Pugeys, qui nobiscum stat in servicio nostro, de villata de Sybeton, aliquas querelas habent prosequendas vel defendendas pro communitate sua in curia domini vestri de Cantuaria, ipsos per tres vel quatuor ex eis, prout superius dictum est, prosequi permittatis, tantum facientes quod dictum fidelem nostrum iterato non oporteat super hoc fatigari. Teste rege apud Westmonasterium vij die Marcii (1255).[60]
> [For the men of Imbert Pugeys—The King to the bailiffs of Boniface, Archbishop of Canterbury, greetings. Since by the law and custom of our realm it has hitherto been the case that the townships and communities of the vills of this our kingdom have been able to prosecute their disputes and complaints by three or four of their inhabitants in our courts and those of others; we order you that, if the inhabitants of the vill of Sybeton, of our dear and faithful Imbert Pugeys, who is in our service at our side, have any disputes in which they are plaintiffs or defendants for their community in the court of your lord of Canterbury, that you allow them to prosecute their case by means of three or four of them as is said above; you should act in such a manner that our said faithful (Imbert Pugeys) will not be further bothered by this matter.]

Imbert Pugeys was one of Henry III's "foreign favourites," being probably a native of Le Puy en Velay, Haute-Loire, and had come over to England with Queen Eleanor about 1235. He served Henry for twenty-five years as yeoman of the Chamber, keeper of the Tower of London, and steward of the Household, holding the last office down to his death in 1263. He was rewarded for his services by lands in various counties where his descendants succeeded him, and his name survives in Stoke Poges, Buckinghamshire, the scene of Gray's *Elegy written in a Country Churchyard.* His rights in Sibton,[61] a knight's fee held of the Archbishop of Canterbury, were derived from his wife, Joan, *née* Aguillon, who held it as part of the dower of her first marriage to Ralph fitz Bernard.[62] He was thus in a strong position to ask for favours, but it is, in fact, the men of the village whose interests seem to be chiefly affected, and it is their rights that are declared by this, apparently unique, statement as to the law and custom of the realm.

Uncorroborated, this incidental statement might carry little weight, but the examples of townships figuring in legal proceedings are numerous enough to lend it credibility. The community of the township of Helpringham appears before the justices in eyre at Lincoln in 1272 by four men to plead against the communities of two other Lincolnshire townships, each represented by four men.[63] The township of Graveley by its attorney brings a plaint against a stonemason for breach of contract in the Court of the Fair of St. Ives in 1275;[64] the communities of the vills of Holbeach and Quappelode enter into a final concord with Thomas de Holbeach before the royal justices in 1287;[65] the bailiff of Headington sues for the king, and for himself, the reeve and the men of Headington against the prior of St. Frideswide's in 1294.[66] The men of Little Hormead, Herefordshire, sue the men of the hamlet of Bordesden, and get 100*s*. damages in 1387.[67] And only two years before the date of this writ the whole communtiy of the vill of Faversham, Kent, pleading by their alderman, had been involved in a lawsuit.[68]

Mr. H. G. Richardson has kindly pointed out to me some even more relevant cases from the rolls of the King's Court. The suit between the villagers of Culham, Oxfordshire, and Sutton, Berkshire, recorded on the Rolls of the Curia Regis for 1212, though it ends in a number of individual appeals, is initiated by a plaint from "the men of Culham," speaking apparently by the mouth of one man; not their lord, the abbot of Abingdon, who remains aloof throughout the controversy.[69] In 1258 one man, acting apparently as the spokesman of the other men of Witley, Surrey, complains that Peter of Savoy has raised the rent of the manor, which it would seem they formerly farmed of the king and now farm of him.[70] The men of Norbiton, Surrey, who have a plaint against a neighbouring township, are advised by the court to proceed by writ,[71] which appears to indicate that the justices not only accept the statement that vills may sue by *querele* and *querimonia,* but also recognize their right to proceed by writ. By far the best instance, however, for bringing out both procedure and legal personality is the case recently discussed by Powicke,[72] recorded on the rolls of the Court *Coram Rege* for the year 1266.[73]

Four days after Evesham, some royalist soldiers came through the village of Peatling, Leicestershire, and were greeted by the villagers with abuse "eo quod fuerunt contra utilitatem communitatis regni et contra barones." Words were followed by violence, and the beaten and wounded men carried back the report of their handling to their lord, Peter de Neville, who sent a larger body of men to demand amends. The men of the village took refuge in the church. As the royalists threatened to burn it down, one of the village wives took it upon herself to arrange that a fine of twenty marks should be paid, and when the men came out of the church, the village reeve confirmed the bargain on behalf of the township, and handed over five villagers as hostages for the payment of the sum in four days' time. The men of the village sent the hostages money for food, but failed to pay the fine, and the hostages remained in prison until the following January, when the case came before the king. Thomas the reeve, Philip the clerk, and four other villagers including the husband of the woman who had taken the first steps to make the fine, appeared "pro se et communitate ville predicte [for themselves and the community of the said vill].” They complained that Peter de Neville had seized the hostages by force to extort money from them, and claimed damages. Peter declared that the bargain had been freely made and properly authorized by the reeve on behalf of the community that had attacked his men. The hostages also claimed damages because they had been made hostages without their own consent and had then been left to lie in prison in wretchedness—*miserrime*—for four months and more. The jury which gave the final verdict found that the township was responsible both for the bargain made with Peter de Neville and for the sufferings of the hostages. The reeve had acted *pro communitate,* in proper form, and the township had sanctioned the bargain by sending money for the hostages' food. So judgement was given against the township, which had to pay the twenty marks to Peter and one mark as damages to each of the five hostages.

The community of the vill of Peatling Magna is seen in this case acting through its traditional representatives, the priest, the reeve, and the four men, suing as a litigant in the king's court, bringing its *querimonium* against Peter de Neville, impleaded by Peter de Neville for breach of contract, sued for damages by the five hostages, and liable as a community for payment of the penalties imposed by the king's court, “to be levied from the lands and chattels of the whole township.”

If we turn back to the statement of 1255 we are inclined less to question the validity of this *obiter dictum* than to ask why it was called for. The *Leges Henrici* had said that the lord of a vill, or his steward, or the priest, the reeve, and the four men, might discharge the obligations of the vill in the shire and hundred courts. Imbert Pugeys was unable to attend the court of the archbishop of Canterbury; it seems that the archbishop's bailiffs were unwilling to recognize the status of his tenants in pleading or defending their cases. It may be that the significant words are *in curiis aliorum,* since a large proportion of the cases noted above were heard in royal courts.

However that may be, the statement seems to clinch observable facts. Maitland, without citing any authority, says: “The men of C., a mere rural township, or a hundred, can sue and be sued; their bailiff or their reeve with four men will represent them . . . But . . . as a group, they have no rights to assert or to defend . . . What is lacking is not a common seal but common property.”[74] Maitland's treatment of the township in *The History of English Law,* even in view of the facts that he himself cites, seems over-legalistic to the student of social and constitutional history. Was he perhaps, in 1899, still fighting the ghost of the Mark? The cases cited above suggest that even from the legal point of view the community of the vill had rights against its own members, as against outsiders. If the statement of 1255 is to be taken as true, the law of the realm gave it procedural rights, and an accepted status in the courts.

By and large, however, the passage is most interesting in the field of constitutional history. It adds one more scrap of evidence to support the contention that representation in England was not a device introduced in the thirteenth century by canon lawyers, but a practice long familiar at the lowest levels, and taken so much for granted as to need no special description. It was a common-sense device, bound to come into existence in a country which combined a strong respect for legal process with a deeply rooted tradition of community. The community of the realm was becoming aware of itself in the thirteenth century; at Great Peatling in 1266, as Powicke points out, it had impinged on the consciousness of a far older community—a community older than that of the borough or the shire—the community of the vill.[75]

NOTES

1. *E.H.R.,* 1941, pp. 174 ff. See also Van Caenegem, *Royal Writs in England from the Conquest to Glanvill* (Selden Society 1959), p. 58.

2. *Select Charters,* p. 414. After 1300 each vill was represented by twelve to sixteen men. Hunnisett, *The Medieval Coronor* (1961), p. 14.

3. Cf. Petit-Dutaillis, *Les Communes françaises,* pp. 117-18.

4. G. C. Homans, *English Villagers in the Thirteenth Century,* p. 330.

5. W. S. Thompson, *Lincs. Assize Roll,* pp. xxiv. 59.

6. *Durham Halmotes* (Surtees Society, 1889), p. 1.

7. *Feudal Aids,* I. xii; P.R.O. Ex. Ac. 15/10.

8. R. Glover, *Kingsthorpiana,* p. 110.

9. See *Liber Memorandorum de Bernewelle,* pp. 238 ff.

10. *Select Charters,* p. 278.

11. *Ibid.,* p. 352.

12. J. F. Willard, *Parliamentary Taxes on Personal Property, 1290–1334,* pp. 55 ff.

13. W. S. Thompson, *Lincs. Assize Roll,* pp. xliii, xlvi.

14. Homans, *op. cit.,* p. 332 (454).

15. Pollock and Maitland, *History of English Law* (1905), I. 564, 567.

16. Madox, *Exchequer,* cxiv, "Of Amercements"—Sections vi, vii, xiv. See also Maitland, *Pleas of the Crown for the County of Gloucester, 1221,* for numerous examples of the criminal liabilities of the township.

17. Pollock and Maitland, I. 611.

18. *Anglo-Saxon England,* p. 294.

19. *Wakefield Court Rolls,* i. 298 (Yorks. Arch. Soc. 1901) cited by Homans, p. 427.

20. W. D. Ault, *E.H.R.,* 1930, p. 212.

21. For a bibliography on by-laws see G. C. Homans, *English Villagers in the Thirteenth Century,* p. 427. Note also the Durham halmotes, and the manuscripts of the dean and chapter of Ely, Sutton Court Rolls, 31 Edward I onward, for which reference I have to thank Mr. Edward Miller. (It should be noted, however, that Mr. Lennard, reviewing Homans, adduced considerable evidence to show that the initiative in the framing of by-laws often came from the lord of the manor. *Econ. Journal,* 1943, pp. 850-6. Dr. Patzelt of Vienna argued to the same effect with regard to the *Weistümer* of German villages).

22. Y.B. [Year Book] 44 Edward III, Trinity Term.

23. Homans, *op. cit.,* pp. 104, 427. Cf. *Records of Templars,* edited B. A. Lees, p. 130.

24. *Kingsthorpiana,* pp. 84–9; cf. pp. 39 f.
25. Pollock and Maitland, I. 619.
26. *Terrier of Fleet,* pp. xli ff.
27. *Ibid.,* p. xli, see also p. 168.
28. *Ibid.,* pp. viii, xlix.
29. See *E.H.R.,* 1926, pp. 98–103.
30. *Records of Templars,* pp. cxciii f.
31. *Ibid.,* pp. cxxxi, 53, 57.
32. *Ibid.,* pp. ccxiii, 130.
33. *Ibid.,* pp. xxxi, cxciii, 101.
34. *R.H.* i. 23. For the more exact description that the villagers failed to give see *V.C.H. Bucks.* iv. 86–7.
35. *Records of Templars,* p. cxciv.
36. *E.H.R.,* 1922, pp. 407–8.
37. *Ibid.,* pp. 409–13. Cf. the regulations for Wymeswold, Leicestershire, made by common assent of the township and of three lords of manors, *Danelaw Charters,* p. lxii, note I.
38. *Estate Book of Henry de Bray* (Camden Society, 1916), p. 43.
39. *Danelaw Charters,* p. lxx, No. 465.
40. *Ibid.,* p. lxi, note I.
41. *Ibid.,* p. lxiii, Nos. 142, 143.
42. *Antiquissimum Registrum of the Cathedral Church of Lincoln,* Linc. Rec. Soc. iii. 311-13. The only other references to the common seal of a township of which I am aware are that noted by Mr. Homans at Bromham, Wiltshire, in 1295, where the villeins are penalized for having taken upon themselves to have a common seal (Homans, p. 332), and those at Kingsthorpe, the common seal of which, attributed to the reign of Richard II, is reproduced on the title-page of Glover's *Kingsthorpiana.*
43. *E.H.R.,* 1922, p. 413.
44. Y.B. 44 Edward III, Trinity Term.
45. *Estate Book,* p. 13.
46. *Annales Monastici,* iii, 378.
47. *Kingsthorpiana,* pp. 3, 36, 54-7.
48. *Ibid.,* p. 26.
49. *Select Pleas in Manorial Courts,* p. 172; also see Maitland's comment on p. 163.
50. *Records of Templars,* p. 128.
51. *Cartulary of Worcester Priory* (Camden Society), pp. 47*a*, 54*b*.
52. M. T. Pearman, *History of the Manor of Bensington,* p. 30.
53. Homans, p. 453.
54. *Pipe Roll 26 Henry III,* p. 319. I owe this reference to Mr. H. G. Richardson.
55. Other examples of hundreds held by the men of a vill are Basingstoke, Hampshire, held by the men of Basingstoke; Elmbridge and Kingston, Surrey, by the men of Kingston; whilst Ainsty, Yorkshire, was held by the mayor and burgesses of York.
56. Homans, p. 336.
57. *Royal Letters,* (R.S.) i. 381-2.
58. *Terrier of Fleet,* pp. 77, 114. Charter of Thomas fitz Lambert of Multon to his free tenants in Fleet and to all the men of the vill, free and villein. Date before 8 Edward I. See also the Bensington Charter mentioned above, p. 78, n. 4.
59. See below, pp. 262–264.
60. *Close Rolls of Henry III, 1254–1256,* p. 173.

61. Sibton in Lyminge; not, as the index to the Close Rolls identifies the name, Siberston near Houghton in Bewsborough Hundred.

62. *Book of Fees,* iii. 490; *Close Rolls, 1237–42,* pp. 72, 79; *1261–4,* pp. 174, 209; *Patent Roll Calendar, 1249–58,* pp. 195, 547, 578, 614, 638; *1259–63,* pp. 198, 203, 233, 266.

63. Assize Roll 481.

64. *Select Pleas in Manorial Courts,* p. 150.

65. *Terrier of Fleet,* pp. 110 f.

66. Madox, *Firma Burgi,* p. 65.

67. *Ibid.,* p. 110. See also instances cited by Maitland from *Durham Halmotes,* pp. 22 (1358) and 33-4 (1364).

68. *Abbreviato Placitorum,* 140.

69. *Curia Regis Rolls,* vi. 390-I.

70. *Select Cases of Procedure without Writ* (Selden Society), ed. H. G. Richardson and G. O. Sayles, pp. 91-2.

71. *Ibid.,* p. 92.

72. *Henry III and the Lord Edward,* pp. 509-10.

73. *Select Cases of Procedure without Writ,* pp. 42-5.

74. Pollock and Maitland, I. 632–3. In the *Pleas of the Crown for the County of Gloucester,* however, he had spoken of "the half-corporate character" of the *villata,* illustrated by the fact that the word governed now a singular and now a plural verb (p. xxv); and in *Township and Borough* he was to say much of its "communalism".

75. I should like to acknowledge here my debt to the many friends with whom I have discussed the significance of this passage—particularly to Sir Maurice Powicke, Professor J. G. Edwards, Professor Postan, Miss K. E. Major, Mr. Edward Miller, and above all, Mr. H. G. Richardson.

MEDIEVAL "SOLIDARITIES"

Flemish Society in Transition, 1127–1128*

Jan Dhondt

A prince has been assassinated. The event—in the Middle Ages—is hardly uncommon. If his designated successor is on the spot, it is hardly more than a minor incident. It is quite otherwise if, at precisely this moment, the indispensable and unquestionable successor is lacking. For it is characteristic of medieval government that the administration, the bureaucracy, if you wish, has not yet become an autonomous power capable of acting by virtue of its own momentum, of absorbing shocks, of crossing those always treacherous interim periods without injury. It is also characteristic that from the seventh to the thirteenth century supreme auhority, despite the fleeting Carolingian parenthesis, is in the hands of the territorial prince—a complex combination of regalian, personal, domainial, and other powers burdening the life of the inhabitants of a region that is large, but not too large. This is the living frame of medieval society; not the kingdom (too large and somewhat unreal) nor the seigniory (too small), but the territorial principality, whether organized or not. It is a question of size. The territorial principality is the optimum dimension, as economists would say, for a political enterprise.

In France and elsewhere the death of a king barely affects the life of the realm's inhabitants (except precisely where he is primarily the "prince"); in the same way the death of a minor knight touches only a small group. In contrast, the death of a territorial prince opens the door

* Jan Dhondt, "Les 'Solidarités' médiévales. Une société en transition: la Flandre en 1127–1128," *Annales, Economies-Sociétés-Civilisations,* 12 (Paris: 1957), 529–560. Trans. by the ed.

to anarchy if he has no successor: it violently throws an entire population's way of life into confusion. An individual drama turns into a social drama. A fight begins, in which all the "powers"[1] of the principality fiercely confront one another. All ties and structures break apart. There, for the historian, is their enormous interest, the nearest thing to a laboratory experiment. Under our very eyes, all collective forces come into play. To be sure, the experiment is not scientifically valid unless minutely observed and described—an exceptional occurrence. But it happened at least once, when Charles the Good, count of Flanders, was murdered at Bruges on March 2, 1127.[2] The event lights up more than a little corner. It illuminates an entire countryside.

The plot and its consequences are a story often told[3]—stereotyped, moralizing tales useless for anyone wanting to grasp the reality of society. There is one exception, however: the narration of Galbert of Bruges. He took down the events day by day, intent (as he tells us) only on describing "general events."[4] The author's habits of mind, his sharp feeling for the concrete, the fact that for mysterious reasons he did not rewrite his story afterward to make it more coherent—and false—all these circumstances give us a unique witness to the inner workings of a medieval society in the grips of a powerful crisis, a crisis strong enough to shake it to its foundations.

I

Often enough, writings on medieval history[5] leave an impression of unreality. Were these men really different from us? The impression undoubtedly comes from the sources, from Sidonius Apollinaris to Suger; still more from the use historians make of them. The documentation is notoriously poor[6] even in the most favorable circumstances; for example, when we are concerned with a sovereign whose biography we possess, we still have only a few badly chosen events for each year of his life. The situation is even worse if we want to study a social group. Regularly we are reduced to the task of linking together facts that are separated by weeks, months, or even years. Never can our fingers grasp the continuous, multiple skein of life. But human history does not unroll along *one* abstract reconstructed line. History is the totality of tangled threads.

For the early Middle Ages we count ourselves fortunate when we can reconstruct a simple line, in reality made up of tiny snippets of very different strings which cross one another but do not extend very far. From the thirteenth century on, and more and more as we come down toward the present, the skein of documentation becomes so thick and full that the historian's task becomes that of untangling the thickest threads to weave his web.

If I allow myself these all too easy and general reflections, it is because Galbert's story, by exceptional luck, gives us a thick bundle of threads; it is a unique document for the understanding of medieval society. Its date increases its value. 1127–1128: the twelfth century is the point at which the Western world turns. Let us say, using old-fashioned words, that in this century the "Middle Ages" ends and the modern age begins. This development, I know very well, does not everywhere occur at the same time, with the same rhythm, by the same process. I am also aware of the precarious value of the tags "Middle Ages" and "modernity." Nevertheless, the twelfth century—break or renewal—is, roughly, the beginning of truly new times.

What we see contrasting in two successive periods can of course be only what predominates. All the elements alive in one period still act in the second, but with different force. No one questions that in every period, from Roman times to our own, there have been traders; nevertheless, the number of merchants, the volume of merchandise, and the proportion of the total quantity of money used for commercial exchange was infinitely less between 600 and 1000 than between 1000 and 1400. What "dominant factors," then, distinguish the pre-twelfth from the post-twelfth centuries?

In the economic and social sectors "Middle Ages" signifies a crushing preponderance of agriculture and agrarian interests. In the "modern" period industry assumes an ever-growing place; it takes a higher percentage of employees from the total population and a higher percentage of invested capital from the total fund of capital. From this comes the growth of cities with the social divisions proper to them: entrepreneurs and wage earners. This gradual overturning of social and economic structures has strong political repercussions: no longer are landed proprietors the only ones to dominate society. They must count on the cities, on the entrepreneurs and their urban following. The social organization of our Middle Ages is characterized by closed groups that are so many brakes on social mobility. A man is born to one group and penetrates only with difficulty into another.

Another contrast: bureaucracy, specialized functions exercised by "clerks" (the word loses its ecclesiastical meaning) and "lawyers." Clerks and lawyers are men who are at home with figures, quantities, and principles of organization and government. Here are the first "managers" in Burnham's sense. Before this the prince, unable to oversee all the population subject to him, delegated his powers to feudal vassals. More and more he now calls on "bureaucrats," the creatures of those who pay them. Since the prince is for technical reasons unable to control them, they quickly become independent in the details of daily life. However, since their pay and the stability of their jobs depend on their master's prosperity, they look out for his interests; in this they differ from the vassals of earlier years.

A final contrast: habits of mind. On one side God rules all; every human act is the expression of the Divine Will. The modern mind is rationalist: instead of accepting explanations in terms of the Will of God, it seeks explanations in terms of permanent rules knowable to the mind, allowing man to foresee and to organize.

"Modernity," we believe, begins in the twelfth (or thirteenth) century and is gradually strengthened. Thus the diverse "modern" characteristics are weak, although slowly growing, in the period with which we are here concerned. The society Galbert shows (to enter now directly into our subject) is essentially turned toward the past, is still "magical," still agrarian; political power is still in the landlords' hands, is still fragmented.[7] The power of the administrative machine is small;[8] oaths take the place of contracts; all those ancient "forces"—personal ties, blood ties, collectivities of persons having different social functions but living in the same territory—still have a "public" value.

Yet, at the same time, society sheds its old skin. Cities fight for political predominance with the "barons of the country"; commercial interests begin to enter seriously into political accounts.[9] A rationalism begins to show itself, although not yet self-consciously. All this will, it is hoped, appear clearly in what follows.

II

The story's "argument":

On March 2, 1127, Charles, count of Flanders, is assassinated in a church of Bruges by some of his vassals. He has only distant heirs. Flanders immediately falls into anarchy. After some hesitation, the "barons" of the county join together and lay siege to the murderers in Bruges. With the help of the King of France, the besieged are finally taken and executed. The Norman prince William Clito, elected Count of Flanders under the pressure of King Louis VI, begins to battle with the cities, who want Thierry of Alsace for prince. A little while later William is killed, and Thierry mounts the Flemish throne.

The event, thus reduced to its bare essentials, is quite simple; but the way it works itself out does not simply follow this one red thread. Galbert's narrative is not the mere tale of a murder,[10] a siege,[11] the punishment of the murderers,[12] and, to end it, a war between pretenders to the throne.[13] Nor is it simply the story of the attempt by the King of France to extend his power over this great fief,[14] or the illumination of one episode among many in the fight between France and England (for the King of England continuously intervened to oppose the aims of Louis VI).[15] Nor is it primarily the story of the different neighboring princes who, of course, rushed in for the spoils.[16] It is the story of a race for a throne (not limited to the two pretenders already named),[17] a headlong race for treasure (the enormous treasury of the Flemish counts);[18] for relics (the body of the assassinated Count, who is considered a martyr); and for the murderers' vast wealth, coveted by the barons of the kingdom. On a different level it is, in addition, the story of a private war (between the assassins, the Erembalds, and their neighbors, the lords of Straten), a fight between clans at the count's court—the Erembalds on one side and various newcomers on the other[19]—for the count's favor and high offices. It is also, in the middle of the tragedy, the story of a family of servile origin (the Erembalds) who have found their way to the top ranks of the county and are threatened with being plunged back into servitude.[20] To all this Galbert's outlook adds yet more: the working out of a plan of divine vengeance against a dynasty that won the Flemish throne by perjury and treason (the accession of Robert the Frisian) and against a family (again the Erembalds) who won their way by adultery and murder[21] and were likewise soaked in the "treason" of Robert the Frisian.[22] There is a final aspect of capital importance: it is the first time the cities claim to play a predominant role in the conduct of the country.

Here then is our skein. In this spider's web, it hardly need be said, individuals do battle with forces stronger than their own wills. They rise or they destroy themselves, all by chance, in this enormous crisis. Such are the honest and courageous Gervais, the only disinterested person it seems, who ends (a moral conclusion) by acceding to the castellany of Bruges;[23] the unfortunate Robert the Young, idol of the people of Bruges, dragged, probably against his will, into the conspiracy against Charles. He leads the heroic resistance of the beseiged until the last and, despite the pleas of the men of Bruges, falls decapitated at Cassel. On the other hand, no women are mentioned except one, the *scorta* who for love or thirst for money lets herself be shut up with the murderers in the beseiged castle of Bruges.[24]

In the midst of this drama, the most engaging individual, the best known, is surely Galbert himself. Uncomplicated, intellectual by the standards of his time, tossed like so many others by the waves of events, he shows us (an exceptional sight for the period)[25] a human being, a man who hesitates from day to day between an easy and total identification with his surroundings and a break with it, however sorrowful and dangerous that break might be. His environment is the crowd of Bruges. He is a part of it; he shares its ideas. I have discussed this last matter elsewhere[26] and, here, want only to make a few essential points. Galbert has both a religious mind and a feeling for the concrete; he reasons and is thus constantly grappling with the serious problem of God's unfathomable Providence, a God who determines the actions of all men but not in the way Galbert thinks justice demands. From this comes his anxiety. Can God be influenced by prayer, sacrifice, and incantations? To Galbert such practices seem unnatural when they seek unjust ends. Yet they take place and sometimes succeed, and this gives new reasons to his anxieties and encourages him to take a clearly anticlerical position. Another puzzle—the crowd's movements. Identifying himself with his milieu, Galbert shares this crowd's "political" conceptions, its now favorable, now unfavorable attitude toward the battling parties. But these movements follow the simplest law—success[27] and group interests. Thus we see Galbert join several parties in succession, whose causes from this moment on become "just." It seems the simplest thing in the world, without explanation, without transition. Despite everything, Galbert is an individualist to the extent—small, to be sure—that an average individual can free himself from his milieu. He has his personal ideas, his personal fears, if you prefer, which lead him one fine day when the fight seems uncertain to try to go it alone. Too bad for his fellow burghers![28] These men do not tolerate such betrayal, of course, and our Galbert must have passed a few bad days.[29] Once the Flemish fight is over, he dives happily back into conformity.[30]

III

Our purpose here is to examine the society Galbert reveals. Our first task will be to break that society down into its component elements, into those groups that are more or less permanent, more or less coherent, groups we shall call "solidarities." Their importance comes from their collective activity—either all the time or for a short period—to obtain a specific object. In either case, collective action is consciously so. To the extent that conscious action orders the course of events, these solidarities—real forces—do the ordering. We shall try to describe these solidarities (about which we have precise documentation) above all from a static point of view. We shall then search out their dynamics, their birth, their life and death. Finally, at the conclusion of this social analysis—all too often portrayed as dominated and explained by blind material forces—we shall try a synthetic examination of the ties among these various solidarities, ties that make of them not a simple sum but a whole.

The study of solidarities starts with a postulate. Only those groups who command a certain ability to exert pressure can influence the course of events: without disputing the possibility that an individual might under exceptional circumstances influence events,[31] we shall not bother to break society into its simplest elements, individuals and families (in the present-day sense of the word). An examination of the solidarities at work in 1127–1128 will give us a rather exact, concrete picture of these medieval groups, the basic architecture of society. It is impossible, as far as the twelfth century is concerned (and perhaps the twentieth as well), even approximately to "weigh" the activities of these various collective forces.[32]

The situation would be simple were society composed of a fairly large number of identical groups. This of course is (and was) not the case. Society at any period is the result of ancient historical forces originating in various periods and circumstances, the result of many diverse impulses. Every period thus exhibits solidarities with very different bases.

Everybody expects to find one solidarity group in the twelfth century: the group composed of a lord-suzerain, his vassal knights, and the able-bodied men of his domains and seigniories. This group we will call the "*potentia*," borrowing the term from Galbert. It is rather precisely a military concept, since only adult males counted in the solidarities of the Middle Ages, for only their activity was evident. This concept of *potentia* is clear enough, provided it is properly understood. An oversimplified view of medieval society deduces from the *potentia* a perfect pyramid—at the top the sovereign, then the territorial princes, then his vassals, down to the free men and serfs subject to the lowest vassals. Let us skip the level of the sovereign. Without question vassalage enveloped all free men, but it did not necessarily envelope them in the classic form of a pyramid. For example, among those who did homage to the count we can recognize no less than four different elements: the heads of the *potentia* (called, it would appear, "princes" and "barons"), simple knights (knights who were vassals of the count or of other "heads of *potentia*" and did not themselves have other vassals), individual merchants,[33] and the cities.[34] This organization was not at all a pyramid; and we must still fit the castellans in somewhere.[35] The picture of a pyramid is surely false. There was no real hierarchy in this world, but rather a juxtaposition of solidarities. Homage, the oath "of security," served when necessary to tie men vertically (simple knights to their barons, for example, and the "heads of *potentia*" to the count); but the real significance of this oath depended on the nature of the ties between the individuals involved. The relationship of a baron who was head of a *potentia* to the count to whom he had done homage could not have been the same as that between the same count and a simple knight. The latter owed all to the count, depended absolutely on him, the baron, who owed him nothing, was largely independent.

A *potentia,* as we have said—this group composed of a baron and his knights and able-bodied men—formed a unit at the orders of its head. The latter was a man whose independent way of acting toward his suzerain makes him clearly recognizable. Under normal conditions his independence might hardly be seen; but in a crisis such as that of 1127–1128, when the material power, administrative organization, and traditional reverence for the count weakened all at once, these *potentiae* affirmed their autonomy. Their autonomous actions run all through Galbert's account—those of the peers or barons of Flanders, the "heads of *potentia*";[36] those of Etienne de Boulare, who was probably not a high-justicer lord, but who nevertheless had forty knights under his orders;[37] those of Gervais de Praat, clearly a lord of only moderate importance, but who had thirty knights and, according to Galbert, "thousands" of foot soldiers.[38] Even if these "thousands" were only a few hundred, they would have been an important force by the standards of the times. There were thus several dozen *potentiae* of this type. The count himself was clearly head of a *potentia,* but, in addition, had the right to call on all the knights and able-bodied men of the county.

The *potentia* was formed by the homage of simple knights to its head. It was dissolved, apparently with great ease, by these same knights' "*effestucatio*" [renunciation of fealty]. It would be erroneous to think that the tie formed by homage was very solid;[39] all depended on the interest the vassal had in observing his oath. But forms at least, were observed. The *effestucatio* was a simple thing. Still, it had to be done.[40]

Quite different was the urban solidarity. The proof is spread out on every page of Galbert's story and in contemporary evidence. These were perfectly autonomous groups, possessing their personal view of general politics and acting quite independently to achieve that view—so much so that almost every urban center had its own candidate to succeed to the countship.[41] The young Count of Holland was momentarily the candidate of Bruges;[42] Count Baldwin IV of Hainaut was the candidate of Audenarde,[43] then of Arras;[44] Thierry of Alsace was preferred by Ghent;[45] Arnold, son of a sister of Charles the Good, was supported by St.-Omer;[46] William of Ypres, by the burghers of his town.[47] Lille formed an urban solidarity,[48] as did Ardenbourg.[49] Apparently, so did Aire, which perhaps preferred William of Ypres.[50] Bruges, Ghent, Ypres, St.-Omer, Lille, Arras, Aire, Ardenbourg, Audenarde—all the main Flemish cities. Only Douai misses the roll call; Galbert never mentions it. These urban solidarities were "communes."[51] The union of their members was affirmed by oath.[52]

But the cities raise a question. To what extent did unanimity truly reign within their solidarities? Within the *potentiae* the same problem existed. The knights could in the last resort use the *effestucatio* to break their ties, but they could also use their counsel to influence the decisions of the *potentia*'s leader. In the "horizontal" solidarities of the towns unanimity would appear, *a priori,* to be even less. Galbert clearly shows many factions within the cities, each with its own aims—a truly volatile public opinion. The power of common interests seems, nevertheless, to have bound these factions strongly together.[53] For the entire city benefited from the advantages it might extort from the prince.[54] Its inhabitants almost always had an enemy in common.[55] Solidarity was expressed in the oath of the commune; it rested on the solid foundations of common interest, especially since this was precisely the moment when the communes were freeing themselves from the direct power of the count.

A few words will suffice for the ecclesiastical solidarities, the conventual solidarities; for if communities of monks and canons existed in Flanders in 1127, their political importance, their impact on events, was null. Too much under the count's authority and, fragmentarily, under the authority of powerful laymen, the Church was incapable of playing an independent role in the temporal sphere. Galbert, however, talks at length about the clergy of the collegiate church of St.-Donatian, and this merits special attention. The canons of St.-Donatian were the first to revolt against the Count's assassins, but for reasons very much their own. They intervened out of charity to save the life of some of the Erembalds' enemies, whom that family wished to slaughter.[56] But they became really angry when the assassins sought to send the body of Count Charles to the abbey of St. Peter of Ghent. The reasons were clear. Charles was thought a martyr;[57] his body was a precious relic. The canons refused to be robbed of it. When the Abbot of St. Peter tried to carry the body off, he was attacked with benches, stools, and candleholders—and was happy to escape alive.[58] The canons' solidarity in defense of their interests was vividly in evidence. Generally, however, the clergy of Bruges totally identified itself with the burgher population, worked with it to fortify the city,[59] excommunicated its enemies over and over again,[60] and even went so far as to take up arms to fight.[61] They were an extension of the urban solidarity. We might add that the social class of knights was likewise not separated from the bourgeoisie by a very high wall.[62] To summarize, the urban solidarity in the early twelfth century encompassed bourgeois and clergy as well as some knights and perhaps even the castellan.[63]

Another type of solidarity often mentioned is the lineage, the family. Galbert's story is more valuable for this than for anything else. His story might be entitled "The Rise and Fall of the Erembalds." He begins it somewhat in the manner of a nineteenth-century Gothic novel. Duva the Dove had inherited the office of castellan of Bruges. She married a man named Bodran, whom she found unsatisfying, and took as her lover (if we trust the gossip that Galbert echoes) Erembald, one of her husband's knights. Erembald became the castellan's intimate friend, while "the Dove" promised her hand to him if he would only put her husband out of the way. The murder done, they married and had many children.[64] All these children attained important positions—one became castellan after Erembald; another (Bertulf), chancellor of Flanders. They collected an enormous fortune;[65] each had a domain and his own fortress.[66] The daughters were married to men of power: castellans,[67] seigniors,[68] even peers of Flanders.[69] The family swam easily in the troubled waters of this period of Flemish history. The fights over succession to the countship handed them the opportunity to strengthen their position.[70] It is easy to believe Galbert when he claims that the Erembald "bloc" formed the greatest power in Flanders after the count.[71] The personal power of the Erembalds moreover had a geographical base—the geographical solidarity of Furnes (where the family originated) was entirely in their service.[72] They also succeeded in seizing a predominant influence in maritime

Flanders, in the section (partly insular at the time) northwest of Bruges.[73] In both these coastal zones, when the moment demanded it, they could mobilize substantial armed forces.

Their impressive power thinly covered a flaw, indeed, a chasm. The Erembalds were of servile origin.[74] This is one of the strangest aspects of the period's social history. It was possible during the eleventh century to gain all this wealth and power while remaining a serf. In reality, as in certain areas of the world today, "wealth washed white"; undoubtedly no one would have dared allude openly to their blemish. But their servile origin had not been forgotten. When rivals finally succeeded in convincing the Count—undoubtedly more than ready to listen to them—to put an end to the Erembalds' all-invading power, they recalled the family's servile past. The tragedy of 1127 sprang largely from this. Determined "to die rather than let themselves be reduced to servitude,"[75] the Erembalds preferred to assassinate the Count who intended at least to take their offices from them, if not to reduce them effectively to servitude.[76] Their desperate plan was put to action, but barely delayed the catastrophe. Besieged, captured, the Erembalds died in atrocious torture. To be sure, their servile origin was only a pretext. The family had succeeded too well. Their very power brought forth a coalition of other family solidarities against them, families whose interests varied. It also brought forth a very different kind of coalition, much more fleeting—a court clique. The Count, undoubtedly, found the Erembalds' power particularly unwelcome; he probably did not have to be alerted to it.[77] Certainly a number of knights, particularly at his court, for various reasons wanted to force the family's fall. To grab their offices was not the least of those reasons. Galbert insinuates that the Erembalds were tough bedfellows to have.[78] Finally, tightly tied to certain geographical groups, the Erembalds found themselves indirectly, but inevitably, grappling with their allies' enemies.

Take Furnes, for example. This maritime people found itself in conflict, it seems, with the dynasty of the castellan of Dixmude,[79] perhaps a geographical solidarity of the neighboring region, certainly a family group. Furthermore—and perhaps tied to this fact—the Erembalds were fighting an important member of this group, Richard, lord of Woumen.[80] In addition, although the details remain unclear, the Erembalds, despite their power in maritime Flanders, seem to have met with hostility from an ill-defined group (urban perhaps) composed of the inhabitants or neighbors of Ardenbourg, a town that had been taken over by Lambert, one of Erembald's sons.[81] A third hostile group were the lords of Straten (now St.-André-lez-Bruges) a few kilometers west of Bruges, probably, as its name suggests, on the great road linking Bruges to Ypres and the southern part of the county. The obvious hatred of the burghers of Bruges for the lords of Straten[82] makes one suspect that these lords interfered considerably with the burghers' commercial traffic; the citizens of Bruges were in conflict with a large number of lords situated south and southeast of the city. Now it happened that one of the Erembalds, established on domains near Bruges, lived very near the Stratens' castle. Private war between the two families was endemic.[83] The Erembalds' destruction of the manor of Straten is even at the origin of the dramatic events of 1127. Furthermore, the families of Straten and of the castellan of Dixmude were allied by marriage.[84] Thus it was not by chance that Straten and the lord of Woumen were two of the most active members of the coalition, the court clique, that wanted to displace the Erembalds and, to do so, raised the question of their servile origin before the Count.

It is clear that the Count's court was divided into two clans—the Erembalds and their opponents. Both clans fought for influence. What determined whether a courtier would join one or the other? The Stratens and the lord of Woumen had obvious hostile motives, but this was not all. Positive goals, the desire to get hold of the Erembalds' offices also played its role. But why did the castellan of Bourbourg, the seneschal Gauthier de Locres, and the chamberlain Gervais de Praat join this coalition?[85] The case of the notary, Fromold Junior, is both clearer and more complicated—clearer because he wanted nothing less than the post of chancellor of Flanders,[86] more complicated because he was related by marriage to the Erembalds.[87] There was nothing extraordinary about it. We know of three individuals, including Fromold, who found themselves opposing their family clans in this fight. The two others were Didier—brother of Isaac and thus nephew of the provost and of Bertulf the chancellor—who was one of the leaders of the army that fought the Erembalds,[88] and Enguerrand of Essen, of the family of the castellans of Dixmude,[89] who was one of the leaders of the conspiracy against the Count.[90] With Fromold and Gervais, the court clique had two important figures at the disposal of their intrigues, for Gervais was one of the Count's most trusted counselors[91] and Fromold was nothing less than his favorite.[92] But the Erembalds were not without influence. Isaac, chamberlain also and a counselor prized by Charles the Good, belonged to their clan[93] as did Guy of Steenvoorde, another of Charles's valued counselors.[94] Bertulf's position as chancellor and his brother Hacket's position as castellan of Bruges, brought them considerable influence. Various other members of the family also contributed, such as Robert the Young, who enjoyed an extraordinary popularity among the people of Bruges.[95] Their group also included Enguerrand of Essen (already mentioned) and William of Wervik. But Wervik and Courtrai had been at odds for a long time.[96] The alliance of William of Wervik won the Erembalds the enmity of the castellan of Courtrai.

Another kind of solidarity, the regional solidarity, although a curious phenomenon, is well attested by Galbert. It was made up of the *potentiae* and the other solidarities existing in the same region, especially the towns.

Undoubtedly these solidarities' true base was not only geographic but historical as well. They appear to be the consequence of ancient administrative solidarities (*pagi*) or new ones (castellanies) rather than simple spatial coexistence. Galbert shows three of these regional solidarities in action—that of "Flanders"[97] (the clearest), that of Furnes,[98] and that of Ghent[99] (this last one less clear). Flanders, as its name shows, was the ancient *Pagus Flandrensis,* both more (because the *pagus* of Ardenbourg was included) and less (since it included only the western part of the *Pagus Flandrensis).*[100] Furnes apparently corresponded to the castellany of Furnes and perhaps to an ancient *centena.* The solidarity of Ghent seems to have included also the *Pays de Waas,* the *Quatre Métiers,* and lands newly won in the eleventh century, which had long lived in symbiosis—from Imperial Flanders to the lands east of the Scheldt. Here we cannot tell if a real regional solidarity existed, or simply an accidental alliance between neighboring powers.

Although the basis of these solidarities was permanent, they had to be "confirmed" before leading to common action, as in the case—clearly shown by Galbert—of the solidarity of Flanders. But there is nothing surprising about this. *Potentiae,* urban communities, and lineages were organically united communities; their community of interests was a matter of course. Regional solidarities, in contrast, were composed of towns and lords, each with its particular and occasionally divergent interests that had to be reconciled before each common action.

Two other types of solidarity remain to be discussed, to be more precise, two types of coalitions of which the second was formed, as it were by accident—the baronial league and the league of "suspects." The league of Flemish peers and barons was a solidarity *sui generis.* It comprised the principal Flemish heads of *potentia* and, probably, the heads of those few quasi-autonomous, high-justicer Flemish principalities.[101] These peers and barons enjoyed a privilege that distinguished them from all the other inhabitants of the county, even from the other lords: they "elected" the count. By implication they "represented the country," a monopoly contested in 1127–1128 by an alliance of communes and knights of lesser rank. But that is another story.[102] This electoral privilege, to which they added a right to "counsel" the count, a right distinct from that of his other vassals,[103] undoubtedly could have made the peers and barons into a "college," into a permanent group. But this possibility was counteracted by the fact that these barons—powerful, independent, with baronies spread throughout the county and almost always in the frontier districts—had few common interests. Their particular interests, tied to their baronies, were much too tenacious. Generally they did not act together. 1127 was an exception, and for a powerful reason. The Count's sudden death left the throne with no definite heir. Its central administration, supposing it might have preserved the comital power, was deeply compromised in the assassination. Flanders was a power vacuum. The barons had to intervene for two reasons. First of all, the country had to be governed and theirs was the only power capable of imposing itself.[104] Second, once their line of duty had been found, their particular—and very different—interests were no less evident: to grab a little, or much, of the Count's treasure;[105] to sell their vote at a high price to the candidates to the throne;[106] and to carry off the Erembalds' enormous property.[107] There is nothing surprising in their program. The Middle Ages was a period when everyone stole more or less nobly. The expedition against the Erembald was an immense pillaging expedition.[108] For the peers at least, it was not only this. They re-established "peace" in Flanders, made the county feel an authority that, for a moment, had been entirely absent. But they did not act simply as barons allied with one another. It was as a "sworn league"[109] that they entered the fray; as an organized solidarity, even though, as with the regional solidarities, their *conjuratio* had a precise and limited objective.

The Erembald party, or more precisely, the "suspects," formed a final solidarity (here we are using the term to mean simply a group that, implicated in one another's actions, fought and suffered together). The Count's murderers were savagely suppressed, the victims extending far beyond the narrow circle of the assassins and their immediate accomplices.[110] For the baronial clique and the new Count and his friends, it was a matter of proscribing as many wealthy people as possible in order to enrich themselves on what was left behind. Interminable inquests followed, organized to track down everyone who might, however distantly (and sometimes far distantly indeed), have been involved in the conspiracy; inquests that in the end tired and annoyed the Flemings.[111] But these persecutions, whose object was perhaps also political—to eliminate the Erembald party from all positions of influence where they might show their hostility to William Clito—wove a web of communal feeling, invisible but real, among all those who felt threatened. How do we know such a group existed and had influence? When Thierry of Alsace entered the competition for the throne with William Clito, he hastened to proclaim, as his first act as Count recognized by part of Flanders, a general amnesty for the assassins' party.[112] William Clito, whose political acumen was not particularly notable, immediately tried (without success) to throw his machine into reverse.[113] To be sure, the "suspect party" was never organized, but it rallied en masse to the banner of Thierry of Alsace. This change in opinion illustrates another aspect of the violent crisis of 1127, difficult to see because so fleeting.

IV

The collectivities acting in Flanders during the critical years 1127–1128 were thus the following: at the lowest level the seignorial *potentiae,* urban communities, lineages, and—marginally—religious communities; at a higher level two groups—the baronial *conjuratio,* which brought together the principal "heads of *potentia*" (who already possessed exceptional rights), and the regional solidarities, which brought together the heterogeneous elements of communes, *potentiae,* and simple knights living in a common geographical area; finally, *de facto* coalitions of individuals—the court clique on the one hand, and the "suspects" on the other.

Among these various groups were both resemblances and contrasts. The durable groups were tied together by oaths; oath of homage within the *potentia;* oath of commune within the urban community; *conjuratio* among the members of a lineage, among the barons of the league, and among those who belonged to a regional solidarity. In contrast, no oath bound the *de facto* groups, the court clique and the "suspects."

We must distinguish two kinds of oaths, however. The oath of vassalage and the communal oath were not limited to a specific action. They were taken once and for all, "for better and for worse." On the other hand, the members of the baronial league, those of the regional solidarity, and even the family solidarity[114] took common oaths to further a precisely determined object. Vassal and urban solidarities were "actual," the others were "potential"; for the general interests of the members of a *potentia* were identical, as were those of the commune. Both had abdicated personal independence for the sake of the community. The members of regional communities, of lineages, of class groups (here, the barons) kept their independence. There was good reason: each belonged at the same time to a *potentia,* or to a town and a region, to a lineage, and even (for the barons) to a class. There was thus a hierarchy of obligations. Even so, the "secondary" solidarities played an important role. The regional solidarities of Bruges and Ghent were constantly recreating themselves.

That these different bases of solidarity existed, especially the "potential" ones, was of great importance. They guaranteed great flexibility of collective organization at the same time as they guaranteed each individual a place in a definite solidarity. Communes and *potentiae* might come together in different ways, but they remained communes and *potentiae.* These different possibilities, by the free play they allowed, offered yet another resource to society. They favored the creation of new solidarities, especially of larger ones. In 1127–1128 a "solidarity of the cities" began to emerge[115]—a foretaste of the later city representation in the assemblies of Estates. The noble "Estate" in these assemblies was prefigured by two different groups: the baronial league, which was really the organization of the principal lords of the county, and the assembly of "knights"[116] (although the reference may concern only the knights grouped in regional solidarities).

The solidarities did not necessarily include the totality of all who might belong to them; indeed, perhaps they never were so inclusive. Individuals who might theoretically have belonged to a group sometimes acted differently from the majority, as we have seen. Similarly, nothing was easier than for someone who had taken an oath to break it and withdraw from his sworn group. This was true even of the oath of vassalage, which, it seems, had become commonplace and emptied of its sacral content. This ought to be emphasized, if only to discourage any rigorously juridical interpretation.

This analysis fits only Flanders in 1127–1128, of course. As it appears, it includes both old and new. How can we grasp a development of which we have fixed only one stage? One point may be considered well established: the commune is a new form of solidarity. Without doubt the cities, as human groups differentiated from the countryside, go far back in the history of Flanders[117] and of neighboring lands.[118] But a reading of Galbert gives the impression (false perhaps?) that these communities had not yet fully acquired two distinctive characteristics of the city: an economic function well distinguished from that of the countryside and a government that has a collective base (whether large or small). As far as the first point is concerned, all students of the subject have been struck by the importance that Flemish cities still attached to the use of communal lands at the beginning of the twelfth century.[119] Communal lands meant a partially rural economy, clearly indicated by Galbert for Ardenbourg (a small town, to be sure).[120] As to the second point: in Galbert's narrative the cities seem to be governed from above, by the count's castellan.[121] They might possibly have already acquired their special law and their *échevinage,* or even a "private" organization peculiar to themselves.[122] Various conflcts between cities and castellans[123] indicate that most probably, however, the emancipation crisis was just on the verge of erupting. Besides, it is common knowledge that outside of Flanders, communes—which contemporaries characterized as "novelties"—appeared at precisely this period.[124]

The communes were thus new forms of solidarity. The *potentiae* apparently were old, as were the regional and familial solidarities. There is good reason to suggest a close tie between these two latter forms; an important family almost of necessity dominated its region and re-enforced its own solidarity in so doing. But the ties between family and region were in constant flux. The fight between the men of Furnes, led by the Erembalds, and the family of the castellans of Dixmude;[125] the conflict that seems to have unrolled in the western part of the *Pagus Flandrensis,* mainly for control of Ardenbourg; perhaps even the rivalry between the Erembalds and the lords southwest of Bruges—were these not all so many stages in a fight aimed at territorial dominion?

It is more difficult, in contrast, to say whether the sworn league of the Flemish barons represented the last phase of a development, the end of an age when the counts of Flanders had to take account of the opposition of the principal Flemish lords; or if it was the first version of the "aristocratic democracy" that would develop in Flanders when the nobility became organized within the Estates. Inasmuch as the Alsatian dynasty absorbed almost all the Flemish high-justicer seigniories during the twelfth century, the first hypothesis seems more probable than the second.

In this long evolution only one form of solidarity, transformed, maintained itself, and became the dominant one—the regional solidarity, led not by a noble family, but by one of the great cities. The cities, bound to one another (the movement, as we have seen, had already begun in 1127), would dominate the county in the fourteenth century. Each city (Ghent, Bruges, and Ypres) would in effect dominate a *quartier,* would be the focal point of a regional solidarity rather different from those of 1127.[126]

V

But what were the ties and forces that bound these different groups together, that prevented them from creating a fragmented society, broken into solidarity groupings? In reality, this society was held together by its common head, the prince.

The point of departure (we are far from it in 1127) was the conquest of different regions by one individual; that is, the joining together, by consent or by force, of pre-existent solidarities. Three arguments were used: pure force, right and law (the conqueror claimed certain rights to dominion), and promises or concessions to those who subjected themselves to the new power. Thus, when Thierry of Alsace conquered Flanders in 1128, the different solidarities—*potentiae,* communes, regions—either rallied to him or refused him.

But the elements that kept the different solidarities united among themselves were far more important than conquest. First of all, the conquest once accepted, tradition created dynastic loyalty. By 1127 the Flemish dynasty had reigned for almost two hundred fifty years, about eight generations. So completely had this dynasty become rooted in Flemish soil that a dynastic historiography began to develop after the tenth century.[127] The dynasty became a subject for both history and popular legend.[128] That the dynasty's authority should be recognized and undisputed throughout Flanders was a general bond among all the country's inhabitants, among all the members of the different solidarities. Galbert called the prince not only *"justius"* [more just, legitimate], but even—a striking phrase—"natural."[129] The fact that they had lived for two and a half centuries under the same dynasty had thus created among the Flemings a conscious idea of their own community. In fact, by the beginning of the twelfth century the next stage had been reached. They no longer needed the prince as a concrete representation of their common belonging; the feeling of community had become immediate, direct. Flanders was a fatherland. The words *"terra"* [country] and *"patria"*[130] were used daily to designate it.

It would not be superfluous, however, to specify what "living in common under the same power" might have meant to them. The curiously bloodless notion of medieval power which historians have, stemming from a literal—and thus restricted—interpretation of their meager sources, creates an insuperable image of a prince who levied taxes, condemned criminals, and summoned the able-bodied to war. This would hardly have created a powerful tie among the inhabitants of a principality. Let us then emphasize that "to live under the same prince" meant to be subjected to the same interference in social life, to feel the same common reactions about the prince's actions—interference and reactions that in the end gave a "specificity" to the inhabitants of a principality which made them different from others. Galbert shows how active this power was, how deeply it penetrated. It presupposed the use of writing, indeed, made it indispensable.[131] The interventions went so far as to prohibit the carrying of arms throughout the county; to fix the prices of foodstuffs; and, at least in time of famine, to decide on an agricultural "plan."[132] A contemporary text formally attributes to Baldwin a profound influence on the county's agriculture, including, among other things, the introduction of viticulture.[133] I have also tried to show elsewhere how this same Count appears to have conceived of and executed an enormous project of creating "social capital" (towns, fairs, castles, chapters) throughout the sparsely populated central part of his county to create a human link between its further reaches.[134]

The government of the counts thus implied many other things than the levy of taxes, the pursuit of evildoers, and the enrollment of inhabitants in time of war. We must, of course, not exaggerate in the other direction. The medieval state did not influence its inhabitants' way of life to the same extent as the modern state, in which the role of solidarities has become absurdly small in comparison with the totality of central authority. In the Middle Ages central power and solidarities were in an unstable equilibrium. The central authority, always threatened by the opposition (at least the potential opposition) of solidarities, could guarantee with assurance neither the security of individuals nor the agreements they concluded among themselves. Powers and individuals thus turned to another form of guarantee, religious or even magic. The religious bases of sovereign power are well known. Between individuals, God functioned, as it were, as a notary for contracts. The oath played the leading role. And when material power did not appear enough to guarantee a group's security and vital interests, it turned to magic.[135]

It was a dangerous situation. The prince was able to keep the solidarities within a "national" framework; but he was not strong enough, his presence was not sufficiently felt, to establish a satisfactory and stable equilibrium between his own power and theirs. The modern era would find a solution by creating a sovereign who emanated both from the prince and from the solidarities. What appears sketchily in Galbert's story is the organization of the different solidarities among themselves—outside of the count and, to an extent, against him. Here was the modern notion of "country," which in practice meant the grouping of "powers" into a separate reality independent of, or even superior to, the count.

The point of departure for this notion lies, undoubtedly, in the one crack in the dynastic system: the choice of a new count. The dynasty's right to reign in Flanders was uncontested; some hesitation remained as to which member of the dynasty should be called upon to do so. To meet this danger, the dynasty itself had carefully created certain "usages" governing the right of succession: indivisibility of the county; male primogeniture; subsidiary succession in the female line, with "representation" called into play in case of extinction of the reigning branch. But the fact that the reigning dynasty proposed these rules did not make them traditional. They had to be accepted by the "powers," by those elements of force—the barons, the principal heads of *potentia,* and later on the communes—whose opposition could bring forth a serious fight. Such a development takes a long time. The indivisibility of the county had to be accepted before a rule of primogeniture could be enforced; but, in the middle of the eleventh century, indivisibility was not yet a firmly established principle, as the serious difficulties accompanying the successions of Baldwin V and Baldwin VI show.[136] The danger was so real that at least one Flemish countess limited the number of her children.[137] By calling on the collaboration of the powers to impose succession by primogeniture, the dynasty recognized the powers' right to oversee the succession. The counts of Flanders in the eleventh and early twelfth centuries were "elected" by the barons, even though they were the eldest or only sons of the preceding count. It was a right of election that was perhaps purely formal in normal times, but very real when no heir was clearly designated. The powers could go so far as to choose among several members of the dynasty, or even outside the dynasty. The "electoral college" thus became a distinct authority independent of the dynasty. From this moment there existed another collective power in Flanders next to that of the count, a power very much formed by "subjects"—the incarnation of the "country's" active forces.

Thus a group of solidarities, the barons, the heads of the principal *potentiae,* succeeded very early in making itself a collective power independent of the count. It was an authority sometimes eclipsed, to be sure, and one that at first intervened only when it came time to determine succession to the countship. But it could be more, and in 1127 the barons formed the only authority in Flanders after the death of the Count. Galbert proclaims this idea with perfect clarity. The "country" (that is, for all practical purposes the barons and the communes—thus the group of principal solidarities) formed a reality superior to the count, able even to judge the count and to depose him if he governed ill.[138] And in fact the country did judge and depose the count.[139] This implied an organization of the country, an organization composed of barons and of representatives for the clergy and the towns.[140] Elsewhere, although the passage is not clear, this organization included barons, knights, clergy, and towns.[141]

It was thus not surprising that collective privileges were granted the entire county in 1128, or that Flemish independence was strongly affirmed, especially with respect to the French crown.[142] Doubtless, these revolutionary theses expressed only the convictions of certain groups—and masked ulterior motives.[143] They nevertheless imply the existence of a "national" consciousness in Flanders, of an idea of the country organized into its different power groups.

From all this discussion comes, I think, at least one clear impression. Medieval society, and that of later centuries, was divided into solidarities of very diverse natures. But this society passed through two successive stages. In the first, solidarities and prince were autonomous elements that met only when opposed or parallel interests brought them together. In the second, solidarities and princes normally collaborated. This collaboration, which forms a community of exploitation, marks the transition from the medieval state to the modern state in which princely power is totally absorbed by much larger solidarities of a new type: social classes, sometimes organized into parties and sometimes not.

NOTES*

1. By "powers" I mean the different social forces, more or less permanent, that are capable of acting in an autonomous fashion in pursuit of their interests —baronial dynasties, towns, regional solidarities, etc.

2. Most of our references are to Galbert's chronicle, of which there are two editions, one in the *MGH (SS* **12**. 561–619) and the other edited by Pirenne [Collection de textes pour servir à l'étude et à l'enseignement de l'histoire, **10** (1891)]. Since the chapter divisions in these two editions are the same, we refer to chapters and not to pages. Unfortunately, Langebek in the edition used for the *MGH* skipped number 59. From this chapter on, therefore, the reader must subtract one number if he is using the *MGH* edition. The other important sources to which we refer are Gauthier of Thérouanne, "Life of Count Charles" (*MGH SS* **12**. 537–561), and the text of the "Inquest" undertaken to punish the murderers, which is inserted in the chronicle of Baldwin of Avesnes (*MGH SS* **25**. 441–442). [Galbert's chronicle has been translated by James Bruce Ross, *Galbert of Bruges, The Murder of Charles the Good* (Columbia Univ., Records of Civilization, Sources and Studies, **61**) (1959).]

3. Apart from Galbert, by Gauthier of Thérouanne, Herman of Tournai (*MGH SS* **14**. 285–286) and Suger (*Vie de Louis le Gros,* Waquet, ed., 1929).

4. Galbert 35.

5. By "Middle Ages" I mean the period from approximately 600 to 1200, a conception I defend below.

6. This poverty is more qualitative than quantitative. Our sources concern

* Except for source and bibliographical references, most of the material in the original notes has been omitted.—Ed.

mainly political history and the individual actions of sovereigns and princes, or the semicollective history of religious communities. Other social groups appear much less often.

7. Although not infinitely so . . . . I have tried to trace the effects of a basically agrarian economy on political fragmentation in my *Etudes sur la naissance des principautés territoriales en France* (1948), esp. chaps. 1 and 5.

8. One ought not exaggerate. . . . It appears that already the prince cannot rule without his administration. See Galbert 35 and 112.

9. Galbert 99, 106. See in general, F. L. Ganshof, "Le droit urbain en Flandre au début de la première phase de son histoire, 1127," *Revue d'histoire de droit* **19** (1951) 407–410. In Galbert, the peasants appear as people good only for pillaging; Galbert 9, 10, 26, 111, 112.

10. Galbert 11–12, 15–19.

11. Galbert 26–75.

12. Galbert 48, 56, 57–58, 80, 81, 84.

13. Galbert 96–122.

14. This has been studied in detail by F. L. Ganshof, "Le roi de France en Flandre en 1127 et 1128," *RHD,* 4me sér., **27** (1949) 204–228.

15. Galbert 49, 99, 101.

16. Galbert 99 and 101.

17. In addition to Thierry of Alsace and William Clito, Baldwin, count of Hainaut; Thierry VI, count of Holland; William of Ypres, a bastard of the comital dynasty; and finally, Arnold, a nephew of Charles the Good.

18. Galbert 18, 20, 29, 39, 41, 49, 61, 75, 83 and 85; Gauthier of Thérouanne 52; "Inquest" *passim.*

19. Galbert 16, 17, 19, 26, 45.

20. Galbert 7, 8, 13; see also Gauthier of Thérouanne 15.

21. Galbert 70.

22. Galbert 71.

23. Galbert 16, 26–28, 54, 98–99, 103–104.

24. Galbert 11, 60, 65, 73, 74, 82, 84.

25. Everyone will naturally think here of the other case: the *De Vita Sua* of Guibert de Nogent. But this noteworthy work has the disadvantage of being a work *a posteriori.* With Galbert, the changes in his thinking are noted day by day, and the very contradictions in his thinking give a strangely human tone to the whole work.

26. Jan Dhondt, "Une mentalité du douzième siècle, Galbert de Bruges," *Revue du Nord* **39** (1957), 101–109.

27. Galbert 33, 36, 45, 51, 52, 65, 67, 73, 74, 88, 93 ff., 96.

28. Galbert 111, 114 ff., 116, 118.

29. The same passages cited above.

30. Galbert 120.

31. It is possible (although disputable) that an individual may play an important role more easily in our own times of liquid, personal wealth (thus, wealth that is independent of its geographical surroundings) and of supertechnology (allowing a man in a position of control over a technological organization to exercise enormous power).

32. This is why historians pay so little attention to it (in the Middle Ages); they suggest that the "active forces" were either the princes and great feudatories or else anonymous forces such as "the peasantry" or the "city proletariat" or "the merchants." There is truth in all of this, but its enormous imprecision makes it extremely unsatisfying.

33. Galbert 25.

34. Galbert 55, 66, 103.

35. Their position is ambiguous. All of Flanders, apart from the high-justicer seigniories, was divided into castellanies administered in the count's name by a castellan. In this sense there was an administrative pyramid (count: castellan : all subjects) placed over the juxtaposition of solidarities. But what is commonly called the "feudalization of functions," which we prefer to call a "tendency toward the creation of *potentiae,*" quickly made itself a force here as well. A *personal* tie was established among all, or almost all, of the inhabitants of the castellany and the castellan. We are sure of this in the early twelfth century only in regard to the cities; the burghers of Bruges took an oath to their castellan: [the castellan speaks to the inhabitants of Bruges] *"fidem et securitatem inter nos firmatam dissolvo"* (—Galbert 59). Even more characteristic is the way the citizens of Bruges spoke of the Erembalds as *"domini nostri"* (—Galbert 25, 45). This, it seems, can be explained only as follows. The family held the charge of castellan of Bruges for several generations. To an extent that our sources do not allow us to determine—but which appears unquestionable—some or all of the inhabitants of the castellany had entered the castellan's *potentia.*

36. Galbert 30, 31, 67.

37. Galbert 100.

38. Galbert 26; see also Gauthier of Thérouanne 30.

39. Galbert 11.

40. Galbert 38, 95, 100, 101, 103, 104, 120.

41. Galbert 96.

42. Galbert 34.

43. Galbert 67, 80.

44. Galbert 96.

45. Galbert 96.

46. Galbert 96.

47. Galbert 79.

48. Galbert 93.

49. Galbert 55.

50. Galbert 67.

51. Galbert 33; see also *Actes des Comtes de Flandre,* F. Vercauteren, ed. (1936), no. 127. The word "commune" is undoubtedly very close to *"amicitia,"* used to designate the community of Aire; G. Espinas, *Recueil de documents relatifs au Droit municipal. Artois.* 1 (1934) no. 20.

52. *Actes des Comtes de Flandre* no. 127.

53. Galbert 25, 28, 118.

54. See Ganshof, "Le droit urbain en Flandre," 387–416.

55. Galbert 20; Gauthier of Thérouanne 43; Galbert 99 and 106, 45 and 113, 59, 94, 95, 98, and 103.

56. Galbert 17–19.

57. Galbert 22, 43.

58. Galbert 22.

59. Galbert 25.

60. Galbert 113, 114.

61. Galbert 116.

62. Galbert 48, 59.

63. Galbert 100, 103.

64. Galbert 71. See J. Dhondt, "Note sur les Châtelains de Flandre," *Mémoires de la Commission départemental des Monuments historiques du Pas-de-Calais* 5[2] (1947), 219–227.

65. Gauthier de Thérouanne 14; Galbert 13, 55; see also the acts of restitution to the church in A. Miraeus and J. F. Foppens, *Opera Diplomatica* (1723–48), 3, 30; A Van Lokeren, *Chartes et documents de l'abbaye de Saint-Pierre au Mont Blandin à Gand depuis sa fondation jusqu'à sa suppression* (1868), no. 214; A. G. G. Wauters, *Table chronologique des Chartes et diplômes* (1866), 2, 170–171.

66. Galbert 9, 10, 26–28.

67. Galbert 49; see also Gauthier of Thérouanne 37.

68. Galbert 7, 58; Gauthier of Thérouanne 37; "Inquest" p. 442.

69. Galbert 89.

70. Galbert 8, 70.

71. Galbert 8, 9, 14.

72. Galbert 25.

73. Galbert 9, 25.

74. Galbert 7 and *passim;* see also Gauthier of Thérouanne 15.

75. Galbert 8.

76. Galbert 19.

77. Galbert 1; see also *Actes des Comtes de Flandre,* no. 108.

78. Galbert 13.

79. Galbert 31, 79, 96, 114; see also Gauthier of Thérouanne 36.

80. Galbert 16.

81. Galbert 55, 108.

82. Galbert 107–109, 114, 120.

83. Galbert 9.

84. Galbert 16.

85. Galbert 16–18.

86. Galbert 19.

87. Galbert 18.

88. Gauthier of Thérouanne 36.

89. Galbert 51.

90. Galbert 11 and *passim.*

91. Galbert 26.

92. Galbert 19.

93. Galbert 28.

94. Galbert 58.

95. Galbert 41, 60, 65.

96. Gauthier of Thérouanne 52.

97. Galbert 51.

98. Galbert 79, 31 and 114; see also Gauthier of Thérouanne 36.

99. Galbert 30, 33, 65, 114.

100. Galbert 51, 101, 113, 120.

101. Galbert 30–31, 33, 52, 67, 89, 91, 98, 100, 102, 114; Gauthier of Théouanne 36. See L. Dhondt-Sevens, "Les premiers seigneurs d'Alost, de Bornem et de Termonde," *Annales de la société royale d'archéologie de Bruxelles,* **46** (1942–43), 161–165.

102. See J. Dhondt, "Les Origines des Etats de Flandre," *Anciens Pays et Assemblées d'Etats,* **1** (1950), 3–53.

103. Galbert 121.

104. Gauthier of Thérouanne 36; Herman of Tournai, *MGH SS* **14**. 286, chap. 31.

105. See above all the "Inquest," *MGH SS* **25**. 441–442; Galbert, 29, 31, 41, 42, 54.

106. Galbert 34, 47, 56.
107. "Inquest" p. 442; Galbert 65.
108. Galbert 9, 20, 33, 45, 63, 83, 85.
109. *MGH SS* **14**. 286: Gauthier of Thérouanne 36; Galbert 34.
110. Galbert 87.
111. Galbert 87, 88, and the "Inquest."
112. Galbert 102, 110.
113. Galbert 101.
114. Galbert 11.
115. Galbert 51–53, 95 ff., 106, 114.
116. Galbert 106.
117. See J. Dhondt, "Initiative comtale et développement urbain en Flandre," *Revue du Nord* **30** (1948), 133, 157.
118. P. Bonenfant, "L'Origine des villes brabançonnes," *Revue Belge de philologie et d'histoire,* **31** (1953) 399–447; J. Dhondt, "L'essor urbain à l'époque mérovingienne," *Mélanges Sapori* (1957).
119. Ganshof, "Le droit urbain en Flandre," p. 412.
120. Galbert 66.
121. Galbert 25, 45, 103.
122. Ganshof, "Le droit urbain en Flandre."
123. Galbert 59, 94, 95.
124. *Gesta Episcoporum Cameracensium, MGH SS* **7**. 498; Guibert de Nogent, *De Vita Sua,* Bourgin, ed.; *Actes des Comtes de Flandre* no. 127, p. 296, chap. 12.
125. Galbert 108.
126. Dhondt, "Les Origines des Etats de Flandre."
127. Witger, *Genealogia, MGH SS* **9**. 302–304; *Gesta Abbatum Sithiensium de Folcuin, MGH SS* **13**. 600–634.
128. J. Dhondt, "De Forestiers van Vlaanderen," *Bull. de la Commission royale d'histoire* (1940), 38–42.
129. Galbert *Introduction.*
130. Galbert 121.
131. Galbert 35.
132. Galbert 1, 3; see also Gauthier of Thérouanne 11.
133. *MGH SS* **15**[2]. 855.
134. Dhondt, "Initiative comtale et développement urbain," pp. 133–156; J. Dhondt in J. A. van Houtte *et al., Algemene Geschiedenis der Nederlanden,* **2** (1950), 120.
135. Galbert 113, 115.
136. See C. Verlinden, *Le règne de Robert le Frison* (1937), 40–73.
137. Herman of Tournai, *MGH SS* **14**. 282.
138. Galbert 95.
139. Galbert 104.
140. Galbert 95.
141. Galbert 106.
142. Galbert 106.
143. F. L. Ganshof, "Les Origines du concept de souveraineté nationale en Flandre," *Revue d'histoire de droit,* **18** (1950) 135–158.

CICERO AND THE ROMAN CIVIC SPIRIT IN THE MIDDLE AGES AND THE EARLY RENAISSANCE*

Hans Baron

Whoever studies the influence of Cicero on later generations will be surprised by the variety of effects which were produced in history by this one figure. Although scholars have frequently investigated this influence, essential aspects of it have remained unexplored.

During the Italian Renaissance, and to some extent even during the Middle Ages, one of these aspects was that of Cicero as a Roman statesman who lived his life in the service of the *Respublica* and wrote his literary works in order to create a culture and a practical philosophy suitable to citizens in the midst of an active life. Although in modern descriptions of medieval and Renaissance culture this part of Cicero's influence is scarcely mentioned,[1] knowledge of it is indispensable for a correct perspective of the growth of humanism.

In the course of history there has perhaps been no other philosophic writer whose thinking was as closely connected with the exigencies of civic life as that of Cicero. When the Roman Empire came into contact with the culture of the Hellenistic world, a tendency prevailed in Greek philosophy to seek the inner independence of the "sage" through tranquil studies

---

* A lecture delivered in Manchester (England) on February 24, 1938 and first published in the *Bulletin of the John Rylands Library,* 22 (1938), 72–97. Partly rephrased by the author, and augmented with a few new references to previously unquoted sources, in 1965. Reprinted by permission of the John Rylands Library and the author.

in a private existence, far from the cares of public life. In Cicero's day, amid the confusion of the civil wars, many Romans were anxious to learn from Greek philosophy that there was another worthy life to be led besides that of a politically active Roman citizen. It was one of the objectives of Cicero's literary work to counteract this trend. His ethics recalled citizens to public life. He set himself the task of adapting the Greek spirit of philosophical investigation to the needs of Roman citizens, who were not to turn away from their responsibility for the common weal.

All the expressions of a politically minded philosophy that could be found in Greek literature—in the works of Plato, Aristotle, Dicaearchus, and Panaitius—were carefully collected in Cicero's writings. Whenever possible, they were given a Roman setting. Corresponding utterances were ascribed to the great Romans of the past. For instance, in his *De Republica* and *Tusculans,* Cicero attributed to the elder Brutus and the Pontifex maximus Scipio Nasica the sayings that "the wise man is never a private individual (*numquam privatum esse sapientem*)"; and that "when the liberty of the citizens is at stake, nobody can remain a private person." In the *De Officiis, prudentia,* the virtue fundamental to a life of study and philosophical contemplation, is described as inferior to *iustitia, fortitudo* and *moderatio,* the virtues of active life. Whoever thinks it the duty of a philosopher to disdain civic ambition for honors in the army and the state, does not deserve admiration but blame. It may be that a man who withdraws from public activities in order to study and write leads a valuable life. But "more fruitful to mankind and more suitable to greatness and renown," so runs the Roman creed of the *De Officiis,* "are the lives of those who apply themselves to statecraft and to great enterprises." Such passages were read together with the famous words in the *Somnium Scipionis* (a fragment of the *De Republica* preserved during the Middle Ages) in which Cicero insists that "nothing on this earth is more agreeable to the God who rules the Universe, than assemblies and societies of man associated by the bonds of law—such as are known as states (*concilia coetusque hominum iure sociati quae civitates appellantur*)."[2] Each of these manifestations of Cicero's Roman convictions was to leave a deep impression on the minds of later readers.

The study of philosophy could only be justified in Roman eyes in the light of the idea that intellectual work was in itself "activity" and that it led to an exertion of human energy no less than did the activity of civic life. Such a conception of intellectual work had by no means been entirely unknown to Greek philosophy. The early followers of Aristotle had already debated the respective merits of the contemplative and the active life. Theophrastus, wishing to extol contemplation, had formulated the impressive paradox that the wise man is never less alone than when he is alone. In solitude his intellect comes into contact with the good men of all times; while he is far from human companionship, he approaches the

Divine.[3] In Rome, Scipio Africanus Maior was said to have referred to the same paradox to justify his own leisure after his great political deeds.[4] In Cicero's *De Republica,* with a slight change in tone, it is used as the key to the true Roman *otium.*† We read there that Scipio Africanus had said of himself, "he had never been less alone than when he was alone"; "he had never done more than when doing nothing."[5] From this Cicero concluded that Scipio, the great statesman, had found in solitary philosophic studies a new source of the highest intellectual activity.

But Cicero continued to probe the problem of active Roman leisure. Ten years later, in the *De Officiis,* he conceived of a different explanation of Scipio's saying, giving it the form in which it was known to the Middle Ages and the Renaissance, when for many centuries the *De Republica* was lost. The Cicero of *De Officiis* realized that the victor of Zama could not merely have pursued studies in his *otium.* If Scipio had engaged in great mental activity in solitude, this could only mean he had devoted his *otium* to considering the vast plans that guided him in building up the Roman Empire: "in his leisure he thought of the things to be done (*in otio de negotio cogitabat*)." Cicero himself, in his long, enforced *otium* during the civil wars, had, it is true, led a life of literary and philosophical leisure in the silence of his country home. But he could boast that he had not used this solitude merely to forget his unhappy fate, or to gain inner peace through contemplation. The chief task of his *otium* had been to labor as a Roman citizen for Rome; he had laid foundations for a Latin literature, preparing the empire of the Latin language after other citizens had built the political Empire of Rome. He now proudly compared his literary, yet Roman *otium* with the statesman-like *otium* of Scipio. "Leisure and solitude," he said, remembering Scipio's dictum, "which serve to make others idle, had in Scipio's case acted as a goad." Cicero wanted his readers to understand that they had also acted for the benefit of Rome and in a way befitting a citizen, in his own writing.[6]

He wanted his readers to see that he himself had fulfilled the ideals he had set up in his early writings. In the *De Legibus* he had already looked upon it as his own task "to bring learning out of the gloomy depths of the study and out of the scholar's leisure, not merely into the sunlight and dust, but also into the fighting line and the center of the conflict." In the *De Oratore* he had shown in the figures of great Romans of the past what culture could mean to a citizen in the midst of his daily life. Cato Censorius was here described as the type of citizen who knew how to unite theory and practice, private and public interests. Legal studies did not prevent him from being a busy lawyer; private business never alienated him from his duties as an orator in the Forum or as a member of the Senate. Marcus Crassus, the leading speaker in the dialogue set forth in

† *Otium*=leisure.—Ed.

De Oratore, had never discontinued his activity in the law courts for theoretical studies, and had yet attained an exceptional degree of intellectual development. He sets up as a model the citizen "who does not give others the impression that he is pursuing philosophical studies, and yet is studying." This, indeed, was and remained Cicero's own highest ideal of civic culture. When, in later years, he defended himself against those who questioned his ability for philosophic work after a life-long political career, he boasted that he was not unprepared, because he, too, "had been studying philosophy most earnestly at the very time when he seemed to be doing so least."[7]

During the Middle Ages, when the bearers of culture were chiefly clerics and monks, which part of Cicero's legacy could be less appreciated than all this Roman craving for activity and for a civic culture? Again, when in the dawn of the Renaissance the citizens of the Italian city-states longed for a laic literature and moral ideals befitting men who led an active life, where could they find a better ally? The most dramatic episodes in the history of Cicero's influence were to develop from these Roman aspects of the *De Oratore* and *De Legibus,* the *Somnium Scipionis* and the *De Officiis.*

Generalization in history is always difficult, and even the contention that the medieval mind was insensitive to Cicero's Roman traits is only part of the truth. To be sure, the civic world of Rome was virtually forgotten for centuries, and we are often amazed to see how fully the historical figure of Cicero the Roman thinker had passed from memory. Even in a clerical or monastic milieu, however, some unmistakable echoes of Cicero's Roman teachings remained. Although they were few and far between, they are yet of great interest, because they reveal both the abiding power of those Roman ideas and the degree to which they were transformed by the medieval mind.

A transformation had already started in the commentary on the *Somnium Scipionis* which Macrobius wrote about 400. Macrobius was a pagan living at the time when Plotinus' philosophy of neoplatonic contemplation was gaining the ascendancy in the ancient world; and Macrobius' intention was to prove that Cicero, in spite of his championship of the active political life, had known that religious contemplation was on a higher plane. Nevertheless this early step in the erosion of the Ciceronian values did not yet bring unlimited triumph for the ideal of contemplation. In Plotinus' neoplatonic conception, the *vita politica* had been merely the ground from which the human mind must quickly ascend to the vision of the Divine and the purification of the soul. Macrobius, however, understood this to mean that the path through the *otiosae virtutes* of contemplation is certainly the higher one, but that the *negotiosae virtutes* also lead man to happiness, so that it is best to pursue both the higher and the lower path. Like Cicero, Macrobius found his models among the great Romans of the past—Numa the king, the two Catos and Scipio Africanus, who all combined *sapientia* and political action. Moreover, Macrobius adopted from Cicero's *Dream of Scipio* the idea that a particular reward awaits good citizens and statesmen in heaven. He stressed the Ciceronian words that "nothing on this earth is more agreeable to God" than life as lived in the *civitates*.[8] Thus some of the distinctively Roman conceptions of Cicero came down to the Middle Ages among the ideas and reflections of a neoplatonic writer. When in the twelfth and thirteenth centuries scholasticism once more had recourse to neoplatonic ideas in building up a powerful synthesis between religion and the politico-social sphere, Macrobius' modification of the neoplatonic flight from life was one of the major sources from which scholastics drew their inspiration.[9] Still later, during the last centuries of the Middle Ages, humanistic readers began to sense the true Roman attitude behind Macrobius' commentation, eventually freeing the Roman core from its neoplatonic disguise.

Another medium of Ciceronian influence throughout the Middle Ages was St. Ambrose's adaptation of the *De Offiiciis* for the use of the clergy. This Christian recasting of Cicero's work presented a different, though comparable effort to extenuate the strongly civic tenor of many Ciceronian teachings. In St. Ambrose's *De Officiis Ministrorum,* the political and social virtues no longer claim pre-eminence. *Sapientia-prudentia,* in open contrast to Cicero's evaluation, now ranks above all the virtues of the active life. Nevertheless, in this adaptation by one of the fathers of the church, no less than in the neoplatonic commentary of Macrobius, many original Ciceronian features outlive the changing times. Since St. Ambrose, more than any of the other church fathers, was a Roman at heart, many a trace of Cicero's Roman patriotism and civic approach to life are found in his guidebook for priests.

Among these traces is the symbol that Cicero had created when he defined the *otium* of Scipio. The Ciceronian praise of true leisure as a regeneration of man's inner strength found response in the heart of the Christian writer. There seemed to be a kindred spirit in the teaching that solitude should serve to rouse the highest mental energy and thus become a means of increasing one's usefulness to one's fellow men. Like Cicero, Ambrose contrasted an *otium* of activity with the despicable leisure of men "who distract their minds from activity in order to indulge in idleness and recreation." But, critical of the pagan world, he declared that it was not Scipio but Moses and the prophets who had been the first to teach a leisure of true activity. While they appeared to be alone and idle, they listened to the voice of God, thus gaining strength to accomplish feats beyond human power.[10]

St. Ambrose was the first of the recorded readers of the *De Officiis* who found inspiration in Scipio's tireless "activity" in solitude for his conception of a living faith in monastic seclusion. In Carolingian times, the abbot Paschasius Radbertus gave the by now familiar Roman aphorism a place in one of the fundamental texts of medieval theology. If Scipio the pagan, Paschasius said in his *Commentary on St. Matthew,* was never less idle than when he was at leisure, because he used his *otium* to think about the exigencies of his *negotia*—"how much less should we, who have been subjected to heavenly discipline, grow weary in our *otium* of meditating on divine matters." To whom, he asked, could Scipio's words be more suitable and more necessary than to monks in the uninterrupted *otium* of the monastery?[11] The end was an ideal in which monastic dedication to contemplation, and scholarly devotion to an industrious life of study, were inseparably linked.[12] When we come to Petrarch, we will find that this trend of medieval thought still had relevance for him.

Usually, however, throughout the early Middle Ages, all vestiges of the Ciceronian civic outlook on life were eliminated outright. Until at least the twelfth century Cicero was viewed as if he had been himself a monastic scholar—a recluse who seemed to teach contempt of marriage and women, and of all the passions and burdens of life in this world.

The first to form this early-medieval conception of Cicero was St. Jerome, the father of scholarly monastic humanism, who in defense of chastity and the solitary life collected all the classical witnesses—genuine and imaginary—against the married state. Jerome ascribed to Cicero the saying that "you cannot devote yourself to a wife and philosophy at the same time (*non posse se uxori et philosophiae pariter operam dare*)." He went back farther and quoted Theophrastus' praise of learning in solitude, which Cicero, in the *De Officiis,* subsequently transformed into a Roman praise of ceaseless activity for the community. Jerome thus preserved for monastic humanists of the Middle Ages the original meaning of Theophrastus' words, that the truly wise man is nowhere less alone than in solitude because the human intellect comes into contact there with the sages of all times and with the Divine. This dictum seemed to Jerome to be in harmony with the alleged Ciceronian warning against family life and women.[13]

The two passages continued to be associated with each other in the literature of the Middle Ages. Up to the twelfth century the typical medieval Cicero remained a teacher of misogyny and flight from active life. Following Jerome, great scholars of the so-called twelfth-century renaissance, like John of Salisbury and Walter Map, continued to attribute to Cicero the opinion that the truly wise must live in solitude and far from household cares.[14] Abelard made Cicero an outright critic of the drudgery of the *vita activa;* he ascribed to him the observation that "the fact that something is toilsome (*laboriosum*), need not necessarily make it *praeclarum* and *gloriosum*"—thus impugning the belief that the laborious life of a secular cleric was worthier of reward than the calm contemplation of a coenobite, or the struggle with the temptations of life more meritorious than monastic seclusion.[15] Even our best evidence of widespread and often enthusiastic interest in Cicero's works in the twelfth century, the well-known *Moralium Dogma Philosophorum,* does not break the bounds of this early medieval trend. Although it literally repeats the Ciceronian decision that *prudentia* is inferior to the three other, more active cardinal virtues, the motive of Cicero's choice remains unperceived. For, of *iustitia, fortitudo* and *temperantia* the last is given precedence because this virtue has the least connection with public life. By means of temperance, says the anonymous author, man rules himself, by courage and justice he rules over family and state; "but it is better for man to govern himself than to exercise any external dominion."[16]

Not till the thirteenth century did Cicero begin to re-emerge as a Roman thinker.

At first sight it may seem strange that it was the thirteenth century which saw the prelude to a new appraisal. At that time, as we know today,[17] the appreciation of classical poets and writers was declining rather than growing. The study of the classical authors was, as it were, restricted to a small anteroom in an imposing edifice, the largest halls of which became the homes of the new theology, jurisprudence, and, finally, science. In ethics and politics, Aristotle, the systematic philosopher, came to the fore, detracting from Cicero's previous authority. On the other hand, the ever growing intellectual curiosity of this century began to throw new light on ancient authors, since more of them were now read than ever before,[18] even though readers in scholastic universities no longer matched the enthusiasm with which in earlier centuries St. Ambrose and the author of the *Moralium Dogma Philosophorum* had taken up some of the views of a book like the *De Officiis.* When compared with the many different moral systems now known—those of Aristotle, the church Fathers, and many recent philosophers—Cicero's ideas little by little became recognized in their unique, but forgotten nature. In the end, his Roman scale of values was perceived for the first time.

If we consult the major encyclopedia of the thirteenth century, the widely circulated *Speculum* of Vincent de Beauvais, we still encounter, to be sure, Jerome's allegation that Cicero had said he could not serve both philosophy and women. In fact, in addition to some misleading statements on Cicero's political career, the Jeromian dictum is used as the chief testimony for characterizing Cicero's personality. Moreover, no attempt is made to comprehend Cicero's doctrines by establishing their interrelationship and the points of emphasis. For instance, in order to document the possible praises of both the *vita socialis* and the *vita contemplativa,* Cicero's various sayings are split up and cited out of context in support of one or the other. But Vincent's encyclopedia hereby shows a knowledge of many of Cicero's works superior to that of the preceding centuries.

Scipio's paradox from *De Officiis* is referred to in Vincent's *Speculum Doctrinale* as well as in his *Speculum Historiale;* and in support of the merits of the active life, Cicero is quoted to the effect that *otium* may be useful to some philosophers, but that "more fruitful to mankind and more suitable to greatness and renown are the lives of those who apply themselves to statecraft and to great enterprises."[19]

One reason for this renewed attention to passages expressing Cicero's civic attitude was that in the thirteenth century civic society was again beginning to play a part, however limited, in literary culture. Although they were usually still clerics, scholars and popular writers learned to look at the world also from the viewpoints of both the citizen and the knight. A cleric writing in civic surroundings would contemplate his studies in a different light from a writer in a monastic cell. He would not feel his work to be a parallel to contemplation and philosophic speculation; he could plan and appraise it as a service to the community, as a counterpart in the intellectual sphere to the political activities of citizens.

As early as 1118 Guido, a cleric of Pisa—at that time one of the most flourishing maritime cities in Italy—had adapted a medieval cosmography to the Mediterranean interests of the citizens of Pisa. He justified his work by saying that, since nature herself had constituted human society, the best part of both human *negotia* and *studia* ought to be devoted to service for the common weal. This was not only his personal opinion, he said; it was confirmed by the teachings of St. Ambrose, who in turn had referred to Cicero's *De Officiis* and other ancient writers as his inspiration. Following their precepts, he was trying to make a contribution to human society through his literary works.[20]

A hundred years later, Italian citizens began to give expression in writing to their moral ideals. In one of the earliest creations of this lay literature, the *Libro della Dilezione di Dio e del Prossimo,* written by Judge Albertano da Brescia in 1238 (i.e. a few decades before the publication of Vincent de Beauvais' encyclopedia), we find the Cicero of the *De Officiis* quoted as a decisive authority in the discussion of the two ways of life between which man must choose. All other spiritual and secular authorities, it is admitted in the book, seem to agree in favoring contemplation and the flight from active life. Christ's preference of Mary to Martha, the teachings of the Son of Sirach and those of the apostles, the stoic contempt of the material world and several statements found in Cicero himself—all these warn us not to consume our human energy in toil for this transient existence. On the opposite side there is only the Cicero of the *De Officiis,* boldly claiming that an existence spent on *"cose comunali e grandi"* should be considered as "more fruitful" than the easy life of contemplation, and that a noble mind should choose unrest and exertion in order to help the world, rather than happiness in untroubled solitude. In the eyes of this layman this single witness alone balances all the other authorities. Man, he concludes, may freely choose between the two ways of life.[21] To the judge of Brescia, the Roman civic spirit and medieval contemplation appear to be of equal value.

The revival of Cicero as a Roman philosopher was thus already in the air when, by the middle of the thirteenth century, scholastic learning reached its zenith. We have a record of the textbooks which were used in the arts faculty of Paris for the baccalaureate examination at that time.[22] "Moral philosophy" was divided into two sections. As far as man was considered with regard to his inner life and moral self-education, the Aristotelian *Ethics* served as a textbook. But in the area where "the human soul lives *in bono aliorum,*" i.e. in social ethics, in addition to the practical study of the *Leges et Decreta,* Cicero's *De Officiis* was the prescribed guide.

The literary work of St. Thomas Aquinas reflects and builds upon this educational plan. In Thomas's *Commentary on the Sentences* as well as in his *Summa Theologiae,* the chapters dealing with the importance of contemplation and the active life point to the Cicero of the *De Officiis* as the sole champion of the *vita activa,* just as the judge of Brescia had suggested a few decades before. By his claim that *iustitia* should be placed at the head of all the virtues and that there was no excuse for disdaining a career in the state and army, Cicero is seen to be in disagreement with all the other authorities acknowledged by St. Thomas. But Thomas, the theologian and great scholar, anxious to establish a fair and even balance, does not consider Cicero's lonely championship a possible counter-poise to the traditionally upheld values. The Ciceronian challenge is absorbed into the synthesis of thirteenth-century thought. An equilibrium, Thomas decides, had long before been achieved by St. Augustine and Gregory the Great, by Aristotle, who in his ethics conceded first place to the *bios theoretikos,* and by Macrobius, who modified Cicero's Roman view with neoplatonic teaching, thus leaving room for a certain "measure of escape from human affairs."[23] The famous Ciceronian maxim from the *Somnium Scipionis*—"nothing is more agreeable to God than the *concilia coetusque hominum iure sociati quae civitates appellantur*"—loses its Roman significance. Its form is taken over, but its meaning is changed by the alteration of the passage to read: "no sacrifice is more agreeable to God than the *regimen animarum,*" that is, the care taken by the Church in its spiritual rule over human souls.[24]

Would this scholastic equilibrium endure when the pendulum swung back to the twelfth century's enthusiasm for certain chosen authors of antiquity, and Cicero again became the object of intense interest? In the second half of the thirteenth and during the fourteenth century the civic world of the Italian city-states came finally to the fore, and the Roman philosopher was soon accepted as a respected teacher of civic conduct.

By that time the Tuscan city-republics had succeeded the more precocious Lombard cities, which were already falling prey to tyranny; but in the case of Tuscany around 1300, our information still comes largely from clerics, in particular from friars whose convents lay within the towns. Among these urban friars, two Dominicans, the Florentine Remigio de' Girolami and Tolomeo of Lucca, former disciples of Aquinas and highly respected in the city-state Tuscany of Dante's day, allow us to observe how the claim that devotion to the community should be the citizen's highest value in life was preached from pulpits, and colored writings on politics and history. Doubtless, the major treasure-trove for these Dominicans remained the recently discovered Aristotelian *Ethics,* understood better than ever before in the surroundings of the Italian Commune, the counterpart of the Greek *Polis*. But side by side with Aristotle, Cicero began to be recognized as the most effective guide to the citizen's social obligations. Tolomeo of Lucca, when dealing with the problem of why God had allowed the pagan Romans of antiquity to build their world-wide empire, concluded that they had been guided, more than any other people, by *amor patriae*. Love of one's country, Tolomeo insisted, was "the most meritorious of all virtues" because "zeal for the common weal" tends toward the same end as the divine command to love one's neighbor as onself. Like the command of God, therefore, the call of the *patria* does not admit of any exception. "This is the reason why Tullius [Cicero] speaking of the *Respublica* states that nothing that might prevent you from answering the summons of your country must be permitted to stand in your way."

Thus Cicero's civic doctrine had at last regained a more profound ethical value. To the Tuscan philosopher, writing in a city-state milieu, one of the characteristics of *De Officiis* was that it "considers the State the most gratifying and most valuable of all human associations" because "all the love of relatives and friends is encompassed by the love of one's *patria*."[25]

An important aspect of the historical Cicero had become visible in these civic circles. In an anonymous Italian biography of Cicero, probably written not long after 1300,[26] we can observe how far the meagre information about Cicero's personality found in Vincent de Beauvais' encyclopedia had by now been expanded. Although details of Cicero's political career remain unknown, Cicero in this early-fourteenth-century biography is clearly a Roman statesman as well as an author. "Even though Cicero devoted himself so whole-heartedly to administrative affairs and the protection of the Republic," says the anonymous biographer, full of admiration, and though Cicero was such a busy lawyer "that it is almost impossible to believe that human strength could suffice for all his labours, he was also filled . . . with such a desire to study and write that it seems wonderful how he was able to develop such tremendous activity in both these spheres."

When this new appreciation of Cicero the Roman citizen encountered the medieval preconceptions, what could be the result but a dramatic struggle? This struggle came about with the advent of Petrarch.

Petrarch was the heir to both the outlook formed in the Italian city-states and older medieval traditions. Although a Florentine citizen, he was born and bred in exile, and during the first half of his humanistic career, before entering the world of the north-Italian tyrant courts, he preferred life in papal Avignon, where he took lower orders, and in the isolated Alpine valley of Vaucluse in southern France to that of a Florentine citizen. At Avignon he was in contact with the Franciscan spiritual movement of his time, as well as with the monastic literature of earlier generations. Thus it fell to his lot to wage the historic battle that was to emerge from the contradictions between monastic persuasions and the reviving memory of Cicero the Roman citizen. This battle grew all the fiercer because Petrarch, in his search for ancient authors and manuscripts, discovered a key to a deeper knowledge of Cicero's personality, a key unknown during the preceding centuries: Cicero's intimate *Letters to Atticus.*

In 1345, when Petrarch made this discovery in the cathedral library in Verona, he saw the historical Cicero face to face for the first time. He saw a Roman who had given up his offices in the state under compulsion, in consequence of Caesar's victory; a citizen who, from his rural retreat, followed political events feverishly, and who (after the murder of Caesar) returned to the confusion of the civil war, to his own ruin. Petrarch, the semi-cleric and hermit of the Vaucluse, shrank back in horror from this discovery. He wrote a letter full of accusation—as strange as it was moving—to the shade of Cicero in Hades. "Why did you involve yourself in so many useless quarrels," he reproached his fallen idol, "and forsake the calm so becoming to your age, your position and the tenor of your life? What vain splendor of fame drove you . . . to a death unworthy of a sage? . . . Oh, how much more fitting it would have been had you, philosopher that you were, grown old in rural surroundings, . . . meditating upon eternal life and not upon this trifling existence here below!"[27]

However much Petrarch admired Cicero's eloquence, his precepts for a cultured life, and his independence from dogmatism, superstition, and the errors of polytheism, Cicero's civic spirit was to him nothing but an offense against monastic values that Petrarch was neither willing nor able to abandon.[28] In all his later humanistic works written in the solitude of the Vaucluse, he stressed the contrast between the vanity of Cicero's political passions and the fruitfulness of Cicero's fleeting withdrawals from politics. In Petrarch's *De Rebus Memorandis,* and even more in his *De Vita Solitaria,* Cicero appears as the historic example of a citizen who, against his own will, became a witness to the superiority of solitude. Petrarch insists that all the literary works of Cicero were written in the *solitudo gloriosa* of his old age. "It was solitude which caused this man's mind to open out; moreover—this is the strange and wonderful thing—it was a solitude obnoxious to him. What, one may think, would it not have accomplished if he had desired it, or, how much should we not long for that which brings such great benefit even to one who is unwilling to endure it?"[29]

The Cicero whom Petrarch, like his medieval forerunners, admired, was the follower of Scipio in his praise of true *otium.* So closely did Petrarch adhere to the medieval tradition at this point that he adopted, side by side with Scipio's commendation of *solitudo,* St. Jerome's and Theophrastus' description of the "wise man" as the one to whom solitude means flight from women, marriage and communal life. Except for Jerome, one may say, the Scipio of the *De Officiis* is the figure of the *De Vita Solitaria* of which Petrarch is fondest. Indeed, Scipio is called the "standard-bearer" (*signifer*) of a new humanistic *otium* because for Petrarch, too, the highest aim of leisure is intense intellectual activity. In the *De Vita Solitaria,* Scipio's paradox from the *De Officiis* is a recurring theme. Scipio's words, said Petrarch, made it clear what he (Petrarch) meant by solitude. He did not mean relaxation or idleness but rather concentrated exertion of all the mental faculties to a higher degree than was possible amid the distractions of civic life. "The body may have its holidays, but the mind must not rest in *otium* longer than is necessary for the attainment of fresh energy." True *otium,* said Petrarch, is the leisure which is "not inactive and without usefulness, but uses solitude to do service to many others."[30]

This was the summit of Cicero's medieval influence, and at the same time it marked the beginning of a development reaching beyond the bounds of medieval traditions. In his *De Otio Religioso* Petrarch endeavored to interpret literary solitude and monastic seclusion from one and the same new angle. A quiet, comfortable life, free from anxiety, he said, would be as harmful to a man in solitary life as to the man of the world. Struggle and exertion are necessary to test the powers of every human being. The decline and fall of the Roman Empire is a lasting proof of the dangers of peace and quietude. When Rome no longer had to struggle for her existence, carefree security and thirst for pleasure and luxury ruined the energy of the Roman people.[31]

By referring to Roman history in order to prove the necessity of inward struggle and exertion in solitude, Petrarch reveals the subtle links which connect his conception of active leisure with the civic world of Rome. Indeed, wherever we observe his humanism, we see his face still turned toward the medieval past, but the ground on which he stands is covered with new seeds—seeds which were only waiting for a propitious wind to carry them to a more favorable soil. Petrarch rejected a life of action in the community and in the family, but he praised activity itself more highly than anyone had since Roman times, and he acknowledged its crucial role for the greatness and history of ancient Rome. As soon as this praise of activity found full response in the circles of citizens who were leading an active life; as soon as the intellectual world of the Italian city-states, which had been developing since the twelfth century, reached final maturity, the time had come for the complete return of the values of Rome. At that point, the slow process of medieval evolution was to develop into a sudden revolution.

The old conception of the Renaissance as a fundamental break with medieval traditions, as a new edifice on changed foundations, was not entirely wrong. It was only erroneous insofar as that break was placed at too early a date. A *revolution* in intellectual life did indeed take place, but not until the end of the fourteenth century, not until the very moment when Petrarch's humanism was transplanted into civic surroundings—first and foremost into the world of Florentine citizens.

Coluccio Salutati, Petrarch's pupil and an ardent Florentine patriot, chancellor of Florence from 1375 to 1406, was the first of the citizen-humanists who now made their appearance. In his youth Salutati had intended to reply to Petrarch's idealization of the *vita solitaria* with a book, *De Vita Associabili et Operativa.* True, this work was never published; but his closer kinship with the Roman civic spirit was soon revealed on another occasion. Just as Petrarch had unexpectedly found himself face to face with Cicero's personality, thanks to his discovery of Cicero's *Epistolae ad Atticum,* so Cicero's personality was revealed to Salutati in 1392 through the discovery of the *Epistolae Familiares.* But whereas Petrarch's first joy had soon turned to increasing disappointment, the Florentine chancellor honored and admired those very characteristics of Cicero which Petrarch had considered unworthy of a philosopher. He admired the part which Cicero had played in political life, his participation in the civil wars, and his thirst for political renown.

Had Cicero himself not said that nobody ought to remain a private individual when the liberty of the citizens was at stake? Salutati understood his master well. Wishing to justify him for taking part in the civil wars, Salutati declared that, according to the *Noctes Atticae* of Gellius, Solon had decreed in Athens that a citizen who in time of civic unrest continued to lead his private life was to be considered unfaithful to his city and expelled. Cicero, therefore, had not been oblivious of the duties of a "wise man" when he took part in the struggle for the liberty of the *Respublica.* He had acted as a true philosopher and as a Roman like Brutus and Cassius, neither of whom thought it permissible for Roman citizens to retire into solitude while the world was in flames.[32]

Two years later one of Salutati's pupils, Pier Paolo Vergerio, wrote, in the name of Cicero, a reply to Petrarch's letter of accusation addressed to Cicero in Hades. It was the true voice of a Roman citizen which spoke this answer "from the Elysia infields." "Why did you forsake the calm so becoming to your age, your position and the tenor of your life"—this was the indignant question which Petrarch had put to his master. "My *otium,*" Vergerio makes Cicero reply, "my age, position and lot intended me to be a man who was to live his life in the midst of activity." Philosophy and culture, as Vergerio's Cicero insists, "were not meant to serve my own self-gratifying leisure, but to be used for the benefit of the community. The most mature and best philosophy has always seemed to me to be the one that dwells in cities and flees solitude (*philosophia quae in urbibus habitat et solitudinem fugit*)." The doctrine which Cicero always upheld was that he is the worthiest "who takes upon himself work for the state and the cares which are demanded by the *salus omnium.*" Vergerio's Cicero maintains that he had lived for the *Respublica* as long as a Roman citizen could work for her. When Caesar set up his tyranny, a Roman citizen was not allowed to ask whether Caesar was a great man or not, or whether he was "full of clemency." He had to face the fact that Caesar made the state, which "the law and the senate" were called upon to govern, dependent on the "clemency" or "cruelty" of a single man.[33]

About 1415 Leonardo Bruni Aretino, Salutati's pupil and Vergerio's friend, and later on successor to Salutati as Florentine chancellor, built up on these foundations his biography of Cicero—the standard biography for the Renaissance.[34] This work was entitled *Cicero Novus* because it was intended to replace Plutarch's *Lives of Demosthenes and Cicero,* which seemed to Bruni to favor the Greek orator. But the title *Cicero Novus* also had a deeper meaning. In contrast to the "old Cicero" of the Middle Ages and of Petrarch, this "new Cicero" of the Florentine Renaissance no longer assumed a contradiction between Cicero's political career, full of calamitous passions, and his fruitful philosophic life in the haven of quiet solitude. It was the trend of thought first revealed by the anonymous Italian biographer in the fourteenth century that now attained fullest expression. The new conception of Cicero was based on the assent of citizens to the ideal union of political action and literary creation found in the Roman's life. "No one seeing Cicero's literary legacy," says Bruni admiringly, "would believe that he had had any time for dealing with men; anyone reviewing his political deeds, his speeches, his occupations, and his struggles both in public and private life, would imagine he could never have had leisure for reading and writing."

Bruni found the explanation in the discovery that Cicero's literary and political activities had been two facets of one and the same life-work: the labors of a Roman citizen for his *patria* and for the Latin Empire of Rome. One must not look upon Cicero's life as if his political activities were followed and, as it were, replaced in his later years by philosophical studies in solitude. Rather, one must understand that the Roman statesman was always guided in all his actions by his civic philosophy. "From the self-same sanctuary of philosophy he took the factual knowledge needed for the administration of the republic and the expressions and phrases used in his writings and for his teaching of others." This double engagement gave Cicero his strength. He became capable, "in spite of the great claims made on him by a state which ruled the world, of writing more than philosophers whose lives are spent in leisure and in study; and, on the other hand, in spite of intense preoccupation with his studies and writings, he was capable of accomplishing more in active work than those people who are unburdened with interest in literary matters." The clue to Cicero's place in history must be sought here. The task of his life was a twofold attainment for Rome. As a consul and orator, Cicero served his state; as a thinker and writer, he created a Latin philosophy previously unknown to the Roman world. "Thus he alone of all men, I believe, has lived up to the two greatest and most difficult tasks."[35]

From that time onward Cicero taught the Italy of the Renaissance two things: the primary task of a man is action and service for his community; and this contact with active life need not distract his intellectual powers, but can stimulate his highest energy. After another generation, we find in Giannantonio Campano's biography of Enea Silvio Piccolomini—Pope Pius II in his later years—these same concepts used to define the significance of one of the great figures of the century. It was amazing, so Campano tells us, that Pius in the midst of all his papal duties should have found time for writing, and *vice versa,* that such a prolific writer as Pius should have found time for action. It is a measure of the greatness of this man of action "that, as a writer, he accomplished more than others who in their lives do nothing but write."[36]

It was in civic circles, however, that these ideas called forth the strongest response .

More than any other Italian city, and perhaps even more than Florence, Venice in the fifteenth century was a counterpart of Rome in the days of Cicero. The Venetian city-state was ruled, like the Rome of Cicero, by a nobility whose lives were spent in the administration of a vast Mediterranean Empire, and who, at the same time, endeavored to combine civic culture with their political work. In 1417, Francesco Barbaro, the patrician champion of humanism in Venice, remarked that admiration of the culture and political teachings of antiquity had begun to pervade the Venetian aristocracy. Although natural efficiency could develop without learning, Roman teachings and examples would make Venetian citizens "wiser and more courageous in ruling their state." Barbaro sent the letter on the administration of the Roman provinces which Cicero had written for his brother Quintus, to a friend who had been appointed governor of Zara in Venetian Dalmatia. Those of us who read Cicero's writings, Barbaro commented, will render better service to our Republic and will be grateful to the Roman writer.[37]

When, in the following year, another member of the Venetian nobility,

Leonardo Giustiniani, delivered the funeral sermon for a great Venetian statesman, Carlo Zeno, he described the life of the deceased citizen in much the same way as Cicero himself would have done. After devoting the best years of his life to the state, Zeno had withdrawn into *otium* and humanistic studies. But in these studies "he exercised due measure, so that he never failed to be available when his counsel was requested for the state or for his friends." He applied *otium ad negotia,* becoming perfect in both, so that he remained useful to his community in old age. It was in this Venetian atmosphere that Barbaro renewed Cicero's own farmula, proclaiming it the task of Venetian citizen-humanists "to bring philosophy out of the gloomy depths of the study and out of the scholar's leisure into the fighting line and the center of the conflict."[38]

Florence, the most flourishing seat of civic culture in the fifteenth century, was destined to carry the effects of the revival of Cicero's Roman genius to their climax.

As early as soon after 1400, Florentines of the old stamp had complained that the younger generation was beginning to gather from Cicero's *De Officiis* that "happiness and virtue were bound up with position and reputation in political life." In the eyes of their elders, these younger men were forgetting the philosophic truth that the "perfect life" is that of contemplation and inner peace.[39] By the 1430's Matteo Palmieri, Bruni's closest follower among the citizens, was to restore the civic attitude of the *De Officiis* in its entirety. Just as St. Ambrose had done at the beginning of the Middle Ages, Palmieri wrote an adaptation of the Ciceronian work that made allowance for the needs of his own century. This adaptation was entitled *Della Vita Civile,* On Civic Life.

It would be interesting to observe in detail how, in this book, the Ciceronian faith in action and in the values of communal life was finally restored.[40] In the concluding chapter, a profound impression is created by combining the vision of the *Somnium Scipionis* with the doctrines of the *De Officiis.* Palmieri transfers Scipio's dream from Roman to Florentine soil. In place of Scipio, Dante (who as the wanderer through heaven and hell is best qualified to report on the reward of souls after death and thus on the ultimate values of life) receives a message from the Hereafter. It reaches him on the battle-field of Campaldino, on the day of one of the greatest Florentine victories. This message is nothing but the Ciceronian teaching from the *Somnium Scipionis.* "I saw in heaven [says Dante's fallen friend, returned to life for a short hour] the souls of all the citizens who had ruled their states justly on earth, and among them I recognized Fabricius, Curius, and Fabius Maximus, Scipio and Metellus, and many others who for the sake of their country forgot themselves and their possessions." "No human work is more valuable than care for the welfare of the *patria,* the maintenance of the *città,* and the preservation of unity and harmony in a rightly ordered community." It is with this passage in imitation of Cicero that the messenger from the Beyond exhorts the Florentine poet.[41]

From the libraries and studies where Cicero's dialogues were read and adapted to Florentine needs, we step out on to the Piazza della Signoria, the center of the political life of Florence. There, in 1427, the *Capitano del Popolo*—a Roman, Stefano Porcari—delivered an oration before the public authorities. The *Capitano* was regularly a citizen from another city who had come to occupy his high office for a limited period, but Porcari, as we know from his own admission, was in his outlook deeply indebted to, and even a spokesman of his present environment; his speech was full of admiration for the state, the prosperity, and the public spirit of Florence. In such surroundings, said the *Capitano del Popolo,* every citizen ought to feel that he owed to the community all his happiness, all his intellectual and material possessions. Even in solitude no good citizen would forget his duty to be grateful. He recalled the example of Scipio Africanus Maior, quoting the paradox, handed down by Cicero, on Scipio's tireless activity in leisure. In this speech in the piazza of Florence, all the distortions and modifications of Scipio's words from the medieval monasteries are forgotten. Porcari, the humanist of the fifteenth century, interprets as follows: Scipio's saying meant that in the silence of his solitude "he was wont to think of the incomparable and glorious gifts he had received from the commonwealth; he then spurred on all his energies, to deserve them by his deeds and persistent efforts."[42]

This moving civic interpretation actually went beyond the ideas expressed by Cicero in his *De Officiis.* But it was in the direction in which Cicero, the Roman statesman, had pointed. Anyone who knows the long historical process which we have been contemplating cannot but recognize the dawn of an age which in many respects was more akin to the world of ancient Rome than had been all the centuries of the Middle Ages. Petrarch's conception of a Scipio who after his victories discovered that philosophical studies in solitude have equal or even higher value for the noble mind than all the victories and honors in the world, had lost its power in the fifteenth century. Either the *otium* of Scipio was now interpreted as that of a citizen who from lonely studious concentration will soon return with added strength to his civic duties,[43] or the old symbol of Scipio's flight into solitude was challenged and replaced by the ideal of a civic culture that needs no scholarly retreat but thrives amid the very activities of daily life.

It was Pier Paolo Vergerio who directed this challenge against the Ciceronian idea of Scipio's "leisure." Vergerio's *De Ingenuis Moribus et Liberalibus Studiis Adolescentiae* (the first comprehensive outline of humanistic pedagogy, written by the author in 1402 after a long sojourn in Florence) called the *otium* of Scipio an example which should not be followed by ordinary men. Perhaps (he said) Scipio Africanus, a man of unique virtues, was able to find his true self in loneliness, after exceptional exertions, and in his old age. "And yet he does not seem to me to be of lesser worth, who . . . knows how to maintain his solitude amid the turbulence of crowds, his inner calm in the midst of action." Vergerio's practical advice was that man should preserve his natural elasticity within the framework of his daily life, by gymnastic exercises, hunting and fishing. In this way he should render any flight into solitude superfluous. The symbol of Scipio, gaining new energy in loneliness, was replaced by the memory of Cato. For Cato, said Vergerio, was able to concentrate on his studies in the midst of public affairs. He had learned to study in the Curia while the Senate was assembling. In this way he fitted himself to give political advice that was beneficial to the *patria* not only for a fleeting moment but for all time.[44]

What was this ideal of the fifteenth-century humanist but the old doctrine of the orator Marcus Crassus in Cicero's *De Oratore?* "What cannot be learned quickly," Crassus had said, "will never be learned at all." A citizen, therefore, should not withdraw from civic duties to scholarly work. His fellow-citizens should not feel that he was devoting himself to study.[45]

In the fifteenth century the time had come for the full restoration of these ideas of the *De Oratore*. In 1421, in the cathedral of Lodi in Northern Italy, a complete text of this Ciceronian work was discovered. From then on the words of Crassus that had been missing, like many other paragraphs, in the manuscripts known to the Middle Ages were again read.[46] This rediscovery of the complete *De Oratore* did not only lead to new doctrines in the pedagogy of the Renaissance, but also helped Florentine citizens in their historical reinterpretation of Dante. Cicero, whose own strength had lain in his power to evoke the great figures of Roman history, was now to teach Florentine citizens how to contemplate the greatest figure of their own past. Just as Scipio the Elder had been the model for Cicero, so Dante came to symbolize the citizen's life for Florence.

Before this revival of Ciceronian thought Dante had not been considered in such light. To the fourteenth century he had been a philosopher who kept aloof from the common world. Giovanni Villani, the Florentine chronicler, had called him "presumptuous and reserved because of his learning, careless of graces as philosophers are," and "not knowing very well how to converse with the unlearned." Boccaccio, Petrarch's follower, had even reproached the Florentine poet for not having remained faithful to the retired life of a philosopher. In his biography of Dante, Boccaccio had interpreted Dante's unhappy fate as that of a philosopher who, in the civic atmosphere of Florence, forgot "what obstacles to a studious life women are" and that philosophy cannot be at home in a mind made restless by political ambition. Thus Dante had forfeited his intellectual peace through marriage and had been drawn into the whirlpool of domestic and public cares which destroyed his life.[47]

The strong revival of civic ideals in the fifteenth century led Leonardo Bruni to reconstruct Dante's political career in the republic and his part in the citizen army during the battle of Campaldino. Bruni's *Vita di Dante* (written in 1436) stressed these facts of Dante's life and pointed out that the Poet, as a true citizen, had had a wife and children. The greatest philosophers—Aristotle, Cicero, Cato, Seneca, and Varro—said Bruni in his *Vita,* had been the heads of families and had served their states. Petrarch had lived only for himself. Dante's life could teach citizens that true intellectual work need not lead man into idle solitude. After the battle of Campaldino Dante "applied himself to his studies with greater zeal than ever; yet he did not neglect intercourse with his fellow-citizens. And it was a marvelous thing: although Dante studied continuously, nobody would have gained the impression that he was studying."

"And here," said Bruni, "I would like to rectify the mistake of many ignorant people. They believe that nobody is a student who does not bury himself in solitude and leisure. Among the stay-at-homes, withdrawn from human society, I have never seen one who could count up to three. A lofty and distinguished mind does not need such fetters. On the contrary, the true conclusion is: whatever does not find expression at once, will never do so."[48]

Thus, with the creation of the new image of Dante, the ideas, even the words of the Crassus of the *De Oratore* had reappeared, not in mere imitation of a literary model but extended and transformed with the naive yet powerful self-confidence of fifteenth-century Florence. These reinforced Ciceronian notions about the proper conduct of citizens would henceforth subtly guide the Florentines whenever they looked at their great men. After the death of Cosimo de' Medici, when Poliziano recalled the great merchant and statesman of Bruni's day in a letter addressed to Pietro de' Medici, he did not only commend Cosimo's proficiency in speech and writing and his untiring energy in countless occupations; he also added as special praise that all the bustle never showed in Cosimo's relations with others. "Never idle, . . . and doing countless things, he did not seem to have anything to do."[49]

The epitome of the Ciceronian citizen, however, remained Dante. Bruni's biography of Dante was circulated more widely and used more frequently by writers than any other literary work of the early Renaissance. Almost everyone who wrote on Dante during the fifteenth and sixteenth centuries stood upon Bruni's shoulders: Gianozzo Manetti in the age of Cosimo de' Medici, Giammario Filelfo and Cristoforo Landino in the period of Platonism, Alessandro Vellutello, the well-known commentator of the *Divine Comedy,* during the first half of the sixteenth century. All these biographers of Dante took over from Bruni the concept of Dante as a symbol of the union of thought and action, of studious and civic life. They were all dependent, through Bruni, on Cicero's *De Oratore*.

Thus, after fifteen centuries, the ideal which Cicero had set up for Roman citizens was restored for modern times—recreated in fifteenth-century Florence in the figure of the Florentine poet.

NOTES

1. This is even true of the two most comprehensive studies of Cicero's influence, Th. Zielinski, *Cicero im Wandel der Jahrhunderte* (4th ed., 1929), and A. Hortis, "M. T. Cicerone nelle opere del Petrarca e del Boccaccio," *Archeografo Triestino,* N.S. VI (1879–80).

2. *De Rep.* II, 25, 46; *Tusc.* IV, 23, 51; *De Off.* I, 6, 19; I, 21, 70–71; *De Rep.* (*Somn. Scip.*) VI, 13.

3. "Sapiens autem numquam solus esse potest. Habet secum omnes qui sunt, qui umquam fuerunt boni, et animum liberum quocumque vult transfert. Quod corpore non potest, cogitatione complectitur. Et si hominum inopia fuerit, loquitur cum Deo. Numquam minus solus erit, quam cum solus erit." These ideas of Theophrastus have been preserved in Jerome's *Adversus Jovinianum;* see n. 13 below.

4. That Scipio's dictum, reported by Cicero (and by Cato before him, in Cato's *Origines*), was suggested by Theophrastus is obvious. It is sufficient to compare Cicero's text (see the next two notes) with the words of Theophrastus in the form just quoted from Jerome, and to remember that Cicero was familiar with the dispute between Theophrastus and Dicaearchus as to the respective merits of *vita activa* and *vita contemplativa.*

5. *De Rep.* I, 17, 27 ("Africanum . . . scribit Cato solitum esse dicere . . . de se . . . numquam se plus agere, quam nihil cum ageret, numquam minus solum esse, quam cum solus esset.")

6. *De Off.* III, 1, 1–4 (". . . numquam se minus otiosum esse, quam cum otiosus, nec minus solum, quam cum solus esset." "Ita duae res, quae languorem adferunt ceteris, illum acuebant, otium et solitudo.")

7. *De Leg.* III, 6, 14; *De Oratore* III, 33, 135; III, 22, 72–83, 89; *De Nat. Deor.* I, 3, 6.

8. *Comm. in Somn. Scip.* I, 8, 3–12; II, 17, 4–9.

9. See H. van Lieshout, *La Théorie Plotinienne de la vertu. Essai sur la genèse d'un article de la somme théologique de saint Thomas* (1926), pp. 124 ff.

10. *De Off. Min.* III 1 (Migne, *PL.* **16**, 145).

11. *Expos. in Matthaeum,* Prologus in lib. XI (*MGH Epp. Karolini Aevi,* VI, 148 f.). Similarly Radbertus makes use of the Scipio paradox in *Expos. in Psalm.* 44, Praefatio (see *ibid.,* p. 148 n. 2).

12. An example from the twelfth century is in Giraldus Cambrensis' *Symbolum Electorum,* Ep. 24 (ed. Brewer, *Rer. Brit. M. Aev. SS.,* I, 281), where the saying "se nunquam minus solum quam cum solus extiterat esse" is, however, surprisingly ascribed to Socrates.

13. *Adversus Jovinianum,* lib. I, c. 47–48 (Migne, *PL.* **23**, 276 ff.) see n. 3 above.

14. Walter Map, *De Nugis Curialium* (ed. M. R. James, *Anecdota Oxonien-*

sia, Mediaeval and Mod. Ser., XIV, 150); John of Salisbury, *Policraticus* (ed. Webb, II, 298). Webb's reference to *De Off.* III, 1, is a mistake; the whole section of the Policraticus is literally taken over from Jerome's *Adv. Jov.* I, c. 47–48. William of Malmesbury, too, in his *Historia Regum Anglorum* (ed. Stubbs, II, 65, "Lucubrabat—sc. Beda— ipse sibi pernox in gratiarum actione et psalmorum cantu, implens sapientissimi viri dictum, ut nunquam minus solus esset quam cum solus esset"), had recourse not to *De Off.* III, 1, as Stubbs believes, but obviously to Jerome.

15. Abélard, *Opera,* ed. Cousin, I, 693 f.; II, 621.

16. Moral. Dogma Phil., ed. J. Homberg [*Arbeten utgivna med Understöd av Vilhelm Ekman Universitetsfond, Uppsala,* **37**], p. 53. The work has more recently been studied by Ph. Delhaye in "Une adaptation du *De officiis* au XIIe siècle," *Recherches de Théologie Ancienne et Médiévale* (1949) but the authorship has not yet been finally established.

17. See L. J. Paetow, *A Guide to the Study of Medieval History* (1931), pp. 442 ff., 484 ff.

18. This has been proved by E. K. Rand, in "The Classics in the Thirteenth Century," *Speculum* IV (1929), and in "A Friend of the Classics in the Times of St. Thomas Aquinas," *Bibliothèque Thomiste* XIV (1930).

19. Speculum Historiale, lib. VI, c. 8 and 11 (ed. Duaci, 1624, pp. 175, 177); *Speculum Doctrinale,* lib. V, c. 41.

True, if the copious *Extracts* taken from Ciceronian works by a certain Hadoardus had really been put together in the Carolingian period, as it was long supposed, the knowledge of Cicero's writings in the early Middle Ages might have been greater than that shown in the thirteenth century in Vincent de Beauvais' encyclopedia. But as R. Mollweide, in *Wiener Studien,* 1911–1915, has proved, these extracts can hardly have been made in the ninth, or tenth century; their compilation must be attributed to the last period of antiquity, probably to learned pupils of St. Jerome in Gaul during the sixth century. See also the confirmation of Molleweide's research by A. Lörcher, in *Bursian's Jahresberichte der klass. Altertumswissenschaft,* 203 (1925), 153 f.

20. Guido's *Historiae Variae,* lib. I, cap. 1–3; in *Ravennatis Anonymi Cosmographia, et Guidonis Geographica,* ed. M. Pinder and G. Parthey (1860).

21. Il libro dell'amore e della dilezione di Dio e del prossimo e dell'altre cose, e della forma dell'onesta vita (Milan, 1830), cap. 65.

22. Discovered by M. Grabmann in a MS. of the *Archivo de la Corona de Aragón*; see M. Grabmann, *Mittelalterliches Geistesleben,* II (1936), 193 f.

23. Comm. in Sent., III dist. 35 q. 1, art. 4; *Summa Theol.* 1–2, q. 61, art. 5.

24. It is true that St. Thomas, in *Comm. in Sent., loc. cit.,* ascribes this saying to Gregorius Magnus, *Super Ezech., Homil. XII.* I have, however, only found the phrase "Nullum quippe omnipotenti Deo tale est sacrificium, quale est zelus animarum" there (Migne, *PL* **76**, 932), which does not show any resemblance to the words of the *Somnium Scipionis.* One must conclude that Thomas, unknowingly, had the latter in mind.

25. "Inde est quod Tullius dicit de republica, quod nulla causa intervenire debet, unde propria patria denegetur." "De hoc autem amore patriae dicit Tullius in lib. *De offic.* [the reference is to I, 57] quod 'omnium societatum nulla est gratior, nulla carior, quam ea quae cum republica perseverat. Unicuique enim nostrum cari sunt parentes, cari sunt liberi, cari sunt propinqui ac familiares, sed omnium propinquitates patria sua charitate complexa est'." Thus Tolomeo of Lucca, about 1302, in the *De Regimine Principum* (by Thomas Aquinas to lib. II cap. 4, but continued by Tolomeo), lib. III cap. 4. For Remigio de' Girolami's admiration of Cicero, cf. Charles T. Davis in the *Proceedings of the American Philosophical Society* CIV (1960), 665 f.

26. It is the *Epythoma de vita, gestis, scientie prestantia . . . Ciceronis* in the famous Cicero Codex in Troyes, from Petrarch's library, partly printed in P. de Nolhac, *Pétrarque et l'humanisme* (2nd ed., 1907), I, 227 ff. De Nolhac (p. 231) gives reasons why the biography cannot have been written by Petrarch himself in his youth, but must be the work of a writer of the early fourteenth century.

27. *Ep. fam.* XXIV, 3.

28. As Denys Hay reminds us in his *The Italian Renaissance in Its Historical Background* (1961) pp. 82–84, Petrarch's encounter with Cicero the Roman occurred only two or three years after Cicero had been viewed in Petrarch's *Secretum* (1342–1343) as an ally of Augustine in his teaching that human ambitions and activities are futile and dangerous to the soul. Petrarch's disgust with Cicero's letters, therefore, was demonstrably a triumph of medieval Augustinian sentiments over the shock of the first humanistic discovery of the true nature of Cicero's Roman world.

29. *De Reb. Mem.*, I, tr. 1, c. 4; I, tr. 2, c. 5; III, tr. 3, c. 13; *De Vita Solitaria,* I, tr. 3, c. 2; II, tr. 8, c. 2 (ed. Altamura, c. 4); II, tr. 10, c. 7 (ed. Altamura, c. 6).

30. *De Reb. Mem.*, I, tr. 1, c. 1 and 2; *De Vita Solitaria,* II, tr. 9, c. 5 and 6; II, tr. 10, c. 9 (ed. Altamura, c. 8); *Ep. sen.* II, 5.

31. *De Otio Religioso,* ed. G. Rotondi (1958), p. 20. (In *Opera* [Basileae, 1581], p. 301). For more details see H. Baron "Das Erwachen des Historischen Denkens im Humanismus des Quattrocento," *HZ* **147** (1932), 6 f.

32. *Ep.* VIII, 7 (Salutati's *Epistolario,* ed. Novati, II, 389); *Ep.* IX, 3 and 4 (ed. Novati, III, 25 f. and 50).

It should be mentioned, however, that even Salutati in the latter part of his life, like Petrarch, shrank back from the full implications of his discovery, as described in detail in the revised edition of the author's *Crisis of the Early Italian Renaissance* (Rev. ed. 1966), pp. 112–118, 148–151. In his later years, though still acknowledging care for the community as the key idea of Ciceronian ethics, Salutati preferred to stress the difference between Christian thinking and any values defended by ancient writers: we Christians "non determinamus humanorum actuum finem voluptate, sicut Epicurii, virtute, sicut Stoici, *humane societatis integritate, sicut Cicero,* meditatione contemptuque mortis, ut Seneca, speculatione, sicut Aristoteles, vel alia humane mentis opinatione; sed illa beatifici obiecti comprehensione, qua beati sumus evo eterno beatudineque perpetua fruituri." (*Ep.* XIV, 19, December 1405; ed. Novati, IV, 135).

33. Vergerio's *Epistolario,* ed. L. Smith, *Fonti per la storia d'Italia* LXXIV (1934), 439 ff.

34. Bruni must have been familiar with Vergerio's fictive letter of Cicero by the time he wrote his biography, because he tells with amusement in his *Ep.* IV, 4, dated Florence, January 2, 1416 (ed. Mehus, I, 111), that "not long ago in Arezzo" he, Bruni, had seen a letter in which Cicero was replying to Petrarch.

35. "Ita solus, ut credo, hominum duo maxima munera et difficillima adimplevit." (Bruni in his *Cicero Novus seu Ciceronis Vita,* in *Leonardo Bruni Aretino, Humanistisch-philosophische Schriften,* ed. H. Baron, 1928, pp. 114 f.)

A scholarly amplification of this biographical outline—revealing, like Bruni's work, the mature historical consciousness of the fifteenth century—was the voluminous biography of Cicero in Sicco Polenton's *Scriptorum Illustrium Latinae Linguae Libri XVIII,* lib. X–XVI. Taking Bruni's notion of Cicero as his starting-point, Sicco endeavored to collect every single fact concerning Cicero's career as a writer, orator and statesman in order to create a biography as comprehensive as Cicero's historical personality itself. To Sicco, as to Bruni, Cicero's literary *otium* in his old age was not a haven which he never should have left, but one to which he returned "when contrary winds and waves had prevented him from sailing to the destination that he had fixed for himself." The activities of the *Forum* and the *Curia* were now replaced by philosophic studies, "ut scribendo saltem prodesset quibus dicendo, ut soleret, bene consulere tempora prohiberent." Ed. B. L. Ullman, *Papers and Monographs of the American Academy in Rome,* VI (1928), 265 f., 407, 408.

36. Berthe Widmer, *Enea Silvio Piccolomini in der sittlichen und politischen Entscheidung* (1963), pp. 20–21, to whom we owe this extension of our fifteenth-century evidence, states rightly that, although Campano's knowledge of the *Cicero Novus* cannot be proved by external evidence, the influence of Bruni's vision is unmistakable.

37. *Centotrenta lettere inedite di Francesco Barbaro,* ed. R. Sabbadini (1884), no. 1.

38. L. Giustiniani's *Funebris Oratio,* in Muratori, *Script. Rer. Ital.* XIX col. 375 f.; *Centotrenta lettere di Barbaro,* no. 95; *Franc. Barbari Epistolae,* ed. Card. A.M. Quirini (1743), Appendix, no. 50.

39. Cino Rinuccini, *Invettiva contro a cierti caluniatori di Dante . . . , Petrarcae . . . Boccaci,* in A. Wesselofsky, *Il paradiso degli Alberti,* I[2] (1867), 314.

40. Such an analysis has in part been made in my essays "La Rinascita dell'-Etica Statale Romana nell'Umanesimo Fiorentino," *Civiltà Moderna* VII (1935) 11 f., 27, and "Franciscan Poverty and Civic Wealth as Factors in the Rise of Humanistic Thought," *Speculum* XIII (1938) 23 f.; see now also A. Buck on Palmieri "als Repräsentant des Florentiner Burgerhumanismus," *Archiv fur Kulturgeschichte* XLVII (1965). The first words of the work, in which Palmieri describes the ideal union of a civic and a studious life, almost literally repeat, without acknowledging it, the introductory words of *De Oratore,* I, 1, 1.

41. *Della Vita Civile,* ed. F. Battaglia (1944), pp. 169 ff., 176.

42. Edited (attributed to a wrong author) in *Prose del giovane Buonaccorso da Montemagno* (1874), p. 18. On Porcari's authorship see G. Zaccagnini in *Studi di Letteratura Italiana,* I (1899), 339 ff.

43. See Guarino da Verona (*Ep.* 681, before 1441; *Epistolario,* ed. Sabbadini, II, 272): when Scipio and Laelius sought relaxation in the country-side, "nec ut laborem fugerent et inertiae sese dederent eos id factitasse constat, sed ut recentiores et ad novum laborem instauratiores se redderent otiabantur."

44. *De Ingenuis Moribus,* ed. Gnesotto, in *Atti e Memorie della R. Accad. di Padova* XXXIV (1918), 119 and 142.

45. *De Oratore,* III, 22, 82–83, 89; see p. 293 above (". . . ut, nisi quod quisque cito potuerit, numquam omnino possit perdiscere").

46. Paragraphs 18–109 of the third book of *De Oratore* had been unknown to the Middle Ages. See R. Sabbadini, *Le scoperte dei codici latini e greci ne' secoli XIV e XV,* I (1905), pp. 100 and 218.

47. Giovanni Villani on Dante in his *Cronaca,* lib. IX, 136. That Villani's view reflects a typical attitude in the Florence of his time is confirmed by what our sources tell us about Dante's friend, the learned poet Guido Cavalcanti, who in Compagni's chronicle is called a "giovane gentile, cortese, ardito, ma *sdegnoso e solitario e intento allo studio*"; in Baccaccio's *Decamerone, novella* VI, 9, he appears as "molto astratto dagli uomini."

Boccaccio's reproaches against Dante are found in his *Trattatello in laude di Dante,* as well as in his *Compendio della origine, vita, costumi e studii di Dante.*

48. Bruni's *Le Vite di Dante e di Petrarca,* in *Leonado Bruni Aretino, Humanistisch-philosophische Schriften,* pp. 53 f. ("E era cosa miracolosa, che, studiando continovamente, a niuna persona sarebbe paruto, che egli studiasse. . . . Anzi è vera conclusione e certissima, che quello, che non appara tosto, non appara mai.")

49. "Non cessat, . . . et cum tam multas res agat, deesse tamen videtur quod agat." This striking testimony is found in a letter already published in Angelo Fabroni's *Magni Cosmi Medicei Vita,* II (Pisa, 1788), 251.

II. Church

RURAL CHURCHES AND RURAL COMMUNITIES IN EARLY MEDIEVAL AUVERGNE*

Gabriel Fournier

I. RURAL CHURCHES IN THE MEROVINGIAN AGE

Beginning in the fourth century the number of rural churches increased both in the villages and hamlets of Gaul where independent landholders lived, and on the great domains of the aristocracy. In the beginning the episcopal cathedral had been the sole religious community of the *civitas,* and the first rural churches were strictly subject to it. They possessed neither their own particular clergy nor their own possessions or special districts; and a part of the faithful's religious activity necessarily took place in the mother church, where all the great holidays were celebrated.[1] But little by little certain churches acquired a growing independence, became the center of autonomous parishes called *"dioceses"*[2] in which all religious

* From Gabriel Fournier, *Le peuplement rural en Basse Auvergne durant le Haut Moyen Age* (Publications de la Faculté des Lettres et Sciences Humaines de Clermont-Ferrand, 2me série, 12). (Paris: Presses Universitaires de France, 1962), pp. 402–409, 411–414, 423–428, 432–433, 436–443, 445–457, 469–473. Trans. by the ed.

services were celebrated. In these churches the principal sacraments were administered; associated with each of them, in particular, was a baptistry separated from the church proper. Most often centered in the *vici*[3] or in fortified places, more rarely on the great domains, endowed with their own property, and usually headed by an archpriest, the earliest rural parishes as they appeared at the end of the sixth century were very large.[4]

Sidonius Apollinaris gives evidence for the existence of rural parishes in Auvergne at the end of the fifth century, when, as Bishop of Clermont, he mentions his visitations of the *dioceses*.[5] At least some of them, dating from the end of the Roman Empire or the Merovingian period, can be identified.

Most of the Auvergnat *vici* appear to have been parish centers in the sixth and seventh centuries.[6] Contemporary texts mention the *dioceses* of Brioude, Riom, and Issoire; and in a number of the *vici* a church of St. John long perpetuated the memory of an ancient separate baptistry (Artonne, Riom, Liziniat, Brioude, Vic-le-Comte, Lezoux, Mauriac). Fortresses were likewise parish centers. Evidence exists for an ancient baptismal group at Ronzières; others probably existed at St.-Jean–St.-Gervais and at Escorailles. In a number of these towns (Artonne, Liziniat, Vic-le-Comte, Brioude, Riom, and Ronzières) the church of St. John kept its baptismal functions until the end of the Old Regime.

Generally the presence of two churches in a town, one of them dedicated to St. John the Baptist, is strong evidence for the existence of an ancient parish.[7] A number of Auvergnat towns belong to this category. . . . In other towns the existence of an ancient baptistry explains why St. John the Baptist has remained the parish patron saint, although the church might today be dedicated to another. . . . For this reason we have some justification for including among the original parishes, those towns where St. John the Baptist has remained the parish patron although no trace of a baptistry remains and the church has another name. . . .[8]

We may estimate—if not with certainty, at least with some degree of probability—that the northern part of the ancient diocese of Clermont had a minimum of twenty parish centers during the Merovingian period. Our list is not exhaustive, but it conforms to what we know of the low density of the earliest parishes.[9] Their distribution, furthermore, was very uneven. Most were to be found along the Roman roads[10] and in the open country that had been inhabited since ancient times, in—or on the edge of—the regions were most of the population was concentrated. The first rural parishes appear to have been sown in a regular manner along the Allier River valley, through which the north-south routes passed. They also seem to have been numerous in the area of Mauriac, crossed by a route going towards the southwest. Their centers were sometimes only six to ten miles apart.

Out of these twenty or so proved or probable parish centers, eight were *vici* and two or three were fortresses; but the nature of the other places remains unknown. To be sure, some of them might have belonged to the former categories. But we know that beginning in the fifth and sixth centuries, domainial chapels were transformed into parishes[11] and it is probable that several of the most ancient Auvergnat parishes had such an origin. This is, for example, the most probable hypothesis for Vensat, where the baptismal group appears to have been formed by two churches constructed on neighboring domains.

At least two churches were built in each of these parish centers. One was used for the parish services. Its name varied from one place to another, but eight or nine of them seem to have been dedicated to the Virgin, like the earliest cathedral. Such a proportion could not have been the result of pure chance and must be explained by the habit of giving the early rural parishes, at the time of their creation as affiliates of the cathedral church, the same name as that of the mother church. Apart from these, most of the parish churches seem in general to have been placed under the patronage of one of the universal saints whose cults very early became dominant in the West. To the nine churches dedicated to the Virgin must be added two consecrated to the Holy Savior in southern Auvergne (Pleaux, Cerzat), one to St. Andrew (Massiac), one to St. Peter (Vic-le-Comte), one to St. Lawrence (Liziniat), one to St. Martin (Blesle), and one or two to St. Gervaisius (St.-Jean–St.-Gervais and perhaps Riom).[12] Dedications to local saints appear to have been exceptional; only the church of Vensat, which probably goes back to a private chapel, had St. Julian as patron. The other church of the parish group, always dedicated to St. John the Baptist and serving as baptistry, was usually constructed close by the parish church (although it might be a certain distance away as at Ronzières, Brioude, and Vensat). Whatever the distance, the two churches formed a single baptismal group, whose memory sometimes lasted very long.[13]

It often happened that a saint other than the patron of the parish church sooner or later became the object of popular devotion. The cult might have originated because of the presence of a tomb (St. Vitalina's at Artonne, St. Austremonius' at Issoire, St. Julian's at Brioude), a donation of relics—or even their passage through the town—(St. Germanus at Moussages, St. Baudilius at Trizac, St. Marcellinus at Cerzat), or an episode in the saint's life that had taken place in the parish center (St. Amabilis at Riom, St. Martin at Artonne). But these cults, which had their *raison d'être* in purely local circumstances, do not appear to have played any part in the origin of the parishes. They reflect, however, the growing place taken by the cult of saints and relics in the religious life of the early Middle Ages and explain the frequent presence, often as early as the Merovingian period, of a third church beside the baptismal group. It was only very late that the saint thus honored ended by supplanting the original patron of the parish, for example at Brioude, Issoire, and Riom.

This is not the place to study the religious life of these parishes. Let us simply note that clergy were permanently attached to each of these churches, where they celebrated all services, including the great liturgical feasts; where they baptized and probably gave the other sacraments as well. At the end of the seventh century, however, the priests at the head of these parishes were still obliged to present themselves before their bishop at Easter,[14] an obligation perpetuating the memory of the times when part of the cult, particularly all the great holidays, were required to be celebrated at the mother church, that is, in the episcopal city.[15]

All rural churches did not have the rank of parish churches; within the limits of each parish other less important churches existed.[16] Among these were the chapels built on the domains of the aristocracy.[17] It was probably one of these that Sidonius Apollinaris visited at a magnate's request, at Chantelle.[18] Gregory of Tours on several occasions also mentions them. . . .

To these chapels built in inhabited areas, we must add those built out in the fields, in a place to which was attached the memory of a saint. . . .[19]

The dedication of several of these chapels to saints such as St. Julian —whose cult began to develop at the end of the fifth century, St. Symphorianus—whose cult spread above all in the second half of the sixth century, St. Saturninus—whose relics crossed Auvergne in the sixth century, St. Cyricus—for whose cult we have evidence at Clermont in the sixth century, as well as the few foundations that Gregory of Tours allows us to date, suggest that if private sanctuaries existed as early as the second half of the fifth century, they began to multiply only at the beginning of the sixth. In the beginning, and according to canon law, these buildings were to serve only for individual or collective prayer, and no clergy were permanently attached to their service. Such, probably, was the chapel built by a peasant in the vicinity of Brioude. Very early, however, bishops apparently allowed mass to be celebrated, at least under certain circumstances. . . .[20]

The gradual Christianization of the countryside also led to an increasing number of monasteries and hermitages. As everywhere in the West, this movement had both an urban and a rural side to it; but only the latter will be considered here.

Gregory of Tours mentions several monasteries existing in Auvergne in his own days—Randan in the north of the Limagne;[21] the monastery (probably St.-Pourçain-sur-Sioule) where St. Pourcainus sought refuge while he was a slave and later became abbot;[22] the *"monasterium Canbidobrense,"* mentioned twice, but whose location cannot be identified;[23] Cournon, six miles from Clermont, also mentioned twice;[24] and Méallet in the mountains near Mauriac.[25]

Gregory also speaks of a number of hermits, some of whom founded lasting monastic establishments. A few, as was common among the early ascetics, did not go far from inhabited areas but sought lonely spots near the towns to withdraw from the confusion of the world without losing all contact with their contemporaries. . . .[26] Others, on the contrary, sought the deep solitude of the woods, despite the ecclesiastical hierarchy's hostility to this form of anarchic monasticism.[27] Recall St. Emilianus and St. Brachio who founded the church of La Cellette and the monastery of Pionsat; such, also, was St. Patroclus who established the monastery of Colombier near Néris.[28] St. Caluppanus, the butt of criticisms from the monks of Méallet whose company he had entered a little time before, withdrew to the well-enclosed and barely accessible valley of Marlhoux, where he fashioned his hermitage from a cave in a steep and isolated rock.[29]

A little later great landowners began to establish monasteries on their properties, building them most often in places that were already inhabited, following a widespread custom in sixth- and seventh-century Gaul.[30] Such were the monasteries of Manglieu, whose foundation is attributed to St. Genesius in the second quarter of the seventh century; Volvic, the work of Avit II who was bishop of Clermont at the end of the seventh century; and Mozat, which appears to have been contemporary with Volvic.[31]

By means of a few texts and some archeological information we can reconstruct the religious topography of a few of these monasteries. The most striking fact is certainly the presence of several churches in the places where these monasteries were located, in particular at Saint-Pourçain, Cournon, Manglieu, and Volvic.[32] These sanctuaries were of two different kinds[33]—either chapels placed around the monasteries, in accordance with a practice inherited from primitive eremitic monasticism, or else part of the monasteries themselves, a development attributable to the liturgy and the way in which the offices were celebrated. The relative dispersion of the chapels around Mozat, and the distance between them, suggests the former type, although the possibility that they were of the latter type cannot be excluded. Most Auvergnat establishments of any considerable size had at least two churches within their walls, a situation recalling the practice on the great contemporary domains. The arrangment of these churches, sometimes next to each other and symmetrically placed (Manglieu and undoubtedly Saint-Pourçain),[34] sometimes irregularly placed (Volvic and undoubtedly Cournon),[35] did not differ from the layout of other ancient monasteries, which almost always had several churches. . . .[36]

Churches were thus quite numerous in the Auvergnat countryside during the Merovingian period. Some very early took on parish functions and can be recognized by the presence of a separate baptistry; almost all the *vici,* some of the fortresses, and perhaps some of the domains were parish centers. The other sanctuaries were chapels built by hermits or laymen, were monastic or pilgrimage churches, or were commemorative monuments.[37] Graveyards were created around these various holy places and slowly became the principal places of burial. Aside from a few hermit chapels and monasteries set up in deserted spots and in the middle of the forests, most of the churches were located in those parts of Auvergne where the rural population was concentrated, especially in the areas through which ran the ancient roads.[38]

These rural sanctuaries, generally giving shelter to a saint's tomb or relics, benefited not only from the prestige attached to holy places and burial grounds, but also from fiscal privileges. Several kings temporarily relieved the churches of Auvergne from taxes; thus they contributed to their wealth and, as a result, to the development of the churches' power. Theodobert freed the region's churches from the tribute they owed the fisc;[39] Childebert did the same for its churches, monasteries, and clergy.[40] The churches also served the surrounding population as places of refuge from danger;[41] in the days of Gregory of Tours, the church of St. Julien of Brioude appears to have been an asylum particularly sought-after.[42]

Holy place, burial ground, beneficiary of fiscal privilege, place of refuge—the rural church in the Merovingian period was a privileged building, called upon to play a determining role in the process of settlement. . . .

II. RURAL CHURCHES FROM THE NINTH TO ELEVENTH CENTURIES

Two important facts mark the history of rural churches in Gaul after the Merovingian period: their number grew considerably, since numerous landowners established new ones on their lands; and most of them, whether new foundations or ancient structures, belonged to the people who owned the land, for whom they represented a source of income like the land itself.[43] The frequency with which the chapter of Brioude and the abbey of Sauxillanges acquired these churches during the Carolingian period (mainly in the tenth century) proves how numerous religious buildings had become in the Auvergnat countryside, and the records of these transactions allow us to describe a few of their characteristics.

All the churches we know of were in the hands of lay or ecclesiastical landowners who owned them outright and could do with them as they did with their other possessions. Sometimes they were considered part of the *indominicatum* [direct domain]—all the churches the priory of Mauriac possessed at the beginning of the ninth century, enumerated in the inventory of its domain about 822, were of this kind; in the localities described, the monks' *indominicatum* consisted of only this building.[44] The same was true for the church of St.-Victor-sur-Massiac, granted in 933 to the chapter of Brioude.[45] Churches were often counted among the lands grouped around a *curtis* or manor. The manors of Huillaux, Sauxillanges, Brassac, Mont-Dore, Fontannes, Anglards, St.-Etienne-de-

Riom, Mercoeur, St.-Victor-sur-Massiac, and Peschadoires each had one or several churches, located either next to the lord's residence or quite near it.[46] When lands were transferred, the church generally followed the other lands of the *curtis* or manor to which it was attached (although it might be separated, as apparently happened at the beginning of the tenth century at Mercoeur, where the church and manor, probably as the result of a division, belonged to different members of the local seignorial family).[47] On occasion, the church represented a foreign element in these vast assemblages of land, incorporated only at the time of its acquisition; the church of Gignat, acquired by the Duke of Acquitaine at the beginning of the tenth century, was a part of the *curtis* of Sauxillanges by 927;[48] the church of Fontannes, granted to the chapter of Brioude at the beginning of the tenth century along with the neighboring *curtis,* had been acquired by Viscount Armand a little before 898.[49] In fact, most of the churches granted to the chapter of Brioude or the abbey of Sauxillanges during the Carolingian period were done so independently of any *curtis* or manor.

As in the rest of Gaul, so in tenth-century Auvergne the institution of the private church, which had spontaneously developed during the seventh century[50] and had later been recognized by Carolingian legislation,[51] was a generalized phenomenon. But the possession of such private churches was not the monopoly of the great landlords; if some were part of those vast assemblages clustered around a manor, others were constructed on less imposing properties by small landholders living in the villages.[52]

Generally the private church had appurtenances that were granted with it,[53] appurtenances defined in several charters as a collection of *mansi,* fields, vineyards, woods,[54] and sometimes mills[55]—landed possessions that might represent everything the donor had in the *villa.*[56] This group of church and appurtenances, even when incorporated into a manor, formed a unit of exploitation to a certain extent similar to the other units into which landlords divided their possessions for ease of operations. The rural church was thus the nucleus of a group of lands and buildings that formed its patrimony and its endowment.[57]

Among these private churches, some went back to ancient Merovingian sanctuaries. They had passed into the patronage and possession of a neighboring lord who, whether heir of the founder or not, assured their protection.[58] It was probably in this way that several of the original parish churches of Auvergne, along with their baptistry and often with a third church, found their way into the hands of great landed proprietors during the Carolingian period. . . . Other private churches were of more recent origin. For throughout Gaul the number of rural churches grew considerably during the eighth and ninth centuries.[59] They were the creations of landowners who provided the land, paid the construction costs, and endowed the new building with its own landed possessions. . . .

These landowners were responsible for the existence of several neighboring churches in the same place. In the earliest parish centers, a third church is often mentioned beside the parish church and its baptistry.[60] There were two churches at Sauxillanges when a monastery was located on the comital domain there in 927,[61] two churches at Chanteuges when an abbey was built there in 936,[62] and three churches at Chauriat when a priory of Sauxillanges was built there in 1016/1025.[63] These multiple churches, often very near one another (numerous examples were also to be found in the cities),[64] undoubtedly were contemporary or successive foundations, the work of one or of several proprietors who wanted to construct a sanctuary for their own use or for that of their tenants, who built to fulfill a vow or to shelter some newly acquired relics.[65] (One cannot exclude the hypothesis that at least in some places, especially in the very ancient parishes, the multiplication of churches might have been in one way or another connected with the procession of the stational liturgy.)

The religious needs of the inhabitants were also taken into consideration. They explain, to a certain degree, both the increased number of churches and their location. Difficulty in traveling to already existing churches brought about the creation of new ones. Individual initiative was limited, however, by the requirement that any new foundation be authorized by the bishop. Before consecrating the church (an indispensable requirement if services were to be celebrated), the bishop inquired about the building's usefulness and the choice of location and also made certain that the endowment would suffice for the upkeep of the building and give a decent living to the man who served it; he also established the tithes that would be due the new foundation.[66] In more than one case, it is true, the construction of a church appears to have preceded the bishop's agreement. This was probably the case at Bousselargues, where the name of the proposed church had not yet been selected when the decision was made to build it. At Chanet the church was probably built despite a first unfavorable decision by the bishop; after it was completed, the founders and the faithful made another attempt to get it consecrated. But these cases themselves prove that any new church had to fulfill certain conditions (concerning mainly the choice of site and the sufficiency of its endowment) in which the interests of the inhabitants and the church were involved; for, in the end, the bishop had to be asked for his approval. If individual proprietors initiated construction by providing the land and paying building costs, the consecration of the church and its use for services depended largely on the religious needs of the surrounding population.

Once the bishop recognized the utility of the new building, the only further condition appears to have been the creation of a sufficient endowment, whose character reflects the proponderant place of the founder in the construction of any new church. To be sure, a significant part of the property and tithes making up this endowment were located in the immediate environs of the new building, within what might be called its territory. But other tithes and lands were given to it, sometimes more than a dozen miles away. This was clearly the case with the churches of Blanède and Chanet, which appear to have been the work of a single landowner whose lands were divided between the valley and the mountains. The endowment of the church of Chanet, established on the edge of the area of fixed habitation, contained land in the valley whose income was less aleatory and also furnished supplementary resources such as wine. The church's original inheritance kept the fragmented character of its founder's. . . .[67]

In the tenth century churches were to be found everywhere in Auvergne. Since, despite a relatively abundant documentation, we know of only a few foundations occurring at this time and since numerous texts speak of already existent churches, many of these buildings probably dated from the ninth or even from the eighth century, the same period when churches multiplied throughout Gaul.[68]

About the place of these churches in the religious life of the countryside we know comparatively little. All those we have spoken of were dedicated to a saint and thus were consecrated.[69] At least part of the cult, the mass and some of the sacraments, could be celebrated there. But according to foundation charters and charters of donation, the possessions of these churches in the tenth century included only land and tithes; no specifically ecclesiastical revenues are ever mentioned. Offerings at the mass, first-fruits, and funerary and baptismal dues are listed among the possessions of churches only after the beginning of the eleventh century.[70] Similarly, only during the eleventh century did people begin to call the territory belonging to the rural churches by the name *parochia*.[71] Found once in the second half of the tenth century as a synonym for *vicaria* and *centena* (a secular administrative district, whose center, to be sure, had long contained a parish church),[72] *parochia* is first used to mean a district belonging to a church in documents dating from 960 and the first half of the eleventh century.[73] The usage does not seem to have become common before the second half of the century. The language of Auvergnat charters thus seems to suggest that specifically parish revenues, deriving not only from the mass but from baptisms and burials as well, came to belong to most of the rural churches only during the course of the eleventh century.

These developments thus parallel the development of the canon law, which only gradually generalized the parishional functions of the rural churches. Many sanctuaries were very early allowed to receive offerings and first-fruits.[74] But in the ninth century, baptism, marriage, and confession, at least in principle, still had to be celebrated in the ancient parish church.[75]

Similarly, right of burial was apparently only gradually allowed most of the rural churches. Despite an ever more general wish to be buried near a church, or even in one,[76] the practice of burying the dead on their own lands had not yet disappeared.[77] A charter from the region of Brioude that appears to date from the eleventh century, granting a *mansus* "where Stephen Dosso was buried," is perhaps a very late witness to this custom.[78] If the practice had not disappeared, it was, in any event, exceptional. In what church, then, were the dead to be buried? By the end of the ninth century the law allowed people to be buried in the church where they had paid the tithe, at least when it was impossible to carry the body to the cathedral church or to a church served by monks or canons.[79] The law was very loose. For all practical purposes, people could be buried near almost any church, and not necessarily either the parish church or the nearest one.[80] It is therefore not surprising that rights of burial, even for people not residing near them, were allowed the most famous monasteries. In the second half of the tenth century numerous donors to the chapter of Brioude and the abbey of Sauxillanges made gifts *pro sepultura* [with a view to burial].[81] One specified that he wished to be buried in the cloister of St. Julian.[82] For a long time this right was counted among the privileges of the abbeys of Sauxillanges and Ebreuil.[83] In a period when funerary rights became one of the fundamental rights of parish churches, this privilege, which prohibited parish priests from preventing their parishioners' burial in the monastic cemetery, must have been a survival of the Carolingian practice that allowed every individual free choice of cemetery —with the preference going to monastic and capitular churches.

Thus, both canon law and the make-up of church property suggest that the private churches of Auvergne succeeded in winning their autonomy from the older parish churches during the tenth century, although the priests who served the older churches continued to claim at least a *de jure* monopoly of the most important religious ceremonies if not of all services. Around these rural churches a group of faithful slowly grew. Within them the rural faithful habitually received at least some of the sacraments and fulfilled their everyday religious duties; to them they paid the tithe; and in their cemeteries they were buried. More and more, these churches came to resemble those of the parish center.[84] The development was completed in the eleventh century. Henceforth the small parish would be one of the most active scenes for rural life as well as its most stable framework.[85]

Although they had parish functions, many rural churches continued in the eleventh and twelfth centuries to belong to laymen who treated them as their own property. We need not go into a development that goes beyond the chronological limits of our study. But several important points may be noted. These private churches and their appurtenances were subject to all kinds of transactions by their owners. In the process, parish rights were divided up; they did not necessarily end in the hands of the person who held the church (which might itself be divided). Churches, like lands, were enfeoffed. It is not exceptional to come across churches in the hands of a vassal, forming the nucleus of a small fief. But in the eleventh and twelfth centuries, as in preceding centuries, numerous proprietors gave their churches to monastic communities. In a few cases this action was perhaps only a restoration of a church that had been usurped, but most of the time the donor gave a church that had never belonged to anyone but to himself and his ascendants.

In this way, at the same time as they acquired parish functions during the tenth and eleventh centuries, more and more of the private churches came into the hands of abbeys and chapters. The donors, by showing their largesse, put their consciences to rest, for the ecclesiastical authorities had never stopped questioning the legitimacy of lay ownership of churches.[86] Furthermore, by granting the church to a monastery or to a chapter of canons, the donors assured better service for the parish, for a monk was thereafter attached to the sanctuary, which became the seat of a tiny priory.[87]

At the same time that private churches were multiplying, new monastic foundations were added to those whose origins went back to the Merovingian period. Whether old or new these foundations occupied a growing place in many towns and villages, taking over more land, sometimes becoming principal lord of their towns and bringing an ever-growing number of churches under their control.

At the beginning of the Carolingian period many ancient monasteries dating from the Merovingian age were rebuilt at the initiative of the kings of Aquitaine, undoubtedly following the crisis brought on by the secularization of monasteries in the eighth century. Others witnessed new activity after welcoming famous relics within their walls. . . . But Merovingian monasteries formed only a small proportion of the establishments existing at the end of the Carolingian period. For during this period the number of monasteries and chapters had also increased in the villages and towns of Auvergne.[88]

During the Carolingian period or immediately thereafter, many of the ancient *vici* became the seats of chapters, monasteries, or priories, whose presence played a decisive role in the reorganization of these towns' topography. By the ninth century Issoire had a monastery, whose origin seems to be related to the resurgence of the cult of St. Austremonius. A monastery was also founded at Mauriac in the ninth century. In 817 Brioude became the seat of a chapter; Liziniat, in 945. From the beginning these chapters were the principal lords of their towns. Chapters also existed in ninth-century Artonne, Riom, Lezoux, and Billom. A large number of ancient parish churches in the former *vici* thus passed into the hands of monks and canons, especially the latter. As for the other churches that often existed within these towns, some fell to the same monastic communities (St.-

Priest at Brioude, St.-Clément at Liziniat, probably St.-Avit at Issoire) while others became secondary priories belonging to other monasteries (St.-Pierre at Brioude, St.-Loup at Billom).

The Carolingian foundations were not limited to *vici;* others were established in less important places.[89] All were the work of great landed proprietors. Most of the time these great lords installed new monastic or canonical communities in churches that already existed on their lands (Moissat, Sauxillanges, Chanteuges, Chantelle, Chauriat, St.-Genés at Thiers). At other times the founding of a monastery was also the occasion for the construction of a new church, either next to the original one and thus in a town that already existed (Sauxillanges, Moissat), or else on uninhabited land nearby (Lavoûte).

Our documentation allows us to reconstruct the plan of these monasteries. They show a gradual abandonment of the multiple churches that had characterized the communities of an earlier period. . . . The monastic church or churches were enclosed by a vast walled circumference (still recognizable in the plans of the villages of Ris, Moissat, and Sauxillanges), which, like those around the more ancient monasteries of Manglieu and Volvic, were similar to the walls that closed off aristocratic residences; at Moissat and Sauxillanges, in fact, they seem to have been the successors of such residences. These walls recall the ones that protected the church and monastic quarters in the *vici* of Brioude, St.-Germain-Lembron, and probably Issoire. Since numerous monasteries throughout Gaul were fortified during the second half of the ninth century,[90] we are probably justified in believing that they functioned as both monastic enclosures and defensive palisades. At Brioude the ancient castle southeast of the cloistral buildings, reconstructed at the beginning of the ninth century, was continuously maintained; it is mentioned in the second half of the ninth century, and its exterior wall is mentioned in the tenth. Elsewhere monastic walls were backed by a *motte* [a fortified hillock], still identifiable at St.-Germain-Lembron, Issoire, and Moissat.[91] Built by a protector or by a vassal of the abbot, these hillocks clearly had a defensive purpose. At Marsat and Blesle the monastery was flanked by a castle (although, because of later radical alterations, it is impossible to tell the original arrangement). In many places, such as Chantelle, Chanteuges, and St.-Flour, the monasteries were built on natural defensive sites that had earlier been used as fortresses and they continued, at least upon occasion, to play a military role. At the end of the eleventh century the original monastery at St.-Flour was destroyed during a war and its land was given in fief by a lord to one of his vassals; Chanteuges at the beginning of the twelfth century was transformed into a castle and became a nest of robbers.[92] These incidents are enough to show that the castles constructed within monastic walls or in their immediate vicinity were not always put there with the abbot's permission. . . .

In the Carolingian period several monasteries, both ancient and more recent in origin, as well as some churches outside Auvergne for their lands in the region, received royal diplomas of immunity that made them privileged communities—the abbey of Manglieu[93] and the chapter of Brioude[94] in the ninth century; the Archbishop of Reims, who received such a diploma from Pepin I for the goods of his church located in Auvergne;[95] St. Martin of Tours, granted one by Pepin in 828 for the *villa* of Marsat, which had just been restored to it.[96] The privilege was much sought after, and when the monstery of Chanteuges was founded in 936 on land belonging to the chapter of Brioude, the founder made sure the new establishment would have it.[97]

Immunity was essentially a judicial and fiscal privilege, which not only freed the immunist from certain levies due the king (such as lodging rights) but above all, by prohibiting all royal officers from entering the land of the immunist, allowed the latter to exercise regalian rights for his own profit.[98] Since the immunist continued to levy royal taxes and dues and to enforce other regalian rights, immunity in theory brought no advantage to the people living on his land. But it did protect them from the exactions of royal and comital officers, who were often hard on their subjects and were not above abusive use of their judicial and fiscal power.[99] The inhabitants of immunist lands thus benefited from the better quality of ecclesiastical organization, which showed its superiority especially after the decay of Carolingian power, when the counts escaped entirely from the control of royal authority. To a large degree the power at the disposal of the immunist churches gave them the material means to defend themselves from an encroaching lay feudalism, to defend both themselves and their men from the lay lords.

The control of commerce, of the movement of men and goods, soon appeared as a derivative of the immunist's exercise of regalian rights. Toward the end of the tenth century or at the beginning of the eleventh, the chapter of Brioude, by virtue of diplomas of immunity reissued at that time, levied river tolls, bridge tolls, road tolls, and taxes on the market held beneath its wall.[100] By means of the immunity the chapter gained control of the commercial activity of the ancient *vicus* of Brioude. The right to hold a market and regulate it is even specifically mentioned in a diploma of immunity granted an abbey of Velay in the ninth century.[101] But whether the right to hold a market was derived from the exercise of regalian rights, whether it came from a special authorization, or was simply usurped, the fact remains that in Auvergne from the ninth century on, numerous markets were linked to the presence of a monastic establishment—Brioude, Sauxillanges,[102] Mozat, Riom,[103] Moissat,[104] Thiers,[105] all known from eleventh- and twelfth-century texts.

Churches were thus much more numerous in the ninth- and tenth-century countryside of Auvergne than they had been in the sixth century.

Most were private churches, built by landowners on their own property; and from the eleventh century on they functioned as parish churches. A number of monasteries were also created. Some of these brought about the construction of new churches, but most were installed in already existing ones. More and more the monasteries acquired the private churches, installed tiny priories in them and performed the parish services.

III. THE ROLE OF CHURCHES IN THE DEVELOPMENT OF SETTLEMENT PATTERNS

The location of churches and monasteries in the countryside to a large extent reflects the pattern of settlement. With few exceptions, most sanctuaries were built in the middle or on the edge of localities with dispersed population, so that their multiplication followed not only the progressive Christianization of the countryside but the progression of land settlement as well. A map of tenth-century churches allows us to chart tenth-century populations before the number of seignorial castles began to increase. Once built, these religious buildings formed poles of attraction for the neighboring population. They played an important role in changing village plans.

Almost everywhere in Gaul the Carolingian period saw houses spring up around monastic establishments, giving birth to monastic towns.[106] Some were of ancient origin; during the tenth and eleventh centuries a number of *vici* regrouped themselves around the monasteries or chapters located within their boundaries.[107] Others grew on the lands of former aristocratic domains. The history of Sauxillanges, Moissat, and Ebreuil, transformed from aristocratic residences into monastic towns, show how closely the birth of the new settlements was related to the transformation in the layout of conventual buildings.

As early as the first half of the eleventh century, houses had been built at Sauxillanges next to the monastery and even within its original walls. At the end of the century this quarter, in which a church of Notre-Dame had been built after the monastery's foundation, and which had its own market, formed part of a town that had spread westward toward another church (St. Martin); the monastic buildings were regrouped around the two original churches, where they remained until the end of the Old Regime.[108]

At Moissat a monastic town developed in the last quarter of the eleventh century around the church of St.-Lomer, which the monks had built a few hundred feet from the ancient church of St.-Pierre. (They had received the latter at the time of the monastery's foundation.) Within the walls of the ancient *villa,* the town, endowed with a market, grew around the church of St.-Pierre, (now turned into the parish church); the monastic buildings were regrouped around St.-Lomer.[109]

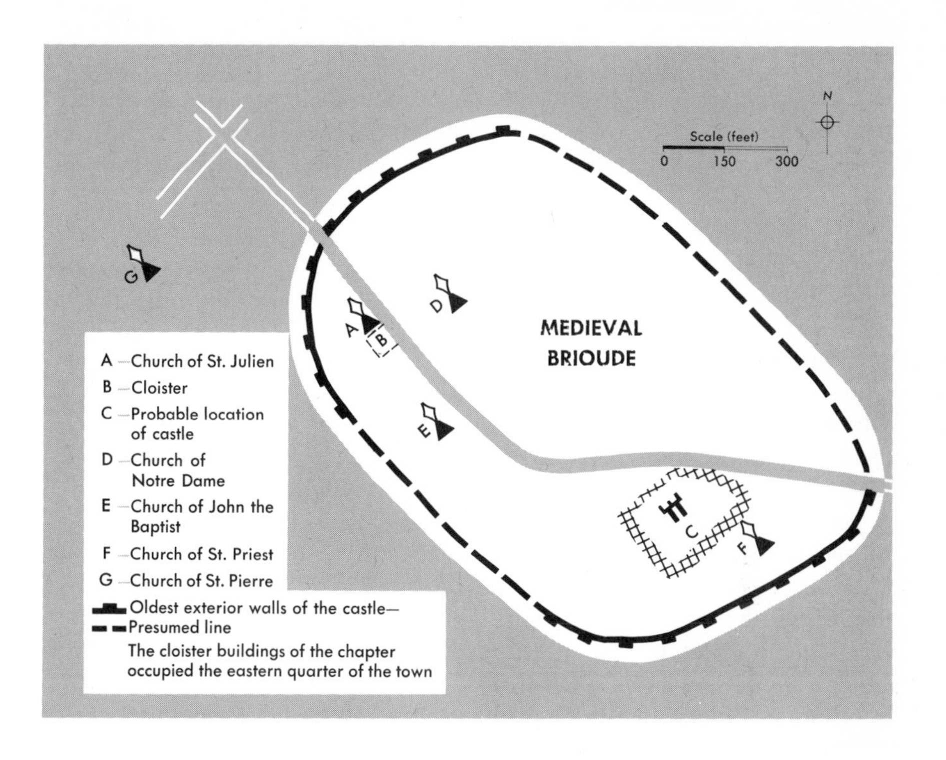
Scale (feet)
0 150 300
N
MEDIEVAL
BRIOUDE
A
B
C
D
E
F
G
A —Church of St. Julien
B —Cloister
C —Probable location
of castle
D —Church of
Notre Dame
E —Church of John the
Baptist
F —Church of St. Priest
G —Church of St. Pierre
Oldest exterior walls of the castle—
Presumed line
The cloister buildings of the chapter
occupied the eastern quarter of the town

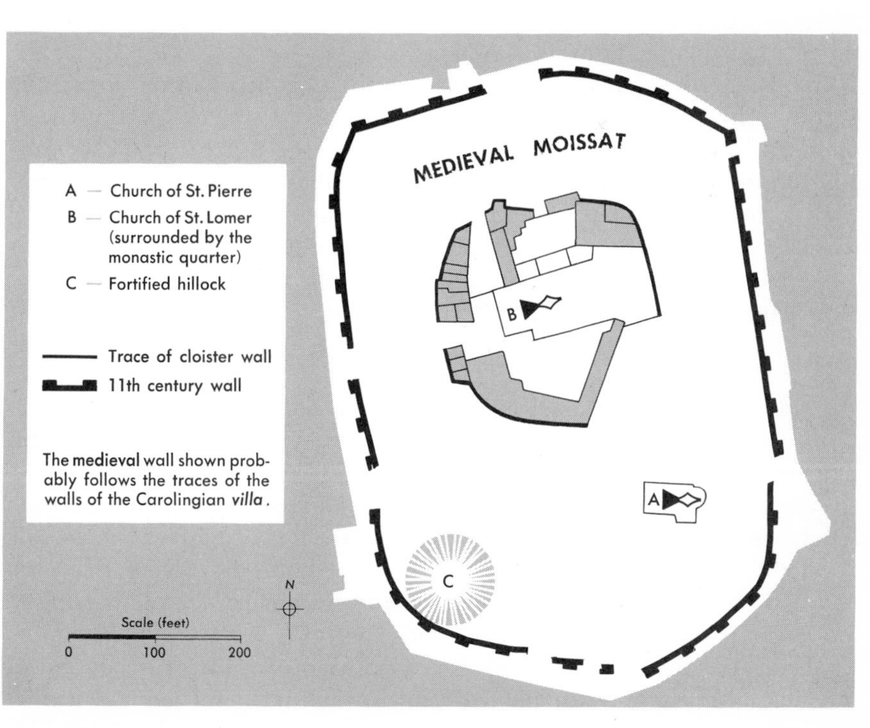
MEDIEVAL MOISSAT
A
B
C
A — Church of St. Pierre
B — Church of St. Lomer
(surrounded by the
monastic quarter)
C — Fortified hillock
Trace of cloister wall
11th century wall
The medieval wall shown probably follows the traces of the walls of the Carolingian villa.
N
Scale (feet)
0 100 200

At Ebreuil the monks apparently found a church already in existence on their installation there, probably the chapel of the ancient royal palace. They built a second to house the relics of St. Leger and by the end of the eleventh century had abandoned the original church to the town's inhabitants.[110]

In all three cases the monks, taking over former comital or royal residences, kept their general layout while adapting them to their conventual needs. However, during the tenth and eleventh century the growth of a town with its own market around one of the early churches, sometimes spreading out beyond the original walls, transformed the original plan. When the monasteries stopped using multiple sanctuaries, or at least reduced their number, conventual buildings were regrouped around one or several of the churches now reserved to the monks, while the other church was given over to the town's inhabitants for their own use.

Apart from these three cases, insufficient documentation makes it difficult to know how villages were reorganized after a monastery was founded in their midst. It is certain only that the development was not everywhere the same nor the results everywhere identical. . . . One must therefore not generalize too much. It is nevertheless certain that the founding of a monastery in an ancient *vicus* or any other village and the tight regrouping of monastic buildings during the tenth and eleventh centuries were events of tremendous consequence. The results recall, *mutatis mutandis,* the transformations of episcopal city plans brought about by the introduction of chapters of canons.[111]

A similar development took place around churches that were only parish churches or tiny priories. Our texts show that constructions were often thrown up in the immediate vicinity of the churches and that each one formed the nucleus of a quarter whose houses sometimes were built right against the sanctuary. . . .[112] Some of these were built on land belonging to the church, so that the texts use the terms *"locus ecclesiae"* or *"villa ecclesiae"* to designate the quarter around the church whose houses were part of its possessions. . . .[113] It sometimes happened, as in the case of the *vicus* of Liziniat (which became St.-Germain), that the name of the church ended by replacing the ancient name of the town. . . .[114] In this way, in a certain number of cases during the tenth century, place names formed from a saint's name replaced a more ancient one, a change that sharply reflected the place taken by the church in the village's development.

The growing number of monastic towns and the regrouping of houses around tiny priories and country churches were but two aspects of a single development: the growing place of the church in the life of the rural population.[115] Auvergne is not very richly documented on this subject, but we may summarize what is generally known.

There was first of all the privileged position of these churches and of the land and people belonging to them. In the ninth and tenth centuries,

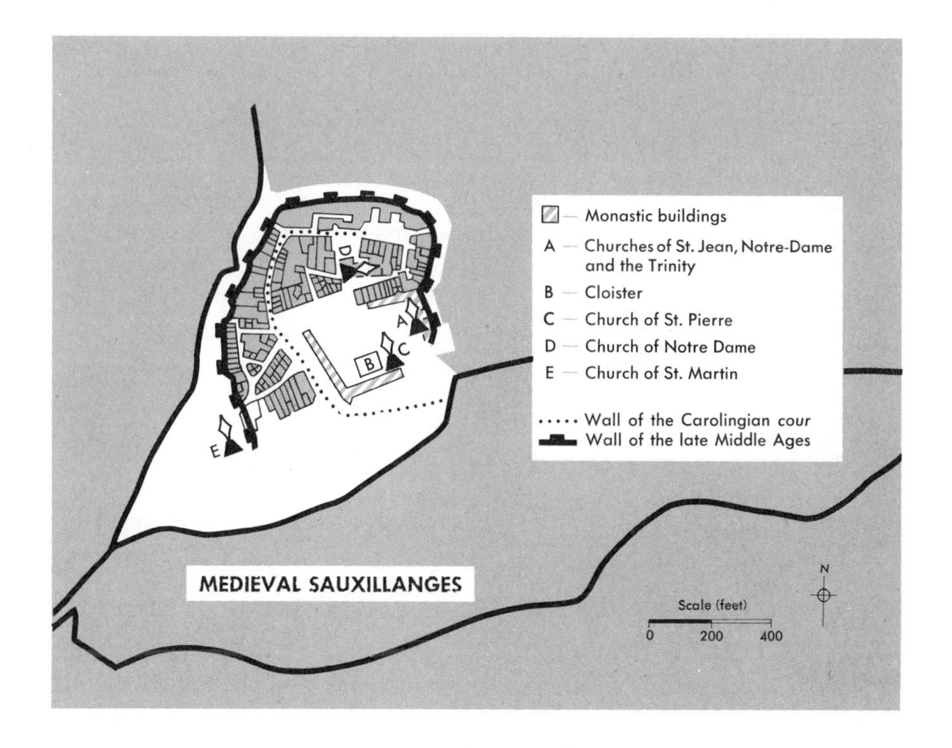

as during the Merovingian period, the churches served everywhere as places of refuge. The church, as a holy building, was inviolable. To break into it was sacrilege; within it people could seek asylum.[116] By the eleventh century these rights had been extended to the cemetery and, more generally, to an area around the church called the "thirty church paces" (*trente pas ecclesiastique*), corresponding to what the age considered the ideal dimensions of a cemetery.[117] From the middle of the eleventh century this area was singled out as enjoying the right of asylum along with the church, provided there were no fortifications within it.[118]

For beginning in the Carolingian period, religious buildings were more and more turned into fortresses—after the monasteries, some of which were fortified by the end of the ninth century,[119] rural churches and their cemeteries.[120] If no fortified churches are mentioned with certainty before the end of the tenth century,[121] during the eleventh the practice became so common that ecclesiastical authorities repeatedly had to prohibit it and withdraw the right of asylum from the buildings thus transformed.[122] For fortification, either by the local clergy and inhabitants or by the local lord for his own use, was too necessary to strengthen the purely symbolic character of a right of asylum that was often violated. The church, furthermore, was usually the most carefully built and the largest building within the village and, with the enclosed cemetery around it, nearly reproduced the layout and the size of contemporary castles. The church tower served as castle-keep, and one had only to replace the cemetery fence with an earth and wood palisade to make the cemetery resemble a castle's inner court. Such constructions are mentioned in the twelfth century.[123]

Under these circumstances, it is not surprising that, given the insecurity of the times, the rural population tended in the eleventh century to gather as near as possible to the church in order to benefit from its right of asylum and its defensive walls. Not only did they find temporary refuge in the cemeteries: they even built their homes there. Cemeteries were colonized, were invaded little by little by houses and markets.[124]

Apart from the churches already fortified by the tenth century, the only Auvergnat documents explicitly mentioning the right of asylum are later than the eleventh century.[125] Two facts, however, are worth mentioning. First of all, many churches occupy the top of a small isolated butte or the end of a mountain spur.[126] The dimensions of these isolated heights—averaging forty to fifty meters in diameter—recall those "thirty church paces," the area protected by the right of asylum; they are also about the same size as many *motte* and bailey castles. The character of these sites suggests that defensive preoccupations were not foreign to the thoughts of those who decided where to build them. Second, the practice of holding the market in the cemetery of the church of St.-Genès, still found at Thiers in the nineteenth century,[127] was surely a survival from medieval times. For medieval men, the land around the church was for the living as well as for the dead.

More generally, the wish to benefit from the advantages of an ecclesiastical seigniory probably influenced much village reorganization, especially around monasteries and priories. Because of their size, their wealth, their privileges, and the extent of their landed holdings, ecclesiastical lords were to be counted among the most powerful. This power turned their lands into economic centers, which explains the frequent presence of markets—and the social classes these markets attracted—next door to the monasteries. Most important, the ecclesiastical lords by fortifying their monasteries and churches, or more simply by defending their privileges, guaranteed to the people living on their land a particularly effective protection from the lay lords of the neighborhood. In the eleventh century the chapter of Brioude received charters of safeguard from their neighboring lords, the form of one of which remains. It guaranteed the security of the church, the town, its market and the neighboring population.[128] At the end of the century the abbey of Moissat persuaded the lord of the town to free the monastic town from the dues he levied there and to move his castle.[129] About the middle of the same century the monks of Sauxillanges freed their churches at Tauves, St.-Hilaire-sous-Monton and St.-

Martial, along with their villages or quarters, from the dues that their neighboring lords demanded;[130] and in 1095 Sauxillanges' papal safeguard was extended to the surrounding town. . . .[131]

Under the circumstances, one can well understand the desire of rural people to fix themselves as closely as possible to churches, which in these troubled times brought them a little security. It was thus the tenth and eleventh centuries that saw the regrouping of settlement in those places that had a church building, a movement which came earlier and more forcefully the more important the sanctuary that formed its nucleus. . . .

A study of the location of churches built prior to the eleventh century shows that the map of parishes was then very similar to what it is today, not only in the valleys but, at least in part, in the mountains as well. The parish framework, with the exception of a few details, was the work of the Carolingian period.[132]

But, contrary to what one might think, the map of small Carolingian parishes provides information neither on the relative size of villages nor on the precise distribution of population. For, as we have seen, despite episcopal control, a large part was played by private initiative and chance in the founding of these rural churches and in the creation of their districts. This explains the eccentricity of some parish divisions;[133] one of the most curious phenomena is certainly the way some *villae* were divided among several neighboring parishes. For it is common to come across lands bearing the name of ancient places which stretch across both sides of a parish boundary. . . .

Thus the construction of new churches, and the resettlement that followed, to a great extent broke apart the ancient framework of rural settlement and changed the relative size of inhabited places. But it is well known that feudal castles also played a role in these changes; and to complete our survey, we must now examine the effects of the increased number of castle chapels.

The frequent lack of concordance between the sites of post-Carolingian castles and their parish churches[134] demonstrates that in many cases the development of a castle town did not bring with it a breakup of the earlier parish. The increasing number of castles built from the tenth century on, and especially in the eleventh, however, could not help but change the ecclesiastical map. As we have seen, already at an early date churches were built within castle walls or next door to them (and sometimes both). Some remained what they originally were—simple seignorial chapels. Others were erected for the sake of the people living around the castle. Both often became the seats of priories or chapters, a development that increased their importance. But some from the beginning, or after a long history, achieved the rank of parish church.[135]

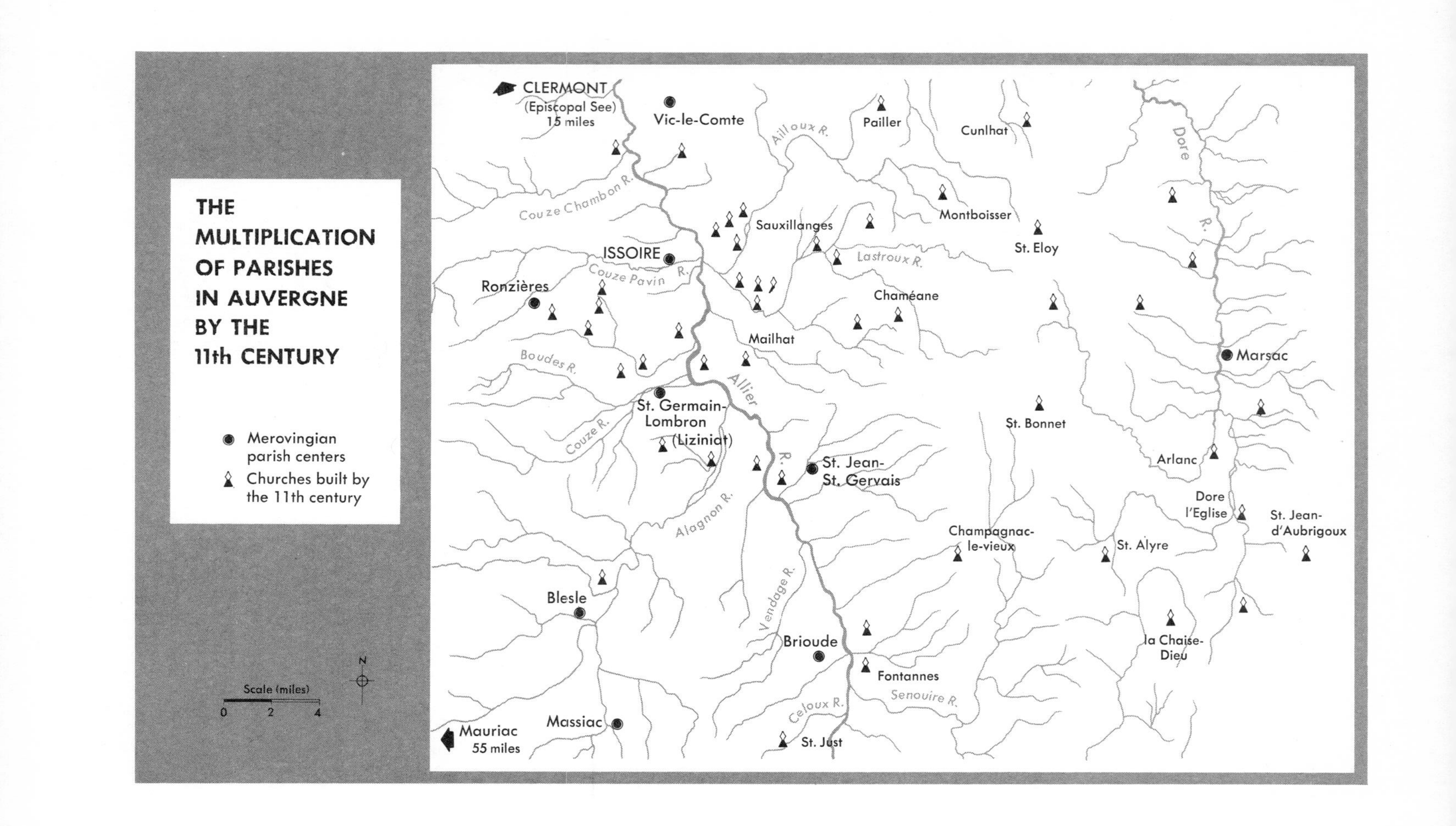
THE MULTIPLICATION OF PARISHES IN AUVERGNE BY THE 11th CENTURY
Merovingian parish centers
Churches built by the 11th century
Scale (miles)
0
2
4
N
CLERMONT
(Episcopal See)
15 miles
Vic-le-Comte
Ailloux R.
Pailler
Cunlhat
Dore
R.
Couze Chambon R.
Sauxillanges
Montboisser
St. Eloy
ISSOIRE
Couze Pavin R.
Lastroux R.
Ronzières
Chaméane
Mailhat
Marsac
Boudes R.
Allier
St. Germain-
Lombron
(Liziniat)
St. Bonnet
Couze R.
R.
St. Jean-
St. Gervais
Arlanc
Dore
l'Eglise
St. Jean-
d'Aubrigoux
Alagnon R.
Champagnac-
le-vieux
St. Alyre
Blesle
Vendage R.
Brioude
la Chaise-
Dieu
Fontannes
Senouire R.
Celoux R.
Massiac
Mauriac
55 miles
St. Just

We cannot go into this evolution in detail, for most of it took place after the eleventh century. . . . But the multiplication of castles after the late tenth century also brought with it an increased number of rural churches. In many cases to be sure, the church predated the castle, which was then attached, along with its town, to the parish church of the older nearby agricultural village. Double villages of this type are frequent in all those areas where settlement went back to Gallo-Roman times. Sometimes, however, the ancient village in whose neighborhood the castle was built did not yet have its own church when the doubling took place, and in this situation, a church was built in the new town, which became the parish center (St.-Just-près-Brioude, for example). On the other hand, the construction of a castle chapel within the limits of an older parish, whose center was the agricultural village under the castle walls, often resulted in fights over the rights belonging to each of the churches. . . . And it occasionally happened that the growing size of the towns served by castle chapels brought—although generally late—the attribution of part or all of the parish functions to the chapel.[136] Thus seignorial castles were also, in more than one instance, the producers of parishes.

IV. CONCLUSION

The place that churches and monasteries had within the villages, and their geographical location prior to the eleventh century, indicates that the multiplication of churches during the Carolingian period was a major element in the history of land settlement. Houses were gathered around these sanctuaries and their cemeteries so that the inhabitants might benefit from their right of asylum and their fortifications (the choice of site is symptomatic). And at least from the beginning of the eleventh century on, new quarters and new villages were thus created. Many churches and monasteries were built in towns of ancient origin; this explains why the site of the parish was sometimes not the same as the site of the seignorial castle, around which people also tended to group in the eleventh century. The map of Carolingian churches reflects the map of land settlement; if churches were especially frequent in the areas that had been anciently settled, they expanded beyond the edges of those sectors in the ninth and tenth centuries, as new land was opened up. After the eleventh century castle churches were also built, sometimes breaking earlier parishes apart. The growth in the number of churches during the Carolingian period, and the place they thenceforth held in village life, explain a practice already documented in the ninth century and more and more common as time progressed—towns were named after their church, sometimes adopting the saint's name as the name of a new village, sometimes choosing it to replace an older name.

NOTES*

1. Imbart de la Tour, "Les paroisses rurales de l'ancienne France," *RH,* **60** (1896), 242–271; E. Griffe, "Les paroisses rurales de la Gaule," *La Maison-Dieu,* **36** (1953), 34–35.

2. In the fifth and sixth centuries *"dioecesis"* had the meaning of parish and *"parochia,"* that of diocese—A. Longnon, *Géographie de la Gaule au VIe siècle* (1878), pp. 36–37.

3. The *vicus* was a rural village; a commercial, artisanal, and religious center with no administrative function. The term disappeared during the Carolingian period.—Ed.

4. Imbart de la Tour, *RH,* **61** (1896), 10–24.

5. Sidonius Apollinaris, *Epist.* **9.** 16.

6. See Griffe, "Paroisses rurales," p. 46 n. 30.

7. See Gabriel Fournier, *Le peuplement rural,* intro. and part 2–*B.*

8. Should we add to this list those places where the cult of St. John the Baptist was held in great honor and the parish church was under his patronage? . . . Given the frequency with which this cult appears, one must be very prudent.

9. Imbart de la Tour, *RH,* **61** (1896), 32–33.

10. See L. Musset, "Arpentage antique en Normandie," *Revue archéologique,* 6me sér., **28** (1947), 35–36.

11. Imbart de la Tour, *RH,* **67** (1898), 7–10; E. Lesne, *Histoire de la propriété ecclésiastique en France* (1910–1943), **1**, 57–59; Griffe, "Paroisses rurales," p. 53.

12. This may be seen throughout Gaul, where the dedication of the oldest parish churches varies little from one diocese to another; the Virgin, St. Peter, St. Lawrence, St. Martin were the most common. See M. Chaume, "Le mode de constitution et de délimitation des paroisses rurales aux temps mérovingiens et carolingiens," *Recherches d'histoire chrétienne et médiévale* (1947), pp. 68–69.

13. See P. A. Février, "Les baptistères de Provence pendant le moyen âge", *Pontificio istituto di archeologia cristiana. Studi di antichità cristiana,* **22** (1957), 424.

14. *Passio praejecti episcopi et martyris arverni, MGH SS rer. merov.* **5.** 229; see Lesne, *Prop. eccl.,* **1**, 53–54.

15. Imbart de la Tour, *RH,* **61** (1896), 16–18.

16. Imbart de la Tour, *RH,* **67** (1898), 1–10; Lesne, *Prop. eccl.,* **1**, 55–59; Griffe, "Paroisses rurales," 52–54; Leclercq, art. "chappelle," *Dictionnaire d'archéologie chrétienne et de liturgie,* **3**1, 415–416.

17. In addition to Leclercq, Lesne, Griffe, and Imbart de la Tour, see E. Salin, *La civilisation mérovingienne* (1949), **1**, 431.

18. Sid. Apoll. *Epist.* 4. 13.

19. See Leclercq, art. "Chapelle," *Dict. d'arch. chrét.,* **3**1, 415; A. Grabar, *Martyrium. Recherches sur le culte des reliques et l'art chrétien antique* (1946).

20. Leclercq, art. "Oratoire," *Dict. d'arch. chrét.,* **12**2, 2359–2361; Griffe, "Paroisses rurales," p. 52.

21. Gregory of Tours, *Historia Francorum* (H. Omont and G. Collon, eds.) 4. 32, 33.

22. Fournier, *Peuplement rural,* app. 2 *A* no. 2.

---

* Except for source and bibliographical references, most of the material in the original notes has been omitted.—Ed.

23. Gregory of Tours, *Liber vitae Patrum (MGH SS rer. merov.* **1.**) 4. 4, **5.** 3.
24. Fournier, *Peuplement rural,* app. 2 *A* no. 1.
25. Gregory of Tours, *Vitae Patrum* **11.** 1.
26. Lesne, *Prop. eccl.,* **1,** 82.
27. *Ibid.,* **1,** 91.
28. Fournier, *Peuplement rural,* **1,** pt. 1.
29. Gregory of Tours, *Vitae Patrum* 1.
30. Lesne, *Prop. eccl.,* **1,** 87–91.
31. See Fournier *Peuplement rural,* app. 2 *A* nos. 3, 4, 5.
32. *Ibid.,* app. 2 *A.*
33. J. Hubert, "Saint-Riquier et le monachisme bénédictin en Gaule à l'époque carolingienne," *Il monachesimo nell'alto Medioevo* [Settimane di studio del Centro italiano di studi sull'alto Medioevo, 4], 114–117.
34. J. Hubert, "Les eglises et bâtiments monastiques de l'abbaye de Manglieu au début du VIIIe siècle," *Bull. de la Société nationale des antiquaires de France* (1958), pp. 95–96.
35. See *ibid.*
36. J. Hubert, *L'Art préroman* (1938) 42–44; J. Hubert, "L'étude de l'ancienne topographie des monastères. Problèmes et méthodes," *Bull. des relations artistiques France-Allemagne* (May 1951); Salin, *Civ. merov.* **1,** 434–437.
37. See J. Lestocquoy, "Le paysage urbain en Gaule du Ve au IXe siècle," *Annales, E.S.C.,* **8** (1953), 162; J. Hubert, "L'évolution de la topographie et de l'aspect des villes de Gaule du Ve au Xe siècle," [Settimane di studio del C.I.S.A.M., **6**], *La città nell'alto Medioevo* p. 545.
38. See Gregory of Tours, *Hist. Francorum* **8.** 30; Imbart de la Tour, *RH,* **60** (1896), 263 n. 1.
39. Gregory of Tours, *Hist. Francorum* 3. 25.
40. *Ibid.* **10.** 7.
41. See G. Le Bras, art. "Asile," *Dictionnaire d'histoire et de géographie ecclésiastique,* 4, 1035–1047; P. Timbal Duclaux de Martin, *Le droit d'asile* (1939).
42. Fournier, *Peuplement rural,* chap. 2 pt. 1; G. Fournier, "Les origines de Brioude," *Almanach de Brioude,* **40** (1960), 19.
43. Imbart de la Tour, *RH,* **61** (1896), 33–44, **63** (1897), 1–41; Griffe, "Paroisses rurales," p. 60; Chaume, *Recherches,* 69 ff.
44. *Polyptyque* of St.-Pierre-le-Vif, *MGH Dipl. imp.,* **1,** *Spuria,* 116–118.
45. Fournier, *Peuplement rural,* app. 1 *B* no. 16.
46. *Ibid.,* app. 1.
47. *Ibid.,* app. 1 *B* no. 10.
48. *Ibid.,* app. 1 *A* no. 4.
49. *Ibid.,* app. 1 *A* no 2.
50. Imbart de la Tour, *RH,* **67** (1898), 2–25; Lesne, *Prop. eccl.,* **1,** 70–78.
51. Imbart de la Tour, *RH,* **67** (1898), 25–33.
52. A. Dumas, *L'Eglise au pouvoir des laïques* [Fliche et Martin, *Histoire de l'Eglise,* **7**], 273–274.
53. *Cartulaire de Brioude,* H. Doniol ed. (1863) [hereinafter *Brioude*], 239, 16; *Cartulaire de Sauxillanges,* H. Doniol, ed. (1864) [hereinafter *Saux.*], 170, 400.
54. *Saux.* 82, 460; *Brioude* 323.
55. *Saux.* 436, 235.
56. *Ibid.* 481.
57. Imbart de la Tour, *RH,* **63** (1896), 23–34.
58. Imbart de la Tour, *RH,* **67** (1898), 2–25.
59. Imbart de la Tour, *RH,* **61** (1896), 33–44.

60. See earlier discussion in sec. 1 of this article.

61. Fournier, *Peuplement rural,* app. 1 *A* no. 4; 2 *B* no. 8.

62. *Ibid.,* app. 2 *B* no. 9.

63. *Ibid.,* app. 2 *C* no. 2.

64. *Libellus de ecclesiis Claromontanis, MGH SS rer. merov.* **7**. 454–467.

65. See Leclercq, art. "Paroisses rurales," *Dict. d'arch. chrét.,* **13**², 2227.

66. Imbart de la Tour, *RH,* **61** (1896), 40–42; Chaume, *Recherches,* pp. 69–71, 84.

67. Chaume, *Recherches,* pp. 83–84.

68. Imbart de la Tour, *RH,* **61** (1896), 33–44; Chaume, *Recherches,* pp. 69–71; Griffe, "Paroisses rurales," p. 60; G. Huard, "Considérations sur l'histoire de la paroisse rurale des origines à la fin du moyen âge," *Revue d'histoire de l'église de France,* **24** (1938), 8–9.

69. P. de Puniet, art. "Dédicace des églises," *Dict. d'arch. chrét.,* **4**¹, 374–405.

70. *Brioude* 331; *Saux.* 476, 297.

71. See Dumas, *L'Eglise au pouvoir des laïques,* pp. 265–266.

72. *Saux.* 376.

73. *Cartulaire de l'abbaye de Savigny,* A. Bernard, ed. (1853), 374; *Saux.* 712.

74. Imbart de la Tour, *RH,* **63** (1897), 38–41.

75. *Ibid.,* pp. 38–41.

76. Lesne, *Prop. eccl.,* **3**, 123–125.

77. *Ibid.,* p. 123.

78. *Brioude* 329.

79. Mansi **18**. A 140, can. 15.

80. Lesne, *Prop. eccl.* **3**, 128; A. Bernard, *La sépulture en droit canonique* (1933), pp. 85–111.

81. *Brioude* 41, 49, 91, 133, 164; *Saux.* 238, 447; see Lesne, *Prop. eccl.* **3**, 132–133 n. 8.

82. *Brioude* 305; see P.-F. Fournier, "Le cimetière médiéval de Saint-Julien de Brioude," *Almanach de Brioude,* **30** (1952), 85–87.

83. *Saux.* 472; L. A. Chaix de Lavaréne, *Monumenta pontifica Arverniae decurrentibus IX°, X°, XI° saeculis* (1880), pp. 106, 233.

84. See G. LeBras in *RHD,* 4me sér., **31** (1953), 590.

85. Imbart de la Tour, *RH,* **63** (1897), 14–37.

86. Imbart de la Tour, *RH,* **67** (1898), 1–53; M. Dillay, "Le régime de l'église privée du XIe au XIIIe siècle dans l'Anjou, le Maine, la Touraine," *RHD,* 4me sér., 4 (1925), 251–294.

87. Dom Benoît, "Les anciennes paroisses monastiques," *Revue du monde catholique,* **104** (1890), 189–205.

88. L. Brehier, "Les origines de l'architecture romane en Auvergne. L'oeuvre des chapitres et des monastères," *Revue Mabillon,* **13** (1923), 8–25.

89. See Fournier, *Peuplement rural,* app. 2 *B*.

90. Lesne, *Prop. eccl.,* **6**, 430–443; J. Hubert, "L'Abbaye de Déols et les constructions monastiques de la fin de l'époque carolingienne," *Cahiers archéologiques,* **9** (1957), 159–162; F. Vercauteren, "Comment s'est-on défendu au IXe siècle dans l'Empire franc contre les invasions normandes?" *XXX congrès de la Fédération archéologique et historique de la Belgique, Annales* (1935), pp. 117–132.

91. Perhaps also at Artonne.

92. See Fournier, *Peuplement rural,* app. 2 *C*. no. 1; *B* no. 9.

93. *Ibid.,* app. 2 *A* no. 3.

94. *Ibid.,* Chap. 2, pt. 1; and Fournier "Les origines de Brioude," 29–30.

95. *Recueil des actes de Pépin Ier et de Pépin II, rois d'Aquitaine (814–848),* L. Levillain, ed. (1926), pp. 66–67.

96. Fournier, *Peuplement rural,* app. 2 *B* no. 4.

97. *Ibid.,* app. 2 *B* no. 9.

98. See M. Kroell, *L'Immunité franque* (1910); F. L. Ganshof, "L'immunité dans la monarchie franque," *Recueils de la Société Jean Bodin,* **1** (2d ed.; 1958), 171–216. Auvergnat documents bring nothing new to the subject.

99. Marc Bloch, *La société féodale,* **2** (1940), 123.

100. Fournier, *Peuplement rural,* chap. 2, pt. 1, and "Les origines de Brioude," 29–30.

101. Levillain, *Actes de Pépin Ier,* pp. 200–204.

102. Fournier, *Peuplement rural,* app. 2 *B.* no. 8, n. 13.

103. Cohadon, "Recherches historiques sur Mozac, son abbaye, son église," *Tablettes historiques de l'Auvergne,* **3** (1842), 41; H. Gomot, *Histoire de l'abbaye royale de Mozat* (1872), p. 249.

104. Fournier, *Peuplement rural,* app. 2 *B* no. 7.

105. G. and P.-F. Fournier, "Remarques sur les origines de Thiers," *Revue d'Auvergne,* **72** (1958), 73.

106. Lesne, *Prop. eccl.,* **6**, 414–424.

107. Fournier, *Peuplement rural,* chap. 2.

108. *Ibid.,* app. 2 *B* no. 8.

109. *Ibid.,* no. 7.

110. *Ibid.,* no. 6.

111. J. Hubert, "La renaissance carolingienne et la topographie religieuse des cités épiscopales," *I problemi della civilita Carolingia* [Settimane di Studio del C.I.S.A.M., 1] (1954), 219–225.

112. *Saux.* 469, 623, 311, 650, 659, 904, 392, etc.

113. *Ibid.* 861, 614, 616, 654, 436, 636.

114. *Ibid.* 235, 550, 557, 566, 561.

115. Imbart de la Tour, *RH,* **63** (1897), 37; Georges Duby, *La société aux XIe et XIIe siècles dans la région mâconnaise* (1953), p. 139 n. 2.

116. Timbal Duclaux de Martin, *Droit d'asile*; Le Bras in *Dict. d'hist. et de géog. eccl.,* **4**, 1035–1047; R. Rey, *Les vieilles églises fortifiées du Midi de la France* (1925), pp. 30–31.

117. As they are given in texts from the end of the ninth century on; Lesne, *Prop. eccl.,* **3**, 127.

118. Timbal Duclaux de Martin *Droit d'asile,* pp. 162–163; J. Flach, "Etude sur les origines et les vicissitudes historiques de l'habitation en France," in A. de Foville, *Enquête sur les conditions de l'habitation en France,* **2** (1894), 47 n. 3; Rey, *Eglises fortifiées,* pp. 26–28; Bernard, *Sépulture en droit canonique,* 51–59.

119. Hubert, "L'Abbaye de Déols," pp. 159–162; Vercauteren, "Comment s'est-on défendu au IXe siècle."

120. Rey, *Églises fortifées,* pp. 11–12, 23–30; Flach, "Etude sur . . . l'habitation," p. 49 n. 1.

121. The earliest mention is in 987; Flach, "Etude sur . . . l'habitation," p. 49 n. 1.

122. Rey, *Églises fortifiées,* pp. 37–39; Timbal Duclaux de Martin, *Droit d'asile,* pp. 162–163.

123. C. and M. d'Elbenne, *Cartulaire de l'abbaye de St.-Vincent-du-Mans,* **1** (1886), col. 155 no. 255; V. Mortet and P. Deschamps, *Recueil de textes relatifs à l'histoire de l'architecture en France au moyen âge* (1911–1929), **1**, 20 n. 7.

124. Rey, *Eglises fortifiées,* pp. 28–29; Lesne, *Prop. eccl.,* **3**, 127–128; Mortet and Deschamps, *Recueil de textes,* **1**, 250–251; Timbal Duclaux de Martin, *Droit d'asile,* pp. 162–163, 169–171; L. Verriest, *Institutions médiévales* (1946), **1** 129–130; R. Grand and R. Delatouche, *L'agriculture au moyen âge* (1950), p. 183; L. Musset, *"Cimiterium ad refugium tantum vivorum non ad sepulturam mortuorum," Revue du Moyen Age Latin,* 4 (1948), 55–60.

125. Chaix de Lavarène, *Monumenta pontifica Arverniae,* pp 443–444; Fournier, *Peuplement rural,* app. 2 *B* no. 9.

126. Rey, *Églises fortifiées,* pp. 29–30.

127. A. Bigay, *L'Abbaye de Moûtier. Essai historique* (1934), p. 46.

128. Fournier, *Peuplement rural,* chap. 4. pt. 2 *A,* n. 25.

129. *Ibid.,* app. 2 *B* no. 7.

130. *Saux.* 861, 561, 380, 403.

131. Fournier, *Peuplement rural,* app. 2 *B* no. 8.

132. Compare Chaume, *Recherches,* 69–71.

133. Chaume, *Recherches,* pp. 83–84.

134. Fournier, *Peuplement rural,* app. 4 *B.*

135. Compare A. de Dion, "Le Puiset aux XIe et XIIe siècles," *Mémoires de la Société archéologique d'Eure-et-Loir* **9** (1889), 71–76; P. Marchagay, "Chartes angevines des XIe et XIIe siècles," *BEC* **36** (1875), 395; Dillay, "Le régime de l'église privée," p. 384 n. 4.

136. See Fournier, *Peuplement rural,* app. 4 *B* nos. 9, 12; and P.-F. Fournier, "L'érection de Villeneuve-Lembron en paroisse," *Bull. historique et scientifique de l'Auvergne* **56** (1936), 148–201.

CONFRATERNITIES OF THE HOLY SPIRIT AND VILLAGE COMMUNITIES IN THE MIDDLE AGES*

Pierre Duparc

Many kinds of associations and many varieties of confraternities were formed in the Middle Ages. Many of them represented town or village communities, above all rural communities. Although these were the basic cells of medieval society, they have not often been studied.[1] What we would like to do here, with reference to the confraternities of the Holy Spirit, is to trace out the shape of this social phenomenon in one region through a study of archival documents and local monographs; we shall then try to draw from that sketch some general conclusions, without waiting for further regional studies to enlarge upon our findings.

The confraternities of the Holy Spirit which we are going to examine have some very special characteristics. They form a homogeneous category and, to avoid all confusion, might be called "village-confraternity-communities of the Holy Spirit."

First of all, they must be distinguished from the pietistic confraternities that took this name, whose appearance resulted from the Counter-Reformation. The Catholic Church in the sixteenth and seventeenth centuries promoted the growth of a large number of confraternities of devotion to bring remedy to a weakened faith and to support a threatened dogma. Among these were the confraternities of the Holy Spirit and of the Holy

* Pierre Duparc, "Confréries du Saint-Esprit et communautès d'habitants au moyen-âge," *Revue historique de droit français et étranger*, 4me série, **36** (1958), 349–367. Trans. by the ed. The *pièces justificatives* added in the appendix have been omitted.

Sacrament, which on occasion became involved in the politics of the times. Our "confraternity-communities," whose aims were different and whose spirit (one might say) was almost secular, were much more ancient; they go back almost to the first centuries of the Middle Ages. We cannot, in fact, date their birth with any precision, but their origins in village customs probably date from before the Carolingian period.

What we are about to describe should likewise not be confused with the Hospital Order of the Holy Spirit and its related groups, founded about 1197 by Gui de Montpellier. A bull of Pope Innocent III in 1204 ordered that the Hospitals of the Holy Spirit should have a confraternity associated with them.[2] But if the date when these hospital-confraternities appeared is quite old, their precise charitable role and their very scattered establishment distinguishes them from the "confraternity-communities."

I

Confraternity-communities of the Holy Spirit at one time existed in large numbers in the parishes of the Alps and the Alpine foothills. We have drawn up as complete a list as possible for the different dioceses of this region—Geneva, the Tarentaise, the Maurienne, the deanery of St.-André in the diocese of Grenoble, and the eastern part of the diocese of Belley—approximately corresponding to the former province of Savoy;[3] and we have supplemented this survey by dipping into the sources for the neighboring Valais (in the diocese of Sion) as well as into studies on the *pays de Vaud*[4] and the canton of Fribourg.[5] About 250 confraternities of the Holy Spirit were discovered: 62 in the diocese of Geneva (out of about 110 parishes), 32 in Tarentaise (out of 77), 37 in Maurienne (out of 100), 28 in the deanery of St.-André in the diocese of Grenoble (out of 58). Traces of confraternities thus can be found in half the parishes of the region.

The number is high, but it is certainly well below the number of confraternities that must have actually existed. For their customary character, their simple—even rudimentary—organization, their grass-roots existence could not have left many written traces. Like most rural communities in medieval France, the confraternities of the Holy Spirit had no official existence and generally remained out of sight to the public authorities. Ecclesiastical authorities were hardly more concerned with them in the Middle Ages, and episcopal visitations mention them only on rare occasions, for they had no religious aim. They attracted attention only when they were the cause of disorder or scandal. It was only in the eighteenth century, when they were in the process of disappearing and when they had been converted and reformed for other goals and activities, that lay and ecclesiastical authorities commonly became concerned with them. For this reason, it is only in the cadastral survey of 1730, made at the order of the King of Sardinia, that we have any mention of the existence and possessions of several confraternities that would otherwise remain unknown.

Confraternities have seldom left any archives; there are a few cases in the Tarentaise, the Maurienne, and the Valais, where they are kept in the communal archives; sometimes they have been placed in the parish archives.[6] In many instances it was only pure chance that allowed us to put a confraternity on our list;[7] in others, we know of them only through research we have done for other purposes in the archives of Savoie and Haute-Savoie, especially the communal archives.[8] For the Middle Ages, testaments and donations predominate among our sources of information, which—aside from these—can come from many different kinds of documents.

What were the essential characteristics of these confraternities of the Holy Spirit? Clearly, they had pious activities—almost all provided masses for deceased members;[9] many organized processions or other devotional practices.[10] But their principal object was to gather together all the members of a rural community, in general all the parishioners, to partake in a common dinner and to distribute foodstuffs once a year at Pentecost. Common meals and general distributions were the dominant traits, appearing in all confraternities without exception, in the oldest sources from the thirteenth century and in the most recent from the eighteenth. As we shall see, however, from the seventeenth century on, shortly before the confraternities were suppressed, both civil and religious authorities tried to give them new functions.

Within these rural confraternity-communities were no distinctions of social classes, at least in the beginning. Numerous noblemen took part in them or left them property;[11] even the Count of Geneva seems to have been a member or associate of certain of them in return for the property whose use he had granted.[12] The local clergy, especially the parish priest, often joined in the banquet and distribution.[13] All the parishioners were admitted; in principle they were brethren of equal standing. Some texts, however, indicate a distinction between "full brethren" and "partial brethren,"[14] a distinction which corresponds to one in other regions between "living brethren" and "dead brethren."[15] From the "partial brother" the confraternity demanded only half the capital or income required of the member who was a "full brother"; in return, the partial member got back only half the ordinary benefits at the distributions and banquets. But these partial memberships seem hardly to have existed except in cases of testamentary gifts when the bequest did not entail any participation by a beneficiary in the banquets. Partial memberships might also have originated in marriages or in settlements outside the parish, by analogy to the rules for use of the commons.

At the banquet table our confraternities might have been described by La Fontaine[16]

> Wolves eat more than anyone.
> One at a confraternity
> Indeed was such a glutton
> He thought it would end fatally.

or by Perrault[17]

> They fight, they have a bout, *(fait frairie)*
> They drink, the more they drink the more they shout.
> And by the time they finish eating
> They talk without anyone agreeing.

Through the ages the tradition of the common meal has in almost all societies been one of the most solid.[18] Seated at table—preferably a well-laden one—the community becomes materially and spiritually conscious of itself. For this reason, in every confraternity of the Holy Spirit precise rules governed the ordering of the common meal, the number and nature of the dishes (beef, pork, or mutton, stew or roast, back-fat, white bread, wine, etc.),[19] and the number of participants (one per hearth, two per household, etc.).[20] But banquet often means excess. Often these long meals and common drinking bouts heated the head, and the brethren, at table or after, gave free vent to their feelings. Often the result was scandalous. And often the ecclesiastical authorities had to step in and warn against the abuses these gatherings engendered.[21] It was one cause of the confraternities' discredit and final suppression.

The distribution of foodstuffs, like the common meal, is not a phenomenon unique to the confraternities of the Holy Spirit. Although less usual, perhaps, than the common meal, general distributions of foodstuffs have also existed in many societies[22] and in the Middle Ages they were undertaken by many kinds of associations.[23] Governed by custom, the distributions made by the confraternities of the Holy Spirit varied greatly but were always considerable; they frequently consisted of bread (the fundamental foodstuff of the times), back-fat, cheese (the produce of a pastoral economy), beans, chick-peas, and, on occasion, wine and salt.[24] The food was distributed to all parish brethren of the confraternity (that is, practically all the parishioners) without distinction of wealth—at least in the beginning. Although these foodstuffs were frequently called "alms," they are not to be confused with acts of charity. In the region under consideration, what we call "alms" was termed—from the Middle Ages until the eighteenth century—*"donne"* or *"donnée"* [gifts].[25] The same was true in many other regions, as these thirteenth-century verses from the *Châtelain de Coucy* prove:

> *A la porte a la gent trouvée*
> *Qui atendoient la donnée.*
> *Maintenant lor a demandé*

S'on lor a encor reins dǫnné. . .
"Pour çou cuidon c'on ait mengié
Et qu'assés tost on nous donra. . ."[26]

In the language of the times the confraternity was not so much the association, the "corporate person," as the reunion itself, the annual meeting when one ate and distributed the foodstuffs. This, in many cases, is the meaning of the expression *"faire la confrairie"* [hold a confraternity];[27] it was the meaning adopted by La Fontaine. And it might happen, because of exceptional circumstances, that a confraternity was not "held" each year.[28]

Naturally, the confraternities of the Holy Spirit also had secondary objects that appear from time to time in the texts, such as giving help to the poor[29] and undertaking public works of communal interest, for example repairing the parish church or building a bridge.[30] Some of these side activities became more and more visible after the end of the Middle Ages, and the progressive tightening of ecclesiastical controls over them turned the confraternities of the Holy Spirit into confraternities for piety and devotion. During the eighteenth century civil and ecclesiastical officials, *intendants* and bishops, diverted the goods of many confraternities to pay for the upkeep of parish churches[31] and schools,[32] or transferred their assets to the rural community[33] or to a devotional confraternity.[34]

How did the confraternities of the Holy Spirit fulfill their role, pay for the banquets, take care of the distribution of foodstuffs? For this they had a special organization and particular resources.

At the head of the confraternity were generally two (although sometimes four or more) administrators called "priors," "procurators," "rectors," or "syndics,"[35] elected directly by the brethren every year in general assemblies,[36] or selected by the syndics and councilors of the community.[37] These administrators received distinctive honorific insignia—a staff or a hat.[38] But the burden of office was sometimes heavy because of the personal expenses they occasionally had to pay—at least after the end of the Middle Ages—and often, like communal syndics, they tried to refuse the honor.[39] Sometimes they were assisted by councilors or surveyors.[40] Their job was to administer the confraternity's goods and income and to account to those who had selected them.[41]

It is not easy to estimate the size of the confraternities' possessions or income, which varied considerably from parish to parish. We have a few fragmentary pieces of information that tell us, in all probability, the minima; these figures are from the late period, the period of decadence, and generally correspond to a devalued income. The income at Aussois was 110 florins in 1700; it was 100 florins at Frétrive in 1670, 426 florins at Lans-le-Villard in 1661, and 400 florins at St.-Jean de La Porte in 1670. The confraternity at Termignon spent 300 florins in 1571; a receipt of 100 florins for money loaned to St.-Pierre de Soucy in 1564 still remains.[42]

What then were the confraternities' possessions? In general they possessed their house, the "house of the confraternity" or "house of the Holy Spirit," or else a granary.[43] There they held their meetings and there they gathered the food required for the dinners and for distribution. In the parish church they often had their own chapel, the chapel of the Holy Spirit (on rare occasions it had another name)[44] endowed with an income for its upkeep and for services; the confraternity had the right to present the chaplain.[45] Here and there the confraternities had mills to make bread for distribution;[46] they also had fields and pastures,[47] vineyards,[48] and sometimes mountains or alps[49]—place names have conserved their memory in "Fields of the confraternity" or "Needles of the Holy Spirit."[50] In the confraternity's house were to be found some furniture and utensils, a trunk for the archives,[51] a processional cross, and a gonfalon or banner.[52] They also collected rents.[53] Most of these possessions were rented by *albergement* contract [a contract involving both an initial payment and an annual rent] that gave the confraternity an annual income.[54]

Where did these goods come from? To be sure, the brethren of the confraternity paid annual dues, either in money[55] or in kind,[56] occasionally —in the high mountains—in the form of *auciège* [a seignorial tax on the use of alpine pastures]:[57] Even in the best circumstances these dues covered but a part of the expenses, however, and would never have allowed the confraternity to put together any significant capital. The wealth of these groups came essentially from donations and bequests. Such gifts, very common until the fifteenth century, were "good works," acts of piety and of social solidarity, of mutual village aid. A brother might leave a field, a mill, a sum of money or an annuity as a bequest, requiring in return continued membership in the confraternity for a certain number of years after his death or in perpetuity[58]—in this way he continued to receive its "spiritual benefits," masses and prayers, while abandoning and distributing to his brothers the material benefits of the dinner and the distribution. Other bequests provided for the maintenance of one or several brethren in the confraternity,[59] often allowing a poor man chosen by the priors or the testamentary executor to take advantage of the banquet and the distribution.[60] Among those who gave to the confraternities were many lords.[61]

The confraternities' possessions enjoyed a special legal status, escaping from the usual perquisites and probably from many *tailles* and other taxes as well;[62] they might have been considered possessions belonging to organizations for pious works, or as property of the church fabric serving the upkeep of the church, and especially the chapel of the Holy Spirit and its chaplain. After an unknown date this character must have favored the formation of a common privileged patrimony. In contrast the situation was reversed in the eighteenth century when, as we have seen, the public authorities tried to reduce the confraternities' possessions.[63]

Can we now go beyond these concrete manifestations, these common banquets and distributions of foodstuffs? Can we discover the real social role of these confraternities of the Holy Spirit and grasp their relationship to the rural communities? Two new aspects, less apparent but equally essential, must be described: to a certain extent they were mutual-aid societies; at their beginning they represented the entire community of inhabitants.

We have already seen that the distribution of foodstuffs was not an act of charity. They were given to all the brethren without regard to wealth. The poor, on their side, benefited from other help, sometimes given by these same confraternities (above all after the end of the Middle Ages), sometimes given by other organizations or in other forms. Thus the brethren, by putting a certain part of their wealth in common and profiting from the common use of bequests, received foodstuffs every year in return. Distributions followed hard upon the payment of dues. The confraternity took on some of the characteristics of a mutual benefit society (as was recognized and proclaimed by some of the confraternities themselves, and has not been overlooked by a number of authors of local studies).[64]

The relations between confraternities and communities of inhabitants were very tight. Often the confraternities were identical with the commune,[65] being nothing but the parish or communal administration. For the confraternity generally included all the inhabitants,[66] and an individual's position as a member of the commons and as beneficiary of the banquet and distribution became one and the same.[67] Often their possessions were not differentiated;[68] the administrators were frequently the same.[69] And episcopal visitations generally list the parishioners as patrons of the chapel of the Holy Spirit in the parish churches.[70] This doubling of one by the other must have been even more general during the earlier Middle Ages, for we have only very late information, from the period of decline. One might thus argue that the confraternities of the Holy Spirit appear to have been the original organization of the rural communities in Savoy and in French-speaking Switzerland.

II

Savoy and French-speaking Switzerland have formed the basis of this study; archives and local monographs have allowed us to find a large number of confraternities in this region and to describe their characteristics. But was this a localized phenomenon, or did confraternity-communities of the Holy Spirit with analogous characteristics exist in other provinces? It would be interesting to map these kinds of associations. Unfortunately, our inquiry is not far enough along to allow it. We will simply note the clues suggesting that the area in which confraternities appeared extended far into the southeast and center of France.

These types of associations existed in all the western Alpine region and the Rhône valley. In Dauphiné local historians have discovered traces of autonomous confraternities of the Holy Spirit, possessing property and distributing general alms on Pentecost—in Grésivaudan and the diocese of Grenoble,[71] in the Viennois and the diocese of Vienne, in the Valentinois, the Dios, the Gapençais, and in the dioceses of Valence, Die, and Gap.[72] They appear to have been particularly active in the high valleys, in the Embrunais or diocese of Embrun—for example those at Savines,[73] Réallon,[74] Baratier, Les Crottes,[75] L'Argentière,[76] and above all at Guillestre.[77] At Guillestre the confraternity lasted until 1801, and students of folklore have left us the details of the annual ceremony as it existed at the dawn of the nineteenth century.

> Each year, when the prior of the confraternity was elected, . . . he was given a torch decorated with flowers; he bought and fattened two steer and a calf and the necessary wheat and vegetables. The day before Pentecost eve, the public officials and former priors came to get the three animals. . . . The cooks, the bakers and all those whose job was to prepare the meal paraded in aprons and white caps decorated with ribbons. The procession, accompanied by a band, went through the streets of Guillestre. Then they slaughtered the animals, prepared the dishes, and the priest came to bless the bread and meat. On Pentecost, all the inhabitants placed themselves around the prepared tables, of which one was reserved for the former priors. In the evening there was a similar celebration. Each meal, ending with the priest saying grace, was followed by a religious service. At midday the *frairet*—bowls of soup and bread—was given to all families without discrimination. The following day there was a similar hand-out, but only to the poor.

The confraternities of the Holy Spirit in Provence were quite similar. They seem to have existed even in cities such as Aix[78] and Marseille;[79] but their existence in such large settlements must have been more troubled than in a rural parish, and their life was dimmed or even disappeared when more developed organisms such as communes and consulates appeared. They were to be found more often in the mountainous region of the bishopric of Digne[80] and the county of Nice.[81] In precisely this region one of them, or at least one of their manifestations, has survived to the present. An investigation *in situ* around 1939 described it in detail, and we reproduce it here as the best illustration of our theme:

> In the village of La Croix, whose amphitheatre of white-bleached houses hugs a steep spur of the mountain north of Puget-Théniers, since time immemorial the population has joined in a common *past* (meal) on Pentecost, the patronal festival of the village. The meal is prepared by the two youngest households in the commune, and the two husbands are named priors for the occasion.
>
> At the beginning of spring the two young couples go from house to

house to ask for wheat; each family gives them an amount in proportion to its own size. The eve of Pentecost they make several ovensful of bread. A second story containing a kitchen and a vast hall is built on top of the parish church which one enters directly from a tiny upper street; the hall is called the "Hall of the Holy Spirit." In the kitchen on the morning of Pentecost the two couples prepare a bean soup called "soup of the Holy Spirit" in two enormous pots holding each about 150 litres. After High Mass, there is a procession of all the people, led by a band, through the village streets to the hall of the Holy Spirit. The priests bless bread and soup. Then follows a picturesque parade of housewives coming with their breadbaskets and soup bowls to receive their portion of bread and soup from the priors to take back to their family table. Every person receives about a pound of bread.

A long table is set up in the hall where the clergy, the public officials and their families take their meal, a meal in which "soup of the Holy Spirit" is an essential part. In the past everyone took part, including numerous friends who had come in from neighboring villages.[82]

The center of France also had its confraternity-communities of the Holy Spirit, as we can see in Forez and Auvergne. Wills from Forez between 1305 and 1316 cite such confraternities for the parishes of Montbrison,[83] Chambéon,[84] St.-Etienne-le-Molard, Marcilly-le-Pavé, Mizérieux,[85] Epercieux-St.-Paul, Cottance, Salt-en-Donzy, Pouilly-lès-Feurs,[86] St.-Didier-sur-Rochefort,[87] St.-Marcellin,[88] St.-Haon-le-Châtel,[89] Villerêt,[90] Ste.-Colombe-sur-Gaud,[91] St.-Germain-Laval,[92] Pommiers, and Souternon.[93] These numerous legacies were saddled with conditions—provisions for distributions, for "gifts" to the poor, and, most often, for maintaining a "brother" in the confraternity, in perpetuity or for a term of years, in either full membership (by a bequest of capital or an annuity equal to the ordinary dues) or partial.[94] The confraternities of Forez were administered by consuls,[95] had their own houses,[96] and counted all social classes, especially the nobility, among their participants.[97]

More varied information for Auvergne allows us to see the common characteristics of the institution there. At Aurillac the confraternity of the Holy Spirit[98] had land-rents whose revenues paid for bread to be distributed to the poor; some annuities were settled on it in the thirteenth century, which indicates that it was already an ancient organization. For the administration of the confraternity's capital, as for consular elections and the collection of the *taille,* the town was divided into three "quarters." From 1337 on at least, the bread to be distributed was stocked in a house kept especially for this purpose. At Riom, where the inhabitants assembled for their meetings in the "house of the Holy Spirit,"[99] the confraternity solemnly celebrated the three days of Pentecost, and gave alms to the poor in its house while the "brethren" dined on bread that had been blessed, called *"céniaux"* in memory of the Last Supper (*la Cène*), and drank wine that had been blessed. Banquets, which had led to wanton riots, had disappeared by the eighteenth century, and the confraternity's decline had even led Henry III to assign its revenues to the local college for its support.[100] At Gerzat, a village in the Limagne, "the people assemble and discuss in the house of the Holy Spirit."[101] Confraternities of the Holy Spirit were noted at Clerlande in 1403,[102] at St.-Julien-de-Coppel in the thirteenth century,[103] at Vic-le-Comte,[104] and at Brioude.[105] At Neschers the "distribution" had a character very similar to the Savoyard "gifts"; in 1703 the Bishop of Clermont found during his pastoral visitation "that a general distribution of what remained (after payment for services, candles and the upkeep of the altar) was made to all brethren of the confraternity both rich and poor on Pentecost day." He concluded by forbidding "the aforesaid custom under pain of destruction of the confraternity and ordering that the surplus be given as general alms to all the poor of the parish."[106]

Indeed, the confraternities of the Holy Spirit seem to have evolved much more rapidly in Auvergne than in Savoy and French-speaking Switzerland. Some were already disappearing in the sixteenth century, their revenues assigned to schools. By the eighteenth century the banquets were suppressed and the distribution of foodstuffs, apart from some bread blessed by the priest which was given to the members, was reserved for the poor. At any rate, the universal appearance of the confraternities and their social role has not escaped historians' notice. The author of a monograph on Gerzat declared, "there was not a village or hamlet, not a town [in Auvergne] that did not have its confraternity of the Holy Spirit,"[107] and a sociologist who has studied these communities has claimed that in Auvergne the patrimony of the community was indiscriminately mixed with that of the confraternity.[108]

III

We shall stop our pursuit of these confraternity-communities here. One could find, and will find, many others. Even so, they appear to have been unknown in many French regions. Let us now try to put them back into the great mass of rural associations, many of which never took any particular form.

It should first of all be clear that these confraternity-communities are not to be confused with the associations established for a special purpose, such as rebuilding a church or a bridge, performing a mystery play, nor, of course, with the professional confraternities.[109]

On the other hand, their identity with the rural community made them similar to those confraternities that took the name of the parish patron saint.[110] They also were undoubtedly similar to a mass of parish confraternities that, without any particular name, represented the communities of rural inhabitants;[111] a passage in the *Livre de Jostice et de*

Plet supplies an important piece of evidence about these anonymous confraternity-communities.[112]

Another side of our confraternities of the Holy Spirit—the charitable side, the side concerned with mutual aid, with its banquet rites—was to be found in many medieval confraternities or "brotherhoods,"[113] both professional and communal, in which aid to needy brethren and common meals were the general rule. By this line they went back to the guilds of the Carolingian period—"the guilds or confraternities" expressly mentioned in a capitulary of 852.[114]

If certain traits of the confraternities of the Holy Spirit made them similar to rural communities and mutual-aid societies, they generally had one peculiarity that we have already noted: they possessed capital, the income from which was divided among all the members. It is tempting to assimilate them on this point to many rural communities who owned commons, pasturage and forests in particular, that brought the inhabitants profit: and we must note that the confraternities of the Holy Spirit were both numerous and active in regions of alpine pasture such as the Tarentaise and the Maurienne. Commons of pasture and estovers were rights of usage, however; the alms distributed by the confraternities of the Holy Spirit were income in kind.

The characteristics of these confraternities perhaps allow us to explain their name, their invocation of the Holy Spirit and their choice of the feast of Pentecost. The Church was mirrored in the microcosm of the parish. The universal mission of the Church, proclaimed on Pentecost day, took parish form in the meetings and common meals. The "gifts" called to mind the *donum Sancti Spiritus* that Peter promised all believers in his Pentecostal sermon.[115] The "love feast"[116] brought to mind that the term *"caritas"* is the most fitting name to call the Holy Spirit.[117]

In conclusion, the importance of phenomena such as the confraternities of the Holy Spirit must be insisted upon. Rural associations and rural communities represented the first forms of social life. Communes and consulates, the objects of so much study and so many theories, were but exceptional forms, both rare and late. No description of medieval society can pass silently over this disproportion between what was permanent and what was accidental.

NOTES

1. This general aspect of social history has not escaped a few authors. See, in particular, G. Le Bras, "Les confréries chrétiennes. Problèmes et propositions," *RHD,* 4me sér., **18/19** (1940–1941), 310–363; R. Grand, "La genése du mouvement communal en France," *RHD,* 4me sér., **20** (1942), 149–173.

2. See P. Brune, *Histoire de l'ordre hospitalier du Saint-Esprit* (1892), with the corrections made by L. Delisle in his review for the *Journal des Savants* (1893).

3. See the *pièces justificatives* to this article, *RHD,* 4me sér., **36** (1958), 554–585 [hereinafter *P.J.* followed by the item number].

4. M. Reymond, "Les confréries du Saint-Esprit au pays de Vaud," *Revue d'histoire ecclésiastique suisse,* **20** (1926), 282–301.

5. J. Niquille, "La confrérie du Saint-Esprit de Fribourg au XVe et au XVIe siècle," *Revue d'hist. eccl. suisse,* **19** (1925), 190–205.

6. A roll of acknowledgments to the benefit of the confraternity of the Holy Spirit at Veyrier (Hte-Savoie) thus came into the papers of the parish priest. But several years ago the priest untied the separate pieces of parchment that made up the roll and was giving them to the children of his catechism class as prizes when we collected the remnants for the departmental archives.

7. As an example, take the parish of Thusy-en-Genevois (Hte-Savoie) for which neither departmental nor communal archives contain any medieval documents, or even more recent documents mentioning a confraternity. The parish priest, however, owned a contract of sale from 1407 to the benefit of the confraternity of the Holy Spirit which served as cover for a parish register of 1606—*P.J.* 1.

8. For the department of Savoie, the manuscript inventories for the communal archives, drawn up by G. Pérouse and kept in the departmental archives —often very detailed—are of great interest.

9. *P.J.* 1: St.-Sigismond; *P.J.* 2: Montgirod; *P.J.* 3: Beaune, Lans-le-Bourg, Orelle; *P.J.* 4: Entremont-le-Vieux.

10. *P.J.* 1: Montmin; *P.J.* 2: Montgirod; *P.J.* 3: Orelle.

11. *P.J.* 1: Beaumont, Boussy, Margencel, Sallanches; *P.J.* 2: Marthod; *P.J.* 3: Fontcouverte, Lans-le-Bourg, St.-Martin de La Porte.

12. *P.J.* 1: Chamonix, Veyrier.

13. *P.J.* 2: Montgirod, *P.J.* 3: Modane.

14. *P.J.* 3: Villargondran, Hermillon, St.-Pancrace, St.-Martin de La Porte.

15. In Forez, see sec. 2 of this article.

16. *Le loup et la cigogne.*

17. *La chasse.*

18. See Fustel de Coulanges, *La cité antique* (1888), pp. 179–183; C. Jullian, *Histoire de la Gaule,* **6** (1920), 283–285.

19. *P.J.* 3: St.-Martin de La Porte, *P.J.* 2: Longefoy.

20. *P.J.* 2: Granier; *P. J.* 3: St.-Martin de La Porte.

21. *P.J.* 2: Marthod.

22. The "potlatch" for example, see Moret and Davy, *Des clans aux empires* (Evolution de l'humanité, 1923), pp. 107–132.

23. *P.J.* 3: Valmeinier.

24. *P.J.* 1: La Chapelle d'Abondance, Morzine; *P.J.* 2: Granier, Landry; P.J. 3: Aussois, St.-Martin de La Porte, Termignon.

25. See the way these two words were defined in the eighteenth century by the parishioners of Longefoy, *P.J.* 2; at Montgirod (*P.J.* 2) and Lans-le-Bourg (*P.J.* 3) *"la donna"* was thought to be the founder's name: P. A. Naz, "Notice historique," *Memoires et Documents publiés par la Société savoisienne d'histoire et d'archéologie,* **10** (1867); G. Pérouse, "Les paroisses rurales d'un diocèse de Savoie au XVIIIe siècle," *Revue d'histoire de l'Eglise de France* (1913), pp. 512–515 does not make the distinction.

26. Vv. 2975 ff.

> [At the gate the people there
> Waiting for alms,
> Now were asked

If they had yet been given anything. . . .
"We thought the eating was over
And that soon we would receive our gift. . ."]

27. *P.J.* 3: Aussois; *P.J.* 2, Landry, Macôt; *P.J.* 5: Sion, Liddes.
28. *P.J.* 2: Marthod; *P.J.* 4: Montmélian.
29. *P.J.* 1: St.-Sigismond, St.-Jorioz; *P.J.* 3: Orelle, Montgirod; *P.J.* 4: Entremont-le-Vieux.
30. *P.J.* 1: Genève; *P.J.* 4: St.-Pierre d'Albigny.
31. *P.J.* 4: Cruet; *P.J.* 3: St.-Martin de La Porte.
32. *P.J.* 3: Lans-le-Villard, St.-Michel de Maurienne, Villargondran.
33. *P.J.* 3: Tessens.
34. *P.J.* 1: Arith.
35. *P.J.* 1: Les Gets, St.-Jorioz, Seythenex, Thonon, especially.
36. *P.J.* 4: Arbin; *P.J.* 2: Macôt; *P.J.* 3: Villargondran.
37. *P.J.* 2: Montgirod.
38. *P.J.* 3: Villargondran (1628).
39. *P.J.* 3: Villargondran (1635).
40. *P.J.* 1: Morzine, *P.J.* 5: Sion.
41. *P.J.* 4: St.-Pierre de Soucy; *P.J.* 1: Talloires.
42. *P.J.* 3, 4.
43. *P.J.* 1: Les Gets, St.-Jean d'Aulph; *P.J.* 2: Granier, La Côte d'Aime, Landry, Montgirod, Tessens, Valezan; *P.J.* 3: Lans-le-Villard, Termignon, Villargondran; *P.J.* 4: Cruet; *P.J.* 5: Liddes.
44. *P.J.* 4: Barberaz.
45. *P.J.* 1: Passy, Vallières, Viuz-en-Salaz; *P.J.* 4: Aix, Chambéry, Cognin La Rochette, Les Déserts, Méry, Montmélian.
46. *P.J.* 2: Granier, Macôt, Planay, St.-Martin de Belleville.
47. *P.J.* 2: Planay.
48. *P.J.* 1: Loisin, Publier; *P.J.* 4: Cruet, St.-Pierre d'Albigny; *P.J.* 2: Valezan.
49. *P.J.* 2: Peisey, Planay.
50. *P.J.* 2: Peisey.
51. *P.J.* 1: Lully.
52. *P.J.* 1: Montmin.
53. *P.J.* 1: Genève, La Chapelle d'Abondance, Le Châtelard.
54. *P.J.* 2: La Côte d'Aime.
55. *P.J.* 2: Feissons, Macôt; *P.J.* 3: St.-Martin de La Porte.
56. *P.J.* 1 and 4: the *cueillette* at Morzine; the *quête* at Entremont-le-Vieux.
57. *P.J.* 1: Entremont, Morzine; *P.J.* 2: Longefoy.
58. *P.J.* 3: Fontcouverte, Lans-le-Villard.
59. *P.J.* 3: Hermillon.
60. *P.J.* 3: St.-Pancrace; *P.J.* 5: Sion.
61. *P.J.* 3: St.-Martin de La Porte; *P.J.* 1: Sallanches.
62. *P.J.* 1: Chamonix; *P.J.* 2: Hauteville-Gondon.
63. *P.J.* 3: Modane, and above.
64. *P.J.* 3: Aussois. F. Bernard, *Histoire de Montmélian* (1956), pp. 129, 281.
65. *P.J.* 1: Domancy, Morzine.
66. *P.J.* 2: Granier.
67. *P.J.* 2: La Côte d'Aime, Granier, Longefoy.
68. *P.J.* 2: Macôt; *P.J.* 3: Modane.
69. *P.J.* 4: Arbin; *P.J.* 2: Longefoy.
70. *P.J.* 1: Manigod, Serraval, Thorens, *P.J.* 4: Fréterive.

71. Not including the northern part of the diocese which formed the deanery of Savoie.

72. L. Fillet, "Histoire religieuse du canton de La Chapelle-en-Vercors," *Bull. d'histoire ecclésiastique et d'archéologie religieuse des diocèses de Valence, Gap, Grenoble et Viviers,* **8** (1887–1888), 218–219; **9** (1888–1889), 17: "Confraternities of the Holy Spirit existed in a great many places in Dauphiné. They had their own goods and their own income; they were governed by their own leaders; and on their feast day—Pentecost—they distributed alms to all the poor who were present." We find such Confraternities at Grenoble and St.-Martin-le-Vinoux [Isère, arr. and canton Grenoble] about 1444, at Montchenu [Drôme arr. Valence, canton Saint-Donat] in 1463, at Alixan [*ibid.* canton Bourg-de-Péage] in 1486 and 1520, at St.-Nazaire en Royans [*ibid.*] and at St.-Lattier [Isére, arr. Grenoble, canton St.-Marcellin] in 1500, at St.-Bonnet-de-Valclérieux [Drôme, arr. Valence, canton Le Grand-Serre] from 1518 to 1732, at St.-Marcel près Die (Drôme, commune de Die] in 1548, at Mirabel aux Baronies [Drôme, arr. and canton Nyons] in 1597, etc. . . . at La Chapelle en Vercors [Drôme, arr. Die] and at St.-Agnan en Vercors" [*ibid.* canton La Chapelle en V.].

73. Hautes-Alpes, arr. Gap. 1391 and 1430: *"juxta pratum confrarie S. Spiritus de Sabina"*; Archives Hautes-Alpes, *E* 36 and 95. In the same commune another confraternity in 1384 at Chérines; Archives Hautes-Alpes, *E* 34.

74. Hautes-Alpes, canton Savines—a vineyard next to that of the confraternity of the Holy Spirit in 1432 at Méans (hamlet of Réallon); Archives Hautes-Alpes, *E* 50.

75. Hautes-Alpes, canton Embrun. In 1432 a vineyard *"in territorio Crotarum seu de Baraterio"* next to that of the confraternity—Archives Hautes-Alpes *E* 52.

76. Hautes-Alpes, arr. Briançon. In 1383 suit over rights and revenues of the confraternity: Letonnelier, *Répertoire des registres du fonds de la Chambre des comptes du Dauphiné* (1947), no. 2025.

77. Hautes-Alpes, arr. Briançon. In 1365: *Inventaire sommaire des archives communales,* P. Guillaume, ed. (1906), p. 15. In 1546: Archives Hautes-Alpes, *E* 668. For the present-day see A. Van Gennep, *Manuel de folklore contemporain,* pt. 1, 4 (1949), 1660–1661.

78. In 1735—nine loads of wheat, free of taxes, granted to the confraternity of the Holy Spirit for the bread distributed at Pentecost. Deliberations of the police office—Archives communales, *FF* 83 f., 231.

79. At the beginning of the thirteenth century the inhabitants of Marseille had to submit to the Bishop and replace their commune with a confraternity of the Holy Spirit that had existed before, at least since 1188. In 1214 the rectors of this confraternity acted as coseigniors of the city—V. L. Bourilly, *Essai sur l'histoire politique de la commune de Marseille* (1925). Was this confraternity originally only a hospital-confraternity? Did the inhabitants radically change its nature after the failure of the commune? Was this confraternity of the Holy Spirit associated in the beginning with the order established by Gui de Montpellier? See Busquet, *Histoire de Marseille* (2d ed.; 1945), pp. 99–103. The confraternity preceded the order; it was already in existence in 1188 and probably much earlier.

80. In the Basses-Alpes at Champtercier, arr. and canton Digne; La Palud, arr. Digne, canton Moustiers Ste-Marie; Barcelonnette; Fours and Les Thuilles, arr. and canton Barcelonnette; Larche, arr. Barcelonnette, canton St.-Paul. Van Gennep, *Manuel,* pp. 1660–1661; 1723–1724.

81. In the Alpes-Martimes at Contes, arr. Nice; Clans, arr. Nice, canton St.-Sauveur; La Croix-sur-Roudoule, arr. Nice, canton Puget-Théniers; St.-Jeannet, arr. Grasse, canton Vence. In Italy at Roccasparvera, province Cuneo. *Ibid.*

82. At La Croix-sur-Roudoule, *ibid.,* p. 1723–1724.

83. Loire. See *Testaments foréziens, 1305–1316* (1951), pp. 1, 147, 209, 313.

84. Arr. et canton Montbrison. *Ibid.,* p. 14.

85. Arr. Montbrison, canton Boën. *Ibid.,* pp. 84, 76, 245.

86. Arr. Montbrison, canton Feurs. *Ibid.,* pp. 265, 13, 48, 72.

87. Arr. Montbrison, canton Noirétable. *Ibid.,* p. 17.

88. Arr. Montbrison, canton St.-Rambert. *Ibid.,* p. 24.

89. Arr. Roanne. *Ibid.,* pp. 97, 216, 260, 262.

90. Arr. and canton Roanne. *Ibid.,* pp. 7, 129, 183, 185, 175–176.

91. Arr. Roanne, canton Néronde. *Ibid.,* p. 56.

92. Arr. Roanne. *Ibid.,* pp. 143, 151, 200, 299.

93. Arr. Roanne, canton St.-Germain-Laval. *Ibid.,* pp. 291, 303.

94. *Ibid.,* p. 74 n. 5.

95. At Montbrison, Cottance, St.-Germain-Laval.

96. At Epercieux, St.-Haon.

97. At St.-Didier.

98. It was later called "Charity of the Holy Spirit," or "Poor man's bread." It has been called "a kind of community service bureau." But it is probable that originally the distributions were not reserved solely for the poor, if one may judge by the case of Neschers (see note 106). See also R. Grand, *Les paix d'Aurillac* (1945), p. CL.

99. In 1375, for example; Archives communales *BB* **7**, 123.

100. See E. Everat, "Les confréries de Riom," *Mémoires de l'Académie de Clermont-Ferrand,* 2me sér., **19** (1905).

101. E. Jaloustre, *Histoire d'un village de la Limagne, Gerzat* (1886). Gerzat, Puy-de-Dôme, arr. and cant. Clermont-Ferrand.

102. Suit against the confraternity of Riom over certain land (Clerlande, Puy-de-Dôme, arr. and cant. Clermont-Ferrand); Everat, "Les confréries de Riom," pp. 33–34.

103. Ms. of 1507 containing thirteenth-century statutes (St.-Julien, Puy-de-Dôme, arr. and cant. Clermont-Ferrand), *ibid.,* p. 30.

104. Puy-de-Dôme, arr. Clermont-Ferrand: *ibid.*

105. Statutes of 1612; *ibid.,* pp. 37–40. Brioude, Hte-Loire.

106. The Bishop also ordered the person keeping the keys to the closet containing the confraternity's archives to return them to the *bailes* of the confraternity—*ibid.,* pp. 8, 40–41. Neschers, Puy-de-Dôme, arr. Issoire, cant. Champeix.

107. In contrast to the "simple Third Order of the hospital order having the same name . . . [these confraternities] originally played a very notable role. They gave birth to the communes; they laid the bases for municipal charters."—Jaloustre, *Histoire d'un village.*

108. E. Sicard, *Notes et hypothèses sur les fraternités. Sociologie et droit slaves* (1952). The author adds that in Auvergne, and in particular at Riom, it is certain that the "house of the Holy Spirit" was transformed into the first town hall; p. 16. The author, concerned only with studying "the sociological problem of fraternities," based his work on comparisons among Normandy, Auvergne, and Dalmatia. His comparisons are both unusual and a bit rapid, and could not lead to conclusions precise enough, or very new, for simple historians or students of law. We feel it is especially dangerous to make no distinction between the different kinds of confraternities, especially in Auvergne. As for Sicard's suggestion that the fraternities might have been at the origin of social conflicts (p. 23), we would have to disagree as far as the confraternities of the Holy Spirit are concerned.

109. At Louvres, for example, before 1270: "A confraternity was created to build a church . . . and to repair the roads and wells of the town and to uphold its rights"—Delaborde, *Layettes du Trésor des Chartes* (1909), **5**, 308–314. See Marc Bloch, *Les caractères originaux de l'histoire rurale française* (1952), p. 176.

110. For example, the confraternity of St.-Michel at Escazeaux (Tarn-et-Garonne, arr. Castelsarrasin, cant. Beaumont de Lomagne), according to the consular accounts of the village from 1306 to 1401, possessed vineyards worked by hired labor under the *bayles'* direction (which produced up to 35 hectoliters of wine); received dues in money and kind (the amount being fixed each year at a general assembly); had a reserve fund that allowed it to lend money to the village consuls, make gifts to the village's lord, and lend money to the church-wardens to build a bell tower on the parish church; lent wheat and flour in times of famine; and held an annual dinner—F. Galabert, *Confréries au Moyen-Age dans le Tarn-et-Garonne* (1897). For the southwest, see J. A. Brutails, "Note sur les anciennes confréries et l'assistance mutuelle dans le sud-ouest," *Revue philomathique de Bordeaux et du Sud-ouest,* **6** (1903): "Some confraternities were nothing more than communities of inhabitants, generally so when they bore the name of the town or of its church." See the same author's introduction to the *Cartulaire de l'église collégiale Saint-Seurin de Bordeaux* (1897), pp. LIV–LVII.

111. Le Bras, "Confréries chrétiennes," pp. 310, 313: "The aim of the confraternities was to satisfy—within a narrow frame—the most pressing needs of body and soul. . . . For a long time in the countryside, the faithful formed communities that were only incompletely organized—kinds of village confraternities." See Brutails, "Note sur les . . . confréries."

112. "The community of the town had a confraternity, possessed a seal and levied taxes; it took this money and placed it in a box. . . ." (ed. Rappetti [1850], p. 9).

113. J. A. Brutails, *La coutume d'Andorre* (1904), p. 42: "The societies of mutual assistance, or *consorcies,* recall those confraternities of France centuries ago, which, in the guise of religious associations, answered the time's demands for mutual aid." The phenomenon has been well studied in Italy: A. Buffa, *Origini e sviluppo della previdenza sociale in Italia* (1934); G. M. Monti, *Le confraternità medievali dell'alta e media Italia* (1927); Sapori, *Studi di storia economica medievale* (Biblioteca storica Sansoni 5) (1940), esp. chap. 16: *"I precedenti della previdenza sociale nel Medioevo."*

114. "Concerning those groups called guilds or confraternities, as we have already verbally ordered and now expressly command in writing, those things which belong to authority and utility and reason should be done. Let absolutely no one, whether priest or layman, go any further [in this matter]. That is, they may meet together in full obedience to religion . . . but we prohibit eating together. . . ."—Labbé and Cossart, *Sacrosancta concilia* **8**. 572.

115. *Acts of the Apostles* 2: 38. See also the late Pentecostal sequence, *"Veni, Pater pauperum / Veni, Dator munerum."*

116. An expression used in particular at Marthod, *P.J.* 2.

117. St. Augustine, *De Trinitate* **15**. 17, 19, 29, 37.

III. State

Ruler and Ruled in the German Empire from the Tenth to the Twelfth Century*

Karl Bosl

What is the essence of government? The question is an old one, in practice as well as in theory. It is a current question as well, because democracies, too, must govern. It has often been said—and is still said by journalists, historians, and political scientists—that in Germany there is no tradition of democracy. It is asserted, with a jealous glance at England and Revolutionary France, that we have too much governing and too little participation in government. The charge is true, but only to a certain degree.

First of all, in what way have the ruled, the subjects, historically participated in government? On what legal titles has this participation been based? In what forms of government has power and authority rested in the hands of a single individual? These questions have not been sufficiently

* Karl Bosl, "Herrscher und Beherrschte im deutschen Reich des 10.–12 Jahrhunderts," *Sitzungsberichte der Bayerischen Akademie der Wissenschaften, Philosophisch-historische Klasse* (Munich, 1963), 2. Reprinted in K. Bosl, *Frühformen der Gesellschaft im mittelalterlichen Europa* (Munich, 1964), pp. 135–155. Trans. by Miriam Sambursky; revised by the ed.

investigated as a unit and their relationships to each other have been treated statically rather than dynamically. Furthermore, historians and political scientists did not formerly view changing forms of government as the consequence of transformations in social structures; because the national state had remained "unfulfilled," they dreamed (as Th. Schieder has recently argued) of an unchanging ideal past that appeared as a perfect form of government. The new approaches of recent constitutional and social history, however, have shown that consultation with the ruled, and participation of the "subjects," were an integral part of medieval government; that our democratic state had an early form in medieval representation, whose rich history in our country still awaits investigation. For these reasons I think that the problem of the relationship of ruler to ruled in the medieval German Empire not only has a certain practical relevance to the present—especially in Germany—but that it can, indeed must, be attacked with new methods that promise a deeper understanding.

Both modest laborers and great scholars have contributed to our understanding of this field, but the work of a few historians on territorial and constitutional history has been particularly significant. These historians have shown how many-layered and ineffective medieval kingship really was; how extensive, intensive, and fundamental was the rule of the nobility. Thus, as the great legal historian Heinrich Mitteis has said, the medieval German kingdom was less a monarchy than an "aristocracy with a monarchical apex." Early in the century Otto von Dungern showed how thin was the stratum that governed the state and society.[1] Otto Brunner gave new sociological insight to the basic notions of land and lordship.[2] And Mitteis (who more than any of his colleagues was concerned with general history) summarized these conclusions for the first time, compared medieval dynamics to modern norms.[3] Since then Theodor Mayer has contributed new material to solve the problem of royal and aristocratic rule;[4] Walter Schlesinger, on the basis of revolutionary research,[5] has dealt with the different forms of kingship and the co-lordship of the aristocracy;[6] and K. Hauck has explored the religious foundations of aristocratic rule.[7] Under the influence of Brunner and Schlesinger—and against Mitteis—historians have come to prefer to speak not of a medieval "state" but rather of lordship and what belonged to lordship. What, then, were the structures that made this lordship possible, the forms in which it was actualized, the conditions that in some places led to royal supremacy and in others to aristocratic rule?

It soon became clear to historians studying these questions that lordship (in this dynamic, unsystematic sense) presupposed a counter-element, a supplement that, following both Gierke and the sources, historians have called "association" (*Genossenschaft*). It was seen that lordship was the decisive power in the Middle Ages and that "association" developed within its framework as an integral part of government, as a part of the structure of political and social life. Already fifty years ago, Otto von Dungern argued that the fight to be allowed to participate in shaping one's own political destiny was fundamental to the history of political development.[8]

"Lordship," a word we meet in the sources (Old High German *hertoum*)[9] and a basic element in the modern state, appeared in many guises. All had in common "the chance a specific command will be obeyed," as Max Weber has said. "Command and prohibition," "coercion and constraint" were the heart of lordship once it passed the age of rude force.[10] To discover the forms it took, one can analyze either those who were ruled or the foundation of lordship itself. One can talk of lordship over tribes, peoples, empires, or countries—that is, over politically stratified and integrated collective groups—of lordship over a household, a farm, a manor, a castle, a town; of lordship over domains, bailiwicks, serfs, and subjects; of lordship exercised in the rural and urban groups, which we call "associations." Lordship, however, was (and is) possible and meaningful only when the ruled obeyed, when they did what was commanded; the more voluntarily this was done, the easier it was to govern.

Otto Brunner has suggested the term "following" for this relationship of obedience that was both voluntary and enforced, for subordination to another's will and command. I should prefer to call it "service."[11] Whether "service" or "following," this obedience was fundamental to the relationship of ruler to ruled. It is a fact of social history—although seemingly a paradox—that lordship created freedom, that service and subordination created liberty.[12] The moral basis on which this service or following rested was fidelity. Solidified by the spread of Christianity, this fidelity eventually became the spiritual and institutional foundation for the relationships among the members of the ruling upper class and between this class and the ruled lower class (which also expressed itself as a community).[13]

Fidelity—*fides, fidelitas, Treue*—was the essential bond between those who commanded and those who obeyed, between the powerful and the weak, *potentes* and *pauperes*,[14] lord and people. It had to be purchased with rights and possessions, with privileges and marks of distinction, and by allowing participation in government action. As punishment replaced revenge and fidelity became an ethical ideal, cases of breach of fidelity tended to decrease (although, to be sure, we know about only the higher strata of society). They did not vanish completely; for there was still self-interest and lust for power to provoke them.

It was the medieval concept of rights that did the most to produce consultation, the right to participate in deliberations, and the duty to take part in commanding. We refer here to the views of Fritz Kern.[15] The discovery of late Roman "Vulgar Law" has shaken the traditional view that Germanic and late Roman laws were sharply distinguished from each other,[16] but we may still assert that a primitive unity of right and justice survived into the Middle Ages. God, in Whom all law is eternal, was considered the source of all law, whether natural, customary, or legislated. One could therefore in God's name oppose the commands of a Christian ruler, although they claimed the title of "law"; one could oppose them even by force of arms. It happened often enough that individuals or an entire subject population (especially the former) opposed a ruler by force of arms, convinced that they were acting justly. This was an important theoretical and objective factor in the medieval relationship of ruler to ruled. Just as breach of peace or violation of right gave rise to enmity, so a ruler's injustice gave rise to resistance. For subjects and ruler were both subject to a higher order, a transcendent, all-embracing *ordo;*[17] they were all members of its spiritual, sacral, secular hierarchy.

To this way of thinking, the lord was not sovereign in the modern sense. He could not be so. He could not institute "positive" law by his own command. For he was accountable to God and his conscience for the legitimacy of his legislation, and from this it followed that the legitimacy of his acts could be contested by everyone concerned. By legal injustice he exposed himself to revenge. Especially from the Investiture Controversy on, the legitimacy of his actions was subject to the inspection of Pope and Church. Thus local powers and churches acted as counterweights to the growth of early princely sovereignty. In modern terms we might say that the Middle Ages recognized only a sovereignty of law above both ruler and ruled. It was in order to oppose a situation where every "partial association" might claim competence to judge right and wrong, and thus the right to resist an unjust ruler, that Jean Bodin defined his concept of sovereignty. Without it, the modern European normative concept of "state" could not have developed. Likewise, the very problem of sovereignty, the question of absolute power in the relations of Church and state, could not be raised before the Investiture Controversy, even though the Church had claimed since the days of Gregory I, an "indirect power" by "reason of sin." For, to the Germanic peoples as to the Greeks, Homer and Hesiod, law was a sacred, a divine heritage—a "sacred knowing about what is right," as my teacher Eduard Schwartz used to define it.[18] For Augustine, "justice," "peace," legitimate power, "just war" were the central concepts of the "mixed constitution."[19]

From the beginning, as far as we can judge, Germanic institutions were dualistic, as perhaps all forms of government are at similar stages in their cultural evolution. Law was not given but found, pointed out. Therein lay a fair portion of individual power. Self-help, feud, the legitimate use of force, so-called "private" execution were the inheritance of earlier times, were the "givens" of society and culture. A medieval ruler could hardly limit self-help, still less prohibit it. Government could oppose self-defense only by assuring protection (*munt*).[20] The strong (*potens*) who gave protection to the weak (*pauperes*) could also call on those whom they protected for help. This was in fact the historical basis of medieval lordship. "Powerful" and "weak," *"potens"* and *"pauper,"* for this reason were the social distinctions known to the early Middle Ages—as the Frankish capitularies and the Mirrors for Princes from Isidor of Seville onward show. The *pauper* was the less powerful man, the weak man, and not a pauper in an economic sense (the "poor people," the *"armen lewt,"* had landed wealth).[21]

But the mutual dependence of the powerful and the weak could not be based on obedience alone. As relationships became more and more differentiated, this dependence required fidelity based on one law and one order: fidelity that equally bound the ruler and the ruled. Whoever broke this sworn fidelity[22] broke the law; resistance to the wrong-doing ruler became a duty, because he had offended a sacred legitimate order. *Fides* meant both fidelity and belief.[23] To be sure, the greater the power and the more effective the protection, the stronger obedience and fidelity became; the weaker the protection, the more loyalty became merely formal. This is why strong kings were so often followed by "feudal anarchy." But although power was so decisive in this culture, it was limited by a very subjectively defined right. All disputes between might and right aimed at legally fixing the end achieved in favor either of the ruler or of the ruled.

Within the framework of lordship, those with equal rights united in "associations." These tended, through a kind of self-government, to develop a lordship-like organization at their summit in order to deal with their lord on an equal footing. Lordship and association were thus not opposites but structural elements that acted now in union, now in conflict with each other. Kingship and noble lordship thus depended on each other and at the same time were in opposition to each other.

Let us now turn directly to the ruler and his people. The king, as we have said, although he was the supreme representative of realm and rule, could not by himself decide what was law; for he and his people were part of a transcendental religious order, an order that, like kingship itself, rested in magic or sacral foundations, whether pagan or Christian.[24] He was king who by birthright came from a family possessing a royal charisma, and who had been elevated to the kingship by election. Inheritance and election were tied together. The right to elect, on the other hand, was a source of the subjects' right to participate in government, for they derived it from the dualistic character of institutions and from the relationship of protection to obedience and fidelity.[25] Hereditary right and right by election, at first hardly distinguished and used side by side, in the course of time became differentiated; the ruled participated more or less significantly in government depending upon which of the two became stronger. The king called his people to arms to defend the country. His victory, a sign of his charisma, gave him prestige, as we know from Otto I's victory over the Hungarians at Lechfeld near Augsburg (the army made the king) and from the election of his father, Henry I. In a Christian sense, the king ruled by grace of God and stood above his subjects by virtue of his office.[26] But over against the king stood the "people,"[27] not as a crowd without a will but as the group of those who had political rights and who acted together in war, in feuds, in the court, and in electing the king. In the course of time the "people" changed. But they were always there, assembled around the king, on court days and in Imperial Diets, in feudal courts and in parliaments.[28]

These institutions were not always derived from preceding ones, nor did they always have equal influence on political decisions. The basic principle was nevertheless that the king, when making a fundamental political decision, had to act together with the "people," had to have their consent. In these assemblies it was the great men of the realm who advised and took part in decisions; the others were merely in attendance. The list of witnesses signing the royal diplomas issued on such days shows who had the right and duty to participate. From the tenth century on it was the same group as that which composed the *Heerbann,* the war troop of a single or of several provinces. It was the magnates, the *potentes,* who, assembled, had the right to co-decide. During the tenth, eleventh, and twelfth centuries the lords of the largest estates, the lords who possessed the greatest rights of lordship, the largest feudal following, the most effective military force spoke the decisive word at these court meetings and Imperial Diets. They were the representatives of the tribal and provincial feudal upper class.

The magnates, however, were lords themselves, independent of royal interference. They were immunists, both lay and ecclesiastic. The centers of their immunities—in part autogenous, in part the gift of the king—were their manors, the centers of their protective lordships over people and of their *Gewere,* of their right to rule and dispose of property. The manor was the focal point of what had once been a household-lordship and was now fragmented into many kinds of lordship—territorial, personal, judicial, ecclesiastical. Whoever possessed a manor and this household-lordship (the *praedium libertatis* of the *Codex Falkensteinensis,* 1160/1170)[29] had full rights within his district. (The citizen subject directly to the state exists only since the days of Enlightened Absolutism and the French Revolution.) The lord had protective power over the people on his manor, his domain, or the territory of his immunity, whether they were attached to the land or not. His subjects owed him support and were bound to him by fealty—even the serfs. The manor had its own special "peace." Lordship, geographically, was the sphere of "enhanced peace," enforced on the tenants, where self-help was excluded and judicial settlement taught. Because lordship had an inner tendency to create this "enhanced peace," it laid claim to the same judicial rights as did kingship. It emulated the king's peace and excluded his officials. The sword-bearing feudal lords thus participated in royal government in a special way; in their immunities they exercised authority by the same right and over the same objects as the king. In modern terms, they were "sovereign."

This primary form of participation in high lordship was so great that the king and his officials could not act within the immunities. The king could not exercise legal power or rights of lordship over the great noble and ecclesiastical landlords. He had no rights over a lord's vassals or a lord's *ministeriales.* This can be seen most clearly in the trial of Henry the Lion in 1180. According to the land law, that is, the law of kingship, Henry could not be deprived of his possessions. This was possible only according to feudal law, by which a fief could be taken from a vassal who had broken his faith.

But, like kingship, noble and clerical lordship developed collective forces and forms of consultation which were similarly many-layered and multiform. Manorial law, applied to the narrow circle of manor house and domain, created the "commons of the court" (*Gerichtsgemeinde*) and forms of village self-government within neighborhood and settlement communities. Lordship and community were bound together by fealty and mutual protection.[30]

Between the king and the great immunities was another political force: the tribes.[31] Together they formed the *regnum Teutonicum,* the German kingdom, brought together by the common will of the nobility, the group that represented the tribes. The unifiers were the nobility not—as Tellenbach thought—the last Carolingians, especially Arnulf of Carinthia.[32] In 918 the nobility of the two strongest and best organized tribes, the Saxons[33] and Bavarians,[34] each elected their tribal king *"rex in regno Teutonicorum";*[35] one with the support of the Alemans, the other with the support of the Lotharingians. By dexterous and patient work, the first Saxon king succeeded in winning the voluntary subjection of other tribal kings to his hegemony. They acknowledged his kingly charisma, although that of the Bavarian king Arnulf was just as clear.

But the invasions that threatened the dying Carolingian realm in the northwest, the east, and the south during the tenth century revived the old tribal will for independence. The most powerful nobles, some of them members of the Carolingian Imperial aristocracy,[36] won positions as independent tribal dukes. They led the defense of tribal territory. Thereby they won the recognition and support of the nobility, for after their victory they were thought to be endowed with divine grace—*"Arnulfus dei gratia dux."* The nobility accepted their jurisdiction, their call to arms, their guarding the peace, and their ecclesiastical overlordship—the four basic elements of ducal rule. On their side, these small-time kings, these "newer" tribal dukes depended on the consent of their territorial magnates, convened at the tribal assembly—in Bavaria, usually at the royal castle in

Regensburg; in Saxony, at Werla castle. There they met to deliberate and decide on tribal affairs. Like the aristocracy of the realm who elected the king, the tribal magnates elected the duke. They gave their consent to his ordinances, decided on wars, sat in judgment in important cases of breach of the peace, and helped to settle important disputes. In 936, at Reichenhall, Duke Arnulf of Bavaria had his son Eberhard elected as his successor in *regnum* (or *regimen,* as it was called in the eleventh century) by a partial tribal assembly.

But the more the emperors, from Otto I on, succeeded in breaking the power of the dukes, the more oppressive became the right of joint government. The dukes' sovereign rights were curtailed; the dukes were bound to the throne by feudal law and the law of office, and their position as intermediary between the king and the immunities was taken from them. For decades, until 1070, until the accession of the Guelfs, Bavaria was administered as a "royal province" by the king himself or by foreign, appointed dukes, that is, by officials. Only one duke of Bavaria became king—the last Saxon, Henry IV. But Henry exhausted the dukedom, the real basis of his power, by giving huge endowments to the new imperial bishopric of Bamberg on the upper Main. From then on there remained only a paltry remnant of his old sovereign rights; during the Investiture Controversy the dukes of Bavaria had to turn to a new path: the institutionalized state. Under the early Hohenstaufen, these newly developed territorial structures were brought under the king by means of feudal law and incorporated into the union of the realm. From the Investiture Controversy onward, however, this unification led inevitably to the same erosion of power from which the dukes had suffered 200 years earlier. From the end of the thirteenth century, only the most powerful prince could hold his own in the office of king.

At the beginning of the tenth century the position of the dukes of Bavaria was nearly a royal one. They succeeded in preserving so many of their ancient sovereign rights and prerogatives over nobility and Church until the thirteenth century that the Wittelsbachs managed, beginning in 1180, to build the most "modern" principality in Germany. The outlying parts of the dukedom had been shorn away; its territory was compact. The dukes succeeded in making their nobility and Church (especially the monasteries) independent of the king and transformed them into territorial "Estates." In 1077 both the regalia [rights of the king] and the *ducatus* [rights of the duke] included the rights of court and taxation, grants for military service, the *fodrum* [animal fodder] in the border districts and the right of ordinance and injunction. The militia was available to king and duke alike (outside of feudal obligations) only in case of *êhafter not,* of territorial necessity; only liegemen joined in "private wars," whether ducal or royal. (The feudal relations between the Bavarian counts and the duke are still not clear.) The duke's judicial power was that of an arbiter, especially in cases of disputes among members of the tribal nobility and among the clergy. To it was joined peace-keeping in the most general sense, by means of military expeditions. His most lucrative rights came from the law of escheat. He even continued to be elected—there is documentary evidence for it—in the period when he was appointed by the king. But the idea of tribal rule came to a definite end with Eike von Repgow's *Sachsenspiegel*. His discussion of tribal rights is embedded in his discussion of the legal system of the realm and the functions of the king who is the apex of this system of rights. The Electors who chose the king were no longer the representatives of the tribes.

The formal and moral ties binding the kings and tribes were homage and the king's provincial "progress."[37] When he ascended the throne at Aachen, the king acquired *potestas* (royal power)[38] and *nomen* (the royal title)[39] but he still had to travel through the tribal territories in order to take on his functions as supreme judge and arbiter. He obtained full lordship only when he presided in court during his first visit to the tribal land. In his "progress" he presented himself before the tribal nobility, for only a limited circle of magnates had in fact elected him. Thus the king's progress was not only a symbolic but also a concrete act of accession to the throne, the real beginning of his rule. He demanded the acclaim, the *collaudatio,* the jubilation of the people, that he needed. He thus came into direct contact with the tribes—and first of all with their nobles, who on this occasion took up their obligations to him.

On the occasion of his "progress," all the members of the tribe did homage to the king, swore an oath of fealty acknowledging the system of royal rights—which was more than simple lordship. At the same time, regard for valid traditions and rights were always demanded of the king in Saxony; obligation to him was always conditional upon his keeping the rights and laws of the territory. The Saxons made this stipulation when they did homage to Henry II and Conrad II. Homage also entered into the relations of the lord of the manor to his peasant tenants, entered into the civic oath of the towns,[40] the oath of the boroughs to their overlords, and the oath of the Estates and subjects of the territories to their territorial lord. Homage was a general phenomenon; feudal homage, a special case.

The transition to feudal forms of "election" was a sign of the feudalization of the realm. In an earlier period the tribes did homage at the time of election and troops were organized by tribal order in the imperial army; in later times, feudal vassals did homage and the army was organized along feudal lines. This transition, one of the most significant events in medieval institutional history, was a sign of the waning importance of the tribes. In this way the king shut out the tribal dukes—and created weighty conflicts of obedience and service for his vassals.

Wipo[41] tells of the heated debate between the Swabian counts and Duke Ernst, the son of Conrad II, over a conflict between fealty to the king and fealty to the duke. The nobles declared they were going to lose their "freedom" if they followed the duke, for they were liege men of the king, the guarantor of their freedom. Since Henry II, the royal "progress" had significantly enlarged the circle of those who paid homage and those who "elected" the king. Not only had the character of the king's election changed, but the royal tribal "following," whose dukes and counts had once made up the realm, was replaced, enlarged, and broken by the feudal homage of a larger stratum of royal vassals. Unused by Henry IV and Henry V, the technique was taken up by Lothar, Conrad III, and Frederic I. (Under the latter three the ecclesiastical princes did no feudal homage.) In this way the kings tried to repair the shaky relations of fealty between themselves and the nobility. For election, which had now become the ruling principle for the elevation to the kingship, was in reality in the hands of a progressively narrower circle of people.

Thus there was in medieval Germany no "monopoly of legitimate power," no unified authority; self-defense, legitimate self-help, and judicial tribunal stood side by side as equivalent possibilities. There was no sovereignty, no state, but only a system of higher or lower orders; of great, medium, and small lordships and lords. Beside the king and under him, the tribal dukes exercised a number of royal rights. They were the principal electors of the king. To the nobility belonged an autogenous rule—neither derived nor delegated—exercised in their immunities by their bailiffs. The Church too possessed its immunities. (This meant, of course, that noble lordship also broke up these special territories.) In fact, the only real direct subjects of the king and his servants (*ministeriales* in the ninth and tenth centuries) were the *principes* with their sovereign rights, the high aristocracy who were royal vassals, and the churches that were under his personal rule or the control of his "advocates."

The statecraft of the king consisted in keeping all these in equilibrium. To execute his policy he could count on the support of his immediate sphere of power and protection, the crown lands and crown domains surrounding the royal palaces and castles, which, again, were immunities.[42] In a wider circle, the king depended on the magnates with their rights of lordship, aid, and protection; on their power in its widest sense. The principle of association, immanent in the whole of German medieval government, constituted the way for the ruling class to participate in royal rule.

Thieme[43] has rightly pointed out that the German kings had to transfer some of their rights and their sources of power to the nobility and the Church in order to use them to realize their policy. The absence of a permanent residence, of a rational centralized administration of the realm, especially a treasury—in short, the absence of a bureaucracy—made this necessary. In exchange the king received, especially from the Church, court attendance and military service; he and his wandering court were lodged, and the scanty apparatus of the court-chancery was supplied with chaplains who acted as officials.[44]

The one way the king's will might have been enforced by powerful officials failed because the officer-dukes, *missi,* counts, and *centenares* themselves had to have delegated or autogenous lordship in order to enforce the ruler's will out in the territories.[45] The limits between office and lordship, the borderline between property and fief, thus became blurred—especially during the Investiture Controversy. From the tenth century on, rich donations to the Church, especially of immunities, had put cathedral chapters and monasteries in a position to serve the king (*servitium regis*). But after the Concordat of Worms they also were involved in lordship. Thus the real power of the king was further eroded, especially as the "church advocateship" in the immunities became a backdoor for the power-hungry bailiff-nobility to participate indirectly in royal rule.

In Germany, feudalism and feudal law[46] likewise remained only a superficial cover for "allodialism," for the rule of nobility. East of the Rhine, where land was first being cleared, where no suprapersonal and rational concepts of law and state survived from Roman times, the idea of service that was so much alive in feudalism led to the idea that lordship was the payment for achievement—as is proved by the rise of the *ministeriales* into the lower ranks of the nobility. The high aristocracy's monopoly of local rule was further strengthened by the right of inheritance, especially the inheritance of offices as fiefs. Feudalism in its developed form was likewise a mutual relationship, with strong associative elements; in Germany it became a particularly important source of participation in government. It was, to be sure, a first attempt to secure the power of kingship, which was threatened in its substance by aristocratic lordship and allodialism by means of a legal and ethical system of personal and material dependence. The *Heerschildordnung* of Frederic Barbarossa was a rationally conceived attempt to organize such a scale of dependencies. Everyone who took part in government, whether profiting from it or serving it, was given a fixed place according to his power and standing—from the king, princes, and lords down to the sixty-shilling knight. This was meant to close the circle of those ruled by the king, his direct subjects. And in this sense the feudal pyramid constituted a stage preliminary to the modern state. We must remember, though, that since tenurial bonds as well as the other dependencies were forms of loyalty, they always included the possibility of legal, legitimate opposition. Although self-help had probably survived under the surface among the lower classes since Frankish times, because the political functions of feudal law were primarily for the fighting classes who retained the possibility of self-defense, self-help and the right to private war remained alive much longer among the higher social classes than in the "enforced peace" of the manor and among the bourgeoisie with their guild and town laws.

At least until the time of the Investiture Controversy, German kingship was so powerful that, although it made use of feudal law, it did not need it. Crown property and authority over the Imperial Church were the decisive instruments of royal power under the Ottonians and early Salians. But the Investiture Controversy destroyed all this. The nobility began to rule independently,[47] and new forms of territorial government appeared. The Roman Church struggled for independence and, in so doing, robbed German kingship of its sacral foundations, undermined its standing in the consciousness of believers. Henry IV tried to renew the foundations of royal power by developing the Crown's domains. The early Hohenstaufen continued this policy by building up imperial estates (*terrae imperii*)[48] around the large imperial palaces (*Pfalzen*) and castles. There they established ecclesiastical feudal estates, given by the Church which had become rich through former donations and had acquired the right of investiture.

Liege vassalage[49] was never successful in Germany; the German *miles,* the vassals of the eleventh century, were still free men. The institution of *"ministeriales"* was thus used—especially by the king, but also by the churches and the high nobility—to govern their vassals. The *ministeriales* rose into the society of the high nobility and joined them in their knightly forms of court culture. They undoubtedly first emerged in the world of the manor, but like those who paid only rents in kind, were not under the jurisdiction of the bailiff but under that of the lord. From the twelfth century onward, they were able to acquire fiefs; thus they penetrated into the circle of the noble feudatories. The most powerful personalities and representatives of this group became rulers equal to the high nobility; the others, whose means were moderate or small, built small domains around their castles, as the nobility had always done, and like the nobility, acquired lordship over land and people; gave protection; and asked for aid, corvées, and taxes in exchange.[50] This group rose by forming an association:[51] the weaker layers of the old nobility and the rising groups of retainers joined in a new lordly class (which has been analyzed by O. von Dungern). The former "servants" of the great lords became partners in their masters' lordship. Essentially they followed the same ascending path as the high nobility of the early and high Middle Ages, who had emerged from the noble officials of the Merovingians and Carolingians, and, in part, like the *ministeriales,* had unfree origins.

Max Weber considered a tendency towards rationality to be a structural element of European civilization and Von Dungern thought that a basic trait was the drive to participate in shaping one's own political destiny; here we must also consider the development of town autonomy. The first stage, ordained and approved by the lord, was the creation of a zone of special peace, of immunity, which in the course of time separated itself more and more from its rural surroundings of noble and royal domains.

The process found its symbolic expression in the town walls.[52] At the same time the towns developed their own laws—a mixture of municipal sovereignty and mercantile law founded on custom. Although the western and central European towns were vastly different from their rural surroundings, in southern Europe they had an even stronger aristocratic-bourgeois character. In the south, the noble remained as such in the town; north of the Alps he became a bourgeois, while the rich patricians became landed nobility by acquiring land. In both zones there developed autonomous communities governed by municipal administrations, especially episcopal. The bishops linked town and country, because they had acquired the titles of "count" in the *contado* and feudal rights over the nobility domiciled there.

But the rise of the bourgeois community diminished the town lord's power; the community itself became lord of the *contado* and ruler in the town council of the seigniory. Collectively enforced rules and collective participation in government in a limited, non-agrarian sphere led once again to rule over others.

In the eleventh century a movement began toward communal self-government, diminishing the former cooperation between town lords and communities.[53] By means of confederations, of communes under the town nobility's leadership, active groups took control of the militia, the law courts, and the town finances and turned the public authority (*consules*) and the town council into their own administrators. The autonomous communities, seeking an "enforced peace," revolted against their episcopal town lords, rebelled against the Hohenstaufen kings, and finally became overlords in their *contado*. The *contado* became municipal territory. The town nobility and the great merchants were the people who did it.

North of the Alps autonomous life developed in the *wik,* the non-agrarian settlement around the cathedral town, the monastery, and the castle. Within it the engine of progress, the carrier of the developing mercantile law (*consuetudo, ius mercatorum*), was the guild, originally a religious brotherhood. From the tenth century on seignorial town and communal *wik* existed side by side, the merchant being joined by the artisan who depended on him (who was not the same as the manorial artisan), both developing the free town economy that found its place, in *wik* or *portus,* next door to the political, military, and cultural center of the *civitas* or *burg*. The two of them developed as neighbors, soon joining their walls. New servile immigrants streamed to them, immigrants who did not become members of the merchants' guild. Thus, within the compass of the town lord's immunity, a community of settlers emerged which gradually expanded into a commune with its own militia and law courts. Within the area covered by mercantile law, around the markets, reigned an "enforced peace," offering refuge from self-help and excluding the right to fight before the tribunal. If the town and its lord were sufficiently powerful, the inhabitants won personal freedom after residence of a year and a day.

Within the community, government was organized by the town's lord until the community won the right to appoint its own authorities. By peaceful compromise—and in battle—the burgesses won the right in the thirteenth century to govern themselves through their own town council. Their instrument was union by oath in the confederation of the *coniuratio,* which then became an association able to negotiate with the town lord. For this reason the civic oath and "oath day" played a decisive role from the thirteenth century on. But the town remained tied to its former lord by an oath of fealty. The town community was thus an organized entity bound by oath, which autonomously governed itself in all essential military, judicial, and financial matters. The extent to which it could decide its political destiny depended on its economic power as well as on the strength or weakness of its lord. Since many German towns were under royal officials, as Frederick II's privilege to Nurnberg makes clear, the decline of German kingship led to the formation of the German "Free Imperial Cities." Other towns remained under princely sovereignty, still dependent on their lord. But the burgesses of these towns also formed autonomous civic communities whose far-reaching rights of self-administration clearly separated them from their lords. Together with nobility and clergy, the towns became Imperial and provincial "Estates," deciding with them on the destiny of their territories and seigniories, especially their financial destiny.

In conclusion, never did an individual in the German Empire of the tenth, eleventh, and twelfth centuries hold the government of any sphere of political or social life concentrated in his own hands. Given the cultural level of the times, rule over larger territories was possible only if supporters and rivals also participated. It was not a peculiarly German characteristic —although it emerged in the development of Germany—that participation in government was immanent in lordship and developed from it, participation that was achieved in collective forms. Around the king, the imperial nobles and the tribal nobility; around the duke, the tribal nobles who supported him; around the aristocratic lord, the *ministeriales* who had risen to ruling positions by service and achievement; around the town lord, the *communitas burgensium;* around the landlord, the *communitas villanorum.* All of them through collective association won the right to help decide their own destiny, won a form of self-government and self-administration. Since tribal lordships made up the kingdom and royal lordship rested on tribal institutions, the great problem remained the king's ability to integrate them into the kingdom. They succeeded. Tribal rule was eroded. But the same process eventually eroded royal power as well. The nobility emerged victorious, gradually transforming its lordship from a purely personal association into an institutionalized state. Here the kings, despite their enormous efforts, could not follow.

Fealty and mutual loyalty were the moral bonds between ruler and ruled, a personal association involving participation in government; protection and aid tested and proved it. Lordship, service, obedience created "liberty"—the word did have a specific meaning in the Middle Ages. The feudal system and feudal law expressed the dualistic character of the basic political and social forms, expressed a political and social situation with vast disparities and differences. "The people," in a constitutional sense, were not lower orders but the nobility and the Church that was ruled by the nobility. *Ministeriales* and bourgeoisie in time became the people. Only in the Imperial Diet with its Curia and in the provincial diets, did this expanding "people" find its first institutional representation. But these institutions had their roots in the beginning of the development we have traced, in the dualism of lordship in early medieval Germany. Here one must start if he wishes to study the tradition and early forms of democratic rule.

The kingdom never developed real forms of subordination. Nor did it ever develop an abstract, rationalized concept of lordship, except in its myths and theology. Each new authority dissolved into participation by collectivization. The kingdom never became a state because it demanded too much of its rulers—too much power, authority, trust, fidelity, right. But this corresponded to the ideas and beliefs of the people. These we have to understand.

In concluding this paper we might adopt this definition: rule and realm in the medieval sense were essentially federal, and not centralizing, structures of political order. Historically, both always contained a collective principle of cooperative decision.

NOTES

1. Otto von Dungern, *Der Herrenstand im Mittelalter* (1908); *Adelsherrschaft im Mittelalter* (1927); "Königsgericht und Reichsfürstenrat zur Zeit Kaiser Lothars III.," *Dopsch-Festschrift, Wirtschaft und Kultur* (1938), pp. 300–329.

2. Otto Brunner, *Land und Herrschaft. Grundlagen der territorialen Verfassungsgeschichte Süd-ostdeutschlands im Mittelalter* (4th ed., 1959); review by H. Mitteis, *HZ,* **163** (1941), 255–281, 471–490.

3. Heinrich Mitteis, *Lehnrecht und Staatsgewalt. Untersuchungen zur mittelalterlichen Verfassungsgeschichte* (1933) (see W. Kienast, *HZ,* **158** [1938], 3 ff.); *Der Staat des hohen Mittelalters. Grundlinien einer vergleichenden Verfassungsgeschichte des Lehnszeitalters* (5th ed., 1955); "Formen der Adelsherrschaft im Mittelalter," *Festschrift für Fritz Schulz* (1951), 226 ff.; *Die deutsche Königswahl. Ihre Rechtsgrundlagen bis zur Goldenen Bulle* (1938).

4. Theodore Mayer, *Fürsten und Staat* (1950).

5. Walter Schlesinger, *Die Entstehung der Landesherrschaft. Untersuchun-*

gen vorwiegend nach mitteldeutschen Quellen (2d ed., 1964); *Mitteldeutsche Beiträge zur deutschen Verfassungsgeschichte des Mittelalters* (1961).

6. W. Schlesinger, "Herrschaft und Gefolgschaft in der germanisch-deutschen Verfassungsgeschichte," *HZ,* **176** (1953), 225–275 [see above, pp. 64–99]; Über germanisches Heerkönigtum," *Vortäge und Forschungen,* **3** (1954), 105–141; "Burg und Stadt, *Festschrift Theodor Mayer. Aus Verfassungs- und Landesgeschichte,* **1** (1954), 97–150; "Die Anfänge der Königswahl," *ZRG GA* **66** (1948), 381–440; "Karolingische Königswahlen," *Festgabe für H. Herzfeld. Zur Geschichte und Problematik der Demokratie* (1959), pp. 207–264.

7. K. Hauck, "Geblutsheiligkeit," *Festgabe für P. Lehmann. Liber Floridus* (1950), pp. 187–240.

8. O. v. Dungern, "Die Verfassungsreform der Hohenstaufen," *Festschrift für Zittelmann* (1913).

9. K. Guntermann, *Herrschaftliche und genossenschaftliche termini in der geistlichen Epik der Westgermanen* (1910); H. Beer, *Führen und Folgen, Herrschen und Beherrschtwerden im Sprachgebrauch der Angelsachsen* (1939).

10. F. Graus, "Die 'Gewalt' bei den Anfängen des Feudalismus und die Gefangenenbefreiungen der merowingischen Hagiographie," *Jahrbuch der Wirtschaftsgeschichte,* **1** (1961), 61–156.

11. Karl Bosl, "Dienstrecht und Lehnrecht im deutschen Mittelalter. Das *ius ministerialium,*" *Studien zum mittelalterlichen Lehenswesen,* Th. Mayer, ed. (1960), pp. 51–94; "Über soziale Mobilität in der mittelalterlichen 'Gesellschaft.' Dienst, Freiheit, Freizügigkeit als Motive sozialen Aufstiegs," *Vierteljahrschrift für Sozial- und Wirtschaftgeschichte* [hereafter *VSWG*], **47** (1960), 306–332.

12. K. Bosl, "Freiheit und Unfreiheit. Zur Entwicklungsgeschichte der Unterschichten in Deutschland und Frankreich während des Mittelalters," *VSWG,* **44** (1957), 193–219; "Vorstufen der deutschen Königsdienstmannschaft. Begriffsgeschichtlich-prosopographische Studien zur frühmittelalterlichen Verfassungs- und Sozialgeschichte," *VSWG,* **39** (1952), 193–214, 289–315.

13. W. Ebel, "Über den Leihegedanken in der deutschen Rechtsgeschichte," *Studien zum mittelalterlichen Lehenswesen,* pp. 11–36; F. Graus, "Über die sogenannte germanische Treue," *Historica,* **1** (1959), 71–121. (See K. Bosl, in *Bohemia Jahrbuch,* **2** (1961), 597–611 and W. Schlesinger, "Randbemerkungen zu drei Aufsätzen über Sippe, Gefolgschaft und Treue," *Festschrift für O. Brunner* [1963].)

14. K. Bosl, "Potens und Pauper," *Frühformen der Gesellschaft im mittelalterlichen Europa* (1965), pp. 106–134.

15. Fritz Kern, *Gottesgnadentum und Widerstandsrecht im früheren Mittelalter. Zur Entwicklungsgeschichte der Monarchie,* R. Buchner, ed. (2d ed., 1954); *Recht und Verfassung* (*n.d.*).

16. E. Levy, *West Roman vulgar law. The law of property* (1951); *Weströmisches Vulgarrecht. Das Obligationenrecht* (1956).

17. L. Manz, *Der Ordogedanke. Ein Beitrag zur Frage des mittelalterlichen Ständegedankens* (1937); H. Krings, *Ordo, philosophisch-historische Grundlegung einer abendländischen Idee* (1941); W. Dyckmann, *Das mittelalterliche Gemeinschaftsdenken unter dem Gesichtspunkt der Totalität* (1937); A. Dempf, *Die Hauptform der mittelalterlichen Weltanschauung* (1925); W. Schwer, *Stand und Ständeordnung im Weltbild des Mittelalters* (1934); B. Jarret, *Social theories of the Middle Ages* (1942).

18. K. Bosl, "Die germanische Kontinuität im deutschen Mittelalter (Adel-König-Kirche)," *Miscellanea Mediaevalia* 1. *Antike und Orient im Mittelalter* (1962), pp. 1–25, reprinted in *Frühformen der Gesellschaft,* pp. 80–105.

19. *"Ordo est parium dispariumque sua cuique loca tribuens dispositio."*

20. A. Waas, *Herrschaft und Staat im deutschen Frühmittelalter* (1938), was the first to try to derive the whole structure of the German state in the early Middle Ages from the *mund.* See also E. Molitor, in *ZRG GA,* **64** (1944), 112 ff. The importance of "protection" in the structure of government is stressed by Brunner, *Land und Herrschaft.*

21. K. Bosl, "Pauper-Potens." In the discussion, Ziegler rightly pointed out that this meaning of *"pauper"* and the pair of opposites *Pauper-Potens* already appears in the Latin Psalms. The best example is to be found in Psalm 71 in the following verses: *"Judicare populum tuum in iustitia, et pauperes tuos in iudicio"; "Judicabit pauperes populi, et salvos faciet filios pauperum et humiliabit calumniatorem"; "Et adorabunt eum omnes reges terrae, omnes gentes servient ei: Quia liberabit pauperem a potente et pauperem, cui non erat adiutor: Parcet pauperi et inopi et animas pauperum salvas faciet."* All the elements discussed in the text above are mentioned here: the mighty (ruler), the weak (subject), the protector (lord), *adiutor* in contradistinction to the *calumniator* who abuses his power. At the time of the dissolution of the ancient municipal constitution of the Roman Empire, the opposites were *honestiores* and *humiliores.* This was changed into the pair of opposites *potentes/pauperes,* probably under Christian influence and the stress of the dissolving order. It infiltrated into the official language of the Frankish realm and is frequent in the *Capitularia* of the ninth century.

22. W. Fritze, "Die fränkische Schwurfreundschaft der Merowingerzeit. Ihr Wesen und ihre politische Funktion," *ZRG GA,* **71** (1954), 74–125; M. David, "Le serment du sacre du XIe au XVe siècle. Contribution à l'étude des limites juridiques de la souveraineté," *Révue du moyen âge latin,* **6** (1950), 5–272.

23. Fraenkel, art. "Fides," *Thesaurus linquae latinae* **6**, 1 (1912/1926), col. 661–691; H. Helbig, "Fideles Dei et regis," *Archiv für Kulturgeschichte,* **33** (1951), 288 ff.; D. v. Gladiss, "Fidelis regis," *ZRG GA,* **57** (1937), 442–451.

24. *Das Königtum. Seine geistigen und rechtlichen Grundlagen,* Th. Mayer, ed. (1956), containing important studies by E. Ewig, O. Höfler, W. Schlesinger, H. Büttner, Th. Mayer, H. Beumann, F. Kempf, M. Hellmann, and O. Brunner; O. Höfler, *Germanisches Sakralkönigtum,* **1** (1952); P. E. Schramm, *Herrschaftszeichen und Staatssymbolik,* **1**, 2 (1954/1955); K. Hauck, "Herrschaftszeichen eines wodanistischen Königtums," *Jahrbuch für fränkische Landesforschung,* **14** (1954), 9–66.

25. W. Kienast, "Rechtsnatur und Anwendung der Mannschaft in Deutschland wahrend des Mittelalters," *IV. Internationaler Kongress für Rechtsvergleichung* (1955), pp. 26–48.

26. Corresponding to the objective ideal of *ordo* of the early Middle Ages, the order of offices in the world was anchored in the world of eternity and not subject to human will. Therefore the office was always in the foreground of all theories of "Estates," clerical or lay. The ordering of office by the will of God was the contrary of the "order by birth" given by God. In a functional, impersonal, church-ordered hierarchy, the clergy would always have had the highest social standing; in reality they had it only if they already owned it by birth. The virtue of *"humilitas"* helped man to take his place in the *ordo*; its sinful counterpart is *"superbia"* [haughtiness]; both were the primary basis of all systems of virtue and sin.

27. J. O. Plassmann, *Princeps und Populus* (1954); "Reich und Gefolgschaft im 10. Jahrhundert," *Germanien,* **15** (1943); G. Herold, *Der Volksbegriff im Althochdeutschen* (1941).

28. H. Weber, *Die Reichsversammlungen im ostfränkischen Reich, 840–918. Eine entwicklungsgeschichtliche Untersuchung vom karolingischen Grossreich zum deutschen Reich* (1962).

29. H. Petz, "Codex Falkensteinensis," *Drei bayerische Traditionsbücher aus dem 12. Jahrhundert* (1880).

30. R. Kotzschke, *Salhof und Siedelhof im älteren deutschen Agrarwesen,* ed. H. Helbig (1953); H. Jankuhn, *Gemeinschaftsform und Herrschaftsbildung in frühgermanischer Zeit* (1939).

31. R. Wenskus, *Stammesbildung und Verfassung. Das Werden der frühmittelalterlichen gentes* (1962).

32. G. Tellenbach, *Königtum und Stämme in der Werdezeit des deutschen Reiches* (1939) (see M. Lintzel in the *Deutsche Literatur-Zeitung* [1941], 505 ff.); H. Zatschek, *Wie das erste Reich der Deutschen entstand* (1940); W. Schlesinger, "Kaiser Arnulf und die Entstehung des deutschen Staates und Volkes," *HZ,* **163** (1941), 457 ff.; G. Tellenbach, "Die Unteilbarkeit des Reiches," *HZ,* **163** (1941), 20 ff.

33. K. Jordan, "Herzogtum und Stamm in Sachsen während des hohen Mittelalters," *Niedersächsisches Jahrbuch für Landesgeschichte,* **30** (1958), 1–2 f.

34. K. Bosl, "Das 'jüngere' bayerische Stammesherzogtum der Luitpoldinger," *Festschrift für Max Spindler* (1955), pp. 145 ff.; "Das bayerische Stammesherzogtum," *Zeitschrift für bayerische Landesgeschichte,* **25** (1962), 275–282; "Die historische Staatlichkeit der bayerischen Lande," *Zeitschrift für bayerische Landesgeschichte,* **25** (1962), 3–19.

35. K. Reindel, *Die bayerischen Luitpoldinger 893–989* (1953); "Herzog Arnulf und das Regnum Bavariae," *Zeitschrift für bayerische Landesgeschichte,* **17** (1954); "Die staatliche Entwicklung Bayerns vom Ende der Agilolfingerzeit bis zur Mitte des 10. Jahrhunderts," *Zeitschrift für bayerische Landesgeschichte,* **25** (1962), 665–678.

36. G. Tellenbach, "Vom karolingischen Reichsadel zum deutschen Reichsfürstenstand," *Adel und Bauern* (1943), pp. 22 ff.; *Studien und Vorarbeiten zur Geschichte des grossfränkischen und frühdeutschen Adels* (1957) (with articles by Fleckenstein, Vollmer, Wollasch, Schmid).

37. R. Schmidt, "Königsumritt und Huldigung in ottonisch-salischer Zeit," *Vorträge und Forschungen,* **6** (1961), 97–233.

38. H. Löwe, "Von Theoderich zu Karl d. Gr.," *DA,* **9** (1952), 380 ff. (*potestas* = ruling authority, in contrast to *potentia* = might.)

39. H. Beumann, "*Nomen imperatoris.* Studien zur Kaiseridee Karls d. Gr., *HZ,* **185** (1958), 515–549; "Zur Entwicklung transpersonaler Staatsvorstellungen," *Vortr. u. Forschungen,* 3, *das Königtum* (1956), 199–209; "Die Historiographie des Mittelalters als Quelle für die Ideengeschichte des Königtums," *HZ,* **180** (1955), 469 ff.

40. W. Ebel, *Der Bürgereid als Geltungsgrund und Gestaltungsprinzip des deutschen mittelalterlichen Stadtrechts* (1958).

41. Wipo, "Gesta Chuonradi," cap. 20 (H. Bresslau, ed. [1955], *MGH SS rer. Germ.* p. 40, A.D. 1027). Compare H. Grundmann, "Freiheit als religiöses, politisches und persönliches Postulat," *HZ,* **183** (1957), 1 ff.; K. Bosl, "Freiheit und Unfreiheit," *VSWG,* **44** (1957), 193 ff., reprinted in *Frühformen der Gesellschaft,* pp. 180–203.

42. K. Bosl, "Pfalzen und Forsten," *Festschrift für P. E. Schramm* (1963); "Probleme der Reichsgutforschung in Mittel- und Süddeutschland," *Jahrbuch für fränkische Landesforschung,* **20** (1960), 305–324.

43. H. Thieme, "Die Funktion der Regalien," *ZRG GA,* **62** (1942), 57–80.

44. K. Bosl, "Würzburg als Reichsbistum," *Festschrift Th. Mayer,* **1** (1954), 161–182; "Aus den Anfängen des Territorialstaates in Franken," *Jahrbuch f. fränk. Landesforsch.,* **22** (1962), 67–88; J. Fleckenstein, *Die Hofkapelle der deutschen Könige.* 1. *Grundlegung. Die karolingische Hofkapelle* (1959).

45. This is most clearly shown by Charlemagne's decision not to send out any more *de infra palatio vassi pauperiores* as *missi* to decide disputes. He thought them to be too weak, cowardly, and corruptible. Instead, he entrusted the task to the magnates. *MGH SS* 1. 38; Katz, *Annalium Laureshamensium editio emendata* (1889), p. 45.

46. F. L. Ganshof, *Feudalism* (1952); "L'origine des rapports féodo-vassaliques. Les rapports féodo-vassaliques au Nord des Alpes à l'époque carolingienne," *I problemi della civiltà carolingia* (Spoleto, 1954); "Das Lehnswesen im fränkischen Reich," *Studien zum mittelalterlichen Lehenswesen* (1960), pp. 37–50.

47. More stress should be put on the fact that Pope Gregory VII, who came from a nonfeudal world, succeeded in separating king and nobility, ruler and ruled, government and participation in it, especially in Germany. In doing so he disturbed a basic structure of early medieval political order and dissolved the functional connection between rulership and community on the highest social level. As a result, king and nobility had to proceed in functionally separate ways —the king creating an Imperial Rule following Roman prototypes, the nobility enforcing and institutionalizing its own rule in the territorial states.

48. K. Bosl, *Die Reichsministerialität der Salier und Staufer, Ein Beitrag zur Geschichte des hochmittelalterlichen Volkes, Reiches und Staates,* (1950/1951).

49. W. Kienast, *Untertaneneid und Treuvorbehalt in England und Frankreich* (1952); see *ZRG GA,* **66** (1948), 111–147; *Die deutschen Fürsten im Dienste der Westmächte,* **1** (1924); **2**, 1 (1931); "Französische Krondomäne und deutsches Reichsgut," *HZ,* **165** (1941), 110 ff.

50. K. Bosl, "Dienstrecht und Lehnrecht."

51. The Pöhlder Annals report in A.D. 1150 of such a *"Res mira et hactenus inaudita."*

52. Schlesinger, "Burg und Stadt," *Aus Verfassungs- und Landesgeschichte, Festschr Th. Mayer* **1** (1956), 97–150.

53. *Studien zur den Anfängen des europäischen Städtewesens,* Th. Mayer, ed. (1958), with contributions by Vittinghoff, Klebel, Petrikovits, Klein, Ammann, Büttner, Dollinger-Léonard, Petri, Schlesinger, Schwineköper, Jankuhn, Johannsen, Ludat.

ESTATES, COMMUNITIES AND THE CONSTITUTION OF THE LATIN KINGDOM*

Joshua Prawer

Studies dealing with the political and social structure of the Crusader Kingdom that have been published during the last decade tend more and more to modify the image hitherto accepted of the Latin establishments in the East. It was an image designed by the great Crusader jurists of the thirteenth century and, in the main, it has been unquestioned by historians, and by students of law and constitution in particular, until our own times.[1] The so-called "Paradise of Feudalism," a figment of the imagination of a biassed jurist of the nobility, John d'Ibelin, is giving place to a balanced and a far more nuanced description of the political system of the Kingdom, one based on contemporary chronicles, acts and deeds, and not on juridical treatises.

As earlier studies have covered the twelfth century principally,[2] the following study will start with the evolution of the Kingdom in the second half of the twelfth, and consider some of its guiding lines of development during the thirteenth century.

I. CROWN AND NOBILITY

The second half of the twelfth century witnessed the gradual enfeeblement of royal prerogatives and a corresponding rise in power of noble families. From the score or so of holders of seigniorial fiefs in the middle

* Reprinted from Joshua Prawer, "Estates, Communities and the Constitution of the Latin Kingdom," *Proceedings of the Israel Academy of Sciences and Humanities,* 2, no. 6 (Jerusalem, 1966), 1–27, 39–42.

of the century, there emerged a higher class of nobility, not more than ten intermarried houses, which succeeded in getting vast estates and political authority into their hands. They revolved around the Ibelins as pivot and mainspring, a family of far-flung possessions, of aristocratic, royal and even imperial marital links and of traditional eminence in the Kingdom. Called in Crusader documents *nobiles, riches homes,* or *barons,* all of them tenants-in-chief of the Crown, this upper group of magnates tended, as its counterparts did almost everywhere, to climb to heights which separated them widely from the rank-and-file of the nobility; the simple knights (*milites, chevaliers*) and even the possessors of smaller seigniorial fiefs were left far behind. The status of the magnates was markedly strengthened during the last years of the reign of Baldwin IV, when fateful issues of succession were fought out between rival claimants supported by royalist and baronial partisans.[3] It was of small consequence that it was the royalist party which temporarily got the upper hand by crowning Sybilla and Guy de Lusignan. It was of much greater moment that the Crown forfeited its prestige, and, although with no overt constitutional changes. its standing was shaken. The respective places of Crown and baronage at the end of the First Kingdom are pithily described in the defiant answer of one of the great barons. The fabulous Renaud de Châtillon, entreated (1186) by the king, Guy de Lusignan, to stop pillaging Moslem caravans in his Transjordan Principality, sent back word *"que aussi estoit il sires de sa terre, come il* (Guy) *de la soe et que il n'avoit point de trive as Sarrasinz"*[4]—he is as much sovereign of his territory as the king is of his own, and he has no truce with the Saracens. It was a rejoinder that not only proclaimed the weakness of the Crown but announced the virtual disruption of the unity of the Kingdom. A grand seigneur did not acknowledge a truce contracted by the State with a foreign Power but resolved to pursue an independent policy. And Renaud de Châtillon was not the only one to do so. At the end of 1186, Raymond, prince of Galilee, entered into a private agreement with Saladin which was harmful to the interests of the State. Inevitably, the Kingdom was approaching total dissolution: this was within a twelvemonth of the disastrous Battle of Hattin.

The vicissitudes of the Crown after the Battle of Hattin may be succinctly told in the language of the agreement concluded between Richard of England and Philip II of France on the eve of the Third Crusade. They divide, in advance, all future conquests of the Crusade, and virtually imply that the State and the Crown of Jerusalem are vacant or have ceased to exist. The future conquerors will decide their fate after the expected victory.[5] The brisk business of offering the Crown to Guy de Lusignan, Conrad de Montferrat and Henry of Champagne (who never accepted it)[6] shows the lamentable depths to which the throne of Jerusalem had sunk.

This once more explains that, during the Fifth Crusade, Pelagius not only displayed little ability and less knowledge in his command of the armies bogged down on the muddy banks of the Nile, but even raised doubts whether captured Egypt belonged at all to the Kingdom of Jerusalem. These doubts subsequently prompted King John of Brienne to press the pope for a promise that the newly envisaged Crusade would assign to the Kingdom all its conquests to come.

The accession of Frederick II to the throne of Jerusalem (1225) turned a new page in the history of the Kingdom. The narrative of his Crusade and of the following "War of the Lombards" have been recounted time and again. But it seems worthwhile to analyse this crucial chapter in the annals of the Kingdom by setting it against the social and political background of Crusader society.

II. THE *ASSISE SUR LA LIGECE* AND THE "ESTATE OF NOBILITY"

We have sought to describe elsewhere the social evolution of the Kingdom during the twelfth century. Our main conclusion purported to clarify and to throw into relief, the double process of the rise and consequent social differentiation of the class of nobility, the second movement already in full swing in the 'thirties of that century. This double process attained its climax in the second half of the century, following the famous *Assise sur la ligece* of King Amalric. The *assise,* which was of primary importance in changing the balance of power between Crown and nobility[7] and of which the repercussions were felt in almost every domain of law and legal procedure, had a revolutionary effect in speeding up the trend of class formation and in shaping the class structure in the Kingdom. It is from this point of view that we propose to review its results here.

The nobility, as a distinct class, existed in the Kingdom from the very outset. Ruled and judged by its own special code of customary law, into which subsequent legislation introduced a body of *assises,* the class as a whole had a well-defined, specific, social and legal status, and its individual members enjoyed a privileged standing, formally expressed in grants of seigniorial and simple fiefs. But it was the tenants-in-chief exclusively, in reality the highest nobility only,[8] who took part in the deliberations of the *curia regis* called the *Haute Cour* of the Kingdom.

The *Assise sur la ligece* theoretically revolutionized this state of affairs. *De iure,* the *hommage lige* was reserved to the king only and nobody could take an oath of *ligece*—and this is diametrically opposed to the European usage—save to the king.[9] From now on, the oath of *ligece* allowed all members of the class of nobles to attend meetings of the *Haute Cour.* Everybody became *home lige* of the king: *"vavassours des riches homes"*[10] became *"ses homes liges qui tienent de ses homes."*[11] All of them are, therefore, summoned: *"que il li viengent aidier ou consellier ou servir à armes, se il en a besoing,"*[12] to give the customary *consilium et auxilium.* Thus the oath constituted a direct legal link between every fief-holder in the Kingdom and the Crown. But the oath of *ligece* not only forged vertical links, meeting at the ideal apex of the feudal pyramid, in the Crown, as the suzerain *par excellence;* it also forged horizontal links, embracing all nobles, that had not previously existed. To quote Philip of Novara:

> *Le rei otroia . . . que tous ses homes liges qui tenoient de li ou de ses homes, queis qu'il fussent, grans ou petits, fusent tenu de fei l'un à l'autre de ce que est dessus escrit, et que chascun d'eaus peust requerre les autres come ces peirs en teil endreit.*[13]

This meant that henceforth all the fief-holders in the Kingdom would not only belong to the class of the nobles, according to the generally accepted view of class division in mediaeval society, but that new and formal links would hold firmly together the internal fabric of the class. These new links would give rise to reciprocal legal obligations of all members to each other. They are all "peers" of each other. The class becomes an "estate" with identical duties and privileges of all members in respect of each other and in its external relations to the Crown.[14] The members of the "estate" are vested, theoretically at least, with the same political vote and authority in the *Haute Cour* wherein all of them take part.

Whoever has studied Crusader sources is aware of the peculiar legalistic way of thinking of the Crusader nobility and so will not be surprised that, instead of the evolutionary process which, by trial and error, elaborated and defined "estates" everywhere else, the Kingdom followed the path of official legislation. It is remarkable that the legal act which brought the formal "estate of nobility" into being belongs to a somewhat early period compared with Europe. Not less characteristic is the fact that the formal "estate" is not founded on an oath binding members to each other, but on a common oath to a party outside their own ranks, the Crown. Thus born, the "estate," permanent though it is and with its preferential place in the Kingdom and in the *Haute Cour,* nevertheless, for purposes of its practical working, like the right to petition the Crown in common, has to go through an awkward procedure of "conjuring" the "peers" of the "estate" every time.

Somehow, the legal "estate of nobles," although stabilized very early in the history of the Kingdom, never went a step further. The Kingdom did take one stride beyond the stage of a *magnum consilium* composed of all the tenants-in-chief by adding *all* fief-holders to its meetings, but it never evolved a system of representation which would have assured the simple knights a permanent standing in the *Haute Cour.* The reason for this arrested evolution should be sought not only in the lack of experience, but in the realities of life in the Kingdom. The main purpose of the *Assise sur la ligece* was to prevent arbitrary confiscation of fiefs without a legal judgment of a Court. Denial of justice was dealt with in all feudal systems by the right of appeal to the jurisdiction of the overlord. The Crusader Kingdom underpinned this procedure by a system of common petitioning of nobles, barons and knights in the *Haute Cour*. In such cases, it was in the interest of the petitioners not only to be represented, but to be present in person. The sheer weight of numbers was of utmost importance in impressing accused and Court. Thus the main purpose of the *Assise sur la ligece* stultified its potentialities and cut short the development of a representative system. Only such a system could have made certain of the permanent attendance of the simple knights at the meetings of the *Haute Cour*. Without it, the *Haute Cour* remained a monopoly of the *grands seigneurs*. Nothing could be more illuminating than the decision of 1182, to levy a general tax on the Kingdom, virtually taken by the higher nobility acting alone, although, in fact, the simple knights, possessing land-fiefs or money-fiefs, were taxed as well.[15]

It needed a different kind of cause and stimulus to start the wheels of the machinery turning and put it beyond the bounds of a *magnum consilium*. We see its operation when one of the great lords, Ralph of Tiberias, charged with treason, sees his fiefs confiscated by King Aimery (the so-called Amalric II) without judgement of the *Haute Cour*.[16] On that occasion, he "conjured" his peers (meaning magnates and knights) against the king.

In another instance, Balian of Sidon, regent of the Kingdom for Frederick II, on an order from that emperor, refused to execute a decision of the *Haute Cour* regarding Toron-Tibnin in favour of Princess Alice against the Teutonic Order. He found himself facing a *coniuratio* of nobility, the barons and knights, who withheld their service as long as he withheld execution of the decision.[17] Henry II of Cyprus and Jerusalem, who kept back a rent-fief from one Philip of Gibelet, was compelled by a *coniuratio* of his knights to grant it to the claimant.[18] The same king narrowly escaped an identical process when petitioned by his knights for the payment of arrears of salaries,[19] an instance that is also significant as evidence of the shortcomings of the *coniuratio* in common petitioning. The petition of the knights of Cyprus was made after the siege of Cérines:

> *la court fu pleniere et que grant partie de ciaus à qui le rei deveit lors vindrent devant le rei en la presence de sa court. Un d'iaus por tos conjura le rei et semonst por lui et por toz les autres.*[20]

This seemed to be a perfect setting for a common petition. It was expounded by one Guillaume Raimond, who *"parla pour tous les autres."* But things turned out differently. John (d'Ibelin) of Beirut, after eulogizing the loyal service rendered by the knights, took especial pleasure to point out their defects as laymen:

car sauve seit vos honors, il semble que vos ne savés mie bien les uz et les assises dou reiaume de Jerusalem.

They should have put their demand forward in the customary way of summons, requests and delays, each claimant demanding individually what was due to him and then threatening the lord legally with relinquishment of service ("*gagier de son service*") and then of fealty. In lieu,[21] the guileless men mustered their courage, chose one of their number to speak in their name and put their demand in common to their overlord. But this, said John of Beirut, was precisely contrary to the customs and *assises.*

No doubt the answer given by this paragon of legality was in strict accordance with prevailing practice, namely, that a claim to a vassal's salary or to a fief should follow the mode of conjuring the lord to fulfill his obligations towards the vassal. In the true spirit of vassalic relations, with their insistence on the direct nexus between lord and vassal, such a claim had to be presented individually and not through a common petition of the vassals. Thus John of Beirut narrowly circumvented a possible use and development of the *Assise sur la ligece.* He must have argued that the competence of the *Assise sur la ligece* was restricted to its primary cause: unlawful confiscation of a fief. Although the *Assise* branched out, and one ramification was the right of all fief-holders to attend the *Haute Cour,* a common petitioning in respect of fiefs seemed to John of Beirut unlawful, or, to put it otherwise, such a case should be determined by the traditional customs obtaining in that regard.

Confined in jurisdiction to confiscation of fiefs, the *Assise sur la ligece* could still play a part even in politics because of the connection, ingrained in the feudal system, between fief-holding and the favored status of the class of fief-holders. Thus it was invoked and activated during the struggle between the representatives of Frederick II and the baronial party led by the Ibelins.[22] This notorious clash has often been described, but, with one exception, only as a narrative of political events. Our main interest is different. We intend to consider it from the point of view of the institutional evolution of the Kingdom.

III. CLASSES AND CORPORATIVE BODIES

Around 1231, the central institution of the Kingdom was still the *Haute Cour,* the undifferentiated *curia regis,* cutting a rather poor figure if compared, for example, with the contemporary *curia* of Henry III of England. Court of justice, advisory council, legislature and political assembly, the *Haute Cour,* despite its undeveloped character, acquired more and more power in direct ratio to the weakening of the Crown. The great offices of the State, the executive organs of the Kingdom, never became powerful in the East, and this is probably the main reason, as far as we can see, why the *Haute Cour* never really sought to control their appointment or functioning. The *Haute Cour* was itself dominated by some half a dozen families and their feudal dependants. The simple knights, the *vavassours,* although theoretically members of the *Haute Cour* according to the *Assise sur la ligece,* were in effect denied all influence.

Their position in the Kingdom, as we have explained elsewhere, was at no time especially flourishing. Dependence on their lords, hardly mitigated by the *Assise sur la ligece,* was stringent. A great many of them, living on rent-fiefs, were very often hardly anything but salaried retainers. If there was a small group of knights who held more than a fief *unius militis* (*fief de son corps* in Crusader terminology), its numbers were always few. Moreover, Crusader legislation of the middle of the twelfth century, which allowed accumulation of fiefs (thereby reversing earlier canon), paved the way for the magnates to swallow up fiefs and replace land-fiefs by rent-fiefs. Both sides, lord and vassal, may well have regarded this arrangement as a convenient answer to their problems. Consequently, the never numerous intermediate class of knights, somewhere between barons and simple knights, was probably disappearing rapidly at the end of the twelfth century. The "estate of nobility" tended to become polarized and clearly split between highest and lowest levels.

Forfeiture of the Kingdom at Hattin and its reconstruction after the Third Crusade did not better the standing of the simple knights. It were truer to say that the Second Kingdom, which comprised no more than a fifth of the former territory, drastically diminished the number of land-fiefs in their possession. Seigniorial dynasties which survived, but had lost their fiefs east of the narrow strip along the sea-shore which was the Second Kingdom, must surely, if they still kept knights, have done so on a basis of salary or rent-fief. And the same will apply to seigniorial families which settled in Cyprus and derived their incomes from the island, quite often as a means of allowing them to hold on to their continental possessions.[23]

In these circumstances, the simple knight, just a paid warrior—although all appearances of genuinely vassalic relations were preserved by jurists and legislation—was in no position to act independently either inside his class or in political life. He might have been proud to be a cut above the Frankish burgesses, and his feelings of superiority might have been bolstered by his so immensely transcending a conquered and contemptible population. But such subjective emotions could not alter the fact that the Kingdom was ruled by the magnates, whereas he, as a part of the *maisnie* of a *lignage,* was completely dependent and could be manipulated by his superiors for their own purposes.

At the time when the magnates, barons and knights were becoming an "estate" in the juridical sense of the word as a result of the *Assise sur la ligece,* other strata of society took on greater importance in the life of the Kingdom. They did not form "estates," but their cohesion and corporative structure made them a factor of consequence in a society where the fabric of State was crumbling. Roughly speaking, there were two types of corporations: the Military Orders, in a steadily rising ascendancy, and the Communes of the great Italian cities. Constituted as they were, the Orders were, in a sense, out of the mainstream of circumstance: their power and resources were chiefly recruited from outside the Kingdom, from their chapters and priories, their fiefs and domains, all over Europe. Their great number (Hospitallers, Templars, the Teutonic Order, St. Lazar, St. Thomas and Montjoie) and their authority should, in theory, have assured them the standing of an "estate," and their chronic quarrels and quick partisanry made them redoubtable adversaries or staunch supporters. But these were not the cohesive qualities that led to the emergence of an "estate." Socially, as their members did by birth, they belonged to nobility.

On a different level, the Communes, that is, the colonies of the Italian cities, and to a smaller degree the Provençal, were corporative bodies. They can scarcely be classified as belonging to one of the traditional social classes, let alone as an "estate". Their standing in the Kingdom was not ordained by tradition, by the origin of their members or—except to a small degree—by their social function. It was fixed once and for all, and statutorily, by the privileges accorded to them by the rulers of the Kingdom in the early history of the conquest. Governed by their own local establishments and judged by their own codes of law, differing from those of noble and burgess alike, the Communes were corporations of which the members, bound by oath to their magistrates, wielded a preponderant influence on the affairs and destiny of the Kingdom. The famous "War of the Communes," raging on the high seas and bringing havoc to Acre, was among the most unedifying episodes of thirteenth-century Christendom. In a way, the State came to a halt when Venice, Pisa and Genoa, seesawing from alliance to alliance, supported by baronial factions and Military Orders, gave vent to their Italian jealousies inside the walls of that city. They behaved and acted, each like an independent political entity, with no regard for the law and order of the State to which they belonged. It was a kind of foretaste of wars to be fought, in centuries to come, between colonial powers on soil not their own.

In the history of the Kingdom in the thirteenth century, one group of corporations is conspicuous by its absence: the cities and their burgesses. It is, indeed, a strange phenomenon. There were Crusader cities, populous, rich and, with few exceptions, surpassing in size their counterparts in Europe, and yet they never became corporative bodies. Stranger still, urban environment, fertile in producing corporative organizations as guilds, for example, seems to have been entirely sterile in the Latin East. It was pointed out long ago that one of the reasons for this complete lack of communal city developments might have been the chronic warfare of the Latin East. It will be impossible to prove or disprove this explanation, but it appears to us that, in the best of cases, it is only a partial one. A city's autonomy is not necessarily a handicap to its fighting power.

To our way of thinking, the major cause should be sought elsewhere. The most characteristic trait of Crusader society is its complete urbanization. We doubt if there was any other area in Christendom where the entire Christian population lived in cities, and in cities only.[24] This intriguing and significant social feature is explained by the exigencies of a minority faced with a permanently hostile majority. To assure its military striking power, the minority gathered itself in walled cities and in castles, and from those centers it kept the countryside in thrall.

The Crusader cities were, consequently, almost the only habitat of the conquerors. And this is probably the principal reason for the absence of urban autonomy. Magnates, knights, Italian Communes, Latin clergy—all lived together in the same cities. So did the burgesses, but the cities were not burgess cities. It was that composition of the urban population, where the burgesses were only one component and surely not the most important, which prevented the rise of any communal movement. No city in the Kingdom or in the Principalities enjoyed any privileges. None had even the most elementary charter. Jerusalem, alone, enjoyed two special privileges for some time: lower duties on imported foodstuffs, and abolition of the property or possession rights of absentee landlords.[25] But it was not only the burgesses of Jerusalem who enjoyed these favours; all the townspeople enjoyed them. The grants were not part of any "city" policy, they were a part of a royal policy to make sure of a stable population in the capital.

This state of things did not preclude the existence of a well-defined class of burgesses, but it never attained the stage of real corporative organization. Burgesses of a given city were a corporation only to the extent that they were subject to a special code of customary law and that a competent jurisdiction operated, following the general pattern of judgement by peers. The *Cour des Bourgeois,* with an appointed viscount as its president, was composed of burgess jurors, also appointed by the city lord. On occasion, this tribunal could submit demands or complaints to the city lord or even take part in administration.[26]

Although, then, the class boundaries were clear, the burgesses nowhere succeeded, not even inside particular cities, in organizing themselves corporatively. This goes far to show why no "estate of burgesses" ever came into being. There was a consciousness of belonging to a common class, but a meeting of delegates of corporate city bodies was needed to engender the attitudes of an "estate" and develop the institutions suited to represent one.

If the presence and overwhelming influence of non-burgess elements are the answer to the question why the cities themselves never become autonomous, it is even more surprising, and puzzling, why no corporate urban bodies, such as guilds, were ever established. The nearest we get to them are streets or quarters settled by men pursuing the same trade, or, more often, by men of common ethnic origin. But there were no guilds, and no guild organizations. The fact that Moslem, Jewish, or local Christian artisans would never have been admitted into a Frankish guild, if there ever had been one, so that no joint craft organization was possible, might be part of the reason. But the main reason, we think, was different. Any guild organization presupposes the possibility of monopolizing the pursuit of a given craft, and it becomes an exclusive and excluding body.

Such an organization might fit well into a settled society with its ideal of *standesmässiger Unterhalt,* but it would hardly do in the Latin Kingdom. We are dealing with a foreign colony, constantly fed and living by and through new contingents. In that set-up, any monopolistic agency would hamper the integration of newcomers in the economy. A guild in the Latin East would be detrimental to further intake and harmful to the interests of State and society. The only exception was medicine. Examination by the bishop and the confrères was a prerequisite to the exercise of that profession:[27] solicitude for public health (or perhaps for the salvation of souls) prevailed over the interest of absorbing more colonists.

In the absence of guilds, the only other comparable form of social cohesion were the Fraternities. The earliest to be found is of foreign origin and, as far as we can see, it was very shortlived: it was the *Societas Vermiliorum* of Pisan origin, a product of the Third Crusade.[28] The existence of other Fraternities is well attested for the middle and the second half of the thirteenth century. But it is only one of them which furnishes us with any details as to the nature and functions of a Fraternity. And it is precisely this one which became a pivot of politics during one of the severest crises that the Kingdom underwent.

IV. THE COMMUNITY OF ACRE

There was no power or factor in the Second Kingdom which could consciously will and direct the evolution of its political régime. In the period of Henry III, Louis IX and Frederick II, it had no captain to chart its fateful courses. After the Crusade of Frederick II, formal sovereignty was vested in an absentee Crown, the Government was run by the emperor's appointees from among the local baronage, and supreme authority exercised by Richard Filangieri, nominated as the emperor's *bailli* for the Kingdom. Frederick II not only left insecure boundaries and a provisional Government, he left a climate of permanent resentment and rebellion.

The first act of Filangieri was to seize the city (but not the castle) of Beirut (1231), the honour, that is, the main fief, of John d'Ibelin, acknowledged chief of the baronial opposition. It is at this stage that there were new constitutional developments, both new theory and new practice. In themselves, they mark an important chapter in the constitutional history of the Kingdom, one which not only denoted a new phase in the general history of the thirteenth century, but, in a sense, more than any other happening, crystallized the image of the Kingdom in historiography and, in the process, obscured its earlier annals. On the other hand, an understanding of these developments can contribute to the study of a basic problem, that of transition from a feudal monarchy to a *Ständestaat*. It is a transition of utmost interest, as it exemplifies a special case conditioned by the social and political framework of the Latin Kingdom.

After seizing Beirut, Filangieri went on to Acre, the veritable capital of the Kingdom, with letters from the emperor. The ordinary procedure for proclaiming the Government's policy and announcing the new appointments of State would have been to summon the *Haute Cour*. But Filangieri and the emperor were not only interested in legal technicality: they wanted to make certain of the loyalty of the population and sway public opinion. Here, Filangieri had recourse to a novel and revolutionary method. Instead of convening the *Haute Cour,* which legally could have been done by Balian of Sidon, till then the *bailli* of the Kingdom, he called a special and extraordinary meeting in the Great Palace of the castle of Acre: *"il assembla tos les chevaliers et les borgeis."*[29] As far as we can see, no institution in the Kingdom was composed of nobles and burgesses. Some burgesses might attend the judicial meetings of the *Haute Cour,* but as individuals, owing the privilege to their knowledge of the law of the realm. Naturally, the two classes would have found themselves together in a military expedition or at a coronation, but never for joint deliberations.

From the institutional aspect, it is hard to classify the gathering. There cannot be the slightest doubt that it was neither a spontaneous occasion nor just a fortuitous rendezvous. Filangieri bore imperial rescripts addressed to the ruling and responsible class of the Kingdom. The *milieu* was the Great Palace of Acre, the customary venue for meetings of the royal Court. The barons were in attendance, the powers-that-be, the nobility and the knights. This could have been brought about within the ambit of State forms: a general session of the *Haute Cour* with the knights taking part according to the *Assise sur la ligece*. What was truly unprecedented was the inclusion of burgesses. They had, till then, no *locus standi* in the *Haute Cour*: inviting them, possibly not altogether formally, served Filangieri's purpose to make the imperial proclamation public and to gain their support. Yet one wonders if the originator of the change was Filangieri himself, or whether he was following the instructions of Frederick II. In this connection one may recall the summoning of burgesses to the meeting of the *curia regis* in Frederick's Italian kingdom (1232), which is almost contemporary with the events in Acre. Even more indicative is it that one of the last acts of the emperor before quitting the Holy Land (May 1229) was to accord privileges (perhaps tax remissions) to the burgesses of Acre and to support the Syrian Christians against the Latin clergy.[30] In the light of this policy, is it not natural to suppose that he expected backing from the popular element and so instructed Filangieri to summon the burgesses to the extraordinary meeting? It is a plausible hypothesis, at least.

It seems to us that there is reason enough to regard the assembly as a meeting of an enlarged *Haute Cour* with the addition of popular elements. But whereas the whole nobility of the Kingdom could have taken part—a fairish number were momentarily in Cyprus—it was only the burgesses of Acre and not of all the cities who came. No unusual significance need be attached to this. Filangieri, still preoccupied with the siege of the castle of Beirut, had little leisure to bid other burgesses to come, and, anyway, politics had always been debated and decided in Acre.

The imperial proclamation may be characterized as a royal decree reminiscent of similar decrees in the contemporary England of Henry III. What Frederick told his hearers was what every gathering or any assembly of estates would have liked to hear. The government will strive *"por maintenir dreit et justice, et por garder en lor raisons les granz et les petiz et les riches et les povres."* And Filangieri added: *"Et je sui prest dou faire par le conseil des prodes homes de la terre."*[31] No wonder that our anonymous chronicler, the author of a *Continuation of William of Tyre,* remarks: "If the behaviour and activities had been as the words in his (the emperor's) letter, the people of the country would have been appeased and would have accepted him as *bailli.*"

While Filangieri was mouthing anew traditional sentiments and well-worn clichés, the Frankish nobility was expounding a theory of Government conceived in terms of historical development, which not only distorted but in a sense falsified all the early history of the Kingdom. The theory was unfolded by Balian of Sidon, the *bailli* in office before Filangieri's arrival.

> I have been charged to tell you in their name and my own—says Balian—that they let you know that, when this land was captured, it was not done by any *chef seignor.*[32] It was conquered by a Crusade and a movement of pilgrims and people foregathered. And when they had conquered it, they made a *seignor* by accord and by election and they gave him the seigniorship of the Kingdom; and then, by accord and recognition of *preudes homes,* they made *establissemens* and *assises,* which they willed that they be held and used in the Kingdom to safeguard the *seignor* and other people and to maintain reason[33] and then they swore to hold it and they made the seignior swear it. And thenceforth all the seigniors of the Kingdom had sworn it until now, and likewise swore it the emperor also.[34]

Three points were underlined by Balian: the popular (or noble, but opposed to royal) origin of the Kingdom; the inviolability of laws sworn by the king and people; a *"contrat social"* binding king and people, confirmed and systematically renewed in the coronation oath. What was said so succinctly by Balian was to be set forth at length, a generation later, by John d'Ibelin of Jaffa, author of the celebrated *Livre de Jean d'Ibelin.* His three introductory chapters repeat the *exposé* of Balian, but the whole work, as far as it deals with the feudal theory of Government, is wittingly based on those assumptions and draws far-reaching conclusions from them.[35] A hereditary monarchy notwithstanding, it is the original constitutional act of election of a lord by peers which forever engages the consciousness of the nobility. John, spokesman of the nobility, sees its era, with power balanced between Crown and itself, as a natural outcome of this primary election; moreover, the theory postulates an uninterrupted continuity of that state of affairs during the century and a half that elapsed between the first election and its own time. The election taken out of context and the oversight of four generations of history thus confound the true historical evolution. The establishment of a strong kingly power and its centralistic tendencies, the ample means at the disposal of the Crown and the favourable circumstances which facilitated centralization—all this was thrust into oblivion.[36] It needs all the acumen of an historian to extract evidence in proof of a situation different from that described by the *Livre de Jean d'Ibelin.* A comparison of the juridical treatise of Philip of Novara, which served as its basis, with the larger and more elaborate work of John d'Ibelin, will demonstrate how a political theory and a prejudiced concept of the Kingdom's history enabled John to conjure up a coherence, an abstraction and symmetry which only a complete detachment from reality could have fashioned. In the light of his concepts, an earlier juridical treatise, the *Livre au Roi,*[37] appears to belong not only to another period but to a completely different State, and yet it was written at the end of the twelfth century in the Kingdom of Jerusalem.

The attempt of Filangieri to generate a favourable public opinion did not succeed. But the institutional machinery which he set in motion, although it failed him, was to figure prominently in the history of the Kingdom. The events that followed are known to us from a unique source, the *Eracles,* and we shall let the chronicler tell the story.

The people having heard Filangieri's refusal to abandon the siege of the castle of Beirut as required by the barons and to bring the case against John of Beirut to the *Haute Cour*—

> The wisest among them and the most farsighted held counsel together and saw that there was no salvation for them save that they be bound together by oath to guard and to maintain their reasons, their rights and the franchises of the Kingdom. Then they remembered that there was in the country a Fraternity, the Fraternity of Saint Andrew, which had its grant from King Baldwin and was confirmed by his privilege. And, later on, it was confirmed by Count Henry (of Champagne) and he made of it a privilege. And this

> Fraternity had *establissemens* devised and fixed in the privileges, and among other *establissemens* was this, that all those who wanted to enter the Fraternity were free to do so and that those of the Fraternity were free to receive them. Then assembled *"li riche home et li chevalier et li borgeis"* and, when they were assembled, they ordered the councillors of the Fraternity to be found and the privileges. And when they came, they caused the two privileges to be read and then swore the Fraternity and then swore most (? many) of the people, who did it right willingly because of the fear of the malice of Marshal Richard (Filangieri); and thus they were all bound to each other.[38].

The events thus described are well known, but in their interpretation we must differ from the accepted views. The starting point is Filangieri's assembly of magnates, knights and burgesses, which declined to accept the imperial policy of administration. This is not yet an assembly of "estates," but it is an assembly in which "estates" take part. Under the real or seeming threat of arbitrary rule, and under the unmistakable threat to rescind or control the franchises of the Kingdom, which included institutions in the sphere of public law and privileges in the sphere of private, it became a revolutionary assembly. Its first thought was to find a formula which would enable the participants to form a legal united front against the imperial menace. It was in perfect compatibility with the incredibly legalistic minds of the Crusader nobility, and in a sense was implied in the feudal system, that even a revolutionary movement should have a legal basis and should be able to pursue its aims within the confines of existing canon and custom.

The result of this deliberation was that the insurgents swore a common oath, which served a dual end: it established a united front against an external danger and, by mutual alliance, assured the safety of each individual inside the new institution.

Historians have linked this oath with similar phenomena known in Europe in the context of urban communal movements. *Coniuratio* would be the right technical expression; it was a *coniuratio* that underlay such movements. The plausibility of this connection seemed all the stronger, seeing that the new institution was, indeed, called *commune* and it was staged in the city of Acre.[39] But this interpretation hardly fits the data at our disposal, nor can it clarify some of the major developments. In our opinion, the right interpretation must be sought in the compass of the customs and institutions of the Kingdom.

The oath taken by the revolutionary movement had nothing to do with a "communal oath." The nearest parallel would be one taken by the insurgent English barons a generation later, during the crisis of the Provisions of Oxford. The commonalty at Oxford swore thus:

> *Ceo jura le commun de Engleterre a Oxenford. Nus . . . fesum a saver a tute genz, ke nus avum jure sur seintes Evangeles, e sumus tenuz ensemble par tel serment, e promettuns en bone fei, ke chescun de nus e tuz ensemble nus entre eiderums, e nus e les nos cuntre tute genz*[40]

In definition and aims, this matches what we are told by our Crusader source: *"que il fussent toz tenus ensemble par seerement de garder et de maintenir les raisons et lor dreitures et les franchises dou reiaume."* One is almost tempted to look for straightforward links between the two events, and it might prove not to be beyond the bounds of reasonable possibility to discover them.

The question arises why the barons of the Latin Kingdom had recourse to this extra-constitutional procedure at all. They had to hand an institution that was not to be found, in similar form, in England—the *Haute Cour* with its conjuration of "peers"; in the given circumstances, this would have suited their needs and attitudes admirably. We believe that it is only by understanding this overt side-stepping of a traditional institution, which the barons always fought to preserve in all its integrity of power, that we can explain events and interpret them aright.

A twofold difficulty faced the insurgents. The *Haute Cour* might have been legally convoked either by the new *bailli,* Marshal Richard Filangieri, or by the "sitting" *bailli,* Balian of Sidon. It goes without saying that Filangieri would not bestow upon an insurrection the favour of legal status. On the other hand, Balian's legal standing was obscure. With the arrival of the new *bailli* appointed by the emperor, his tenure of office should have come to an end. True, the legal minds of the Ibelins argued that the emperor had no right to undo by script what was done *viva voce* in the *Haute Cour.* Still, the position was doubtful. And there was a further difficulty, not legal but actual, which the Ibelins could not surmount. As it turned out, Balian, expounder of the constitution of the Kingdom to the imperial envoy, did not join the extreme faction of baronial resistance. He belonged to a small group of nobles who cooperated with the Military Orders and the Communes of Venice and Genoa in mediating between the rival parties. Even assuming that a meeting of the *Haute Cour* convoked by Balian had been legal, Balian himself was, then, by no means a certain bet.[41]

There was yet another problem of the utmost moment, the problem of the burgesses. Granted, for the sake of argument, that the *Haute Cour* could have been convened, it would still have been no more than a meeting of barons and knights, at most of the "estate of nobles", duly constituted as a body sworn in through the *Assise sur la ligece.* But, at this juncture, the baronial opposition urgently needed a far larger popular backing than the upper "estate" alone could assure. At its zenith, the "estate of nobles" hardly exceeded a count of some thousands,[42] whereas Acre by itself probably exceeded forty thousand, and perhaps had as many as sixty thousand inhabitants, and Filangieri, as Frederick II before him, was apparently wooing the populace.

How to gain the allegiance of that element, and, at the same time, mould it institutionally—this was the main problem of the baronial opposition. It was not just a problem of engineering a declaration of allegiance, which could have been done spectacularly by vociferous acclamation. What was wanted, and by those members of the baronial faction who had a legal training, was an institution, parallel to the *Haute Cour,* that would bring solidly together people of different classes. The barons and knights already formed an "estate"; the popular element did not, and could not, so long as the Kingdom had failed, as the first step, to evolve an "estate of burgesses," or a corporative urban organization, which might be put forward as its popular, non-noble sector. Consequently, the barons could not simply add "representatives" of the burgesses to the "estate of nobility." Moreover, for reasons already given, they could not use the *Haute Cour* for such a purpose, because it was not "constitutionally" possible to convene it. The way out was found in the Fraternity of Saint Andrew. By taking the common oath of the Fraternity, every man was bound by its rule and also each to the other, as our chronicler explicitly says—after taking the oath: *"et lors furent toz tenus les unz as autres."* This could not have been put more neatly.

Before analysing the institutional results of the "oath of Saint Andrew," it will pay us to look more closely into what is known about the Fraternity. It clearly belongs to the First Kingdom, as its rule, or its foundation, was confirmed by a privilege of one of the Baldwins. Of the five Baldwins known, it is scarcely possible that either the first or the last can have been the author of the privilege, and we are inclined, although lacking proof, to infer that the Fraternity was established by Baldwin IV (1174–1185) or perhaps earlier, and confirmed by Henry I of Champagne (1192–1197). The seal of the Fraternity, fortunately extant, adds some details to our knowledge.[43] On one side are depicted two figures, marked by the letters: S. P[etrus]—S. A[ndreas] and surrounded by an inscription: ELEMOSINA. FR[ATER]NITATIS. ACCO[NENSIS]. Saint Peter holds the traditional keys and a volumen, and Saint Andrew the Gospel. The reverse includes the conventional design of the Church of the Holy Sepulchre with its conical open roof and, beneath it, the Holy Sepulchre itself. The sun and the moon flank the design. On the rim is the inscription. IN.HONOR[EM]. D[E]I. ET XR[ISTIA]NITATIS.

The connection with Jerusalem or the Holy Sepulchre is enigmatic. Allowing that the Fraternity was established with Jerusalem still in Crusader hands, during the First Kingdom, it is difficult to explain the conjunction of a reproduction of the Holy Sepulchre with a Fraternity of Acre. We prefer to conclude that the image pertains to the king of Jerusalem. As a matter of fact, pieces of money struck by one of the Baldwins bear it.[44] The two Saints, Peter and Andrew, are a riddle in themselves. We know the name of the Fraternity, from written sources, as eponymous of Saint Andrew alone.[45] Remarkably enough, none of the two Saints had a church dedicated to him in Jerusalem, whereas Saint

Andrew had one in Acre. But in all probability we should not link the Fraternity with any contemporary church. On the other hand, these two fisher Saints would have a special appeal for a sea-faring city like Acre and its citizens. The official name, according to the seal, was "The Charity of the Fraternity of Acre—to the Honour of God and of Christendom." Unless we surmise that the seal belongs to a different Fraternity, which is rather improbable, we must take it that "Fraternity of Saint Andrew" was the name in vogue or that the seal belongs to our period and that the name, while it stresses the Fraternity's new institutional status as the *Fraternity of Acre,* is still joined with an image reflective of the Fraternity's first patrons.

The primary aim of the Fraternity, as of many others, must have been charity and social welfare. If it was chosen by the leaders of the revolution for their remoter purposes, that might have been because of its popularity, but, more likely, because of the character of its privileges, that whoever wished might enter it. The royal privilege it enjoyed is further proof of the general attitude of misgiving on the part of the authorities, lay and ecclesiastic, towards any sworn corporation. The subsequent confirmation by Henry of Champagne might have been one of property, if the Fraternity had any, or, what is more probable, followed the line taken by the Italian Communes, which eagerly sought confirmation of their ancient privileges on the establishment of the Second Kingdom as the upshot of the Third Crusade. What was, doubtless, extraordinary in the rules of the Fraternity was that everybody (which presumably meant every Frank) could be admitted to membership. The Venetian Marino Sanudo, a contemporary of the fall of Acre (1291) and for some time resident in the city, was already struck by the liberality of that privilege.[46] And it was precisely this rule which the insurgent Frankish nobles found so meet for their purpose. It enabled nobles, knights and burgesses to form a legal body, bound together by a common oath, assuring mutual security and competent to act as a *persona iuris.* If we were to look for a technical term to describe the body thus created, we would, in accordance with contemporary usage, employ the expression *communitas* or *universitas.* There is no need to add that this *communitas* has nothing to do with any "communal movement," despite the noun *communitas* which it shared with many other corporative bodies.

It is a purely academic speculation whether, following the oath, the Fraternity of Saint Andrew was still a Fraternity. If the seal described was engraved in 1232, then the name "Fraternitas Acconensis" is living testimony to a change from the archaic organization. Our written sources do not again mention the Fraternity; the name *commune* takes its place and this should be translated into contemporary French as *le commun* as in the Provisions of Oxford, and as "commonalty" in English.[47]

It is only in this context that we can rightly understand Philip of

Novara, who tells how John of Beirut, in Cyprus during the rebellion in Acre, wrote letters to certain nobles and to his kinfolk in Acre *"et envoia unes letres au comun des homes de la terre."*[48] Had he written Latin, he would in all probability have employed the expression *communitas hominum terrae,* as that was the exact institutional meaning of the corporative body brought into existence by the oath to the Fraternity of Saint Andrew. No wonder that the ambassador Godfrey de la Tor sent to Pope Gregory IX is described: *"et por ce se mist li roi Henri en la communauté des gens de roiaume de Jerusalem."*[49]

Not long afterwards, the same Pope, in an effort to establish peace between Frederick II and the barons, addressed a letter (8 August 1234) thus: *"Nobilibus viris baronibus et civibus Acconensibus,"* but a few lines later the double addressee becomes *"Universitas Vestra."*[50] In a second letter, in 1235, he calls the new revolutionary body *"Universitas Acconensis."*[51] If additional proof is required that *Acconensis* in the two texts has no special urban or "communal" attribution, it is furnished by the rebellious movement itself. In a letter written in 1241, the senders describe themselves as *"barons et chevaliers et citeens del reaume de Jérusalem."*[52] The *cives Acconenses* are simply replaced by *cives regni Hierosolymitani,* as the French title would have been put in Latin. In the letter itself, the trinity of senders became *gens de la terre,* meaning the "commonalty of the land."

Let us now attempt to review what is known about the organization of the rebellious "community." For it is in the details of organization that we can trace some truly urban or "communal" influences, explained, simply, by the fact that the new institution was established inside the walls of Acre and confronted day by day with the practical example of the Italian cities. Unfortunately, only a few glimpses into its inner organization are possible. The most spectacular feature is the *companae,* the bells of the "community," sounding the tocsin of alarm when need arose, and perhaps as a summons to assembly. It does not appear that a special *campanile* was built. In all likelihood, it was the bells of the cathedral, the *Sainte Croix,* that were rung. At the time Frederick II sent the bishop of Sidon in 1234 to Acre to mediate peace, the bishop persuaded Balian of Sidon and the connétable, Montbéliard, to make peace on the basis of a division of the bailliship between Filangieri in Tyre and a local baron, Philip of Maugastel, in Acre. When all was ready for renewal of the oath of fealty to the emperor in the cathedral, it was the irruption of the Ibelin lord of Caesarea that turned the tables. "He entered," Philip of Novara recounts, "into the cathedral church of the Holy Cross and ordered that the bell of the commune be pealed. When they heard this in the Fraternity of Saint Andrew, they took to their arms and all shouted: Death (to the bishop of Sidon, Balian of Sidon and the connétable)!"[53] It was this *campana* which the barons, knights and citizens of Acre proposed to demolish if they came to agreement with the emperor.[54] Our quotation might, perhaps, prove that a special bell was hung in the belfry of the cathedral for the use of the "commune," so as not to confuse the bells tolled for religious purposes with those used by the "community."

As long as the Fraternity existed, it may be supposed that a man who entered it after taking the oath became a member for life. This was hardly enough for the revolutionary community. Two years after its establishment, there was a general renewal of the oath and, at the same time, a new election of the community's head, the mayor.[55] Some further data on inner organization can be extracted from the peace proposals offered by the barons to Frederick II in 1243, in which *les conseles et les cheuetaines de la commune* are mentioned, and from a more itemized enumeration of offices in a letter of Pope Gregory IX of 1235. Here we find the phrase:

> *Communiam dissolvant, campanam deponant et amoveant consules et capitaneos ab eis post ortam discordiam ordinatos. . . . In civitatem Acconensem interdicti et in sindicos praedictorum civium et nobilium et maiorum consulum universitatis Acconensis ac eorum fautores et consiliarios excommunicationis sententias promulgavit.*[56]

Unhappily, the text is not easy to interpret. If we take *consiliarii* in the proper technical sense of "counsellors," we may detect in it an earlier layer of organization from the first days of the Fraternity, which, as we saw, had its own "counsellors," and these were possibly carried over into the later "community." But as the noun appears in the conjuncture of *fautores et consiliarii,* adherents and counsellors, we hesitate to assign a precise technical meaning to it. Nor are other names of office exact. Gregory IX mentions "syndics," which, in this case, can only mean "representatives." But whom do they represent? Plainly enough the non-noble *cives,* but, according to our text, also the nobles. Then the phrase degenerates into obscurity. Whereas we understand the phrase: *sindici praedictorum civium et nobilium,* we do not grasp: *sindici . . . maiorum consulum.* The latter suggests *maiores consules,* which means at least two major consuls and presupposes minor consuls, which would point to a somewhat elaborate machinery if we add the "captains" and "counsellors." Besides, John of Beirut is called *maire* and not "consul," and he was definitely the chief man in the organization. It might be held that the *capitanei* = *cheuetaines* are military officers, but the *maiores consules* are really baffling. Did Gregory IX, Italian that he was, mix up northern *maiores* with southern consuls? It is possible, but we are now in the realm of conjecture.

For ten or, maybe, even twelve years (1231–1243), the period of the "Wars of Frederick II against the Ibelins," the "commonalty of Acre," or the "commonalty of the Kingdom of Jerusalem," abided as an institutional reality and a legal personality in the political history of the Kingdom. As far as we can ascertain, it is referred to for the last time in our sources by Marsiglio Ziorzi, the Venetian *bailli,* who reports to his metropolis on the wresting of Tyre from imperial hands. Among the participants in that engagement he lists the Military Orders, the Commune of Acre, the Communes of Venice and Genoa.[57] This happened in 1243. The year is not an accident, but fits perfectly into the institutional history of the Kingdom. It coincides with the revival of the *Haute Cour,* which heard the claimants to the Crown of Jerusalem[58] and accepted the Princess Alice and her husband, Ralph of Soisson, as the rulers of the Kingdom. It was, therefore, the year that signalized a return to normal working of the Kingdom's institutions. In this context, there was, from the baronial point of view, neither place nor need for the "commonalty of Acre" nor any special need for the popular support given by the burgesses to the Government.

The last official act of the "community" is the offer of peace drawn up by John (d'Ibelin) of Jaffa on 7 May 1241, and sent, it seems, to Richard of Cornwall, brother of Henry III of England, asking for his mediation.[59] The Ibelins there suggested the appointment of Simon de Montfort, earl of Leicester, as *bailli* of the emperor. Being the emperor's brother-in-law and well connected with the local nobility—the great local baron Philip of Montfort was his nephew—Leicester was an excellent choice. It is not unreasonable to suppose that the barons had approached him, and got his agreement to the nomination, during his Crusade to the Holy Land (1241) with Richard of Cornwall. There was no imperial answer. In this offer of peace (*forme de la pais*), there is one phrase which draws our special attention:

> *Et nos gens de la terre . . . esterons la campane et les conseles et les cheuetaines de la commune, sauf ceaux qui esteient auant que l'emperere fuist seignor des païs.*

This is not a sentence from a chronicle, it is from a legal document written by the finest jurist of the Latin East, John of Jaffa. Consequently we can assume very circumspect phraseology, where nothing was left to chance. Even so, the words are astonishing. Frederick II became king of Jerusalem by his marriage to Isabelle of Jerusalem in 1225. He had been regent of the Kingdom since the birth of his son Conrad in 1228. He was crowned in 1229. But the *commune* was not established before 1231! What, then, did John of Jaffa imply by saying that they would abolish the heads of the *commune*[60] "excepting those who existed before the emperor became lord of the land"? The only explanation we can suggest is that, in the mind of John d'Ibelin of Jaffa, a *communitas regni* existed long before the establishment of the "community of Acre" as a legal personality, before the inception of the oath of that "community." As a matter of fact, it had existed since the founding of the First Kingdom and the election of Godfrey by the warriors of the First Crusade, or, to use John's own words in the introductory chapter to his legal treatise: "when the princes and barons who captured it (the city of Jerusalem) elected as king and lord of the Kingdom of Jerusalem the Duke Godfrey." This line of thought would not be out of place in the middle of the thirteenth century,[61] although it certainly was amiss in 1099. But it was conceivable and even logical for a John of Jaffa, who shaped a political theory and insinuated into it a changelessness of political practice in the Latin Kingdom from the day of its birth down to his own generation.

It is very tempting to ask if the events of the Latin East had any actual, and not only theoretical, impact beyond its frontiers. It was the late M. Powicke who suggested that Simon de Montfort might have taken the idea of a Government-by-council, as proposed by the Provisions of Oxford, from his own Crusade.[62] We would subscribe to Powicke's hesitancy, as the Latin Kingdom was never ruled by barons in permanent attendance on the king, nor was there a permanent council in the sense of the "Provisions" or any direct appointment of officers of the Crown by a council, not even the *Haute Cour*. The institutional patterns of the two States were too divergent for a practice evolved in the East to have been imported into, and applied in, the West. But it is not impossible that another event influenced Montfort. We refer, as already hinted, to the common oath taken by the rebellious barons in Acre and the oath taken by their equivalents in Oxford. Such a mutual oath of security, giving rise to a corporative body in opposition to an authority which was deemed to have overreached itself and perverted justice, could have been applied successfully even to an institutionally different political make-up.

Furthermore, the famous summons of the burgesses of "York, Lincoln and other boroughs of England" to the parliament to be held in January 1265 might have reflected another of Simon's experiences on the Crusade. He had then witnessed the organization of a baronial opposition to established authority. As a royalist, but at the same time an ardent legitimist, he might have identified himself with the Syrian barons' "offer of peace" to Frederick II, and perhaps agreed, on the spur of the moment, to be the agent of establishment of peace in the tottering Latin Kingdom. It might have been the memory of the united *communitas regni* of that Kingdom, consisting of barons, knights and burgesses, which, in the hour of crisis, precipitated his famous decision to summon burgesses to a *commune consilium* and assure his party of a popular backing.

[In Part V, omitted here, the author describes the formation and activities of the "Community of Antioch," formed in 1193 or 1194 to oppose the occupation of the city by Leo II of Armenia. Although called a "commune" in a contemporary source, it was not an urban but a "state" organization (a *communitas*), composed of knights and clergy as well as burgesses. It took an active part in the politics of the principality of Antioch until 1219. In Part VI, also omitted here, the author discusses the "Community of Tripoli," formed after the death of Bohemond VII in 1288. Again, although called a "commune," it was not an urban movement. It was led by a baronial faction, and demanded of the new Countess "a constitutional government in the medieval sense of the term." It disappeared when the city fell to the Sultan of Egypt in 1289.]

VII. THE AFTERMATH

Was there any tangible change in the régime of the States in the aftermath of the *communitates* movement? Tripoli is naturally out of the question. Antioch's internal history is not known enough for us to draw conclusions. It is only in the Latin Kingdom that such results can be sought.

It is not our intention, here, to embark upon a detailed study of the mid-thirteenth century evolution of the Kingdom. We would like to apply ourselves to one aspect of it only. The virtual disappearance of the royal power and the paralysis of the Kingdom's institutions, generally speaking, induced a dislocation of the social framework.[63] One marked outcome, to our way of thinking, was a widespread urge to find protection in small corporative bodies which could, on occasion, wield influence even in politics. This development, as might have been foreseen, is especially conspicuous among the burgesses of the Crusader Kingdom, and, under their influence, in their emulation by the Syrian Christians.

It was only in exceptional circumstances that burgesses came into direct contact with the Crown, barring the cases when the king was also lord of a city.[64] But in the middle of the thirteenth century we observe an entirely new trend. It is the sudden flourishing of *Fraternitates*. Until about 1240, we know of the actual existence of only two, but after that they figure frequently in our sources.

In 1261, after the death of Plaisance, when Hugh (the future Hugh III of Cyprus and Jerusalem, 1267–1284) and Hugh of Brienne claimed the *bailliage* of the Kingdom in one of the most remarkable feats of oratory before the *Haute Cour*:

> Godfrey de Sargines and the Legate and the Masters (of the Military Orders) and the (European) *Communes* and the Fraternities agreed that the *bail* (Hugh of Cyprus) should have the *bailliage* of the Kingdom before the count de Brienne; and all the knights who were liegemen were on one side, and recognised through the *Assise* of Jerusalem that the *bailliage* belonged to the *bail,* as he was older than the Count de Brienne. And then Godfrey de Sargines (who had been *bail*) laid down his office and was the first to do homage to the *bail,* and then all the men and burgesses and Fraternities.[65]

This text is explicit enough to show that the Kingdom really entered a new phase of evolution. Juridically speaking, the meeting described is that of the *Haute Cour*. But it is no longer the *Haute Cour* of the First Kingdom, nor even that following the *Assise sur la ligece*. Since about 1240, if not earlier, the representatives of the corporative bodies, of the Military Orders and Italian and other *Communes* had been present. But now we have also the presence of the Fraternities, spokesmen of the corporative bodies of the burgesses. *Pari passu* with that presence a new custom emerged: an oath of homage of the Fraternities and of the burgesses to the *bailli,* an oath unknown, or at least not generalized, in the First Kingdom.

Seven years afterwards, in 1287, when the same Hugh of Lusignan, now already Hugh III of Cyprus, came to the *Haute Cour* of Jerusalem, sitting in Acre, to claim the crown of the kingdom and was opposed by "Damoiselle Marie," daughter of Bohemond VI of Antioch, the same evolution is once more exemplified, and the terms in which it is described vividly illustrate the general direction of evolution. After donning the Crown of Cyprus, Hugh appeared in Acre—

> to claim the Kingdom of Jerusalem from the men and people of Acre, the Legate and members of the Orders (or monasteries), and the Master of the Temple, and the Teutonic Order, the "consul" (or council) of Pisa, and the *bailli* of Venice and the Fraternities, and all the people of Acre who were there. And the said king spoke to the men of the *Haute Cour* of Jerusalem who were gathered there in the presence of those named above.[66]

The last phrase proves that, in fact, it is still the "estate of nobility" which composes the *Haute Cour*. Representatives of the corporative bodies are present but take no part in the proceedings. It seems patent that their presence added nothing to the legality of the meeting, though it certainly gave force to the deliberations. And yet something is already changing. After hearing the claims of Hugh III and Marie—

> the said men of the Kingdom went to one part and after a short while returned and made say for the commonalty and with the consent of all, by one of them, that is, Sire Jacques Vidan, that, following the clear request made by the king, they were all ready to give him their homages and their taxes and services as was the custom to do to the lord of the Kingdom.[67]

The "commonalty" (= *la comunauté*) mentioned in the text is still the "commonalty" of the nobility, as is clear from the rest of the text.[68] But a notable modification is seen in the composition of the bodies which owe homage or perhaps an oath of fealty to the king. Our source goes on to say that, after the king's coronation oath, administered to him by Jacques Vidan—

> the liegemen of the Kingdom who were there of the said Kingdom of Jerusalem made their homage, and first of all Godfrey, and the lord of Tyre and he of Toron, and all the rest of the men who were there; and after that he received the homage of others who were obliged to offer it, and after he received the oaths of the Fraternities and of all the others who were obliged to give him oaths.[69]

Only this new development can explain the fact that a king of Jerusalem left the country because of his quarrels with the nobility and the Fraternities.[70] The Fraternities[71] became a normal part of the Kingdom's "estate"-building apparatus and a new factor in its political life.

Taken, then, as a whole, the evolution of the thirteenth century did not bring the Crusader State down to the common denominator of "communal movements." For that, it lacked primary urban and social premises, but it brought the State to the common denominator of formation of "estates" and *communitates,* the normal transition from feudal monarchies to *Ständestaaten*. Still, the Latin States never reached the point of a full-fledged variation in their constitutional history. Perhaps a hundred years more of existence were needed to produce one.

NOTES

1. On the position of research in the field of the history of institutions, see Cl. Cahen, "La Féodalité et les institutions politiques de l'Orient latin," *XII Convegno "Volta," Accad. Naz. dei Lincei,* Roma 1956, pp. 167–194; H. E. Mayer, "Probleme moderner Kreuzzugsforschung," *Vierteljahrschrift für Sozial- und Wirtschaftsgeschichte,* L (1964), pp. 505–513; J. A. Brundage, "Recent Crusade Historiography—Some Observations and Suggestions," *Catholic Historical Review,* XLIX (1964), pp. 493–507.

2. See J. Prawer, "The *Assise de Teneure* and the *Assise de Vente*—A Study of Landed Property in the Latin Kingdom," *Economic History Review,* IV (1951), pp. 77–87; idem, "Les Premiers temps de la féodalité dans le royaume latin de Jérusalem," *Revue d'histoire du droit,* XXII (1954), pp. 401–424; idem, "La Noblesse et le régime féodal du royaume latin de Jérusalem," *Le Moyen Age,* LXV (1959), pp. 41–74; idem, "Etude sur le droit des *Assises de Jérusalem*: Droit de confiscation et droit d'exhérédation," *Revue historique de droit français et étranger* (= *RHDFE*), XXXIX (1961), pp. 520–551; XL (1962), pp. 29–42; J. Richard, "Pairie d'Orient latin: Les quatre baronies des royaumes de Jérusalem et de Chypre," *RHDFE,* XXVIII (1950), pp. 67–89; R. B. Patterson, "The Early Existence of the *Funda* and *Catena* in the XIIth Century Latin Kingdom of Jerusalem," *Speculum,* XXXIX (1964), pp. 474–477. The new approach was already indicated by J. Richard, *Le Royaume latin de Jérusalem,* Paris 1953, and the main conclusions of newer studies are well integrated in H. E. Mayer, *Geschichte der Kreuzzüge,* Stuttgart 1965.

3. An excellent and penetrating account was given by M. W. Baldwin, *Raymond III of Tripolis and the Fall of Jerusalem (1140–1187),* Princeton University Press 1936.

4. *Le Livre d'Eracles* in: *Recueil des Historiens des Croisades, Historiens Occidentaux* (= *RHC, HOcc.,* Paris 1844–1895), II, p. 34 (henceforth *Eracles*).

5. *Itinerarium Regis Ricardi,* in: W. Stubbs (ed.), *Chronicles and Memorials of the Reign of Richard I* (*Rerum Britannicarum Medii Aevi Scriptores,* Vol. XXXVIII, London 1864), Vol. I, Lib. II, Ch. 9, p. 150; *L'Estoire de la Guerre Sainte par Ambroise* (edited by G. Paris), vers. 365 f.

6. J. Prawer, "L'Etablissement des coutumes du marché à Saint Jean d'Acre," *RHDFE,* XXIX (1951), especially pp. 341–343.

7. J. Prawer, "La Noblesse et le régime féodal du royaume latin de Jérusalem," *Le Moyen Age,* LXV (1959), pp. 41–74.

8. This means that, although the numerous knights of the royal domain—all tenants-in-chief of the Crown—had a right to participate in the meetings of the feudal *Haute Cour* as direct vassals of the Crown, it was only the barons, tenants of seigniorial fiefs held from the Crown, who had an actual voice in its deliberations.

9. *Le Livre de Jean d'Ibelin,* Ch. 195, in: *RHC, Lois,* I (henceforth Jean d'Ibelin), pp. 313–314: *"Et qui fait homage de chose qui seit ou reiaume à autre que au chief seignor, il le deit faire en la maniere dessus devisiée, mais que tant que il ne li deit pas faire ligege; por ce que nul home ne peut faire plus d'une ligece; et que toz les homes des homes dou chief seignor dou reiaume li deivent faire ligece par l'assise; et puisque l'on li deit la ligece, l'on ne la peut à autre faire sanz mesprendre vers lui."*

10. Philippe de Novare, Ch. 40 (*Lois,* I, p. 517).

11. Philippe de Novare, Ch. 51 (*Lois,* I, p. 526).

12. *Loc. cit.*: "That they come to aid or counsel or serve with arms if the need arises."

13. *Ibid.,* p. 527: "The king granted . . . that all his liegemen, who hold from him or from his men, whoever they are, great and small, should be held to faith one to another in regard to what was written above and that each of them could require others as his peers in such a place (= such circumstances)." See also Jean d'Ibelin, Ch. 140 (*Lois,* I, pp. 214–215).

14. On the general problem of "estates" see E. Lousse, "La Formation des ordres dans la société médiévale," *L'Organisation corporative du Moyen-Age à la fin de l'Ancien Régime,* Louvain 1937, pp. 63–90; idem, "Parlementarisme ou corporatisme," *RHDFE,* XIV (1935), pp. 638 f.

15. Willelmus Tyrensis, *Historia Rerum in Partibus Transmarinis Gestarum* (= WT), XXII, 23: *"Convenerunt regni principes universi . . . de rerum statu . . . consilium habituri."* And in the official document: *"Haec est forma colligendi census, qui de communi omnium principum, tam ecclesiasticorum quam saecularium, et de assensu universae plebis regni Hierosolymorum, pro communi utilitate ejusdem regni, contra imminentes necessitates, colligi debet."* In the French translation even the implied assent of the *universa plebs* disappeared: *"Ce est la forme de cueillir la cense qui est establie par l'otroi des prelaz et des autres barons por le besoign du roiaume de Jherusalem," Guillaume de Tyr et ses continuateurs* (edited by P. Paris), Paris 1880, XXII, 22 (II, 45).

16. Philippe de Novare, Ch. 42 (*Lois,* I, p. 518); Jean d'Ibelin, Ch. 203 (*ibid.,* I, p. 325).

17. Jean d'Ibelin, Ch. 203 (*Lois,* I, p. 326).

18. *Loc. cit.*

19. *Ibid.,* Ch. 239 (*Lois,* I, p. 384); cf. Chs. 236–237.

20. "There was a plenary court (or the court was full) and a great number of those to whom the king owed (payment) came before the king in the presence of his court. One of them "conjured" the king for all of them and summoned him for himself and for all the others."

21. This interminable procedure is described minutely by Jean d'Ibelin in Ch. 237 (*Lois,* I, pp. 381–382).

22. Philippe de Novare, Ch. 52 (*Lois,* I, p. 528); Jean d'Ibelin, Ch. 203 (*ibid.,* I, p. 325).

23. See the speech of John of Beirut before Frederick II in *Les Gestes des Chiprois* (edited by G. Raynaud), Genève 1887, § 127, pp. 41–42. Beirut was fortified and garrisoned out of John's income from Cyprus.

24. By Christian we naturally refer to European Christians, i.e., to the Frankish population. The only exception were Crusader castles, some of them as large as cities (for instance, Crac des Chevaliers, Safad) and a few villages which the Crusaders tried to colonize. The process of colonization was never very successful and in the thirteenth century, it seems, was halted entirely. Cf. J. Prawer, "Colonization Activities in the Latin Kingdom of Jerusalem," *Revue belge de philologie et d'histoire,* XXIX (1951), pp. 1063–1118.

25. J. Prawer, "The Settlement of the Latins in Jerusalem," *Speculum,* XXVII (1952), pp. 490–503.

26. When we find military service due to the Crown listed according to cities (Jean d'Ibelin, Ch. 271), it is not the corporate body of a city which owes it, but the lord of the city. A good indication of the non-corporative character of the cities is furnished by the taxation experiment of 1182. It is not the *Court of Burgesses* which is responsible for imposing and collecting the tax, but four specially selected citizens in each city (WT, XXII, 23).

27. *Livre des Assises des Bourgeois,* Ch. 298 (*Lois,* II, p. 169).

28. For more details see our study "Social Classes and Social Stratification in the Crusader Kingdom—The Franks," to be published in *The History of the Crusades* (edited by K. M. Setton), IV.

29. *Eracles,* Lib. XXXIII, Ch. 23 (*RHC, HOcc.,* II, p. 388).

30. J. L. A. Huillard-Bréholles (ed.), *Historia Diplomatica Friderici II,* III, Paris 1852, p. 137 and p. 140, n.1.

31. *Eracles,* Lib. XXXIII, Ch. 23 (*RHC, HOcc.,* II, p. 389).

32. *Chef seignor* is the normal designation of the king in the jurists' treatises. It stresses the element of suzerainty in the competences of the Crown.

33. *Raison,* meaning: to each his reason, that is, his rights.

34. *Eracles,* Lib. XXXIII, Ch. 24 (*RHC, HOcc.,* II, pp. 389–390).

35. It is of importance and interest that Jacques d'Ibelin, pleading against Hugh III of Cyprus before Prince Edward of England in Acre in 1271, took a far more historical view of the origin of the Crusader laws and institutions. What he says should really guide modern research, if it finally cuts loose from Jean d'Ibelin: *"Cest reaume fu conquis par Latins et par genz espessiaument qui esteient de la corone de France et de pluisors provinces d'outre les mons; donc deit on creire que il n'establirent mie usages ne divers ne estranges: on deit miaus creire qu'ils pristrent les usages de leur pays ou de leur veisins."*—"Document relatif au service militaire," *Lois,* II, p. 431.

36. See J. Prawer, "Les Premiers temps de la féodalité dans le Royaume Latin de Jérusalem—Une Reconsidération," *Revue d'histoire du droit,* XXII (1954), pp. 401–424.

37. *Livre au Roi,* published by Beugnot in *Lois,* I, pp. 607–644. This treatise deserves yet to be studied in detail.

38. *Eracles,* Lib. XXXIII, Ch. 26 (*RHC, HOcc.,* II, pp. 391–392). The chapter is to be found translated into English by J. L. La Monte, *The Wars of Frederick II against the Ibelins in Syria and Cyprus by Philip de Novare,* New York 1936, pp. 122–123, note. Our translation differs in some details.

39. This was the line of thought of J. L. La Monte, "The Communal Movement in Syria in the Thirteenth Century," *Charles Haskins Anniversary Essays in Mediaeval History,* Boston-New York 1929, pp. 117–131, the only detailed study of the subject. It is in the main accepted by Cl. Cahen (see below) and unanimously followed in all general histories of the Crusades. A different interpretation was suggested by J. Colson, "Aux origines des assemblées d'Etats—L'Exemple de l'Orient latin," *Revue des études byzantines,* XII (1954), pp. 114–128. This interpretation comes near to our own, but we think that the author tried to read more into the events than our sources warrant. Moreover, the machinery of the movement cannot be described without due regard to the infrastructure of the State and society and these were entirely neglected by the author.

40. W. H. Stubbs (ed.), *Select Charters*[7], Oxford 1890, p. 398.

41. Balian was ready to execute an imperial order against a decision of the *Haute Cour.* See above, n. 18.

42. The number of knights serving the Crown was around six hundred. Cf. R. C. Smail, *Crusading Warfare,* Cambridge, 1956, pp. 88 ff.

43. Published by G. Schlumberger, "Neuf sceaux de l'Orient latin," *Revue de l'Orient latin* (= *ROL*), II (1894), p. 178 and Pl. I:1.

44. See G. Schlumberger, *Numismatique de l'Orient latin,* Paris 1878.

45. *Eracles,* Lib. XXXIII, Ch. 29 (*RHC, HOcc.,* II, p. 395); Marino Sanudo, *Secreta Fidelium Crucis* in: Bongars (ed.), *Gesta Dei per Francos,* Hanover 1611, p. 214 calls it *Fraternitas Sancti Iacobi,* evidently a mistake.

46. *Loc. cit.*: *"Cui* (i.e., *Fraternitati*) *regali privilegio, ut cuncti intrare volentes libenter possint recipi, concessum erat de gratia singulari."*

47. There is a large number of studies regarding the "commonalty" or "community" of the realm. We refer especially to the excellent exposition (with abundant bibliography) by G. Post, "The Two Laws and the Statute of York," *Speculum,* XXIX (1954), pp. 417–432.

48. *Eracles,* Lib. XXXIII, Ch. 28 (*RHC, HOcc.,* II, p. 393).

49. *Eracles,* Lib. XXXIII, Ch. 40 (*RHC, HOcc.,* II, p. 406).

50. *Monumenta Germaniae Historica* (= *MGH*), *Epistolae Saeculi XIII e Registris Pontificum Romanorum Selectae,* I, Berlin 1883, No. 594.

51. *MGH, Epistolae,* I, No. 656 p. 554 (1235).

52. *Archives de l'Orient latin* (= *AOL*), I, p. 402.

53. *Gestes des Chiprois,* § 205, p. 113: *"il entra dedens la mere yglise de Sainte Cruis, et comanda à souner la campane de la commune. Quant a la frarie de saint André ler sot, il furent as armes et crierent tuit: 'Muire! Muire!'."* Jean d'Ibelin (*Lois,* II, p. 399) has a different expression: *"si que y ot si grant remor que la campane dou comun sona."* Attention should be paid to the parallel expressions: *"la campane de la commune"* and *"la campane dou comun."*

54. In 1241, in a letter to the Emperor: *"et osterons la campane," AOL,* I, p. 403.

55. *Gestes des Chiprois,* § 206, p. 113: *"Le seignor de Baruth ala à Acre, et tant ordena et fist que les sairemans des Poulains furent tous refreichis, et qu'il fut maire de nouveau."*

56. *MGH, Epistolae,* I, No. 656, p. 544; cf. a letter of 1236, *ibid.,* No. 674, p. 571.

57. G. Tafel & G. M. Thomas, *Urkunden zur älteren Handels- und Stadtsgeschichte der Republik Venedig,* II, *Fontes Rerum Austriacarum,* XIII, Wien 1856, pp. 354–355.

58. *Documents relatifs à la successibilité au trône et à la régence,* in: *Lois,* II, pp. 397–422.

59. Published by R. Röhricht in *AOL,* I, pp. 402–403.

60. It is impossible to argue that John referred to the restitution of the 'Fraternity of St. Andrew' to its erstwhile position. Frederick II could not care less about the whereabouts of a welfare Fraternity.

61. See the inspiring study of G. Post, "The Two Laws and the Statute of York," *Speculum,* XXIX (1954), pp. 417-432.

62. M. Powicke, *The Thirteenth Century, 1216–1307, The Oxford History of England,* IV, Oxford 1953, p. 134 and note 1. There is a slight contradiction between the text and the note.

63. See our study: "Classes and Social Stratification of the Latin Kingdom," scheduled to be published in Vol. IV of the *History of the Crusades* (edited by K. M. Setton).

64. The *Assise sur la ligece* stipulated that the king could require an oath from burgesses in cities not belonging to the Crown, if he had doubts as to the loyalty of their lord. Actually, Amalric took such an oath from the burgesses of Sidon and Beaufort after the war against the lord of Sidon, when the *Assise sur la ligece* was promulgated.

65. *Documents relatifs à la successibilité au trône et à la régence,* Ch. 11 (*Lois,* II, pp. 414–415): *"Messire Joffroy de Saugine, et le legat, et les maistres, et les comunes, et les frairies s'accorderent que le baill ost le baillage dou royaume avant que le conte de Braine; et tous les chevaliers homes liges furent d'une part, et coneurent, par l'assise dou royaume de Jerusalem, que le bailliage montoit audit bail, pour ce que il estoit ainsné dou conte de Braine. Et lors messire Joffroi de Saugines se depouilla et ala premier faire homage au baill, et puis tous les homes et borjois et frairies."*

66. *Ibid.,* Ch. 12 (*Lois,* II, p. 415): *"A requerre le royaume de Jerusalem as homes et à la gent de Acre, le legat et les gens de religion, et le maistre du Temple, et l'Ospital des Alemans, et le concile de Pise, et le baill de Venise et les frairies, et tous les homes d'Acre que là se troverent. Et le dessus nomé roy dit as homes de la Houte Court de Jerusalem que là estoient assemblés en la presence des dessus només."* The speech is quoted in Ch. 13.

67. *Ibid.,* Ch. 13 (*Lois,* II, p. 416): *"Les devant dis homes dou royaume alerent d'une part, et au chief d'une presse se retournerent, et firent dire par la communauté et par l'otroy d'eaus tous, par l'un d'eaus, ce est assavoir par sire Jacque Vidan, que selon clere requeste que le roy lor avoit fait, il estoient tous apareillés de faire li lors homages et lors redevances et services si com l'on estoit usé de faire à seignor dou royaume."*

68. *Ibid.,* Ch. 16 (*Lois,* II, p. 418): *"Adonc les homes liges revindrent devant le roy, et parla por la communauté de tous sire Jacques Vidan . . ."*

69. *Ibid.,* Ch. 17 (*Lois,* II, p. 419): *"les homes liges qui là estoient dou dit royaume de Jerusalem li firent homage, et tout premierement messire Joffroy, et le sire de Sur, et celui dou Touron, et tout le remanant des homes que là se trouverent; et puis aprez receut les homages des autres qui li estoient tenus à faire, et aprez receut les seremens des frairies et de tous les autres qui serement li devoient."*

70. *RHC, HOcc.,* II, p. 474.

71. The existence of fraternities was not limited to Acre. In 1264 Philip de Montfort, lord of Tyre, had to promise to the Genoese that property in their quarter in Tyre will not be given: *"communitatibus nec frateriis pro hospitando, neque pro alio re facere"*—*AOL,* II B, p. 226.

THE THEORY OF DEMOCRACY AND CONSENT IN THE FOURTEENTH CENTURY*

Antonio Marongiu

Quod omnes tangit. What touches all must be approved by all. The juridical and political principle that this concise maxim so happily expressed was neither a hothouse flower nor a rhetorical flourish[1] nor the far-fetched fantasy of obscure thinkers; it was the successful and realistic expression of a widespread notion of group life and, thus, an expression of the spirit of the age. As Paul Viollet authoritatively pointed out long ago, *Quod omnes tangit* was a living reality, a principle that was, so to say, in the air.[2]

Recent studies have greatly expanded our knowledge of the use of *Quod omnes tangit.* Indeed, our knowledge of its use in the course of some thirteenth-century events may be considered fairly exhaustive: the 1222 convocation by the common decision of Emperor Frederick II and Pope Honorius III of a "general court" of the Holy Roman Empire to decide on a Crusade;[3] the convocation in 1244 of another "general court" of the Empire by Frederick II;[4] another convocation of the court of the Empire in 1274 by the Emperor, or "King of the Romans," Rudolph of Hapsburg;[5] the writ of summons to the famous Parliament of 1295 by Edward I of England.[6] On the whole, however, the studies of this principle[7] do not go much beyond the limits of the short period I dealt with in my study of this maxim in the thirteenth century.[8]

---

* Antonio Marongiu, "Il principio della democrazia e del consenso (*Quod omnes tangit, ab omnibus approbari debet*) nel XIV secolo," *Studia Gratiana post octava decreti saecularia,* **8** (Bologna: Institutum Gratianum, 1962), 555–575. Trans. by Dr. Giuseppe Galigani; revised by the ed.

Some have remarked, with considerable justification, that principles do not really move by themselves. It is men, striving to achieve particular goals, who use principles to justify and provide moral support for their actions.[9] It is now necessary, I think, to take another step forward[10] in the study of this principle of democracy and consent, to search out whatever can be found about its life in the fourteenth century.[11] This kind of research is anything but easy, for the useful data are very scattered and difficult to collect. Because of this difficulty and because more aspects of the fourteenth century remain unexplored than is true of the thirteenth century, this essay will be little more than an exploration, even though it is the result not of improvised research but of attentive study over many years.

As in my previous studies, I shall deal with *Quod omnes tangit* as a political principle. I shall not be concerned, at least for the moment, with its value as a legal maxim, a maxim of private, procedural, or administrative law.[12] It is, of course, important to note that the canonists defined *Quod omnes tangit* more precisely—and somewhat more restrictively. Following the *Glossa ordinaria* to Gratian's *Decretum*[13] and a decretal of Pope Innocent III (1198–1216) included in the *Liber extra* of Gregory IX (1234),[14] they specified[15] that only those things that concern everyone directly or personally (*uti singuli*)—and not as members of a collective body or organized community (*ut universi*)—must be submitted to the deliberation and consent of all.[16] (In this form *Quod omnes tangit* has been preserved in the present *Codex iuris Canonici:* can. 101 § I, *n.* 2. The present formulation is the following: *Quod autem omnes, uti singulos, tangit, ab omnibus, probari debet.*) Originally put forward by Justinian[17] simply as a formal justification for a narrowly circumscribed ruling, the maxim has come down to us as one of those programmatic rules that express a general concept of law.

In surveying the evidence we must bear in mind the historical realities of the period; we must examine not only theory but real life, the way institutions really worked. On the same level of comparative public law, we should also try to verify the principle's validity, or rather its scope of application, in different areas of collective deliberation. The debate over Edward I's famous convocation of Parliament, his reasons for it, and the ends he pursued make these clarifications particularly necessary. For, where Stubbs[18] praised the king for transforming *Quod omnes tangit* into a constitutional principle, others (for example C. H. McIlwain and G. Haskins) maintained that, although it was indeed novel, it was limited to the field of taxation.[19]

Chronologically speaking,[20] the first authoritative fourteenth-century acknowledgment of *Quod omnes tangit* seems to have been the reference to it by William Durandus the Younger, the nephew of the famous *Speculator,* in his treatise *De modo generalis concilii tenendi et de corruptelis in ecclesia reformandis.* In his hands the principle became exceptionally important; it became the justification and foundation of conciliar theory in its broadest sense. The supreme power in the field of Christian doctrine and Church discipline would be entrusted to an ecumenical council, superior to the Pope, kings, and princes.[21] "*Contra . . . concilia et iura* (the *iura* decided by the Council?) *nihil possunt dominus papa et reges ac principes de novo statuere, vel concedere, nisi generali concilio convocato; quum illud quod omnes tangit secundum iuris utriusque regulam, ab omnibus debeat communiter approbari.*"[22] [Neither the lord pope nor kings nor princes may legislate anything against the councils or laws without calling a general council; for according to the rules of both (Roman and Canon) laws what touches all must be approved in common by all.] Such a clear statement of the democratic principle was truly exceptional. It was to remain so.

With Marsilio of Padua we are more sure of the date, since the *Defensor Pacis* was already finished by June 24, 1324. One fundamental proposition of this great political work is that law[23] must spring from popular will, that is, from *civium universitas* [corporation of the citizens] or the *valentior pars* [weightier part][24] that represents it (*quae totam universitatem repraesentat*). Here in full are two passages of great interest for our topic:[25]

> 1. *que . . . omnium possunt tangere commodum et incommodum ab omnibus sciri debent et audiri ut commodum assequi et appositum repellere possint;*
> 2. *illius veritas cercius iudicatur, et ipsius communis utilitas diligencius iudicatur, ad quod tota intendit civium universitas intellectu et affectu.*
>
> [T]hose matters . . . which can affect the benefit and harm of all ought to be known and heard by all, in order that they may be able to attain the beneficial and avoid the opposite.
> [T]hat at which the entire body of the citizens aims intellectually and emotionally is more certainly judged as to its truth and more diligently noted as to its common utility.]

Some have asserted that Marsilio, "since he was all wrapped up in Aristotelian ideas," was unaware of *Quod omnes tangit*.[26] These passages seem to me to indicate clearly, on the contrary, how much importance he attached to the principle. He accepted it, not on the authority of others, but because he recognized its utility and advantage. By using it, he showed—and perhaps increased[27]—its already considerable importance. He presented it and freely elaborated on it, going well beyond the formula. This should conclusively refute those who quite arbitrarily see in *Quod omnes tangit* a precious rhetorical flourish and nothing else.

Consider another great political theoretician of the fourteenth century, the learned and subtle "bachelor of Oxford"—the *venerabilis inceptor*—William of Ockham.[28] He drew from the constitution of the English kingdom (which he knew by personal experience) an ideal model of political and religious organization.[29] He advocated the creation of a council or parliament[30] to be the direct or indirect (*per procuratores et alios gerentes*) voice of the members of the Christian community. Both laity and clergy were to be included, for they all are equally involved: *"quod omnes tangit ab omnibus tractari et approbari debet"*[31] [what touches all should be discussed and approved by all]. In this spirit the assembly could fulfill its mission—to represent and defend the interests of the members of the community against the person endowed with the supreme power, and to make provision for any necessary reforms. This would furthermore achieve what he called[32] *"principatus ministrativus"* [administering, or administrative, rule] that is, constitutional monarchy: a form of government which he contrasted to (and, of course, preferred to) absolute power, which he called *"principatus dominativus"* and even *"principatus bestiarum"* [rule over animals]. *Quod omnes tangit* was thus for Ockham the foundation of the best organized community, one in which the king—and the public power in general—can demand of the citizens whatever is strictly necessary to fulfill his institutional aims, but in which he cannot deprive the people of either their freedom or their property and rights.

That is not all. In this nonconformist Franciscan's opinion, the principle of democracy and consent was mixed with that of representation.[33] Once it is settled in principle that everyone participates, it becomes necessary and legitimate to appoint popular representatives with the necessary mandate; for it is materially impossible for everyone to attend the great assembly.

Unfortunately Ockham was not a jurist. On the contrary, in W. Ullmann's[34] opinion, as far as canon law was concerned he knew only the *Glossa ordinaria* to the *Decretum* and the *Liber extra* of Gregory IX. He did not clearly state how such representation could be effectively and legally created; above all, he never explained how it should function in order to remedy the defect he himself had pointed out—the impossibility of having all the clergy and laity attend in person. Certainly, if representation meant for him (as my French colleague G. de Lagarde[35] infers) not collective delegation, but only individual delegation by members of the community—that is, one person substituting for another—then all Ockham's argument becomes an obscure way of saying he doesn't know what to say.

Be this as it may, his *Dialogus de potestate imperiali et papali* ranked *Quod omnes tangit* among the fundamental principles of social life, not only from a structural point of view, but particularly for its moral and political value. If it is necessary to take steps in the case of a heretical pope, it is not up to individuals or small committees to make the relevant decision; all members must do so. *"Quod omnes tangit ab omnibus tractari debet: sed causa papae haeritici omnes tangit Christianos. Ergo per omnes Christianos vel congregationem, cuiusmodi est concilium generale, tractari debet.*"[36] [What touches all must be dealt with by all. But the case of an heretical pope touches all Christians. Thus it must be dealt with by all Christians or by their congregation, that is by the general council.]

Ockham did not stop here. *Quod omnes tangit* was a principle not only of procedure, but also of life. It is much more than a rule of human or positive law. It is a principle of natural law, even of divine law; for the latter teaches that the leaders of society must be elected by the members of the community themselves. "*Universitati mortalium nullus praefici debet nisi per electionem et consensum eorum; quod omnes tangit debet tractari per omnes, quod autem aliquis praefici aliis omnes tangit, igitur per omnes tractari debet.*"[37] [None ought to be set over a group of human beings except by their election and consent; for what touches all should be dealt with by all; but for someone to be set over others touches all, and thus should be dealt with by all.] Can the idea of democracy be better expressed?

In the *De iuribus regni et imperii Romanorum* of Lupold von Bebenburg[38] the principle appeared again. Despite the title of his essay, Lupold was a supporter, not of the rights of the Empire, but rather of democratic ideals. His work appeared in the same period (not later than 1340 and perhaps shortly before) and in the same political and ecclesiastical environment as Ockham's; and it is significant that for him, as for Ockham, *Quod omnes tangit* was a principle of natural justice: "*Aequitas et ratio naturalis dictat apud omnes, quod, quando per aliquod factum praeiudicatur pluribus, quod id per omnes illos comprobari debebit, et sic illud videtur esse di iure gentium.*" [Equity and natural reason state to all men that, whenever a thing is done that affects several people, it should be approved by all of them; and this is the case according to the law of peoples.] From this he drew two conclusions: (1) that whenever a people lacks a king they may elect one according to the law of peoples; (2) that the king must rule with the consent and collaboration of his people in essential matters, that is in those matters which concern all.[39]

Conciliar polemics and the struggle between the Avignonese papacy and Lewis of Bavaria (who crowned himself Emperor in Rome) gave considerable impetus to this literature.[40] But the subject was thoroughly and autonomously treated in Spain as well. There it drew from various sources—classical, Biblical, Roman, Greek, and "modern."

One of its greatest representatives was the famous Alvaro Pelayo, who in Bologna had been the pupil of the great canonist Guido of Baisio (known as "The Archdeacon") and was in direct contact with, among many others, the equally famous Bolognese jurist, Johannes Andrea. For a long time, and on various occasions, he lived in Italy and even held an important office in the papal court at Avignon. *De planctu ecclesiae* is perhaps the best known of his writings. But for our purposes, his political-pedagogical work, the *Speculum regum,* written between 1341 and 1344[41] is of greater interest, especially where it deals with evil kings and princes and considers the nature of their errors and abuses (*in quibus peccant*). Kings, says Pelayo, must not venture to decide the most important and serious matters and problems of the realm by themselves (*sensu proprio*) or together with only a few councilors (*cum paucis assessoribus*). On the contrary, the decision must be taken together with the majority of the country: "*Quia maiora negocia regni expediunt sensu proprio vel cum paucis suis asesoribus* (*sic*), *cum tamen maiorem partem regni super hoc eorum interest et quod omnes tangit ab omnibus debet approbari.*"[42] The main point is this: what concerns all can be decided only by all.

We find the same doctrine in the treatise *De vita moribus et regimine principum*,[43] written about fifteen years later by the Spanish infante Don Pedro, son of Jaime II of Aragon and uncle of King Pedro IV the Ceremonious. Don Pedro, however, emphasizes not the legislative function, government or taxation, as do the others I have mentioned, but a possible declaration of war—a just war, of course! Starting from biblical and learned examples, he ends with *Quod omnes tangit*. Isidore of Seville states in the ninth book of the *Etymologiae*, so his argument goes, that to carry on war successfully it is necessary to have the advice of many people, especially those with the most authority and power. The sayings and examples of the saints and wisemen of ancient times, who have so laudably preceded us, agree with this, he says. And the maxim *Quod omnes tangit ab omnibus debet approbari*[44] represents a widespread opinion, constantly affirmed by saints and the learned. Since the pros and cons of the war obviously concern not only the king but also the community as a whole (*rempublicam regni*), it can be neither declared nor concluded without the advice of those whom the matter (*negotium*) concerns; without the aid of those who are to fight and who, in good fortune or bad, share with their king the burden and brunt of the war.

It was a piece of bravura for Nicholas Oresme, a bishop and counselor of Charles VI of France, to insert *Quod omnes tangit* in the middle of his translation of Aristotle's *Politics* about 1370. His work is more a paraphrase than a translation of the Stagirite, adapted to the situation and institutions of his time. He is anything but inclined to allow popular participation in public affairs; but for legislation he makes an exception. Universal consent is necessary, he says, to create or change laws, for what touches all must be approved by all: "*ce qui touche tous, doit etre approve de tous.*"[45]

Twenty years later—in 1392 to be precise—Francis Eximeniç,[46] the encyclopedic writer whom the late Ferran Valls-Taberner called "the brightest figure of Catalonian jurisprudence in the late fourteenth and early fifteenth centuries," again took up the ideas of Don Pedro. He did this not in his most famous treatise, *Crestia* (least of all in the twelfth book of his treatise, the *Libre de regiment de princeps e de communitats,* where he sets out the best of his thoughts), but in his letter of 1392[47] to the infante, Don Martino, who was about to embark for Sicily to take the throne. Among many other things, he exhorted the young prince not to declare war without the consent of his subjects. (*"Senyor vos placia esser amador de las communitatz e de la cosa publica e de no pendra guerra sens lur consentiment."*) To his mind, too, war required consultation and consent. *Quod omnes tangit* was implicit. It was unnecessary to express it.

It could be freely expressed, however (although neither in the canonical nor in the vernacular formula), as we can see in a Spanish didactic poem, the *Rimado de Palacio* written by the adventurous Pedro Lopez de Ayala.[48] One of the chapters is entitled *"Del governamiento de la Republica."* He writes, in effect, that when important matters are brought up, the king must not act without consulting the council; for where there are many heads, there is also much wisdom (*"Do ha muchas cabeças ha mas entendimiento"*). What deserves our attention above all is what he says about the council, the assembly to which the king must resort in order to be enlightened (vv. 286 ff.):

> *E sean con el rey al concejo llegados*
> *Perlados, cavalleros, doctores e letrados*
> *Buenos omes de villas, que hay mucho onrrados*
> *E pues a todos atanne, todos sean llamados.*
>
> [There should come with the king to his council
> Men of excellence, knights, theologians and lawyers,
> Good man of the towns, who have much honor,
> For since it touches all, all are to be called.]

The last line translates *Quod omnes tangit* almost literally.

It would be impossible to collect all the fourteenth-century references to the principle here. We will end this section with an important passage in a work by Henry of Langenstein (*Henricus de Hassia*), a German follower of Ockham. In his *Consilium pacis, de Unione et Reformatione Ecclesiae* of 1391,[49] Langenstein stated that the new and dangerous situations that arise within the Church must be considered and decided in councils: diocesan problems on the provincial level; universal problems, by a general council. For this is what *Quod omnes tangit* requires. (*"Casus novi et periculosi emergentes in Dioecesi aliqua per concilium particulare sive provinciale emendantur; igitur casus novi et ardui, totum mundum concernentes, per generale Concilium discuti debent; quod enim omnes tangit, ab omnibus tractari debet et convenit."*)

Quod omnes tangit remained a living principle in the political theories of the following century, in the writings of Jean Gerson and Nicholas of Cusa, for example; but their works would take us beyond the chronological limits of this essay. Let us turn rather to the practical effectiveness of the principle, to its place in the reality of politics, administration, and legislation.[50]

In England *Quod omnes tangit* continued to exist as a legal and political principle. In the year 1300, for example,[51] Edward I quoted it in reply to Boniface VIII; he could decide, he said, on matters concerning the general interests of his kingdom (*statum eiusdem regni*) only after hearing everybody's opinion (*consilium omnium, quos res tangit*).[52] This principle was singularly confirmed in 1310, during the reign of Edward II. Unable to oppose the barons' coalition and what was almost a national revolt caused by general hostility to his Gascon favorite, Piers Gaveston, the king had to allow a baronial commission to review all that had been done in his name during the immediately preceding period, and to propose whatever they felt necessary to remedy errors and abuses. The commissioners (*Ordinatores*) carried out their task perhaps too seriously and ended by summoning King and nobles to London in order to submit the text of their proposals to the latter's judgment (*"ut coram eis vel infirmarentur vel approbarentur; quod enim omnes tangit ab omnibus debet approbari"*). The assembly, all members present (*"omnibus itaque quorum interesse vertebatur adunatis"*), approved and imposed its decisions[53] on the king, who tried in vain to cavil, pleading *"excusationes frivolas et fictas."*[54]

The principle appeared once again in England—not openly, but nevertheless enforced by the irresolute king himself, in the original French text of the famous Statute of York of 1322:

> *les choses que serrount a establir pour l'estat du roialme et due poeple, soient tretes, accordees, establies en parlementz, pur nostre seigneur le roi, et par l'assent des prelats, countes et barouns et la communaulte du roialme: auxint come ad este acustume cea enarere.*[55]
>
> [. . . those things that are to be established for the status of the realm and the people are to be discussed, agreed upon, and established in parliament, for our lord the king, and with the consent of the prelates, counts and barons and the community of the realm, as has been customary.]

In September 1336 the Archbishop of Canterbury, Primate of the kingdom, used the same principle to justify his calling two convocations of the English clergy[56] in order to examine and grant the new king's request for financial subsidy. According to the writ of summons,[57] the request had to be discussed by everybody (*"cum omnes tangant, per omnes debeant pertractari"*).

In Italy, the history of *Quod omnes tangit* during the thirteenth century shows that it had already been welcomed by the communes and incorporated into their laws.[58] But during the fourteenth century it met with serious obstacles because of the spread of seignorial governments. Still it was not quite forgotten. It appeared, for instance, in a Bolognese document of 1315 instituting a Guelph party council: *"illos status reipublicae cura spetialior comitatur, quos tangit singularius"*[59] [to them is specially given the care of the estate of the commonwealth, which touches every individual]. And it was stated in exemplary fashion in the document constituting the Gonzaga seigniory in Mantua in 1360.[60] The Council of the

Elders was of the opinion that the seigniory should be created, but naturally decided to ask for the decision of the people gathered in general council:

> *Dignum est ea que omnes tangunt ab omnibus comprobari, et cum dispositio civitatis Mantue et districtus populi et universitatis eiusdem spectat de iure ad populum mantuanum et ad universitatem civium predictorum ut per ipsos et ipsorum decreto, arbitrio et voluntate firmentur et roborentur et ab ipsis effectum plenarium consequantur. . . .*[61]
>
> [It is fitting that those things that touch all be approved by all; and since the ordering of the city of Mantua and the territory of its people and corporation belongs to the people of Mantua and the corporation of its citizens in such a fashion that whatever they order, decide and will should be confirmed and affirmed and fully executed. . . .]

Thanks to Cardinal Aegidius de Albornoz, who had been Governor of Castile under King Alfonso XI, *Quod omnes tangit* appeared clearly as a principle of politics and financial law in one of the provisions of the Constitutions for the March of Ancona, sometimes called (after the legislator's name) "the Aegidian Constitutions" [published in 1357]. In the chapter *"De statutis et ordinamentis terrarum"* the Constitutions sought, among other things, to eliminate or at least reduce the new tyrants who were swarming over the countryside and to control the way the more or less lawful administrators and lords exploited the inhabitants. What is gathered from *universitates et singuli* [from each and all] in the form of collections and *tributa* must be employed exclusively for purposes of public utility, since (the text reads) *"interest locupletes habere subiectos et sicut rationi congruit ut quod omnes tangit ab omnibus approbetur . . ."* [it is important to have wealthy subjects and, as reason accords, it is important that what touches all be approved by all].[62]

But, as far as we know, the most solemn and noteworthy evidence for the persistence of the principle in the fourteenth century is to be found in Portugal. It is associated with the memory of one of the greatest events of Portuguese history, the Cortes of Coimbra in 1385, recently commemorated by my colleague Professor Marcello Caetano.[63] This Cortes brought Portugal not only a new dynasty—with the accession to the throne of Don João, the popular Mestre de Avis—it also brought the country a new political regime, a constitutional regime. The Cortes' composition is well known: representatives of the high clergy, seventy-two *fidalgos,* and proctors of thirty-one towns who took an equal part in the assembly's deliberations, both in separate and in common sessions. It is not our purpose to examine here the nature of this assembly's decisions and its acclamation of the new king; actually the members present simply allowed the prince to call himself king (*"quod ipse nominaret se Regem"*), and the question was consciously avoided. But the unanimous determination to change the rules of succession to the throne had been preceded, not only by revolt, which was the basis for the constitutional innovation, but also by the *Cortes'* discussion of the *capitulos de agravamento*—the lists of grievances against the misrule of the late King Don Fernando. The people's representatives had in particular complained that the king had surrounded himself with bad counselors; that he had not listened to the complaints and appeals of the people; and that he had decided on questions of importance for the community, such as war and monetary reform, without discussing them in the Cortes. They wished, they said, never to see this repeated. The decision of the Cortes itself was directly, immediately inspired by these protests.

The passage that reaffirmed the moral and pragmatic value of the principle *Quod omnes tangit* appeared in the midst of others. But it was more than one element of a series; the principle appears to be the common motif, the presupposition of all the other elements, the leading note, the spirit with which the *Cortes* (and, earlier, the three Estates) had faced and resolved the problems of the life of Portugal as a society and the question of who was to hold the supreme political power. But beneath the political principle lay the Portuguese Cortes' very principle of existence in terms of an organized community and of representative function. To conclude their debates—and sanction them—the Cortes repeated, *"hé direito quea as cousas, que a todos pertenencem, e de que todos sentem carrego, sejam a ello chamàdo"*[64] [there is a law that there are things that belong to all and that all feel responsible for, be they thus called]. It recalled for the future that, in the past, the people had been deprived of this privilege by the former king. The people had indeed been deprived, but they had not forgotten; the principle had not disappeared. It could not.

The new King replied in circumstantial and precise terms. He was entitled to the power and would defend it. His words, however polite and compliant, lacked a sense of the whole. For the moment he sought to please the Cortes. He made promises. He wanted, above all however, to keep his own freedom to marry whomever he might choose without interference. On this he would not yield and he cited precedent: "marriages must be free, since the kings before him married freely; for this reason he cannot be obliged nor can he promise" . . . anything; but he will inform everybody as soon as possible. For the rest, the present war was a war of defense and other wars would not be waged without the consent of the Cortes (or of the people). As to the problems of peace, the administration of the commonwealth, whenever there is something to be decided (*que he compridorio*), he would summon the people *"para com seu acordo delles tomar aquello que for seu serviço e pela honra delles todos"* [in order to be in agreement with them to take whatever may be for his service and for the honor of all].

Quod omnes tangit, despite its modest origin, thus appeared where it belonged. This short essay is simply meant to remind the reader that this was so, above all in what we call the world of ideas, of general theories and doctrines, of politics and public law. From a mere technical principle of formal law it had attained a more dignified level. But it was still only a normative sentence. In order for the concept to display its real effectiveness, society had to intervene directly.

On the other hand—and I mention it only as a last detail of classification—none of the people discussed were jurists, although, to be sure, they were not complete outsiders to the world of law and particularly to the world of canon law. They acknowledged the principle's importance; but they certainly had no power to give it normative value, as a legislator could have done. They were mainly witnesses and interpreters of the thought of their time, sensitive interpreters and witnesses of great human and historical value. They still belonged to the Middle Ages. They were therefore under the divergent influences both of a traditional ideal of sovereignty constantly in touch with the people and of the antithetical ideal of a monarchy that, once it had been invested with full powers by the people, would be complete and absolute, subject to no legal ties. The political situation was not the same everywhere. Changes in social relations did not take place everywhere on the same scale.

In the field of political polemics, *Quod omnes tangit* seemed to the supporters of the democratic tradition to be much more than an abstract rule; it was a rule of life, a precious gift to be preserved and handed down to future generations. For the zealots of royal power and *plena potestas,* it was a chimerical and a slightly dangerous ideal, which perhaps inspired a wholesome awe; one had to pass over it without giving the impression of denying or opposing it. In politics and administration it remained an excellent watchword, a typical expression of democracy, the expression of political leadership based on wisdom, agreement, and collaboration. In the end, the value that each time and place attached to *Quod omnes tangit,* as a theoretical notion and as a rule of behavior, reflected the degree to which authority was concentrated in the supreme power of the state in comparison with the other elements of society.

NOTES

1. This is what D. Pasquet thought (*Essai sur les origines de la Chambre des Communes* [1914], pp. 201–202); the late P. S. Leicht effectively showed him wrong ("Un principio politico medioevale," Accademia nazionale dei Lincei, *Rendiconti della Classe di scienze morali,* ser. 5, **29** (1920) now in *Scritti vari di storia del diritto italiano,* **1** (1943), 129 ff.); I hope my argument against Pasquet's opinion may be considered conclusive (*L'istituto parlamentare in Italia dalle origini al 1500* [1949], pp. 68 ff.). I deal with this matter in my book *Il parlamento in Italia nel medio evo e nell'eta moderna,* chap. 1, sec. 2 ("the principle of the cooperation by subjects and their consent in assemblies, *Q.o.t.*) (1962), pp. 34 ff.

2. *Histoire des institutions politiques et administratives de la France,* 2 (1898), 199. R. W. and A. J. Carlyle write that the success of *Q.o.t.* was not the result of casual or isolated forces in one country or another, but was the logical development of the fundamental principles of medieval political culture (*A History of Medieval Political Theory in the West,* 5 (1928), 139–140).

3. The reference to *Q.o.t.* is evident, even if the principle is only paraphrased: *"Ut prosecutio dicti negotii quod christianos tangit communiter universos cum deliberatione in tanto negotio necessaria ordinetur et universi et singuli eo magis proprium ipsum negotium reputantes quo cum ipsorum consilio et deliberatione ordinatum fuerit, ad illum prosequendum animentur."* [. . . that further action on this matter, which concerns all Christians alike, be decided with the deliberation required for such a matter; and, considering it very much their own concern, all of those with whose counsel and deliberation the decision is taken should be pressed to carry it out.] The text is in J. L. A. Huillard-Bréholles, *Historia diplomatica Friderici II Romanorum imperatoris et Siciliae regis . . .* (1852 ff.) 2, pt. 1, 241.

4. The text is in Huillard-Bréholles, *Historia diplomatica . . . ,* **6**, pt. 1, 168. I examined the document for the first time in "Note federiciane," *Annali Univ. Macerata* **18** (1951), and more fully in *Studi medievali* **18** (1952) [1954]; see also G. de Vergottini, *Studi sulla legislazione imperiale di Federico II in Italia, Le leggi del 1220* (1952), 247 ff.

5. The text is in *MGH Const.* 3. 49–50. This document is discussed in my book, *L'istituto parlamentare,* 71 ff.

6. The text of the document, famous at least in the English-speaking world, can be found in F. Palgrave, *The Parliamentary Writs of Military Summons,* 1 (1827), 30 and in W. Stubbs, *Select Charters and other Illustrations of English Constitutional History* (H. W. C. Davis, ed. 1913), p. 479. (The analogous writ of 1294, Davis, *Select Charters,* p. 476.) The myth of the "Model Parliament" [against which see my remarks in *L'istituto parlamentare,* pp. 48, 112] does not seem to enjoy the popularity it once did. Lady D. M. Stenton, *English Society in the Early Middle Ages, 1066–1307* (1955), p. 56, in fact writes that "despite his 'Model Parliament' of 1295, when Edward I died the constitution of Parliament was very far from settled. The Commons, that is the knights and burgesses, were not yet a necessary part of a true parliament; nor is there any evidence of their talks together from which the House of Commons ultimately grew." Although G. M. Trevelyan, *A Shortened History of England* (1959), does not neglect the English constitutional history of the time, he does not even hint at any "Model Parliament." On the contrary, on p. 157 he remarks, "When Edward I died he was on the way to make himself absolute master of England and of Scotland both"; thus Trevelyan does not seem to think Edward imbued with much democratic spirit! Besides, it is dubious whether that assembly of 1295 was a real parliament or a "Great Council," following the classification recently proposed by H. G. Richardson and G. O. Sayles, *Parliaments and Great Councils in Medieval England* (1961).

7. Y. M. J. Congar, "Quod omnes tangit, ab omnibus tractari et approbari debet," *RHD,* 4me sèr., **36** (1958), summarizes them all.

8. A. Marongiu, "Il principio fondamentale della democrazia nel XIII secolo," *Paideia,* **1** (1946), 257 ff.

9. H. F. Jolowicz, "The Stone that Builders Rejected: Adventures of some Civil Law Texts," *Seminar,* **12** (1954), 34 ff. An essay of more general interest by the same author is *Roman Foundations of Modern Law* (1957).

10. This short essay corrects, develops, and supplements with notes a French article entitled *"Q.o.t.* principe fondamental de démocratie au XIV siècle," read at Stockholm (during the XI International Congress of Historical Science, in August 1960) to the *Commission internationale pour l'histoire des assemblées d'état.* The French text appears in the *Album Helen Maud Cam* (1961), 101 ff.

11. Indeed, it was defined as the principle of consent by the late Miss M. Clarke in her important book *Medieval Representation and Consent* (1936).

12. See the important contributions of G. Post: *"Plena Potestas* and Consent in Medieval Assemblies, A Study in Romano-Canonical Procedure and the Rise of Representation," *Speculum,* **18** (1943); "A Romano-Canonical Maxim *Quod omnes tangit* in Bracton," *Traditio* (1946); "The Theory of Public Law and the State in the 13th Century," *Seminar* (1948); "A Roman Legal Theory of Consent, *Quod omnes tangit," Wisconsin Law Rev.* (1950) [Now reprinted in G. Post, *Studies in Medieval Legal Thought* (1964)]. The *Summa "Reverentia sacrorum canonum"* is a little earlier than Innocent's decretal; it is ascribed by S. Kuttner to the period between 1183–1184 and 1192 (*Repertorium der Kanonistik, 1140–1234,* **1** (1937), pp. 194 ff.); in the passage *"A fide devius,"* it states that the Pope himself, or the metropolitan or the bishop themselves, in case of heresy must be judged by the community of the faithful: *"Quod forte videtur quia heresis omnes ecclesie iudices tangit et quod omnes similiter tangit ab omnibus, sicut si bonum est debet comprobari, ita si malum est improbari"*; [. . . because heresy concerns all the judges of the Church; and since that which concerns all in a similar way, if it is good, should be approved by all, so that which is evil should be condemned by all.]; as, it adds, can be deduced from the Code of Justinian (5. 59, 5). The text of the passage is in B. Tierney, "Pope and Council—Some New Decretist Texts," *Medieval Studies,* **19** (1957), 216. Some more references in G. Post, "A Romano-Canonical Maxim," and Y. M. Congar, *"Q.o.t."*

13. Gloss to the *Decretum,* **1**, 1, *dist.* 96, *c.* 4.

14. *Decret. Gregorii IX,* **1**, 23, 7, 6. It refers, purely and simply, to Roman law (below, n.15): *"quum juxta imperialis sanctionis auctoritatem ab omnibus quod omnes tangit approbari debeat, et quum commune eorum decanus officium exerceat, communiter est eligendus, vel etiam amovendus."* [. . . since, according to the authority of Imperial law, what touches all should be approved by all, and since the rural deal exercises their office (i.e. that of the bishop and the archdeacon) in common, he is to be elected by their common decision and removed by their common decision.] This resort to Roman sources by the ecclesiastical legislator was neither new nor out of the ordinary. Pope Lucius III (1181–1185), in fact, said (*Extra,* **5**, 32, **1**), *"sicut humanae leges non dedignantur sacros canones imitari, ita et sacrorum statuta canonum priorum principum constitutionibus adiuvantur."* [. . . just as human laws have not found it unworthy to imitate the sacred Canons, so the laws of the sacred Canons are aided by preceding princely legislation.]

15. It is difficult to say when or by whom the position of a person as an individual was first distinguished from that of a person as a member of an organized community: texts in O. Gierke, *Das deutsche Genossenschaft,* **3**, *Die Staats- und Korporationslehre des Alterthums und des Mittelalters und ihre Ausnahme in Deutschland* (1881), pp. 306, 322 ff., 367, 433, and elsewhere.

16. See now, O. Giacchi, "La regola *Quod omnes tangit* nel diritto canonico (*c.* 101, 1, *n.* 2 *C.J.C.*)," *Studi in onore di G. Del Vecchio,* **1** (1953); and G. Leone, "De juribus singulorum jure proprio et non jure collegii," *Ephemerides juris canonici,* **11** (1955); A. Toso, "Quod uti singulos omnes tangit," *Jus Pontificium* (1938).

17. C.V. 59, 5: *"Etenim absurdum est solvi tutelam non consentiente, sed forsitan ignorante eo qui tutor fuerit ordinatus. . . . Necesse est omnes suam auctoritatem praestare: ut quod omnes similiter tangit, ab omnibus comprobetur."* [For it is absurd that a wardship should be dissolved without the consent—indeed without even the knowledge—of the person who has been appointed guardian . . . . It is necessary for all to lend their authority, for what touches all should be approved by all.]

18. In his famous work *The Constitutional History of England* (1st ed.; 1873; 4th ed., 1896, pp. 133 and 369) he attributed to the king himself the merit of having changed *Q.o.t.* "from a mere legal maxim into a great constitutional principle."

19. C. H. McIlwain, *The High Court of Parliament and its Supremacy: an Historical Essay on the Boundaries between Legislation and Adjudication in England* (1910); *Growth of Political Thought in the West* (1932) and the chapter *"Medieval Estates"* from the *Cambridge Medieval History,* **7** (1932); G. H. Haskins, *The Statute of York and the Interest of the Commons* (1935), and *The Growth of English Representative Government* (1948).

20. He died in 1328. The work we quote probably belongs to 1311 (the date of the Council of Vienne): the text is from the Paris edition of 1671, pt. 2, *t.* 41, p. 151.

21. On his attitude toward papal power, see P. Torquebiau, "Le gallicanisme de Durand de Mende le jeune," *Acta Congressus iuridici internationalis, Romae, 1934,* **3** (1936), 268 ff. and B. Tierney, *Foundations of Conciliar Theory, The Contribution of Medieval Canonists from Gratian to the Great Schism* (1955).

22. Venitian ed. of 1561, **1**, 4, p. 11.

23. Defensor pacis, **1**, 12 and *passim.* In the *Defensor minor* (**12**, 1) he speaks of *"universitas hominum."*

24. D.p., Dictio **1**, 12, 5 and *Dictio* **2**, 19, 2.

25. D.p., Dictio **1**, 12, 7 and 5 [Trans. by A. Gewirth (1956), pp. 445, 446].

26. As has been maintained by P. S. Leicht, "Un principio politico medioevale," p. 11. More recently, Congar, *"Q.o.t.,"* pp. 239, 241, says that, although *Q.o.t.* is never found in Marsilio, "he often touches on the idea itself," and Congar explains that Marsilio does not quote it by alleging the limited legal learning of the author. The problem of the extent of Marsilio's knowledge of law is rather complex; he may have studied at Orléans, and P. R. Meyer, *Étude sur Marsile de Padoue jurisconsulte et théologien du XIVe siècle* (1870), has made a law professor of him. F. Battaglia, *Marsilio da Padova e la filosofiia politica nel medio evo* (1928), p. 710, argues (among other things) that, *"ignaro com'è di diritto romano,"* Marsilio never quotes the *lex de imperio* or *lex regia* to which Frederic II alluded. In my opinion, if Marsilio had quoted them it would have meant that he was not acquainted with Roman law. (Is the *lex regia* among the Justinian texts?) In fact, Marsilio was directly acquainted with many legal texts, at least of canon law (see Battaglia, *Marsilio da Padova* p. 34, and, C. W. Previté-Orton, "The authors cited in the *Defensor pacis," Essays in History Presented to R. L. Poole* [1927], pp. 405–420), and he might have learned the principle from them. On the other hand, *Q.o.t.* was very common: why should Marsilio himself not have been acquainted with it and write as if he knew it? It is preferable to think, as Battaglia himself does ("Modernità di Marsilio di Padova," *Studi in memoria di O. Vannini* [1955], p. 14), that Marsilio "echoes" and paraphrases *Q.o.t.* This is also the view of P. Torelli, "Capitanato del popolo e vicariato imperiale come elementi costitutivi della Signoria Bonacolsiana,"

Accademia Virgiliana (Mantova), Atti e Memorie **14–16** (1923), 155, who writes that *Q.o.t.* found in Marsilio its final affirmation, in a form which, although faithful to the Justinian one, is not literally identical. Marsilio, having assimilated the principle, attached to it a value it had not possessed in its primitive formulation and which, as a matter of fact, was contrary to the concept of the imperial Roman state.

27. If Battaglia's assumption (*Marsilio da Padova*), according to which *Q.o.t.* reached Nicolas of Cusa through Marsilio, is true.

28. On his political thought the following works are fundamental: A. Amman, *La doctrine de l'église et de l'état chez Occam; étude sur le "Breviloquium"* (1942), and R. Scholz, *Wilhelm von Ockam als politischer Denker und sein "Breviloquium de principatu tyrannico"* (1944); see also note 29.

29. I do not know whether we may assume that Ockham really considers the rights he thinks belong to the members of the community and to political organizations to be the foundation for a democratic regime, or at least a device to limit the otherwise full authority of those holding supreme power in a political regime not very different from the one we today call "constitutional." Although he expresses a superior ideal of justice, he apparently neglects to advocate a real transformation of the system then in force; see my *L'istituto parlamentare in Italia dalle origini al 1500,* p. 303. M. Grignaschi holds virtually the same opinion; "La limitazione dei poteri del 'Principans' in Guglielmo d'Ockam e Marsilio da Padova," *Commission internationale pour l'histoire des assemblées d'états, Etudes,* **18** (1958) pp. 35 ff., 41. Grignaschi thinks that, although William of Ockham "formulated a complete theory of privileges and 'liberty,' " in which the communtiy and the councils could paralyze royal or imperial authority, these privileges were valid only insofar as they were profitable for common welfare (*bonum totius communitatis*); if Ockham was an acute observer of reality, he was at the same time "a total stranger to any plan for political reform" (Grignaschi, "La limitazione . . . ," p. 46). J. Lecler, "Les théories démocratiques au Moyen-Âge," *Etudes,* **225** (1935), 26 has judged Marsilio and Ockham realistically. "Their bold ideas about the origins and nature of society are followed, in the end, by only timid conclusions containing nothing that might disturb royal power." Lecler considers them the best supporters of imperial and royal authority.

30. In his famous *Dialogus de potestate imperiali et papali* (or *Dialogus inter magistrum et discipulum de imperatorum et pontificum potestate*), **6**, chap. 84, 85 (M. Goldast, ed. *Monarchia S. Romani Imperii sive Tractatus de iurisdictione imperiali seu regia et pontificia seu sacerdotali. . . ,* **2** [1614], 603 ff.)

31. He quotes (Goldast, *Monarchia,* **2**, p. 604) the texts of the *Glossa ordinaria* to Gratian's *Decretum* and of the *Liber Extra* (see footnotes 13, 14), and specifies that "the rule *quod omnes tangit ab omnibus tractari debet* is to be understood as meaning if it can be done by all and there appears to be no manifest reason why anyone should be excluded." Ockham refers to *Q.o.t.* several times. In another passage of his *Dialogus,* 3, *tract.* 2, *lib.* 3, *c.* 6 (*ibid.,* p. 934) on the subject of papal elections, he writes, "Those persons over whom someone is to be placed as ruler have the right to elect and to place someone over themselves" for "what touches all must be dealt with by all; but placing someone to rule over others concerns all: therefore it must be done by all." He also uses it elsewhere. See L. Baudry, "La lettre de Guillaume d'Occam au Chapitre d'Assise," *Revue d'histoire Franciscane* **38** (1926), 207, and C. Bramton *Guillelmi de Ockham epistula ad fratres minores* (1926); Ockham, *Opera Politica* [*Octo questiones de potestate papae*] J. G. Sikes, ed. (1940), p. 65; *Compendium errorum papae Iohannis XXII,* in Goldast, p. 974; R. Scholz, *Unbekannte Kirchenpo-*

litische Streitschriften aus der Zeit Ludwigs des Bayern (1327–1354), **2** (1914), p. 443 [*An rex Angliae, pro succursu guerrae possit recipere bona ecclesiarum,* chap. 8 from ms. Vat. Lat. 4115]. William of Ockham's several references to *Q.o.t.* are mentioned more than once by G. de Lagarde, "L'idée de représentation dans les oeuvres de Guillaume d'Ockham," *International Bulletin of the Committee of Historical Sciences,* **9** (1937), 584, and by Congar, "*Q.o.t.,*" pp. 244, 250 ff.; according to the latter, Ockham is, as far as *Q.o.t.* is concerned, a world all by himself; he employs it as a weapon against the papacy.

32. *Dialogus,* (Goldast, ed. p. 350, and in *Archivum franciscanum historicum,* W. Mulder, ed., **16** [1923], 477).

33. This is what G. de Lagarde believes (see *n.* 31).

34. In a review of H. S. Offler, *Guillelmi de Ockham opera politica, E.H.R.* **72** (1957), 309.

35. Lagarde, "L'idée de représentation," pp. 440 ff. and esp. p. 448.

36. I[a] pars, **6**, *c.* 70 (Goldast, ed. p. 584).

37. See *n.* 31.

38. H. Meyer, *Lupold von Bebenburg—Studien zu seinen Schriften—Ein Beitrag zur Geschichte der staatsrechtlichen und kirchenpolitischen Ideen und der Publizistik im 14. Jahrhundert* (1909).

39. *De iuribus regni et imperii romani* (Argentorati, 1664), *c.* 17.

40. F. P. Bliemetzrieder, *Literarische Polemik zu Beginn des grossen abendländischen Schismas* (1910) and O. Borhak, *Staatskirchliche Anschauungen und Handlungen am Hofe Kaiser Ludwigs des Bayern* (1933).

41. On Pelayo see R. Scholz, *Unbekannte kirchenpolitische Streitschriften* (1911), 202 ff., and J. Beneyto, *Los origenes de la ciencia politica en España* (1949), 100 ff.

42. The text is in Scholz, *Unbekannte Streitschr.,* **2**, 517.

43. F. Valls-Taberner, "El tractat 'de regimine principum' de l'infant Pere d'Arago," *Estudis franciscans,* **37** (1926).

44. The text is in Valls-Taberner, "El tractat," *Est. francisc.,* **37** (1926), *c.* 24, p. 116.

45. *Le livre de politique d'Aristote* (Paris, 1482), lib. **3**, chap. 17 (*t.* **1**, fo. 96) was brought to my attention by M. Grignaschi, "Nicolas Oresme et son commentaire à la "Politique d'Aristote," *Album Helen M. Cam.,* **1** (1960), 111, 112.

46. "Les doctrines politiques de la Catalunya médiéval," *Obras selectas,* **2** (1954), 213; see also F. H. Probst, "Francesco Eximeniç ses idées politiques et sociales," *Revue hispanique* (1918); J. Beneyto, "Los origenes," 106 ff., and *Historia de las doctrinas politicas* (1948), 120 ff., 137, 140 ff.; and A. Lopez-Amo y Marin, *El pensamiento politico de Eximeniç en su tratado de 'Regiment de princeps'* (1946).

47. *Carta de fra Francesch Eximeniç al infant Martì . . . . donantli consells;* text in A. Rubió y Lluch, *Documents per l'historia de la cultura catalana migeval,* **2** (1921), 401.

48. "*Rimado de palacio:* este libro fiço el honrrado caballero Pero Lopez de Ayala estando preso e llamase *El libro de Palagio,*" *Bibl. aut. españ. Poetas castellanos anteriores al siglo XV,* (P. J. Pidal, ed. 1864).

49. The text is in J. Gerson, *Opera omnia* (Ellies du Pin, ed., Antwerp, 1706), **2**, *c.* 823.

50. The interpretation of Jean Faure, a French jurist and high magistrate of the middle of the century, is partly political and partly legal. In his *In quattuor libros Institutionum eruditissima Commentaria* (Venice, 1582) r. *De pena temere litigantium,* p. 173, *nn.* 6 ff., he explains that when the people to summon are *multi, Q.o.t.* can be fulfilled even without summoning all the people concerned. For instance, in the case of a controversy concerning a whole territory and a religious order, if a community is concerned, only the heads are summoned. Or, if the clergy are to be summoned, the *prelati* are summoned in their place, and the *barones seu habentes iurisdictionem terrarum et villarum* instead of the inhabitants. This system, he states, is followed by French court (*curia Franciae*), which, to levy subsidies (*collectae*), convenes the *praelatos, barones et villas notabiles* in an assembly. Therefore he implicitly states that the assemblies of the "Three Estates" are the realization of *Q.o.t.*

51. See Marongiu, *L'istituto parlamentare,* p. 75 (where, however, owing to a singular slip, I spoke of a controversy over Ireland instead of Scotland).

52. *Consuetudo est regni Angliae in negotiis tangentibus status eiusdem regni requiratur consilium omnium quos res tangit;* in fact Edward submitted the text of the Papal bull to the barons of the kingdom summoned to parliament at Lincoln: text and information in Stubbs, *The Constitutional History of England,* **2**, 158, 159.

53. They were the *Noveles Ordenances;* text in *Statutes of the Realm,* **1**, 157 ff. (5th year, Edw. II, A.D. 1311).

54. A detailed account can be found in the almost contemporary *Monachi cujusdam Malmesberiensis, vita Eduardi II* (W. Stubbs, ed. *Rerum britannicarum medii aevi scriptores, Chronicles Edward I and Edward II,* **2** [1883], 170 ff.).

55. *Statutes of the Realm* (15th Edw. II), **1**, 189. Many scholars have dealt with this important text: see G. T. Lapsley, "The Interpretation of the Statute of York, 1322," *E.H.R.* **66** (1941); B. Wilkinson, "The Coronation Oath of Edward II and the Statute of York," *Speculum,* **19** (1944) and G. Post, "The Two Laws and the Statute of York," *Speculum,* **29** (1954). According to Post, the procedure "reaffirmed, but did not create, a constitutional as well as political principle of royal government." See now also D. Clementi, "That the State of York of 1322 is no longer ambiguous," *Album Helen M. Cam.,* **2** (1961), 93 ff.

56. On the *Convocations,* for lack of more recent writings, see: T. Lathbury, *A History of the Convocation of the Church of England, being an Account of the Proceedings of Anglican Ecclesiastical Councils from the Earliest Period* (1853).

57. The text is in *Lords' Report on the Dignity of a Peer,* 4, 463.

58. Both in practice (at Florence: see A. Gherardi, *Le consulte della repubblica fiorentina dall'anno 1280 all'anno 1298,* **1** [1898], p. 175) and in theory (in the anonymous *Oculus pastoralis—Libellus erudiens futurum rectorem populorum* and in the *Liber de regimine civitatum* by John of Viterbo). On this literature, which Torelli, "Capitanato del popolo," with mild irony called "literature of the *podestà,*" see Leicht, "Un principio politico," and my *L'istituto parlamentare,* pp. 69 ff.

59. I have corrected (by substituting *cura* for *circa*) the otherwise incomprehensible text quoted in V. Vitale, *Il dominio della parte guelfa in Bologna, 1280–1327* (1901), p. 237, doc. 29.

60. The text is in Torelli, "Capitanato," p. 151.

61. Although Torelli does not use Pasquet's polemical tone (the latter had stated in his *Essai sur les origines* that *Q.o.t.* was part of "the baggage of philosophical considerations and rhetorical flourishes into which the clerks of the English Chancery liked to dip from time to time, especially when writing to the clergy, whom they thought more able than the laity to enjoy these stylistic embellishments") he does say they are "ready-made phrases, that is, pure rhetoric."

I do not agree with Torelli. In fact I am not ready to share his opinion on the illusory value of tradition, nor do I think that the problem is properly handled on such a basis. In his opinion, the Mantuan document by which Guido Gonzaga was allotted the siegniory "smelled of the formulary and not of living thought," but to expect to find the latter and not the former in a notarial or chancery act is perhaps to expect too much. He questions both the spontaneity of this grant of power (which is not of interest here) and the existence of *"un operante concetto di libertà e sovranità popolare, che di fatto era ben morto."* In fact, if it is true that our communes, by now ruled by *signori,* had lost their freedom, it is not true that the concept had also been lost nor that—in this case —once the Bonacolsian seigniory had died out, the commune of Mantua and its people would not become once again *sui iuris* and able to make decisions for themselves. It is therefore not a matter of traditions unfelt but of reality.

62. *Costituzioni egidiane* (P. Sella, ed. 1912), lib. 2, *r.* 19, p. 91.

63. "As Cortes de 1385," *Revista portuguese de história—Homen. Gama Barros* (1941).

64. The text is in *ibid.* doc. *n.* 4. p. 79.

The Theory and Practice of Representation in Medieval England*

Helen Maud Cam

Though representation is an old, not to say, hackneyed subject, we can never get away from it. It is the basis of our Anglo-American assumptions about democracy, though little used by the Greeks who invented the word democracy and repudiated by Rousseau, the prophet of modern democracy. Representative institutions are the background of Stubbs' great book. His design of the growth of the English constitution proceeds from the history of the things represented to that of the series of events by which the principle and practice of representation were incorporated in the national assembly. I use the word *things* (which we are at such pains to eliminate from the undergraduate essay) advisedly, for the problem, as I should like to pose it, is "*What* is represented, and why?"

In the last twenty years the study of this ancient subject has been reinvigorated from two new sources, each of them originating outside England. The first is the one with which I am most intimately concerned, since it is embodied in an international commission of which I have the honour to be president. In 1933, at the International Congress of Historical Sciences held at Warsaw, a Belgian scholar, M. Émile Lousse, whom we are happy to have with us today, propounded to the assembled historians a project for a concerted study of the formation of assemblies of estates. The *Ständestaat,* the *état corporatif*—the realm of estates— had long been a subject of study in Germany; two articles by Otto Hintze, published in the

* Reprinted from Helen M. Cam, *Law-finders and Law-makers in Medieval England* (London: Merlin Press, 1962), pp. 159–175.

Historische Zeitschrift in 1929 and 1931, had set forth the theory that the evolution of estates was the clue to the later medieval history not merely of Germany but of all Western Christendom. This view, in tune with the new corporatism which Italy and Germany were translating into fact and which La Tour du Pin had been preaching in France for many years, appeared to the historians at Warsaw worthy of scientific investigation; and in 1935 the international commission for the study of assemblies of estates came into being, with M. Coville as its president and M. Lousse as its secretary and driving force.

Conferences were held year after year, mostly under the auspices of the French *Société d'Histoire du Droit;* volumes of studies by French, Swiss, Belgian, Hungarian, Italian and English scholars were published, on various aspects of the history of estates,[1] and the first volume of Professor Lousse's own book on corporative organization and representation came out in occupied Belgium in 1943.[2] It was followed in 1949 by Signor Marongiu's book, *L'istituto parlamentare in Italia dalle origine al* 1500,[3] and two months ago by Mr. Richardson's and Professor Sayles' book on *The Irish Parliament in the Middle Ages.*[4] Owing largely to Professor Lousse, the commission on estates, unlike some other children of the *Comité International des Sciences Historiques,* justified its existence by its activity and it was reconstituted at the Paris conference two years ago. With representatives of fourteen nations involved, it can fairly claim to be an international undertaking.[5]

This digression is not altogether irrelevant. In our study of English medieval history, we are, perhaps, too ready to stay on our island. Considering the very close relations between England and Rome, and England and France during the greater part of the Middle Ages, our reluctance to look overseas and study parallel developments for enlightenment, is rather less than scientific. If English and American scholars have been roused to protest by some of the statements made about English institutions in the volumes I have mentioned, the result has, I think, been only beneficial; but I have the impression that considerably more attention has been paid to them in the United States than in England. The outcome should be, I think, first a stimulus to the use of the comparative method; secondly, a re-examination of our own views. It is attack that compels one to define and justify assumptions that may never have been formulated.

Some of Professor Lousse's criticisms in detail can be answered fairly readily. He does very much less than justice to Stubbs, whose learning stands on a rock, however much his interpretations may be affected by the ebb and flow of circumstance. M. Lousse went so far as to say that Maitland, "who taught at Cambridge," did not think much of Stubbs (an Oxford professor) and published a course of lectures in opposition to him, where he showed his knowledge of Western Christendom (in opposition to Stubbs' insularity), by referring to the idea of the three estates of those who pray, those who fight and those who work. The fact is that Maitland expressly referred his Cambridge students to Stubbs' fifteenth chapter, not only for the phrase he quotes but also for a fuller discussion of the history of estates in France, Germany, Sicily, Aragon, Castile, Naples, and the Netherlands, than he, Maitland, had time to give.

The conception of estates of the realm is indeed not a new one to American and English students of history, for whom McIlwain's chapter in the seventh volume of the Cambridge Medieval History has amplified Stubbs' sketch. The classification of society into those who pray, those who fight, and those who labour, is a medieval commonplace, to be found in Alfred the Great and Aelfric, in Langland and Wyclif, in Gerson and Nicholas of Clamangis; it is familiar in Germany in the three categories of *Lehrstand, Wehrstand, Nährstand.* Dumézil[6] indeed would say that it goes back to the origins of the Indo-European peoples and is one of their basic social and religious conceptions, being reflected in the three Hindu castes of priests, fighters and cultivators—Brahmans, Kshatriyas, Vaisyas; in the Druids, warriors and agriculturists of primitive Celtic society, in the three tribes and three deities of primitive Rome—Jupiter, Mars, Quirinus; in the three Scandinavian deities, Odin, Thor and Freya. A cruder but more recent expression of it is in the inn-sign of the Four Alls, on which are depicted side by side, the parson saying "I pray for all"; the soldier saying "I fight for all"; the labourer, "I work for all," and the king, "I rule all."[7]

Such a view of society is functional, vocational; it does not of itself indicate the common consciousness or common action that goes with the idea of estates of the realm, or the *Ständestaat.* There may well be division of function in the lord's household or the king's realm; but so long as the functionaries are the tools of their lord, as Alfred called them, and so long as the horizontal principle of the associations of like with like has not yet triumphed over the vertical principle of loyalty to and dependence upon the lord, so long society is still in the feudal stage. It is changing economic conditions, what we used to call "the rise of the middle class," that produces the sense of common interest with one's equals, common aims, common action against one's enemies (often one's superiors), and that leads to the formation of associations and the organization of societies by estates. To take one instance: such a stage is reached when the English bishops begin to regard themselves, and be regarded primarily, as members of the clerical estate, rather than as tenants in chief, owing service at the king's court "like the other barons"—*sicut barones ceteri,* as the Constitutions of Clarendon phrase it. Stubbs notes the corresponding moment in Aragon as occurring in 1301.

For Professor Lousse the process of association is clear cut and deliberate. It follows a regular pattern of mutual oaths—*conjurationes* or *communiones;* of pacts like that of the citizens of London in 1193 or of the community of the baronage of Oxford in 1258. M. Petit-Dutaillis in his last book[8] insisted that it is in this mutual oath that the *sine qua non* of the French commune consists, not in any specific privilege or status. For M. Lousse, however, there is a second stage; the *corporation,* whether urban, mercantile, or noble, that has been constituted by oaths, must secure legal status; it must obtain a charter of privileges from the governmental authority in order to become an estate and not merely a group. A number of corporations may combine to appeal for privileges and thus establish themselves as an order. He has a rich collection both of pacts and of charters of privileges to bear out his contention. But it is here that the formula begins to look foreign to the student of English institutions.[9]

Confronted with the charge of obstinate insularity and national pride, which M. Lousse hurls against him, the English historian examines the tendencies of English social and constitutional evolution to see how they look in the light of the continental formula. Yes, there are gilds; yes, there is at least one sworn commune; yes, there are charters to boroughs, and charters of liberties to the barons, and to the clergy (though the English historian is a little startled to find the Constitutions of Clarendon and the Statute of Mortmain listed among the concessions of liberties to the English church). Yes, there is—but only for a fleeting moment—a *communitas bachelerie.* But the only lasting associations and corporations that we are aware of in England are the gilds and companies, the universities and colleges, and the religious houses and orders. There is no closed or sworn order or fraternity of nobles, and even less of knights; there are no charters to groups of towns. The associations of magnates for the obtaining of privileges are occasional and ephemeral; they are not part of the permanent order of English society. As with Pirenne's formula for the growth of towns, so with M. Lousse's formula for the corporative state; England is the square peg that will not fit into the round hole.

There are two main reasons for this, as it seems to me—the economic and the political—or rather one that combines the two and is even more basic—the chronological. It is the timing in Engand that differs from that of the Continent. Owing to the circumstances of the Norman conquest, which wedded military efficiency to the fairly advanced institutions of the Anglo-Saxon monarchy, England had something like 100 years' start of France in the evolution of a royal administrative system. Neither the great feudatories who confronted the Capetian dynasty, nor the imperfectly feudalized regionalisms of the Empire, were present to impede the growth of Anglo-Norman and Angevin authority; the beginnings of the *Beamtenstaat,* the bureaucracy, which, on the Continent, came to be the dominant character of the great monarchies and princedoms of the fourteenth and fifteenth centuries, are traceable in England from the twelfth century onwards.

But if England is administratively and politically ahead of the Continent, she is economically behind. She has her commercial and industrial features

—we all know about the tribe of foreign merchants in the port of London in the days of Ethelred—but compared with the ferment in the valleys of the Po, the Rhine and the Scheldt, or even in northern France, her urban and industrial developments are on a small scale. Weaker and less institutionalized central authorities on the Continent are confronted by denser populations, with more urgent economic problems and more substantial resources, which in their turn, it may well be, stimulate the nobles into a more class-conscious solidarity. The pacts, the corporations, and the orders of the Continent are the product of conditions that do not obtain in England.

Nevertheless, this new angle of vision is illuminating, and we need be in no hurry to reject the light it may give us. Certain old commonplaces and recent interests take a fresh colour, for instance, the rise to prominence of the expression *communitas* in the thirteenth century, commented on by Stubbs, Jolliffe and Powicke, among many others. Tait in his book *The Medieval English Borough,* as he relates the appearance of the mayor in the English borough to the wave of communal sentiment coming from France, points out that John, who had sanctioned the commune of London on his brother's behalf in 1191, appealed fourteen years later to the commune of the realm, the *communa liberorum hominum,* for the defence of the kingdom against a threatened French invasion in 1205. You will remember how the phrase and possibly the sentiment was turned against John in 1215 when the twenty-five guarantors of Magna Carta were empowered as a last resort to grieve and distrain the king *cum communia totius terrae.* When, under John's son, the expression *communitas regni* or *communitas terrae* recurs more and more frequently, it should have for us now overtones evoked by the continental events to which Lousse and Petit-Dutaillis have been calling our attention. The oath taken by the *comune de la tere* at Oxford in 1258 is absolutely in the continental tradition.

Or again there is the petitionary process, so intimately bound up with the judicial and legislative activities of early parliaments, so fruitfully studied in recent years by H. L. Gray, H. G. Richardson, G. O. Sayles, G. L. Haskins, D. Rayner and A. R. Myers. This may profitably be examined afresh in relation to the rich material furnished by Lousse in his fourth chapter. We are still very much in the dark as to the genesis of the petitions, whether singular or common, that were presented to the king and his council in the thirteenth and fourteenth centuries. Who drew up the Petition of the Barons of 1258? and how were the *Monstraunces* of 1297 drafted? or the complaints of the rectors of Berkshire in 1240? In the ninth chapter of *Henry III and the Lord Edward,* Powicke has suggested that "the growing coherence of the clergy probably influenced the *communitas* of the barons and made it more conscious"; it seems not improbable that the clerks who drafted the *gravamina* of their own order had the lion's share in moulding the petitionary technique, with its immense potentialities for the future.

In M. Lousse's attack on the *parlementarisme* of Stubbs he was not in 1943 aware of the formidable allies he possessed. He ignored all the undermining of the seventeenth- and eighteenth-century conceptions of primitive democratic institutions by the erection in 1893 of the high court of parliament as a royal and judicial elder brother who had ousted the younger brother, the embryonic house of commons, from the place of honour. But Stubbs' picture—not quite as black and white as some allege—has had to face criticism from a third quarter.

In the same year that M. Lousse's book came out there appeared two important articles by Mr. Gaines Post of the University of Wisconsin on "*Plena Potestas* and Consent" and on "Roman Law and Early Representation in Spain and Italy,"[10] in which he demonstrated, with a wealth of learning, how great was the contribution of Roman and Canon Law to the theory and practice of medieval representation. Medieval representation, he says, was constructed of heterogeneous materials on a foundation of feudal law, local institutions, royal curias, ecclesiastical synods, and the growth of royal and papal authority, but in both ideas and procedure its architects were greatly aided by the revival of Roman Law in the eleventh and twelfth centuries. In his articles on *plena potestas* Mr. Gaines Post has convincingly linked the early summoning of representatives to assemblies in Spain and Italy with the Roman lawyers' device of the plenipotentiary attorney representing his principal in a court of law: a conception that fits in very neatly with the *persona ficta* of M. Lousse's corporations.

In face of all these attacks, are our English knights of the shire and burgesses to retire meekly into the background, saying, as they did to king and lords in 1348, "As to your war and its array, we are so ignorant and simple that we know nothing about it nor can give any counsel in the matter"?

It was a deceptive reply and a pregnant negative; the rolls of parliament show that they took four days of discussion to arrive at it. We also should not be in a hurry to write off the representative element in the English parliaments as irrelevant in the thirteenth and fourteenth centuries. *Sustine modicum,* as the senior clerk said to his junior in the exchequer in 1177 when he asked him a tricky question; *Sustine modicum: ruricolae melius hoc norunt*—"Wait a bit; let us ask the country folk."

There are really two issues: What is represented by the representatives? And what is the origin of the device of representation? M. Lousse alleges that it is a corporation or association that is represented, and one recognized if not created by royal charter. Mr. Gaines Post very rightly emphasizes the authoritarian and legalistic aspects of the device as used by twelfth- and thirteenth-century rulers, and, as Stubbs and others have done before him, points out ecclesiastical precedents. But the earliest reference to representation in England occurs in a slightly old-fashioned record of local custom that can be dated soon after 1110, whilst the earliest instance of political representation outside England is in the year 1136, in Italy. There is no need to deny the influence of the Church; it must have been operative in England at any date after A.D. 600. On the other hand, "representation" is a far from unequivocal expression, as is made clear, for instance, in de Lagarde's brilliant analysis of its various significations in the days of Ockham.[11] But long before jurists and scholastics began examining into the bearing of the word, representation, the thing itself, was already on the scene as an obvious common-sense solution of constantly recurrent problems. If you want to get the opinion of a crowd, whether of children or of adults, you will in effect say, "Don't all talk at once—who will speak for you?" If an agreement on action has been arrived at by a group of people, one man will naturally be empowered to act for them. If a job has to be done for which a body of persons will be held responsible, it is mere common sense for them to arrange among themselves that one or two shall do it and leave the others free to get on with the work of food production, or business, or whatever it may be. These problems, you will note, arise when there is an active community upon which some external demand is made. That is all that is needed to produce some form of representation.[12] The precise nature of the link between community and representative, and between the community and the source of the external demand will be worked out in practice and defined, as becomes necessary, by custom and, in due course, by written law, and last of all, perhaps, in theory.

So we are driven back to our starting point—what is the community that is represented? This is where Stubbs comes into his own and the obstinate insularity of our "nationalist" historians is vindicated. In English sources, the oldest unit to be represented is the vill, in 1110; the next is the shire and hundred, in 1166; the next is the cathedral chapter, in 1226; the next is the diocesan clergy, in 1254; the next is the "community of the land"—otherwise the barons—in 1258; and the next, the borough in 1265.

The representation of the clergy is clearly inspired by canonist doctrine, and can be associated with Innocent III's enunciation of the principle that links representation with consent—*quod omnes tangit ab omnibus approbetur.* In the case of the borough we have a corporation of Lousse's sort; boroughs owe the privileges which make them boroughs to a royal grant; and the practice of summoning representatives of towns to assemblies had precedents in Italy and Spain from 1162 on, representatives who, from 1214 onwards, come as plenipotentiaries with power to bind those who send them, a device which, as Mr. Post has shown, is directly traceable to papal influence.[13]

But with the earlier instances we are in a different world. The vill, the hundred and the shire are not voluntary associations privileged by royal charter, nor is the community of the barons who, at Oxford, have to elect twelve of their number to attend the parliaments that are to meet thrice a year, to treat of common needs and common business with the king's council. (One of the twelve, it should be noted, is a bishop, who on "functional" principles has no business there.) The twelve are to have power to act on behalf of the community of barons; and the *purpose* of the device is to save the pockets of the barons who cannot afford such frequent journeys to court: *Ceo serra fet pur esparnier le cust del commun*—a sound and practical reason.

It is a reason, moreover, that links up with that given in the *Leges Henrici,* in its account of the attendance of the representatives, of villagers at the shire and hundred moots. In theory, it implies, all the village might be expected to come; but either the lord of the village or his steward can discharge the obligation of the whole vill; failing that, the reeve, the priest and four of the better men of the vill should attend in place of (*pro*) all the village. Again, a common-sense delegation to one or two of a common responsibility. Whether this was a new practice under Henry I, or a recording of ancient custom, as Stubbs assumed, there is nothing to show; both William the Conqueror and Henry I stressed their preservation of the customs of Edward the Confessor, but we know that they also introduced new practices.

The first reference to representation of the shire, however, does sound like a new practice. In 1166 Henry II provided that if criminals arrested under the new procedure of the jury of indictment could not be brought before a royal justice in their own shire, they should be sent to the nearest royal session in some other shire, and with them, the sheriff was to bring two lawful men of the hundred and township where they had been arrested to bear the record of the shire and the hundred as to why they had been arrested. Neither shire nor hundred court kept a written record of their proceedings; only the oral testimony of "credible men of the court," the ancient "witness of the shire," could be produced to prove what had occurred. And this record, it must be remembered, binds those whom they represent, in the sense that the whole shire may be penalized for the action they report. This is not the same relationship as that of a jury which commits no one beyond itself. Nevertheless, when the jurors give their information to the king's inquisitors in 1086, Domesday Book notes that the "hundred says" so and so, and Stubbs does not seem to be going too far in bringing the jury into his picture of the origins of representation.

We may fully accord to Mr. Edwards the essential importance of the formula of *plena potestas* that rivets the power of the representatives to bind those who send them;[14] we may fully accept Mr. Post's demonstration that that formula is of Roman origin, like the *plene instructi* of the clerical proctors; but it is clear that the conception in England is older than the adoption of the formula. The burgesses summoned to the council of 1268 had to bring with them letters from their community declaring that they would hold as accepted and established whatever these men should do on their behalf; the community of the barons in 1258 had agreed to hold as established whatever the twelve whom they had elected should do; and men who bore the record of the shire might in fact involve the shire in an amercement if they reported an irregular action of the shire court.

I do not wish to insist on this point; no doubt the barons at Oxford had clerical advisers and colleagues; Bracton, himself a clerk learned in the Roman law, undoubtedly worked with them. But I wish to recur to my point—*what* was represented?—and to insist on the old standing of the communities of shire, hundred and township.

The districts called the shire and the hundred, as they existed in 1166, were not so very ancient, perhaps not more than 200 or 250 years old. But the communities of shire and hundred succeeded to the traditions of the folkmoots; the assemblies in which, as the tenth century hundred ordinance said, men did justice to each other, and folk right, the law of the people, was declared; the *popularia concilia* whose existence, as Stenton reminds us, is attested in the days of Coenwulf of Mercia. The continuity of the twelfth-century shire and hundred courts from those assemblies of the tenth century in which the men of the court had done justice to each other under the presidency of ealdorman or reeve is unbroken down to that thirteenth-century session when the sheriff of Lincolnshire had to give up the attempt to do business and close the court because the country gentlemen went on strike and refused to do their duty as doomsmen. Neither Stubbs' assumption (based on a mangled text) that Henry I was reviving a moribund institution, nor Mr. Jolliffe's that Henry II recreated it, is warranted by any objective evidence. For business, for justice, and for publicity the shire court maintained its vitality, though it may well have been livelier and more active in a county of many small freeholders, like Lincolnshire, than in a county that contained many large liberties, like Dorset.

This is not to deny that the policy of the Norman and Angevin kings helped to keep the shire and hundred alive. They preserved them not merely by edicts that compelled the sheriffs to observe ancient custom, but even more by giving them work to do. The hundreds had had thief-catching duties; William the Conqueror gave them a concern with homicide by the institution of the *murdrum* fine, besides calling on them for information as to the holding of land, well before 1086. Henry II involved them in the reporting of suspects and Henry III gave them military and police responsibilities, for the keeping of watches and furnishing of armour, and demanded more and more information as to royal rights and private liberties and official misdoing from the hundred juries. The shire found itself involved in the extension of royal justice and the enlargement of the scope of royal revenues: invited by John to send delegates to discuss the affairs of the realm with the king; invited by Henry III to send delegates in 1227 to report on the sheriff's observance of Magna Carta and in 1254 on the willingness of the shire to contribute to the expenses of the king's wars in France.

Who, in fact, ran the shire court? From M. Lousse's angle, it was the *petite-noblesse—de smalre heeren—les seigneurs bassains—the Kleinadel* —though he visualizes them in isolation, each on his own estate, only taking common action in free knightly associations—*Ritterbunde*. The nearest he can get to a shire is a *"localité rurale— une agglomeration plus ou moins dense."* In the three-fold cord of English traditional institutions, he can distinguish only the royal and feudal, he is not aware of the communal. It is true that, broadly speaking, the thirteenth-century shire is the field of the gentry, the knights, the squirearchy. The magnates have ceased to attend it, probably well before 1259; but, though the knights or gentlemen will undoubtedly take the lead in county doings, they will be working with freemen of ungentle blood, yeomen, *valetti,* who may represent the shire at parliaments if knights are not available. All the freeholders of the shire contribute to the expenses of their representative at a fixed rate. And there are no water-tight class barriers—the burgess may be a squire, the agriculturist may buy a town house, the squire's son may marry a villein's daughter, the same man may represent borough and county by turns. And above all, the locality counts. Devonshire will petition the king to have a Devon-born sheriff; and at Oxford the barons will demand that the sheriffs shall not only be landholders, but residents in the shire they administer. The *pays,* the *patria,* the *country,* as the county was still called in Jane Austen's days, of the country gentlemen is the dominant *motif;* however he may link up with his fellows in the house of commons as an estate of the realm, it is not an order or estate that he represents, but a locality, and the house of commons, when it finally comes into existence, is not a house of *roturiers,* of the non-noble, but a house of communities, urban and rural.

It is this fact, together with the fluidity of social relations in England, that might lead us to maintain the position that Lousse condemns in Stubbs and in other English historians; to reassert *"le caractère absolument exceptionnel du parlement anglais."* It is the survival of the shire that is unique; and it is the shire that makes the English parliament absolutely exceptional.

And at the lowest level of all, the community of the vill has still in the thirteenth century a perfectly definite place in the national system as a community that bears joint responsibility, that can and does take common action in its own interests, that is still represented, as it was 1110, by its priest, reeve, and four men, or something very like it, and that is declared, in a royal document of the year 1255, to be entitled to prosecute its plaints in the courts by three or four of its own men—as the later legal theory of corporations would phrase it, "to sue and be sued." The very fact that this legal status was lost in later days strengthens the case for the antiquity of the tradition of responsibility and representation in the oldest and smallest community.

How far are we justified in maintaining that this relationship of the ancient communities to representation and to the king's court is absolutely unique and peculiar to England?

The latest contributor to the history of the estates strongly disputes the claim of uniqueness. Mr. Russell Major in his book on *The Estates-General of 1560,* published in 1951 by the Princeton University Press, argues that many of the differences alleged between English and continental representative assemblies did not in fact exist. In France, as in England, the different orders co-operated. The same local assemblies gave mandates to the representatives of the different orders, who were not organized as three distinct houses in the estates-general until well on in the sixteenth century. The class antagonism so often insisted on was not, he maintains, in existence to any degree sufficient to account for the difference in the ultimate fate of the two nations; "the line between noble and non-noble was so vague as almost to defy definition."[15]

> A deputy to the estates-general was usually elected and empowered by all three estates, but even when named by a single order of society, local ties bound him as strongly to the other orders of his community as his class tie bound him to members of his estate from other parts of France . . . he represented a particular region whose privileges and autonomy he was carefully instructed to maintain.

Further, the men elected were very often men of considerable experience in local government; and they were not only instructed but paid by those who sent them to the national assembly.[16]

For Mr. Major the key to the different history of the national representative institutions of France and England lies in the strength, not the weakness of local feeling—the regionalism which prevented effective common action from being taken in a meeting of the estates-general, or even in the estates of the Languedoil, and made the provincial estates, rather than the estates-general, the source of financial supply for the Crown. The explanation of the greater effectiveness and ultimate survival of the English parliament as against the fading-out of the continental estates is to be found, he maintains, in the policy of the monarchy. Everything turned on the question whether a national representative assembly was or was not of use to the king: if it was, he convoked it; if not, he used the provincial estates in France, the provincial *cortes* in Spain. Mr. Major, whether or not we accept the validity of his arguments, drives us back to look at our facts and our arguments once more, and to ask the question, "What is represented and why?" with renewed determination.

Mr. Chrimes, following on the heels of Maude Clarke, has collected instances to show the emergence of the *term,* "estates of the realm" in

England in the fourteenth and fifteenth centuries.[17] It is most conspicuous in connexion with the depositions of kings—Edward II, Richard II, Edward V. On the occasions when the king's parliament cannot function, the ingredients that go to make a parliament without a king combine to constitute something like a Convention Parliament of the seventeenth century. The lawyers, like Thirning in 1399, see that, legally speaking, a parliament needs a king. The politicians, like the prior of Canterbury in 1326,[18] see that it is desirable to spread the responsibility for revolution as widely as possible, and to involve in the act of changing the succession as many of the elements of society as can be brought in. Preachers will produce texts and similes to underline the conception of a hierarchical order of society; it is a commonplace; but the estates, though they may be a way of thinking, do not seem to be really of outstanding practical significance. Nor can we get away from the fact that the practice of representation does not apply to the two higher estates. However much the Church contributed to the prevalence of the canonist theory, the position of the clergy in parliament does not conform to it. The bishops and abbots are not elected representatives of the clerical order; the diocesan clergy are not in parliament but in convocation. The lay peers of England are not elected by their fellows, they are summoned by the king.

It looks, then, as if we must go back to our traditional formulas, though modified by examination and comparison into something rather different from the Stubbsian pattern. Parliament is both "an assembly of estates and a concentration of local communities," but we couple with this formula the phrase that comes from across the Atlantic: "self-government at the king's command." It was the effective centralization of power under the Angevins that made possible the preservation and utilization of local institutions and local sentiment by the monarchy, which in its turn made possible the growth of the conception of the community of the realm, to which Stubbs directed our attention, and on which Sir Maurice Powicke has so recently insisted. The episode of the villagers of Great Peatling, which Mr. Richardson dug out of the plea rolls for us, with its many-sided social, legal and political implications,[19] may be cited once more in this connexion. In 1265 the villagers of this small Leicestershire township could act as a body to meet an emergency; they could, as a community, enter into a contract and be penalized for breaking it; they could sue and be sued, not only by the magnate whose followers they had mishandled, but by individuals of the community itself, and pay damages to them. But Sir Maurice Powicke[20] links up this local episode with political thought on a national scale when he quotes from the record the words by which the men of Peatling Magna justified their attack on the men of a royalist magnate. It was because "they were against the barons and the welfare of the community of the realm"—*contra utilitatem communitatis regni et contra barones*.[21] The fact that in 1265 peasants could speak like this—that the community of the vill was aware of the community of the realm—gives us in a nutshell the clue to the history of representation in England. From such a beginning there could develop what, by Tudor times, was a political commonplace—the conception that all England was represented in the house of commons. A man was there not only for his own locality but for something much more; he was "a publick, a Councellor to the whole State."[22] Though, as Burke was to say long after, the local units were but "inns and resting places," national consciousness had been bred in the *"patria,"* the country, the neighbourhood, and it was there that the foundations were laid which preserved the institutions of representation unbrokenly in the countries of Anglo-Saxon tradition when they perished elsewhere.

NOTES

1. *Études présentées à la Commission Internationale pour l'histoire des assemblées d'états;* I., Paris, 1937; II-VIII, Louvain, 1937, 1939, 1940, 1943, 1949 (henceforth cited as *Études.*)

2. *La Société d'Ancien Régime,* Louvain, 1943.

3. Rome, 1949.

4. Philadelphia, 1952.

5. By 1962 twenty-four volumes of the *Études* had been published, and the membership included representatives of twenty-one nations.

6. Georges Dumézil, *Jupiter, Mars, Quirinus.* Paris, 1941.

7. Cf. *La société d'Ancien Régime,* p. 103.

8. *Les communes françaises,* Paris, 1947.

9. In the second edition, however, of *La Société d'Ancien Régime* (1952) M. Lousse refers to the *pays,* which he considers has some points in common with the English shire, and indicates that the local community, as well as the social group, has its part to play.

10. *Traditio,* i. (1943) pp. 355–408; *Speculum* (1943), pp. 211–232.

11. *Bulletin of the International Commission of Historical Sciences,* No. 37 (Paris, 1937), pp. 425-51.

12. Compare M. V. Clarke, *Medieval Representation and Consent,* pp. 335–47.

13. Note also the letter of Pope Clement IV to Charles of Anjou in 1267, cited by P. S. Leicht, *Études,* II. (1937), p. 99.

14. See also H. Koenigsberger on "The Powers of Deputies in sixteenth-century Assemblies," *Études,* XXIV. (1962), pp. 211–243.

15. This fact is abundantly illustrated in the thirteenth- and fourteenth-century records of Forez, as Professor Perroy has recently demonstrated. See "Social mobility among the French *Noblesse* in the later Middle Ages," *Past and Present,* April 1962.

16. *The Estates-General of 1560,* pp. 73–5.

17. S. B. Chrimes, *English Constitutional Ideas in the Fifteenth Century* (Cambridge, 1936), pp. 105–26.

18. M. V. Clarke, *Medieval Representation and Consent* (London, 1936), pp. 177–8.

19. See above, pp. 263–264.

20. *Henry III and the Lord Edward,* pp. 509–10.

21. As Mr. Post has pointed out (*History,* 1953, pp. 289–90), the phrase *utilitas communitatis regni* indicates the far reaching influence of baronial propaganda, itself reflecting clerical thought. See Powicke, *op. cit.,* p. 387.

22. Quoted by Louise Fargo Brown in "Ideas of Representation from Elizabeth to Charles II," *Journal of Modern History,* xi. (1939), 27.